Disraeli

Disraeli
from an engraving after a photograph by Mayall

DISRAELI

by Robert Blake

B
B356
1967

c. 1

ST. MARTIN'S PRESS
New York

TO THE MEMORY
OF MY FATHER

Contents

Part One: Early Years

Disraeli's birth – His erroneous account of his ancestry – Character of his grandfather and father – The Basevis – The Jews in England – Disraeli becomes a Christian – His education – Autobiographical hints in his novels – Uneasy relation with his mother – Ambitiousness – Solicitor's clerk – John Murray – James Meredith – A continental tour – Disraeli abandons the law

Disraeli's financial speculations – Their disastrous outcome – His mining pamphlets – Joins with Murray in founding a daily paper – Negotiations with Lockhart at Chiefswood – Disraeli taken in by Dr Maginn – Second visit to Scotland – Failure of the paper – Disraeli's later efforts to suppress his own part – Vivian Grey – Plumer Ward and the Austens – Mrs Austen in love with Disraeli – Colburn agrees to publish – Appearance of the novel – Its autobiographical nature – Importance of reading pre-1853 editions – Fury of the reviewers – Murray's anger at being lampooned – His breach with the D'Israelis – Mrs D'Israeli's letter – Harm done to Disraeli by Vivian Grey – Disraeli's Italianate character

Disraeli and the Austens visit Switzerland and Italy – Rowed on Lake Geneva by Byron's boatman – Nervous breakdown on return to England – A blank period – Recovery – The Young Duke – Acquaintance with Bulwer Lytton – Criticism of the novel – Disraeli and Meredith go on Mediterranean tour – Gibraltar, Spain, Malta – James Clay – A debauched Wykehamist – Disraeli explores the

Part Two: Front Bench

Part Three: Top of the Greasy Pole

Illustrations

Maps illustrating the Eastern question appear on pages 572 and 573.

Acknowledgements are due for the following plates: to the Radio Times Hulton Picture Library for the frontispiece, 6, 7, 8, 9, 10, 11a, 12; to the National Trust and Michael R. Dudley for 1, 2a, 4, 5, 11b; to Sir John Wheeler-Bennett, KCVO, for 2b; to Sir Francis Sykes, Bt, for 3.

Preface

Disraeli died in 1881. His literary executor was his private secretary, Montagu Corry (Lord Rowton), who seems to have contemplated writing a biography of his chief. Certainly no one would have been better qualified to 'Boswellize' Disraeli. But when he died in 1903 nothing had been done. In the interval not only had several unofficial lives – mostly of dubious value – appeared, but also the official biography of Gladstone, whose death had occurred only five years earlier, in 1898. In the circumstances the Beaconsfield Trustees, of whom Lord Rothschild was the key figure, were anxious to have something done as soon as possible. After offering the job for a fee of £20,000 to Lord Rosebery, who declined it, they chose W. F. Monypenny, a distinguished *Times* journalist. He began work in 1906. His first volume, covering the years 1804–37, appeared in 1910, and the second (1837–46) in November 1912. But he was in failing health and died a few days later. The Trustees then invited G. E. Buckle, who had recently resigned the editorship of *The Times* as a result of disagreement with Lord Northcliffe. The remaining four volumes were published at intervals over the next eight years, the last two appearing together in 1920.

The six-volume work, running to at least one and a quarter million words, is rightly described in the notice of Buckle in the *Dictionary of National Biography* as both 'a quarry and a classic'. Not least of its virtues is the great quantity of Disraeli's letters published there for the first time. All subsequent writers about Disraeli must acknowledge their debt to Monypenny and Buckle. Perhaps one day some wealthy foundation will finance a complete edition of the correspondence of the best letter-writer among all English statesmen. Till that day the official biography remains the nearest equivalent.

It is now sixty years since that work was begun and nearly half a century since it was completed. During that time there have been studies of aspects of Disraeli's career and of English history in which use has been made of his papers, and Professor B. R. Jerman in his *The Young Disraeli* (1960) has exploited them in order to unravel details of Disraeli's early life. There have also, of course, been numerous biographies based on printed sources. But there has been no attempt at a fresh appraisal of his whole career, based on the papers and on the information which has subsequently become available. This biography is an attempt to fill this gap.

Politics was the breath of Disraeli's life and it is the political side of his career which is most in need of re-examination, although other aspects, too, such as his reckless and raffish youth, need to be reconsidered. It is impossible to deal with the political background otherwise than at some length. This is therefore a long book, but perhaps the reader will console himself with the thought that it is not as long as Monypenny and Buckle.

Christ Church, Oxford   R.B.
July 1966

Acknowledgements

I would like first of all to express my gratitude to Her Majesty the Queen for her gracious permission to make use of material from the Royal Archives at Windsor Castle. I would also like to thank Mr Robert Mackworth-Young, MVO, the Librarian, and Miss Price Hill, MVO, the former Registrar, for all the help which they personally gave me.

The Disraeli Papers are now at Hughenden, in the custody of the National Trust, which owns the house. I must thank the Trust for permission to use and quote from the papers and to reproduce several pictures among the plates. I am most grateful to Mr Rogers and his colleagues at Hughenden for their unfailing courtesy and kindness. The papers were being catalogued by Mr R. W. Stewart while I was engaged on this biography: I would like to thank him for the help that he has given me; also for letting me see his unpublished work on Disraeli's early literary career, and for compiling the list of Disraeli's writings which appears in Appendix II.

I must acknowledge the kind permission of the Beaconsfield Trustees to quote from Disraeli's unpublished letters.

I must also express my gratitude to Sir Francis Sykes, Bt, for permitting me to quote from the letters of Henrietta Lady Sykes and for lending me the portrait of her by Maclise which is reproduced as Plate 3.

I would like to thank Lord Derby for his kindness in lending me the papers of the 14th Earl of Derby, and Mr Montagu Lowry-Corry for lending me those of Lord Rowton. I am also most grateful to Sir John Murray, KCVO, for giving me access to the Murray Papers and permitting me to quote from Monypenny and Buckle's *Life of Disraeli*.

I have to thank the following for their kind permission to quote from material which is in their possession or of which they own the copyright: the Marquess of Salisbury, KG (Salisbury Papers); Lady Cobbold (the Lytton Papers); the Trustees of the British Museum (Papers of Sir Robert Peel, Lord Cross, Lord Iddesleigh and Benjamin Austen); the Hon. Jacob Rothschild (letters of Mrs Brydges Willyams).

I would like to thank Sir John Wheeler-Bennett, KCVO, for permission to reproduce the drawing of Disraeli by Count d'Orsay (Plate 2b), and Mr Hugh Carey for presenting me with the cartoon by 'Vincent' which is reproduced as Plate 9.

I wish to express my gratitude to Dr G. Kitson Clark for allowing me to read a part of his forthcoming work on Peel and the Corn Laws, and to Dr F. B. Smith for allowing me to consult his unpublished Cambridge Ph.D. thesis, *The Making of the Second Reform Bill*.

Finally let me thank Mr James Wright for his careful editing of my typescript; the Earl of Birkenhead and Mr E. T. Williams for undertaking the arduous task of reading the proofs; and Mr F. T. Dunn for compiling the index.

Note on Sources

Works which appear repeatedly in the footnotes have been given the following short titles after their first appearance, e.g.:

M. & B., for Monypenny and Buckle's *Life of Benjamin Disraeli*

Morley, for Morley's *Life of Gladstone*

Jerman, for B. R. Jerman, *The Young Disraeli*

Correspondence, for R. Disraeli (ed.), *Lord Beaconsfield's Correspondence with his Sister, 1832–52*

Zetland, for Lord Zetland, *The Letters of Disraeli to Lady Bradford and Lady Chesterfield*

Part I

EARLY YEARS

CHAPTER I

Background and Boyhood

1804–24

1

Benjamin Disraeli's career was an extraordinary one; but there is no need to make it seem more extraordinary than it really was. His point of departure, though low by the standards of nineteenth-century Prime Ministers, was neither as humble nor as alien as some people have believed. It is possible to overestimate the obstacles in his way and underestimate the assets he possessed.

He was born in London on December 21, 1804, at his father's house, 6 King's Road, Bedford Row (later renamed 22 Theobald's Road), near Gray's Inn. He was the second child and eldest son of Isaac D'Israeli, author of the *Curiosities of Literature*, a volatile, kindly, sceptical literary man of comfortable private means and of Italian Sephardi[1] Jewish origin. Benjamin's mother was Maria (Miriam) Basevi, whose family was of the same origin and equally prosperous. He had an elder sister, Sarah, born in 1802, whose fiancé died tragically in 1831. She never married and devoted herself to her parents and her eldest brother. She died in 1859. Of his three younger brothers Naphtali was born and died in 1807, Ralph (Raphael) was born in 1809, James (Jacobus) in 1813. The last two became conscientious and dull public servants. James, a Commissioner of Excise, died in 1868 leaving no heirs. Ralph, who became Deputy Clerk of Parliament, outlived all the family, dying in 1898. His son inherited Benjamin's Buckinghamshire estate and country house, Hughenden, near High Wycombe. With his death in 1936 the male line of the family became extinct.

Throughout his life Benjamin Disraeli was addicted to romance and careless about facts. His account of his ancestry, though wrong in almost every detail, is interesting both for the light that it throws

---

[1] The Jews are divided into two principal groups: the Sephardi whose liturgy is said to descend from that of the Jews settled by Nebuchadnezzar in Babylonia, and the Ashkenazi whose liturgy is supposed to descend from that of the revived community established in Palestine by Ezra and Nehemiah. Spanish, Portuguese and Italian names predominate among the former. German, Polish and Russian among the latter.

3

and the influence that it had upon his character and beliefs. It
appeared in 1849 as a memoir prefacing the collected works of his
father, to whom he was devoted. Disraeli maintained that his
father's family had been expelled from Spain in the great exodus of
1492 and had settled in Venice, where they 'dropped their Gothic
surname and, grateful to the God of Jacob who had sustained them
through unprecedented trials and guarded them through unheard-of
perils, they assumed the name of Disraeli, a name never borne before
or since by any other family in order that their race might be for
ever recognised'. In Venice they flourished 'as merchants for more
than two centuries under the protection of the lion of S Mark'.
Then towards the middle of the eighteenth century his great-grandfather sent the younger of his two sons, Benjamin, to England,
'where the dynasty seemed at length established through the recent
failure of Prince Charles Edward and where public opinion appeared
definitively adverse to the persecution of creed and conscience'.[1]
The other son, so Disraeli alleged, remained in Venice as a banker
and became a friend of Sir Horace Mann, the British envoy in
Florence.

The learned researches of Dr Cecil Roth and the late Mr Lucien
Wolf have revealed this account as largely mythical[2]. There is no
evidence at all that the family came from Spain. The name, which
was Israeli until the elder Benjamin changed it to D'Israeli, is
neither unique nor Spanish nor Italian: the D', which sounds like a
nobiliary particle, is probably the Aramaic *di* used by the Sephardi
Jews in their Synagogal names in place of the Hebrew *ben*, and
meaning 'son of'. The name Israeli is Arabic and was used by the
Moors in Spain and the Levant to distinguish Jews holding public
office or otherwise coming into contact with the non-Jewish population. The Spanish or Italian version would be Israelita, and it is
most unlikely that a Jewish refugee escaping from the Spanish
Inquisition to Venice would have advertised his Hebrew origin by
adopting an Arabic name. Nor is the name unique even in the form
of Disraeli, which was apparently adopted by Benjamin, the
younger, very early in life.[3] A Huguenot family of that name
flourished in London for much of the eighteenth century, and died

[1] Isaac D'Israeli, *The Curiosities of Literature* (new edition, 1881), Memoir viii–ix.
[2] Cecil Roth, *Benjamin Disraeli, Earl of Beaconsfield* (New York, 1952), ch. i.
Lucien Wolf, *The Times*, December 21, 22, 1904, on Disraeli's centenary.
[3] He told Lord Rowton in 1873 that his father had changed it for him before he
went to school: Hughenden Papers, Box 26, B/X/B/26.

out in 1814 in the person of one Benjamin Disraeli, a rich Dublin moneylender who had no connexion whatever with his famous namesake.

The story of a Venetian ancestry is equally untrue. No record of the name appears in any Venetian records before 1821. The elder Benjamin, Disraeli's grandfather who migrated to England, did, indeed, have two sisters who settled in Venice in middle age and kept a girls' school in the ghetto, but there is no other connexion with Venice, and the elder brother who was alleged to be a banker and a friend of Sir Horace Mann seems to have been conjured up by Disraeli's imagination. At all events his name is unknown to the Venetian archives and appears nowhere in the gigantic correspondence of Sir Horace Mann.

Disraeli could easily have ascertained from a glance at his own family papers that his grandfather came from Cento near Ferrara, which belonged to the Papal States. It is impossible to trace the family back beyond his great-grandfather, Isaac Israeli, of whom very little is known. He or his forebears probably came to Italy from the Levant. Isaac Israeli's son, Benjamin, was born in 1730 and emigrated to England in 1748. His motive is unlikely to have been anything so profound as confidence in the Hanoverian dynasty or admiration of the English way of life; it was probably, in Mr Wolf's words, 'a humdrum but entirely creditable desire to find the best market for his knowledge of the straw bonnet trade'. In 1756 he married Rebecca Furtado, who died eight years later. It was this connexion which gave rise to the belief that Disraeli had some relationship with the grand Spanish family of Lara. Rebecca's brother-in-law was one Aaron Lara, a prosperous London broker, and Disraeli himself enumerates among the leading Sephardi families flourishing in England in his grandfather's time the Laras, 'who were our Kinsmen'. In fact, this family of Lara was Portuguese and quite unconnected with the Spanish family of the same name. It is wrong to suggest, as some have, that Lara was the 'gothic name' which the D'Israelis originally bore. In any case, Disraeli had no blood relationship with his grandfather's first wife. There was one daughter of this marriage, who subsequently emigrated to Italy and whose descendants are still there.

The following year Benjamin the elder married again. His second wife, Sarah Shiprut de Gabay Villa Real, was the youngest daughter of Isaac Shiprut, a rich city merchant, whose mother hailed, not from the famous Portuguese family of Villa Real, as the younger Benjamin believed, but from a family of the same name in Leghorn.[1] The marriage brought Benjamin D'Israeli the elder both money and credit, and did much to re-establish his somewhat shaky finances. He became a stockbroker and left £35,000 when he died in 1816 – a comfortable fortune, but scarcely one that could ever have put him, as his grandson maintained, into the category of a potential Rothschild.

There was in Disraeli's day, and long after, a notion that the Sephardi Jews were more 'aristocratic', whatever that may mean, than the Ashkenazi who came from central and eastern Europe. Disraeli was undoubtedly a Sephardi. There was also a belief that of the Sephardi the most aristocratic branch was the descendants of the Spanish or Portuguese Jews, whether those who professed their faith openly and were expelled in 1492, or the so-called Marranos or secret Jews who lived as nominal Christians adopting 'gothic' surnames, but were eventually forced to leave by the racialist persecution of the Inquisition. Disraeli never made it quite clear which of these branches he thought he belonged to. The point is not important, since there is no proof at all that he belonged to either. What matters is that he believed that his origins were highly aristocratic and the belief had no small effect on his political outlook and his political career.

He appears to have taken very little interest in his mother and to have disliked the Basevi family. But it is curious to notice that, by one of those ironies which so often attend human vanities, he had a far more picturesque and romantic descent through her than through his father. Here, indeed, he really might have claimed a genuine ancestor in one of the Jews who left Spain in the great exodus of 1492, and what is more a far more distinguished ancestor than he ever dared to invent for the Disraelis. Her father, Naphtali Basevi, had married another of his race, Rebecca Rieti. Rebecca's mother came from a family called Aboab Cardoso. The Cardosos had been settled in England since the end of the seventeenth century – which gives Disraeli four generations of English-born ancestors, not merely one, as his enemies maintained. The Cardosos claimed, probably with justice, a direct lineal descent from Isaac Aboab, the last Gaon of Castille, who in 1492 led a contingent of 20,000 compatriots into Portugal, where he had obtained permission for a

[1] Roth, *Beaconsfield*, 8.

temporary stay from King John II. Disraeli would have made much of this if he had known the facts.

2

The elder Benjamin was a genial, friendly, conformist who remained to the end of his days a devout member of the Sephardi congregation at Bevis Marks in London. His wife, Sarah, was, however, a rebel. She hated the faith to which her ancestry caused her to belong. She was, her grandson says, 'a demon', and 'so mortified by her social position that she lived until eighty without indulging in a tender expression'. She was evidently not a very agreeable grandmother. Her religious doubts, however, had advantages for her only son. Her mother, Esther Shiprut, Disraeli's great-grandmother, was so grieved at this infidelity that she cut her daughter out of her will and left her fortune direct to Isaac, who thus became a man of independent means at the age of twenty-five. Esther was luckily not to know that Isaac would later behave even more badly from her point of view than Sarah did, leave the family faith altogether and have his children brought up as Christians.

Isaac was born on May 11, 1766. He seems in his early years to have shown some signs of the rebelliousness that was to character-ize his eldest son. He once ran away from home and was found in a suitably romantic posture lying on a tombstone in Hackney church-yard. His father did not understand this sort of thing. His solution to the problem was to give him a pony. Later, when there seemed the ominous possibility that parental influence would oblige him to go into trade, Isaac wrote a poem 'against commerce which is the corruption of man'. Clever youths are often out of sympathy with their fathers. Some eighty years later Isaac's famous son remarked to his private secretary, 'that his father never understood him, neither in early life when he failed to see his utter unfitness to be-come a solicitor, nor in latter days when he had got into Parlia-ment.'[1] It is a matter in which experience seldom teaches a lesson.

Isaac, thanks no doubt to the prospect of his grandmother's fortune, escaped 'the corruption of man' and was allowed to travel and write. Influenced by a free-thinking tutor in Amsterdam, he soon dropped his boyish romanticism and surveyed life through the

[1] Hughenden Papers, Box 26, A/X/B/13, Memorandum by Montagu Corry, December 14, 1873.

eyes of Voltaire rather than those of Rousseau. He produced various
verses and other trifles, but it was in 1791 that he first made his
name with a genre of literature which he continued to exploit for the
rest of his life. In that year he published *The Curiosities of Literature*,
a fascinating anthology of anecdotes and character sketches about
literary men, together with random observations on history and
literature, written in a dryly elegant style. Although Isaac was
modest enough to issue it anonymously, indeed to present the copyright to his publisher, John Murray, it was at once a great success.
The author's name soon became known and Isaac found that he had
achieved fame. Fortune arrived simultaneously, for his grandmother
died that same year.

Already Isaac's mode of life had become established: a constant
worker in the British Museum during the morning and in his own
ever-expanding library during the afternoon, he would cover innumerable slips of paper with notes and extracts in his tiny crabbed
handwriting. The first volume of the *Curiosities* went into twelve
editions. It was followed by five more volumes, the last appearing
in 1834. *A Dissertation on Anecdotes, Calamities of Authors, Quarrels
of Authors* were variations on the same theme. As an anecdotalist
and anthologist Isaac D'Israeli had scarcely a rival in his own day
or since.

He did not confine himself to anthology and anecdote. He wrote
a number of novels and stories, the last appearing in 1811 and
entitled *Despotism, or the Fall of the Jesuits*. None was successful;
and they are wholly forgotten today. He also tried his hand at
history. Here he followed in the Tory footsteps of Hume, and
his *Commentaries on the Life and Reign of Charles I* (5 volumes,
1828–30) earned him in 1832 an honorary DCL from Oxford, still
loyal to the glorious memory of Charles the Martyr. It was a serious
work of historical research and the author made use of much then
unpublished material, but, naturally enough, it has long been
superseded by modern scholarship.

In 1795 Isaac became mysteriously but seriously ill, and for three
years he lived in Devonshire recuperating. Benjamin was to have a
similar breakdown even earlier in life. By the time Isaac was thirty-
five most of his friends regarded him as a confirmed bachelor, but
on February 10, 1802, he married Maria Basevi. The Basevis were
a distinguished and talented Jewish family settled in Verona since
the end of the sixteenth century. Maria's father, Naphtali, had set

up in London as a merchant in 1762. He became President of the Jewish Board of Deputies in 1801. His wife's uncle, Solomon Rieti, was the creator of the celebrated pleasure gardens by the Thames at Ranelagh. His grandson, Nathaniel, was the first Jewish-born barrister to practise in the English courts. Another grandson, George Basevi, Benjamin Disraeli's first cousin, was an able architect, pupil of Sir John Soane and responsible for designing the Fitzwilliam Museum at Cambridge. He met his death in 1845 by a tragic accident, falling from the scaffolding round Ely Cathedral, where he was inspecting the work on the bell tower. Maria herself does not seem to have possessed any special talent other than the far from contemptible one of making a happy home for her husband and children.

Benjamin Disraeli was thus born into a family neither obscure, undistinguished, nor poor. 'It is really nonsense', wrote the Duke of Argyll,[1] 'to talk of a man in such a position as a mere "Jew Boy" who by the force of nothing but extraordinary genius attained to the leadership of a great party. The only impediments in his way were not in any want of external advantages but his own often grotesque and unintelligible opinions.' The Duke was no friend of Disraeli and he overstated the case, but there was more in it than is usually admitted. His father's *réclame* in the literary world was considerable, and Isaac seems to have been personally liked by other writers. Scott, Byron, Southey and Samuel Rogers praised him. John Murray was his intimate friend. He had no financial worries and his family could rely on servants, good food, a comfortable house and a generous, though not lavish, upbringing. In character Isaac was not perhaps the ideal father; but who is? He was inclined to be over-indulgent to his children. He was nervous and retiring. He was at times fussy and too readily put off by trifles. During the crisis of 1832, when there seemed danger of a run on the banks, he wrote to his son to say that he was thinking of coming up to London to take out some gold – as long as it was not raining.[2]

Isaac never took any active part in politics, but his views were Tory all his life. The literary world was by no means remote from the political in the early nineteenth century. Of course, the company frequented by Isaac was separated by a wide gulf from the grandees who dominated the Cabinet or led the Opposition, but John

[1] George Douglas, Duke of Argyll, *Autobiography and Memoirs* (2 vols, 1906) i, 280.
[2] Hughenden Papers, Box 7, A/I/B/427, May 14, 1832.

Murray's dinner parties included a fair number of those hard-working lesser figures, under-secretaries and the like, such as Croker,[1] Barrow[2] and Wilmot Horton,[3] for whom political gossip was the principal theme of conversation. Benjamin Disraeli's background was more helpful and relevant to his later career than is sometimes realized.

3

In one respect, however, Disraeli suffered from a potentially fatal handicap. He was a Jew. The handicap did not arise from social or religious persecution. England at the beginning of the nineteenth century was a tolerant place, and its Jewish inhabitants were numerically far below the figure at which, sociologists tell us, an alien minority risks becoming the object of hatred to their fellow citizens. The Jewish religion with its strange observances and eccentric taboos inspired curiosity rather than detestation. The handicap lay in the fact that the law prohibited non-Christians from entering Parliament. Until 1829 Jews, along with Roman Catholics and Dissenters, were excluded by the Test Acts, which preserved the higher positions in public life for members of the Church of England. In 1829 this monopoly was broken so far as the Christian sects were concerned, but the parliamentary oath continued to be taken 'on the true faith of a Christian', and Jews were still excluded – a barrier not removed until 1858.

No such ban applied to people who were merely Jewish by race, provided that they were ready to take the oath. As early as 1770 Sampson Gideon the younger, who later became a peer, was returned for Parliament. Sir Manasseh Lopes entered the House in 1802, Ralph Bernal in 1818, and, most famous of all, the great economist, David Ricardo, in 1819. All four were members of the Anglican Church, but their racial origin was well known, and it was evidently not an insuperable bar.

Fortunately for Disraeli the difficulty soon vanished. Isaac had never taken his faith at all seriously, although he paid his dues and conformed outwardly. But in 1813, greatly to his annoyance, he was elected Parnass or Warden of the Congregation of Bevis Marks – a

---

[1] John Wilson Croker, 1780–1857. Politician and writer.
[2] Sir John Barrow, 1764–1848. Politician and geographer.
[3] Sir Robert John Wilmot Horton, 3rd Bt. 1784–1841. Politician.

position somewhat analogous to that of an elder in the Scottish Kirk. Under the rules of the synagogue, refusal of office entailed a fine of £40. Isaac declined either to accept or to pay. 'I lament the occasion', he wrote, 'which drives me with so many others out of the pale of your jurisdiction. . . . Do not shut out the general improvement of the age; . . . a society has only to make itself respectable in these times to draw to itself the public esteem.'

In fact, however, he did not resign at once. Probably he was anxious not to hurt the feelings of his father. The authorities of the synagogue for their part do not seem to have pressed the matter of the fine. But four years later, in March 1817, as a result of a renewed financial wrangle, he finally left the Congregation. Benjamin the elder had died in the previous year, and there was no one else whose susceptibilities would be damaged, for Isaac's mother detested Judaism. The Basevi family withdrew at the same time.

Isaac was content to remain outside any formal religious organization, but his close friend, Sharon Turner, a solicitor and antiquary, persuaded him with some difficulty that this would not do for the children. On July 11 the two younger boys were taken by Turner to be baptized at S Andrew's, Holborn, by the Reverend W. H. Coleridge, a nephew of the poet. But oddly enough – and contrary to his own later recollection – Benjamin was not baptized till July 31 (by the Reverend J. Thimbleby), and his sister a month after that, on August 28. Dr Cecil Roth suggests that Benjamin and Sarah, being old enough to have some ideas of their own, may have dug their toes in and refused to accompany their father's friend on the earlier occasion[1]. This is possible, although Benjamin seems to have had no memory of such reluctance: in his own account he says, wrongly, that all four children were baptized on the same day.

Benjamin had taken, or been pushed into taking, far the most important decision of his boyhood. From now onwards he was a practising member of the Church of England as by law established. Had he remained a Jew, his later political career would have been impossible. He would never have become leader of the Conservative party if he had been obliged to wait till his middle fifties before entering Parliament.

There is something of a mystery about the exact chronology of his education. At a very early age he went to a dame's school at Islington kept by a Miss Roper. He himself declared that he was sent

1 *Beaconsfield*, 12–13.

there to learn to speak, but this is scarcely credible. After that, though it is not quite clear when, he moved to a boarding-school at Blackheath whose headmaster was a Nonconformist minister by the name of Potticany. He remained there until he was nearly thirteen, but he never mentions it at all in any of his reminiscences. At this school, according to the recollection of some of his schoolfellows, he was allowed to stand at the back of the hall during prayers, and he was apparently given some kind of instruction in Hebrew once a week by a visiting teacher.

In the autumn term of 1817, after he had become a Christian, he was sent to another school; no doubt there was some connexion between the two events. To have returned to Blackheath after the change of religion might have been embarrasing. The new school was Higham Hall in Epping Forest. Its headmaster was a Unitarian minister, the Reverend Eli Cogan, and it catered for about fifty or sixty boys from what was then termed 'the middling class', sons of prosperous but unaristocratic fathers – for example, the four sons of Baron Gurney, the judge, went there. The choice of school is not in itself surprising, but it becomes so when we remember that Isaac soon afterwards sent both his younger sons to Winchester. Why he had his eldest and cleverest boy educated at a rather dim little place like Higham Hall and his two younger and duller sons at one of England's greatest public schools is far from clear. The reason cannot have been financial. Isaac's father had died the previous year, leaving a substantial sum, and Isaac signalized his increased prosperity by moving in 1817 to a larger house in Bloomsbury Square. 'Both my brothers,' wrote Disraeli many years later in an autobiographical fragment which is in some respects far from reliable, 'were at Winchester for wh: I was intended. This is the reason for my being often described as an alumnus of that public school'.[1] But he does not say why the intention was frustrated. Perhaps he gives us a hint in *Vivian Grey*. 'Mr Grey was for Eton but his lady was one of those women whom nothing in the world can persuade that a public school is anything but a place where boys are roasted alive; and so with tears taunts, and supplications, the point of private education was conceded.' Did Maria Disraeli for once intervene? The first and only Wykehamist Prime Minister was Addington. It is odd to think how near Disraeli came to being the second.

[1] Hughenden Papers, Box 16, A/X/B/1, March 27, 1860.

He only stayed at Higham Hall for two or three years – once again the chronology is obscure – but it evidently made a deep impression on him. In his words to Lord Rowton, 'the whole drama of public school life was acted in a smaller theatre'.[1] It is hard to believe that the vivid descriptions of schoolboy life given in *Vivian Grey*, *Contarini Fleming* and *Coningsby* do not have some basis in personal experience. Nearly everything else in Disraeli's novels has, and *Contarini Fleming* is described by the author as a 'Psychological Auto-Biography'. Although this does not mean that the story must be taken as literally true, nevertheless it is worth considering. Contarini Fleming is the son by his Venetian first wife of Baron Fleming, a diplomat in some unspecified northern court, too deeply immersed in business to bother about his family. The Baron has married again. His second wife is conventional, cold, scrupulously fair, but utterly insensitive to the feelings of Contarini, who is a moody, emotional, poetical genius. There are two sons by the second marriage. 'They were called my brothers but Nature gave the lie to the repeated assertion. Their blue eyes, their flaxen hair, and their white visages claimed no kindred with my Venetian countenance.' Glad to escape an uncomprehending stepmother and dullard brothers whom he dislikes, Contarini goes to school, but in retrospect he hates it.

> Our school boy days are looked back to by all with fondness. Oppressed with the cares of life we contrast our worn and harrassed existence with that sweet prime, free from anxiety and fragrant with innocence. I cannot share these feelings. I was a most miserable child; and school I detested more than ever I abhorred the world in the darkest moments of my experienced manhood.

Nevertheless at first things go well. Conscious hitherto of not only being different in appearance but inferior to his fair-haired northern companions, he finds to his surprise that he has a talent for wit and persiflage which astounds them all. 'It seemed that I was the soul of the school. Wherever I went my name sounded, whatever was done my opinion was quoted.' The hero in *Vivian Grey* has the same experience.

Then Contarini falls in love. In those pre-Freudian days it was possible to write about schoolboy romances in a way which could

---

[1] Hughenden Papers, Box 26, A/X/B/31.

scarcely be imitated today. The object of his passion is a boy called Musaeus.

> It seemed to me that I never beheld so lovely and so pensive a countenance. His face was quite oval, his eyes deep blue: his rich brown curls clustered in hyacinthine grace upon the delicate rose of his downy cheek and shaded the light blue veins of his white forehead.
> I beheld him: I loved him. My friendship was a passion. Of all our society he alone crowded not round me. He was of a cold temperament, shy and timid. He looked upon me as a being whom he could not comprehend, and rather feared. . . .
> Musaeus was lowly born, and I was noble; he poor and I wealthy; I had a dazzling reputation, he but a poor report. To find himself an object of interest, of quiet and tender regard, to one to whose notice all aspired, and who seemed to exist only in a blaze of cold-hearted raillery and reckless repartee, developed even his dormant vanity. He looked upon me with much interest, and this feeling soon matured into fondness.
> Oh! days of rare and pure felicity, when Musaeus and myself with our arms around each other's neck wandered together amid the meads and shady woods that formed our limits! I lavished upon him all the fanciful love that I had long stored up; and the mighty passions that lay yet dormant in my obscure soul now first began to stir in their glimmering abyss.

There follow lovers' quarrels, passionate scenes and frenzied letters, but term, alas, draws to an end. One last walk on the evening before, and even Musaeus sheds a tear. 'The bell sounded. I embraced him as if it sounded for my execution, and we parted.' But the holidays induce a different mood. Musaeus comes to stay. Contarini now finds him a bore, and on returning next term, plunged in despondency and gloom, only 'supported by my ambition which now each day became more quickening', severs all relations with him. The rest of the school, astonished at this change, take up the cause of Musaeus, and rather surprisingly march *en masse*, all two hundred of them, to remonstrate with Contarini, who is brooding in solitude on a gate in a remote part of the grounds. The leader of this curious deputation gets a short answer from Contarini. They fight, Contarini, of course, winning; and he hurls his enemy's 'half-inanimate body' on to a dunghill. A similar fight, though for different reasons, occurs in *Vivian Grey*. Soon afterwards, tormented, unhappy, at odds with himself for reasons that he cannot analyse, Contarini runs away from school. The remainder of the novel does not for the moment concern us.

What light does all this throw on Disraeli's adolescent life? No one can be sure, but from other straws in the wind it is reasonable to guess that some of it corresponds to reality. It is clear that he did not get on well with his mother. To transpose her for fictional purpose into that recognized object of dislike, a stepmother, would be a natural precaution. Precisely what went wrong with their relationship no one can now tell. But something went wrong. There is no record of his ever talking about her after her death, and no reference to her in the numerous autobiographical fragments which survive among his papers. Indeed, one might almost think that he wished to obliterate her memory. In the somewhat imaginative memoir recounting his family history, from which quotation has been made earlier, her name is never even mentioned. This strange omission did not go unnoticed. Sarah D'Israeli protested. 'I do wish,' she wrote, 'that one felicitous stroke, one tender word had brought our dear Mother into the picture.' Disraeli's answer, if any, has not survived. Perhaps Maria D'Israeli gave her two younger sons, with whom Benjamin had little in common, more affection than he felt they deserved. Perhaps like Contarini's stepmother she did not recognize his brilliance. 'Tho' a clever boy . . . no prodigy', was her verdict in writing to John Murray after the quarrel occasioned by the publication of *Vivian Grey*.[1] She came round in the end. In March 1847 Disraeli, now well on the way to the leadership of the Tory party, made a brilliant speech. 'Mama at last confesses,' wrote Sarah to Disraeli's wife, 'that she never before thought Dis was equal to Mr. Pitt. So you see it pleases all variety of hearers or readers.' But it was too late. She died a month later, and if silence may thus be interpreted her son was not reconciled. One faintly pathetic piece of evidence survives to suggest that Disraeli never quite brought himself to accept this lack of the love and affection which he thought his due. It is a sonnet, a very bad one, headed 'To My Mother nursing me on her birthday 1838'.[2] Whether or not she saw it there is no means of knowing. Twenty-two years later he sent it on December 8, 1860, in a letter marked 'immediate' to his brother, Ralph. There is nothing to explain why. This is the only known evidence that Disraeli ever even thought about her after she died.

[1] See below, p. 45.
[2] Hughenden Papers, Box 9, A/I/E/5.

Yet the more his character, particularly in his relation with women, is examined, the more clear it becomes that he felt this deprivation deeply. All his life he seems to be searching for a substitute for the mother who was somehow missing. His wife, his mistresses, his friends were almost always older women who could, or he hoped that they could, supply that need.[1] It is impossible to doubt that some very real experience lay behind these early passages in *Contarini Fleming*, and that Disraeli with his intense vanity, his supreme egoism, craved from his mother a degree of admiration and adulation which was never forthcoming.

Nor can there be much doubt that Contarini's schooldays are in some measure based on the author's experience. The theme of schoolboy friendship is one to which Disraeli returns on other occasions. It is difficult to believe that he had not felt such sentiments himself. There is a famous passage in *Coningsby*:

> At school friendship is a passion. It entrances the being; it tears the soul. All loves of after-life can never bring its rapture, or its wretchedness; no bliss so absorbing, no pangs of jealousy or despair so crushing and so keen! What tenderness and what devotion; what illimitable confidence; infinite revelations of inmost thoughts; what ecstatic present and romantic future; what bitter estrangements, what melting reconciliations; what scenes of wild recrimination, agitating explanations, passionate correspondence; what insane sensitiveness and what frantic sensibility, what earthquakes of the heart and whirlwinds of the soul are confined in that simple phrase, a schoolboy's friendship. 'Tis some indefinite recollection of these mystic passages of their young emotion that makes grey-haired men mourn over the memory of their schoolboy days. It is a spell that can soften the acerbity of political warfare, and with its witchery can call forth a sigh even amid the callous bustle of fashionable saloons.

One is reminded of Byron's famous meeting near Bologna with his Harrow friend, Lord Clare.[2] That Disraeli wrote from his heart on this occasion is evident. It is probable that at Higham Hall he first felt the pangs of love, and felt them intensely; and that either there or at Blackheath he first became conscious of being different – 'the Venetian countenance'. It is more than likely that he suffered some

---

[1] See below, p. 99.

[2] The sceptic, aware of Disraeli's penchant for plagiarism, might be tempted to wonder whether this is another instance. But, in fact, the passage in question, from Byron's 'Detached Thoughts', was first published in 1900 in R. E. Prothero's six-volume *Letters and Journals of Lord Byron*.

sort of rebuff on this account, possibly connected with one of these schoolboy romances. The great fight which figures in both *Vivian Grey* and *Contarini Fleming*, or some similar episode, may have really occurred. Disraeli's black curls, hooked nose, dark eyes and pale complexion must have contrasted oddly with the pink cheeks and fair hair of his companions. It is unlikely that the contrast went unobserved either by him or by them. The young Disraeli when we begin to know anything definite about him, from the age of twenty onwards, is a youth of immense ambition, consumed with an almost insolent determination to make his mark. The conquest of a hostile or indifferent world – military metaphors recur constantly when he writes about politics and society – is the theme of his life, and it remained so till in his old age he had finally triumphed. It is hard to say what gave the impetus to this ambition, if indeed any single experience did so. But it is certain that throughout his adult life he was conscious of dwelling apart from other men and it is probable that this awareness first came upon him when he was a schoolboy. Perhaps we need not look beyond it for the clue to his extraordinary determination to climb to the top. If he could not 'belong', he could at least rule. To the end of his days he remained an alien figure, never truly merged in the social and political order which after a lifetime of vicissitudes he had so strangely come to dominate at last.

4

Disraeli left Mr Cogan's establishment some time in 1819 or early 1820. For the next year or so he worked at home. He had the run of his father's vast and learned library, and it was during this time of his life that he began to acquire the wide if somewhat shallow knowledge of history and literature that was to characterize his thought and writing all his days. At the same time he endeavoured to turn himself into a classical scholar, but it is doubtful whether he ever really attained the knowledge of classical authors which he was inclined to claim in later life. During 1820 he kept a diary of his studies. His numerous errors of grammar, syntax, and accidence suggest that in Greek he never advanced very far. On the other hand he had a tolerable knowledge of the Latin language and literature. Disraeli probably was quite genuine in his love of the classics, but, like Stanley Baldwin, he rested that love upon somewhat shaky foundations. However, he knew enough to bandy Latin quotations in the House of Commons, and, luckily, it was not the form to do so in Greek.

In November 1821, shortly before he was seventeen, he became articled to a firm of solicitors, Messrs Swain, Stevens, Maples, Pearce and Hunt of Frederick's Place, Old Jewry. The premium paid by his father was 400 guineas. According to Disraeli's autobiographical note already mentioned, the firm was the principal rival of the famous City firm of Freshfields, and its 'partners divided though in unequal portions fifteen thousand per annum'.

Maples, who was his father's friend among the partners, had a daughter, and it was hinted that a match might well be acceptable to both families. The daughter was, so Disraeli says, 'by no means without charm, either personally or intellectually'. There is no very reliable first-hand evidence of how Disraeli conducted himself as an articled clerk. Maples's son, writing to Lord Rowton in 1889, said:

> I have heard my father say that Mr. Benjamin D'Israeli was very diligent very obliging and useful in the business and that he then already displayed more than ordinary talents. He served nearly four years' articles in 6, Frederick's Place but at the end of that period my father represented to Mr. Isaac D'Israeli that his son's talents were too great for a Solicitor's Office and advised Mr. Isaac D'Israeli that his son should follow some profession where he would have greater opportunities of distinguishing himself and suggested that he should go to the Bar.[1]

Recollections of this sort are liable to be coloured by later events. It is hard to imagine Disraeli being particularly efficient in the humdrum work which must have come his way. A contemporary letter from his father rings more truly:

> 15th October 1824 Old Ship Hotel, Brighton.
> My dear Ben,
> Your sister received your letter this morning which no doubt proved highly amusing – but I wished besides amusement you had combined for my use a little business-like information . . .[2]

And, as we saw earlier, Disraeli recognized in retrospect 'his utter unfitness to become a solicitor', although he did not regret the experience.

[1] Hughenden Papers, Box 10, A/II/B/1, February 1889.
[2] ibid., Box 8, A/I/C/11.

Indeed, he writes of his time as an articled clerk:

> It would be a mistake to suppose that the two years and more that I was in the office of our friend were wasted. I have often thought, though I have often regretted the University, that it was very much the reverse. My business was to be private secretary of the busiest partner of our friend. He dictated to me every day his correspondence which was as extensive as a Minister's, and when the clients arrived I did not leave the room but remained not only to learn my business but to become acquainted with my future clients. . . . It gave me great facility with my pen and no inconsiderable knowledge of human nature.
>
> Unfortunately, if indeed I ought to use the word, the rest of my life was not in harmony with this practice and business. . . . I became pensive and restless and before I was twenty I was obliged to terminate the dream of my father and his friend. Nothing would satisfy me but travel. My father then made a feeble effort for Oxford, but the hour of adventure had arrived. I was unmanageable.[1]

As for the young lady, she and Disraeli remained good friends, but nothing came of the family's hopes of a match. 'She said to me one day and before I had shown any indication of my waywardness, "You have too much genius for Frederick's Place: it will never do." '

We must envisage the young Disraeli during these years from seventeen to twenty as a precocious, moody, sensitive and somewhat affected youth, conscious of great powers, but uncertain how or where to use them, vaguely dissatisfied with his mode of life, much given to solitary reading and imaginative flights of fancy. Whether, at this early stage, like Vivian Grey, he had 'a devil of a tongue', and 'a certain *espirit de société*, an indefinable *tact*', there is now no means of ascertaining. It is, however, certain that the picture given in that novel of the society which Vivian frequented, thanks to his father, Horace, who had always found himself 'an honoured guest among the powerful and the great', does not correspond to reality. Isaac did not move in society at all. His friends were minor politicians, scholars, authors, publishers and fellow frequenters of the British Museum. It was a porty, snuffy, rather donnish world, whose leviathan was John Murray, the friend and literary executor of Byron and the second of that great dynasty of publishers. He seems to have taken to the young Disraeli, whose

[1] W. F. Monypenny and G. E. Buckle, *The Life of Benjamin Disraeli, Earl of Beaconsfield* (6 vols, 1910–20), i, 32–33. Hereafter referred to as M. & B.

precocious talent he was one of the first to recognize. While still scarcely more than a boy Disraeli was allowed to be a guest along with his father at some of John Murray's celebrated dinner parties.[1] When he was only seventeen the publisher consulted him on the merits of a play. Disraeli's answer is one of his earliest surviving letters.

August 1822

Dear Sir,

I ran my eye over three acts of 'Wallace'[2] and as far as I could form an opinion I cannot conceive these acts to be as effective on the stage as you seemed to expect. However it is impossible to say what a very clever actor like Macready may make of some of the passages. Notwithstanding the many erasures the diction is still diffuse and sometimes languishing though not inelegant. I cannot imagine it a powerful work as far as I have read. But indeed running over a part of a thing with people talking around is too unfair. . . . Your note arrives. If on so slight a knowledge of the play I could venture to erase either of the words you set before me I fear it would be *Yes*, but I feel cruel and wicked in saying so. . . .

Yours truly
B. D.[3]

In 1824, possibly encouraged by Murray, Disraeli wrote his first novel. It was a political satire entitled *Aylmer Papillion*. He sent it to Murray except for two chapters which he had mislaid. Murray evidently thought little of it, but perhaps did not quite like to say so. Sensing this reluctance, Disraeli wrote urging him not to bother about it, 'and as you have had some small experience in burning manuscripts perhaps you will be so kind as to consign it to the flames'.[4] Murray seems to have followed this advice. All that survives of *Aylmer Papillion* are the chapters which Disraeli had mislaid. They are crude and jejune. There is no need to regret the destruction of the others.

Two glimpses of the young Disraeli at this period of his life or a

[1] They evidently impressed him. See M. & B., i, 37–39, where his notes on a party in November 1822 are reproduced. Tom Moore was present and discoursed on Byron. Disraeli later used the whole passage almost verbatim in *Vivian Grey*.

[2] By C. E. Walker, first published in London in 1820. It is not clear whether Murray contemplated republishing or producing it.

[3] Murray Papers. This seems to be the first example of his change in spelling his name.

[4] ibid. An allusion to the famous destruction of Byron's Memoirs only a month earlier.

little earlier have come down to us. Mrs Maples recalled that even then his dress excited notice. He often dined with her and used to dress 'in a black velvet suit with ruffles and black silk stockings with red clocks, which was very conspicuous attire on those days'.[1] And William Archer Shee, son of the President of the Royal Academy, remembered juvenile parties given by Mrs Disraeli in Bloomsbury Square. He was only ten or eleven. Disraeli was some seven years older, and, not unnaturally, found them tedious.

> He took little notice of the small fry around him but walked about and dawdled through the quadrilles in tight pantaloons, with his hands in his pockets, looking very pale, bored, and dissatisfied, and evidently wishing us all in bed. He looked like Gulliver among the Liliputians, suffering from chronic dyspepsia.[2]

Disraeli's health seems to have caused some anxiety at this time, and in 1824 Isaac, partly because he was worried on this score, decided to vary his usual summer holiday at an English watering-place and to take Benjamin at the end of July for a six-week tour of Belgium and the Rhine valley.

The rest of the family were left behind, but father and son were accompanied by one of Benjamin's closest friends, William George Meredith, a young man who had just come down from Brasenose. While he was still at Oxford an unofficial engagement had been contracted between him and Sarah Disraeli. Both families approved. There was indeed no reason why the engagement should not have been published and the young couple duly married, for Meredith's parents were rich and he had no need to earn his living. But he had an even richer uncle who had given it to be understood that William would be his heir and who appears to have had some sort of objection to the match. Accordingly, and as events turned out, tragically, it was agreed to postpone matters for the time being. Meanwhile the intimacy of the two families was very close. The Merediths had a London house at Nottingham Place in addition to a country seat in Worcestershire. William, and his sister Georgiana, were constantly visiting the Disraelis. The young men wrote plays and sketches,[3]

[1] M. & B., i, 39. Quoting a letter from Mrs Maples's son, Frederick, to Lord Rowton, February 1889.

[2] Quoted in Wilfrid Meynell, *The Man Disraeli* (revised edition, 1927), 21.

[3] One of these called *Rumpel Stiltskin* 'A Dramatic Spectacle' survives, and has been published by Michael Sadleir for the Roxburghe Club. It is dated 'Oxoniae 1823'. Disraeli is said to have written the songs, Meredith the rest. It must be Disraeli's earliest surviving literary work.

the girls illustrated them, and the two families acted them. Meredith was a more prosaic character than his erratic friend, but he was by no means untalented. He became a Fellow of the Royal Society at twenty-seven and in 1829 published a reputable book on recent Swedish history.

The tour was a great success. It was Disraeli's first visit outside England, and his letters to his sister describing what they saw, did and ate – especially the last – have survived and make excellent reading.[1] Even at that early age Disraeli was very much of a gourmet. 'Our living for the last week', he writes from Antwerp, 'has been of the most luxurious possible, and my mother must really reform her table before our return.' A diary which he kept for the tour carries us without a break from a description of Rubens's pictures in Antwerp to one of the *vol-au-vent* of pigeons at their hotel. The features of Brussels which struck him were the magnificence of the cathedral, the sweetness of the oysters, and the excellence of the *pâté de grenouilles*, which was, he said, 'sublime'. In Mainz he dwells on the pleasures of wine. 'The governor allows us to debauch to the utmost and Hochheimer, Johannisberg Rudesheimer, Assmanshausen, and a thousand other varieties are unsealed and floored with equal rapidity.' The letters show a sharpness of observation and a satirical eye which anticipate the author of *Vivian Grey*. They also show much of the brashness, conceit and affectation which critics were to discern in the same work.

Disraeli maintained in retrospect that it was during his tour of the Rhine that he decided to give up the law as a career. 'I determined when descending those magical waters that I would not be a lawyer.' As with many of Disraeli's recollections, this is slightly misleading. He did indeed abandon the plan to become a solicitor. He did not return to Frederick Place and he gave up his articles in 1825. But whether as a compromise with his father's 'feeble effort for Oxford', or for other reasons, he made the gesture of reading for the Bar and was admitted on November 18, 1824, as a student of Lincoln's Inn.[2] But it is probably true that in his own mind he had abandoned either branch of the law by the autumn of 1824, and that he was already brooding on a brisker means of securing fame and fortune.

[1] Copious extracts appear in M. & B., i, 42–53.
[2] M. & B., i, 115, wrongly puts the date as April 1827. Gladstone became a student of the same Inn later, but neither of the two great rivals was called to the Bar.

CHAPTER II
'The Hour of Adventure'
1824–6

1

The two years which followed Disraeli's return from his tour of the Rhine saw the first great crisis of his life. The 'hour of adventure' had indeed arrived and he plunged with a recklessness which, when every allowance is made for his temperament and youth, remains astounding. His fortunes fluctuated with wild rapidity. But in the end his luck failed, and at an age when most of his contemporaries would hardly have left the university he found himself burdened with a load of debt and a dubious reputation, which were to affect his career for many years to come.

His frame of mind in the autumn of 1824 may perhaps be reconstructed from *Vivian Grey*.[1]

And now . . . this stripling who was going to begin his education had all the experience of a matured mind – of an experienced man; was already a cunning reader of human hearts; and felt conscious from experience that his was a tongue which was born to guide human beings. The idea of Oxford to such an individual was an insult . . . THE BAR – pooh! law and bad jokes till we are forty; and then with the most brilliant success the prospect of gout and a coronet . . . THE SERVICES in war time are fit only for desperadoes (and that truly am I); but, in peace, are fit only for fools. THE CHURCH is more rational . . . I should certainly like to act Wolsey; but the thousand and one chances against me! And truly I feel *my* destiny should not be on a chance. Were I the son of a Millionaire or a noble I might have *all* . . .

Such was the general tenor of Vivian's thoughts, until nursing himself almost into madness, he at last made, as he conceived, the GRAND DISCOVERY. 'Riches are power', says the Economist:— and is not *Intellect*? asks the philosopher. And yet while the influence of the Millionaire is instantly felt in all classes of society, how is it that 'Noble Mind' so often leaves us unknown and unhonoured?

[1] *Vivian Grey* (1st edition, 1826), Bk I, ch. 8 and 9 (7 and 8 in revised edition, 1853).

The answer, Vivian concludes, is that men of intellect do not study the human nature of ordinary mankind.

> . . . Yes we must mix with the herd; we must enter into their feelings; we must humour their weaknesses; we must sympathise with the sorrows we do not feel; and share the merriment of fools. Oh yes! to *rule* men we must *be* men . . . Mankind then is my great game.

Vivian conveys part of these sentiments to his father, who warns him against trying to 'become a great man in a hurry'.

> . . . Here dashed by the gorgeous equipage of Mrs. Ormolu, the wife of a man who was working all the gold and silver mines in Christendom. 'Ah! my dear Vivian,' said Mr. Grey, 'it is *this* which has turned all your brains . . . This thirst for sudden wealth it is, which engenders the extravagant conceptions, and fosters that wild spirit of speculation which is now stalking abroad . . . Oh my son the wisest has said 'He that maketh haste to be rich shall not be innocent.' Let us step into Clarke's and take an ice.[1]

But the ice cooled the blood of neither the fictitious nor the real Vivian Grey. Disraeli was determined to make a fortune and impatient to become independent of his family. He had already begun to speculate on the Stock Exchange together with a fellow solicitor's clerk called Evans. The two young men now resolved to play for higher stakes. A third partner by the name of Messer, the son of a rich stockbroker, went in with them. For some time past the stock market had been booming; and at this particular moment the most promising field seemed to be that in which Mr Ormolu specialized, the shares of mining companies, those of South America in particular. Finance and politics were closely connected, for everything depended on the success of the rebellions in these former Spanish colonies. Canning's famous dispatch in March 1824, and his known desire – contrary to the opinions of the King and Lord Eldon – to recognize the new republics made him the hero of the whole commercial interest.

At first Disraeli and his fellow financiers had speculated for the fall. Their instinct was right, for most of the companies concerned were thoroughly unsound. But when the republics were at last recognized, just after Christmas 1824, there was such a boom that

[1] Bk I, ch. 9 (8 in 1853 edition).

they lost their nerve and became 'bulls' at precisely the wrong moment. It was hardly surprising. The Anglo-Mexican Mining Association's shares rose from £33 on December 10 to £158 on January 11, and those of the Colombian Mining Association, whose prospectus was drafted by Messrs Swain, Maples & Co., from £19 to £82. Both were promoted by J. & A. Powles, a leading firm of South American merchants, and Disraeli came into active contact with J. D. Powles, the principal partner. His optimism may well have encouraged Disraeli's speculations. But mid-January saw the high point of the mining-share market. No great profit was to be made thereafter, and from April onwards values began gradually to fall. The adverse balance against Disraeli and his partners, who were, of course, operating on the margin throughout, rose from £400 at the end of 1824 to £7,000 by June 1825. Of this about half had been paid by Evans in cash. It is uncertain how much of this debt was Disraeli's, for the surviving accounts are obscure and do not show the proportions.[1] Even if we assume that his share was one-third, the sum far exceeded his means. It was the origin of the financial embarrassments that were to encumber him for the rest of his life. He did not settle finally with Messer till 1849, and then only in response to a quasi-blackmailing letter.[2]

Powles had the strongest motive for encouraging public confidence in the South American boom now that limited liability had resulted in wide ownership of shares, but at this juncture official warnings began to come from the Government. Lord Liverpool, the Prime Minister, advised caution, and Lord Eldon threatened promotors with the penalties of the Bubble Act of 1820. Powles accordingly wrote a pamphlet to counteract these jeremiads. But his style was that of most businessmen. No one read it. He accordingly enlisted Disraeli. In so far as the latter had any regular employment since leaving Messrs Swain other than speculation on the Stock Exchange, it was as reader and assistant to John Murray. He edited a life of Paul Jones for Murray, which came out at the end of 1825 and performed other services. Murray was involved in some sort of partnership with Disraeli in mining shares and was not unwilling to publish on commission pamphlets in their favour.[3] Early

[1] Hughenden Papers, Box 17, A/V/A/1–9.
[2] See below, p. 268–9.
[3] Hughenden Papers, not catalogued, copy of declaration, n.d., that the mining shares and all other certificates 'in this iron box' are held by Murray and Disraeli in proportion of two-thirds and one-third respectively.

in March there appeared Disraeli's first authentic work, an anonymous pamphlet of nearly a hundred pages, entitled *An Enquiry into the Plans Progress and Policy of the American Mining Companies*. Couched in grave tones of apparent impartiality and appealing to high principles of liberty and national prosperity, it was in reality an elaborate puff for South American mining companies in general, and those promoted by J. and A. Powles in particular. A second pamphlet rapidly followed, called *Lawyers and Legislators*, or *Notes on the American Mining Companies*. Disraeli attacked the recent dicta of Lord Eldon, and denounced Alexander Baring and John Cam Hobhouse, who had presumed to cast doubt in the House of Commons upon the soundness of the prevalent gambling mania.

He ended on a lofty note, describing himself as

> one whose opinions are unbiased by self-interest and uncontrolled by party influence, who, whatever may be the result, will feel some satisfaction, perchance some pride, that at a time when . . . Ignorance was the ready slave of Interest, and Truth was deserted by those who should have been her stoutest champions, there was at least one attempt to support sounder principles, and inculcate a wiser policy.

Disraeli's third and final mining pamphlet was entitled *The Present State of Mexico*. The main part of the text was a translation of a report laid before the Mexican Congress by Don Lucas Alaman, Minister for Home and Foreign Affairs, who was being paid, on the side, by the mining companies in order to look after their interests. He was described by Disraeli, who contributed a high-flown introduction, as a 'pure and practical patriot'.

It is impossible to say how far Disraeli believed in the correctness of his own statements in these pamphlets. What is certain is that the companies which he puffed were worthless concerns based on fraud or at best folly. For one destined to be a master of the art of fiction, this literary début was perhaps not inappropriate, but it was an odd beginning for a future Chancellor of the Exchequer.

Thirteen years later Gladstone's first book appeared, also under the imprint of John Murray. It was entitled *The Church in its Relations with the State*.

2

Disraeli now proceeded to involve himself in a new and in the end equally disastrous venture. John Murray had toyed for some years with the idea of starting a daily newspaper as well as his highly successful *Quarterly Review*. In retrospect he doubted whether he would have taken the plunge but for Disraeli, to whose 'unrelenting excitement and importunity' he later described himself as having 'yielded'.[1] But by then everything had gone wrong. An experienced Scottish businessman of forty-six would not have acceded to the importunity of a flamboyant youth of twenty if he had not already been more than half converted to the project on his own account. The new paper was to be Canningite, of course. Perhaps it was expected to achieve what the pamphlets had failed to achieve. Powles was in on the business from the start and a letter from Disraeli among the Murray Papers shows the publisher's interest in mining shares. 'Be easy about your mines – we were more behind the scenes than I even imagined.'[2] On August 3 a memorandum was drawn up under which Murray agreed to supply half and Powles and Disraeli one-quarter each of the capital required to start the new paper.[3] How Disraeli supposed that he could produce the money is one of the puzzles of the affair. It is no less strange that Murray and Powles should have relied on him – he was legally still an infant – and one can only explain the transaction in the light of the commercial euphoria that swept London at the time.[4]

Equally strange was the dilatory manner in which Murray now proceeded. He planned to start publication on November 1, but it was not until the second week of September that anything was done about the managerial side of the new paper. Disraeli posted up to Edinburgh on September 12 to persuade J. G. Lockhart, Sir Walter Scott's son-in-law, to become . . . what? It is far from clear. Evidently not editor, for this was regarded as socially degrading in the case of a daily paper. He was apparently to be manager, and contributor, too, with perhaps some form of editorial control. It may be that Disraeli was none too clear about the matter himself.

[1] See below, p. 47.
[2] Dated simply 'May, 1825', Murray Papers.
[3] Samuel Smiles, *Memoir of John Murray* (2 vols, 1891), ii, 186.
[4] There are many obscurities in the history of the founding of the newspaper. I am obliged to Mr R. W. Stewart for allowing me to consult his unpublished account of the episode, which clears up some of them.

He bore with him a letter from a lawyer called Wright, who seems to have advised Murray on these matters and had already written direct to Lockhart giving the erroneous impression that Canning wished Lockhart to edit the new paper.[1] When Disraeli called on Lockhart at Chiefswood, his house near Melrose, Lockhart showed such palpable surprise that he had to explain it away by saying that he had expected Isaac D'Israeli. Letters from Wright and Murray had already made it obvious who Disraeli was, but Lockhart, a stiff, formal, middle-aged young man, was probably too astounded at the sight of this exotic boy to conceal his feelings. However, he treated Disraeli with civility, introduced him to Sir Walter at Abbotsford, and put him up at Chiefswood for over a fortnight.

Disraeli kept Murray informed of negotiations in a series of letters which only add to the mystery of the story. He devised a code (which he sometimes forgot to keep). 'M from Melrose' was Lockhart, 'The Chevalier' Sir Walter, 'O' was 'The Political Puck', i.e. Disraeli himself, and 'X' was 'a certain personage on whom we called one day, who lives a slight distance from town and who was then unwell'.[2] It is usually assumed that 'X' was Canning, but it is hard to believe that if so Disraeli would have said nothing at all about such a visit in his various published and unpublished reminiscences. On the other hand, if 'X' was not Canning, who was he?

In his third letter to Murray, probably written on September 21 he launched into what seems a world of pure fantasy. Lockhart is to be found a seat in Parliament. He must when he comes to town be convinced that 'through Powles all America and the Commercial Interest is at our back . . . that the Ch.[3] [Church] is firm; that the West India Interest will pledge themselves; that such men as Barrow &c &c are *distinctly in our power* . . .' Lockhart is 'not to be an Editor of a Newspaper but the Directeur General of an immense organ, and at the head of a band of high bred gentlemen and important interests . . .' There are references to 'X' and to Disraeli's ability to organize 'in the interest with which I am now engaged, a *most immense party* and a *most serviceable one*'.[4] This sounds as if some sort of Canningite faction was envisaged, but it may well have existed only in Disraeli's imagination. The project of

[1] Lockhart Papers (National Library of Scotland).
[2] Smiles, *Murray*, ii, 189.
[3] Murray Papers. Samuel Smiles, *Memoir of John Murray* (2 vols, 1891), ii, 191, conjectures 'Chevalier', but this makes nonsense.
[4] Murray Papers. Nearly all of the letter appears in M. & B., i, 64–66.

a seat for Lockhart is never mentioned again and the whole story becomes even odder when at the end of the month Lockhart, with his father-in-law's full support, wrote a letter to Murray refusing what had not been offered – the editorship of the new organ,[1] although from the start Wright had made it quite clear that they were not asking him to take on that post.

It is hard to avoid the impression that, in spite of his own account to Murray, Disraeli had somehow muddled matters. Although Murray regarded him as his 'right hand' and praised him highly to Lockhart as 'a good scholar, hard student, deep thinker . . . and a complete man of business . . . worthy of any degree of confidence that you may be induced to repose in him',[2] a letter from Wright to Lockhart rings more truly.

> . . . whatever our friend Disraeli may say or flourish on this subject, your accepting of the Editorship of a newspaper would be *infra dig* . . . but not so as I think the accepting of the Editorship of the *Quarterly Review* . . . Disraeli who is with you I have not seen much of, but I believe he is a sensible clever young fellow; his judgment however wants sobering down; he has never had to struggle with a single difficulty nor to act in any affairs in which his mind has necessarily been called on to consider and choose in difficult situations. At present his chief exertions as to matters of decision have been with regard to the selection of his food, his employment, and his clothing and, though he is honest and, I take it, wiser than his father, he is inexperienced and untried in the world, and of course, though you may, I believe, safely trust to his integrity, you cannot prudently trust much to his judgment . . .[3]

Meanwhile, without telling Disraeli, Murray offered Lockhart the editorship of the *Quarterly*, a very different proposition, which brought him hurrying down to London. He was to have £1,000 a year and several hundreds more for articles, and he also agreed to contribute to the new daily in return for a minimum of £1,500. He quickly clinched this excellent bargain.

Disraeli was now busy in London making arrangements for the daily paper – and none too soon. It could not now come out in November, but might at the New Year. His cousin George Basevi was to be architect for the new offices in Great George Street.

[1] Smiles, *Murray*, ii, 196.
[2] Walter Scott, *Familiar Letters* (2 vols, 1890), ii, 405.
[3] Lockhart Papers, October 3.

Disraeli conferred with lawyers and printers, engaged correspondents. 'Private intelligence from a family of distinction in Washington' was to come 'by every packet'. 'Mr. Briggs the great Alexandrian merchant' would answer for Egypt. A Herr Maas whom he had met at Coblenz would send gossip about English travellers in Germany. The Provost of Oriel (Copleston) would be correspondent for the universities.[1]

Disraeli was proud of one *coup*. He secured the services of Dr Maginn as their representative in Paris. But the doctor, an entertaining Irish scamp who also wrote under the pseudonym of Morgan O'Doherty, was a most undesirable choice. He drank like a fish, was in debt to Murray, and later, writing for Westmacott's *Age*, engaged in the worst sort of blackmailing journalism. He took Disraeli in by first professing grave doubts and then appearing to be suddenly converted. 'The Dr. started in his chair like Giovanni in the banquet scene and . . . ended by saying that as to the success of the affair doubt could not exist,' Disraeli complacently told Lockhart. 'In brief the Dr. goes to Paris and Murray acquits him (this au secret) of his little engagement.'[2] Alas, it was a case of the biter bitten. Maginn's blarney defeated Disraeli's eloquence. He went to Paris, ran up new debts to replace those cancelled by Murray, drank much, and wrote little. Brought back to London to edit the lighter side of the paper, which certainly needed enlivening, he gave offence by his frivolities and hastened its demise.

That Disraeli with his youthful exuberance should have been wildly optimistic about the prospect is scarcely surprising. More remarkable is the enthusiasm of his hard-headed elders. Powles appears to have been confident. Murray, though he had occasional misgivings, wrote to Scott that he was 'certain . . . of inevitable success', and to a friend, William Jerdan, that 'I have never attempted anything with more considerate circumspection'. Isaac D'Israeli, too, was sanguine enough at the time, though he denied it later. Writing to Murray on October 9 he says:

. . . never did the first season of blossoms promise a richer gathering. But he [Benjamin] has not the sole merit for you share it with him in the grand view you take of the capability of the new intellectual Steam Engine. You have already secured such Coadjutors as no publisher has had before . . . You will put out

[1] Murray Papers.
[2] Lockhart Papers, Disraeli to Lockhart, October 1825.

the other lights without any wish to do them that disservice but merely by outshining them.[1]

Scott was less enthusiastic. From the very beginning he seems to have been mildly sceptical about the newspaper and, though he approved of his son-in-law editing the *Quarterly*, he had no confidence whatever in the consistency or determination of Murray.[2]

Half-way through November, Murray sent Disraeli on a second mission to Abbotsford. 'The most timorous of all God's booksellers' had become nervous about the appointment of Lockhart,[3] which he had endeavoured to keep dark for the time being, not even informing the current editor, J. T. Coleridge. But the story leaked out and a cabal of the *Quarterly*'s old guard led by Barrow were on the warpath. Disraeli's task was to persuade Sir Walter to reassure them. Scott, as he puts it in his journal, was not very willing 'to tell all and sundry that my son-in-law is not a slanderer or a silly thoughtless lad', but he did in the end write a sort of open letter to Murray.[4] Disraeli seems to have botched his job as an ambassador, for he spilled the story to Lockhart himself, who was back in Scotland and was naturally perturbed to find his position less safe than he believed. He wrote at once to Murray, who was furious with Disraeli, but the quarrel was soon composed, and Disraeli defended 'the Emperor' to Lockhart:

Do not think Murray's conduct in this last affair wavering and inconsistent. His situation has been very trying. You and he have never rightly understood each other . . . When such connections were about to be formed between two men, they should have become acquainted, not by the stimulus of wine. There should have been some interchange of sentiment and feelings. The fault I know was not yours; the result however was bad. All men have their sober moments, and Murray in his is a man of pure and honourable, I might say elevated, sentiments.[5]

What with Murray's hesitation, Disraeli's inexperience, and Powles's financial distractions which were soon to end in disaster, it

[1] Murray Papers.

[2] H. J. C. Grierson, *Letters of Sir Walter Scott* (Centenary edition, 12 vols, 1932–7), ix, 290 and n. 296.

[3] Lockhart was a controversial character. His satirical lampoons in *Blackwood's* a few years earlier had caused Murray to terminate his partnership in that journal – which makes his choice of Lockhart for the *Quarterly* all the odder.

[4] Sir Walter Scott, *Familiar Letters* (2 vols, Edinburgh, 1890), i, 21.

[5] Grierson, ix, 290 n.

is hardly surprising that the new paper's birth pangs were prolonged.

Although there might have been a public for a new Tory organ, if
it had been well run, Murray and his allies had entered on to the field
with little or no idea of the difficulties involved. It was all very well
Murray's declaring to Lockhart that '*The Times* has offended everyone so much last week that Mr. P. told us there was scarcely a knot
of merchants – Rothschild was at the head of one knot – which did
not talk of setting up a paper'.[1] People have often said this, but *The
Times* somehow goes on. A rival organ, to have a chance, had to be
well organized, lively and interesting. At this stage the partners
had not even decided its name, Lockhart upon whom they obviously
depended for articles and advice, had not yet arrived in London,
there was no real editor, and the printing presses seemed unlikely
to be ready in time.

In the end Disraeli christened the paper. 'I am delighted, and
what is more satisfied with Disraeli's title – the *Representative*',
wrote Lockhart, now at last in London, to Murray on December 21.
'If Mr. Powles does not produce some thundering objection, let this
be fixed in God's name.'[2] But already the prospect of success had
begun to recede. At the end of October the market in South American mines slumped. At the end of November a prominent Plymouth
bank failed. By the middle of December panic reigned in the city
and a large number of people were ruined. Among them were
Powles and Disraeli; ruined, moreover, at precisely the moment that
they were required to provide their proportion of the capital of the
Representative. Powles failed because he had made personal loans
of £120,000 to the various South American republics and lost every
penny. According to a letter from his daughter to Monypenny, he
later recovered and paid his creditors twenty shillings in the pound
plus interest at 5 per cent.[3] Moreover, his friendship with Disraeli
was resumed in the 'fifties when the latter, as his papers show,
corresponded with him as a leading City Conservative. But in the
late 1850s he failed again, this time irretrievably.

Smiles in his life of Murray states categorically that Disraeli and
Powles did not pay their share of the capital for the *Representative*.[4]
It is hard to see how Disraeli ever could have done so. But whereas
Powles seems to have continued to correspond with Murray in the

---

[1] Lockhart Papers.   [2] Smiles, *Murray*, ii, 206.
[3] Hughenden Papers, Box 301.   [4] Smiles, ii, 207.

capacity of a partner for another two months, Disraeli abruptly vanished from the counsels of the *Representative*. The reason for this difference is far from clear. Perhaps Murray continued to have hopes of money from Powles, after he had ceased to have any hope from Disraeli.

The paper, which did not begin publication till January 25, was a total failure from the start. Its first number was atrociously edited, three exclusive items of news were so concealed that no one could find them, and the leaders were, in the words of Crofton Croker, one of Murray's writers, 'tedious to a degree and intolerably long'. Such attempts as were made to brighten up later numbers failed dismally. 'Lord's mercy,' wrote Scott to his daughter, Mrs Lockhart, 'its jokes put me in mind of the child's question whether a pound of feathers or a pound of lead is the heaviest.' The economic depression no doubt made such a venture hopeless, but it is unlikely that the *Representative* would have been a success even in more propitious circumstances. Left with sole responsibility, and harassed by worries, Murray sank into gloom and refused to answer letters. Even the general election of the early summer did nothing to revive the paper's fortunes. It ceased publication on July 29, 1826, Murray having lost £26,000.

Disraeli did not look back on his part in the paper with any satisfaction. When he became celebrated frequent attempts were made by his enemies to assert that he had been the editor of a journal that had miserably failed. This, of course, he could and did deny with truth. But he considered it unnecessary to explain what his real connexion was with the paper, and no one could have guessed from his denials that he had been Murray's 'right hand' in promoting it, nor that he had been for a time part-proprietor of 'the new intellectual steam engine'.[1] In after years he jotted down some reminiscences about his two visits to Scotland, with a vivid description of Sir Walter at Abbotsford, and an account of how after the second visit he travelled down to London with Constable, the great publisher then 'on the point of a most fatal and shattering bankruptcy',[2] but he gives no hint whatever of the mission which

[1] See letter to a Mr L'Espinasse, March 27, 1860, Hughenden Papers, Box 26, A/X/B/1, in which Disraeli denies editing the paper and attributes the allegation to Lockhart, who, he says, was the editor and 'an expert in all the nebulous chicanery of these literary intrigues'. He also denied that his father's breach with Murray had anything to do with him. It is a very misleading letter.

[2] See M. & B., i, 77–78, where the passage is printed in full.

took him to the north. He did not believe in dwelling upon failure,
and he was good at burying the past.

3

Disraeli's feelings on being excluded from any further part in the
Representative may only be conjectured: it must have been a disagreeable shock. A few weeks earlier he had been the associate of
city magnates, the ambassador to Abbotsford, the borough-monger
fixing up Lockhart with a seat, the ally – at one remove – of Canning; he was now simply a young man out of work and in debt. But
he possessed resilience and energy. He had failed to acquire wealth
or power, but he might still acquire fame – and some much-needed
cash – by the use of his pen.

The exact genesis of *Vivian Grey* is uncertain. Years later
Disraeli maintained that it had been completed before he was
twenty-one, i.e. before December 21, at Hyde House, a place near
Amersham rented by his father for the autumn of 1825. But this
is incredible. No one, however energetic, could have written a novel
of 80,000 words in four months, when swamped with business, as
Disraeli was from August to December, and the second volume
(Books 3 and 4 of the ordinary editions of today) is in large part a
thinly disguised account of that very business; it must have been
written afterwards – in the early months of 1826. 'As hot and hurried a sketch as ever yet was penned,' Disraeli himself described it.[1]

Hyde House did have a connexion with the novel. Its owner,
Robert Plumer Ward,[2] had published anonymously during 1825
Tremaine or the Man of Refinement, which was the model upon
which Disraeli based his own book. Isaac D'Israeli rented Hyde
House through a solicitor, Benjamin Austen, whose wife Sara was
an ambitious, clever, attractive and childless blue stocking.[3]
Husband and wife were both in the secret of *Tremaine* and Austen
acted as Ward's agent in placing the book with the publisher Col-

[1] Contarini Fleming wrote 'Manstein', which evidently disguises *Vivian Grey*, in
seven days, but there is no need to take this literally. The evidence from which
Mr Lucien Wolf concludes that Disraeli did not begin till after February 14 also seems
unconvincing. But the book, particularly Volume ii, shows every sign of having been
hastily written.

[2] 1765–1846. Minor politician and novelist; son of John Ward, a Gibraltar merchant,
and Rebecca Raphael, who was of Spanish Jewish descent.

[3] The part played by the Austens in Disraeli's life has been treated very fully by
B. R. Jerman in his *The Young Disraeli* (1960).

burn, another of his clients. *Tremaine* was perhaps the first-so-called 'society novel' to be published in England, and it has a certain historical importance; by inspiring both Disraeli and Bulwer it set the tone which was to dominate English novel-writing for over twenty years. The mark of this particular form of novel sometimes called 'silver-fork fiction' was not merely that the characters came from high life. There was nothing new in that. The feature of *Tremaine*, of the novels of Theodore Hook, and Mrs Gore, and of the early novels of Disraeli and Bulwer was that they described, or purported to describe, the beau-monde correctly – their clothes, their houses, their furniture and their conversation. Accuracy and verisimilitude were at a premium for the first time.

The years after Waterloo were a period of immorality, ostentation, luxury, extravagance and snobbery – or, to be accurate, for such generalizations are rash, they presented this aspect to the observer of the square mile that constituted the heart of fashionable London. A whole class of new rich sought to mingle on equal terms with an aristocracy that possessed power, prestige and wealth unsurpassed in Europe. Novels which depicted with seeming familiarity, and often under thin disguise, the behaviour of persons in the grand world were certain to be popular – among the outsiders because they wished to read about the insiders, and among the insiders because they liked to read about themselves.

The publisher who cashed in on this vogue was Henry Colburn, a shrewd man of business and an adept at the art of 'puffery'. The essence of this was to publish the book anonymously, hint that the author moved in the highest circles of society, suggest a 'key' for the characters (often a bogus one) and, if the author really was a man of fashion, discreetly allow his name to leak out at a suitable moment after the novel had been launched. This technique, together with the genuine merits of the book, made *Tremaine* the novel of the year.

No leakage was needed for the Disraeli family to know its authorship. Isaac read his landlord's novel in manuscript. The Austens formed another link, and it was natural that when Benjamin decided to try his luck at literature he should have written a 'silver fork' novel modelled on *Tremaine*, and, using Sara Austen as reader, amanuensis and agent, should have published it with Colburn. She seems to have plunged into the business with the greatest enthusiasm. In order to keep the author's name secret even from Colburn, she copied the manuscript in her own hand. She made suggestions and criticisms. She negotiated the contract. It is hard to believe that she was not at least half in love with Disraeli. A letter from her has survived in which after some polite commonplaces in ordinary writing she abruptly changed into a cipher:

> I cannot continue my note thus coldly. My shaking hand will tell that I am nervous with the shock of your illness. *What is the matter?* For God's sake take care of yourself. I dare not say for my sake do so, nor can I scold you for your note now you are ill. So indeed I must pray. Do everything that you are desired. If without risk you can come out tomorrow, let me see you at twelve or any hour which will suit you better. I shall not leave the house till I have seen you. I shall be miserably anxious till I do . . . May God bless you and grant your recovery to my anxious prayers; my spirits are gone till you bring a renewal of them . . .[1]

For years afterwards she was his willing slave and her husband his less-willing creditor. In 1834 he airily demanded some research into the subject of the south-west wind for 'a grand simile' in a poem he was writing. 'Get it up by the 16th,' he ends his letter. 'My dear Ben,' Sara replies, 'I am always most happy to have an opportunity of being useful to you.'

In the latter half of February, Disraeli submitted a part of his manuscript to her for the first time. She was delighted with it. 'I have now gone through it twice and the more I read the better I am pleased . . .' 'Trouble', she added, 'is an odious word which shall henceforth be banished from our vocabulary.'[2] This letter was written on February 25, and haste was all the more necessary because Sara Austen knew that a second novel by Ward – *De Vere or the Man of Independence* – was on the way (it was, in fact, not published till the following year) and it was important for Disraeli to get in first. Colburn accepted the manuscript before he saw it, but having done so was enthusiastic. He agreed to pay £200 and at once set his puffing machine into action. He controlled the *New Monthly Magazine* and had an interest in *Literary Gazette*, and Theodore Hook, the editor of *John Bull*, was in his pocket. He also had an interest in the *Sunday Times*. Through these and other organs news of an impending novel, 'a sort of Don Juan in prose'

[1] Hughenden Papers, Box 12, A/IV/D/2, n.d. Deciphered and published by R. W. Stewart, 'The Publication and Reception of Vivian Grey', *Cornhill Magazine*, October 1960.

[2] ibid., Box 12, A/IV/D/4, dated '25th'.

written by a Society personage, began to circulate early in April.

There is nothing to show that Colburn 'puffed' *Vivian Grey* more than was his normal practice with any new novel, and there is no evidence to suggest, as has often been alleged, that Disraeli personally took any part in the process. But *Vivian Grey* undoubtedly received plenty of advance publicity. One day, so Cyrus Redding, the *New Monthly*'s editor records in his autobiography, he called on Colburn in his office in New Burlington Street. 'By the by', said the publisher, 'I have a capital book out – *Vivian Grey*. The authorship is a great secret – a man of high fashion – very high – keeps the first society. I can assure you it is a most piquant and spirited work, quite sparkling.' On April 22, in the same week that saw the publication of Scott's *Woodstock* and Fenimore Cooper's *The Last of the Mohicans*, the much-advertised novel appeared in two anonymous octavo volumes.

4

To understand the effect of *Vivian Grey* upon Disraeli's reputation and career it is important to read the original edition of 1826.[1] Most modern readers are acquainted with it only in the drastically revised version of 1853 which is the basis of nearly all the subsequent editions. In the course of time Disraeli became much ashamed of his first novel. He would have liked to exclude it altogether from the 1853 edition of his collected works, but he compromised by pleading indulgence from the public and cutting out not only phrases and locutions but chapters, scenes, and characters which he felt betrayed the author's youth, brashness and general impudence – particularly those which showed that he was not in 1826 the man of the world which he later became.[2]

Few people at twenty-one can be expected to write anything but an autobiography. *Vivian Grey* is the story of the *Representative* transposed from the journalistic to the political key. Vivian himself is the young Benjamin; his father, Horace, is Isaac. Whatever ingenious defenders of Disraeli may say, there can be no doubt that

[1] The easiest way of doing this today is to obtain the excellent Centenary Edition (1905), edited by Lucien Wolf, who prints the first edition of 1826 and provides a spirited, though not always accurate, biographical introduction. In an appendix Wolf indicates the main changes made by Disraeli in 1853. Unhappily the Centenary Edition appears to have been discontinued after one more novel, *The Young Duke*.

[2] Disraeli similarly 'bowdlerized' some of his other early novels, in particular *The Young Duke* and *Henrietta Temple*.

Vivian with his recklessness, lack of scruple, devouring ambition and impudent effrontery is a self-portrait. Some years later, in that curious fragmentary diary which he kept between 1833 and 1836, Disraeli wrote:

> In *Vivian Grey* I have portrayed my active and real ambition. In *Alroy* my ideal ambition. The P.R. [Psychological Romance, the alternative title of *Contarini Fleming*] is a developm^t of my Poetic character. This Trilogy is the secret history of my feelings – I shall write no more about myself.[1]

No doubt he had in mind the *Vivian Grey* of the first three books – not the rather absurd figure of melodrama who figures at the end of the fourth – but otherwise this seems as plain a statement as one could need, written in a diary which Disraeli probably intended no one to see in his lifetime, moreover written seven years later when he had had plenty of time to reflect. Against this, the disclaimers, which appear in the preface to the second part of *Vivian Grey*, published in the aftermath of the uproar caused by the first, carry no great weight.[2]

Vivian's schooldays, his deep reading in his father's library, his refusal to go to Oxford, his 'devil of a tongue', his discovery that 'there is no fascination so irresistible to a boy as the smile of a married woman' – all are pure Disraeli. Then he resolves to make his fortune:

> At this moment how many a powerful noble wants only wit to be a Minister; and what wants Vivian Grey to attain the same end? That noble's influence . . . Supposing I am in contact with this magnifico, am I prepared? Now let me probe my very soul. Does my cheek blanch? I have the mind for the conception; and I can perform right skilfully upon the most splendid of musical instruments – the human voice – to make these conceptions beloved by others. There wants but one thing more – courage, pure, perfect courage; – and does Vivian Grey know fear? He laughed an answer of bitterest derision.[3]

His magnifico is the Marquess of Carabas, who holds a grand sinecure, but has lost all effective power. This prosy, politically

---

[1] Hughenden Papers, Box 11, A/III/C.

[2] For the contrary argument, see Lucien Wolf's introduction to *Vivian Grey*, xxxvi–xxxix, and for a compromise view Monypenny (i, 87–91), who is at much pains to argue that the Vivian Grey who lapses into a heartless villain at the end of Book IV is not a self-portrait. Surely no sensible person would argue otherwise.

[3] *Vivian Grey*, Bk I, ch. 9 (8 in the 1853 edition).

disappointed and – in the original edition of the book – tipsy mediocrity is induced by Vivian, whose charm captivates him, his wife, his friends and his toadies, to engage in the formation of a new party, reminiscent of that 'most immense party' in Disraeli's letters to John Murray, which will restore him to power. One of its members is 'Lord Beaconsfield – a very worthy gentleman but between ourselves a damned fool'. It is, however, essential to have a leader in the House of Commons. Vivian does not undertake this role himself, just as Disraeli did not seek the editorship of the *Representative*, but he offers to go on a mission to persuade one Cleveland, who after a brief but brilliant career in Parliament has forsaken the world for the 'luxuries of a *cottage ornée*, in the most romantic part of the Principality [of Wales]'.

Cleveland, who is clearly Lockhart,[1] just as Carabas, despite all denials, must be Murray, gives Vivian a reception which is 'cold and constrained in the extreme'. But before long all is well, Cleveland is persuaded, the new party is on the point of being formed, when Mrs Lorraine, the Marquess's equivocal sister-in-law (alleged without much basis to be a portrait of Lady Caroline Lamb), whose amorous advances have been repulsed by Vivian, ruins the whole plan by poisoning the minds of the chief plotters against the author of the plot. Even as Vivian discourses on 'political gastronomy' to the Marquess, letters arrive from the other members of the party repudiating their allegiance, and finally the Marquess himself receives his dismissal from the sinecure office which he holds. He rounds in a fury on Vivian, who departs to take vengeance on Mrs Lorraine, falsely telling her that he has counteracted her machinations, and is about to become a MP. The result is gratifying.

> When he had ended she sprang from the sofa, and looking up, and extending her arms with unmeaning wildness, she gave one loud shriek, and dropped like a bird shot on the wing – she had burst a blood-vessel.

He then kills Cleveland in a duel and the story ends with a tongue-in-the-cheek passage which Disraeli deleted in the 1853 edition: 'I fear me much that Vivian Grey is a lost man; but I am sure that every sweet and gentle spirit, who has read this sad story of his

---

[1] In the original MS the name is Chiefston, evidently an allusion to Lockhart's house, Chiefswood, which could be fairly described as a '*cottage ornée*'.

fortunes, will breathe a holy prayer this night, for his restoration to society and to himself.'

The plot is highly improbable and too thin to sustain a book of that length. Disraeli, conscious of this, inserted a good deal of irrelevant padding to fill it out. The result is a novel which, in point of form and construction could scarcely be worse, but its vitality and vigour makes it remarkably readable even today. It is infused with an extraordinary compound of reckless satire, youthful worldliness, cynical observation, grandiloquent sentiment, sheer fun and impudence; and the irrelevant digressions, the superfluous minor characters, the inessential scenes and episodes are what give it its flavour.

Vivian Grey had an instant *succès de scandale*. It was discussed in society. There was much speculation about the identity of the characters – and above all about that of the author. Some people were delighted and some furious, but few were bored. Early in May, Plumer Ward wrote to Mrs Austen:

> All are talking of *Vivian Grey*. Its wit, raciness, and boldness are admired; and you would have been not ill-pleased with the re-marks upon particular passages and characters – the dinner at Château Désir particularly, Mrs. Millions,[1] all the women, the two toadies, and universally Stapylton.[2] From the Nugents' account it is much spreading in London, excites curiosity and also resentment . . . It certainly frightens a great many people who expect to be shown up; and you must really be careful of discovering the author . . .[3]

But such secrets are not easy to keep. As long as the author's name remained unknown the reviewers were cautious. Some did indeed observe that there were solecisms and social blunders which could hardly have been made by a man of fashion. One of these was Jerdan, editor of the *Literary Gazette*, who noticed that 'the class of the author is a little betrayed by his frequent references to topics of which the mere man of fashion knows nothing and cares less'. Mrs Austen did her best to prevent the truth emerging. 'Don't be anxious about V.G.', she writes excitedly to Disraeli. 'We'll blind them yet. I have not committed you by even a look – it's only a

---

[1] Mrs Millions was a take-off of Mrs J. D. Powles.

[2] Stapylton Toad, MP, a minor character in the book, a solicitor and borough-monger of obscure origin. It is not clear who was the model, if anyone.

[3] The Hon. E. Phipps, *Memoir of Plumer Ward* (1850), ii, 147.

guess which may be averted'[1] It seems, however, that Jerdan, who knew Murray well and hence the saga of the *Representative*, had somehow guessed the real author, and when once the secret was out the fury of the reviewers knew no bounds.

No doubt in an ideal world critics would be indifferent to the name of an author. A book should be judged on its merits and is equally good whether written by Mr X, Lord Y, or some famous literary figure: likewise if it is bad. But the world is not ideal, and there are passages in *Vivian Grey* which no one could have read in quite the same light after knowing that the author was a youth of twenty-one who had never moved in society. Disraeli found himself the object of a series of ferocious personal attacks. Reviewers in those days were not the urbane and courteous figures which they have become today. Their lives were conducted in a whirlwind of splenetic fury and ceaseless vendettas. Disraeli had to suffer, moreover, not only for his own faults, but for the animosity which Colburn had acquired by his notorious methods.

Blackwood's Magazine[2] denounced 'the shameful and shameless puffery' which had pushed the book forward. The writer was branded as 'an obscure person for whom nobody cares a straw', and the book described as 'a paltry catchpenny'. The *Monthly Magazine*[3] said of the author:

> . . . we shall probably never have to mention his name again. He would perhaps make a useful assistant to old D'Israeli in cutting out paragraphs to manufacture into some other half dozen dull volumes, and add to the 'calamities of authors'; he is evidently incapable of anything better, and his only chance of escaping perpetual burlesque is to content himself with 'wearing his violet-coloured slippers', 'slobbering his Italian greyhound',[4] and sinking suddenly and finally into total oblivion.

Many critics dwelt on a defect of the book, which was particularly mortifying for someone with the ambitions of the young Disraeli, his numerous social blunders or, as one critic put it, 'his most ludicrous affectation of good breeding'. This side of *Vivian Grey* is one that can only be appreciated by those who read the 1826 edition, for Disraeli, who knew the manners of the beau-monde well enough

---

[1] Hughenden Papers, Box 12, A/IV/D/11.

[2] July 1826. Ironically the *London Magazine*, before the author's identity had been established, attributed it to one of the 'Blackwood *click*'.

[3] August 1826.

[4] Disraeli omitted this passage from the 1853 edition.

by 1853, cut most of the solecisms out when he revised the novel. But in the original version there are expressions which almost remind one of the *Young Visiters*: the Marquess 'dashed off a tumbler of Burgundy'; 'the cuisine of Mr. Grey was *superbe*'; 'Her Ladyship . . . was now *passata* although with the aid of cachemeres [*sic*] diamonds and turbans, her *tout ensemble* was still very striking', etc.

The *Literary Magnet* went one stage beyond anyone else. It roundly declared that 'this spark', together with Mrs Austen, had conspired to defraud Colburn, that they had passed off the manuscript as being written by Plumer Ward, and thus secured twice as high a publisher's advance as Disraeli would otherwise have got. Stories to this effect were widely circulated in London literary circles, and it is not inconceivable that Mrs Austen, without uttering any positive falsehood, may have allowed Colburn to gain an incorrect impression about the authorship of the book.

Slashing criticism is disagreeable, even when it can be discounted as the product of malice. The attack in *Blackwood's* particularly dismayed Disraeli. Five years later he described in *Contarini Fleming* the effect of those hostile observations from 'the great critical journal of the north of Europe'.

> With what horror, with what blank despair, with what supreme appalling astonishment did I find myself for the first time in my life the subject of the most reckless, the most malignant, and the most adroit ridicule. I was sacrificed, I was scalped . . . The criticism fell from my hand. A film floated over my vision, my knees trembled. I felt that sickness of heart that we experience in our first scrape. I was ridiculous. It was time to die.

5

There was one quarter in which *Vivian Grey* did its author nothing but harm – the literary and political circle centred round John Murray. He considered that he had been grossly caricatured and that his confidence had been abused. He had good reason to think so. Coming on top of his previous causes for exasperation, *Vivian Grey* must have been the last straw. When it appeared the *Representative* was still in publication, running its sole remaining and solvent proprietor into ever-increasing losses. Murray had already begun to persuade himself that he would never have undertaken the venture but for Disraeli's 'unrelenting importunity'. Then there was his default over the capital. Monypenny in a valiant effort to defend Disraeli underestimates the degree of offence which the book was bound to give. 'Murray,' he says, 'apparently fancied that he had been satirised in the character of the Marquis, though it is not easy to detect the slightest resemblance between them.'[1] But no impartial reader who knew the inner story of the *Representative* could fail to see John Murray as the Marquess of Carabas, any more than he could fail to see Lockhart as Cleveland, Horace Grey as Isaac D'Israeli, Mr and Mrs Millions as Mr and Mrs Powles, etc., and some reviewers did, in fact, comment on these resemblances.

Here again, to appreciate the position it is essential to read the 1826 edition. Murray was a genial host and enjoyed the wine that circulated liberally at his table. In the original edition of *Vivian Grey* we find the Marquess depicted as a timorous and tipsy nincompoop, and it is possible that a scene such as the following, though a crude caricature, was not so very remote from what sometimes occurred at Murray's dinner-table while the *Representative* was being hatched.

We are at dinner at Château Désir, where the new party is being launched. The Marquess addresses the assembly more or less coherently for a sentence or so, then:

> Here the bottle passed, and the Marquess took a bumper. 'My Lords and Gentlemen, when I take into consideration the nature of the various interests, of which the body politic of this great empire is regulated; (Lord Courtown the bottle stops with you) when I observe, I repeat, this, I naturally ask myself what right, what claims, what, what, what – I repeat what right, these governing interests have to the influence which they possess? (Vivian, my boy, you'll find Champagne on the waiter behind you.) Yes, gentlemen it is in this temper (the corkscrew's by Sir Berdmore), it is, I repeat, in this temper, and actuated by these views, that we meet together this day.'[2]

It is significant that in 1853 this and every other allusion to the Marquess's drunkenness was omitted and the whole scene rewritten. But in 1826 John Murray's friends would have had little difficulty in convincing him that the description of the Carabas dinner party was an impudent lampoon and an outrageous breach of trust.

---

[1] M. & B., i, 75.
[2] *Vivian Grey* (1st edition), Bk II, ch. 17 (16 in the 1853 edition).

Moreover, at the very moment of the publication of *Vivian Grey*, Disraeli involved himself in another affair, which, whatever the true facts, undoubtedly enraged Murray and his circle even further. This was the production of a satirical weekly journal called the *Star Chamber*. It only lasted for nine numbers from April 19 to June 7, 1826, and then abruptly ceased publication. *Vivian Grey* appeared three days after the first number, and it is perhaps significant that the printers, who were also printers for Murray, declined to print the second number, which accordingly had to be transferred elsewhere.

Disraeli's part in the journal has always been something of an enigma. He denied on several occasions in later life that he had edited it, but he certainly contributed.[1] The nominal editor and proprietor was one Peter Hall, a Brasenose friend of Meredith through whom he met Disraeli. Meredith was also a contributor. It is difficult to avoid the conclusion that Disraeli was the moving spirit. Nothing that we know of Hall, who later became a parson and edited an antiquarian magazine called *The Crypt*, or of Meredith, who seems to have been a serious-minded, rather grave, young man, suggests that they could have written the satires and lampoons with which the new journal abounded. Whether Disraeli wrote the *Dunciad of To-day*, a long satirical poem which appeared in the later numbers of the magazine, it is impossible to say for certain.[2] But if he did, then Murray had even more cause for annoyance, for it contains a number of wounding hits at him and his friends.

At all events a bitter and prolonged battle now broke out between Murray and the Disraeli family. Writing more in sorrow than in anger, Isaac said:

> In conversation with my son this day I find him so sensibly hurt at a sudden change of your conduct towards him that I cannot but deeply sympathize with his depression . . . I well know your late disappointment but the sole error does not rest with him. You were all inexperienced and it happened that the youngest

[1] He avowedly contributed the *Modern Aesop*, and one or two reviews, but the allegation that the *Star Chamber* was used to puff *Vivian Grey* has no foundation.

[2] Disraeli denied, somewhat indirectly, authorship of the satire, in his preface to Part II of *Vivian Grey*, but this cannot be regarded as conclusive. For a discussion of this question, and the *Star Chamber* generally, see Michael Sadleir, *Benjamin Disraeli: The Dunciad of Today* (1928). Contrary to Monypenny and Lucien Wolf, he decides on internal evidence, style, diction, etc., that Disraeli not only wrote this poem but was the chief inspirer and effective editor of the short-lived journal. He is probably right, although in the absence of any external evidence we cannot be sure.

was most. Without due and proper preparations you expected what with every precaution it might be difficult to provide you with. Time was that you consulted me on such things – I was near you, but I will not say anything about myself . . .[1]

Isaac was curiously forgetful of the recent past. His letters to Murray in the previous autumn were very far from those of a sage counsellor waiting only to be asked in order to warn. Evidently he made no impression on Murray, for on May 21 we find Benjamin writing thus to Mrs Murray:

Mr. Murray has overstepped the bounds which the remembrance of former friendship has too indulgently conceded him, and he has spoke and is now speaking of me to the world generally in terms which to me are as inexplicable as they appear to be out-rageous. Under these circumstances one course apparently is only left to me, and that is of a decided and deplorable nature . . .[2]

Monypenny conjectures that this was a threat of legal action, but from all that we know of the young Disraeli a challenge seems more likely. Nothing, in fact, happened. On the same day Mrs D'Israeli wrote a long and revealing letter to John Murray himself.

May 21   Bloomsbury Sq.

Dear Sir,

Having learnt that my son has written to Mrs. Murray this morning I am now doing what had I pleased myself I should have done some time since, which is to write to you to request an explanation of your conduct which the kindness and pliability of Mr. D'Israeli's character could never obtain, for while you were expressing great friendship, we were constantly hearing of the great losses Mr. Murray had sustained through the mis-management and bad conduct of my son. Surely, Sir, were this story truly told it would not be believed that the experienced publisher of Albermarle Street could be deceived by the plans of a boy of twenty whom you had known from his cradle and whose resources you must have as well known as his father and had you con-descended to consult that father the folly might not have been committed.

You might then Sir perhaps would have found tho' a *clever boy* he was no 'prodigy' and I must say I believe the failure of the *Representative* lay much more with the Proprietor and his Editor than it ever did with my son but I feel your disappointment and can forgive your irritability, yet I must resent your late attack

[1] Murray Papers, dated '3rd', and it must be May 3.
[2] loc. cit.

on Benjamin. What can you mean by saying as an excuse for not meeting D'Israeli that *our son had divulged and made public your secrets* this surely you must know is not truth – and can you as the father of a family think yourself justified in hurting the character and future prospects of a young man to whose Father you subscribe yourself his faithful friend and to whose Mother her most obliged.

I now must beg an explanation of this enigma . . . I really cannot believe John Murray who has so often professed such strong friendship for D'Israeli should be now going about blasting the character of that Friend's son because he had formed in his imagination a *perfect being* and expected impossibilities and found him on trial a mere mortal and a very very young man.

I fear I have made this letter too long and that you will destroy it instead of reading it pray for old friendship do not do that but give me the explanation I so ardently require.

> And believe me ever your
> sincere well wisher
> Maria D'Israeli[1]

Isaac was by no means as supine on this occasion as his wife's letter would suggest. He too bombarded Murray with letters demanding explanations and withdrawals. Like Mrs D'Israeli, he ignored *Vivian Grey* and concentrated on the *Representative*; and he continued to display a singular obliviousness about his own attitude before the ill-fated paper came out. He did, however, deem it wise to repudiate the *Star Chamber*.

He withdrew from a trusteeship which he had undertaken on behalf of his old friend. He returned the books which Murray had given him. He even wrote to Mrs Murray on October 4 threatening to produce a pamphlet on the whole question. This alarmed his friend Sharon Turner, the man who had insisted on the baptizing of his children. He was a friend of Murray also, and he expressed incredulity at Isaac's resolve.

> After reading Benjamin's agreement [with Murray and Powles] of 3rd August, 1825 [he wrote] and your letters to Murray on him and the business, of the 27th September, the 29th September, and the 9th October, my sincere opinion is that you cannot with a due regard to your own reputation, *write* or *publish* anything about it.[2]

He pointed out that Murray would be bound to reply, and that the

---

[1] Murray Papers.   [2] Smiles, *Murray*, ii, 217.

ensuing scandal would damage the D'Israelis far more than it would Murray. At the same time he wrote to Murray trying to persuade him that no one could see any resemblance between him and the Marquess of Carabas. Isaac took his friend's advice and no pamphlet appeared, but there was no genuine reconciliation.[1]

Murray was never again on terms of friendship with either father or son. He did indeed publish two of Benjamin's books later.[2] But there was no cordiality – a purely business relationship of 'Dear Sirs' and letters written in the third person. Murray's final view was expressed in a letter of October 16 to Sharon Turner. After denying that he was annoyed because of the financial loss incurred by 'yielding to [Disraeli's] unrelenting excitement and importunity . . .'[3] he went on in a passage, most of which is omitted for some reason by Smiles in his life of Murray:

> So my complaint against Mr. D'Israeli's son arises solely from the the untruths which he told and for his conduct during, (of which in part I made the discovery subsequently) and at the close of our transactions, and since, and particularly from his outrageous breach of all confidence and of every tie which binds man to man in social life in the publication of *Vivian Grey*. From me his son received nothing but the most unbounded confidence and parental attachment; my fault was in having loved, not wisely but too well. May his parents never have occasion to repent in bitterness the fatal moment when they expressed their approbation of *Vivian Grey*.[4]

This letter shows that Murray had a grievance about Disraeli's conduct over the *Representative* as well as over *Vivian Grey*. But it is not clear what the alleged untruths were. Disraeli came to believe that Lockhart had poisoned Murray's mind, and it is possible that he gave a damaging version of Disraeli's efforts as ambassador to Chiefswood in the autumn. It may be that Croker, Stewart Rose and others lampooned in the *Star Chamber* did their bit, too. But since there was apparently no overt quarrel before the publication of *Vivian Grey*, it seems likely that Disraeli's alleged misconduct

[1] Smiles, ii, 218, says that there was, on the strength of a letter to Murray from Isaac at the end of 1826. But the letter to which he refers is cold and formal in tone and there appears to have been no further correspondence between the two men on the old familiar basis.

[2] *Contarini Fleming*, which was a financial failure, and the *Gallomania*, to which other authors contributed – both published in 1832.

[3] Smiles, ii, 217.

[4] Murray Papers.

over the *Representative* was exaggerated in retrospect by an angry
and much-tried man. What is certain is that Murray had far more
cause for indignation about the novel than Disraeli's partisans have
been ready to concede.

There can be little doubt that Disraeli's career was seriously
affected not merely by the character of the book but by the offence
which it gave to powerful people whose help would have been useful
to him in the 'thirties, when he struggled to make his way into
politics. He acquired a reputation for cynicism, double dealing,
recklessness and insincerity which it took him years to live down.
Murray, Croker and Lockhart were influential persons in the
respectable Tory world. Croker was an intimate friend of Peel until
their famous breach over the Corn Laws. Lockhart for twenty-eight
years edited the *Quarterly*, which was as much the organ of the Tory
'establishment' as the *Edinburgh* of the Whig. He persistently
ignored Disraeli. As late as 1848, when the latter had been a major
political figure for at least two years, and a conspicuous one for a
good deal longer, his name had never even been mentioned in the
Quarterly. Lockhart's attitude of unrelenting hatred is well exemplified by his comment on *Coningsby*: 'That Jew scamp has published
a very blackguard novel.'[1]

In that same 'blackguard novel' Disraeli certainly got his own
back on Croker, whom he held up to immortal ridicule in the
character of Rigby, Lord Monmouth's toady, creature and general
factotum. But he never succeeded in squaring accounts with
Lockhart, although he was under no delusion about his animosity.
They must occasionally have met socially. The only recorded
instance, in 1836 at a dinner party given by Lord Lyndhurst, who
wanted Lockhart to review Disraeli's *Vindication*, was not a success.
'He never spoke a word,' wrote Disraeli to his sister. 'He is known in
society by the name of Viper but if he tries to sting me he will find
my heel of iron.'[2] In fact, Disraeli's one effort to use his heel of iron
had not come off. In a venomous exchange of letters on the subject
of *The Young Duke* in 1832 it was Lockhart who scored, not his
opponent.[3]

For all Disraeli's precocity and genius, he was remarkably blind
to the adverse effect that such a book was bound to have upon his

[1] Andrew Lang, *Life and Letters of J. G. Lockhart* (2 vols, 1896), ii, 199.
[2] M. & B., i, 322.
[3] See below, p. 82.

reputation in the world in which he wished to rise. No one now would regret the publication of *Vivian Grey*, but it is to be doubted whether it did him any good whatever in his lifetime, apart from the seven hundred much-needed pounds that it brought him.[1] The notion that he achieved instant social celebrity and at once became a 'lion' in the drawing-rooms of London is a complete myth, although it has been often repeated. His ascent into society did not even begin for another six years, when he came back from his tour of the Near East in 1832.

Vivian Grey haunted Disraeli to the end. In vain he tried to explain it away as 'a juvenile indiscretion', 'a kind of literary *lusus*', 'a youthful blunder'. In vain he tried to suppress it altogether, and, failing that, to make it reputable by altering the text. It was no use. He might try to laugh it off. He could not live it down. The book went into edition after edition. It seemed to possess the same inextinguishable vitality as its hero. Half a century later the Prime Minister and leader of the Tory party found his first novel quoted against him from the platform to prove that he had never been a true Conservative, and from the pulpit to denounce his moral character. Seldom can a juvenile indiscretion have had more lasting consequences than *Vivian Grey*.

The story of the *Representative* and *Vivian Grey* has been told at some length not only because of its effect on Disraeli's career but because of what it reveals about his character. Much has been written about Disraeli's Jewishness. He later became intensely interested in it himself to the point of being something of a bore on the subject. No doubt it should not be underestimated. But if national or racial stereotypes are to be introduced at all – and they are perilous guides – it is not so much the Jewish as the Italian streak in Disraeli that predominated. The Jews who were rising to the top in Disraeli's day tended to be silent, prudent, high-principled persons of impeccable integrity, who acquired vast wealth, became Masters of Hounds and bought up the Vale of Aylesbury. Their quintessence is represented by Disraeli's later friend Baron Rothschild, who on grounds of principle stood again and again for Parliament until the ban on Jews was removed, and then, having at last got there, sat for fifteen years without opening his mouth.

[1] Part II of *Vivian Grey* produced £500.

The 'hour of adventure' and the story of Disraeli's early life in the next few chapters show how far removed he was from this sort of image. But the traits associated, though perhaps not always fairly, with the Mediterranean character are much more in evidence. Disraeli was proud, vain, flamboyant, quick-witted, generous, emotional, quarrelsome, extravagant, theatrical, addicted to conspiracy, fond of backstairs intrigue. He was also – and this is certainly un-Jewish – financially incompetent to a high degree. His great object both at this time and later was to be someone, to attract notice, to cut a dash – *'far figura'*, as the Italians say. It would not be just to attribute all these characteristics to any particular nation. But they are not those that leap to the mind in connexion with either Jews or Englishmen, and it is probably significant that Disraeli should have made the hero of *Contarini Fleming*, the most autobiographical of his novels, half-Venetian. Of course, some of his qualities were those of the romantic generation to which he belonged. His impulsiveness, his recklessness, his emotional fluctuation between euphoria and depression are features to be found in the artist's temperament at all epochs, but it was particularly fashionable to display them just then. Byron was the hero of the hour. The day of good form and the stiff upper lip was yet to come. All the same it remains true that Disraeli, unlike his family, was a most untypical English Jew. Throughout his life people remarked upon the indefinable but indubitable impression that he gave of being a foreigner, whether it was the pride of a Spanish grandee, the ingenuity of an Italian juggler, or the plausibility of a Levantine on the make.

CHAPTER III

The Grand Tour

1826–32

1

In order to recover from the strain of that feverish year Disraeli went on a tour of the Continent with the Austens in August. His letters to his family are cheerful, vivid and racy as ever.[1] No hint of despondency at the events of the past creeps in. 'I have not had a day's, nay an hour's illness since I left England', he wrote to his father when they reached Geneva, and Mrs Austen, writing from Dijon to his sister, Sarah, confirmed the fact. 'The real improvement in your brother's health and looks quite surprises me. He seems to enjoy everything, *pour ou contre*, and has just said high mass for a third bottle of burgundy.'[2] The party first went to Paris. 'I never was so struck with anything in the whole course of my life', he wrote; thence via Dijon to Geneva. Here Disraeli enjoyed a notable experience. He was a passionate admirer of Byron, who had died two years before and whose influence upon a whole generation it is hard to exaggerate. Byron was the symbol of adventure, liberation, romance and mystery. His extraordinary combination of literary genius, worldly cynicism, theatrical melancholy, aristocratic disdain and political liberalism, together with the rumour not only of a multitude of sexual triumphs but also of what used to be called 'nameless' vices, had made him even in his lifetime the object of perennial fascination which he has remained ever since.

Isaac D'Israeli knew Byron personally and had exchanged letters with him. The poet professed himself a great admirer of the *Curiosities of Literature*. It is therefore easy to understand how excited Benjamin was to meet at Geneva, Maurice, Byron's famous and handsome boatman who had rowed him on the lake during the great storm described in the third canto of *Childe Harold*. Disraeli arranged to have himself rowed on the lake every night by Maurice, and was able to hear from his lips numerous Byroniana which he

[1] See M. & B., i, ch. 7, for copious extracts.
[2] ibid., i, 96.

retailed to his father. One night there was a storm and Maurice sent
for him.

> As it was just after dinner and Austen was with me I was obliged
> to take a companion, but as we had discussed a considerable
> quantity of Burgundy, I was soon freed from his presence, for he
> laid down on my cloak, and 'ere half an hour was passed was fast
> asleep, never disturbing us save with an occasional request to
> participate in our brandy bottle. As for myself I was soon sobered,
> not by sleep, but by the scene. It was sublime – lightning almost
> continuous, and sometimes in four places, but as the evening
> advanced the lake became quite calm, and we never had a drop
> of rain. I would willingly have staid out all night, but we were to
> leave next morning at five and nothing was packed up . . .[1]

There is something singularly appropriate about the young
Disraeli re-enacting on Lake Geneva with Byron's boatman Byron's
experiences. All his life Disraeli, like Bismarck whom he resembled
in so many ways, dwelt in the long shadow of the Byronic myth. He
was fascinated by every detail of Byron's career. Later he actually
acquired Byron's gondolier, Battista Falcieri ('Tita'), in whose arms
Byron died at Missolonghi, as a man-servant, and imported him to
his father's country house. Later still, he came very near to renting
Byron's former rooms in Albany from another Byronic figure, his
friend and fellow novelist, Bulwer Lytton. One can only regret that
Disraeli and Byron never met. It would have been a memorable
occasion indeed.

From Geneva the party crossed the Alps to the Italian lakes. On
the way they paid a visit to the monastery of the Great St Bernard.
Half a century later Disraeli told Lord Rowton that the principal
interest which the monks took in him was to ask how the recently
constructed Thames Tunnel was working. Disraeli had to admit that
he had never seen it. He indulged in a virtuous reflection to the
effect that travel only teaches us what we ought to know of our own
country, and he made a resolution to see the tunnel as soon as he
returned. 'But do you know,' he said to Lord Rowton, 'I have never
seen it yet.'[2]

The remainder of the tour need not detain us, though it is interesting to notice that in a letter to Isaac, Disraeli, referring to Guercino
as 'a native of a little town a few miles from Bologna, *Cento* which

[1] ibid., i, 99, to Isaac D'Israel, September 2.
[2] Hughenden Papers, Box 26, A/X/B/14, note by Corry, dated 1871.

perhaps you remember', apparently had no idea that it was his grandfather's birthplace. It is clear that neither in Cento nor in Venice, which he also visited, did he make contact with any of his relations living there at the time. He probably did not even know of their existence. After visiting Bologna, Florence, Pisa, Spezzia, Genoa and Turin, the party returned home via Lyons and Paris. The tour lasted some two months and Disraeli's share of the expenses came to £151.

He returned to England in a state of continued excitement – a sort of feverish aftermath from the hectic months of the *Representative* and *Vivian Grey*. He had already begun, and in the autumn of 1826 he finished, a sequel to his now notorious novel. Once again Sara Austen acted as critic, amanuensis and agent. Colburn gave him £500 for it, but the increased advance was in inverse proportion to the merits of the book, which was rightly described by Gladstone as 'trash', when he read it half a century later for the first time. Money was a matter of paramount importance to Disraeli. His total debts far exceeded anything he could hope to earn, but ready cash could help to pay for the more pressing. There was one which, though not pressing in a legal sense, Disraeli was determined to pay off as a matter of pride: that was the £150 which he owed Murray for the mining pamphlets. On March 19 he had the satisfaction of writing a frigid business letter to his former patron and partner, enclosing the money.

After completing Part II of *Vivian Grey*, Disraeli collapsed. He was utterly exhausted, and the delayed effects of the strains to which he had subjected himself during 'the hour of adventure' at last began to show. He was seriously ill, and it was over three years before he managed to recover. The exact nature of the malady is obscure. One of the doctors who treated him called it 'chronic inflammation of the membrane of the brain', whatever that may mean. Today it would perhaps be described as a nervous break-down. Throughout his youth, indeed until his marriage, Disraeli was addicted to what are nowadays known as psychosomatic illnesses. Crises in his affairs frequently gave him violent headaches and caused him to take to his bed.

This period of his life is, as Monypenny puts it, 'almost a blank'. He managed to produce a novel called *Popanilla*, which appeared early in 1828, a satire on contemporary society modelled on the lines of *Candide*. It is very slight, but it takes off the more absurd extravagances of the Benthamites in an amusing fashion. It also laughs at the Corn Laws and the colonial system. John Bright is said to have greatly admired it, but it attracted little attention at the time or since.

Disraeli's health was poor throughout these years, and he seems to have had no clear plan for a career. He ate dinners at Lincoln's Inn during the Michaelmas Term of 1824 and the Hilary Term of 1825. He did nothing in 1826, but in 1827 he seems to have taken the law rather more seriously, for he 'performed exercises' in May, and ate dinners in the last three terms of the year, and in all four of 1828. Thereafter his interest lapsed. In 1831 he petitioned to have his name removed. During all this time he wandered about with his family in search of surroundings where he could shake off his affliction – Fifield in Oxfordshire, Lyme Regis, various parts of Buckinghamshire. As time went on he gradually improved. In March 1828 he wrote to Sharon Turner: 'I am at present quite idle, being at this moment slowly recovering from one of those tremendous disorganisations which happen to all men at some period of their lives, and which are perhaps equally necessary for the formation of both body and constitution. Whether I shall ever do anything which may mark me out from the crowd I know not . . . I am one of those to whom moderate reputation can give no pleasure, and who in all probability, am incapable of achieving a great one.'[1] The last few words are untypically despondent, but the scorn for a 'moderate reputation' is the quintessence of Disraeli, indeed the key to his character and career.

Earlier that year his father, worried, so he wrote to a friend, at 'the precarious health of several members of my family' – Mrs Disraeli was often ill, too – decided to move permanently out of London. For him, with his devotion to the Reading Room of the British Museum and his enjoyment of the literary society which only London could supply, this was something of a sacrifice. But the place which he chose, Bradenham, a beautiful red-brick Queen Anne house on the well-wooded slopes of the Chilterns a few miles from High Wycombe, was and is wholly delightful. With the church in its own grounds, it dominated the tiny village, and its owner inevitably undertook the role of a country squire, however incongruous this may seem for a scholarly recluse like Isaac D'Israeli. There he lived for the twenty years of life which remained to him.

[1] M. & B., 116.

Thither his son repaired to spend nearly every autumn until his marriage. He was devoted to the place, and his description of it in the last novel that he ever wrote, *Endymion*, is one of the most charming passages from his pen.[1] But not all his memories of it were happy. When he was old and famous he took the reigning Lady Derby for a walk from Hughenden to Bradenham, which had long since gone into other hands. 'It was there that I passed my miserable youth,' he told her. 'Why miserable?' 'I was devoured by ambition I did not see any means of gratifying.'[2]

2

In spite of the pessimistic tone of his letter to Turner, Disraeli, helped by the treatment of a Dr Buckley Bolton, was, in fact, rapidly recovering his health towards the end of 1829. A renewed activity was infused into his life, and sanguine schemes to advance his career began once more to revolve in his mind. Two of these were promptly rebuffed by Isaac. One was a plan, incredible though it may seem, for Disraeli to set himself up as a country gentleman – his father of course advancing the money. But Isaac made it clear that he would not help. 'The Governor is fairly frightened,' Disraeli told Austen. His other plan also failed to meet with Isaac's approval. He had become deeply interested in the East. For some time past he had been busy on the manuscript of a novel about the twelfth-century Jewish hero, David Alroy. At the same time he had convinced himself that only a lengthy absence from England – a sort of Grand Tour of the Mediterranean and the Near East – would restore him to health. A prolonged visit of this kind was bound to be expensive, and once again Isaac, who presumably was asked to pay, dug in his toes. There was only one solution, as he told Austen:

> I fear I must hack for it. A literary prostitute I have never yet been, though born in an age of literary prostitution, and though I have been more than once subject to temptations, which might have been the ruination of a less virtuous young man. My muse is still a virgin but the mystical flower, I fear, must soon be plucked. Colburn, I suppose, will be the bawd. Tempting Mother Colburn![3]

[1] *Endymion*, ch. 2.
[2] Quoted, Meynell, *The Man Disraeli*, 30.
[3] Quoted by Jerman, *The Young Disraeli*, 91.

Disraeli's virtue soon succumbed, for almost at once he abandoned *Alroy* and began to write *The Young Duke* – a novel of
fashionable life well calculated to appeal to the public for which
Colburn catered. He finished it with his usual speed, and by the end
of March 1830 was up in London in order to place the manuscript
with Colburn.[1] 'I am confident of its success,' he wrote to Meredith,
'and that it will complete the corruption of the public taste.' At the
same time he consulted a new friend with whom he was destined to
have a close alliance for many years – the youthful novelist, Lytton
Bulwer, whose *Pelham*, largely inspired by *Vivian Grey*, had caused
a sensation two years earlier. Bulwer was also a great admirer of
Isaac D'Israeli, and had exchanged letters with him even before the
publication of *Pelham*. It was therefore natural that he and the
young Disraeli should strike up an acquaintance, first by correspondence and now in person.

In many ways Bulwer and Disraeli were made for each other.
Bulwer might laugh in *Pelham* at the more absurd aspects of the
Byromania, as indeed Disraeli did in Part II of *Vivian Grey*, but he
was, like Disraeli, an admirer of Byron. While still an undergraduate
at Cambridge he had actually been for a short time the lover of Lady
Caroline Lamb. When three years later, in 1827, he made his
disastrous marriage, his conduct towards his wife combined many
of the more deplorable characteristics of Byron's towards both
Caroline Lamb and Lady Byron. Indeed, there are times when one
feels that Bulwer's life was only a macabre repetition of Byron's,
but conducted with one woman, on a less grand level, and in slower
motion. Lady Byron and Lady Caroline Lamb belonged to the
cream of fashionable society. Rosina Wheeler, whom Bulwer
married, was the daughter of a raffish and disreputable Irish proto-
suffragette. Lady Byron left Byron within a year of marriage. It was
nearly nine years before a formal separation took place between the
Bulwers. Whereas Lady Caroline Lamb relapsed into semi-insanity
almost as soon as Byron finally broke with her, it was not till 1858
that Bulwer, provoked by Rosina's appearance on the hustings in
his constituency, had her locked up in a mad-house. In only one
respect did Bulwer's life rival the hectic tempo of Byron's. Lady
Caroline Lamb published her deplorable novel, *Glenarvon*, lampoon-

[1] According to Lucien Wolf in his edition of *The Young Duke*, Disraeli spent three
months of the winter 1829–30 obtaining 'copy' for his new novel in London, and
leading a life of extravagant dissipation. He gives no evidence to support this theory,
and it seems unlikely to be true.

ing both Byron and her husband, only two years after her last encounter with Byron. Rosina was scarcely longer in producing hers – *Cheveley or the Man of Honour*, a similar satire on Bulwer. But these events lay in the future. In 1830 Bulwer seemed a busy and happy man, worried only by shortage of money.

The Young Duke consists of a series of highly coloured scenes from what Disraeli then imagined to be fashionable life. 'What does Ben know of dukes?' his father is reputed to have asked. Certainly the young Duke of St James bears small resemblance to any other duke in fact or fiction, except perhaps the Duke of Dorset in *Zuleika Dobson*. The style is artificial, full of far-fetched witticisms, convoluted antitheses, elaborate epigrams. After praising Disraeli's 'wit, terseness, and philosophy of style and the remarkable felicity with which you make the coldest insipidities of real life entertaining and racy – one would think you had been learning at Laputa how to extract sunbeams from cucumbers', Bulwer continues:[1]

> You do not seem to me to have done justice to your own powers when you are so indulgent to flippancies . . . At all events if you do not think twice and act a little on this point I fear you are likely to be attacked and vituperated to a degree which fame can scarcely recompense, and which hereafter may occasion you serious inconvenience. Recollect that you have written a book [*Vivian Grey*] of wonderful promise – but which got you enemies. You have therefore to meet in this a very severe ordeal both of expectation and malice.

Although Disraeli left in a good many passages of the sort to which Bulwer objected, such criticisms coming from a man who was anything but stuffy and whose egotism, foppery and affectation were at least equal to Disraeli's own did make him pause. He even appears to have contemplated scrapping the book altogether. Bulwer at once hastened to reassure him,[2] Colburn offered £500 in easily discountable post-dated bills, Austen offered an advance, and Disraeli clinched the deal. The eastern voyage at last became possible.

The Young Duke was not published until the following April, when Disraeli was still on his Grand Tour. The reaction of the critics, despite Colburn's puffery, was more friendly than Bulwer had feared. It is indeed an enjoyable book, despite all its absurdities

[1] Hughenden Papers, Box 104, B/XX/Ly14, April 10, 1830.
[2] ibid., B/XX/Ly/15, April 14, 1830.

of manner and diction, and it has a better, though hardly less improbable, plot than *Vivian Grey*. The Duke may be 'a sublime coxcomb', but one wants to read on about him. The famous gambling
scene is so exciting that we forget its intrinsic implausibility. The
heroine, May Dacre, is one of the most charming of Disraeli's
women. The villain, Sir Lucius Grafton, is a well-drawn portrait,
and comes to life more effectively than does any of the other
characters.

'The book,' wrote Sarah Disraeli to her brother, 'is reviewed in
all weekly and Sunday papers – all with excessive praise.' Not quite
all, however: Disraeli, as in *Popanilla*, had inserted a passage satiriz-
ing the Benthamites, and he did not go unanswered. In their organ,
The Westminster Review (pilloried in *The Young Duke* as the 'Screw
and Lever Review'), an unambiguous verdict on the novel appeared:
'To parasites, sycophants, toad-eaters, tuft-hunters and humble
companions, it will be a book full of comfort and instruction in their
calling.'

Disraeli's own later attitude to his third novel resembled his
attitude to his first. He disliked it in retrospect, and regretted having
written it. In the 1853 edition of his works it is expurgated almost
as drastically as *Vivian Grey*.[1] In the preface to his collected novels
which appeared in 1870 he does not mention it at all. It was
certainly not the sort of production with which a Tory statesman
would care to be associated, but authors are not always the best
judges of their work. Posterity can treat *The Young Duke* in the
spirit in which it was originally written, and enjoy the impudence,
freshness and vitality of a book which was never meant to be taken
seriously.

In London at the end of March 1830 Disraeli was at the top of his
form, determined to make a really sensational impression. He blossomed out like a rosebud in water. His dress of a 'blue surtout,
a pair of military light blue trousers, black stockings with red
stripes, and shoes "caused a sensation in Regent Street". "The
people," he complacently told Meredith who soberly recorded it all
in his diary, "quite made way for me as I passed! It was like the

---

[1] Including a surprisingly Rabelaisian passage to which Professor Jerman draws
attention in his *The Young Disraeli*, 101, and which ends, after a discussion of the
'amatory' properties of oysters and eggs: 'Why then cure us [of indigestion]? Why
send us forth with renovated livers, to lose our souls through salad and sex?' This
would not have gone down too well as a dictum from an ex-Chancellor of the Exchequer in 1853.

parting of the Red Sea, which I now perfectly believe from experience . . ." ' Meredith added that he was in excellent spirits 'full as usual of capital stories, but he could make a story out of everything'. It was on this same visit that Disraeli met Bulwer personally for the first time. He dined with him at his house in Hertford Street. The others present were Henry Bulwer (Lytton's brother), Charles Villiers[1] and Alexander Cockburn.[2] Henry Bulwer, years later, recalled how Disraeli outshone everyone else in conversation. He also remembered his dress – 'green velvet trousers, a canary coloured waistcoat, low shoes, silver buckles, lace at his wrists, and his hair in ringlets'.

3

Disraeli's tour of the Near East was one of the formative experiences of his youth. Its importance does not lie merely in the effect that it had upon his novels and romances, although he certainly could not have written *Contarini, Alroy, Tancred* or even *Lothair* but for the sense of atmosphere which he absorbed during these sixteen months of travel. Nor does it lie in the impetus given to the somewhat bizarre, and, if the truth be admitted, woolly, Oriental philosophy which he professed from time to time – 'the great Asian mystery'. The significance of the Eastern tour lies rather in the way that it affected his attitude on critical issues of foreign and imperial policy, which, as chance would have it, were to dominate public affairs during his premiership forty-four years later.

Historians do not always sufficiently weigh the influence of the emotions, prejudices and sympathies of early youth upon the choice of sides made by statesmen later, when they are confronted with the great political questions of the hour. But who can seriously doubt, for example, that Winston Churchill's attitude to the Indian question in the 1930s was conditioned by his experience as a cavalry subaltern in the Punjab thirty-three years earlier; or that Lloyd George's sympathy with the smaller nations had some connexion with the grievances that Welshmen in his youth felt against English rule?

[1] Charles Villiers, 1802–98. Brother of the 4th Earl of Clarendon who became Liberal Foreign Secretary. A staunch advocate of free trade and an associate of the Benthamites. MP for Wolverhampton from 1834 till his death.

[2] Alexander Cockburn, 1802–80. Lord Chief Justice of England from 1859 to his death. He was a roué in his youth. See A. Ramm, *Political Correspondence of Mr. Gladstone and Lord Granville*, 1868–71, Camden, 3rd Series, LXXXI, 1.

So, too, with Disraeli. No doubt a man of Jewish race, and of a faith which, if not Jewish, was certainly not in any orthodox sense Christian, would be naturally inclined to sympathize with the Turks under whose rule the Jewish merchants and bankers of the Levant were tolerantly, indeed generously, treated. But Disraeli's prejudices were even more strongly confirmed by his Eastern tour. In the light of the great struggle with Gladstone in the 1870s, there is something wonderfully prophetic about Disraeli actually planning to volunteer for the Turkish Army, which was in the process of crushing the Albanian revolt of 1830, although he arrived too late for the war and could only congratulate the Grand Vizier on his victory.

The details of the tour may best be read in the series of vivid and amusing letters which Disraeli wrote to his family and friends at home. They are perhaps the best that he ever wrote: they have a zest, a vitality and a self-revealing egotism which seldom fail to fascinate.[1]

In spite of occasional complaints about his health, he was evidently on the way to recovery, and the farther south he went the better he felt. All his life, to a greater degree than those of most people, Disraeli's health and spirits were influenced by climate. It was perhaps a part of his Italianate character. He adored sunshine, and its absence plunged him into a gloom which the average Englishman seldom experiences. On his Mediterranean tour Disraeli expanded and blossomed as never before, and in one respect at least the effect was lasting. The neurotic illness which had afflicted him since the failure of his first venture vanished for ever. By the time he returned to England he was completely cured.

Disraeli did not set out alone. His companion was Meredith, whose engagement to Sarah had just been officially announced, the obstructive uncle having at last withdrawn his opposition. The tour was intended to be Meredith's last fling as a bachelor, and the marriage was due to take place on his return. Disraeli and his companion left London by steamer on May 28 and arrived in Gibraltar towards the end of June. *Vivian Grey*, he declared, was there regarded

as one of the masterpieces of the nineteenth century. You may

---

[1] Unfortunately there is no single collection of them. Some appear in *Home Letters*, 1830–31, badly edited by Ralph Disraeli (1885). Others, including letters to Austen and Bulwer which were not available to Ralph Disraeli, are to be found in M. & B., i, ch. 9.

feel their intellectual pulse from this. At first I apologized and talked of youthful blunders and all that, really being ashamed; but finding them, to my astonishment, sincere, and fearing they were stupid enough to adopt my last opinion, I shifted my position just in time, looked very grand, and passed myself off for a child of the Sun just like the Spaniard in Peru.[1]

Thus early did Disraeli discover the important truth that, up to a point, the world will take a man at his own valuation. Undue modesty was not destined to be one of his handicaps during the remainder of the tour – or, for that matter, of his life. His behaviour in Gibraltar shows this well enough. He lectured the Governor, Sir George Don, on morals and politics. He at once laid siege to Lady Don, and with his extraordinary facility, which was to stand him in good stead later, for conquering elderly ladies soon had her at his feet, and was ordering Ralph to send her a copy of *The Young Duke* with the author's compliments.[2] Nor did he fail to cut a dash with the garrison. His clothes were, so he said, the 'admiration and envy of many subalterns', and he was the first person to carry a morning and an evening cane, changing them over when the gun fired.[3] The two travellers thoroughly enjoyed themselves, taking excursions, attending routs and dinner parties and quaffing Sir George Don's favourite summer drink, 'half champagne and half lemonade'. Bores were duly put in their places. When the Judge-Advocate-General, 'who is a true lawyer, ever illustrating the obvious, explaining the evident and expatiating the commonplace', claimed an acquaintance with Isaac D'Israeli and tried to saddle Benjamin with his mother, who was 'deaf dumb and blind', as a travelling companion, 'I gave him a lecture on canes, which made him stare, and he has avoided me ever since'.[4]

Disraeli and Meredith had intended to go on to Malta almost immediately, but, seduced by the charms of Spain, they delayed their move for two months and travelled on horseback through Andalusia. They returned by Malaga and the sea to Gibraltar at the end of July. Before they left Granada they visited the Alhambra, and Meredith records how the old lady who acted as their guide was convinced that Disraeli was a Moor.

At the end of August, after a rough, slow and disagreeable

[1] M. & B., i, 138, to Isaac, July 1, 1830.
[2] He wrongly expected it to be published almost at once.
[3] M. & B., i, 140.
[4] ibid., 142.

passage, they reached Malta. There they met an old acquaintance,
James Clay who had been at Winchester with Ralph Disraeli and at
Oxford with Meredith. Clay was a handsome youth with the complexion of a ripe peach. He had two other assets – he had chartered
a fifty-five-ton yacht, *The Susan,* and had acquired Byron's former
servant, 'Tita' Falcieri. Clay was an amusing and witty companion,
but, although he later became a Liberal MP and an authority on
whist[1] – achievements which seem respectable enough – he was at
this stage of life a shameless roué and an unceasing pursuer of
women. A letter to Disraeli, part of which is unprintable even in this
liberal era, written on the latter's birthday sixteen months later,
after they had parted at Malta on their return home, shows the
sort of person that he was, and the activities in which they both
engaged.

Venice, Lazaretto
December 21, 1831

Dear Disraeli

Many returns of this day to you under kinder Gods than, I fear,
rule your destiny at present. Between us we have contrived to
stumble on all the thorns, with which (as Mr. Dickens, the Winchester Porter, was wont poetically to observe) Venus guards her
roses; for while you were cursing the greater evils I contrived to
secure the minor . . . the latter was quickly cured, and I am in
high cue for a real debauch in Venice . . .

. . . Yesterday being *my* birthday I drank our very good
healths, a ceremony I shall repeat today. After dinner a capital
batch of letters (yours included) arrived, which I placed before
me with a bottle of superb milk punch (the Fusiliers gave me a
dozen) and another of claret. I drank and drank again and read
and re-read my letters until it became impossible to distinguish
one correspondent from another. On reading what I thought your
handwriting, I found an exhortation to marry and settle, and
when I took up, as I believed a letter from my mother I read that
'Mercury had succeeded to Venus' – a most extraordinary communication from an elderly gentlewoman. This morning a splitting
headache and two empty bottles informed me that for the first
time in my life I had got really drunk solus cum solo . . .[2]

Not surprisingly the D'Israeli family strongly disapproved of this
debauched Wykehamist. In a note on the few letters of Clay found
among Disraeli's papers Sir Philip Rose writes:

---

[1] *A Treatise on the Game of Whist by J.C.,* published as an appendix to J. L.
Baldwin, *Laws of Short Whist* (1864).

[2] Hughenden Papers, Box 122, B/XX/C/240.

Clay was a thoroughly bad unprincipled man. D's family had a horror of him and dreaded his influence over D. He was at Brasenose[1] with Meredith, and was, I think, a contemporary of Ralph D. at Winchester, with whom he was intimate. Miss D. who probably knew Meredith's opinion of Clay expresses in one of her letters her astonishment at her brother making a travelling companion of Clay. It was a bad connexion for D. and one which gave him no pleasure in retrospect, and in after years he felt relieved that politics had to some extent divided them.[2]

It is noticeable that Disraeli wrote rather defensively to his family on the subject of his friend, and felt it necessary to dwell at some length on his virtues as a travelling companion. But, whatever Rose believed, their relations remained intimate long after this. They were in secret communication over the Reform Bill of 1867, and during Clay's last illness in 1873 Disraeli called every day at his house.

Whether or not Clay's presence counteracted such faint restraining influence as Meredith possessed, Disraeli was apparently determined to create an even greater sensation in Malta than in Gibraltar. He called on the Governor, a brother of Lady Caroline Lamb and 'exceedingly exclusive', reduced him to fits of laughter, and secured an instant invitation to a party. He dined with the 73rd Foot in Andalusian dress – an action which even he admitted to have been a 'buffoonery'. Meredith described the clothes in which Disraeli paid a round of calls in Valetta – 'his majo jacket, white trousers, and sash of all the colours in the rainbow'. Half the population followed him, so Disraeli reported to Meredith, 'putting a complete stop to all business'.[3]

The high point in his antics was reached, however, when he went to watch a game of rackets.

To govern men you must either excel them in their accomplishments, or despise them. Clay does one; I do the other, and we are both equally popular. Affectation tells here even better than wit. Yesterday at the racket court sitting in the gallery among strangers, the ball entered, and lightly struck me, and fell at my feet. I picked it up, and observing a young rifleman excessively stiff, I humbly requested him to forward its passage into the court, as I really had never thrown a ball in my life. This incident has been the general subject of conversation at all the messes today![4]

[1] Clay was actually at Balliol, not Brasenose.
[2] Hughenden Papers, Box 27, A/XI/A.
[3] M. & B., i, 155.   [4] M. & B., i, 154–5.

One can well believe it, but whether the conversation flattered
Disraeli is quite another matter. Sir William Gregory, a Liberal MP
and Governor of Ceylon, whose autobiography abounds in disagreeable remarks about Disraeli, records Clay as saying years later
that although Disraeli was a delightful companion while they were
alone, 'when they got into society his coxcombry was insupportable
. . He made himself so hateful to the Officers' Mess that while they
welcomed Clay they ceased to invite "that damned bumptious Jew
boy".'[1]

Towards the end of September 1830, Disraeli and Meredith left
Malta for Corfu as passengers on Clay's yacht – the cautious Meredith, who possibly may not have liked Clay overmuch, having
vetoed a proposal that the three should charter her jointly. Disraeli
was, of course, dressed up to the nines as usual: 'You should see me
in the costume of a Greek pirate', he wrote to Ralph. 'A blood-red
shirt, with silver studs as big as shillings,[2] an immense scarf for
girdle, full of pistols and daggers, red cap, red slippers, broad blue
striped jacket and trousers.'

From Corfu they proceeded to Yanina, then capital of the
Turkish province of Albania, hoping, as we saw earlier, to participate
in the Grand Vizier's campaign against the rebels. On the way up
from the coast they found themselves benighted at a desolate
military post in the mountains. The Bey in charge of it spoke no
language which they could understand. They sat on a divan, feeling
intensely hungry, but unable to communicate at all.

> The Bey sat in a corner, I unfortunately next, so I had the onus
> of mute attention; and Clay next to me, so he and M. could at
> least have an occasional joke, though of course we were too well-
> bred to exceed an occasional irresistible observation. Clay wanted
> to play écarté, and with a grave face as if we were at our devo-
> tions; but just as we were about commencing, it occurred to us
> that we had some brandy, and that we would offer our host a
> glass, as it might be a hint for what should follow to so vehement
> a schnapps. Mashallah! Had the effect only taken place 1830
> years ago instead of in the present age of scepticism, it would
> have been instantly voted a first class miracle. Our mild friend
> smacked his lips and instantly asked for another cup; we drank
> it in coffee cups . . .
> . . . a most capital supper was brought in, accompanied, to

[1] Sir William Gregory, *An Autobiography* (1894), 95.
[2] 'Sixpences', according to Meredith.

our great horror by – wine. We ate, we drank, we ate with our fingers, we drank in a manner I never recollect . . . The room turned round; the wild attendants who sat at our feet seemed dancing in strange and fantastic whirls; the Bey shook hands with me; he shouted English – I Greek. 'Very good,' he had caught up from us. 'Kalo, Kalo,' was my rejoinder. He roared; I smacked him on the back. I remember no more. In the middle of the night I woke. I found myself sleeping on the divan rolled up in its sacred carpet; the Bey had wisely reeled to the fire. The thirst I felt was like that of Dives. All were sleeping except two who kept up during the night the great wood fire. I rose lightly, stepping over my sleeping companions and the shining arms that here and there informed me that the dark capote was a human being. I found Abraham's bosom in a flagon of water. I think I must have drunk a gallon at the draught. I looked at the wood fire and thought of the blazing blocks in the hall at Bradenham, asked myself whether I was indeed in the mountain fastness of an Albanian chief, and, shrugging my shoulders went to bed and woke without a headache.[1]

At length they reached Yanina and had an audience with the Grand Vizier, Redschid Ali, 'an approved warrior, a consummate politician, unrivalled as a dissembler'. 'I bowed with all the nonchalance of St James's Street to a little ferocious, shrivelled, careworn man, plainly dressed, with a brow covered with wrinkles and a countenance clouded with anxiety and thought.'[2] The Grand Vizier was most civil to them. 'The delight of being made much of by a man who was daily decapitating half the province,' wrote Disraeli gleefully to Austen from Nauplia.[3]

After leaving Albania they wandered in leisurely fashion through the Ionian Sea towards Athens – 'a cloudless sky, a summer atmosphere, and sunsets like the neck of a dove', writes Disraeli. But depression at times set in: 'I wander in pursuit of health like the immortal exile in pursuit of that lost shore which is now almost glittering in my sight. Five years of my life have been already wasted and sometimes I think my pilgrimage may be as long as that of Ulysses.'[4] Was this a genuine relapse of spirit after the excitement of Yanina, or was Disraeli only expressing the feelings which he deemed appropriate to one who voyaged where once Ulysses had? It is the enigma and fascination of Disraeli's personality that we can

[1] M. & B., i, 160–1, to Isaac, October 25.
[2] ibid., 162.
[3] Jerman, 114, November 18.
[4] M. & B., i, 164.

never be sure. Pose and sincerity are inextricably interwoven. What
begins as a theatrical gesture becomes a real expression of feeling,
and even the sincerest sentiments take on an air of the stage when
Disraeli utters them.

The travellers spent a week at Navarino, visited Corinth, Argos
and Mycenae, and finally on November 24 arrived at Athens. There
they remained until early December, and, so Disraeli claimed in a
letter to Isaac, were the first Englishmen to whom the Acropolis had
been opened for nine years[1] – owing to the war of liberation which
had devastated Greece. From Athens they sailed for Constantinople.
Disraeli's thrill as he approached that magical and mysterious city
may be readily conceived.

> It is near sunset and Constantinople is in full sight; it baffles all
> description, though so often described. An immense mass of
> buildings, cupolas, cypress groves, and minarets. I feel an excite-
> ment which I thought was dead.[2]

Disraeli had by now become almost intoxicated with the glamour
of the East. It was an unforgettable experience for him, and,
although he seemed to live so lazily compared with the virtuous
Meredith, or the unvirtuous Clay, he was in reality absorbing
impressions which remained with him to the end of his life: the
sound of the muezzin from the minaret in Arta, the wild throb of the
drum which preceded a train of Arabian camels carrying corn
through Yanina for the Grand Vizier's army, the Turkish pipes with
their diamond mouthpieces, the coffee perfumed with roses and
sipped from cups encrusted with precious stones, the fantastic
costumes in Constantinople – 'the meanest merchant in the Bazaar
looks like a Sultan in an Eastern fairy tale' – the Bosphorus covered
with 'long thin boats as swift as gondolas, and far more gay'.

In Constantinople, Disraeli and Clay remained for nearly six
weeks, until the middle of January. Meredith, however, left them
at the end of December in order to explore Asia Minor, 'respecting
which', Disraeli wrote to Sarah, 'he was very mad, although I
believe it to be a country equally unsatisfactory to the topographer,
the antiquarian, and the man of taste'.

From Constantinople they sailed to Smyrna, where they met
Meredith again, but he refused to accompany them on their visit to
Jerusalem, preferring a 'trip to the unseen relics of some unheard-of

---

[1] M. & B., i, 165.   [2] ibid., 168.

cock and bull city' in the hinterland. It was agreed that they should all three meet again in Egypt, whence they would return home via Malta and Gibraltar. Meanwhile Disraeli and Clay, after spending a day in Cyprus, headed for the Holy Land and cast anchor in the port of Jaffa. From there 'a party of six well mounted and armed we departed for Jerusalem'.

> I was thunderstruck. I saw before me apparently a gorgeous city. Nothing can be conceived more wild, and terrible, and barren than the surrounding scenery, dark, stony, and severe . . . Except Athens I never saw anything more essentially striking; no city except that, whose site was so pre-eminently impressive . . .[1]

The weather, although it was the end of February, was mild and summery. Every night they dined by moonlight on the roof of the house where they were staying. It was one of the most memorable of all Disraeli's experiences. His mystical belief in the mysterious heritage of his race, his romantic love of high-sounding historic names, his exotic imagination, all were heightened by the week which he passed in Jerusalem – 'the most delightful in all my travels', and eloquent passages in his novels testify to the permanent impression which it left upon him.

On March 12 Disraeli and Clay arrived in Alexandria, where Meredith joined them again. In Egypt, Disraeli was to linger for several months. He travelled across the desert to Rosetta, where he first saw the 'mighty Nile'. 'A grove of palms', he observed, 'is the most elegant thing in nature.' Thence he went by boat to Cairo, and then in the same boat up the river to Thebes and back – a three weeks' voyage which he greatly enjoyed except for the experience of a simoom.

Back in Cairo he led a life of agreeable sloth. True, there were tiresome vexations. His Cypriot servant, who wore a dress of crimson and gold with a white turban thirty feet long, suddenly gave notice, and he was reduced to a barefooted Arab in a blue shirt. 'How are the mighty fallen!' he wrote to Sarah. Then Clay and 'Tita' both became ill simultaneously, because, so Disraeli maintained, they refused like him to live indolently 'à la Turque', but insisted on shooting and swimming from morning to night. This was a nuisance, for Clay saved Disraeli a great deal of trouble. 'Indeed I am

[1] *Home Letters*, 118–9.

greatly indebted to him for much comfort. You know that, though I like to be at my ease, I want energy in these little affairs of which life greatly consists. Here I found Clay always ready; in short he saved me from much bore.' Clay put the matter somewhat differently. Disraeli, he told Meredith, was a person who 'ought never to travel without a nurse'.[1]

In general, however, Disraeli was well content with life in Cairo. He found the climate delightful, and his health was excellent. He smoked a hookah cooled in a wet silken bag. His coffee was boiled with spices, 'and I finish my last chibouque with a sherbert of pomegranate'. One day, wandering in the gardens of Mehemet Ali's palace, he actually encountered that formidable character in person, surrounded by black eunuchs in scarlet and gold, 'playing chess with his fool'. He was duly presented, and this led to a further audience later, at which Disraeli was consulted, so he said, upon the question of introducing parliamentary institutions into Egypt. Mehemet Ali was delighted at the idea of having a parliament. ' "I will have as many Parliaments as the King of England himself. See here!" So saying his Highness produced two lists of names . . . "See here!" said he, "here are my Parliaments; but I have made up my mind, to prevent inconvenience, to elect them myself." '[2]

It was during this period that Disraeli made the acquaintance of an Italian doctor by the name of Paul Emile Botta who was travelling in the Near East at this time. Three years later in his journal he described the great impression which Botta made upon him.

But the man from whom I have gained most in conversation is Botta, the son of the Italian historian, whom I knew in Egypt, travelling as a physician in the Syrian dress – the most philosophic mind that I ever came in contact with. Hour after hour has glided away, while, *chibouque* in mouth, we have disserted together upon our divan, in a country where there are no journals and no books. My mind made a jump in these high discourses. Botta was wont to say that they formed also an era in his intellectual life . . .[3]

Unfortunately we have no evidence of the nature of these high discourses. Only two letters of any length from Botta have survived; one is an entertaining but unprintable description of the sexual

[1] M. & B., i, 175.

[2] *Vindication of the English Constitution* (1835), 103. The story may be a later embroidery on Disraeli's part. It does not appear in any of his contemporary letters.

[3] Hughenden Papers, Box 11, A/III/C.

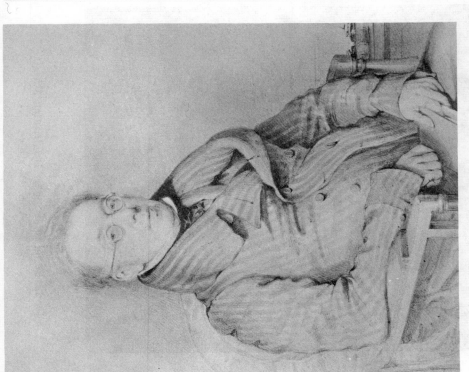

Isaac and Sarah D'Israeli, 1828

Drawings by Daniel Maclise now at Hughenden Manor.

Disraeli

from a drawing by Count d'Orsay, 1834

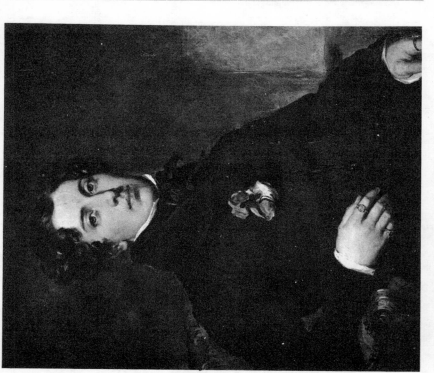

James Clay

from the oil painting at Hughenden Manor
by A. S. Wortley

customs of the Arabs, written to Disraeli with a wealth of intimate detail after his return to England; the other dwells on the pleasures of smoking opium.[1]

Towards the end of June, Meredith, who had stayed on at Thebes long after the others, returned to Cairo, and plans were duly put in train for their return to England. Then there occurred a tragedy which came as a fearful blow to Disraeli, and an even more disastrous one to his sister. Meredith was taken ill with smallpox and died on July 19. The shock to Disraeli was all the greater because the disease was not diagnosed as being an acute form of the malady, and the patient appeared to be making such good progress under the ministrations of the excellent doctor who had treated Clay that his friends felt no anxiety. Indeed, Clay had left for Alexandria to make arrangements for their passage home, and was away when Meredith died.

Gaetani [the doctor] assured me that all would go well [wrote Disraeli to his father], that it was of a kind that was never fatal, that it must take its course, that he would not even be marked. Our poor friend had no pain and never lost confidence for a moment. Each day the suppuration advanced and yesterday, the 19th July, Gaetani came as usual in the morning and examined him and said that all was well and that in all probability to-morrow the eruption would commence disappearing . . . About five o'clock one of his attendants came running into a room where I was conversing with a son of Botta, the historian, a very scientific traveller and a surgeon, and told me that his master had fainted. I took Botta along with me, who opened a vein – the blood flew but not strongly, the body was quite warm. The terrible truth apparent to all never occurred to me. But I will not dwell on my own horrible sufferings, and so much now depends on me that I feel I must exert myself. I would willingly have given up my life for his . . . Oh my father when I think of this I am nearly mad. Why do we live. The anguish of my soul is great. Our innocent lamb, our angel is stricken. Save her, save her . . . My dear father I do not know whether I have done all that is necessary. It requires great exertion not to go distracted. I have sent a courier to Clay. Mr. Botta has been very kind to me as I could not sleep and dared not be alone and my anguish was overpowering. I wish to live only for my sister.[2]

The news of Meredith's death struck Bradenham like a thunderbolt. Sarah saw her world collapse in ruins about her, and was

[1] ibid., Box 12, A/IV/F/1 and 2.
[2] ibid, Box 12, A/IV/E/29, July 20, 1831.

prostrated by the blow. She was now twenty-eight and she resolved henceforth to live only for her family. No question of marriage ever arose again. Hitherto she had looked on her brother with the ordinary scepticism of an elder sister. But her feelings now became, in the words of Sir Philip Rose, 'a passion bordering upon romance'. During the next few years, when he was struggling for social, literary and political fame, she was his most intimate confidante. At times he was forgetful, and inevitably he did not carry out his resolution to live only for her. It would have been unnatural if he had, nor would she have wished for such a sacrifice. But his appreciation of her devotion was sincere and genuine. Moreover, that devotion was not mere idolatry. She alone of the family, apart from Isaac, came near to being his intellectual equal. She was clever, witty and amusing, and her best letters are almost as good to read as Disraeli's own. Until his marriage she played as important a part in his personal life as anyone, by her constant and judicious admiration and encouragement.

There is one final ironical twist of events to record. The rich uncle, whose caprice had prevented Meredith from marrying Sarah many years before, died in London at almost the very same moment as his nephew and heir in Cairo.

CHAPTER IV

'I struggle from Pride'
1832–3

1

The tragedy of Meredith's death determined Disraeli to travel back to England by sea, then the quickest route. He abandoned his original plan to return via Naples and Rome, and, as it turned out, he was never to visit either city. Towards the end of October, having left Clay at Malta, he arrived at Falmouth and travelled up to London, but he did not at once repair to Bradenham. The reason was a curious and little-known episode. Our source for it is a memorandum by Sir Philip Rose, who had before him letters which have now disappeared.[1]

On board ship Disraeli had struck up a close friendship with one Henry Stanley, a young man of his own age and a younger brother of the Secretary for Ireland, Edward Stanley, the future 14th Earl of Derby and Prime Minister. They went to London together. On arrival Henry Stanley disappeared. His family were naturally worried, and, to quote Rose, 'he was eventually run to earth at Effie Bond's, the Keeper of the Hell in St. James's Street where he had taken up his quarters and to which it was alleged Disraeli had introduced him' the charge being that Disraeli had some pecuniary interest in bringing a young man of high family to be fleeced by the proprietor. Rose goes on to say that they had apparently gone together to this unsavoury abode 'and as Disraeli was known to have had money relations with the Bonds the rest was assumed'. Or rather it would be correct to say assumed by Edward Stanley, for, according to Rose, the letters showed that Henry's father and brother-in-law 'had no complaint against Disraeli and not only

---

[1] Rose's memorandum was published in full by C. L. Cline, *Journal of Modern History*, Vol. II, No. 4 (December 1939), 509, but seems to have attracted very little notice. In the Hughenden Papers it can be found in Box 27. The letters were either destroyed or returned to the Stanley family. In correspondence with Lord Esher (Royal Archives, Queen Victoria, X33/332–42, October–November 1907), Lord Rothschild mentions that it had been necessary to 'remove' certain papers concerning 'Colonel Stanley'. The episode of Henry Stanley and Disraeli is not mentioned at all by Monypenny or Jerman.

acquitted him of all blame but were grateful for his interference and aid'. Disraeli's well-meant efforts to extricate his friend were interpreted by Edward Stanley as the cover for a sinister plot, and he 'professed to believe that while Disraeli was working day and night to discover his missing relative he was all the time party to a conspiracy to entangle him and in league with the Bonds'.

The disappearance of the letters makes it impossible to give a final verdict on the affair, but there is no reason to doubt Rose's opinion: '. . . the Hon. Henry's own letters shew that Disraeli had given him the best and most disinterested advice.' Disraeli undoubtedly had financial dealings with the brothers Bond just as he had with many other shady figures, but he never acted dishonourably in personal matters and it is most unlikely that he would engage in an intrigue of this sort. Rose surmises that Edward Stanley's feeling was 'rather the resentment of a proud man at a stranger . . . having cognizance of a brother's misconduct, rather than any real distrust or belief that his brother had been led into difficulties by Disraeli'. But this did not make the allegation any the less damaging to Disraeli. In the small tight-knit politico-social world of London in the 1830s, where everyone knew every scandal, Edward Stanley's opinion of Disraeli became notorious; and people were more likely to side with the heir to Knowsley than with Disraeli.

It is improbable that Disraeli had any idea at first of the misconstruction put on his actions. His sister wrote to him on November 13. 'Do not, however, think of hurrying down here, while you can be of such essential service in London. I am very sorry for Henry Stanley and it would give me much future pain, as I am sure it would you, if any fatal mischief should happen by your deserting them.'[1] Later, Disraeli must have become conscious of Edward Stanley's hostility. Rose says that he never mentioned the matter to him, 'but I was aware of it from one of his brothers who accounted for Lord Derby's [Stanley's] dislike of Disraeli on this ground. Whether there was any explanation between Lord Derby and Disraeli which satisfied the former I cannot say, but I have the impression that something did pass on the subject.'

It seems likely that Derby in the end was persuaded that his accusation had no substance, but this could only have occurred many years later when political alliance made a certain degree of

---

[1] Hughenden Papers, Box 7, A/I/B/414.

personal intimacy essential. Meanwhile, the episode contributed to that 'storm of political hate and malice' of which Disraeli complained to Peel ten years later. Much of it was of his own making, but this was not. The most that can be said by the moralist is that such charges are among the occupational risks of leading the sort of life Disraeli led.

Disraeli was in no mood to worry. He was in a state of vigour and euphoria. The mysterious psychological malady which vexed him before his departure to the Near East had vanished. True, Clay's jest about Mercury and Venus was justified, but that famous specific seems to have been effective. 'I am pretty well,' he told Austen on January 6, 1832, 'having just left off a six weeks course of Mercury which has pulled me down, but head all right and working like a tiger.'[1] Early in the new year, after a visit to Bradenham, he took lodgings in London at 35 Duke Street, which running as it does southwards from Jermyn Street, parallel to S James's, was admirably situated in the heart of fashionable London. From there Disraeli prepared once again to assault the social and political heights which had defied him six years earlier.

By the early 1830s life in the great world had already acquired the pattern which was to remain basically unchanged for the rest of the century. The parliamentary session usually opened in February and, with interludes at Easter and Whitsun, lasted till August. Everyone who was anyone lived in London during those six months. It was not until August that the great exodus began. From then onwards, except in the rare event of an autumn session, London was deserted by the world of politics and fashion. People went abroad or to the country, and the rest of the year was spent in hunting and shooting, and in a round of country-house visits. Only when Christmas was over was it time to renew the struggle which had been in semi-abeyance for the last four months.

For the next six years Disraeli's life conformed to this pattern in most respects – though not all. Thanks to his friend Bulwer he had no difficulty in launching himself into society, not into the most exclusive houses, but into the salons of such people as Lady Blessington, Lady Charleville, Mrs Norton and Lady Cork, who sought to attract the fashionable up-and-coming figures of literature and politics. From February to August he was occupied in an exhausting round of routs and dinner parties, varied by sporadic political

[1] British Museum, Add. MSS, 45908.

pamphleteering and attempts to get into Parliament. With the end
of the session he would repair to Bradenham, and there amidst the
autumnal beech trees he would recuperate from the strain of high
life and endeavour to make progress with whatever book he was
writing at the time.

He did not, however, get many invitations to country houses.
There has always been a distinction drawn by hostesses between
those whom they invite to balls or even dinner parties in London
and those whom they ask to stay in the country. The latter constituted a smaller and more 'eligible' circle. Disraeli was not, on any
view, an eligible young man. He, therefore, had to be content with
domestic life at Bradenham for the four or five months which
elapsed between the end of one session and the beginning of the
next.

It is unlikely that he regretted this necessity. English country-
house life was dominated by a sort of philistine masculinity which
could never have been very agreeable to him. Sport of one kind or
another was the chief subject of activity by day and discussion by
night, and, although Disraeli is recorded as having hunted on one or
two occasions, everything suggests that sport was not his *métier*. As
for the evenings, they were almost as bad. Disraeli only really shone
in feminine society. It was with a sinking feeling that he anticipated
the dread moment when the hostess would give the signal for the
ladies to depart and he would be left at the dinner-table with the
men while the decanter circulated and the conversation droned endlessly on about poachers, pheasants and the Poor Law; or, worse
still, descended into competitive rounds of bawdy anecdotage – that
most tedious of all forms of talk, and one which Disraeli particularly
disliked.

At all events, whether or not he minded, Disraeli in those early
days seldom received invitations to the great country houses.
London was a different matter. There his progress was rapid, though
perhaps not quite so rapid as his letters, which are our main source,
suggest. It should never be forgotten that he was writing for an
adoring sister who was spurring him on and who now lived for his
success. No doubt he did become under Bulwer's patronage a well-
known figure in certain salons. His novels, good looks, exotic dress,
amusing, if at times insufferably affected, conversation, all helped
his climb up the social ladder, but it was neither as speedy nor
as sensational as one might believe from his letters. To many men he

remained, to quote the happy expression of Mr Raymond Mortimer, 'a dandified young bounder'. But he had the women on his side, and that was a help.

2

During 1832 Disraeli began – or possibly resumed, for the facts are obscure – an affair with a woman called Clara Bolton, wife of a doctor who practised in Park Lane and had treated him for his mysterious illness before he left England for the East. The evidence for this episode is principally a bundle of letters from her to Disraeli endorsed by Sir Philip Rose with the comment: 'By his family she was looked on as D's mistress.'[1] The letters all written in 1832 do not in themselves give any conclusive proof of their relationship, although they undoubtedly suggest an intense and possessive interest in him and his activities, rather like that of Sara Austen. She frequently offers him a bed or 'a crib' at her house, No. 3 King Street,[2] off S James's, and she pours out a flood of excited social and political gossip. But there is not the unequivocal eroticism that one finds in the letters from Henrietta Sykes, the woman who supplanted her in his affections a year later. However, Mrs Bolton may merely have been more cautious. Rose, who was a boy of seventeen at the time and a near neighbour of the Disraelis, is unlikely to have been wrong.

We know tantalizingly little about her. No portrait seems to have survived, nor is there much reliable evidence to determine what sort of person she was. Such comments upon her as appear in Disraeli's papers are either from his sister, Sarah, who evidently did not like her, or from Henrietta Sykes, who was obviously jealous, for by the time she came on the scene Clara Bolton was not only Disraeli's ex-mistress but her husband Sir Francis Sykes's current one.[3] Mrs Bolton evidently was not in any sense deceiving her own husband. Dr Buckley Bolton seems to have been a thorough *mari complaisant*, and, according to Rose, made a profit in some way out of his wife's liaison with Sykes[4] – a situation possibly confirmed by an entry of August 1834 in Disraeli's cryptic diary written well over a year after

---

[1] Hughenden Papers, Box 27, A/XI/A.
[2] She sometimes writes from 21 Alexander Square, Brompton, but this does not seem to have been her regular address.
[3] See below, p. 101.
[4] Hughenden Papers, Box 27, A/XI/A.

he had broken with her: 'Bolton and his wife – a decoy duck.'[1] It is not easy to judge the social nuances of a hundred and thirty years ago, but Mrs Bolton's letters[2] do in some indefinable way give the impression of brassiness and a certain vulgarity. One suspects her of name-dropping at times. The way she refers on one occasion to getting franks from 'Lord Johnny' [Russell] does not quite ring true, and on other occasions she clearly boasted of friends and accomplishments which did not correspond to reality.

Yet she was evidently not stupid and she moved in circles which had some claim to being both intellectual and cosmopolitan. We hear of Fanny Burney's son, the Reverend Alexander d'Arblay – 'a really talented orthodox creature, a beautiful poet I never heard so fine a preacher' – reciting Racine to a gathering of foreigners at her house. She asks Disraeli to help him in his canvass for 'the duty' at the Foundling Hospital. Moreover, Disraeli was not the only man of genius who was attracted by her. The famous Danish clergyman, philosopher and educationalist, N. F. S. Grundtvig, met her when on a visit to London in the summer of 1831, and she inspired in him a deep though wholly platonic love. A conversation with her, so he said, opened his eyes 'as if by a miracle' to 'the natural human life'. They never met again, but she remained his muse and inspiration for years afterwards, and she appears in one of the most important of his books, *Nordens Mythologi* (1832), as Proserpine to his Pluto.[3] There must have been more to her than one would deduce by reading her letters or the letters about her in Disraeli's papers.

It is not clear exactly when the affair with Disraeli began. The Boltons apparently knew the Disraelis in London before the move to Bradenham, but not at all well. In March 1835 Sarah Disraeli wrote to her brother apropos of an inquiry about Mrs Bolton made by Isaac King, the local parson, on behalf of the English chaplain in Rotterdam, where she had arrived and was living alone, 'the object it seems of great curiosity and, as the pious man gently indicates, of much scandal'. Sarah continued:

Amongst other rhodomontade she has said that she has a Sunday School supported entirely at her own expense, and another in

[1] ibid., Box 11, A/III/C.

[2] ibid., Box 13, A/IV/G. There are fifteen of them.

[3] For this information I am obliged to Pastor Thanning, whose doctoral thesis on Grundtvig for the University of Copenhagen (1963) is the latest and most authoritative study of Grundtvig's life and work.

conjunction with the Disraelis. She has talked of Isaac King, I suppose, as if she were an intimate associate . . . Isaac sent me the dispatch . . . to beg me to tell him how to answer it & everything I could say in her favour. I wrote in reply that I knew nothing whatever about her; that you had wished us to show some attention in return for great attention received during a long continued illness from Mr B., that her visit here was the result, that it had proved a little longer than we expected & that it had so happened that we had never seen either her or her husband since; now nearly five years ago.[1]

'Nearly five years' carries us back to the spring or early summer of 1830, just before Disraeli left for his tour of the Near East. One wonders whether the affair began at Bradenham then; this might explain why she stayed longer than expected. On the other hand, Sarah does not write as if conscious of any such relationship. It seems on balance more probable — though the point is of no great importance — that the affair was confined in time and place to London in 1832, and that the members of the family who, according to Rose, 'looked on her as D's mistress' were one or both of his brothers. They were more likely to be well-informed on such a matter than his parents or sister. Whatever the truth, the liaison was over by the end of that year. When Mrs Bolton reappeared in Disraeli's life a few months later it was in a very different and far less agreeable role.

3

In manners and style the 1830s constitute a period of extravagance, affectation, frivolity and artifice. As Mr James Pope-Hennessy puts it, 'There is something about the reign of William the Fourth which inexorable chronological fact alone prevents one from calling *fin de siècle*.'[2] Time and time again the stories we read about Disraeli's demeanour, dress and conversation remind us not so much of the grave sedate bourgeois England that he was destined to govern as of the England which flourished ten years after his death — the England of the *Yellow Book* and Oscar Wilde. Wilde acknowledged his debt. It was no accident that he chose the title of *Dorian Gray* for one of his most extravagant books, and his own famous epigrams

---

[1] Hughenden Papers, Box 7, A/I/B/463, n.d. but almost certainly March 1835.

[2] James Pope-Hennessy, *Monckton Milnes: The Years of Promise* (1949), 88, an excellent account of social and literary London at this time.

might well, without incongruity, have appeared in the pages of a
Disraeli novel. Indeed, who, without actual knowledge, would guess
offhand which of them was author of which of these epigrams?

'My idea of an agreeable person is a person who agrees with me.'

Or this:
'A little sincerity is a dangerous thing,
and a great deal of it is absolutely fatal.'

Or this:
'Every woman should marry – and no man.'

Or this:
'I rather like bad wine. One gets so bored with good wine.'

A feature of both epochs was the cult of that now-vanished
phenomenon – the dandy. It was as a dandy, perhaps even more
than as a novelist, or politician, that Disraeli first became famous in
the 1830s. What exactly was dandyism? It seems to be a characteristic of an era of social flux, when aristocracy is tottering or uncertain, but when radicalism has not yet replaced it with a new set
of values. It flourishes in a period when manners are no longer rigidly
fixed, but have not yet degenerated into mere anarchy, so that there
is still a convention to rebel against, still a world to be shocked and
amused by extravagance and eccentricity. The dandy must have a
framework within which to operate. The social grades must still
exist, but it must be easy for those with sufficient courage, carelessness or sheer brazen determination to climb from one to another.

The 1830s constituted just such a period. The British aristocracy
was not, in fact, tottering to its fall, but a great many people thought
that it was. The Reform Bill of 1832 seemed to the whole Tory party
from the Duke of Wellington downwards, and to many Whigs also,
the death knell of the old order. Few had the prescience of Earl Grey,
who declared that the measure would in reality prove to be a
bulwark of aristocracy. As time went on and the threatened revolution never took place, the upper classes began to recover their poise.
By the 1850s England was governed by an alliance between the
landed aristocracy and the middle class – and it was the latter which
was the junior partner. An era of seeming stability had arrived, and
the dandy vanished, giving way to that very different and less
attractive character – the 'heavy swell'.

The dandy of the day was Alfred, Count d'Orsay, who lived with the widowed second wife of the last Earl of Blessington in circumstances which occasioned much scandal. The Earl, who seems to have been as much in love with him as Lady Blessington, had made a will leaving his entire fortune to whichever of his two daughters d'Orsay married. In 1827 d'Orsay, by now Lady Blessington's lover, married the younger, Harriet, on condition laid down by her stepmother that the marriage should not be consummated for four years, till she was nineteen. In 1829 the Earl died. In 1830 Lady Blessington and her lover returned from Italy bent on the social conquest of London, and moved into their famous house in Seamore Place. Almost at once Harriet left d'Orsay, and the late Earl's family began to contest the will. Not surprisingly, Lady Blessington was ostracized by all respectable women. But although the women cut her the men did not. She was an admirable hostess, her dinners were delicious, and Seamore Place soon became the fashionable salon for those who combined literary leanings, aristocratic birth or pretensions, with slightly radical politics, and did not worry too much about respectability. It was, of course, just the place for Disraeli and Bulwer. Indeed, it seems in retrospect to have epitomized – almost embodied – one aspect of the spirit of the 1830s. D'Orsay had every qualification for dandyism – wit, looks, extreme egotism, a certain cold-heartedness, a dubious or at least questionable social background (like Brummell), fantastic extravagance (which ultimately ruined both him and Lady Blessington), and above all an impeccable sense of just how far he could go without breaking all the conventions of dress and becoming merely *outré*.

If d'Orsay represented one facet of the times, Lady Blessington, who wrote society novels and edited annuals bound in watered silk and filled with atrocious poems by people like the unfortunate 'L.E.L.',[1] represented another. It fully accords with the spirit of the day that the brilliant façade of her salon masked a most rickety financial background: the litigation over the late Earl's will had made her income anything but sure, and her literary activities were a ceaseless but ultimately vain attempt to bridge the gulf between her diminishing means and d'Orsay's ever-increasing expenditure. Disraeli could sympathize, for his own situation was, on a smaller

[1] See below, p. 80. L.E.L. stood for Laetitia Elizabeth Landon, now wholly forgotten but praised at the time as a poetical genius. She was in, fact, an indifferent versifier, and Sir Harold Nicolson is surely right in singling out her *réclame* as one of the most conspicuous examples of misjudgement on the part of contemporary critics.

scale, very similar. Certainly he found the atmosphere of Seamore Place congenial, and we must envisage many an evening spent there, in the celebrated red and gold drawing-room which contained Marie Antoinette's Sèvres and ormolu clock from the Petit Trianon, or in the boudoir-library with its famous collection of curiosities – Madame de Sevigné's smelling-bottle, Madame de Maintenon's pin-cushion, Louis XIV's snuff-box, Madame du Deffand's scissors. There Disraeli would listen to the conversation of some of the more amusing and raffish figures of the day, and observe the dress and demeanour of London's greatest dandy.

It is probably true, however, to say that Disraeli himself never became the complete dandy as exemplified by d'Orsay. He was, after all, despite his egotism, interested in other things. His very vanity concealed an inner insecurity which showed itself in sudden impetuous actions, such as challenging the Irish leader, O'Connell, to a duel,[1] and in bouts of gloom and despondency – traits far re-moved from the sang-froid of the true dandy. In any case he never really possessed d'Orsay's knack of knowing the limits to which one might go in matters of dress.

His extravagant appearance, his mordant wit, his arrogant demeanour and his flamboyant conversation made Disraeli far from popular in some quarters. Certainly he had plenty of invitations, but his hostesses were not the highest in society, and there was a whole set of aristocratic and intellectual grandees into whose presence he never moved – the circle which centered around Holland House. Even in the salons where he was accepted he did not always behave in a conciliatory manner. One of his more irritat-ing mannerisms was to put his thumbs into the armholes of his fantastic waistcoat and preface his remarks with a drawling 'Allah is great' – doubtless in order to remind the company of his Oriental experiences. If he was bored, he showed it. Mrs Bulwer wanted him to take down to dinner Mrs Wyndham Lewis, who, little though he guessed it then, was to be his future wife. 'Oh anything rather than that insufferable woman, but Allah is great', and he walked over and languidly offered her his arm.[2] He was well aware that literature was not the passport to the highest social success, and he treated his fellow authors, apart from Bulwer, with indifference. At a soirée at Bulwer's 'I avoided L.E.L. who looked the very personi-

---

[1] See below, pp. 124–6.
[2] Louisa Devey, *Life of Rosina, Lady Lytton* (1887), 412.

fication of Brompton', he tells his sister.[1] At another one he relents and 'at the end of the evening I addressed a few words to her, of the value of which she seemed sensible'.[2] When Bulwer wanted to introduce him to the then well-known society novelist, Mrs Gore, 'Oh my dear fellow, I cannot really, the power of repartee has deserted me.'[3] But Bulwer was firm and the introduction was made. We can have less sympathy with another victim of Disraeli's arrogance. Mrs Norton's husband, the Hon. George Norton, was a peculiarly odious character. Disraeli was dining with the Nortons one night, and his host proceeded to praise his own wine. Disraeli agreed. 'I have got wine twenty times as good in my cellar,' said Norton. 'No doubt, no doubt,' replied Disraeli, looking round the table; 'but, my dear fellow, this is quite good enough for such canaille as you have got today.'[4]

Inevitably there was no lack of malicious and disagreeable remarks about Disraeli's ancestry. He was known in some quarters as 'the Jew d'esprit'. Mrs Bulwer, (not, it must be admitted, a reliable witness where her husband's friends were concerned), tells a story of Disraeli and Samuel Rogers, the rich, formidable and acidulated old literary potentate, who was born in 1763, and lived to see the beginnings of the Crimean War. Disraeli had been sitting on a cane-seated chair, and when he stood up the marks were palpable upon his bottle-green velvet trousers. 'Who is that?' asked Rogers. 'Oh, young Disraeli, the Jew', replied Mrs Bulwer. 'Rather, the wandering Jew with the brand of Cane on him,' said Rogers.[5] Disraeli, who partly overheard, did not conceal his irritation. Perhaps it was this episode that made him write in his diary for 1834.

> Rogers hates me. I can hardly believe, as he gives out, that V. G. [Vivian Grey] is the cause. Considering his age I endeavoured to conciliate him, but it is impossible. I think I will give him cause to hate me.[6]

The hostility which Disraeli had inspired in influential quarters of the literary world appeared soon after his arrival in London. He was a candidate for election to the Athenaeum Club, of which his

[1] Ralph Disraeli (ed.), Lord Beaconsfield's Correspondence with his Sister, 1832–52 (1886). Hereafter described as Correspondence.
[2] ibid., 6.
[3] ibid., 2.
[4] M. & B., i, 232.
[5] Devey, Lady Lytton, 412.
[6] Hughenden Papers, Box 11, A/III/C.

father had been a founding member. Bulwer, whom he asked to lobby on his behalf, was politely pessimistic:

> I think there is some chance of your not coming in because you have written books people have talked about. Had you compiled some obscure quarto which nobody had read you would be sure of success. But *il faut souffrir pour être célèbre.* These quiet fellows too have a great horror of us Novel writers. They fancy – the Ninnies – we shall clap them in a book. 'Suspicion is the badge of all our tribe.' For my part if I had not got into all my Clubs (at least the respectable ones) before I had taken to Authoring I should certainly be out of them all at this time.[1]

Bulwer was right. Disraeli was blackballed. He and his family attributed this rebuff to Croker, and it became one more count in their indictment against him.

Towards the end of 1832 he had another quarrel whose origins went back to the days of the *Representative*. Lockhart had already been trying to ridicule Bulwer, whom he described privately as 'a horrid puppy', but in the ensuing battle of words Bulwer was victorious. Lockhart now had a go at Disraeli. In the *Quarterly* of December 1832 he – or his reviewer – made an adverse comment on *The Young Duke*. Disraeli at once wrote:

> Sir
>   I have long been aware of the hostile influence (to use no harsher term) which you have exercised over my literary career, but I have hitherto passed it by unnoticed because of a great dislike of literary squabbles and because I feel confident that if I possess any genuine power I must prevail against even my most ungenerous opponents.
>   In the recently published number of the Quarterly Review you have by one of those side-wind sneers for which I have often been indebted to you, held me up to ridicule as using a phrase in a book called The Young Duke which is not to be found in that work . . .[2]

And he proceeded to demand an explanation. The phrase in question – 'to wine with' someone – actually occurred in *Vivian Grey*, and was no doubt just the sort of social solecism of which Disraeli least wanted to be reminded. But in such disputes an injured author seldom comes off best. Lockhart denied malice and

[1] ibid., Box 104, B/XX/Ly/9, n.d.
[2] Hughenden Papers, Box 134, B/XXI/L/243, December 1832 draft.

offered to publish a correction showing the true origin of the quotation.[1] This did not suit Disraeli, who replied that public satisfaction was not what he wanted. (If not, what did he want? one wonders.)

> The reputation [he continued] that depends upon such punctilios must indeed be delicate . . . I applied to you with the conviction that the critic who to attack the recent work of a writer quoted a phrase in a very distant and juvenile production could only have been influenced by a very ungenerous, not to say malignant motive. It appears that I was mistaken.[2]

Disraeli's only close friend among the literary set was Bulwer. It is disappointing that so few of their letters have survived at either Hughenden or Knebworth. But they may well have been indiscreet. In August of 1832 we find him bringing Bulwer to Bradenham for a week. 'He is to do what he likes,' Disraeli warns Sarah, 'and wander about the woods like a madman.' As we saw earlier, Bulwer was a great admirer of Isaac D'Israeli. Early in the following year the two young dandies went to Bath, where they enjoyed to the full the sensations of being lionized. 'I like Bath very much,' writes Disraeli; adding almost ingenuously, 'Bulwer and I went in late to one public ball and got quite mobbed.'[3]

In his diary Disraeli records the value which he set on Bulwer's society. 'I have not gained much in conversation with men. Bulwer is one of the few with whom my intellect comes into collision with benefit. He is full of thought, and views at once original and just.'[4] The two friends, as radical young men often do, sought consolation for the hostility of the respectable world in a sense of mutual rebellion against mediocrity and stuffiness, a semi-conspiratorial alliance against the dull and the conventional. On September 1, 1833, when Disraeli was back in Bradenham after another exhausting season, into which he had not only packed politics, literature and social climbing, but the beginnings of a passionate love affair, he wrote in his diary:

> My disposition is now *indolent*. I wish to be idle and *enjoy* myself, muse over the stormy past and smile at the placid present. My career will probably be more energetic than ever, and the world

---

[1] ibid., Box 134, B/XXI/L/244, December 29, 1832.
[2] ibid., Box 134, B/XXI/L/245, draft.
[3] *Correspondence*, 15.
[4] M. & B., i, 235.

will wonder at my ambition. Alas! I struggle from Pride. Yes! It
is Pride that now prompts me, not Ambition. They shall not say
that I have failed. It is not Love that makes me say this. I
remember expressing this feeling to Bulwer as we were returning
from Bath together, a man who was at that moment an M.P.,
and an active one, editing a political journal and writing at the
same time a novel and a profound and admirable philosophical
work. He turned round and pressed my arm and said in a tone,
the sincerity of which could not be doubted: 'It is true, my dear
fellow, it is true. We are sacrificing our youth, the time of
pleasure, the bright season of enjoyment – but we are *bound* to
go on, we are *bound*. How our enemies would triumph, were we
to retire from the stage! And yet,' he continued in a solemn voice,
'I have more than once been tempted to throw it all up, and quit
my country, for ever.'[1]

4

By the time Disraeli wrote this he had made his first attempts to get
into the House and had failed. Whether it was ambition or pride
which pushed him towards politics does not greatly matter. It was
probably both, and added to them was the desire to make a splash.
'We came here for fame,' he told Bright many years later. To create
a sensation, to occupy the limelight, to act a part on the greatest
stage in the world, these were the springs of action that thrust
Disraeli onwards. Obscurity, mediocrity, failure, were what he
dreaded. To be in Parliament was to be *someone*. And if these
feelings were not sufficient spur, there was the example of Bulwer.
Here was a man who had achieved far greater literary *réclame* than
Disraeli and who had been sitting since the summer of 1831 as a
Radical MP.

Politics had probably been Disraeli's goal ever since the affair of
the *Representative*. A letter from Austen in July 1830 suggests that
the idea of standing for Parliament had been mooted before he left
for the East. While he was away the country was convulsed by the
greatest political crisis since the fall of the Fox–North Coalition.
Disraeli followed the course of the Reform Bill with fascination.
Afterwards he maintained that he first began to understand politics
by reading long out-of-date numbers of *Galignani's Messenger*, a
then well-known journal, while detained in prolonged quarantine at
Malta on his way home. He arrived in London the day Parliament

[1] loc. cit.

was prorogued as a result of the House of Lords rejecting the second
Reform Bill. 'The times are damnable,' he wrote to Austen, 'I take
the gloomiest view of affairs, but we must not lose our property
without a struggle . . . In the event of an election, I offer myself
for Wycombe.'[1]

In what political interest was he to offer himself? The letter suggests a Tory inclination, or at any rate hostility to the Whigs and
Reform. Moreover, family tradition in so far as there was any
pointed that way. Isaac was a mild Tory and most of his friends
belonged to the same side. On the other hand, Disraeli was a natural
rebel at this stage of his career and long after; and his exemplar,
Bulwer, was emphatically on the side of Reform. There may have
been a further consideration. Disraeli's great object was to get in,
and the tide was obviously flowing fast against the Tories. No one
who was ambitious would commit himself to the losers. Soon after
his return to England, Disraeli began to 'nurse' High Wycombe in
the Radical interest.

But it showed his lack of any fixed ideas that he chose this
moment to collaborate in the production of an anonymous anti-
Whig publication brought out by Murray in April 1832, entitled:
England and France: or a Cure for Ministerial Gallomania. It was
three hundred pages long and combined a melodramatic account of
the July Revolution with a vituperative attack on the Government's
pro-French foreign policy. The other collaborators were Baron
d'Haussez, a reactionary legitimist refugee and ex-Minister, and a
certain Baron de Haber, an enigmatic figure whose name turns up
from time to time in Disraeli's more dubious enterprises. He was a
financier of sorts and is described by Smiles in his life of Murray as
'a mysterious German gentleman of Jewish extraction'.[2] Whatever
distinctions Disraeli made in his own mind, the authors of such a
publication were bound to appear as enemies of the whole Reform
cause. At the last moment he began to be uneasy, especially when
Croker, who to Disraeli's great annoyance had been given by Murray
the task of reading the proofs, wanted to restore some high Tory
sentiments which he had erased. 'It is quite impossible that anything adverse to the general measure of Reform can issue from my
pen or from anything to which I contribute', he wrote to Murray,
adding that within the last four months he had rejected an offer to

[1] M. & B., i, 203.
[2] Smiles, *Murray*, ii, 347.

be returned for a Tory borough and within the last four hours an offer to join 'the Conservative Club'.[1]

The Tory borough which is not named or mentioned anywhere else in Disraeli's papers was probably a myth. But any Tory association was undeniably awkward just then. When the book appeared Sarah observed: 'I long to see you that you may read me many riddles. The principal one is how you will reconcile your constituents to your politics,' and she added that one Huffam, Disraeli's main supporter, in Wycombe, 'is in a great fright that you are going to betray him by proving yourself a Tory after he has for so many months sworn to all Wycombites that you were not one'.[2] Disraeli had intended to keep the authorship dark, concealing it even from his former confidante, Mrs Austen. He was beginning to be bored with the Austens now, and to cut their dinner parties. But she guessed his part, though he continued to deny it, and she passed the story on to his cousin George Basevi, between whom and the Disraelis there was no love lost. 'George Base', as Isaac called him, sent the news to Bradenham, asking whether Disraeli 'was mad'.[3]

Disraeli's time was fully occupied just now. In May, *Contarini Fleming* was published by Murray. Disraeli persisted in regarding it as his best novel, but it was a financial failure at the time and has never 'taken' since. Its autobiographical interest is great, but as a novel it is curiously stilted and lifeless, after the early part about Contarini's boyhood. Although the profits were exiguous, Disraeli exaggerated when he said that they did not even cover the cost of publication.[4] It is fair to add that the market for novels generally was a bad one in the early 'thirties, perhaps because public attention focused on politics. By far the best things which Disraeli wrote during the next three years were two short pieces which appeared in Bulwer's *New Monthly Magazine*. These were *Ixion in Heaven* in December 1832 and February 1833, and *The Infernal Marriage*, July to October 1834. Light satires modelled on Lucian, they have a freshness, wit and daring which still charm. Isaac considered them to be his son's most original contribution to literature.[5]

[1] ibid., 344–5.   [2] M. & B., i, 210–11.
[3] Hughenden Papers, Box 8, A/I/c/28, Isaac to Benjamin, April 1832.
[4] See C. L. Cline, *Notes and Queries*, August 1942, 69.
[5] In 1842 William Aytoun, the Scottish poet and parodist, produced an amusing burlesque of *Ixion in Heaven*, entitled *Endymion; or a Family Party of Olympus*. The two works bound up together were republished in 1927 by Eric Partridge as number one of the series, *Nineteenth Century Highways and Byways* – an entertaining example of that unusual genre, the satire satirized.

In the middle of May, Disraeli met Sir Robert Peel for the first time. It was at a dinner party given by Lord Eliot, later the 3rd Earl of St Germans. They sat next to each other and Disraeli noticed that Peel 'attacked his turbot almost exclusively with his knife, so Walker's story is true'.

Disraeli continued in his letter to his sister: 'I can easily conceive that he could be very disagreeable but yesterday he was in a most condescending mood and unbent with becoming haughtiness. I reminded him by my dignified familiarity both that he was ex-Minister and I a present radical.'[1]

But perhaps he overdid the dignified familiarity. For once in a while we have another account than his own of the impression Disraeli made on an important personage. Sir William Fraser, writing many years later, records Lord St Germans's account of the dinner.[2] Disraeli 'probably from nervousness did not recommend himself to Sir Robert Peel'. He asked Peel to lend him some papers to help him in a book that he was writing. 'From his appearance or manner Sir Robert Peel seemed to take an intuitive dislike to him. He "buried his chin in his neckcloth," to use Lord St Germans's own expression; and did not speak a word to Disraeli during the rest of the meal.' A raffish *outré* literary dandy of radical opinions and foreign appearance was not likely to hit it off with a person like Peel, rich, reserved, quintessentially English, yet – for all his Harrow and Christ Church background – uneasily established.[3]

On June 7 the Reform Bill became law and an election on the new register was certain before the end of the year. Disraeli at once began to canvass High Wycombe. 'I start in the high Radical interest,' he wrote to Austen, 'and take down strong recommendatory epistles from O'Connell, Hume,[4] Burdett and *hoc genus*. Toryism is worn out & I cannot condescend to be a Whig.'[5] The sitting members were two Whigs, Sir Thomas Baring and Robert Smith, son of Lord Carrington, who lived at Wycombe Abbey and possessed much electoral 'influence' locally. Since they were both reformers, and so was Disraeli, it was difficult for him to find any very plausible

---

[1] M. & B., i, 205, May 15, 1832.
[2] Sir William Fraser, *Disraeli and His Day* (1891), 187.
[3] After Disraeli's death a garbled version of this episode was current – and actually published – to the effect that Peel had walked out of the room offended at blasphemous language by Disraeli about Jesus and Mary Magdalen. Corry was asked to deny it. Corry Papers.
[4] Joseph Hume, 1777–1855. Radical politician.
[5] M. & B., i, 211.

issue on which to fight them. He had, it is true, letters of support
from leading Radicals, but that of Hume proved to be a boomerang.
He had muddled up Wycombe with Wendover,[1] where the sitting
members were Tories. As soon as he discovered the mistake he
hastened to throw over Disraeli and assure Smith and Baring of his
support in a letter which they were quick to publish. This was
awkward, but it did not depress Disraeli unduly.

> Whigs, Tories, and Radicals [he wrote to Austen from the Red
> Lion at Wycombe], Quakers, Evangelicals, Abolition of Slavery,
> Reform, Conservatism, Corn Laws – here is hard work for one
> who is to please all parties. I make an excellent canvasser and am
> told I shall carry it if the borough be opened.[2]

At this moment a further complication occurred: Sir Thomas
Baring resigned in order to contest an unexpected vacancy for
Hampshire and there was a by-election in Wycombe on the old
unreformed franchise – one of the last ever held in Britain. Despite
Disraeli's refusal to 'condescend to be a Whig', his friend Bulwer
tried hard to persuade the Whig party managers to let him in unopposed.[3] It is hardly surprising that they declined and put up
instead Colonel Grey, a younger son of the Prime Minister. Great
excitement followed. Disraeli lived in a whirl of activity, speeches,
letters, canvassing. He had his spies in London, in particular Mrs
Bolton.

> All information, however trifling [she wrote on June 9 in a breath-
> less letter full of underlinings], is of use at an election *but never
> betray* me for my informers are my *most* particular friends – I
> think the Carringtons are playing a deep game . . . Take care
> what you say to a Mr. Hughes – he is one of their set and was at
> my door on Thursday morning giving the history of your doings
> to Charles Gore. Pray try and outwit these people. I begin to
> tremble – Grey boasts in fine style at the Travellers – I assure you
> you are creating a sensation – at your father's club[4] you are
> terribly abused – think of my telling you all these reports so

---

[1] The muddle was not as silly as it sounds. Smith had sat for Wendover at one
time, and Lord Carrington, unlike his son, was a strong Tory – one of the twenty-two
'stalwarts' who voted to the bitter end against the Reform Bill. It would be natural
to assume that father and son were on the same side.

[2] M. & B., i, 212.

[3] 'Don't abuse Ministers . . . I'll try all I can to prevent opposition.' Hughenden
Papers, Box 104, B/XX/Ly/13, Bulwer to Disraeli, June 17, 1832.

[4] The Athenaeum.

entirely out of my line – all I mention are *facts* I have *first* hand, so you may depend upon them.[1]

But there was nothing which Disraeli could do. The electorate was tiny. Only thirty-two people recorded their votes. In vain Disraeli, dressed in his most flamboyant style, stood above the portico of the Red Lion in the main street of Wycombe, and made his celebrated opening speech. He pointed to the head of the lion – 'When the poll is declared I shall be there' – then to the tail – 'and my opponent will be there.' In vain he asserted on the hustings that he had never taken a penny of public money, that he had no Plantagenet blood in his veins, that he was sprung from the people, that he preferred the happiness of the many to the happiness of the few. It was the few who had the votes. When the poll was declared he was defeated by twenty to twelve.

Disraeli made a strong speech of defiance to show that he did not intend to take his defeat lying down – so strong that it provoked a local magnate, Lord Nugent,[2] to send a rather absurd challenge, because of some imagined personal aspersions. The seconds, Disraeli's being a Captain Angerstein of the Grenadier Guards, however, managed to compromise the matter, and prevent an actual duel. But there was one alleged remark of Disraeli's upon which his enemies fastened. 'The Whigs', he was supposed to have said, 'have cast me off, and they shall repent it.' Disraeli denied having used the words, and he probably had not said anything quite so damaging. But it is permissible none the less to wonder what his attitude to the Whig party would have been if Bulwer's application had been successful.

The by-election of June was a mere overture to the real struggle. On December 3, Parliament was dissolved. In High Wycombe the electorate had increased from a figure of not much more than thirty to one of 298.[3] Disraeli issued his address as early as October 1. He wore, he said, 'the badge of no party and the livery of no faction'. He supported the secret ballot, triennial parliaments, repeal of 'the Taxes on knowledge' (ie the paper duties), rigid economy, and amelioration of 'the condition of the lower orders'. He also favoured

[1] Hughenden Papers, Box 13, A/IV/G/4.

[2] Lord Nugent was a brother of the Duke of Buckingham, and, unlike most of the Grenville family, a strong Whig.

[3] It was a two member seat and each elector had two votes, though he was not obliged to cast both.

commutation of tithes and such changes in the Corn Laws as will 'relieve the customer without injuring the farmer'.

> Englishmen [he ended], behold the unparalleled Empire raised by the heroic energies of your fathers; rouse yourselves in this hour of doubt and danger; rid yourselves of all that political jargon and factious slang of Whig and Tory – two names with one meaning, used only to delude you – and unite in forming a great national party which alone can save the country from impending destruction.[1]

In spite of his contemptuous equation of Tory and Whig there are already signs in this, the second of Disraeli's four unsuccessful attempts to get into Parliament, that he preferred the Tories to the Whigs. It is not as surprising as it might seem. In the absence of a candidate of their own party a number of Wycombe Tories were inclined to give him their support, for they detested the Whigs so bitterly that in order to unseat one of them they were even willing to vote for a Radical whose views, theoretically at least, lay even farther to the Left. Disraeli was shrewd enough to take advantage of this paradoxical situation. Indeed, this local union of opposite extremes against the centre was to be the pattern which he sought to repeat on a national scale twenty years later when he tried to convince Derby, an ex-Whig, that a Conservative-Radical alliance was the answer to their problems. He spoke at Wycombe in favour of the Corn Laws, and he now began, for the first time, to propound his doctrines of primitive Toryism; the principles of Sir William Wyndham and 'my Lord Bolingbroke', who, he maintained, advocated a purer form of constitutionalism, which had since been subverted and overlaid by the misrepresentations of the Whig aristocracy. It is doubtful whether his audience understood what he was talking about. But Disraeli expected to win. He even had a special chair made in his colours – pink and white – in which he hoped to be carried by his supporters after victory was announced. His optimism was unfounded. He was once more at the bottom of the poll, the figures which were declared on December 12 being: Smith 179; Grey 140; Disraeli 119.

The Radicals of the 1830s, to whom Disraeli proclaimed allegiance, should not be confused with those who bore the same name in the high noon of the Victorian era – the earnest, thoughtful, hardworking and respectable group which looked for leadership to

[1] M. & B., i, 218.

Cobden and Bright. On the contrary, they were an erratic, frivolous, colourful and picturesque collection of independent MPs with no coherent political philosophy and counting as adherents a large quota of cranks and eccentrics of every kind. The general election of 1832, like the elections of 1906 and 1945, was one of those great political upheavals, which resemble some volcanic eruption deep down below the bed of the sea and bring floating to the surface all manner of strange marine life seldom seen by the ordinary observer. If the Parliament of 1832–4 could contain such characters as Molesworth who had fought a duel with his Cambridge tutor, John Gully, the prize-fighter and bookmaker, or a dandy like Bulwer, there seemed some chance that Disraeli might get in, for all his oddities.

General elections in those days were spread over two or three weeks and a defeated candidate could often have a try elsewhere. Disraeli now proceeded to issue an address to the County of Bucks. There was only one anti-Whig candidate, Lord Chandos, who was one of the sitting members and the eldest son of the Duke of Buckingham, against two Whig reformers. There was nothing radical about Chandos, who was known as 'the farmers' friend', and was an extreme high Tory, but apparently – or so Disraeli maintained many years later – he approved of Disraeli's intervention. Disraeli's address to the county was, therefore, distinctly more Tory in tone. He came forward as a supporter of 'the protected industry of the farmer' and declared that he would resist 'that spirit of rash and experimental legislation which is fast hurrying this once glorious Empire to the agony of civil convulsion'.[1] But, unknown to him, a Mr Scott Murray, had agreed to stand as a Tory along with Chandos, and Disraeli deemed it prudent to withdraw. He had the consolation of seeing Scott Murray defeated, although Chandos was elected by a comfortable majority.

This was Disraeli's last effort in the election of 1832, but before long another chance seemed imminent. A vacancy was expected in the borough of Marylebone, and in April 1833 Disraeli issued yet another address. Once again he trimmed his sails to the prevailing wind. An urban constituency like Marylebone required a more radical approach than Buckinghamshire. We hear little about the land or about 'rash experimental legislation', and a great deal about the candidate's independence, his popular views, his contempt for the aristocracy, and his position 'as a man who has already

[1] M. & B., i, 221.

fought the battle of the people'.[1] Alas, it was a waste of print and paper: the expected vacancy did not occur.

Much ink has been expended by pious Conservatives seeking to discern a consistent political creed running through these and later effusions of Disraeli before he finally got in. It is an unprofitable task. Disraeli himself took a far more light-hearted view of his own activities. When the question of his contesting Marylebone first arose a newspaper published an imaginary conversation which Disraeli quotes without comment in a letter to Sarah. 'Someone asked Disraeli in offering himself for Marylebone, on what he intended *to stand*. "On my head," was the reply.'[2]

Naturally the fact that Disraeli had first tried to get in with Whig consent, that he had then stood as a strong Radical, then as a Radical with a slight Tory tinge, that he had then issued an address whose tone was near-Tory with a slight Radical tinge, and finally issued one as a strong Radical again, did not go unobserved by his enemies. He, therefore, deemed it wise to publish a pamphlet justifying his position. It was entitled *What is He? by the Author of Vivian Grey*.[3] The title was explained by an extract from an alleged letter 'of an Eminent Personage' who was supposed to have said: 'I hear that *** is again in the field; I hardly know whether we ought to wish him success. What is he?' The letter was attributed to the Prime Minister, but, as Monypenny rightly observes, the eminent person was 'just as likely to have been a figment of Disraeli's imagination'[4] – indeed much more likely, for after all it was Grey's own son whom Disraeli had twice fought, and the Prime Minister, if he bothered about the matter at all, could easily have found out about this eccentric adventurer into the political field of High Wycombe.

The pamphlet was an argument for a national party – a coalition between Tories and Radicals.

A Tory and a Radical I understand; a Whig – a democratic aristocrat I cannot comprehend. If the Tories indeed despair of restoring the aristocratic principle, and are sincere in their avowal that the State cannot be governed with the present machinery, it is their duty to coalesce with the Radicals, and permit both political nicknames to merge in the common, the intelligible, and

[1] M. & B., i, 225.
[2] *Correspondence*, 18–19, April 8, 1833.
[3] Reprinted in W. Hutcheon (ed.), *Whigs and Whiggism* (1913), 16–22.
[4] M. & B., i, 225.

the dignified title of a National Party. He is a mean spirited wretch who is restrained from doing his duty by the fear of being held up as insincere and inconsistent by those who are incapable of forming an opinion on public affairs.

Finally, after detailing some rather unconvincing points for the policy of this new national party, Disraeli ends in resounding style:

Let us not forget also an influence too much underrated in this age of bustling mediocrity – the influence of individual character. Great spirits may yet arise to guide the groaning helm through the world of troubled waters; spirits whose proud destiny it may still be at the same time to maintain the glory of the Empire and to secure the happiness of the People!

With the vanishing of his chance at Marylebone, Disraeli's political activities fell temporarily into abeyance. Society, love, debts and literature dominated his life for the next eighteen months, and it was not until the end of 1834 that he again stood for Parliament.

CHAPTER V

Henrietta

1833-4

1

Isaac Disraeli and Sarah were naturally anxious to see the erratic genius of the family safely and suitably married as early as possible. They hoped that he might be successful with Ellen Meredith, the younger sister of his dead friend, William. He did, in fact, propose to her early in May 1833,[1] but she refused him. The rebuff does not seem to have disconcerted him. On May 22 he wrote to Sarah:

> By the bye would you like Lady Z—— for a sister-in-law, very clever, 25000l, and domestic? As for 'love' all my friends who married for love and beauty either beat their wives or live apart from them. This is literally the case. I may commit many follies in life, but I never intend to marry for 'love', which I am sure is a guarantee of infelicity.[2]

Lady Z—— was Lady Charlotte Bertie,[3] aged twenty-one, a daughter of the Earl of Lindsey. Sarah did not approve of her. She expressed doubts about the money and adjured him to remember 'what improvident blood more than half fills her veins'.[4] She urged him not to give up Ellen Meredith, but to try again. Nor was Sarah the only person to push Disraeli in the direction of matrimony. Mrs Bolton, curiously enough, also had a candidate. In November of the previous year she pressed the case for a Miss Trotter, who was a patient of her husband and a friend of Lady Francis Leveson-Gower. Mrs Bolton described her, rather unpromisingly, as 'a splendid wreck and now in great misery'. But she went on to say

> No one thing could reconcile me more to this world of ill nature than to see her your wife. All her fine feelings are thrown back

---

[1] Jerman, *The Young Disraeli* (1960), 186.

[2] *Correspondence*, 20.

[3] She had a shadowy connexion with the Austens, her mother (*née* Layard) being a sister of Peter Layard, who was Austen's brother-in-law and father of Henry Layard, the assyriologist and diplomat.

[4] Jerman, 187.

and she – with all her brilliant qualities and splendid fortune there – she is a lone solitary creature.[1]

Nothing came of the suggestion. As for Lady Charlotte, she seems to have enjoyed Disraeli's company. She first met him in the box of a friend, Lady Sykes, at the opera on May 18. She wrote in her diary:

> . . . He is wild enthusiastic and very poetical . . . The brilliance of my companion infected me and we ran on about poetry and Venice and Bagdad and Damascus, and my eye lit up and my cheek burned and in the pauses of the beautiful music [*Tancred*] my words flowed almost as rapidly as his . . . He tells me that repose is the great thing and that nothing repays exertion. Yet noise and light are his fondest dreams, and nothing could compensate to him for an obscure youth, not even glorious old age. I cannot understand his trying to get into Parliament . . .[2]

But the matter went no farther. Lady Charlotte became engaged to Josiah John Guest, MP, who was nearly thirty years older, very rich, one of the proprietors of the Dowlais ironworks, and a partner of Wyndham Lewis, whose wife pressed the match. Many years later Disraeli had the pleasure as Prime Minister of recommending their son for a peerage.[3] Lady Charlotte Schreiber (as she later became, marrying her children's tutor after Guest's death) was a notable Victorian 'character', who had ten children, wrote books on iron, translated the *Mabinogion* and became a great collector of china, fans and playing-cards. One suspects that she would not have suited Disraeli. In any case, whatever he might say to appease his family, he was not interested in matrimony at this moment. For in the summer of 1833 he became deeply involved in an illicit love affair which was to dominate his life for the next three years.

The person in whose box Disraeli met Lady Charlotte Bertie was Henrietta, wife of Sir Francis Sykes, third baronet, of Basildon in Berkshire. 'She is a fine woman, and very pleasant and good natured', wrote Lady Charlotte in her journal. Disraeli fell in love with her and she became his mistress about this time or a little later. She was the eldest daughter of Henry Villebois of Marham Hall in Norfolk and Gloucester Place in London, a rich man and a partner

---

[1] Disraeli Papers, Box 13, A/IV/G/9, n.d.
[2] Quoted by Jerman, *The Young Disraeli*, 187–8, from the manuscript diaries in the possession of Viscount Wimborne.
[3] The first Lord Wimborne.

in the great brewing firm of Truman and Hanbury.[1] Sir Francis was
the grandson of the first baronet (1730–1804), an able and respected
servant of the East India Company, who made some £300,000 in its
employ and was a close friend of both Clive and Warren Hastings.
Sir Francis's father, the second baronet (1767–1804), only held the
title for a few weeks, he and his wife and youngest son dying of
scarlet fever in Germany within ten days of each other and less than
two months after the first baronet's death. He was a much less
worthy character than his father, being both dissipated and extravagant in his youth. He later became more respectable, marrying a
daughter of the first Lord Henniker and entering Parliament.

His son, the third baronet (1799–1843), an orphan at the age of
five and a delicate child as a result of the scarlet fever which carried
off his parents, was brought up by the Duchess of Chandos, his
maternal great-aunt. In 1821 he married Henrietta. They had three
sons and a daughter.[2] Sir Francis owned Basildon, a fine house
though scarcely a 'Palladian palace', as Disraeli called it, and a
house in Upper Grosvenor Street. He did his best to provide for his
family in spite of a diminished patrimony. He was evidently an
intelligent man, as his privately printed *Scraps from a Journal*
(1836) shows. But his health was weak – his letters to Disraeli
abound with medical details – and his character was not very
strong. He had, moreover, made a disastrous marriage to a head-
strong, wilful and passionate woman whom he could not easily
control.

A conspiracy of silence has till recently concealed the story of her
liaison with Disraeli, although it was well known at the time. The
evidence consists of a series of badly written, ungrammatical semi-
legible love letters – some eighty altogether – from her to him, and a
memorandum by Disraeli's solicitor, Sir Philip Rose, summarizing
the story and advising Lord Rowton, Disraeli's literary executor,
to destroy them.[3] Happily he did not, and they survive among the

---

[1] Rye, *Norfolk Families* (2 vols, 1911–13), ii, 968. Henrietta's brother became High
Sheriff of Norfolk and MP for West Norfolk. One of her sisters, Maria, who appears
later in this story, married first Lord Glentworth, then a Colonel Baillie. She died at
the age of 100 in 1903. The other, Emily, married Colonel Bathurst, a grandson of
Bishop Bathurst of Norwich. Their son inherited the Villebois estates.

[2] Francis, b. 1822; Frederick, b. 1826; Henry, b. 1828; and Eva, b. 1830. None of
the three brothers had any male heirs. They inherited the title in succession and on
the death of Henry in 1916 it passed to the descendants of the Rev. William Sykes, a
brother of the third baronet, but a very different and much stronger character. It
remains in that branch of the family today.

[3] Hughenden Papers, Box 27, A/XI/A/8.

Hughenden papers. Inquiries have failed to discover Disraeli's letters to her. The family probably destroyed them after her death. Monypenny refers to the affair so briefly and in such guarded language that it is impossible to infer what really happened. He does not even reveal the lady's name. Although numerous books about Disraeli have appeared since the official biography, it was not until 1960 that the silence was broken by an American scholar, Professor B. R. Jerman in his book, *The Young Disraeli*.[1]

Henrietta was a woman of striking appearance, as the picture by Maclise shows. The first part of the novel *Henrietta Temple* is clearly based on this love affair, and Disraeli's feelings for her are vividly described.

> There is no love but love at first sight. This is the transcendant and surpassing offspring of sheer and unpolluted sympathy. . . . An immortal flame burns in the breast of the man who adores and is adored. . . . He laughs alike at loss of fortune, loss of friends and loss of character. The deeds and thoughts of men are to him equally indifferent. He does not mingle in their paths of callous bustle or hold himself responsible to the airy impostures before which they bow down. He is a mariner who, in the sea of life, keeps his gaze fixedly on a single star; and if that do not shine, he lets go the rudder, and glories when his barque descends into the bottomless gulf.[2]

Disraeli first met Henrietta in the early spring, probably April. By June the affair was in full swing. On June 24 Disraeli apologizes to Austen for not seeing him. 'The truth is, my dear fellow, but this is an explanation which I offer only to you – I have for the last ten weeks been only *nominally in Town*. The engrossing nature of my pursuits I leave to your imagination . . .'[3] This is very probably an allusion to Henrietta. Early in June, Disraeli decided to bring Henrietta to Bradenham for a short visit on the 9th, and persuaded Sarah to send a formal invitation. The prospect of this fashionable figure from the grand London world descending upon the Disraeli household filled his sister with alarm.

Life at Bradenham was normally of a quiet and somewhat Jane

---

[1] The story in this and the succeeding chapters is based directly upon Disraeli's papers, but the main outline is the same as Professor Jerman's, and although we differ in some details I should like to pay tribute to his skill in unravelling this and many other obscure matters in Disraeli's early life.

[2] *Henrietta Temple*, Bk II, ch. 4.

[3] British Museum, Add. MSS., 45908, f.70.

Austenish hue – anyway when Benjamin was away. Sarah's letters to him are filled with such episodes as their brother Jem's (James) indignation at Benjamin's ingratitude for all that he had done for the latter's bay mare, or her fear that 'the Governor will get into a scrape' with the Bishop of Bristol 'about the Sabbath', or the odd conduct of Mr King, the Rector of Bradenham, in inviting the D'Israelis to dinner along with the Norrisses and the Dashwoods, despite the bad relations of the three families. 'It was so like the Kings who owed us all three a dinner and were determined to make one do.'

The visit bristled with difficulties. For example, there was the cook, Mrs Adams, who, as early as April, had been described by Isaac to Benjamin as 'sunk into childishness'. Indeed, Isaac with reckless optimism tried to enlist his son's aid in procuring a new one – 'The great difficulty is to get one who will *live in the country*', he wrote. Disraeli was scarcely the man to cope with such domestic matters, as his sister well knew, and Sarah soon followed up her father's letter: 'It is too bad of the Governor to torment you about cooks.' And so, in June, Adams was still there, but would 'get furious' if the visitors came down any later than the 9th. And what were they to do to entertain Henrietta?

> I am so afraid that it will rain [wrote Sarah] & then Lady Sykes will die of ennui for how can we amuse her of an evening as it is & then the long mornings too. She will hate us. Let us know as well as you can tell what établissement travels with her & with you.
>
> Send the claret directly as we want that at any rate & it will not be good if it have not time to settle – Durrants is very good – one doz. – but do not take a moment about it. The champagne had better come from Favene – let them pack it cool if such a thing be possible. I write in the greatest haste.[1]

But the visit seems to have been a success and Jem, then aged nineteen, was delighted when Henrietta offered to send him some antlers. A month later, in early July, we find Disraeli writing from Southend, where Sir Francis and Henrietta had taken a house. At the beginning of August they parted for the time being, and Disraeli returned to Bradenham. The first letter from Henrietta which has survived and can be dated accurately was written to him on August 16. It leaves no doubt about their relationship by then.

[1] Hughenden Papers, Box 7, A/I/B, June 4, 1833.

12 o'clock Thursday night

It is the night Dearest the night that we used to pass so happily together. I cannot sleep and the sad reality that we are parted presses heavily upon me – very very heavily. I love you indeed I do, and I am thankful that you cannot quite share my sorrowfulness of feeling. The returning to *our* House and seeing the solitary chair and knife and fork and the bright fire blazing as if from cheerfulness spoke more forcibly to me than any language could do. . . .

. . . The dear head is it better? That it were pillowed on my bosom for ever. I would be such an affectionate old Nurse to my child and kiss and soothe every pain. You are in bed my love asleep from being tired and worn out. It is a comfort I know your room and the white couch and that when you write and say: 'I have been walking on the Terrace or the Common,' all will be present to my imagination. I am blinded – Good Angels guard my dearest. A thousand and a thousand kisses. Good night. Sleep and dream of – your Mother.[1]

The signature is revealing. Disraeli needed not only a mistress but an adoring mother, someone to look after him in illness, sympathize with him in adversity, encourage him when he was in a mood of despondency, admire him when he was successful. His loves and friendships were almost invariably with women older than himself: Sara Austen; Clara Bolton; Henrietta; his wife; Mrs Brydges Williams. He sought the maternal solicitude which his mother never gave him – or not to the extent which he demanded. Henrietta 'would be such an affectionate old Nurse to my child, and kiss and soothe every pain'. She corrects him as if he were her young son. 'I hope my child you do not neglect the comb or the teeth. I shall scold you if you do, but above all I *charge* you *not* to smoke *much*. It leaves a strong flavour and last night at the Opera it was spoken of.' The same pattern is repeated a few years later with Mary Anne Lewis, his future wife. 'No one attended the funeral [of her brother] except your child,' he writes. And again, 'How is his darling? When will she come to see her child?' She was twelve years older and really could provide the quasi-maternal affection that he wanted. Hence the success of the marriage. Henrietta was not so well suited to satisfy this element in Disraeli's temperament. She could not give him material security, for she had no money of her own and was married to someone else; and, however much she might play up to the maternal role for which Disraeli cast her, she

[1] Hughenden Papers, Box, 13, A/IV/H/1.

was basically a passionate, emotional, jealous, highly sexed woman who wanted a lover. Here are some typical letters:

My pensive love did the deep feeling of last night banish all thoughts but those of rapture and love and is there no reaction? . . . I fain would tell you all I feel for you but alas words are denied me. *Love me* my Soul *love me* & be assured that the measure of my idolatry for you is full to the brim. Every breath I draw is yours, even *now* your kisses live on my lips and face and I feel the passion of your embrace . . .[1]

Sometimes she had doubts about him and wanted to be re-assured.

Best beloved do you love me? Do you indeed? How often have I asked you that question, how often been soothed by your assurance of devotion to me. I do not doubt you, oh no, I dare not − it would drive me mad − I have faith, the most implicit faith in all you have said and sworn and I know we shall meet with the same love we bear each other now. Dearest exert your-self for my sake and let our parting be as short as possible and I will bear it as best I can . . .

How I wish I was very clever for your sake. I do not fear your criticism. I have just sense enough to feel my deficiency & to wish we were more on a par . . . My sisters have been here, nosy things going on . . . [illegible] between H and her love. I have felt too unwell to leave my bed and was obliged to declare I had the cholera. My best blessing is with you Darling of my heart. Adieu. Think of me.[2]

Sometimes their love-making gave her belated fears which she wanted him to dispel, though it is hard to see what he could say.

I suffered last night from a fit of horror. I will hide my head in the dear bosom and ask you a question. Do you think any misery can occur to us *now* from all the loved embraces? I fear we are very rash people & when I think I shake − answer please a little yes or no & I beseech you not to be angry with me for who have I to communicate all my thoughts and fears but you my Soul . . . Can you come at 4. I hope to be there before that time. Remember yes or no.[3]

One cannot easily imagine Mary Anne, who for all her fantastical manners was cool and practical at heart, indulging in effusions like

[1] Hughenden Papers, Box 13, A/IV/H/82, n.d.
[2] ibid., A/IV/H/1.
[3] ibid., A/IV/H/66.

Henrietta Sykes
from a painting by Daniel Maclise, 1837

Mary Anne Disraeli
from an oil painting by J. G. Middleton

these. Nor does it require the wisdom of hindsight to guess that for Disraeli a liaison of this sort could not last for very long. At heart he, too, was cool and practical. He was not going to sacrifice his life for love.

The conduct of the affair was made easier than it might have been by the irregularities in the private life of Sir Francis. Clara Bolton[1] had now become his mistress, with the connivance of her husband, the doctor, who, according to Sir Philip Rose, 'was said to derive a pecuniary benefit from the connexion'. At first her presence on the scene caused trouble, for she still seems to have been intensely jealous about Disraeli, but in the end it made possible a *modus vivendi* between husband and wife.

Matters came to a head at the end of August. While Henrietta was writing from London the first letter quoted above, her husband was away shooting.

> A million and more of thanks [she wrote to Disraeli on August 17] for the dearest letter . . . I will do as you tell me, live for Hope, but I own to the task being difficult every thought is so entirely yours and latterly I have been utterly dependent upon you for amusement for everything . . . I hope the Grouse will be eatable[2] – A *most* kind letter from My Lord saying it was 4 in the morning and he had despatched me the first birds he had slaughtered . . . and the day brought Mrs. Bolton but I was not downstairs and dared not exhibit myself had I been. Such eyes, red, yellow, anything but blue. Dearest, Dearest Ammin[3] how he would hate my ugly self.[4]

Meanwhile trouble impended. Scarcely had the grouse and Mrs Bolton arrived but Sir Francis Sykes himself appeared unexpectedly in London, instigated, so Henrietta suspected, by Mrs Bolton. He at once made a scene, asked whether she had been seeing Disraeli, and when she admitted doing so for an hour or two every day, forbade her ever to meet him again.

> I said there was no probability as you were away for six months – evidently he expects that I should refuse giving the promise and

---

[1] See above, p. 75.

[2] She had sent some to Bradenham.

[3] Henrietta frequently used this as a term of endearment. Ferdinand Armine is the hero of *Henrietta Temple*, of which Disraeli had written the first volume already. He did not resume and finish the novel until 1836, after he had parted from the real Henrietta for good and all.

[4] Hughenden Papers, Box 13, A/IV/H/2.

then there would have been the excuse for a fracas. I shall be calm
for so much is at stake – fear not for me, I am prudent. I think
Madame [Mrs Bolton] recalled him – he was most severe about
my not seeing her – and she is at the bottom of all this.[1]

But Henrietta did not interpret prudence as silence. The mysterious Baron Haber had seen Sir Francis at Mrs Bolton's the previous
night (August 19) and had told Henrietta. She resolved on a counter-
attack, and after drafting and destroying several notes, decided to
go round to Mrs Bolton's house in person. There she had a stroke
of luck. She found her husband's carriage standing outside the door,
which was open.

I walked in [she writes to Disraeli][2] *sans* knocking, and up to the
drawing room *sans* being announced. Fancy their consternation.
I really thought Francis would have fainted. Lady S., as stiff as
a poker and perfectly cool: 'Mrs. Bolton I have called upon you in
consequence of a scene which I am perfectly aware I owe entirely
to you, and I am here to have an understanding as from what has
passed there can be no discourse between us 3. [You and] Sir F.
are aware of my more than intimacy with Disraeli. It has suited
all parties to be a great deal together, not certainly from the
intimacy of the ladies, for I have never expressed a friendship for
you. I have never been even commonly ladylike in my conduct to
you and when together Disraeli and I Francis and you formed to
[*sic*] distinct parties, and it can be proved that we did. Consequently in Sir Francis' absence there was no change in me, and
should he leave London to-morrow your doors I *would never* enter
– nothing should induce me, but I will give Francis the sanction of
my presence[3] on the strict condition of his not violating by unjust
and ungenerous threats ties which he himself has sanctioned and
which both himself and yourself *know* have been necessary to
carry on your own game . . . Before I leave this house the solemn
promise must be given *never* to mention Disraeli's name as a bug
bear.'

This attack threw the enemy into confusion. Mrs Bolton at first
tried to fight back. She declared that Henrietta had caused 'as much
of pain as of *surprise*' to her.

'Disraeli,' [she went on, as reported by Henrietta], 'is a heartless
wretch. I have stuck up for him for years – our acquaintance has

[1] Hughenden Papers, Box 13, A/IV/H/14.
[2] ibid., Box 13, A/IV/H/88, n.d. The letter is printed in full by Jerman, *The
Young Disraeli*, 200–2. The date must be August 22 or 23.
[3] Professor Jerman reads 'precedence', but this makes no sense.

been of 9 years standing. Here are his letters vowing undying, unspeakable, obligationship, but I repay them now with scorn. As for you and I [*sic*] I have too much dignity to wish our acquaintanceship on any other footing than you have placed it. Disraeli has influenced his *dear* family to desert me, witness his father never having called on me . . .'

She then added for good measure that, through Disraeli, Henrietta's character was gone.

'I heard from good authority (Fitzgerald, I suppose) that no one would visit you next year on his account, and he will leave you, he has left you. I know him well, he is everywhere despised.'

But Mrs Bolton could not sustain the battle. Henrietta ends her account to Disraeli,

Sufficient for you and I that we are victorious. Madame cried and wrung her hands. F. cried and begged me to be merciful. I did *not* cry and had apologies from both.

The air had been cleared and from then onwards Sir Francis accepted the situation. There was as yet no question of a separation. Henrietta agreed to go to France with him on a tour for eleven days. Disraeli was summoned from Bradenham to say good-bye on August 28, and the following day the Sykeses left for the Continent. After they had gone she wrote advising him to 'live as plainly and industriously as possible – *no fruit, no made dishes* – how you are laughing but my advice is nevertheless good and to be followed, Sir. Remember *I* am to order you to obey.' Then she wanders into an amorous rhapsody:

Think of the happy ten minutes on the sopha . . . and how delicious would be the wandering of Henrietta and himself through the friendly domain and the happiness of returning to the peaceful cot and reposing in each other's arms – it would be bliss, my Ammin, bliss beyond compare and hope whispers it will be realized – most idolized, I love you, I adore you, I worship you with fond idolatry . . .[1]

In Calais she met the Bulwers beginning on their ill-fated journey to Naples – a holiday intended to restore their fragile marriage but destined to shatter it beyond repair. They told her that Disraeli stooped so much that walking in front of them he looked like fifty.

[1] Hughenden Papers, Box 13, A/IV/H/5.

'I was in a rage but it is true. *So remember.*' The Bulwers had a bed in the back of their travelling-carriage, and Henrietta writes: 'I built castles in the air of *our* travelling.'[1]

A day or so after she had left for Calais, Disraeli began to jot down his reflections and experiences in a notebook. Although it has become known to students of Disraeliana as 'the Mutilated Diary',[2] even that name suggests a degree of coherence and order which is lacking. It is, rather, a sporadic record of his feelings, his thoughts and people whom he met. It ends abruptly with the commencement of his parliamentary career four years later.

Disraeli begins, on September 1, 1833, with the oft-quoted words: 'I have passed the whole of this year in uninterrupted lounging and pleasure.' After a reference to his political efforts he goes on:

> . . . and one incident has indeed made this year the happiest of my life. How long will those feelings last? They have stood a great test, and now absence, perhaps the most fatal of all. My life has not been a happy one. Nature has given me an awful ambition and fiery passions. My life has been a struggle – with moments of rapture – a storm with dashes of moonlight – Love, Poetry . . .

At this point two pages are torn out of the book and we resume with an incomplete sentence

> . . . achieve the difficult undertaking. With fair health I have no doubt of success but the result will probably be fatal to my health.

The incident was undoubtedly his love affair with Henrietta, and the missing pages probably refer to this, too. What was the 'great test' which his feelings had stood? We can but conjecture – perhaps the Bolton episode. The whole passage is a strange one. 'How long will these feelings last?' The question is one which a man would scarcely ask if he was swept away by a passionate love affair; it is possible to suspect that even from the start he was less in love with her than with the idea of being in love and of being loved. A grand passion was an inseparable part of that Byronic tradition which so often sounds, with a slightly hollow note, in Disraeli's life. 'That beautiful pale face will be my fate', wrote Lady Caroline Lamb, and, as if echoing the words, Henrietta writes to Disraeli: 'Your pale face is before me my Beloved.'

It is clear from the diary that Disraeli was in a curiously un-

[1] Hughenden Papers, Box 13, A/IV/H/6.
[2] ibid., Box 11, A/III/C.

settled state of mind. He was contemplating yet another method of making his name in the world: he planned to write nothing less than an epic poem on the subject of the French Revolution, and intended to devote the autumn at Bradenham to this great work. But he made little progress. Early in the fourth week of September Henrietta returned to London. On September 25 he suddenly left Bradenham to be with her.

It is not clear, in spite of the visit in June, quite how much the D'Israeli family knew about the liaison at this stage. It is hard to believe that they knew nothing. Isaac was unworldly, but not as unworldly as all that. At any rate, whether or not he correctly understood the reasons he was worried about his son's erratic behaviour and wrote him a letter of unusual seriousness.

Wednesday
[Sept. 25, 1833]

My dear Benjamin,

You may imagine that my distress was not less than my surprise on learning this morning of your sudden departure – without giving last night the slightest hint to any of us.

All such violent movements in the quiet of domestic habits alarm me – I would ease my mind by the hope that nothing of any painful nature has drawn you off so unexpectedly, but I cannot conceal from myself that they betray that unsettled state of your mind which occasions me the greatest anxiety.

If this however should only prove to be a freak you will easily forget the few words I have written and perhaps hereafter you may yet discipline your mind, too long the creature of Imagination.

Believe me, my Dearest son, that I who can sympathize with all your feelings – and all your Errors – I have still most at heart our combined happiness. I am but too deeply sensible how this has been risked! – and how much must be repaired! – it is a work well worthy of Ourselves, should we ever discover how to set about it. It ceaselessly occupies my thoughts – but I who am offering my advice stand in great need of an Adviser.

Your ever affectionate Father
I. D'Israeli

I will not trouble you with any errands for you are an indifferent messenger. I hope we shall see you in a day or so.[1]

Disraeli soon returned to Bradenham. Meanwhile a further complication arose. Henrietta's father, Mr Henry Villebois, had cut

[1] Hughenden Papers, Box 8, A/I/C/46.

Henrietta and Disraeli in the street when he was last in London. Unfortunately the gesture was wasted, as the lovers were too engrossed in each other to notice him. He was obliged to inform Henrietta through one of his other daughters that he intended, so Henrietta reported to Disraeli, to go on cutting her until 'my intimacy with you ceased'. He said that 'Francis' conduct was everything unprincipled and Mrs. Bolton no fit companion for either of us'. Henrietta went on:

> in fact that extreme fear for the consequences, and wretchedness, had almost broken his heart and he was ill and it only remained for me to continue my present dishonourable flirtation to send him to the grave but he trusted to my making the sacrifice for all our sakes, more particularly for yours and so on. I wrote back to say how little I had seen of you, that I was *agonized* by his displeasure but so long as Francis allowed me your society I should enjoy it &c &c. . . .[1]

She then proceeded to invite Disraeli to stay at Southend in November. Sir Francis, now apparently reconciled to the relationship, added his solicitations in cordial terms.

> Dear D'Israeli
>   Lady Sykes has taken possession of the house at Southend for nearly a fortnight – we like it very much – the weather is favourable for all out door amusements . . . I like it much more at night as the appearance is grand mysterious and wild . . . we hope we shall have the pleasure of your company down here – there is a very good bedroom with the dining room attached to it, with a fire in it. . . .[2]

There was only one snag. Presumably as a *quid pro quo*, he insisted upon the Boltons being regular guests, too. This seems reasonable enough in the circumstances, but naturally Henrietta disliked having as a constant guest a woman who had been her lover's former mistress. Indeed, she had already sought reassurance on this very point, and wrote to Disraeli in the same letter quoted above,

> And so it is all over with B – is it not so – tell me. Write to me as soon as you can (to-morrow, do) – the fracas did good, not anything now but praise –. I have seen no one excepting always the Boltons – we are going to-morrow to Gravesend about Francis' yacht.[3]

[1] ibid., Box 13, A/IV/H/8, October 11, 1833.
[2] ibid., A/IV/H/10, October 30.
[3] ibid., A/IV/H/8, October 11.

And again she writes a week later from Southend

> Mrs. Bolton, thank Heaven, is off to Chertsey. The Lamberts
> appear to dote on her. She told me she intended going to Braden-
> ham to see her *dear* friends. What's to be done? For she has im-
> pudence for anything . . . I think, beloved Ammin, you will like
> the quiet of this place. The greatest drawback will be the *damnable*
> Boltons. They poison love, my greatest source of enjoyment.[1]

Disraeli seems to have arrived early in November, but there was no
question of the Boltons making any overt trouble. 'My word is law,
my look is a command,' Henrietta wrote early in December, just
after Disraeli's return to Bradenham, 'but I am hourly nay every
minute annoyed by the coarse vulgarity of the one, and the hypocrisy, the low cunning of the other.'[2] Disraeli too must have been
embarrassed by the situation. Poulter's Grange, Southend, during
the month of November, certainly contained a curious household:
Sir Francis, weak and affable; Dr Bolton, ill-bred and familiar; Mrs
Bolton, brassy and overdressed;[3] Henrietta, condescending and
grand; Disraeli, silent and cryptic. It suited all parties concerned to
preserve a veneer of civility, but beneath it passions seethed.

2

Disraeli passed the whole of November at Southend, returning to
Bradenham at the end of the month. He had made some progress
with the *Revolutionary Epick*, and indeed it was becoming more than
ever necessary that he should finish the book, if only to recoup his
finances. These had long been in a state of confusion. To some extent
he was able to stave off the most pressing demands, and to earn
enough for current expenses, by his pen. But the last of his books
to make much money had been *The Young Duke*, for which he had
received and spent the advance as long ago as 1830. Since then he
had published *Contarini Fleming* in May 1832, and *Alroy* along with
the *Rise of Iskander* in March 1833.

Contarini Fleming, as we saw, was a complete failure. Author and
publisher shared the profits, which amounted to only £18 each.
Alroy, whose opening chapter, as Disraeli himself admitted, made

---

[1] Hughenden Papers, Box 13, A/IV/H/9, October 18, 1833.
[2] ibid., Box 13, A/IV/H/12, December 6, 1833.
[3] ibid., 'Mrs B. is a mass of splendour – where the money to pay it [comes from]
is an awful question.'

just as good sense if one read it backwards, was oddly enough more profitable – anyway to the author, if not to the publisher. Murray declined it, but Saunders and Otley gave an advance of £300, which enabled Disraeli to pay off his debt to Austen. Most modern critics would attribute some merit to *Contarini*, perhaps a little to *Iskander*, and none whatever to *Alroy*, which is written in a deplorable sort of prose-poetry and is perhaps the most unreadable of his romances. The contemporary public found all three equally obscure, and Disraeli by now badly needed the money which only a real popular success could give him. It was destined to come neither soon nor easily. Over a year later, early in 1835, we find the American gossip writer N. P. Willis writing: 'd'Israeli cannot sell a book *at all*, I hear.' Not until December 1836 did he manage to catch the attention of the public again – with *Henrietta Temple*.

If his income had declined, his expenditure had increased. His wardrobe, 'ruinous' in 1830, had certainly become no less so in 1833; there had been election expenses, and finally there was Henrietta. To conduct a love affair with a lady of fashion was bound to be costly. Moreover, in Henrietta's case it was also extremely distracting. She was possessive, tearful and exhausting. Being in love with her was a full-time occupation when she was present, and a considerable drain on the emotional and mental resources even when she was not. When one is trying to compose an epic poem it is presumably tiresome to have to spend hours writing love letters.

Desperate for money, Disraeli resolved to consult his old friend Austen, who had just lent him another £300 when he passed through London at the end of November on his way back to Bradenham from Southend. Disraeli now asked him to lend an additional £1,200, which he said would cover his outstanding debts, in return for an assignment of his copyrights. These, with the exception of *The Young Duke*, which was due to fall in shortly, belonged to Disraeli, and he proposed to bring out a complete edition of his romances, 'by which if I sell 4000 in monthly volumes I shall make £1,500'. In addition the appearance of 'the Epic poem and a novel' (presumably *Henrietta Temple*) would produce at least £1,000. The loan would give him the necessary tranquility of mind to complete these two works within six months. 'I entreat you my dear friend not to look upon this letter in the light in which such appeals are usually and justly viewed.'[1]

---

[1] The correspondence about this loan is printed in full by Jerman, 207–11 and 214.

But Austen felt it was a time to deliver a rebuke. Rightly or wrongly he considered that Disraeli had 'dropped' him in the course of climbing into a more upper-class world than that inhabited by sedate London solicitors like himself. On December 1 he wrote and said so, adding that after 'many hours of most anxious and painful consideration' he had decided to refuse the loan, although he would not insist on calling in the £300 existing debt. Could not Disraeli appeal to his relatives?

This rebuff seems to have come as a genuine surprise to the recipient. 'I awoke from a dream,' he wrote to Austen on December 3, 'I really thought that you would have done anything for me and that's the truth.' He repudiated the charge of having dropped his old friend.

> Illness, different countries, different pursuits and circles, all these are causes which may render men *little intimate* who are nevertheless great friends . . . I was so circumstanced last year that my acquaintance I utterly neglected, the relations to which you allude I never went near and I disregarded an entrance which offered itself to me to the most brilliant society of the metropolis.[1]

He went on to say that his debts were solely due to electioneering expenses, doubtless forgetting that he had told Austen the year before that the cost to him of the Wycombe election had been 'a mere trifle'.[2] He ended:

> Now for my father. In the most important step of a man's life, though this should be breathed scarcely even to you, I have opposed his earnest wishes, and I have based my dutiful opposition upon my independence. I do not wish by extraordinary money applications to one who was always very generous to me to revive a most painful subject. As for my relations I have never been on terms of intimacy or friendship with a single member of the whole brood. Friends my dear Austen are not made every day nor do the habits of my life which are either passed in the dazzle of existence or complete solitude, allow me to make them. It is in youth only that these connections are formed and yours was my last. Had the friend [Meredith] who in his gloomier hours never found me wanting been spared to me I should not have had to write this humiliating letter. Farewell . . .[3]

[1] No doubt the last sentence refers to his love affair, but it is not clear what the entrance was to Society, which he disregarded. Perhaps it was a myth.

[2] Austen did not forget. See Jerman, 212, for his reply. 'I recollect your telling me when I cautioned you about electioneering expenses that you had managed for a mere trifle.'

[3] See Jerman, 208–10, for the whole letter.

Disraeli's reason for not wishing to apply to Isaac may have been
because he had rejected some sort of matrimonial project, favoured
by the family; or it may have been merely an excuse. Henrietta was
duly shocked by Austen's heartlessness.

> May I say [she wrote on December 6] Austen's letter was brutal.
> You asked him for *no* favour, your copyright was a generous offer
> on your part and Austen's taunt was unmannerly, as a man's
> ceasing to visit when he is in love is not an unusual occurrence,
> is it?[1]

Disraeli remained at Bradenham to compose his poem, though he
was evidently much distracted by his difficulties. Henrietta's letters
poured in:

> Of all the evils of life to be harassed about money is the most
> provoking.
>   Loving you as I do I cannot but grieve at our separation. I
> went into your room today, arranged your wardrobe, *kissed* the
> Bed, swallowed my tears and behaved as a heroine – dearest
> dearest Ammin – I do think my fate is a cruel one – born to love
> you does add to my sorrow & still I am grateful that I do – I live
> for Thursday, remember to tell me all. Today's letter was the
> kindest, the dearest – write me many such . . . 125 lines [of the
> poem], I scarcely believe it. Dearest I am astonished and delighted
> and congratulate you. Tell me every word your Father says about
> it. Is he not delighted?[2]

The answer to the last question was doubtful. Isaac thought that
the style resembled that of Pye,[3] but we do not know whether
Disraeli passed this opinion on to Henrietta. And so the letters
continue. On Christmas Eve she writes:

> . . . The blissful hours we have spent! Never let them be effaced
> from your mind. Sometimes I fear novelty will wear off & satiety
> succeed to your present feelings – can it ever be? Last evening I
> amused myself turning over all your Duke St. wardrobe – washing
> the brushes etc & I felt a gush of happiness even for the old
> slippers – you may laugh for I did at my folly, still I hate to think
> it is folly, for I could not wish to love you less and I should if I
> felt not so.[4]

[1] Hughenden Papers, Box 13, A/IV/H/12, December 6, 1833. My transcription
differs from Jerman's, 215.

[2] ibid., Box 13, A/IV/H/11, December 4, 1833.

[3] The worst Poet Laureate in English history with the possible exception of Alfred
Austin.

[4] Hughenden Papers, Box 13, A/IV/H/14, December 24, 1833.

The end of the year saw an unexpected and welcome change in their fortunes. Disraeli called on the Austens after Christmas, and Austen, whether cajoled by his wife who still adored Disraeli, or persuaded by Disraeli's personal charm, lent him the £1,200 at 2½ per cent for a year.[1] For the time being Disraeli was safe.

3

Disraeli spent most of the spring of 1834 at Southend finishing off the *Revolutionary Epick*. Before he went he rather reluctantly agreed to repay the Austens' kindness by giving the first part of the poem a trial run at a literary party of Mrs Austen's on January 16. The scene was recalled many years afterwards by Mrs Austen's nephew, Sir Henry Layard.[2] Disraeli was dressed in his most fantastic and affected costume, his shirt collar turned down in Byronic fashion, his shoes enlivened by red rosettes, his hair elaborately curled and highly scented. He stood with his back to the fire and recited in theatrical tones the opening canto. He then had to go, and as soon as he was out of the room Samuel Warren, one of the other guests, who was an excellent mimic and later wrote a best-selling novel called *Ten Thousand a Year*, proceeded to declaim a sort of parody which he had improvised for the occasion. The whole party dissolved in laughter, and there was at least one literary circle in which Disraeli's poem was ridiculed even before it was published.

At Southend, Disraeli seems to have made rapid progress despite the claims of Henrietta.

I pass my days in constant composition [he wrote in mid-February to Sarah.] I live solely on snipes and ride a good deal. You could not have a softer climate or sunnier skies than much abused Southend. Here there are myrtles in the open air in profusion.[3]

On one occasion he even hunted. As he modestly puts it,

I hunted the other day with Sir Henry Smythe's hounds and, although not in scarlet, was the best mounted man in the field

---

[1] Jerman, 217.
[2] An article in the *Quarterly Review* for January 1889.
[3] *Correspondence*, 23.

riding Lady Sykes's Arabian mare which I nearly killed: a run of 30 miles and I stopped at nothing. I gained great *Kudos*.[1]

His good progress with the poem may partly be explained by the fact that Henrietta was not there all the while, for in the same letter he observes that his only companion is her daughter Eva, who 'is a most beautiful child and prattles without ceasing' – it was one of Disraeli's most amiable traits that he was devoted to children – and that the Sykeses were away indefinitely. 'Solitude at this moment,' he observes, 'suits me very well.'

Not that his solitude was entirely undisturbed. Disraeli's family suddenly seems to have taken to literature. Sarah wrote a short story and pestered her brother into getting it accepted, only to complain bitterly at the low payment which she got for it. The pen of Ralph, too, was not idle. 'I suppose you will be at Southend for some time,' he mournfully observed,[2] as he sent his brother first a work entitled 'Preparatory Schools and Public Schools by an Old Wiccamist' and secondly 'a slight humorous sketch'. He had, however, some doubts whether his brother had perused either very carefully. For example, against the words 'Until the son is 12 years it is the mother alone who must find him a preparatory school' Benjamin had marked an obscure squiggle. What did it mean? And in a passage beginning, 'Of what use is all this knowledge of Latin and Greek . . .?' a blank had been left for Benjamin to insert a list of suitable books, but the blank remained – blank. As for the humorous sketch, Benjamin said that 'the design and execution are not felicitous'. 'Do you like its foundation?' asked his persistent brother, adding, 'But I do not think you have *much looked* into it, though I perceive one slight alteration.' Disraeli's family loyalty was deep, but it must have been strained at times.

The first book of the Epick was published in March. Disraeli asked permission to dedicate it to the Duke of Wellington, who courteously declined. In his preface the author declared that he awaited the public's verdict to decide whether to publish more, '. . . and if it pass in the negative I shall, without a pang, hurl my lyre to limbo'. However, although the verdict was anything but

---

[1] M. & B., i, 246. It is typical of the way in which that cautious Wykehamist Civil Servant, Ralph Disraeli, edited his brother's letters that in his version *Correspondence*, 23) 'pink' is substituted for 'scarlet', the allusion to the ownership of the Arabian mare is cut out, and the last sentence is eliminated altogether.

[2] Hughenden Papers, Box 9, A/I/E/54.

favourable, this did not stop Disraeli from bringing out two more volumes in June. These fell equally flat. True, there were encouraging cries from his family and friends – Isaac conceding that his apprehensions about the resemblance to Pye were unjustified. True, that ancient and celebrated lion-huntress, Lady Cork, who had once been addressed by Dr Johnson as 'dearest dunce', was so enthusiastic that she instructed her maid to bind the volumes in crimson velvet at the cost of seventeen shillings. But nothing could conceal the fact that Disraeli was not a poet. His style is feeble, derivative, and wholly devoid of inspiration.

4

In April 1834 one of the difficulties of Disraeli's private life was temporarily removed: Sir Francis Sykes departed on a prolonged tour of Europe. He did not return until late in 1836. Mrs Bolton vanished from the scene, too, and we next hear of her as occupying a somewhat equivocal status in Rotterdam.[1] Disraeli and Henrietta were able to carry on their love affair without further interruption from that quarter. Sir Francis seems to have fully condoned their relationship and wrote friendly letters to both of them during his sojourn on the Continent. Disraeli now lived openly with Henrietta and virtually took up residence in the Sykes's London house in Upper Grosvenor Street. They went everywhere together, and enjoyed to the full a London season of unusual brilliance. 'What a happy or rather amusing society H and myself commanded this year,' he wrote in his diary. 'What delicious little suppers after the opera.'

Disraeli's letters to his sister at this time sound more than ever like a gossip column in a glossy weekly journal. In a single week in June he went on Monday to the Duchess of St Albans's, on Tuesday to the opera with Lady Essex, on Wednesday to the Duchess of Hamilton's. A month later he made his début at Almacks. He dined regularly with Lady Blessington at Gore House. D'Orsay was his friend, and he writes in his diary: 'I am as popular with the first-rate men as I am hated by the second-rate.'

He met the celebrities of the day; he was sought out by the aged Beckford, the owner of Fonthill and author of *Vathek*, who was drawn from his habits of a recluse to meet this rising literary and

[1] See above, pp. 76–7.

social star; he had a long talk with O'Connell, with whom he was later to quarrel so bitterly; he was introduced to Lord Hertford, celebrated alike for his wealth, arrogance and profligacy – the Lord Steyne of *Vanity Fair*, the Lord Monmouth of *Coningsby*. At Lady Cork's he meets the Duke of Wellington, at Lady Blessington's Lord Durham, at Mrs Norton's Lord Melbourne.

The last of these encounters has achieved a well-deserved fame. It took place in the early summer. Grey was still Prime Minister. Melbourne, who had been Home Secretary since 1830, was not generally regarded as his successor, although he was, of course, one of the leading figures in the Cabinet. He was an intimate friend of Mrs Norton. One evening, at her tiny house in Storey's Gate, Disraeli came in, and Mrs Norton introduced him to Melbourne who was intrigued by his unusual appearance, and his equally unusual conversation, and suddenly asked him, in an abrupt but kindly tone: 'Well now, tell me what do you want to be.' 'I want to be Prime Minister', replied Disraeli. Melbourne was not easily surprised, but this reply surprised even him. He decided that such absurd ambitions should be discouraged. 'No chance of that in our time. It is all arranged and settled', he said, somewhat in the tone of Hilaire Belloc's Duke,[1] 'Nobody can compete with Stanley . . . If you are going to enter politics and mean to stick to it, I dare say you will do very well, for you have ability and enterprise; and if you are careful how you steer, no doubt you will get into some port at last. But you must put all these foolish notions out of your head; they won't do at all. Stanley will be the next Prime Minister, you will see.'[2]

Disraeli never forgot this curious conversation. Forty years later he told Lord Rowton that he could still repeat every word that Melbourne had said.

During this gay summer season Disraeli made one new friendship which was to be more important for his future than any of the encounters so far described. At a dinner party given by Henrietta on July 10 he met for the first time the former Tory Lord Chancellor, Lord Lyndhurst.[3] The latter was over sixty, Disraeli was not yet

---

[1] 'We had intended you to be
The next Prime Minister but three:
The Stocks were sold; the Press was squared;
The Middle Class was quite prepared'. *Lord Lundy*.
[2] W. M. Torrens, *Memoirs of . . . Viscount Melbourne* (new edition, 1890), 275.
[3] John Singleton Copley, 1st and only Earl of Lyndhurst, 1772–1863. Lord Chancellor 1827–30, 1834–5, 1841–6. Chief Baron of the Exchequer 1831–4.

thirty, but the two men took an instant liking for each other.

Lyndhurst comes down to history as a somewhat enigmatic figure, and the enigma is not made any easier of solution by the existence of two violently conflicting biographies,[1] and by the fact that Lyndhurst himself before his death destroyed most of his papers. Nevertheless, there is enough surviving evidence from contemporaries to leave us in little doubt that, although Lyndhurst was a man of brilliant parts and considerable legal ability, he did not inspire trust. The licence of his conversation, his ribaldry and cynicism, his general levity of demeanour were ill calculated to give him a reputation for seriousness of purpose, high principles, and that Roman *gravitas*, which Englishmen were beginning to expect from their statesmen. It was not enough to have a good brain. In a brilliant portrait of Lyndhurst, Walter Bagehot wrote: 'Few men led a laxer life; few men, to the end of their life, were looser in their conversation; but there was no laxity in his intellect.'[2] This was, indeed, true. But it did not save Lyndhurst in an increasingly serious-minded era from the suspicion that there was something basically unreliable about his character and his principles.

Bagehot alludes to the laxity of his life, and Bagehot was a man who weighed his words carefully when he wrote them. For Lyndhurst, who managed to preserve an astonishingly youthful appearance long into his middle age, was a notorious pursuer of women. He is said to have been the prototype of Gilbert's 'highly susceptible Chancellor' in *Iolanthe*. Lady Tankerville once, so Disraeli records, 'asked Lyndhurst whether he believed in platonic friendship. "After, but not before," was the reply.'[3] And Disraeli wrote in an appraisal after his friend's death: 'He was wonderfully fond of the society of women, and this not merely from his susceptibility to the sex, which was notorious, but because he was fond of them in every relation of life . . .' The passage ends with a description of Lyndhurst's face which in its upper part was 'that of Olympian Jove . . . The lower part of his countenance betrayed the deficiencies of his character, a want of high purpose, and some sensual attributes.'[4]

---

[1] Campbell in his *Lives of the Lord Chancellors* is hostile. Sir Theodore Martin, who was commissioned by Lady Lyndhurst to redress the balance, is panegyrical. Neither should be regarded as reliable.

[2] Walter Bagehot, *Biographical Studies* (1880), 329.

[3] Hughenden Papers, Box 26, A/X/A/57.1.

[4] ibid., Box 26, A/X/A/60, 3.

Although Disraeli had by now made the acquaintance of a good many men of power and influence, Lyndhurst was the first with whom he became on terms of real intimacy. Most accounts agree that Lyndhurst's conversation was reckless in the extreme, and remarkably indiscreet. Disraeli soon found himself the recipient of high secrets. He had that delicious sense of being on the inside of great events, of knowing what *really* lay behind this or that celebrated political transaction of the immediate past. Nor was this the only advantage that he derived from his new friendship. Lyndhurst may not have been trusted everywhere, but he was a man of much influence, and high enough in the councils of the Tory party to help Disraeli in his political ambitions. He himself saw in his young friend's literary talents a valuable weapon in the war of political journalism which raged between the parties. A useful bargain might well be tacitly struck. A great magnifico of a very different calibre from the Marquess of Carabas had found his Vivian Grey. Disraeli was in effect Lyndhurst's secretary and man of confidence for the next two years.

His own political position was still doubtful. He remained in theory a Radical, and, both before and after meeting Lyndhurst, looked to the leader of the Radicals, Lord Durham, for patronage and advancement. On June 15 he met Durham for the first time at a dinner party given by Lady Blessington at Gore House. She skilfully guided the conversation so as to show Disraeli to Durham at his best, and he appears to have made an impression upon that great magnate.

But, however sparkling he was at Lady Blessington's dinner-table, he does not seem to have convinced Durham that he would be an asset to the Radical party. At all events nothing came of the meeting.[1] This was all the more annoying since it was clear that a political crisis impended. Despite, or perhaps because of, their huge parliamentary majority, the Whig party was beginning to dissolve into fragments. As early as March 1833 Durham had left the Cabinet. In May 1834 the right wing headed by Stanley, Graham and the Duke of Richmond resigned. In July the intrigues of Brougham drove the elderly Prime Minister, Grey, into resignation,

---

[1] Disraeli claimed in a memorandum written nearly thirty years later (see M. & B., i, 263) that Durham offered to return him to Parliament, but this seems to conflict with Durham's rather unhelpful reply (ibid., 267) when Disraeli asked him point-blank for his support at Aylesbury. Perhaps Durham had made some non-committal observations which Disraeli misconstrued.

and William IV, somewhat to the public surprise, selected Melbourne as his successor. Thus matters stood when Parliament went into recess in the late summer of 1834.

At the beginning of August, Disraeli repaired to Bradenham, melancholy, ill, and despondent at being away from Henrietta. His intimacy with Lyndhurst had much increased, and the latter's readiness to help him was enhanced by the activities of Henrietta. Her letters leave no doubt that she used her influence with him to forward Disraeli's interests. The question is what the basis of this influence was. Did Disraeli, as was believed in some circles at the time, encourage her to become Lyndhurst's mistress in order to secure Lyndhurst's patronage for himself? On this point it is necessary again to quote Sir Philip Rose's memorandum.

> The positive assertion at the time [he writes] that Lady Sykes was the mistress both of D. and also of Lord Lyndhurst was evidently true, but by which of the two she was introduced to the other there is no evidence to show. The allegation at the time was that D. had introduced her to Lord L. and made use of the influence she acquired over Lord L. to forward his own advancement. I can well remember the scandal in the county at this connexion and especially at the visit of Lady Sykes to Bradenham accompanied by Lord L. and the indignation aroused in the neighbourhood at D. having introduced his reputed mistress and her Paramour to his *Home* and made them the associates of his *Sister* as well as of his father and mother. It did him much harm at the time and to show how unfavourable impressions linger long afterwards I have had it thrown in my teeth by influential county people within very recent years [he was writing in 1882] that this was an act which would never be forgotten and which all D's subsequent career could never obliterate.[1]

Rose goes on to add, however, that the letters suggest that the pressure for the invitation came from the D'Israeli family rather than from Benjamin himself, and that it might have been embarrassing for him to refuse.

Examination of these papers and others which Sir Philip Rose probably had not seen enables us to clear up some points. It was Henrietta who first introduced Disraeli to Lyndhurst, and, whatever the circumstances in which she first met the latter, it was not the result of any initiative on Disraeli's part. He therefore can be acquitted of that charge. Was Henrietta, as Rose believed,

[1] Hughenden Papers, Box 27, A/XI/A/8.

Lyndhurst's mistress? The letters do not prove conclusively that she was, but she travelled with him on the Continent – along with some members of his family, it is fair to add – in the autumn of 1834.[1] With a man of Lyndhurst's reputation this makes for the probability of such a connexion, but not certainty.

Did Disraeli approve of, and connive at, the close friendship which prevailed between his mistress and the ex-Lord Chancellor? He was apparently invited to go on the continental visit, but refused. This might suggest that he did not approve. But Henrietta's decision to accompany Lyndhurst was a sudden one prompted largely by the threat of her sister Maria descending upon her in Park Lane and trying to cajole her, on grounds of the notoriety of her affair with Disraeli, into quitting London and living with her father in Norfolk. Disraeli might have been genuinely unable to go at such short notice. Moreover, he had no money at all just then.

> Dearest love you will see by the accompanying disagreeable letter why I am so anxious to leave it [London] on the 25th. Lord Lyndhurst arrived in town last night. I can make him do as I like so whatever arrangement you think best *tell me* and I will perform it only to my father I cannot go. I should lose my senses . . . I shall never be happy till clasped to your bosom . . . Ld Lyndhurst is anxious you should be in Parlt. Seriously he is a most excellent being and I am sure I can make him [do] what I please – even the Durhamites – he is a gt friend of Brougham.[2]

And she enclosed the 'disagreeable letter' from her sister Maria, which warned her that she would be socially ostracized 'if you allowed him [Disraeli] to be actually Master of your House', and implored her to go to Norfolk with her father.[3]

A few days later Henrietta announced her resolve to accompany Lyndhurst abroad adding,

> I like Lord L. very much. He is very good natured and I only wish he had the power to serve us but he is too unambitious and only thinks of driving away care. He has a magnificent house.[4]

And shortly after that she thoughtfully observed: 'He is a perfect fool where women are concerned.'[5]

---

[1] Lyndhurst's first wife died at the beginning of the year.
[2] Hughenden Papers, Box 13, A/IV/H/85, n.d.
[3] Hughenden Papers, Box 13, A/IV/H/21, September 20, 1834.
[4] ibid., Box 13, A/IV/H/23, September 25.
[5] loc. cit.

The notorious visit to Bradenham, which seems to have caused such a scandal in Buckinghamshire county society, did not take place until July 1835, and it was followed by another that autumn when Henrietta and Lyndhurst again visited Bradenham together. The true relationship between the three cannot be determined with certainty. One thing, however, is certain; the episode did him nothing but harm in the locality where he was trying to make his political way. Sir Philip Rose goes further and says that when Disraeli was passed over for office by Peel in1841 the Lyndhurst – Sykes imbroglio was 'reported' to be the cause. If such reports were current, they were probably ill founded, since Peel had, as we shall see, other and stronger motives for acting as he did in 1841. But there can be no doubt that the affair damaged Disraeli and that it made its contribution, along with many other episodes, to the understandable aura of distrust which hung around his name for so many years.

CHAPTER VI

Distraction and Disappointment
1834-7

1

The autumn of 1834 saw a new political crisis and a new chance for Disraeli. Althorp, leader of the House of Commons, had inherited his father's peerage and Melbourne felt obliged to insist on Lord John Russell as his successor. This occurred just as Disraeli was in the middle of weaving a plot reminiscent of *Vivian Grey*, whereby Chandos, with whom he was on friendly terms, was to join with Lyndhurst in resuscitating the old Country party.[1] On November 14 William IV, unwilling to accept Russell, dismissed Melbourne and sent for Wellington. The Duke recommended him to send for Peel, who was in Rome at the time. It would take a month to bring him back. Meanwhile Wellington and Lyndhurst formed a two-man caretaker government, the political world hummed with intrigue and everyone made plans for the inevitable general election.

Disraeli first made an overture to Lord Durham, but there was nothing doing. The Radical Earl would not give tangible help, although he wished Disraeli luck – 'these are times which require the presence in Parliament of every true and honest politician'. This was not good enough. In no way perturbed at swinging to the opposite side of the political compass, Disraeli applied to Wellington and Lyndhurst. The latter did his best, consulting Greville who had told him that Lord George Bentinck, Tory MP for King's Lynn, needed 'a good man to assist in turning out Billy Lennox'.[2] Lyndhurst suggested Disraeli, adding that he was a friend of Chandos and, incorrectly, that Durham was trying to get him a seat. Greville commented dryly in his journal on December 6: 'His political principles, must, however, be in abeyance, for he said that Durham was doing all he could to get him by the offer of a seat, and so forth; if, therefore, he is undecided and wavering between Chandos and

---

[1] See M. & B., i, 262-5, for Disraeli's account of these abortive intrigues.

[2] Lytton Strachey and Roger Fulford (ed.), *The Greville Memoirs* (8 vols, 1938), iii, 117. Lord William Lennox, son of 4th Duke of Richmond, M.P. King's Lynn, 1832-4.

Durham, he must be a mighty impartial personage. I don't think such a man will do, though just such as Lyndhurst would be connected with.' Nevertheless he passed the suggestion on to Bentinck, for he noted next day: 'Disraeli he won't hear of.'[1] It would have required second sight to predict that within a dozen years they were to be intimate allies engaged in driving Peel out of office for ever.

There was now nothing for Disraeli but to make a third assault on Wycombe as an independent Radical, but it is interesting to notice that on this occasion at the instigation of Lyndhurst the Tory managers contributed £500 toward his election expenses.[2] They appear to have had some misgivings, but Lyndhurst informed them that Disraeli would withdraw at once if the money was not forthcoming. Presumably it was considered worth while to ensure a contest even if the anti-Whig candidate sailed under Radical colours.

On December 16 Disraeli delivered a lengthy speech at Wycombe, which he considered sufficiently important to issue in pamphlet form immediately afterwards.[3] He could not, he said, condescend both to be supported by the Tories because they believed he was a Tory and the Liberals because they thought he was a Liberal. He stood for repeal of the Malt Tax to relieve agriculture, and for the abolition of Irish tithes, though he was against lay appropriation, which all too often meant aristocratic robbery. 'I know the love that great lords, and especially Whig lords have for abbey lands and great tithes: I remember Woburn and I profit by the reminiscence.' He favoured abolition of Church rates if only for the sake of the Establishment itself, which 'I consider . . . a guarantee of civilization, and a barrier against bigotry'. He also supported the reform of municipal corporations. As for Peel's Government, he was noncommittal; it should be given a chance. He would have no truck with the argument that it was wrong to accept reforming measures from the party which had once opposed reform. The Whigs had a poor record for consistency, too, and anyway did consistency matter? 'The truth is, gentlemen, a statesman is the creature of his age, the child of circumstances, the creation of his times.' He laughed at the

[1] ibid., 118.
[2] N. Gash, *Politics in the Age of Peel* (1953), 436. In an autobiographical note written in 1860 (Hughenden Papers, Box 26, A/X/B/1) Disraeli says that he 'stood for the Boro at the request of Sir Robert Peel'.
[3] *The Crisis Examined by Disraeli, the Younger*, reprinted in William Hutcheon (ed.), *Whigs and Whiggism* (1913), 23–40.

objection to a rising politician that at a former period of his career
he advocated a policy different from his present one. 'All I seek to
ascertain is whether his present policy be just, necessary, expedient.'
The Whigs, he maintained, had aimed at power for life, and would
have succeeded if they had been able to pack the House of Lords as
they had packed the House of Commons. 'I think we may feel that
we have some interest in maintaining the prerogative of the Crown
and the privileges of the Peers.' Finally he let himself go in an
entertaining comparison of the late Government to the performance
of Mr Ducrow, a then celebrated circus performer who rode six
horses at the same time. Unfortunately one by one they fell ill and
donkeys were substituted instead.

> Puffing, panting, and perspiring he pokes one sullen brute,
> thwacks another, cuffs a third, curses a fourth, while one brays
> to the audience, and another rolls in the sawdust. Behold the late
> Prime Minister and the Reform Ministry – the spirited and snow
> white steeds have gradually changed into an equal number of
> sullen and obstinate donkeys; while Mr. Merryman, who, like the
> Lord Chancellor, was once the very life of the ring now lies his
> despairing length in the middle of the stage, with his jokes
> exhausted and his bottle empty.[1]

It was all in vain. He was beaten for the third time, the figures being
Smith 289, Grey 147, Disraeli 128.

Disraeli evidently decided after his latest setback that independent radicalism was no longer a winner, if it ever had been. He must
join one of the two great traditional organized parties. His choice
could not fail to be the Tories. Indeed, it already was, and if Lyndhurst's overture to Bentinck had come off he would by now have
been a Tory MP. The Whigs were out of the question. His political
efforts had inevitably been based on a stout anti-Whig programme,
if only because the constituency where he stood had as its sitting
members two Whigs; and in the last contest he had accepted financial aid from the Tory managers. Monypenny's suggestion that he
was converted by the Tamworth Manifesto, Peel's proclamation of
a new and more liberal form of Toryism, will not hold water.[2] Peel
had not even returned to England by December 7, when Disraeli's

---

[1] This was a hit at Brougham, who had caused much scandal by a 'progress' in the
north, during the course of which he played hunt the slipper with the Great Seal at a
party, and arrived drunk at the Edinburgh races in his Chancellor's full robes.
[2] M. & B., i, 276.

negotiations for a Tory seat at King's Lynn fell through. The manifesto was not issued till the 16th.

As soon as the news of his defeat came through on January 7, Disraeli wrote to the Duke of Wellington: 'I am now a cipher, but if the devotion of my energies to your cause, *in* and *out* can ever avail you, your Grace may count upon me who seeks no greater satisfaction than that of serving a great man.' The Duke replied with guarded courtesy in the third person: 'He very much regrets the result of the election at Wycombe.' To mark his conversion to the Tory cause Disraeli had his name put down for the Carlton Club, his proposer and seconder being respectively Lords Strangford and Chandos. The former, a diplomat *manqué* and an Irish poetaster, was a great admirer of *Contarini Fleming*. His son George Smythe was to be closely linked with Disraeli in the Young England movement. It was some time before Disraeli got in, and after his experience at the Athenaeum he was somewhat apprehensive, busily lobbying Lady Blessington and others for their influence. But he was duly elected in March 1836, one of fifty out of four hundred candidates. By then Strangford was a member of the selection committee, and Chandos was chairman. As Strangford observed, 'The Devil's in the fire if you don't get in.' From early 1835 onwards Disraeli became a regular diner-out in Conservative houses. One party out of many deserves resuscitation. It was given by Lyndhurst. There Disraeli met for the first time W. E. Gladstone, 'the rising hope of those stern and unbending Tories', MP for Newark since 1831 and one of Peel's Junior Lords of the Treasury. Disraeli noted that the dinner was 'rather dull but we had a swan very white and stuffed with truffles, the best company there'.

The general election greatly improved the position of the Conservative party, but Peel was still in a minority. Following the conventions of an earlier day, he tried, nevertheless, to carry on, but after six defeats in as many weeks he had to resign. The King was obliged in April 1835 to take back Melbourne as Prime Minister with Russell as leader of the House. He regarded the Whigs with bitter hostility for the remainder of his reign. The change of Government gave Disraeli a fresh chance. In those days acceptance of office involved vacating one's parliamentary seat. Henry Labouchere, Member for Taunton, was one of those included in the new ministry, and it was decided at Tory headquarters to put up £300 and send Disraeli to fight the by-election. Bonham, the Tory agent, described Disraeli to a local Tory solicitor 'as a Gentleman for whom all the Conservative Party are most anxious to obtain a seat in the H. of Commons . . . He is the son of Mr. D'Israeli well known in the literary world, and is himself a very able man.'[1] In a later letter he ended: 'At all events I am satisfied that we have sent you a good Candidate.'[2] This was a big step forward, for Disraeli was now the official nominee of his party, and even if he lost was likely in the long run to get a safe seat, provided he put up a good performance. He had, however, to endure a good deal of abuse on the ground of being a turncoat. Even the unpolitical d'Orsay wrote urging him to proclaim that 'though a Tory you are a reforming one, because it is generally understood that you committed yourself in some degree to the other party'.

A vivid account of his appearance and manner of speaking survives from the pen of a contemporary journalist. He was more dandified than ever, loaded with glittering chains on his waistcoat and rings on his fingers. 'Altogether he was the most intellectual looking exquisite I had ever seen.' But the observer was impressed by his powers of speech. 'The dandy was transformed into the man of mind, the Mantalini-looking personage into a practical orator and finished elocutionist.'[3] Disraeli was defeated by 452 to 282.

The Taunton by-election resulted in the most famous of all Disraeli's personal quarrels. He was reported in the Press as having stigmatized O'Connell, with whom the Whigs had recently concluded a parliamentary alliance, as 'an incendiary and a traitor'. In fact, he had not said this. He had merely quoted what the Whigs themselves had once said about O'Connell, and the most reliable version of the speech in question is that he described the Whigs as 'that weak aristocratic party in the state who could only obtain power by leaguing themselves with one whom they had denounced as a traitor'.

However, O'Connell saw the garbled version and was greatly enraged by it. At a meeting in Dublin he let himself go in one of the most ferocious pieces of invective which the annals of British politics can furnish.[4] He dwelt on Disraeli's 'superlative black-guardism', 'impudence', 'assurance' and 'gratuitous impertinence'.

[1] Quoted by Gash, *Politics in the Age of Peel*, 462.
[2] ibid., 463.
[3] M. & B., i, 282, quoting *Pen and Ink Sketches of Poets, Preachers and Politicians* (1846).
[4] M. & B., i, 287–8, quoting the *Courier*, May 6, 1835.

Disraeli himself was 'a vile creature', 'a living lie', 'a miscreant' and 'a reptile'. He declared that he had himself once been asked to support Disraeli, and that the latter by turning his coat and becoming a Conservative showed that he possessed 'perfidy, selfishness, depravity and want of principle'. He ended:

> His name shows that he is of Jewish origin. I do not use it as a term of reproach; there are many most respectable Jews. But there are as in every other people some of the lowest and most disgusting grade of moral turpitude; and of those I look upon Mr. Disraeli as the worst. He has just the qualities of the impenitent thief on the Cross, and I verily believe, if Mr. Disraeli's family herald were to be examined, and his genealogy traced, the same personage would be discovered to be the heir at law of the exalted individual to whom I allude. I forgive Mr. Disraeli now, and as the lineal descendant of the blasphemous robber who ended his career beside the Founder of the Christian Faith, I leave the gentleman to the enjoyment of his infamous distinction and family honours.

These outrageous remarks received wide publicity. A challenge was the only answer, but, since O'Connell had vowed, after killing a man in a duel, never to fight another, the correct procedure was obscure. However, O'Connell's son, Morgan, had recently challenged a Tory peer, Lord Alvanley, whom he deemed to have insulted his father. Disraeli argued that the converse ought to apply and wrote to challenge Morgan O'Connell. The latter replied that he was not responsible for his father's words. Disraeli then sent an open letter of over 1,000 words to the elder O'Connell and had it inserted in all the newspapers.[1] As a piece of writing it shows some of Disraeli's commonest defects, being too turgid and repetitive, but its tone was quite as offensive as his enemy's and, given the circumstances, one need not feel any undue sympathy for O'Connell.

It would have been better to have left the matter at that, but Disraeli followed up with a second letter to the younger O'Connell.[2] He inferred, he said, that the latter would only fight if his father had been insulted. This was to say that 'I *have* insulted him'. The letter ended:

> I shall take every opportunity of holding your father's name up to public contempt. And I fervently pray that you or someone of his blood, may attempt to avenge the inextinguishable hatred with which I shall pursue his existence.

[1] M. & B., i, 289–92.   [2] ibid., 292.

Disraeli now called upon d'Orsay to act as his second in the duel that seemed inevitable. D'Orsay as a foreigner was unwilling to interfere in a political duel. So he picked upon Henry Baillie, a mutual friend, for the task, but personally arranged all details. The duel did not come off. The police intervened and Disraeli was bound over to keep the peace. The affair made him notorious and gave him all the publicity that even he could wish for. His family was much alarmed at what seemed to them an excess of vindictiveness and ill temper, but Disraeli was unashamed. 'Row with O'Connell in which I greatly distinguished myself', he wrote in his diary for the year 1835.

2

The early summer had now arrived. Sir Francis Sykes was still abroad. Disraeli and Henrietta once again plunged into the gaieties of the season, with Lyndhurst as a frequent companion, guest, or host.

> Agreeable partys [sic] this season at Henrietta's [he writes in his diary] Strangford, Stewart de Rothesay, Burgersh.
>   Political parties at Lyndhurst's and masqued ball, my intimacy with the Londonderrys. Rosebank.

Almost every year saw a move upwards in Disraeli's ascent of the social ladder. Lady Londonderry was the stepmother of his friend, Lord Castlereagh. Famed for her opulence and her arrogance, she was a great Tory hostess. Disraeli first met her on July 19 at the grand fancy-dress ball to which he refers in the diary. She went as Cleopatra 'in a dress literally embroidered with emeralds and diamonds from top to toe'. She asked Castlereagh to introduce Disraeli and the encounter seems to have been a success. A few days later he was invited to dine at Rosebank, her country villa by the Thames. Disraeli was determined not to lose this valuable entrée into Tory society.

As for the ball, it was a splendid affair. Henrietta was dressed to look like one of Reynolds's ladies, Mrs Norton was a Greek, and Disraeli's dress was 'very good', although we are not told what it was. At half past two Lyndhurst, who went as a Marshal of France, gave a supper at his house in George Street 'to eighty of the supremest *ton* and beauty . . . and everybody looked blue who was not going to Lyndhurst's'.[1] Nevertheless it seems as if Disraeli had not relished the ball in anticipation. At all events a tear-stained letter from Henrietta which probably refers to it would suggest some sort of trouble:

> Wednesday 3 o'clock
> You are quite right to do as you please and keep an old faithful friend waiting for dinner. As for this morning I was alone during the whole time consequently choice only could influence you – you never wished to go to the Ball and now you have the opportunity of staying away. I will not be drawn off and on as you would a glove – if I cared for you less I suppose I should not grieve at the appearance of neglect.
> Henrietta Sykes[2]

However this does not appear to have been more than a passing tiff. The episode came only a few days after the celebrated visit *à trois* to Bradenham, which created such a scandal among the Buckinghamshire squirearchy, and since the visit was repeated only a couple of months later there was evidently no lasting quarrel.

Throughout 1835 Disraeli's intimacy with Lyndhurst increased. He became the latter's agent, go-between and general factotum. His mind buzzed with ingenious expedients. Might the situation after Peel's resignation perhaps be saved by an alliance of Peel and Lyndhurst with Melbourne and the right-wing Whigs? Mrs Norton acted as agent for Melbourne, Disraeli for Lyndhurst, and *pourparlers* began. But the plan was wrecked by the Lichfield House compact under which O'Connell had promised Russell the support of his followers in return for Whig benevolence towards Irish reform. Nothing came of Disraeli's proposal, except that Melbourne consulted Lyndhurst on the best way of getting rid of Brougham. Then, in the late summer another exciting possibility appeared. Was there not a chance that the King would again dismiss Melbourne, and if so, that Peel would this time refuse to accept office? In that case Lyndhurst would clearly be the man. Some such development seems to have been seriously envisaged by Lyndhurst himself, who claimed to have had a hint from Windsor, and he promised Disraeli a seat in the House if it came off.[3] It is hard to see how all this could have been taken seriously, but ultra-Tory intrigue was rife both then and

---

[1] Disraeli to Sarah, quoted M. & B., i, 302–3.
[2] Hughenden Papers, Box 13, A/IV/H/53.
[3] Sir Theodore Martin categorically denies the whole story, but Disraeli's evidence cannot be dismissed. See M. & B., i, 301–2, for his full account.

later, and the influence of the reactionary Duke of Cumberland may well have been at work on his brother, the king, and induced him to *say* foolish things if not to do them. Nothing happened, and a year later similar manoeuvres took place. 'Great courage and eminent services of the Duke of Cumberland', Disraeli records in his account of another series of equally abortive intrigues on behalf of Lyndhurst, and he finishes: '. . . a large party in the country would hail L's accession to the Premiership with satisfaction. His firmness and courage have won all hearts . . .' In fact, Lyndhurst carried little weight outside the House of Lords. He was never a serious contender for the Premiership and his moral and political character were not such as to inspire public confidence. However, Disraeli plunged merrily into the battle, wrote scurrilous anonymous articles for the *Morning Post*, packed with praise of Lyndhurst and abuse of the Whigs, hurried from dinner party to party at his patron's side, and generally enjoyed himself in the bustle of political conspiracy.

With the close of the 1835 session Disraeli embarked upon his first serious contribution to political literature. During the autumn at Bradenham he wrote, and in December published, one of his most famous books, an open letter of two hundred pages to Lord Lyndhurst. Usually known for brevity's sake as the *Vindication*, its full title is 'A Vindication of the English Constitution in a Letter to a Noble and Learned Lord by Disraeli, the Younger'. Its publication marks an important stage in Disraeli's progress as a political thinker. The letter was first and foremost a defence of the House of Lords, then in bad odour with the reformers for having tried to reject the Municipal Corporations Bill during the previous session. Much of the defence is ingenious rather than convincing, for example that it is no more anomalous for certain people to be entitled by heredity to become legislators on reaching the legal age than for others to be similarly entitled by heredity to exercise the franchise; and at times he comes near to saying that the House of Lords is more 'representative' than the House of Commons, a proposition implausible even then, though perhaps less so in an age of limited suffrage than it would to today.

But the real interest of the book lies in its adumbration of nearly all Disraeli's most well-known and characteristic ideas about history and politics. Here we have the anti-Whig theory of English history that the Tory party had been the truly democratic party, the party of the majority, ever since the reign of Queen Anne; that the Whigs were the oligarchical anti-national party which obtained power by a *coup d'état* and retained it in 1835 by 'the same desperate and treasonable compact', made by the Parliamentarians in the reign of Charles I, but with 'Irish Papists' instead of 'Scotch Presbyterians'. We have, too, Disraeli's admiration for Bolingbroke as the prophet of a reinvigorated Toryism, his contempt for doctrinaires and abstract theories, especially those of the Utilitarians, his deep respect for traditional institutions, and his reverence for landed property and all that goes with it. All these ideas are to be found in more vivid form in his later writings, especially *Coningsby* and *Sybil*. The *Vindication* is at times diffuse and ornate, both extravagant and slightly absurd. For example, he reproves those who doubted whether bishops should sit in the House of Lords thus:

> . . . certain persons at the present day who inherit all the faction of Pym and Hampden, though none of their genius, being as like to them as Butler's Hudibras is like to Milton's Satan, have, in a manner at once indecent and unconstitutional, and which, if I have any knowledge of the laws of my country, subjects them to a praemunire – soiled the notice book of the proceedings of the next session of the House of Commons with a vile and vulgar menace of this exalted order.[1]

There are too many sentences of this sort to put the book among the better specimens of Disraeli's prose. Nevertheless it remains his only serious treatise on the subject and we can assume that he meant what he said here, whereas in his novels we may never be quite sure.

The theory of the Whigs as the 'anti-national' party was not as paradoxical as it sounds. At that particular moment, and for the next six years, their narrow majority rested on an alliance with O'Connell, and on a heavy majority of the Scottish seats. In England they were actually in a minority. Of course, it was quite another matter to convert this temporary phenomenon into a general law of history. The picture of the Tories as the 'Democratic' party is harder to swallow, and indeed it depends on what is meant by the word. The Whigs had extended the franchise from a small minority of adult males to a rather larger one, and the resulting constituency gave them a great victory in 1832. In an age of widespread territorial 'influence', open voting, and inadequate laws against bribery or intimidation, it by no means followed that a further extension

[1] *Vindication*, 134.

would further damage the Tories. The opposite might be the case if the extension was judiciously made. The Chandos clause giving the vote to the fifty pound tenant-at-will and Lyndhurst's successful move to retain the Freeman's vote are the examples of Tory democracy chosen by Disraeli. Technically he was quite entitled to use the word, but one does not require much perspicacity to see what the authors of those amendments had in mind. It was certainly not 'one man, one vote'.

The *Vindication* seems to have been reasonably successful. Lyndhurst considered it 'masterly', and Peel, to whom Disraeli sent a copy 'with a cold dry note',[1] knowing that he was 'by reputation the most jealous frigid and haughty of men and as I had reason to believe anything but friendly to me', replied with a friendly letter of thanks, remarking that he had bought a copy as soon as it came out and 'was gratified and surprised to find that a familiar and apparently exhausted topic could be treated with so much of original force of argument and novelty of illustration'. Disraeli showed it to Lyndhurst, who 'thinks this is *much* considering the writer'.

Disraeli followed up the *Vindication* by a renewed burst of journalistic activity, on this occasion choosing *The Times* as his organ. He had been introduced to Barnes, the great editor, by Lyndhurst. The paper's policy was to support Peel and attack the Whigs, and early in 1836 Disraeli, under the pseudonym of 'Runnymede', wrote a series of open letters to some of the leading politicians of the day. The tone is not quite as scurrilous as in the articles for the *Morning Post,* and there are some memorable if extravagant phrases. Melbourne is adjured to 'cease to saunter over the destinies of a nation and lounge away the glories of an empire'; Palmerston is the 'Lord Fanny of diplomacy . . . cajoling France with an airy compliment and menacing Russia with a perfumed cane'; and when Lord Cottenham succeeds Brougham as Lord Chancellor it is 'the great transition from humbug to humdrum. We have escaped from the eagle to be preyed upon by the owl'.

But in general the tone shows Disraeli nearly at his worst. A visitor from foreign parts who learns that Lord John Russell is leader of the House 'may begin to comprehend how the Egyptians worshipped – AN INSECT'. Lord William Bentinck, the ex-Governor-General of India was standing in the Whig interest for

---

[1] *Correspondence,* 108, Disraeli to Sarah Disraeli, January 1836.

Glasgow. The author predicts that he is unlikely to survive the session. 'Congenial Cheltenham will receive from now glorious Glasgow the antiquated Governor and the drivelling Nabob.' As for O'Connell, Disraeli reaches depths of verbose invective which suggest that the famous attack at the time of the Taunton election had cut deeper than he ever admitted. O'Connell is 'the hired instrument of the Papacy; as such his mission is to destroy your Protestant society, and, as such, he is a more terrible enemy to England than Napoleon'. People have accused him of hypocrisy 'humbling himself in the mud before a simple priest'.

> There was no hypocrisy in this, no craft. The agent recognized his principal, the slave bowed before his lord; and when he pressed to his lips those robes, reeking with whisky and redolent of incense, I doubt not that his soul was filled at the same time with unaffected awe and devout gratitude.[1]

Throughout these letters Disraeli evinced a virulent racial and religious prejudice towards Ireland. This was, indeed, to be one of the least commendable features of Victorian politics, especially among the unenlightened masses who saw their standards threatened by hordes of alien papist immigrants accepting low wages and living in filthy conditions. It is, however, surprising to find Disraeli going so far, even though it is true that the attitude fitted with his theory in the *Vindication* of the Whigs as the anti-national party and the Tories as the party of England. It is also true that the Lichfield House compact had aroused something of the same furious Tory indignation that was to be evoked in later years by Gladstone's alliance with Parnell or Asquith's with Redmond. Nevertheless Disraeli cannot in retrospect have reflected with pride on a passage like this – or at least one hopes not:

> . . . [The Irish] hate our free and fertile isle. They hate our order, our civilisation, our enterprising industry, our sustained courage, our decorous liberty, our pure religion. This wild, reckless, indolent, uncertain and superstitious race have no sympathy with the English character. Their fair ideal of human felicity is an alternation of clannish broils and coarse idolatry. Their history describes an unbroken circle of bigotry and blood . . . My lords, shall the delegates of these tribes, under the direction of the Roman priesthood, ride roughshod over our country – over England – haughty and still imperial England?[2]

[1] Letter viii, February 2, 1836.   [2] Letter xvi, April 18, 1836.

It is not surprising that Barnes became at times alarmed at the savagery and libellousness of some of his new protégé's contributions and that he frequently watered them down before publication. It is also not surprising that Disraeli never publicly acknowledged his authorship, although he was sufficiently proud of his work to have the letters published in book form in July 1836 together with a tract entitled *The Spirit of Whiggism* which reproduces in abbreviated form the argument of the *Vindication*. It was dedicated to Peel, to whom one of the open letters, couched in terms of grandiloquent flattery, had been addressed.

Disraeli continued to write occasionally for *The Times* during the next few years. In the summer of 1836 O'Connell attacked Barnes and threatened in the same letter to the Press to describe 'with hideous details' the 'private life' of Lord Lyndhurst. The draft of a reply exists at Hughenden.[1] O'Connell is stigmatized as 'a tyrant, a swindler, a poltroon and a profligate . . . There is no human being . . . who if he were acquainted with all the circumstances of this creature's life . . . would not shrink with disgust and horror from the loathsome portrait of this insolvent satyr.' Barnes evidently regarded this as too strong in spite of his own dislike of O'Connell, and the reply in *The Times* (August 29, 1836), though vigorous, is toned down. Barnes frequently returned Disraeli's later pieces for revision. On at least one occasion the author took offence and protested. He received a snub. After observing that he must be at least fifteen years older than his contributor, the editor went on:

> Judge then my surprise at receiving a letter from you in which with the didactic and patronizing air of a tutor to a child ten years old you condescend to inform me who is the author of a well-known line and to give me a sort of elementary lesson on the meaning of the word Irony. I am perfectly convinced that you intend no offence nor am I apt to be offended, but really such a tone is inexpressibly ludicrous . . .[2]

Barnes frequently had to remind Disraeli that personalities, particularly from an anonymous source, are to be avoided. But the distinction between personal character and political or literary conduct was one which Disraeli, like most young men, never found easy to draw.

---

[1] Hughenden Papers, Box 138, B/XXI/0/2.
[2] *The History of the Times* 1785–1841 (1935), 441.

3

The eighteen months between January 1836 and July 1837 were perhaps the most hectic and turbulent that Disraeli had so far known. His debts had increased and his creditors became even more pressing. He had fobbed off Austen with £450 in January 1835, but a year later the solicitor was once again beginning to lose patience. Disraeli had persuaded himself that he was on the point of bringing off some sort of financial *coup* as London agent for Baron de Haber, with whom he had already had some dealings over the publication of the *Gallomania* and who turned up again, as we saw, in connexion with the Sykes–Bolton affair. Haber's headquarters were at The Hague, but the transaction in question seems to have been the promotion of a loan to the Swedish Government. There is some obscure correspondence to Disraeli in February from J. S. Brownrigg, another financier, who declined to float a Swedish loan of £100,000 at 5 per cent.[1] Disraeli's commission from Haber was to have been £1,000, and he writes to Austen as if it was already his. His debts, he says, are £1,300, but his assets are scarcely less if the commission is counted in.[2] Austen was sceptical, and a sharp exchange ensued, ending with Austen's terse request. 'So pray put an end to this correspondence by removing the cause of it.'[3]

The reader who wishes to study the whole of this history of prevarication and excuses should consult Professor Jerman's admirable work. It need hardly be said that Disraeli's venture in the foreign money market was, as Austen expected, an unredeemed disaster; he not only failed to lay his hands on a penny of the £1,000 commission but landed himself more heavily in debt than ever before. By May his affairs were in an alarming condition. Austen had, moreover, been correct in guessing even before this latest crisis that the total of Disraeli's debts far exceeded the figure that he admitted. The situation now became much worse. But Disraeli still refused to apply to his father.

At about this time he found a new ally in his difficulties. The firm of solicitors who acted for Sir Francis Sykes were Messrs Pyne and Richards, and William Pyne, one of the partners, now became Disraeli's principal stand-by during the next two years. It would be interesting to know more about him, for it seems clear that without

[1] Hughenden Papers, Box 120, B/XXI/B/1080–5.
[2] Jerman, 265–6.
[3] British Museum, Add. MSS, 45908, f.118.

his aid Disraeli might well have had to face bankruptcy at this time.[1]
One of the duties of Messrs Pyne and Richards was to pay over the
allowance of £1,800 per annum which Sir Francis now made to
Henrietta for the upkeep of herself and their London house while he
was on the continent. When a year later he finally broke with
Henrietta he claimed that his solicitors had during 1836 and 1837
paid £2,000 over and above the authorized allowance. Professor
Jerman surmises that this may have been the money which tided
Disraeli over his financial crisis. There is no conclusive proof, but it
is quite likely that Pyne, at Henrietta's instigation, did something
of the sort.[2] If so, Disraeli's cryptic note for 1836 in the mutilated
diary – 'The singular good services of Pyne to me' – would appear to
be more than justified.

Although Pyne staved off the immediate dangers, Disraeli's life
for the next year was extremely embarrassing. 'Peel has asked me
to dine with a party today of the late Government at the Carlton',
he writes to Pyne in July. 'Is it safe? I fear not.' His letters show his
usual fluctuations of optimism and despair. In September he tells
Pyne, 'I have no pecuniary cares for the next three months.' In
November he thinks that 'between £3000 and £4000 might be poured
into my coffers by May'. But in December he has to ask whether he
can risk appearing at a Buckinghamshire Conservative dinner,
where he is to propose the toast of the House of Lords. 'I trust there
is no danger of my being nabbed as this would be a fatal *contretemps*
inasmuch as, in all probability, I am addressing my future constituents.' In January 1837, however, he talks of buying the estate
of Chequers Court 'not under £40,000, perhaps £10,000 more as
there is timber'.[3] But this was probably a joke.

Meanwhile Austen continued throughout 1836 to press for the
settlement of Disraeli's long-overdue debt. He threatened at one
stage to go to law over the matter, but Disraeli knew that he could
twist him round his little finger. He finished *Henrietta Temple* in time
for Christmas, and its sales must have given him enough money to
repay some of the loan. But none of it went to Austen. In January
1837 he assured Austen that only the failure of a bank prevented

[1] Disraeli's letters to Pyne were available to Monypenny, who copied extracts and
quoted at some length, i, 354 *et seq*. Inquiries have failed to elicit their present where-
abouts, and quotations here are taken from Monypenny's notes, of which most but
not all were published in the biography. Pyne's letters to Disraeli do not appear to
have survived. There is none in the Hughenden archives.

[2] Jerman, 282.

[3] M. & B., i, 351–3, for letters to Pyne from which these extracts are taken.

him from paying up. Finally in February he gave way and applied to Isaac, who settled the greater part of the debt, probably not more than £700, though for some reason about £30 was still left outstanding. Austen proceeded to press for this, too, but Disraeli waited until the publication of *Venetia* in May before paying the last instalment.

This was the end of his connexion with the Austens. He had no further dealings with the husband. A later letter of his to Mrs Austen has survived – a reply in 1839 to one from her written months earlier in praise of his *Tragedy of Count Alarcos*. But their friendship was already part of the past. In December 1837 she told Crabb Robinson that she had broken with Disraeli because he deceived her about the fictitiousness of the characters in *Vivian Grey*.[1] Whether or not Disraeli deceived her, it certainly was not the cause of their friendship fading away. The truth is that Disraeli had a streak of ruthlessness towards those who had served him well. If they could no longer do so, he was no longer interested. With Parliament and marriage he was moving into a world where the Austens could be of little help to him. One may suspect that he had long regarded them as bores. As the years passed by he came to regard them as something even less pleasing; reminders of a time when he had been raffish, struggling, debt-ridden and dependent, of the period in his life which he sought to blot out by tearing pages from his diary, by expurgating the social solecisms and Byronic extravagances from his early novels. As for the Austens, it is not surprising to find the ever-loyal Sir Philip Rose writing that they 'seemed to be suffering under a morbid feeling of slight and neglect'.

Benjamin Austen died in 1863. If Disraeli noticed the fact at all, he made no comment that has been preserved for posterity. He did not write to Sara. She lived on and on, a prisoner of increasing deafness and mental infirmity. She even outlasted her former protégé, dying in 1887 at the great age of ninety-two. Six years earlier her nephew, Sir Henry Layard, had called on her, anxious to know whether she was much afflicted by the death of Lord Beaconsfield which had occurred the day before. 'No,' her aged companion said, 'Not much – Nothing hurts her much now – She often confuses so much that she says *Gladstone* is her great friend.'[2]

---

[1] Jerman, 296, quoting Crabb Robinson's diary, from the MS in the Dr Williams Library, Gordon Square.
[2] Jerman, 34, quoting from the Layard Papers.

4

Money was not Disraeli's only trouble. There was Henrietta. True, in the spring all seemed well. 'This spring', he writes in his diary on September 17, 1836, 'Henrietta moved to Park Lane which she furnished with lavish and enchanting taste.' But in the same diary a year later we read:

> Autumn of 1836 – Parted for ever from Henrietta. Returned to Bradenham at the latter end of August; concluded *Henrietta Temple*, of which one volume had been written three years. It was published early in December and was very successful.[1]

What led to this final breach? Sir Philip Rose refers to the liaison as having 'materially affected D's health and nearly shipwrecked his career'. He goes on: 'Few other men could have had the necessary force of will to escape from such an entanglement.' Certainly Henrietta's letters suggest a neurotic possessiveness which must have sorely tried a man with the intense egotism of Disraeli.

> 1 o'clock In bed
> Has he thought of his Henrietta this morning and wished her to be snugly placed by him in that comfortable couch sipping coffee and kisses at the same time . . . I love you even to madness, and do not suppose that I set [out] to show the power I have over you. I swear I suffer the torments of the damned when you are away and although there is nothing I would not sacrifice to give you a moment's enjoyment I cannot bear that your amusement should spring from any other source than myself. Are you angry, love, at my selfishness. You never answer questions and I sometimes think I bore you by writing . . . it appears an age since we parted and I would that we were never separated a moment. Is it vain to suppose you would love me better and better the longer we were together? I feel I am not the vain frivolous being I am set down to be and with you for my guiding star what would I not do to retain and cherish the love I've gained . . .[2]

There are dozens of letters in the same vein, and it is easy to imagine that what at first flattered Disraeli's vanity came in the end to be a maddening distraction.

But, despite Sir Philip Rose, it is far from clear that Disraeli really had the strength of mind to break off the affair of his own

---

[1] Hughenden Papers, Box 11, A/III/C., n.d. must be after August, 1837.
[2] ibid., Box 13, A/IV/H 86, n.d.

accord. Perhaps he would never have brought himself to do so if Henrietta had not provided him with an excuse by succumbing to the advances of the painter David Maclise, a notorious philanderer, handsome, big, and full of Irish charm. He had been a friend of Disraeli for many years and had first drawn his portrait as long ago as 1828. Exactly when Henrietta first became involved with Maclise is by no means clear. Nor is it clear when Disraeli first heard about the matter. Evidently it cannot have been before September 17 or he would hardly have written the passage in his diary quoted above. He knew all about it by December. Did Henrietta's unfaithfulness cause the final parting, or was she seeking consolation from a new lover because Disraeli had already left her? Or was the truth more complicated – a half-hearted resolution on Disraeli's part, hardened and confirmed by Henrietta's yielding to Maclise?

We are unlikely ever to know the answers to these questions, and they do not greatly matter. The last recorded occasion on which Disraeli saw Henrietta was in August. She was ill at Basildon,[1] and Disraeli characteristically made this an excuse for delay in answering Austen's letters. 'I have suddenly been called down here', he writes on August 13 from Basildon, 'by the dangerous illness of a friend.'[2] It is tempting to wonder whether even then he was trying to end the affair. It would have been thoroughly true to form if Henrietta on receiving a letter of dismissal had at once thrown a fit of illness. But this is mere speculation. What is certain is that the two lovers parted in the autumn of 1836 and that the fact that Disraeli had been supplanted was well known to his intimates by Christmas. Clear evidence on this point comes in a letter to Bulwer, dated 'Thursday' and almost certainly written on December 22. Disraeli was negotiating at the time for Bulwer's rooms in Albany, once occupied by Byron.[3]

Quite Private.   Thursday.

My dear Bulwer,

When I wrote to you the other day certain domestic annoyances that had long been menacing me and which I trusted I might at least prevent from terminating in a disgraceful catastrophe had

---

[1] Sir F. Sykes's country seat near Reading.

[2] British Museum, Add. MSS., 45908.

[3] '. . . a curious coincidence of successive scribblers', wrote Disraeli to Pyne on January 8, 1837, 'the spell, I suppose, growing weaker every degree and the inspiration less genuine, but I may flare up yet and surprise you all'. Nothing came of this transaction in the end, and Disraeli never lived in Albany.

burst upon my head with triple thunder. I fled to a club for solace and then from what I heard it seemed to me that the barriers of my life were simultaneously failing and that not only my love was vanishing but friendship also. You have unfortunately been a sufferer; you will therefore sympathize with one of too irritable a temperament and whose philosophy arrives generally too late.

I confess to you my dear fellow that I am and have been for some time in a state of great excitement.

I am ready to take the rooms when you please and am obliged by all your kindness. Write when you wish me to settle the business. I shall be glad to be there as soon as possible but wish you *entirely to consult your own convenience.*

My dear E.L.B. our friendship has stood many tests. If I analyze the causes I would ascribe them in some degree to a warm heart on my side and a generous temper on yours. Then let it never dissolve for my heart shall never grow cold to you and be yours always indulgent to

Your affectionate friend,
Yr. D.

Arranging his correspondence many years later, Bulwer wrote on the margin of this letter, 'I believe this refers to Lady Sykes who exercised an influence over him – and was implicated in an affair with David Maclise – then his friend.'[1] Two days later, on Christmas Eve, Bulwer wrote to Disraeli that 'he was pained sincerely at the affliction you have undergone'.[2]

On Boxing Day Lady Blessington wrote a long letter of condolence:

If you knew how warmly and sincerely I enter into all your feelings, feelings I can so well understand you would not refrain from seeking consolation where it can best be found, with true and attached friends. I got your letter of Saturday only yesterday – I am glad you have written to Lord L. and that you will never permit *anything* to make a division between him and you, as nothing could have a worse appearance upon the public or be more likely to give rise to reports injurious to you both. Be assured that I never speak of you or let others speak, in any manner that could be disagreeable or injurious to you.

Of the lady, my respect for my sex, would always preclude me from speaking lightly. Many and many a time have I defended

---

[1] Knebworth Papers. The letter but not the marginal comment is published in his grandson's biography of Bulwer, where it is misdated, being attributed to the year 1832. The Earl of Lytton, *The Life of Edward Bulwer, First Lord Lytton* (2 vols, 1913) i, 370.

[2] Hughenden Papers, Box 104, B/XX/Ly/29, December 24.

her, necessarily and successfully, and from respect to consistency I shall not now censure her, though my opinion is changed. Our mutual friend Mr. Bulwer is the only person before whom I ever spoke of her since my change, which change took place from the reports continually in circulation relatively to her forming *her* attachments . . .

She went on to chide him for being oversuspicious and touchy about the reviews of *Henrietta Temple*, and then reverted to the real Henrietta.

. . . I quite agree with you that it is best to let the whole affair of the Lady drop into oblivion and not refer to it. Yet are you quite sure that you have not done her an injustice? How often are we imposed upon by appearances – I should like to think better of her than to suppose that she is so unworthy as to burst asunder ties cemented by long years of affection, were she not under some mistake or illusion relative to you . . .[1]

Was he, she wondered, quarrelling about straws?
Disraeli replied from Bradenham on January 12.

. . . I really grieve if I said anything which deserved the lecture you gave me, though I am almost glad I merited it if only for its kindness. I was rather harassed when I was last in town as you know and have a disagreeable habit of saying everything I feel: but I love my friends and am not naturally suspicious or on the alert to quarrel about straws . . .[2]

On December 26 he writes to Pyne from Bradenham, having arrived just before snow made the roads impassable.

. . . I assure you when I reached the old hall, and found the beech blocks crackling and blazing, I felt no common sentiments of gratitude to that kind friend whose never tired zeal allowed me to reach my house, and is some consolation for the plague of women, the wear and tear of politics, and the dunning of creditors . . .[3]

On December 31 he wrote:

The Park Lane affair is not very agreeable to brood over &, view them as we please, these are domestic convulsions wh: strike one to the centre.[4]

[1] Hughenden Papers, Box 119, B/XXI/B/580, December 26, 1836.
[2] M. & B., i, 355.
[3] ibid., 352.
[4] Hughenden Papers, Box 301.

But as time went by Disraeli seems to have become more reconciled to his lot. On January 8 he ends another letter to Pyne:

> I am on the whole savagely gay and sincerely glad that I am freer of encumbrances, in every sense of the word than I was this time last year.[1]

By March she has, in another letter to Pyne, entered the category of 'malignant mistresses' whom, along with 'ungrateful statesmen', he feels he can almost defy.[2]

This is not quite the last we hear of Henrietta. At the end of 1836 Sir Francis Sykes returned from over two years' absence in Europe. His behaviour is one of the most puzzling features of the whole story. After Henrietta's discovery of his relations with Mrs Bolton he appears to have completely acquiesced in his replacement by Disraeli, to whom he wrote in terms of trust and friendship; nor does he seem to have minded his wife's association with Lyndhurst, although the latter's reputation must have been notorious to anyone who had ever moved in society. True, he made no proper financial provision. But this was the result of improvidence rather than ill will, for when Disraeli wrote to him in Venice early in 1835, pointing out the difficulty of Henrietta keeping up a proper establishment and educating the children, the absent baronet put matters straight by authorizing the allowance of £1,800 p.a. already mentioned.[3] In replying to Disraeli he said that he was 'fully convinced of my wife's honor and integrity which stands undefiled, though her conduct has been foolish'. A few days later he sent a letter to Henrietta, dictated to an amanuensis, for he was ill, but he ended in his own hand, 'I cannot use another's pen to write of my affection to you.'

But however *complaisant* his attitude may have been towards Disraeli or Lyndhurst, he was to take a very different line towards Maclise. No open breach occurred on his return. Shortly after the publication of *Henrietta Temple*, Henrietta wrote what was probably her last letter to Disraeli. It is undated, but must have been written in December or January, and throws some light on her relations with Sir Francis:

> What can I say sufficient to convey to you my deep admiration of your book and the extreme pleasure I felt in reading it. You

[1] M. & B., i, 353.

[2] Hughenden Papers, Box 301.

[3] Disraeli's letter has not survived, but the gist of it may be inferred from Sir Francis Sykes's reply. Jerman, 247, February 18, 1835.

know I am not very eloquent in expressing my feelings, therefore I must fail to convey to you a tythe part of the extreme gratification I have in your brilliant success. Your complete triumph is echoed by everyone I come near.

I think it due to myself to tell you that you were mistaken in supposing that I had not received letters from Lord L. When I wrote to you I had had 2. Since, I have received several but I refrained from answering them as I felt convinced by your manner he had said something of me, and to no one will I stoop. I am aware of your correspondence with him and I hear of you from Miss Copley.[1]

It is possible that I may go abroad with Francis – he is perfectly recovered and *tolerably* kind to me – he is not in the slightest degree aware but that the sole reason for your absence from London is your application to your books and frightened me by projecting a trip to Bradenham.

All your daggers and things are safe. I do not like to return them to Bradenham.[2]

God prosper you,

H.

Henrietta evidently believed that Sir Francis still knew nothing of the affair with Maclise. Whether his kindness was genuine or feigned we cannot tell. It is possible that he was biding his time. During the first half of 1837 Maclise painted the family group, from which Henrietta's portrait is reproduced. But later in the year Henrietta and her lover were caught *flagrante delicto*, in bed together at the house in Park Lane, and in July Sir Francis instigated proceedings for 'criminal conversation' against Maclise. He ran into unexpected difficulties, for Pyne and Richards refused to act; according to *The Times* report, 'upon the ground that they apprehended that the result of the proceeding would not be productive to the plaintiff of any great "glory" or advantage'. Presumably both his condonation of the liaison with Disraeli and his own relations with Clara Bolton might have been brought out in court with damaging consequences. As a result of this refusal Sir Francis appointed another firm, Messrs Lake, Wilkinson and Co., to look after his affairs. It was a dispute over the bill from Pyne and Richards that caused the allegation referred to earlier of a payment of £2,000 over and above Henrietta's allowance. The case was referred back for further evidence, and was either withdrawn or

[1] Lyndhurst's daughter.
[2] Hughenden Papers, Box 13, A/IV/H/68, n.d.

settled out of court. The proceedings against Maclise were dropped. Perhaps Disraeli, who was now in Parliament, could regard the outcome as yet another of Pyne's 'singular good services'. His own comments on the case survive in the mutilated diary, where he writes, 'During the election occurred the terrible catastrophe of Henrietta nearly one year after we had parted.'[1] And in a letter to his future wife, then Mrs Wyndham Lewis, written early in August, he says, after inviting her and her husband to stay at Bradenham:

> All here is quiet and happy. Not a word about the painful subject which, it is tacitly agreed, shall be consigned to oblivion with the hope that there may never again be an occasion to recollect it.[2]

Although no legal action was taken against Henrietta, she was irretrievably disgraced, and she no longer moved in society. Sir Francis died in 1843. Mrs Bolton died in France in September 1839.[3] Henrietta died three years later than her husband, on May 15, 1846, the very day on which Disraeli made one of his most brilliant speeches against the Corn Laws and, to quote a contemporary critic, 'resumed his seat amid cheers which for duration and vehemence are seldom heard within the walls of Parliament'. He must have been aware of her death, but we know nothing of his reaction. For nearly ten years she had been dead as far as he was concerned, but the memory of the affair never faded from his mind. A quarter of a century later, when something reminded him of Basildon,[4] he wrote in his reminiscent jottings – half playing with fire, one suspects – 'I passed there in 34 & 35 some romantic hours . . . the house a Palladian palace.' Although he did so much to expunge his early life from the pages of history, he could not bring himself to destroy Henrietta's love letters. They survive still and tell their strange half-tragic, half-comic story to a generation no less intrigued by Disraeli than his own, but perhaps more tolerant and less censorious.

[1] Hughenden Papers, Box 11, A/III/C.
[2] ibid., Box 1, A/I/A.
[3] *The Times*, September 27, 1839. 'Lately at Harvre-de-Grace, Clarissa Marion, wife of George Buckley Bolton, Esq., of Pall Mall.'
[4] Hughenden Papers, Box 26, A/X/A/59. Disraeli was reminded of the place by the eccentricity of its owner, Morison, of Tod, Morison & Co., who bought it from Sir Francis for £140,000. He died 'worth I believe four millions and received during the last years of his life twelve shillings a week from his bailiff for working in his own garden at Basildon'.

CHAPTER VII

Parliament and Marriage
1837–41

1

Disraeli's love affair left one legacy for which posterity should be grateful. During the late summer and early autumn of 1836, which he spent at Bradenham, he finished *Henrietta Temple*. It was published by Colburn early in December and was financially his most successful effort since *Vivian Grey*. Like that novel, it is in two sections inspired by very different sentiments. The first part, which was written three years earlier, is a vivid account of Ferdinand Armine, the handsome, empty-headed, debt-ridden, impoverished heir to an ancient line, falling passionately in love, not with the wealthy cousin who could restore his fortunes, but with the beautiful and poor Henrietta Temple. Armine bears no resemblance whatever to Disraeli. Henrietta, who is only eighteen, bears little to the real Henrietta, except for her physical description, and her letters to Ferdinand. These are so like those of the real Henrietta that one is tempted to think that Disraeli transcribed them verbatim.[1] But if the characters are fictitious, their experience is not. The account of love at first sight has an authentic ring of personal passion[2] seldom found elsewhere among the novels. Philip Guedalla is surely right when he observes in his introduction to the 'Bradenham' edition: 'The rustle of real petticoats is more audible than in any other part of Disraeli's work.'

The second half of the novel is in sharp contrast to the first. Passion has vanished. In the first volume Disraeli could write of the lover: 'To violate in her favour every duty of society; this is a lover, and this is love.' In the second part he observes: 'A female friend, amiable, clever, and devoted, is a possession more valuable than parks and palaces; and without such a muse, few men can succeed

---

[1] *Henrietta Temple*, Bk IV, ch. 1 and 2.

[2] Disraeli evidently thought later that he had overdone the passion. In the 1853 edition of his novels, *Henrietta Temple*, like *Vivian Grey* and *The Young Duke*, was subjected to a good many changes and excisions.

in life, none be content.' From a story of passionate romance the novel has become an urbane comedy of manners. The best characters are those drawn from real life; and the portraits of Lady Bellair, who is Disraeli's old friend, Lady Cork, and of Count Alcibiades de Mirabel, a delightful picture of d'Orsay to whom the book was dedicated, have an attractive sparkle which redeems the improbabilities of the story.

Disraeli needed money badly and quickly. *Henrietta Temple* produced some, but not enough. He promptly started another novel, *Venetia, or the Poet's Daughter*, based on the lives of Byron and Shelley. The work was begun at Bradenham, but in the middle of January 1837 he left for London and stayed off and on for the next few weeks with d'Orsay, whose house at Kensington was adjacent to the famous Gore House, which belonged to Lady Blessington. 'Saw of course much of the Countess B. whose magnificent mansion adjoined his elegant residence', he wrote in his diary with that Ouidaesque touch that is never very far from his style. Disraeli was anxious to obtain local colour from the Countess, who claimed that she had known Byron well. In reality – not that this mattered for Disraeli's purpose – Lady Blessington's version of their acquaintanceship was highly misleading, and she much exaggerated her own intimacy with the great man.[1]

He had not been there long when a by-election occurred for the county of Bucks. He travelled at once all night to Aylesbury to canvass for the Tory candidate, but the effort affected his health. While talking to some friends on February 16 outside the George Inn he was struck by some sort of fit or seizure and fell down in a coma. He was taken to Bradenham, where he soon recovered, but there was an unfortunate by-product. The news got into the papers, *The Times* describing it as 'a melancholy accident', and thus alerted his numerous creditors, whose concern with his health was anything but disinterested. Demands rained upon him, and for the second time he was obliged to reveal some part of his plight to his father. This action received the grave approbation of d'Orsay, who wrote: '*Je suis bien aise pour votre intérêt présent et futur que vous vous soyez décidé à avouer à votre père l'étendue de votre scrape. Car les plasterings-*

---

[1] See Doris Langley Moore, *The Late Lord Byron* (1961), 465–84, for an analysis of Lady Blessington's *Conversations with Lord Byron*.

According to Sarah Disraeli, Tita 'declares that Ld Byron never saw Lady Blessington but three times'. Hughenden Papers, Box 7, A/I/B/453, February 2, 1833.

*over se demolissent toujours et'vous en auriez été victime continuelle-
ment . . .'*[1] Disraeli wrote to Pyne on March 8, 'I ventured to say
£2000 might be required. He looked blue'.[2]

Whether Isaac paid all this or not, Disraeli continued to be in dire
straits for money. He returned to d'Orsay's house, but in early
March was back in Bradenham, endeavouring to finish *Venetia*.
There matters came to another crisis. 'Of all things in the world
preserve me from the Sheriff's officer in my own county', he wrote
to Pyne,[3] and the story goes that he had on one occasion to hide in a
well to escape the attentions of that tiresome functionary. This was
in spite of having paid his creditors, as he told Austen, 'upwards of
£1500 since December'. On April 23 he wrote to Pyne: 'I conclude
from your interview that the game is up and that our system has
failed. I assure you that the only feelings I have are regret for your
unavailing exertions, which I feel *no professional remuneration can
compensate*, and gratitude for the generous zeal with which you have
served me . . .'[4] The nature of the system which had failed is unknown, perhaps something to do with the affairs of Henrietta and
Sir Francis.

Whatever the truth in this matter, the setback was not fatal.
Disraeli for the third time had recourse to Isaac, who evidently
produced enough to prevent disaster. It is clear that Disraeli did so
on each occasion with much reluctance, and that he never told his
father, even if he knew himself, the total sum of his debts. He gave
various excuses to Austen for his unwillingness: his refusal to take
Isaac's advice on matrimony, fear for Isaac's health, Isaac's disapproval of extravagance. One can probably add another: the
thought of his sceptical old mother knowing about his scrape, and
of the inevitable gossip among her Basevi relatives, whom he disliked and who disliked him. Perhaps, too, there was a touch of
pleasure in pain, a certain enjoyment of the intrigues and subterfuges forced upon him, a feeling that a load of debt was one of the
accepted features of the dandy and the man of the world; something,
along with a fashionable mistress and membership of Almack's,
which marked him off from the Austens, Basevis – or for that matter
the other D'Israelis – of this world. In *Tancred*, Fakredeen is 'fond
of his debts', and exclaims 'The two greatest stimulants in the

[1] M. & B., i, 357–8.
[2] Hughenden Papers, Monypenny's notes.
[3] M. & B., i, 359.
[4] ibid.

world, Youth and Debt! What should I be without my debts, dear
companions of my life that never desert me . . .'[1]

Disraeli's financial methods certainly ensured that the 'dear
companions' never deserted *him*. The original sum which he lost on
the Stock Exchange was comparatively small, perhaps some two or
three thousand pounds. By 1841 he owed at least £20,000, although
his father had on three occasions come to the rescue. This increase
was partly the result of habitual extravagance and overspending,
but it was also the result of constant borrowings, renewals, assign-
ments, annuities, etc., at enormous rates of interest. It is probable
that most of these ruinous expedients could have been avoided if
he had at any moment drawn up a true account of his position and
given it to his father.

Venetia came out in May. It brought in some money, but not as
much as *Henrietta Temple*. It is an awkward and artificial work,
fatally marred by its whole concept – a fictionalized account of
Byron and Shelley put back in the period of the American War of
Independence. This involves such liberties with history that contemporary readers simply could not accept it. It is as if someone
had produced in recent times a book about T. E. Lawrence or Rupert
Brooke in the setting of the Crimean War. Professor Jerman may be
right in seeing in it Disraeli's last tribute to the Byronic myth which
had enthralled him since his boyhood, a final protest against the
respectable world with which he now had to come to terms. Whatever the motive, the novel, apart from the opening chapters with
their charming picture of Venetia's childhood, is not a success. Lord
Cadurcis (Byron) never comes to life, and though it is reasonable to
find Marmion Herbert (Shelley) on the side of the American rebels,
it is too much to swallow when we read of him as a successful
general.

Contemporary critics were severe on the portrait of Lady
Caroline Lamb who had been the Prime Minister's wife, and
on the introduction of Herbert's Italian mistress. Nor did they
fail to observe one of Disraeli's most deplorable pieces of plagiarism
when he lifted the well-known passage from Macaulay's essay on
Byron beginning 'We know no spectacle so ridiculous as the English
public in one of its fits of periodical morality . . .' with no acknow-
ledgement other than 'it has been well observed that . . .'

On June 19 the old King died. Disraeli accompanied Lyndhurst

[1] *Tancred*, Bk V, ch. 3.

to Kensington Palace for the accession of Queen Victoria, and his famous description of the scene in *Sybil* is based on Lyndhurst's account of it. He was confident that his efforts for the party would at last be rewarded; and he was right. The death of the monarch automatically caused a general election. Several offers came; the most promising of them seemed to be Maidstone, where the representation in the old Parliament was split between Wyndham Lewis, Conservative, and a Liberal who in the end decided not to stand again. The local Tories sent a deputation to the Carlton Club to seek a second candidate, and Disraeli was nominated. Liberal withdrawal did not prevent a contest, for the editor of the Radical *Westminster Review*, Colonel Perronet Thompson, decided to stand. But the Conservatives had a big lead, and, despite the cries of 'Old Clothes!' and 'Shylock!' which greeted him on nomination day, Disraeli was returned with a majority of 200 over the Radical colonel. The poll closed on July 27 and the figures were: Wyndham Lewis, 706; Disraeli, 616;[1] and Thompson, 412. Maidstone was reckoned to be one of the most venal constituencies of the day. Wyndham Lewis was a rich man, but Disraeli ran into difficulties at once. It would appear from the correspondence that Wyndham Lewis advanced him part of the money, and had some trouble in getting it back. Although Disraeli produced £500 on account before the end of the year, matters were still dragging on early in 1838. But he had from the start an enthusiastic supporter in Mrs Wyndham Lewis. 'Mr. Disraeli will in a very few years be one of the greatest men of his day', she wrote to her brother. 'His great talents backed by his friends Lord Lyndhurst and Lord Chandos, with Wyndham's power to keep him in Parliament will ensure his success. They call him my Parliamentary protégé.'[2]

Disraeli was in the House at last. No one could say that he had had an easy passage. It was his fifth election in five years. He had endured much abuse in the course of them; and if he had brought it upon himself by his own cynicism and bravado, the experience was not the less disagreeable. Now he was filled with elation. 'I franked your letter', he writes triumphantly to his sister, and later in the same paragraph, 'What fun, and how lucky after all I should esteem myself'.[3] The new Parliament was not due to meet until November.

[1] Maidstone, like most boroughs, was a two-member constituency.
[2] M. & B., i, 376.
[3] ibid., 378.

Disraeli repaired once again to Bradenham for the autumn and
spent a peaceful three months in what he called 'desultory political
reading' varied by a visit from the Wyndham Lewises. On November 12 he wrote his last entry in the mutilated diary:

> My health wonderfully renovated: were it not for the anxiety the
> state of my affairs occasionally causes me I should laugh at ill-
> ness. My life for the past year has been very temperate; my
> nervous system consequently much stronger. I am now as one
> leaving a secure haven for an unknown sea. What will the next
> twelve months produce?[1]

The King's death had cut short the normal session, and accordingly Parliament met again in the autumn – an unusual procedure
in those days. It soon became evident that the Whigs could carry
on, and the confident prophecies of a Tory ministry proved premature. Disraeli made his maiden speech, one of the most celebrated
in history, on December 7. It was fully in accord with the streak of
reckless courage in his character, combined with love of the limelight, that he should have resolved to take the House by storm, and
to try to make himself famous at his first attempt. F. E. Smith is the
only person who has ever succeeded in this hazardous task, and he
did not have to face the organized rowdyism of a section of the
House. Disraeli's effort was a failure which came near to disaster.
'D'Israeli made his first exhibition this night,' wrote Greville,
'beginning with florid assurance, speedily degenerating into ludicrous absurdity, and being at last put down with inextinguishable
shouts of laughter.'[2]

The subject which he chose, the validity of certain Irish elections,
was bound to inspire the wrath of the Irish members, who were
determined to avenge their leader for the great row over the
Taunton election. Moreover, Disraeli caught the Speaker's eye
immediately after O'Connell had sat down. If ever time and circumstances pointed to trouble, this was the occasion. The earlier part of
Disraeli's speech as reported in *Hansard*[3] does not sound particularly
absurd. Perhaps such expressions as 'majestic mendicancy' for
O'Connell's protection fund, and the charge that 'the strain of
borough mongering assumed a deeper and darker hue' in Ireland
were somewhat extravagant for a maiden speech, but what inspired

[1] ibid., 382.
[2] Fulford and Strachey (ed.), *Greville Memoirs*, iii, 404.
[3] *Hansard*, 3rd Series, xxxix, 802–7.

ridicule was evidently the manner of delivery rather than the matter. Towards the end, by which time he had great difficulty in making himself heard at all above the hisses, hoots, laughter and catcalls, Disraeli did launch into one of his worst pieces of affected and carefully prepared euphuism; and it was just as well that the final sentence was drowned by the uproar. Indeed, the conduct of the Irish may be regarded as a blessing in disguise. If Disraeli's peroration had been listened to in silence it might have blasted his Parliamentary reputation for ever. As it was, he inspired a certain sympathy for his courage if for nothing else when, having been on his feet for precisely the time that he intended, he shouted in a voice heard high above the hubbub: 'I will sit down now, but the time will come when you will hear me.'

That Disraeli had made a fool of himself somehow – and not solely because of the ruffianly conduct of the Irish – is too well attested for doubt. Stanley, who spoke immediately afterwards, made no reference at all to the episode. Yet even he, prejudiced as he was against Disraeli, could scarcely have avoided some mention of the behaviour of the Irish, whom he detested, if it had been simply a case of a new member on his own side being unfairly howled down. Hobhouse describes Disraeli's speech as 'such a mixture of insolence and folly as I never heard in my life before'.[1] According to Monckton Milnes, 'Disraeli nearly killed the House', and 'Peel quite screamed with laughter'.[2] On the latter point there is a conflict of evidence. One parliamentary reporter said that Peel 'cheered him in the most stentorian tones'.[3] Chandos told Disraeli, who passed it on to Sarah, that Peel refused to regard the speech as a failure. 'I say *just the reverse*. He did all he could under the circumstances. I say anything but failure. He must make his way.'[4] But this is somewhat indirect evidence. Peel might well have wished afterwards to console a new member for a setback.

That the Irish uproar was a stroke of luck rather than ill fortune was confirmed by R. L. O'Sheil, an Irish MP with long experience and no love for O'Connell. Bulwer told Disraeli that O'Sheil, over-hearing 'a knot of low Rads' abusing him in the Athenaeum,

[1] Lord Broughton (J. C. Hobhouse), *Recollections of A Long Life* (6 vols, 1909–11,) v, 112.

[2] Pope-Hennessy, *Monckton Milnes*, i, 100.

[3] M. & B., ii, 12, quoting Grant, *British Senate in* 1838, ii, 334. Perhaps Peel both laughed and cheered during this curious scene.

[4] *Correspondence*, 79, December 8, 1837.

rounded on them and declared that 'if there had not been this interruption Mr Disraeli might have made a failure. I don't call this a
failure, it is a crush.' Bulwer invited Sheil to meet Disraeli, and the
old Irishman gave sagacious counsel. 'Now get rid of your genius
for a session. Speak often, for you must not show yourself cowed,
but speak shortly. Be very quiet, try to be dull . . . and in a short
time the House will sigh for the wit and eloquence which they know
are in you . . .'[1]

'As interesting a rencontre as I have ever experienced,' Disraeli
told Sarah, and he took this sensible advice. His next speech was a
short unadorned comment upon a technical point in connexion with
a Bill about copyright. Disraeli knew his subject well, and was
listened to with attention. He did not speak again until March 1838,
when he defended the Corn Laws against his old friend, Charles
Villiers. He thought that this had been a success and told Sarah:[2]
'. . . all the squires came up to shake hands with me and thank me
for the good service. They were so grateful and well they might be,
for certainly they had nothing to say for themselves.'

2

On March 14, 1838, Disraeli's rich senior colleague in the representation of Maidstone suddenly died. He came from an old Welsh landed
family in Glamorgan, but the greater part of his wealth derived
from his position as a partner in the Dowlais ironworks.[3] He was
entitled to a fifth share of the profits. These were apt to fluctuate
widely. In 1829 they were below £5,000. In 1837 they were only just
short of £100,000. Wyndham Lewis left his widow a life interest in
a part of his fortune unconnected with Dowlais, yielding an income
of between £4,000 and £5,000 a year, and in his house in London,
No. 1 Grosvenor Gate (now No. 29 Park Lane). His interest in the
ironworks was bequeathed to his brother.

Mary Anne Wyndham Lewis was born in 1792, daughter of
Lieutenant John Evans, RN, and his wife Eleanor, formerly Miss
Viney of Gloucester. She came from respectable middle class
parentage. The Evans family had been for many years farmers in

---

[1] *Correspondence*, 81–82, Disraeli to Sarah, December 11, 1837.

[2] ibid., 103, March 16, 1838.

[3] I am indebted to Mr D. H. Elletson's study of Mrs Disraeli in *Maryannery*
(1959), for the information about the Wyndham Lewis and Evans families on which
the first part of this chapter is based.

Devon. On the Viney side she had an uncle of some distinction who served under Wellington and became a major-general. On neither side was there any money to spare, and matters were made no better by her father's death at sea when she was only two. Her mother married again in 1810, but her second husband, a Mr Thomas Yate, does not seem to have been a man of means either. They lived at Clifton, near Bristol, and it was at a ball in Clifton that Mary Anne met Wyndham Lewis. He at once fell in love with her. From a worldly point of view the match was highly desirable, especially as she had an extravagant ne'er-do-well brother in the army, to whom she was devoted; and in 1815 she and Lewis were married at Clifton parish church.

Mary Anne at once found herself elevated into a richer and grander world than anything to which she had been accustomed. Wyndham Lewis expected things to be done in style. She became a leading hostess in South Wales, and from 1820 onwards, when her husband first entered Parliament, entertained lavishly in London, too. He was fond of money, but never stinted it where she was concerned. When in 1827 they moved into the house at Grosvenor Gate she gave a great ball. 'My company were most of the first people in London,' she wrote to her brother, 'the Duke of Wellington said it was like fairy land, the best ball he had been at this season, but are you not dazzled at your little Whizzy having received the Noble Hero at her house.'[1] Two years later, when she gave a party to watch a military review in Hyde Park, she could boast of ninety guests, 'half of them Lords and Ladies'.[2] In fact, her marriage with Wyndham Lewis seems to have been happy enough, apart from her failure to have any children and his reluctance to purchase promotion for her brother.

Mary Anne was forty-five when her husband died, and her character was fully formed. She was an incessant talker – what in the language of the day was termed 'a rattle' – and of a flirtatious disposition. She was impulsive, warm-hearted, kind and affectionate; palpably not from the top flight of society, even perhaps by their standards slightly 'common'. It was characteristic that she found one of her closest friends in Rosina Bulwer, whose social status was equivocal, too. Mary Anne did not lack shrewdness and a certain native wit, but she was remarkably uneducated and often made

[1] Elletson, *Maryannery*, 83.
[2] ibid., 84.

absurd remarks. To Disraeli himself we owe the story that she could never remember who came first, the Greeks or the Romans; while Rosina Bulwer would recount a malicious tale of how when the conversation had turned on the subject of the great Dean Swift, Mary Anne had asked who he was so that she could invite him to one of her parties.[1]

Disraeli had first met her on April 27, 1832, at a soirée of Bulwer's. He described her to Sarah as 'a pretty little woman, a flirt and a rattle, indeed gifted with a volubility I should think unequalled and of which I can convey no idea'. And he went on to add: 'She told me she "liked silent melancholy men". I answered "that I had no doubt of it".'[2] His only other recorded opinion of her in these early days was, as we saw, even less flattering: if Rosina Bulwer is to be believed, he described her as 'that insufferable woman'.[3] The circles in which they moved did not often intersect during the next five years, and her rash espousal in 1836 of the cause of Rosina during the quarrel which finally broke up the Bulwer marriage could not have endeared her to Disraeli.[4]

Naturally, however, they saw much more of each other when Disraeli became member for Maidstone and in the autumn of 1837 she and her husband stayed for a week at Bradenham. Disraeli's letters to her suggest, as Monypenny puts it, 'a sort of mock devotion'. With Wyndham Lewis's death that situation could not continue. It is clear that she sought sympathy and support from Disraeli in her bereavement and he gave her advice on the legal problems arising from her inheritance. Her brother, who was seriously ill, died in the same year and she appears to have been on distant terms with her husband's relations.

> Upon my honour, dear kind Dizzy [she wrote from Glamorgan while on business over her husband's estate], you are the only person I have written to (except on business) since I left town . . . I am glad you pass so much of your time with Lady L. . . . because the more you go to there or to any other married lady the less likely you are to think of marrying yourself . . . I hate

[1] Devey, *Lady Lytton*, 412.
[2] *Correspondence*, 6–7.
[3] See above, p. 80.
[4] The deed of separation between the Bulwers was actually signed by Rosina in Wyndham Lewis's house at Grosvenor Gate. Mary Anne's ill-founded gossip about Rosina having discovered Bulwer with a woman in his rooms in Albany brought upon her a severe letter of rebuke from Bulwer himself, which she is unlikely to have readily forgiven. Disraeli's relations with Bulwer seem to have cooled off for some years after his marriage; it may be that Mary Anne was responsible.

married men . . . I would much sooner you were dead . . .
Selfish, yes I am.[1]

Precisely when Disraeli first contemplated marrying her is
obscure. Sir William Gregory in his autobiography has a story that
it was suggested to him in jest by d'Orsay and Disraeli accepted the
idea, which seemed new to him, with alacrity.[2] This may or may not
be true. What is quite certain is that, anyway in the first instance,
Disraeli's motives were essentially practical. Mrs Lewis was remarkably youthful for her years, but it is hardly conceivable that the
garrulous *naïveté* of a widow twelve years older than himself would
have appealed to a sophisticated man of the world like Disraeli if
she had had neither money nor position. He had arrived at a moment
in his career when a good marriage was, if not essential, at least highly
useful. The commonly accepted opinion then and ever since that he
married her for her money is, therefore, plausible enough, and
appears to be confirmed by a sentence from the famous letter which
he wrote to her during his courtship after a quarrel. 'I avow, when
I first made my advances to you, I was influenced by no romantic
feelings.'

His intimate friends certainly took it for granted. 'My good D'Is,'
wrote d'Orsay. 'When I read in the beginning of your letter the
tragedy is finished I thought you were married but on reflection I
suppose that if it was so you would have said the comedy. How is it
that you leave her in London by herself?'[3]

Yet when every allowance is made for interested motives there is
something about Disraeli's conduct that does not quite fit with a
purely cynical purpose. For one thing he took to poetry (as with
Henrietta), in his case a sure sign of love; and the tragedy which
was finished was his five-act blank-verse drama *Count Alarcos*, a
work almost as destitute of literary merit as *The Revolutionary
Epick*. It is part of the ambivalent mixture of romance and irony
in his outlook that one can never be sure what he was thinking
about anything. The dandies and men of the world among whom he
moved assumed that he was marrying for money. Perhaps they even
convinced him, and it may have been true at first; to deny it now
would make him appear a romantic simpleton. But it is difficult to

[1] Quoted, *Maryannery*, 109.
[2] Gregory, *Autobiography*, 93. There are several variants of this story which
certainly would not have lost in the telling.
[3] Hughenden Papers, Box 125, B/XXI/D/301, n.d.

read his letters to her without feeling that there was more to it than that.

If he is telling the truth in the extraordinary letter which finally brought her to accept him, he did not know at first that she had only a life interest in her husband's fortune. He soon found out, but he persisted all the same. It is undeniable that the restrictions on her use of capital made a great difference to a mere fortune-hunter in those days before the Married Women's Property Act. If her money had been hers absolutely, it would have been his after marriage and he could have paid off all his debts. Although as things turned out she was able to help him, the fact would not have been self-evident to begin with. Moreover, she was twelve years older, and likely to predecease him. If so he would obtain nothing, for not only her fortune but her London house was entailed to relatives of her first husband.

Disraeli needed a home, affection, security. He had reached the age which most men of sense reach sooner or later when, as he put it, he 'shrank from all the torturing passions of intrigue'. Feminine sympathy, admiration, idolatry, were essential to him.

Once again, as with Henrietta, there is the search for a missing mother. 'Tell me that you love your child', he writes, and he often uses similar words. It is hard to believe that he was concerned solely with money. Some of his letters have, it is true, a histrionic ring. Signed with his 'mystical mark', which looks like the outline of a misshapen turnip, they often refer to his trembling hand, streaming eyes and pale lips. But this was part of his manner; it need not be regarded as a pose.

> I pass my nights & days in scenes of strange & fascinating rapture. Till I embrace you I shall not know what calmness is. I write this to beg you to have your hand *ungloved*, when you arrive, so that you may stand by me, & I may hold & clasp & feel your soft delicious hand as I help your mother out of the carriage; now mind this, or I shall be insane with disappointment . . . A thousand & 1000 kisses. More, more, come, come, come.[1]

On other occasions he is more matter of fact. 'My dearest love, I have been obliged to betake myself to bed & wish you were with me there.'[2]

Disraeli first avowed his love at the end of July. She insisted that

[1] Hughenden Papers, Box 1, A/I/A/60, December 30, 1838.
[2] ibid., Box 1, A/I/A/54, December 5, 1838.

a year should elapse from her husband's death before she gave any answer. It has been surmised that Mrs Bulwer implanted doubts in her mind. Whether or not this was so, Disraeli certainly regarded Rosina as an enemy.

> I cannot express to you what an aversion I have taken to that woman. She is thoroughly vulgar & I think quite heartless. You must not mistake her jolly good nature as an evidence of feeling: it is merely the impulse of the Irish blood. Indeed she is so thoroughly a daughter of Erin that I never see her without thinking of a hod of mortar and a potatoe. Nature certainly intended that she should console her sorrows in Potteen . . .[1]

At some stage Mary Anne admitted her love for him, but she remained adamant about the year. His suitorship was by no means smooth or easy. There were quarrels, tiffs and scenes. There was trouble over one of his grand friends.

> I do not know what you mean by passing '*so much*' of my time with Lady Londonderry. I do not pass any more time with her than Lady anybody else.
> I hope you are amused at Clifton. You do not appear to have time to write; at least not to me.[2]

He often recurs to the absence of letters.

> Above all persons you who alone occasion our painful separation are the last who shd grudge me the only solace under such circumstances. It does indeed appear to me more than unaccountable that a person who can have found time to write to her lawyer or trustee & probably to many a corpulent bear or seedy second rate dandy should have allowed nearly a week to elapse witht sending a line to the individual to whom she professes herself devoted . . .[3]

And if she could be jealous of his fashionable acquaintance, he could rage against the 'ignoble prey', as he later called them, whom she encouraged. 'Fortunate Berkeley, thrice happy Stapleton cursed Neale! What is it to you whether he takes snuff or not.'[4] And he sent her a poem beginning 'Dark Doubt my heart invokes . . .' each stanza ending 'I have no hope'.

---

[1] ibid., Box 1, A/I/A/69, n.d. Probably early summer, 1838.
[2] ibid., Box 1, A/I/A/68, n.d. Probably autumn, 1838.
[3] ibid., Box 13, A/I/A/57, December 23, 1838.
[4] ibid., Box 13, A/I/A/39, October 18, 1838.

Early in their acquaintanceship she lent some money to Disraeli to help him out of a difficulty. There was trouble at Maidstone soon after Wyndham Lewis's death. A petition was brought against his successor, and in the course of proceedings it was alleged that Disraeli had promised bribes in 1837 which he had failed to pay. The electors of Maidstone did not mind the first charge. They lived on bribes. But to promise and not to pay was much more serious; the accusation might ruin his chances of re-election. Unfortunately the petition was withdrawn before he could vindicate himself. He therefore sent a letter on June 5, 1838, to all the newspapers in his best polemical style personally attacking the barrister for the petitioners, who, he urbanely observed, displayed 'the blustering artifice of a rhetorical hireling, availing himself of the vile license of a loose tongued lawyer, not only to make a statement that was false, but to make it with a consciousness of its falsehood'. This was too much for the Bar. A rule *nisi* for a criminal information against him was made absolute, and Disraeli had to plead mitigation of sentence. Under an appearance of contrition, he repeated most of his charges, but the Attorney-General prudently accepted the plea as 'an ample apology'. Inevitably these proceedings involved substantial costs and it was for those that Mrs Lewis made him a loan.

Doubtless she had no lack of warning from those who disliked him that he was an adventurer out for money. The year was not up till the Ides of March, and she continued to hold him off. Meanwhile Disraeli began to sense the invidiousness of his own position. His friends expected the news of his engagement at any moment. He must either get a favourable answer or break things off altogether. To continue on the present basis would incur the charge of being a rich middle-aged widow's paid lover. On February 7 he resolved to put matters to the test. He called at Grosvenor Gate and pressed her with the strongest words at his command to marry him. There followed a furious row. She flung the loan in his face, called him 'a selfish bully' and ordered him never to return to her house. Disraeli went back to his lodgings in Park Street and wrote a letter of over 1,500 words – it must have taken him at least two hours – and dispatched it that night. The letter is a remarkable production which has never been printed in full.[1]

He wrote, he said, 'as if it were the night before my execution'. Everyone was talking of their forthcoming union except her. A

[1] It is given in Appendix I; Hughenden Papers, Box 1, A/I/A/89.

friend had even offered him 'one of his seats for our happy month. The affair was then approaching absurdity'. She must 'as a woman of the world which you are thoroughly' recognize the difference between their positions.

> The continuance of the present state of affairs cd only render you *disreputable*; me it wd render *infamous* . . .
> This reputation impends over me . . . ere a few weeks I must inevitably chuse between being ridiculous or being contemptible. I must be recognized as being jilted, or I must at once sink into what your friend Lady Morgan has already styled me '*Mrs. Wyndham-Lewis's De Novo*'.

He admitted that he had not been influenced by love when he made his first advances. But his heart was touched when he found her in sorrow. He felt that she was 'one whom I cd look upon with pride as the partner of my life, who cd sympathize with all my projects & feelings, console me in the moments of depression, share my hour of triumph & work with me for our honor & happiness'. As for her fortune, it was far less than he or the world had believed. What use was a mere jointure to him? 'Was this an inducement to sacrifice my sweet liberty & that indefinite future which is one of the charms of existence?' In the course of time he would succeed to that financial independence which was needful. 'All that society can offer is at my command. . . . I wd not condescend to be the minion of a princess. . . . My nature demands that my life shd be perpetual love.' He ended on a note of sombre prophecy:

> For a few years you may flutter in some frivolous circle. But the time will come when you will sigh for any heart that could be fond and despair of one that could be faithful. Then will be the penal hour of retribution; then you will recall to your memory the passionate heart that you have forfeited and the genius you have betrayed.

Most women on receiving such a letter would have broken off the affair at once. But Mary Anne, eccentric and unsophisticated as she was, saw that there was something behind this theatrical extravagance. She realized, perhaps for the first time, that even if his feelings for her could not be described as love in the ordinary sense, at least they were not purely mercenary. 'For God's sake come to me', she wrote. 'I never desired you to leave the house, or implied or thought a word about money . . . I am devoted to you.'

And so all was well at last. She accepted him, and they were married
very quietly at S George's, Hanover Square, on August 28, the day
after the session ended. Bulwer and Lyndhurst were among the few
present. A prolonged honeymoon was spent at Tunbridge Wells and
on the Continent. They did not return to England until November.

The marriage was a great success. To say that they lived happily
ever after would be an exaggeration, but it is as near the truth as it
can be of any marriage. Disraeli behaved towards her with a devotion and respect which was considered exemplary, even by Gladstone. Her social blunders, strange remarks, extraordinary gaffes,
soon became famous, and her oddities did not diminish with time.
But it is surely wrong to suggest as Monypenny does, that 'fortunately Disraeli was bizarre enough himself to be blind or indifferent
to many of her peculiarities'. On the contrary, Disraeli's novels
and letters show him as a man who was highly sensitive to the
conventions and manners of the great world and extremely acute
in observing the nuances of conduct among others. If he appeared
indifferent to Mary Anne's peculiarities, it was not because he failed
to notice them but because he had made his bargain and he meant
to keep it. To this rule he adhered with iron determination. No one
who jested about her in his presence did so again. Whether his
motive was gratitude, as is suggested by the well-known snub
which he gave George Smythe,[1] or love, or simply self-respect, he
never compromised, nor by the slightest sign betrayed the consciousness that Mary Anne was in any way different from the great
ladies in whose salons they moved.

In some of these salons he was no longer so welcome as he had
been. An attractive amusing bachelor was much more of a social
asset than the husband of a very odd, not very grand, widow of
middle-class origins. Lady Londonderry and Lady Jersey, both
appear to have cut the Disraelis off their lists. He was unperturbed.
He probably guessed that they would change their attitude sooner
or later – and of course they did.

As for Mary Anne, she sank her existence in his. She gave him
just the love, devotion and worship he needed, and she protected
him from the tiresome domestic details he detested. She believed
passionately in his genius. She did everything she could for him.

[1] The story is that Smythe in Disraeli's presence once spoke disrespectfully of her.
Disraeli gave him a look such as he had never given before. 'George, there is one word
in the English language, of which you are ignorant.' 'What is that?' 'Gratitude,
George.' Gregory, *Autobiography*, 94.

But she could survey him with a certain detachment as well as affection. She once drew up a list of the contrasting qualities, as she saw them, of him and herself. Famous though it is, no biography should omit it.

It begins with a characteristically inconsequential couplet at the top of the page 'His eyes they are as black as Sloes, But oh! so beautiful his nose.' and the list runs thus, his being on the left, hers on the right:

Very calm	Very effervescent
Manners grave and almost sad	Gay and happy looking when speaking
Never irritable	Very irritable
Bad-humoured	Good-humoured
Warm in love but cold in friendship	Cold in love but warm in friendship
Very patient	No patience
Very studious	Very idle
Very generous	Only generous to those she loves
Often says what he does not think	Never says anything she does not think
It is impossible to find out who he likes or dislikes from his manner. He does not show his feelings	Her manner is quite different, and to those she likes she shows her feelings
No vanity	Much vanity
Conceited	No conceit
No self-love	Much self-love
He is seldom amused	Everything amuses her
He is a genius	She is a dunce
He is to be depended on to a certain degree	She is not to be depended on
His whole soul is devoted to politics and ambition	She has no ambition and hates politics

So it is evident they sympathize only on one subject: Maidstone like most husbands & wives about their Children.[1]

In the first few years of their marriage there were occasional differences. The main trouble was money. Disraeli did not wish her to know how deep he was in debt, and she was understandably annoyed at the successive revelations which took place. He could not touch her capital, but he seems to have made use of the improvement of his credit, resulting from his marriage. Perhaps he

[1] Hughenden Papers, Box 4, A/I/A/583; Monypenny (ii, 68) omits the couplet at the top and the sentence at the bottom.

went rather farther than that. 'Mrs. D is aware that I am about raising a sum of money but is ignorant of the method', he wrote to Pyne from his honeymoon. A year later he writes: 'A writ from Ford delivered in my absence to my lady & other circumstances have at length produced a terrible domestic crisis.' About this time the shadowy figure of Pyne fades out and for a while Disraeli had to attend personally to these matters. He refers to Pyne being 'always invisible', and to his 'general inability to prosecute business'.

Early in 1841 he put his affairs into the hands of H. S. Ford of Henrietta Street, whose writ had caused the domestic crisis. Ford did not prove satisfactory, and two years later he transferred to a solicitor called Wright, of Wright, Smith and Shepherd. To him he gave a memorandum which sheds some light on his dealings with Ford.[1] The details are hard to follow, although it is interesting to notice that Disraeli borrowed at 40 per cent to pay a bill of £800 which he had been foolish enough to back for d'Orsay. It seems that Ford agreed to make a temporary advance at 5 per cent to repay all Disraeli's most pressing creditors on condition of becoming his family solicitor and being introduced to Mrs Disraeli. How far she was in the picture one cannot say. She agreed to charge her life estate with a loan of £5,000 on the certain anticipation of a legacy of that amount, but apparently Ford was to merge his costs, which were £250 for this and £200 for another loan, into the general bill, 'engaging that no attendance, conference or transaction directly or indirectly having reference to this loan should appear'. It looks as if Disraeli was being somewhat disingenuous. And what are we to make of an even more surprising transaction? The curious may discover at Hughenden a list of the contents of the house at Grosvenor Gate from 'the three foot feather bed bolster and pillow' in 'the Attic Story Further Room West' to the 'Ormolu Time Piece representing Apollo in a Chariot attended by Cupid' in the drawing-room, set out in a deed as security for the renewal of another loan from Ford from March 16 to April 14, 1842.[2] Did Mary Anne know? It is impossible to be sure.

Naturally enough, involved as he was in these embarrassing financial matters, Disraeli was anxious about his mail arriving when he was absent. It was all too liable to contain something disagreeable. Mary Anne was greatly offended when, staying at

[1] Hughenden Papers, Box 17, A/V/B/45, March 6, 1843.

[2] ibid., Box 17, A/V/D/2. It came to £2,871, of which £871 was a bill of d'Orsay's.

Bradenham in February 1842 while Disraeli was in London, she discovered that Sarah was forwarding his letters without showing them to her.[1] Much recrimination and hurt feeling ensued. Disraeli's marriage by no means ended his intimate correspondence with his sister. There, an occasional flicker of humour even appears about Mary Anne, and Sarah co-operated in the little subterfuges by which he endeavoured to keep his money affairs secret. Yet it should not be thought from all this that Mary Anne was ungenerous. She paid in the end at least £13,000 towards his debts. Nor was there any question of a permanent quarrel with Sarah. On the contrary, Mary Anne got on excellently with the family at Bradenham for most of the while, and they with her.

The saga of all that she did to make his life happy has been told in many books. The stories about her solicitude for him are famous, how she endured in silence the pain of her hand crushed in a carriage door because she feared the knowledge might upset him before a speech; how for the same reason she persuaded Lady Salisbury to place her as far away from him as possible at dinner at Hatfield, for she had cut her face and she knew that he had lost his eye-glass and so would not see. There are many others. No wonder that Disraeli could dedicate *Sybil* 'to one whose sweet voice has often encouraged, and whose taste and judgement have ever guided, its pages; the most severe of critics but – a perfect Wife!'

3

It is hard to say how much success Disraeli really had during the Parliament of 1837–41. His own glowing accounts to his sister and his wife cannot be regarded as conclusive. He was incurably optimistic and he wanted to impress an adoring audience. He certainly made some speeches which read well today. There was his notable attack on the new Poor Law in 1839, arising out of the Chartist petition. He condemned the substitution of centralized relief for the old system based on local administration. It was one of his favourite themes throughout his career that the Tory party should always oppose the centralization, and favour the distribution, of power. But it is doubtful whether this weighed much with the country

[1] Hughenden Papers, Box 2, A/I/A/173, Disraeli to Mrs Disraeli, February 25, 1842.

gentlemen against the fact that the new system was indisputably cheaper than the old. In criticizing the new law he was criticizing his official leaders who had supported it. He risked their disapproval again by being one of only three to vote against a Bill advancing money for a police force at Birmingham where the Chartist Convention was sitting. In 1840 he was one of five who opposed the harsh treatment given to some of the Chartist leaders. This was the time when the 'Condition of England' was beginning to disturb many thoughtful men, and Disraeli can be counted among them, even if he was concerned more with the dramatic than the practical aspect of the problem. Politically he could be described at this time as a Tory radical standing well to the left of centre.

But what eludes us today is the impression which he actually made on the House of Commons. If it had been as great as he obviously believed, would we not have heard more about it in the memoirs and letters of the day? Yet they are almost totally silent, except upon the fiasco of his maiden speech. Perhaps this very silence is significant, like the dog that did not bark in the Sherlock Holmes story.

Although Disraeli could not possibly be described as an orthodox Tory at this or any time, he wished to stand well with Peel. There is no hint in his speeches or writings of the major defects in Peel's conduct and outlook from 1832 onwards, which he was to expose in *Coningsby* and *Sybil*. On the contrary, in *The Times*, under the pseudonym of 'Laelius', he supported Peel and reproved the Queen for her attitude over the Bedchamber Crisis – 'Madam, it cannot be . . .' and in a long encomium he described his leader as 'a man unrivalled for Parliamentary talents, of unimpeached integrity . . . guided by principles but not despising expedients . . . most courageous when in peril; most cautious in prosperity.'

What did Peel think of Disraeli? The answer probably is that he seldom thought about him at all, and when he did regarded him as a bit of an oddity, perhaps something of a blackguard, but clever and worth encouraging. He would have known that he was a protégé of Lyndhurst and Chandos, both of whom were somewhat questionable characters, though people whom Peel did not wish to offend. Disraeli's first meeting with him had not been a success, but that was quite a time ago. Peel now was as civil as might be expected, and asked him to dinner; on one occasion all the other guests were men who had held office, although it is very doubtful whether we should magnify this, as Monypenny does, into the equivalent of a meeting of 'the shadow cabinet'. But Disraeli, sanguine and ambitious, may well have done so.

This was in 1840, and it was clear that the Whigs, kept in office only by royal favour, could not last much longer. They managed to limp through that year, but at the end of May 1841 they were defeated by one vote on a motion of no confidence. At the ensuing general election the Conservaties had a majority of between seventy and ninety. Disraeli had been obliged to find another seat. He could not satisfy the cupidity of the electors of Maidstone, and his old friend, Lord Forester, helped him to secure the nomination for Shrewsbury. This was reckoned to be safe enough, but the election was not all plain sailing. A vigilant though anonymous foe placarded the town with a list of the judgements out against Disraeli, amounting to £22,000. The details may have been incorrect, but his papers show a sum of roughly that amount registered against him two years later. Disraeli, however, stigmatized it as 'utterly false', declaring that he would never have stood had he not possessed 'that ample independence which renders the attainment of any office in the state, except as the recognition of public service, to me a matter of complete indifference'. He was duly elected, although for months afterwards proceedings for bribery hung over him, and it was not till the following April that the good news arrived of his agent having 'swopped' Shrewsbury for Gloucester where a Whig member was in similar jeopardy.

Meanwhile he was in a state of excited anticipation. Melbourne, sticking it out to the end, waited for Parliament to meet. There was much discussion in the Tory party whether to treat the re-election of the Speaker or an amendment to the Address as the issue on which to eject the Government. Peel and most of the leading figures were against opposing the Speaker, and their decision not to do so is one of the landmarks in the development of the Speakership as a non-partisan office. But there was a dissident minority in the party, and a letter in *The Times* signed 'Psittacus' set out their views. In a letter to Peel, Bonham commented on 'the most extraordinary and bitter abuse less at the Carlton than elsewhere (I hear) on the part of Disracli who is the Psittacus of the Times, and of whom you will doubtless hear more.'[1]

Disraeli denied the charge, writing on August 17 to Peel:

[1] British Museum, *Peel Papers*, Add. MSS., 40486, f.7.

On arriving in town today I met Bonham who informed me with
that morose jocularity that he sometimes affects that the party
was flourishing notwithstanding any attempts 'to stir up discussion about the Speakership'.

As I have been in Bucks during the month & with the exception
of Ld Lyndhurst have not even spoken to any member of the new
Parliament I was somewhat surprised at this salute & learnt on
enquiry that I was the author of a letter to the 'Times' Newspr
signed 'Psittacus' . . .

I confess my mortification that after having occasionally for
nearly ten years exercised my pen when I thought it cd serve the
interests of our party I shd be esteemed the author of a paper
which I remember as one absolutely deficient in the commonest
rules of composition . . .[1]

Whether he was telling the truth is another matter. He made other
denials on similar occasions, when we know that they were false.
But the important point is that he was evidently suspected of being
a trouble-maker – a charge which was bound to diminish whatever chance he had of receiving office.

On Friday, August 27, the Government was defeated on an
amendment to the Address. On Monday, August 30, Peel kissed
hands. By Saturday all the major and most of the minor offices were
filled, but no summons came to Disraeli. In desperation he wrote on
Sunday, September 5, to Peel. His letter ended:

. . . I have tried to struggle against a storm of political hate and
malice which few men ever experienced, from the moment, at the
instigation of a member of your Cabinet,[2] I enrolled myself under
your banner, and I have only been sustained under these trials by
the conviction that the day would come when the foremost man
of the country would publicly testify that he had some respect for
my ability and my character.

I confess to be unrecognised at this moment by you appears to
me to be overwhelming, and I appeal to your own heart – to that
justice and that magnanimity which I feel are your characteristics
– to save me from an intolerable humiliation.

Believe me, dear Sir Robert,
Your faithful servant
B. Disraeli[3]

This letter has sometimes been criticized as unduly importunate. It

[1] ibid., f.119.

[2] Presumably Lord Lyndhurst.

[3] C. S. Parker (ed.), *Sir Robert Peel from his Private Papers* (3 vols, 1891–9), ii,
486–9, gives the whole correspondence. See also M. & B., ii, 118–20.

may seem so to those who imagine that politicians regard office in the same way as schoolboys are supposed to regard selection for the first eleven, an honour to be won on merit and to be lost without complaint. No one who has studied the political papers of any Prime Minister will suffer from that delusion. On the contrary, Disraeli's letter will be seen as differing in eloquence only from the kind of plea which every Prime Minister receives from many disappointed applicants. Nor is there any reason for surprise that Mary Anne, on the strength of her own support for Peel and perhaps of her friendship with his sister, should have written, too.

> . . . Literature he has abandoned for politics. Do not destroy all his hopes, and make him feel his life has been a mistake.
>
> May I venture to name my own humble but enthusiastic exertions in time gone by for the party, or rather for your own splendid self? They will tell you at Maidstone that more than £40,000 was spent through my influence only.
>
> Be pleased not to answer this, as I do not wish any human being to know that I have written to you this humble petition.[1]

Peel's reply to Disraeli seems either evasive or based on a misreading, since it is largely devoted to a discussion of something which Disraeli never claimed, viz. that a member of the Cabinet had held out hopes of office to him. What Disraeli actually said was that he had joined the party at the instigation of a member of the Cabinet. He never implied that anyone had made a promise to him, nor was he willing to let Peel get away with this misconstruction. He sent a dignified letter of clarification which closed the correspondence.[2]

Although much has been written about Peel's possible motives in passing over Disraeli, there is really no mystery if we look simply at contemporary evidence and forget about the claims made after Disraeli had become famous and Peel had been vanquished. There is only a problem if it is assumed that Peel's natural instinct was to promote Disraeli, and that someone or something made him change his mind; according to one version, the party hacks, the Tadpoles and Tapers, whom he satirized in *Coningsby*;[3] Stanley,

---

[1] Parker 486–7. There is no proof that Disraeli knew of the letter from his wife, which is dated the night before his own, but it strains credulity to suppose that there was no collusion.

[2] ibid., 487–9.

[3] George Smythe in *The Press*, January 7, 1854.

according to another;[1] the affair with Henrietta, according to a third.[2] But there is not the slightest evidence in Peel's papers that he ever contemplated office for Disraeli, nor does Disraeli's name figure on the lists drawn up by Bonham, from which Peel worked.[3] Why should he have bothered about Disraeli anyway?

Like all Prime Ministers of that era, Peel had to give office to those with great territorial 'influence', and to those who had long served without reward. 'I have not four Parliamentary Civil Offices at my disposal in respect to which I can exercise a discretion,' he wrote.[4] There were eight peers, two heirs to earldoms, three baronets, one knight, and only one plain 'Mr' in his Cabinet; all, except the Duke of Buckingham, had held office before. Eleven ministers outside the Cabinet had been in office in 1834–5. Only four men were included who had entered the House since 1835, and there were special reasons in each case. Of course, Disraeli was a genius. He could 'floor them all'. Peel's career and the whole future of the party might have been very different if Disraeli had been in. But by the standards of his day Peel was acting perfectly reasonably in ignoring Disraeli, just as Disraeli, by the same standards, was acting quite unreasonably in expecting anything else.

[1] A story of Monckton-Milnes who probably knew about the Henry Stanley affair. See above, p. 71–73.

[2] Sir Philip Rose.

[3] I am grateful to Dr Kitson Clark, whose knowledge of the Peel Papers is unsurpassed for drawing my attention to this point and for letting me read his unpublished chapter on Peel's formation of his government, on which this and the next paragraph are largely based.

[4] British Museum, Add. MSS. 40487, ff.64–65, Peel to the Duke of Buccleuch.

CHAPTER VIII

Young England
1841–5

1

Disraeli was much mortified at his rebuff. Although he kept the facts of the application and refusal a profound secret, he was bitterly disappointed. It would be oversimplifying matters to say that his eventual conflict with Peel was directly caused by this episode, but his attitude to his leader naturally became more critical. There is nothing like full employment to suppress doubts; but he had time on his hands, time to reflect, brood, wonder. As early as February 1842 something of this state of mind appears in a letter to his wife. He feels, he says, 'utterly isolated', and he goes on: 'Before the change of Government political party was a tie among men, but now it is only a tie among men in office.'[1] Already in his mind a subtle transition was taking place. Peel and the other ministers were ceasing to be 'we' and becoming 'they'.

There was no immediate breach. Partly because he suspected, probably without any justification, that there was a move afoot to drive him into rebellion, Disraeli bent over backwards to display his orthodoxy during the first year of the new Parliament.[2] He kept away from the agricultural malcontents, Sir R. Vyvyan and others, who, encouraged by the resignation of the Duke of Buckingham, (Chandos), early in 1842 withdrew their support from Peel. At the end of the session Disraeli was regarded as sufficiently 'sound' to be asked by Fremantle, the Chief Whip, after Peel had spoken in an important debate, to reply 'to any man of note who rose on the opposite benches'.[3] But it was too much to expect that Disraeli would keep this up for long, and behave as a docile party man awaiting his turn for promotion. Bored, restless, vaguely discontented, fascinated by new and esoteric ideas, he soon gravitated to another small and rebellious section of the party, very different in

[1] M. & B., ii, 125.
[2] ibid., quoting letter to Mrs Disraeli, February 26.
[3] ibid., 136.

character from the dull Duke and his empty-headed supporters. This was the group known later as 'Young England'. Their influence on him was scarcely less deep than his on them.

The history of Young England has all the charm and nostalgia which attend tales of forlorn hopes and lost causes, like the Jacobitism that they themselves worshipped, like the Fourth Party which, forty years on, modelled itself upon them. The success of such movements of protest cannot be measured by their immediate political failure. They must, rather, be regarded as symbols and examples that lend an imaginative glow to the dull course of party politics; showing that there are other ways to fame than conformism, diligence and calculation; showing that a gesture, however absurd it may seem to contemporaries, may sometimes live longer than many Blue Books. Neither Young England nor the Fourth Party achieved anything significant, but their memory will always beckon to those incurable romantics for whom political life is something more than a humdrum profession.

George Smythe, eldest son of Disraeli's former friend Lord Strangford, was Young England's Bonnie Prince Charlie and Lord Randolph Churchill rolled into one. Brilliant, reckless, dissipated, he burned himself out and died early, leaving rather the memory of what he was than the record of what he did. It seems to be agreed by all his contemporaries that he was a youth of extraordinary talent and charm. First at Eton, then at Cambridge, he dominated an exclusive coterie of intellectual patricians who, under the combined influences of Clarendon's *History*, Bolingbroke's *Patriot King*, Kenelm Digby's *Broadstone of Honour*, Scott's novels, and the *Tracts for the Times*, sought to revive a Toryism not the less potent for having never existed outside their imagination. If Strafford, Laud and Bolingbroke were his political mentors, his hero in all other things was Byron. The ghost of the great poet may often be seen walking in Smythe's career. There is the same mixture of cynicism and romance, the same hatred of cant, the same contempt for prudent middle-class morality, the same disregard for money, the same inverted puritanism, the same irresistible good looks, the same impulse towards self-torment.

The parallel must not be pressed too far. Byron was a genius. Smythe was not more than talented. His verses, novels and political writings are forgotten now, or only remembered for absurdities like his plea to revive 'touching' for the 'King's Evil' as a means of reviving the monarchy. Moreover, he never matured. Old for his years at Eton and perhaps at Cambridge, he then stopped. He was in spirit the eternal undergraduate. Disraeli described a speech of his early in February 1842 as having 'ability though puerile', observing earlier in the same letter to his wife that it was as 'unprincipled as his little agreeable self'. This was before he sniffed the incense of Smythe's hero-worship. In *Coningsby* we have a more flattering picture. Coningsby himself is Smythe, though as so often with Disraeli's heroes – Tancred, Lothair and Endymion are the same – he is curiously uninteresting, essentially passive, someone to whom things happen. A livelier portrait appears in *Endymion*, where Smythe features not as the hero but as Waldershare, whose 'versatile nature became palled even with the society of duchesses . . .'

> Waldershare was profligate but sentimental; unprincipled but romantic; the child of whim, and the slave of an imagination so freakish and deceptive that it was impossible to foretell his course. He was alike capable of sacrificing all his feelings to worldly considerations or of forfeiting the world for a visionary caprice.[1]

Smythe was undoubtedly 'profligate'. He was wildly extravagant and always in debt. He was involved in a series of disreputable amours, and although women fell for him like ninepins he only made a respectable marriage to the heiress of his father's dreams a few weeks before his death from tuberculosis, hastened by excessive potations of brandy. His temper and impetuousness were fatal disadvantages. In 1852 he fought the last duel on English soil against his colleague in the representation of Canterbury; at the ensuing election he only received seven votes. Well before then he had had his political career blasted by a scandal which, though not his fault, stamped him as a failure.

It is always difficult to see at a long distance of time exactly what it was that made such a person so fascinating to his contemporaries. Much of it must have been in that most elusive of qualities, conversational wit and the humour that depends on the time and mode of utterance. Disraeli wrote once:

> George Smythe was very rich when he had made up his mind to marry an heiress and gave instructions to all the ladies who were and had been in love with him to work for his benefit. 'Family,' he used to say, 'I don't care in the least for: would rather like to

---

[1] *Endymion*, ch. 22.

marry into a rich vulgar family. Madness no objection. As for
Scrofula why should I care for it more than a king. All this ought
to be a great pull in my favour.' Strange to say he succeeded and
married an heiress – but literally on his death bed.[1]

Disraeli was entranced by him and forgave all his vagaries.[2]
Smythe died in 1857 at the age of forty-one, two years after he had
succeeded as 7th Lord Strangford. 'I once heard that you had said
of me that I was the one man who had never bored you', he wrote
to Disraeli shortly before his death. And in the preface to the 1870
edition of his novels Disraeli described him as 'a man of brilliant
gifts, of dazzling wit, of infinite culture, and of fascinating manners'.
But perhaps the truest epitaph was Lord Lyttelton's – 'a splendid
failure'.

If Smythe was both leader and spoilt child of Young England,
the person who represented its quintessence was not he but his
closest friend of Eton and Cambridge days, Lord John Manners,
second son of the 5th Duke of Rutland. He is too often ridiculed as
the author of the couplet which has become notorious:

'Let wealth and commerce, laws and learning die,
But leave us still our old Nobility.'

Manners cannot be discounted so easily. The formidable Whewell,
fellow of Trinity when Manners was an undergraduate and subsequently master for twenty-five years, once said: 'I had rather be
Lord John Manners than any young man who has passed through
the University.' Manners, who figures in *Coningsby* as Lord Henry
Sydney, was a person of handsome appearance, the highest integrity,
considerable ability and of the utmost good nature. He collected
friends as readily as Smythe with his mordant and reckless wit made
enemies.

The romantic Toryism that he espoused was absolutely consistent. The 'worldly considerations' of a Waldershare were unknown
to him. No man was ever such an assiduous devotee of lost causes.
He visited the Carlists in Spain, and composed a sonnet in honour
of the unfortunate pretender. He toured Lancashire and decided
that monasticism was the cure for Manchester. To him the only
redeeming feature of the new social order in the north was the one

---

[1] Hughenden Papers, Box 26, A/X/A/61.1.
[2] It would be interesting to know what happened to Smythe's letters to Disraeli.
In 1873 Disraeli told Corry that he had found enough for three volumes, but in the
Hughenden Papers today there are only five letters remaining.

which most people severely condemned. 'There was never so complete a feudal system as that of the mills; soul and body are or
might be at the absolute disposal of one man, and that to my mind
is not at all a bad state of society,'[1] he characteristically wrote to
his brother, Lord Granby. Was the Provost of Eton in favour of
abolishing Montem? Lord John was ready to organize a London
committee of Old Etonians for resistance. Did Ambrose Phillipps De
Lisle[2] suggest an Anglican union with Rome – 'the present Clergy
to retain their wives and livings, appointing Curates to administer
the Sacrament'?[3] Lord John could be relied on to promote the
unhopeful cause.

Both Manners and Smythe were profoundly influenced by Frederick Faber, a leading disciple of Newman. Young England was the
Oxford movement translated by Cambridge from religion into
politics. Both stemmed from the same origin – an emotional revulsion against the liberal utilitarian spirit of the time. The whole
contemporary medieval revival which reached its apogee in the
famous mock tournament organized by Lord Eglinton in 1839[4] was
part of the same phenomenon, and there is something very appropriate in Lord John Manners leading many years later yet another of
his forlorn hopes, the struggle for a Gothic design for the new
Foreign Office. Alas, he had that robust Regency figure, Palmerston,
against him; and the battle of the styles, conducted on strict Conservative versus Liberal party lines, ended, as so often with Lord
John's battles, in a victory for his opponents.

Viewed in its widest context, Young England, like Tractarianism
and the Gothic revival, was the reaction of a defeated class to a sense
of its own defeat – a sort of nostalgic escape from the disagreeable
present to the agreeable but imaginary past. The aristocracy to
which Smythe and his friends belonged was losing its ascendancy.
It still possessed great power and influence, but the writing was
discernible upon the wall, spelled out already by the Reform Act of
1832, soon to be underlined by the repeal of the Corn Laws. Just as
the Oxford movement set up for its ideal the revival of a pure,
uncorrupted, pre-Reformation church which had never existed, in
order to counter the Erastian and latitudinarian tendencies of the

[1] Charles Whibley, *Lord John Manners and his Friends* (2 vols, 1925), i, 106.
[2] A rich young Catholic landowner, the original of Eustace Lyle in *Coningsby*.
[3] Quoted by Whibley, *Lord John Manners*, i, 253.
[4] Disraeli, being on his honeymoon, did not attend; his account in *Endymion*, chs.
59 and 60, is second-hand and inaccurate.

day, so Young England resuscitated a no less mythical benevolent feudal system to set against the radical, centralizing Benthamism which seemed to be carrying all before it in the 1830s and 1840s.

Yet if this may be its social explanation, and if one may easily laugh at some of its more absurd follies, the movement should not be dismissed as wholly ineffective. It was not a bad thing that some generous young men of high birth should declare the owners of property to have duties as well as privileges. It was not a bad thing that there should be a section of the Tory party concerned with the harshness of the Poor Law. It was not a bad thing that the 'haves' should not be all grouped on one side against the 'have-nots', and that the landed classes should be encouraged first to put their own house in order and then to flay the abuses of the 'millocracy'. And if the movement was mixed up with a good deal of ecclesiastical flummery, medieval bric-à-brac and gothic rubbish, did this really do anyone any harm?

Disraeli was not the man to take it too seriously. He certainly owed to Smythe parts of his theory of history as outlined in *Coningsby* and *Sybil*. In the *Vindication* he had merely traced the Tory apostolic succession to Bolingbroke. Now he goes back to the Stuarts, to Laud and Strafford. In *Sybil* even the Reformation is looked at with a jaundiced eye and there is much nostalgia for monasteries and the Old Faith. But he was careful not to translate any High or Roman sympathies in his writings into practical politics. He was well aware of the unpopularity of Puseyism. Any move on his part in that direction was intended only to please his new friends. 'Dizzy's attachment to moderate Oxfordism', wrote Smythe with perception, 'is something like Bonaparte's to moderate Mohammedanism'.[1]

Disraeli had known Smythe from boyhood through his acquaintance with Lord Strangford. At a dinner party in February 1841 he first met Manners, who wrote in his journal: 'D'Israeli talked well, but a little too well.'[2] The misgivings implied in this comment soon diminished. Manners and Smythe, who were both in the House of Commons by the end of 1841, looked increasingly to Disraeli for a lead. Also in the House was another Cambridge friend, Alexander Baillie-Cochrane[3] (Buckhurst in *Coningsby*). He was the fourth

[1] Whibley, *Lord John Manners*, i, 153.
[2] ibid., 84–85.
[3] Not to be confused with Henry Baillie, a man of Disraeli's own age, a brother-in-law of Smythe and an intermittent supporter of Young England.

member and the dimmest of what Lord John called 'our *partie carrée*'. On March 11, 1842, Disraeli wrote to his wife, who was at Bradenham: 'I already find myself without effort the leader of a party chiefly of the youth and new members.'[1] But the alliance was not formally consolidated until the next year's session.

During the autumn recess in 1842 the Disraelis repaired to Paris and took up residence for a couple of months in the Hôtel de l'Europe in the rue de Rivoli. They were duly entertained by the Parisian *haute monde* and they met princes, dukes and counts galore, invested with all the glamour of ancient titles and high-sounding historic names. 'But', Disraeli wrote to Sarah, 'where are the territories? There are only 100 men in France who have ten thousand per ann. Henry Hope and De Rothschild could buy them all.'[2] The court was in mourning for the death of the Duke of Orléans, and so Mary Anne could not be presented, but Disraeli himself had several audiences from the King.

His object was not merely social. He had completely reversed the attitude to France expressed in his *Gallomania* of ten years earlier, and now sought to promote an entente between the two nations. He submitted a lengthy memorandum to the King.[3] Palmerston, who dominated the policy of the late Government, had, so Disraeli argued, been anti-French. The new Government was better disposed, but spoke with an uncertain and confused voice. If pressure could be brought on Peel and Aberdeen, a clear pro-French policy might emerge. This was where Young England came in:

> The Government of Sir Robert Peel is at this moment upheld by an apparent majority in the Commons of 90 members. It is known that among these 90 are between 40 and 50 agricultural malcontents who, though not prepared to commence an active opposition, will often be absent on questions which, though not of vital, may yet be of great importance to the Minister. It is obvious therefore that another section of Conservative members, full of youth and energy and constant in their seats, must exercise an irrestible control over the tone of the Minister . . .

[1] M. & B., ii, 130.
[2] ibid., ii, 148. Henry Hope was a supporter of Young England and MP for Gloucester. *Coningsby* is dedicated to him and was written at his country seat Deepdene. He was very rich, having inherited large fortunes of Dutch origin from his father and uncle. His brother Beresford Hope, also a wealthy Conservative MP, brother-in-law of the 3rd Marquess of Salisbury, was a cordial enemy both of Disraeli and Young England.
[3] M. & B., ii, Appendix, 409–13, taken from a draft in the Hughenden Papers.

Evidently Young England, as envisaged by Disraeli at this moment, was to be something more than a *partie carrée*. On his figures at least fifty would have been needed to produce any results. Nothing came of all this. Disraeli was in a mood of euphoria in Paris, and the heady exhilaration produced by that enchanting capital had given him an optimistic and oversimplified view of the dark politics of fog-ridden London. 'Disraeli's salons', wrote Baillie-Cochrane to Manners, 'rival Law's under the Regent. Guizot, Thiers, Molé, Decazes and God wots how many deiminores are found in his antechamber, while the great man himself is closeted with Louis Philippe at St. Cloud and already pictures himself the founder of some new dynasty with his Manfred love-locks stamped on the current coin of the realm.'[1]

The formation of the new party did indeed proceed rapidly in Paris, but not on the grandiose lines contemplated by Disraeli. Manners and Smythe had been in Geneva together in the summer and had made their plans. From Geneva Smythe proceeded to Paris, where he found not only Disraeli but Baillie-Cochrane. Manners returned to London and the letters which he received from his two friends are a fascinating commentary on the role of Disraeli.[2] Both favoured from the first a small, exclusive, intimate group acting in concert. They would not spurn outside supporters, but those in the innermost councils must be few. On October 19 Smythe, back in London, wrote to Manners

> *Most private*. Dizzy has much more parliamentary power than I had any notion of. The two Hodgsons are his, and Quintin Dick. He has a great hold on Walter and 'The Times'. Henry Hope who will come in soon is entirely in his hands. He was in Paris, and I had an opportunity of judging. You understand me? We four vote, and these men are to be played upon and won and wooed, for the sense in which we esoterics may have decided.[3]

The difficulty was Cochrane, who favoured keeping the party down to three and Disraeli at arm's length.

> You see Kok does not know him well, and sometimes dreads his jokes, and is jealous of his throwing us over. But even if he did, it is always better to be *in a position* to be thrown over than to be *nothing at all*.

[1] Whibley, *Lord John Manners*, i, 141.
[2] ibid., 138, *et seq*.
[3] ibid., 143.

The truth was that Disraeli had never at any time in his life been an easy man to know; and as he grew older he became no easier. It was hard to penetrate the façade which he now presented to the world. In his youth he had been overeffusive and oversensitive. He was vulnerable and had shown his vulnerability in his love affairs, his debts and his quarrels. He had made a fool of himself in his maiden speech. He knew that he had to preserve an iron control over his voice and countenance if he was to avoid revealing the passion and ambition which seethed in his mind. Hence his assumption of that magniloquent half-ironic half-serious manner which so disconcerted those who expected the ordinary self-deprecatory candour of the English upper class. The rhetorical quasi-Gibbonian sentences flowed, with their hyperbole, their satire, their mordant and witty asides, from a face as expressionless as an antique mask. How could the hearer tell whether these orotund extravagances were seriously meant? Indeed, did Disraeli himself really know?

Smythe was not disconcerted. He was too cynical, too much on the make. He had experienced at twenty-four the debts, amours, and dissipations which it had taken Disraeli ten years longer to run through. Despite the gap in age they understood each other profoundly: they were birds of a feather. It was otherwise with Manners and Cochrane. Smythe might laughingly refer to the new party as the 'Diz-Union', but his friends were less happy.

> . . . the impression [wrote Cochrane] which he conveys to others of his great personal influence in the House is calculated to embarrass all our movements, because no man can indulge in such contemplations of self-aggrandisement without at least in the words of Thiers, 'prenant ses voeux pour des realités' . . . D'I's head is full of great movements, vast combinations, the importance of numbers, cabinet dinners, the practice of dissimulation! in fact of the vaguest speculations, the mere phantasmagoria of politique legerdemain . . .[1]

Manners, too, seems to have been uneasy. Six months later he noted in his journal: 'Could I only satisfy myself that D'Israeli believed all he said, I should be more happy: his historical views are quite mine, but does he believe them?'[2]

Does he believe them? The question echoes emptily down the years. We can answer it no more certainly today than Lord John Manners could then.

[1] Whibley, *Lord John Manners*, i, 148–9.   [2] ibid., i, 149.

2

Whatever the misgivings felt by some of them, the quartet became firmly established during the session of 1843. Lord John Manners had already provided a sort of manifesto in his pamphlet – 'A Plea for National Holy-Days', which inspired a certain amount of ridicule among the ill disposed. The four Young Englanders sat together behind the Treasury Bench. They consulted on every topic, concerted their speeches – when they could agree – and generally enjoyed all the pleasures of conspiracy, intrigue and a common sense of the ridiculous. Others voted with them on occasions: Henry Baillie, W. B. Ferrand, Peter Borthwick, Henry Hope and Stafford O'Brien. Monckton Milnes hovered around, half fascinated, half frightened and intensely jealous of Smythe, who, as he rightly suspected, regarded him as a figure of fun; John Walter allowed his house, Bearwood, to be the headquarters of many a meeting, and saw to it that *The Times* gave them generous treatment. But the quartet remained a quartet. Like the Fourth Party, they did not seek recruits and like it, too, they made a splash out of all proportion to their weight and numbers.

For a number of reasons the times were favourable to a dissident group in the party, anxious to draw the maximum of attention to itself. Peel had a safe majority, but he was not overpopular with his supporters. He was never good at managing men and although he had a warm heart he hid it behind a cold repellent façade. A certain pepperiness in his character had, moreover, begun to appear, and was to increase over the next four years. He has often been described as the last Prime Minister to exercise a detailed control over all the departments of state. The truth is, rather, that he was the first as well as the last, and that he was unwise to do it. The strain of unremitting work made him touchy and irritable. At times he scarcely bothered to conceal his contempt for the more wooden-headed of his supporters.

Throughout 1843 and 1844 Peel's party still for the most part gave him solid support, but did so with increasing reluctance and resentment. A gap was opening between the rank and file – the old Country party, which had ever been the backbone of Toryism, and the Government men, the ministers and under-secretaries whose brains were as indispensable as the votes of the back benchers. It was an excellent opportunity for clever rebels to gain applause. The ministry was running into difficulties. There was much industrial and agrarian discontent. The economic depression which had vexed the country from 1836 onwards showed no real sign of lifting. In 1842 the Chartists made another great demonstration and brought a second petition to the House in May. From another quarter – middle-class radicalism – came the threat of the Anti-Corn Law League headed by Cobden and Bright. And all the while the problem of Ireland rumbled away in the background.

It was, indeed, Ireland which first drew Young England into open revolt. Smythe, Manners and Cochrane voted against the Government in July 1843 on Smith O'Brien's resolution demanding an inquiry into the condition of Ireland. Disraeli was absent on this occasion, but on August 10 took the opportunity of the third reading of an Irish Arms Bill to deliver a contemptuous indictment of Government policy. He intended, he said, to abstain: 'There are some measures which to introduce is disgraceful and to oppose is degrading.' He ended by urging the Government to penetrate to the real heart of the problem and 'put an end to a state of things that is the bane of England and the opprobrium of Europe'. The front bench did not relish these remarks from someone whose powers of trouble-making were known to be formidable.

They did not take Smythe and Manners very seriously, but Disraeli was in a different category. Sir James Graham, Home Secretary and a close friend of both Peel and Stanley, wrote to Croker at the end of August.

With respect to Young England, the puppets are moved by Disraeli, who is the ablest man among them; I consider him un-principled and disappointed and in despair he has tried the effect of bullying. I think with you that they will return to the crib after prancing, capering, and snorting; but a crack or two of the whip well applied may hasten and insure their return. Disraeli alone is mischievous, and with him I have no desire to keep terms. It would be better for the party if he were driven into the ranks of our open enemies.[1]

Disraeli was curiously insensitive about his effect upon others. It was typical of him that, after a session in which he had greatly offended his leaders and while he was in the middle of writing a novel which held up to ridicule the whole policy of official conservatism,

[1] Louis J. Jennings, *Memoirs . . of . . Croker* (3 vols, 1884), iii, 9.

he should have asked first Stanley and then Graham for a government post for his brother, James. It is true that he had already in 1841 procured through Lyndhurst a clerkship in Chancery for Ralph, but his political position was then rather different; moreover, Lyndhurst was a friend, whereas Graham and Stanley were not. Both sent the usual polite letters of refusal, but privately Graham was indignant. 'His letter', he wrote to Peel, 'is an impudent one and is considered by me doubly so when I remember his conduct and language in the House of Commons towards the end of the last session.' Peel replied on December 22, 1843.

> I am very glad that Mr. Disraeli has asked for an office for his brother. It is a good thing when such a man puts his shabbiness on record. He asked me for office himself and I am not surprised that being refused he became independent and a patriot. But to ask favours after his conduct last session is too bad. However it is a bridle in his mouth.[1]

A few weeks later he withheld the customary circular letter which he sent to all his supporters asking for their attendance in the coming session. Disraeli at once protested. The omission, he wrote on February 4, was 'a painful personal procedure which the past by no means authorized'. And he alluded to Peel's 'want of courtesy in debate'. Peel replied in a conciliatory tone. 'My reason for not sending the usual circular was an honest doubt whether I was entitled to send it . . . It gives me, however, great satisfaction to infer from your letter – as I trust I am justified in inferring – that my impressions were mistaken and my scruples unnecessary.'[2] He disclaimed any intention of being discourteous. There the matter rested for the moment, and Disraeli made a point of giving support to the Government during the early part of the session of 1844, doing so, moreover, on Irish policy which had previously brought him into conflict with Peel.

The occasion was an Opposition vote of censure against the Irish administration. Disraeli persuaded the rest of Young England to vote with him, and during the debate made one of his most celebrated speeches, perhaps the first in which he caught the ear of the House of Commons and established himself as something more than a clever literary man. One passage in particular will always be remembered.

[1] C. S. Parker (ed.), *Peel*, iii, 424–5.
[2] M. & B., ii, 185–8, for these letters in full.

I want to see a public man come forward and say what the Irish question is. One says it is a physical question, another, a spiritual. Now it is the absence of aristocracy, then the absence of railways. It is the Pope one day, potatoes the next. Consider Ireland as you would any other country similarly situated. You will see a teeming population which, with reference to the cultivated soil, is denser to the square mile than that of China; created solely by agriculture, with none of the resources of wealth which develop with civilisation; and sustained, consequently, upon the lowest conceivable diet, so that in the case of failure they have no other means of subsistence upon which they can fall back. That dense population in extreme distress inhabits an island where there is an established Church which is not their Church and a territorial aristocracy the richest of whom live in distant capitals. Thus you have a starving population, an absentee aristocracy, and an alien Church, and in addition the weakest executive in the world. That is the Irish question.[1]

Peel responded to Disraeli's support by referring to 'the very able speech of the hon. member for Shrewsbury'.

But the *rapprochement* did not last long. In May, *Coningsby* was published. Disraeli's description of the Tamworth Manifesto as 'an attempt to construct a party without principles', and of the 'Conservative Constitution' as a 'Caput Mortuum' cannot have pleased Peel and his friends. In the middle of May a fierce parliamentary battle took place on the Government's Factory Bill. Ashley, the great philanthropist, with the support of all Young England, except Smythe, who could not always withstand his father's adjurations to vote for Peel, managed to defeat in committee the Government's proposal merely to limit the hours of work for boys under eighteen to twelve per day; Ashley considered that ten should be the maximum figure. Peel, however, brought in a new bill, and virtually forced the House to rescind its previous decision by a personal threat to resign. Disraeli did not have a chance of speaking on this occasion, but he did not forget.

A few weeks later Peel repeated the performance on another issue. He wished to equalize the tariffs on colonial and foreign sugar by lowering the latter, but a group of pro-colonial Tories had combined with the anti-slavery members of the Opposition to carry an amendment reducing the duty on colonial as well as foreign, ie largely slave-grown sugar, thus preserving the differential

[1] *Hansard*, 3rd series, LXXII, 1016.

which had always existed between them, to the annoyance of free traders. Disraeli voted with the majority.

Peel was determined to get his way and have the vote rescinded. He summoned a party meeting and stated his case in a speech which even Gladstone said 'was thought to be haughty and unconciliatory'.[1] There was only a handful of overt dissentients, Disraeli and Ferrand among them, but Peel himself realized that his attitude was resented, for he told Gladstone as he left the room 'that it was the worst meeting he had ever attended' and he warned the Queen that the Government was in danger. Despite this awareness he seems to have made a scarcely less imperious speech in the House, and Disraeli obtained great applause by a defiant declaration that he had no intention of 'changing my vote within forty-eight hours at the menace of a Minister'. The situation was saved for Peel by a brilliant speech from Stanley. 'The Prince Rupert of Parliamentary discussion', as Disraeli once called him, did not on this occasion return to find 'his camp in the possession of the enemy'. The Government survived by twenty votes, and Queen Victoria wrote with relief on June 18 to the King of the Belgians of its narrow escape from the danger caused by 'the recklessness of a handful of foolish half "Puseyite", half "Young England" people'.[2]

Young England was causing perturbation in other high circles, too. The King of Hanover urged the Duke of Rutland and Lord Strangford to discipline their sons. The Duke did not know Disraeli even by sight, but Lord Strangford at one time had been a friend and admirer. Recently, however, his attitude had changed. Passionately anxious to see his son in office, he rightly regarded the latter's hero-worship of Disraeli as an impediment.

> It is grievous [the Duke wrote to Strangford in the grave and stately style of the old school] that two young men such as John and Mr. Smythe should be led by one of whose integrity of purpose I have an opinion similar to your own, though I can judge only by his public career.[3] The admirable character of our sons makes them the more assailable by the arts of a designing person. I will write to John tomorrow and I shall enquire of him whether there

[1] John Morley, *Life of W. E. Gladstone* (3 vols, 1903), i, 644.
[2] A. C. Benson and Viscount Esher (ed.), *The Letters of Queen Victoria*, 1837–61 (3 vols, 1907), ii, 19.
[3] Strangford may have been regaling the Duke with some details of Disraeli's private life.

is any truth in the report of his having engaged himself to a great dinner at Manchester under the presidency of Mr. Disraeli.[1]

Alas, it was almost true, although the Duke perhaps could take some comfort in the fact that the function was a 'literary tea' and that party politics were eschewed. The meeting – it was of young artisans of the Manchester Athenaeum – took place in October, Smythe, Manners and Disraeli all making speeches of much fervour. Disraeli prided himself on one much quoted passage:

> Knowledge is like the mystic ladder in the patriarch's dream: its base rests on the primeval earth, its crest is lost in the shadowy splendour of the empyrean; while the great authors who for traditionary ages have held the chain of science and philosophy, of poesy and erudition, are the angels ascending and descending the sacred scale, and maintaining as it were the communication between man and heaven.[2]

And it was in this same speech that Disraeli made another observation which has become famous: 'The youth of a nation are the trustees of posterity.' Charles Whibley in his *Lord John Manners and his Friends* discerns in the meeting of the Manchester Athenaeum the high water mark of their success, and Monypenny describes it as 'the culminating point in the glory of Young England'.[3] Even the doubting elders felt less uneasy. The King of Hanover, despite his disapprobation of people putting any ideas, even Tory ones, into the minds of the lower orders, admired Smythe's speech, and Strangford and the Duke were proud, too, of their sons' efforts.

Disraeli was busy now on *Sybil*, a sequel to *Coningsby*. It was even more hostile to Peel and all his works. Much of *Sybil* is devoted to the conditions of the working class in the great manufacturing capitals. Disraeli probably obtained a good deal of local colour in the course of a prolonged stay in the north, which followed his speech at Manchester. He and Mary Anne visited Lord Francis Egerton at Worsley Hall, and W. B. Ferrand, MP, at Bingley in the West Riding. Ferrand, a man of most intemperate language, was a stout ally of Young England and a great expert on the malpractices of manufacturers and millowners.

From Bingley, the Disraeli's went to Fryston, one of the seats of

---

[1] E. B. de Fonblanque, *Lives of the Viscounts Strangford* . . . (1877), 224–5.
[2] M. & B., ii, 247.
[3] loc. cit.

old Mr Pemberton Milnes, the father of the busy, voluble and ubi-
quitous 'Dicky' Monckton-Milnes. They probably owed their invitation to the father, who enjoyed irritating his son. The latter's attitude
to Disraeli and Young England was ambivalent. Like Disraeli, he
had sought and been refused office in 1841, although, unlike Disraeli,
he proclaimed his ill treatment to all the salons of London. Therefore, in order to show that he was no mere doormat, he was inclined
to skirmish on the flanks of Young England. On the other hand, he
cordially detested Smythe, of whom he was intensely jealous, and
who, according to a memorandum left among Disraeli's jottings,
'hated him with a sort of diablerie and treated him with a fantastic
insolence which requires a great pen to picture'.[1]

It is seldom that impressions of the ceaseless country house visits
of those days are recorded. It so happens that two reminiscences of
that particular one have survived the years. Gathorne Hardy (later
Lord Cranbrook but then an unknown young barrister), records how
Disraeli's conversation struck him as 'too much striving to be
epigrammatic': moreover, he adds, vanity prevented him from
talking freely 'lest he should lose ground'.[2] The other witness was
Lady Elizabeth Spencer-Stanhope, a daughter of the famous Coke
of Holkham, 1st Earl of Leicester in the new creation. Charades, she
remembered, were acted, Richard Milnes distinguishing himself as
Sarah Gamp. She was not previously well disposed to the Disraelis,
but she was delighted at his half-foreign manner and at the way in
which he helped her to dress her truffles; and Mary Anne won her
heart, despite a peculiarly fantastical dress, by giving her the real
story of the great row between Bulwer and his wife.[3]

The Disraelis returned to the south for Christmas and in the
middle of January attended the last grand party given by their old
friend, the Duke of Buckingham, who entertained the Queen and
the Prince Consort at Stowe. 'The whole scene', wrote Disraeli
to his sister on January 20, 'sumptuous and a great success for
the Duke.'[4] But it was very cold. 'Fancy, dear shivering Dizzy,

[1] Hughenden Papers, Box 26, A/X/A/33. The greater part of this acid memorandum, though not this particular sentence, is quoted in M. & B., iii, 51–53. Its purpose
is not quite clear, but evidently by the time Disraeli wrote it, probably 1863 or there-
abouts, he had come to regard Milnes with much dislike. See below, p. 206, for a
possible explanation.

[2] A. E. Gathorne Hardy (ed.), *Gathorne Hardy; a Memoir* (2 vols, 1910), i, 53.

[3] Pope-Hennessy, *Monckton-Milnes*, i, 195–6. Disraeli's explanation, which he
had from Henry Baillie, was that Bulwer 'wants *bonnes fortunes*'. Hughenden Papers,
Box 26, A/X/A.26.

[4] *Correspondence*, 203.

and cross looking Mary Anne', wrote the latter, also to Sarah, 'in black velvet, hanging sleeves looped up with knots of blue, and diamond buttons.'

However, when the Queen had left, 'all became joy and triumph to us'. Peel was very cordial 'and remained talking for some time'. Graham and Aberdeen were civil, and the Duchess of Buckingham told Mary Anne 'that her Majesty had pointed Dizzy out, saying *"There's Mr. Disraeli."* Do you call all this nothing?'[1] It was the swan song of the Duke. His finances were already tottering. This lavish entertainment was the last straw. Within three years he was forced to leave the country, owing a million pounds.

3

The session of 1845 saw Disraeli in open rebellion against Peel. Why did he finally break with his leader? It is hard to see any notable change in Peel's policy. Nor is there any real evidence that Disraeli perceived the impending split in the Conservative party. It may be, as Monypenny suggests, that the very process of writing *Sybil* had brought home to him the utter incompatibility of his outlook and that of Peel. Perhaps he realized, too, that all chance of preferment at Peel's hands had finally vanished, that he had passed the point of no return, and that, however frail the hope, he had to stake his career upon the ruin of Peel's. It would not be surprising if he was in a mood of some desperation by this time. He had been in Parliament for seven years, and he had done nothing of real importance. It is true that people listened to him with attention, and sometimes took what he said seriously. But they found many of his ideas eccentric and incomprehensible. Above all, they did not trust him personally. And no wonder. Here was an insolent, mysterious, half-foreign adventurer with a libertine past and a load of debt, who had married a rich widow for money. We may be sure that garbled versions of his past relations with Henrietta and Lyndhurst lost nothing in the telling. The truth was disreputable enough. Then there were powerful enemies: some, like Stanley, made through no fault of Disraeli's; others, like Murray, Lockhart, Crocker and the world of the Tory literary establishment, made by his own reckless youthful indiscretions. *Vivian Grey* and *The Young Duke* constituted heavy millstones round the neck of anyone who wanted to become a

[1] M. & B., ii, 249.

respectable political figure. Disraeli could do nothing about them. They were there for all to read, and they told their tale.

Moreover, time was working against him. He was forty, old in those days for first entry into office. A whole group of able, hard-working and younger men were ahead of him in the official hierarchy: Gladstone, Sidney Herbert, Lincoln, Dalhousie, Cardwell, Canning;[1] all members of the Government, whether in or outside the Cabinet, all born between 1807 and 1813, all Oxonians – mostly products of Eton and Christ Church. How could he hope to displace these distinguished figures who represented the very cream of the upper-class English political world. No doubt is was some consolation to be hero-worshipped by the patrician youths of Young England, and to be the dominant figure in their exclusive coterie. Yet even this had not led to acceptance by their families. The Duke of Rutland regarded him as 'a designing person'. Lord Strangford had thrown him over. He was not, like Smythe, Manners, Cochrane, a mere youth in his twenties. They could afford to wait, to indulge in eccentric poses and rebellious gestures, secure in the knowledge that they had plenty of time to make their peace with their leaders, but Disraeli could afford no such leisurely delay. The sands were beginning to run out, and in his less sanguine moments he must have known it. At all events, whether his motive was despair at his own prospects, belief in his own principles, long-sighted appraisal of the future, or – perhaps most probable of all – love of revenge, Disraeli enlivened the session by a series of bitter and memorable attacks on Peel.

The first arose as a result of the demand for a parliamentary inquiry into the alleged opening of a Radical MP's letters in the post under a warrant from the Home Office. Disraeli observed that Peel 'displayed an unusual warmth', adding: 'I am aware that it by no means follows that the right hon. gentleman felt it . . . but in a popular assembly it is sometimes expedient to enact the part of the choleric gentleman.'[2] In the same speech he was rash enough to imply that Bonham, the agent of the Conservative party, who held a sinecure position in the Ordnance, had been concerned in the Despard plot of 1802.

Peel made a devastating reply on the second point. Bonham was only sixteen in 1802 and the story arose out of the fact that in 1799

---

[1] The son of the Prime Minister and Govenor-General and first Viceroy of India.
[2] *Hansard*, 3rd series, lxxvii, 906, February 10, 1845.

his half-brother, Colonel Bonham, who was fifteen years older and a
violent radical, had been confined in the Tower for a time on
unspecified charges, habeas corpus being in suspense. Disraeli had
to make an unreserved apology. Peel seemed to have scored on the
first charge, too.

> The hon. gentleman has a perfect right to support a hostile
> motion . . . but all that I ask is that when he gives that support
> to the motion, let him not say that he does it in a friendly spirit.
>> 'Give me the avowed, the erect, the manly foe;
>> Bold I can meet, perhaps may turn the blow;
>> But of all plagues, good Heaven, Thy wrath can send
>> Save, save, O save me from the candid friend.'[1]

Disraeli bided his time to answer this, but his reply when it came
was devastating. The lines of Canning which Peel quoted were ill
chosen, not because of their content, but because of their author.
Peel's relations with Canning had been the most controversial episode
in his career. Had he not, so his enemies argued, refused in 1827 to
join Canning and engaged in a factious opposition which drove the
great man to his premature death, ostensibly because Canning
favoured Catholic emancipation? And had he not, only two years
later, when back in office, carried precisely that measure which he
had denounced while Canning was Prime Minister?

With the sarcastic drawl and impassive countenance which had
now become his manner, Disraeli congratulated Peel on his felicitous
use of the art of quotation, and on his introduction of the great
name of Canning.

> That is a name never to be mentioned, I am sure, in the House of
> Commons without emotion. We all admire his genius; we all, at
> least most of us, deplore his untimely end; and we all sympathize
> with him in his fierce struggle with supreme prejudice and
> sublime mediocrity – with inveterate foes, and with – 'candid
> friends'. The right hon. gentleman may be sure that a quotation
> from such an authority will always tell. Some lines for example
> on friendship, written by Mr. Canning, and quoted by the right
> hon. Gentleman! The theme – the poet – the speaker – what a
> felicitous combination! Its effect in debate must be overwhelming;
> and I am sure, were it addressed to me, all that would remain for
> me would be thus publicly to congratulate the right hon. Gentle-
> man, not only on his ready memory, but on his courageous
> conscience.[2]

[1] ibid., 998, February 21.   [2] ibid., lxxviii, February 28.

He sat down amidst tremendous cheers, and, according to his letter
to Sarah recounting the triumph, Peel was 'stunned and stupified,
lost his head, and vacillating between silence and spleen, spoke
much and weakly. Never was a greater failure.' Disraeli seldom
underestimated his own successes, but he seems on this occasion to
have been right. The Prime Minister hated ridicule and was very
sensitive to attacks. Disraeli knew that he had got Peel's measure
at last.

Twice more during the session he repeated the performance. The
first occasion was a debate on the Corn Laws. Peel's arguments in
defence of these had long dissatisfied the more ardent protectionists.
He had never defended the principle upon which the agriculturists
considered them to be based; which was, broadly speaking, the
importance of retaining the ascendancy of the landed interest as a
dominant group in society. Peel preferred to rest the case on arguments of expediency, the necessity of being self-supporting in the
event of war, the harm done to numerous vested interests if complete free trade were suddenly introduced. Moreover, for a long time
he had believed in the fallacious doctrine that wages varied with
the price of bread, and that repeal of the Corn Laws would cheapen
bread only in order to enable the manufacturers to pay lower wages
and make larger profits – a view which seemed to be confirmed by
the alacrity with which the manufacturers rallied to the Anti-Corn
Law League.

But the fact was that wages did not vary with the price of bread.
In 1839–41 wages were low and bread expensive; in 1843 wages
were unusually high, and bread was unusually cheap. By the spring
of 1845 Peel had come to an important decision: the Corn Laws
could not be defended; they were artificially keeping up the price
of a basic necessity for the poor and no corresponding benefit was
being gained. But he recognized that, however guarded his own
words had been in 1841, a large majority of his party believed that
he and they were pledged to uphold the Corn Laws. He resolved,
therefore, to wait until 1846 and at some stage during that session
announce his conversion to free trade. The life of the 1841 Parliament would then be nearing its end. Convention in those days
dictated a six-year term for Parliament, unless something extraordinary occurred, and a dissolution before that was regarded as
premature. Peel could go to the country in 1847 as an open free trader;
by then accusations of bad faith would be harder to sustain.

Peel's conversion was kept a close secret, only two other members of the Cabinet being privy to it. One was his closest friend, Sir James Graham. The other was Sidney Herbert. When in March 1845 Cobden launched one of his attacks against the Corn Laws, Peel convinced by his reasoning, turned to Herbert who was sitting beside him and said, 'You must answer this, for I cannot.' Herbert did his best, but in the course of his speech used an unlucky expression about agriculturists 'whining for help'. Disraeli did not miss the opportunity. He drew an entertaining picture of the contrast in Peel's attitude to 'the Gentlemen of England', when he was in Opposition and when he was in office

> They were his first love and though he may not kneel to them now as in the hour of passion, still they can recall the past; and nothing is more useless and unwise than these scenes of crimination and reproach, for we know that in all these cases where the beloved object has ceased to charm it is in vain to appeal to the feelings. You know that this is true. Every man, almost, has gone through it. My hon. Friends reproach the right hon. Gentleman. The right hon. Gentleman does what he can to keep them quiet; he sometimes takes refuge in arrogant silence, and sometimes he treats them with haughty frigidity; and if they knew anything of human nature they would take the hint and shut their mouths. But they won't. And what then happens? What happens under all such circumstances? The right hon. Gentleman being compelled to interfere sends down his valet who says in the genteelest manner 'We can have no whining here'.[1]

Disraeli went on to observe that protection seemed to be in the same position as Protestantism in 1828.

> Dissolve if you please the Parliament you have betrayed and appeal to the people who, I believe, mistrust you. For me there remains this at least – the opportunity of expressing thus publicly my belief that a Conservative Government is an Organized Hypocrisy.

This final sentence brought a storm of applause and not only from the Opposition benches. A contemporary journalist describes Peel's reaction – 'nervous twitchings . . . and his utter powerlessness to look indifferent or conceal his palpable annoyance' – together with 'the delirious laughter' of the House.[2] As for Sidney Herbert, he was furious and never forgave the comparison with the valet.

---

[1] *Hansard*, 3rd series, lxxviii, 1028, March 17.   [2] Quoted, M. & B., ii, 322.

Disraeli's third and last attack during the session was prompted by an Irish controversy: Peel's proposal to increase the government grant to the Maynooth seminary for the education of Catholic priests from an annually voted subvention of £9,000 a year to a permanent subsidy of £26,000.

The uproar was tremendous. Over 2,000 petitions against the Bill were presented to Parliament. Peel feared that the Government might fall. Gladstone, who had earlier written a book in which he denounced the original Maynooth grant, felt obliged to resign, although in fact he was now in favour of Peel's measure. His speech of explanation was so involved and obscure that Disraeli decided that he had no future in politics. Young England was divided, Smythe and Manners supporting Peel, Disraeli opposing. Even Radical opinion was not unanimous. Cobden favoured the grant, but Bright voted against it on the ground that no state support should be given to any religious denomination, Protestant or Roman Catholic. As for the high Tory Protestants led by Sir Robert Inglis, their disapprobation was eloquent. Colonel Sibthorp said that he would rather lose his head 'than forget I am a Protestant, born a Protestant, bred a Protestant, educated a Protestant – and God grant that I may die with similar feelings, and in that faith'.

Disraeli's speech against the Maynooth grant was one of his most memorable *tours de force*. It is often quoted, and it is so much more readable than any of the others, except perhaps Macaulay's splendid oration in support of the Bill, that we tend to forget what a poor case he had. He ought on his own principles to have been in favour of the grant. Smythe and Manners were truer to the generous concepts of Young England than was its leader. Disraeli had shown in *Sybil* much sympathy for 'the old faith'. Surely he should not have grudged £17,000 p.a. to improve that 'miserable Do-the-Boys-Hall', as Macaulay described Maynooth. Gladstone may have been obscure, Peel prosy and humdrum; but they both spoke for tolerance and generosity, whereas Disraeli defended a fundamentally indefensible position. But he was not really concerned with the merits of the case. He wished to have another hit at Peel and this was an opportunity not to be missed. His argument was essentially *ad hominem*. To appreciate the full flavour one must read the whole speech, but the most famous passage is worth quoting on its own:

If you are to have a popular Government – if you are to have a Parliamentary Administration the conditions antecedent are, that you should have a Government which declares the principles upon which its policy is founded, and then you can have the wholesome check of a constitutional Opposition. What have we got instead? Something has risen up in this country as fatal in the political world, as it has been in the landed world of Ireland – we have a great Parliamentary middleman. It is well known what a middleman is; he is a man who bamboozles one party and plunders the other, till, having obtained a position to which he is not entitled, he cries out, 'Let us have no party questions, but fixity of tenure.' I want to have a Commission issued to inquire into the tenure by which Downing Street is held . . . I hope I shall not be answered by *Hansard* [Peel's speech had been full of quotations from *Hansard*] . . . What dreary pages of interminable talk, what predictions falsified, what pledges broken, what calculations that have gone wrong, what budgets that have blown up! And all this too, not relieved by a single original thought, a single generous impulse, or a single happy expression! Why *Hansard*, instead of being the Delphi of Downing Street is but the Dunciad of politics.[1]

Returning to the actual subject, Disraeli urged the Roman Catholics to be wary of accepting the proffered boon from 'polluted hands', from 'the same individual whose bleak shade fell on the sunshine of your hopes for more than a quarter of a century'. And then at last he came to his peroration.

Let us in this House re-echo that which I believe to be the sovereign sentiment of this country; let us tell persons in high places that cunning is not caution, and that habitual perfidy is not high policy of State. On that ground we may all join. Let us bring back to this House that which it has for so long a time past been without – the legitimate influence and salutary check of a constitutional Opposition. Let us do it at once in the only way in which it can be done, by dethroning this dynasty of deception, by putting an end to the intolerable yoke of official despotism and Parliamentary imposture. (Loud cheers.)[2]

It was a wonderful performance, delivered, we are told, without hesitation and without notes; and Disraeli held the House completely. He had prophesied that the time would come when they would hear him. That time had come now.

[1] *Hansard*, 3rd Series, lxxix, 565–6, April 11.   [2] ibid., 568–9.

CHAPTER IX

The Trilogy
1844–7

1

In May 1845 Disraeli published *Sybil* exactly a year after the appearance of *Coningsby*. They are his most famous novels. Together with *Tancred* (1847) they form a trilogy so closely tied up with the political and religious ideas of the early 1840s that this is a convenient point at which to consider Disraeli as a novelist. It is indeed a subject to which a whole book could be devoted, and it is surprising that no one has yet produced a critical edition of the novels. The trilogy was not, of course, his last excursus into the field of fiction. Many years later he wrote *Lothair* (1870), deemed by some to be his masterpiece, and *Endymion* (1880), which will always be read if only for its fascinating retrospective commentary on political history during Disraeli's formative years. But they do not mark any new development in his art. They are in a sense predictable. In contrast the trilogy made up by *Coningsby*, *Sybil* and *Tancred* is quite different from anything he had written before. A wide gulf separates them from his silver fork novels and historical romances of the 'twenties and 'thirties.

Disraeli's novels must be seen in their proper perspective. Their merits ought not to be overstated. It should be said at once that he was not a great novelist in the sense that Scott, Dickens, Thackeray and George Eliot were, or even a very good novelist like Trollope. He is too slapdash, too limited in his sympathies, too fond of verbal extravagances and absurd plots. Yet although one would not put him in the top class of nineteenth-century novelists, one would not put him in the second either. At one time examiners in the Oxford Final Schools, when puzzled by a candidate who had touches of brilliance mixed with incongruous errors and follies, used to award him the mark of alpha/gamma. Disraeli is the alpha/gamma novelist of the Victorian age, but his alpha element is not to be derided. In *Coningsby* he produced the first and most brilliant of English political novels, a genre which he may be said to have invented, and in *Sybil* he produced one of the first and one of the most famous social novels. He would be remembered for these if he had written nothing else and never become a minister.

But neither he nor his novels would be remembered in quite the same way. The fact is that he did become leader of the Tory party and Prime Minister of England. It is impossible to dissociate our minds from what we know about his life. Although this is true to some extent of any novelist, it is much more true of Disraeli than of, say, Jane Austen. When we read the acid analysis of Peel's Conservatism in *Coningsby* we cannot forget the overthrow of Peel, largely at Disraeli's hands, only two years later. When we read Fakredeen's advice to Tancred to persuade the Queen of England to sail away to India with her fleet and her treasure and make Delhi her capital instead of London, we cannot forget that it was Disraeli who put through the Royal Titles Act making Queen Victoria Empress of India. And apart from these and other fulfilments, however shadowy, Disraeli's trilogy cannot be fully understood without reference to contemporary events and ideas. This again is true in a certain degree of all novels, but one can get much more from reading Scott, Dickens, Thackeray, the Brontës or Trollope without that sort of knowledge than one can from Disraeli. *Coningsby*, *Sybil* and *Tancred* make a trilogy of *romans à thèse*, and it is impossible to appreciate them fully without an understanding of what Disraeli's thesis was.

Fiction with a propagandist purpose was a feature of the eighteen-forties.[1] The decade was one of social, religious, political anxiety and doubt: 'the condition-of-England' question, the problems raised by the Oxford movement, a general disillusionment with Whig and Tory party politics. The dominant figure was Carlyle at the height of his fame. It is not clear whether Disraeli ever read Carlyle. He did not read much contemporary literature apart from the works of friends like Bulwer – and very few of his friends belonged to literary circles, which he tended to despise. He appears to have read little in the way of poetry after Byron and little in the way of novels after Scott. 'When I want to read a novel, I write one,' he is supposed to have said to someone who asked him whether he had read *Daniel Deronda*. Dickens to him is 'Gushy' briefly referred to in *Endymion*, and Thackeray is almost viciously

---

[1] See Louis Cazamian, *Le Roman Social en Angleterre* (Paris, 1904), for a full discussion of the subject.

lampooned at some length as St Barbe in the same novel, but there is nothing to suggest that he was familiar with their books. Even if Disraeli never read Carlyle he must, however, have been aware of the ideas that Carlyle was disseminating. *Sartor Resartus* was republished in 1838 and its mockery of Bulwer's *Pelham* helped to kill the society novel. In the same year Carlyle made a scathing attack on the Waverley novels. Nothing can destroy Scott, but Carlyle had effectively destroyed another literary dead end, imitation of Scott. In 1840 *Chartism* appeared, and in 1843 *Past and Present*, both of them highly relevant to the theme of *Sybil*.

The influence of Carlyle, increased social awareness consequent upon the agitation over the new Poor Law and the Chartist movement, the theological dilemma epitomized by Newman, all combined to make fashionable a new form of literature, the novel-with-a-message. It was the most characteristic type of fiction in the 'forties. To mention only a few of the propaganda novels written in that decade, there was Mrs Gaskell's *Mary Barton* (1848); Kingsley's *Yeast* (1848); Newman's *Loss and Gain* (1848); Froude's *Nemesis of Faith* (1849). On occasions the fashion could be carried to disconcerting lengths, eg Mrs Frewin's somewhat off-putting title, *The Inheritance of Evil or The Consequences of Marrying a Deceased Wife's Sister* (1849),[1] and the degree to which some people sought for a social message in the most unlikely quarter is shown by a reviewer of *Wuthering Heights* who decided that the moral of the book must be to 'show what Satan could do with the law of Entail'.[2] Towards the end of the decade the novel-with-a-purpose began to be the object of satire. Both Thackeray and Trollope made fun of it, and Thackeray's hits at Disraeli were no doubt part of the reason for St Barbe.

Two other general points should be made about Disraeli's novels. He never attempted, like Dickens, Thackeray and Trollope, to bring them out in numbers. Both the assets and the liabilities of this form of serialization are missing in Disraeli, who adopted the normal 'three-decker' form, simultaneous publication in three separate volumes at a guinea and a half for the set. Nor was he a best-seller. Both *Coningsby* and *Sybil* sold about 3,000 copies of the three-volume edition, Disraeli's share of the profits, which were divided equally between author and publisher, being about £1,000

[1] Cited by Kathleen Tillotson, *Novels of the Eighteen-Forties* (1954), 15.
[2] ibid., 117 n.

in each case. *Tancred* sold less well, 2,250 copies, and Disraeli received £750. He made some further profit, but not much, from the cheap single-volume reprints which appeared later. It was not until *Lothair* and *Endymion* that he had a real financial success, but novels written by an ex-Prime Minister would be almost bound to create something of a sensation. By 1870 Disraeli was a national, and by 1880 a European, celebrity of the first magnitude. In the 1840s, he was neither and, though he was read with keen interest in society and parliamentary circles, he did not appeal to the great middle-class public which doted on Dickens. He neither understood nor sympathized with its aspirations and never once in his trilogy does he portray a member of that social group with any degree of conviction.

2

In his preface to the fifth edition of *Coningsby* in 1849 Disraeli made clear his propagandist purpose.

> It was not originally the intention of the writer to adopt the form of fiction as the instrument to scatter his suggestions, but, after reflection, he resolved to avail himself of a method which, in the temper of the times, offered the best chance of influencing opinion.

He sets out the purpose of the trilogy in the General Preface to the collected edition of his novels in 1870, writing of *Coningsby or the New Generation*, to give its full title:

> The derivation and character of political parties; the condition of the people which had been the consequence of them; the duties of the Church as a main remedial agency in our present state; were the principal topics which I intended to treat, but I found they were too vast for the space I had allotted to myself.
> They were all launched in 'Coningsby' but the origin and condition of political parties, the first portion of the theme, was the only one completely handled in that work.
> Next year (1845), in SYBIL, OR THE TWO NATIONS, I considered the condition of the people, and the whole work, generally speaking, was devoted to that portion of my scheme . . .
> In recognizing the Church as a powerful agent in the previous development of England . . . it seemed to me that the time had arrived when it became my duty to . . . consider the position of the descendants of that race who had been the founders of Christianity. Familiar as we all are now with such themes, the House

of Israel being now freed from the barbarism of mediaeval misconception, and judged like other races by their contributions to
the existing sum of human welfare, and the general influence of
race on human action being universally recognized as the key of
history, the difficulty and hazard of touching for the first time on
such topics cannot now be easily appreciated. But public opinion
recognised both the truth and sincerity of these views, and, with
its sanction, in TANCRED OR THE NEW CRUSADE, the third
portion of the Trilogy, I completed their development.

It is probably best to regard the trilogy as expressing two distinct
themes. *Tancred* is the vehicle for Disraeli's own highly idiosyncratic
views on race and religion, which are also set out in his life of Lord
George Bentinck. They really have little connexion with the ideas
in *Coningsby* and *Sybil*. It is in these two novels that Disraeli's Tory
theory of history and the doctrine of Young England are expounded.
They are more read and more readable than *Tancred*, and they have
had far more influence.

Disraeli's thesis, he says, was derived from his reading as a boy
in his father's library and from the training which he had 'from
early childhood by learned men who did not share the passions and
prejudices of our political and social life'. He probably owed much
of it to his father. The influence of the ideas in Isaac's *Genius of
Judaism* (1833) can be clearly detected in *Tancred*, and the royalist
sympathies of his *Commentaries on the Life and Reign of Charles I*
(1828–30) are echoed in both *Coningsby* and *Sybil*. Viewed in its
widest aspect, the theory of England's social and political development expounded in these two novels can be seen as one reaction –
the most picturesque and articulate example – against the Whig
interpretation of history which with the Whig political triumph of
1832 bid fair to become the accepted orthodoxy of the day. Put
briefly Disraeli's Tory interpretation was that the Whigs were a
'factitious aristocracy' whose fortunes originated in the 'unhallowed
booty' obtained at the time of the Reformation by 'the plunder of
the Church'. Their principles were those of 'exclusion', by which
Disraeli meant exclusion from power of all other interests or institutions: the Crown, the Church, the 'People'. The Church had protected the people. The Crown tried to do so. Ship money was a
direct tax levied on the rich, but the Whigs preferred customs
and excise, which fell mainly on the poor. 'Rightly was King
Charles surnamed the Martyr; for he was the holocaust of
direct taxation. Never yet did man lay down his heroic life for so

great a cause: the cause of the Church and the cause of the Poor.'[1]

The object of the Whigs was to establish 'a high aristocratic republic on the model of the Venetian'. This would have been achieved in 1640 but for the Puritans. 'Geneva beat Venice.'[2] In 1688 the struggle was renewed. James II did not really mean to re-establish popery but by seeming to mean it played into his enemies' hands. Had it not been for this folly 'we might have been saved from the triple blessings of Venetian politics, Dutch finance, and French Wars'.[3] By Dutch finance Disraeli apparently meant the National Debt. However, the Venetian constitution did not at once prevail. The reigns of William III and Anne saw a hard-fought battle between the Venetian and English systems. Only on the Queen's very death-bed did the former prevail. A new dynasty was brought in on terms dictated by the Venetian party. George I was a doge. So was George II. George III tried vainly to escape.

> He might get rid of the Whig magnificoes, but he could not rid himself of the Venetian constitution. And a Venetian constitution did govern England from the accession of the House of Hanover until 1832.[4]

But throughout these years there was an element in the English political class which sought to preserve the 'English system'. Disraeli's Tory apostolic succession is not always the same. An inclusive list would contain the names of the Jacobite, Sir John Hynde Cotton, of Sir William Wyndham, Bolingbroke's lieutenant, and of Bolingbroke himself, a character who fascinated Disraeli and to whom, indeed, Disraeli himself had many similarities. From Bolingbroke the line goes through Carteret, Walpole's enemy, to Shelburne, who was Carteret's son-in-law, and thence to the younger Pitt. Disraeli rightly sensed that there was something mysterious about Shelburne and tries to restore him from being 'one of the suppressed characters of English history', but, although he took the trouble to inquire of Shelburne's son, the 3rd Marquess of Lansdowne, and received a courteous reply, there was not enough information to make the restoration very convincing. With Pitt, Disraeli is coming near to his own time. It is essential for his thesis to argue that the Tory party which dominated England between

---

[1] *Sybil*, Bk IV, ch. 1.
[2] *Coningsby* Bk. VII, ch. 4.
[3] *Sybil*, Bk I, ch. 3.
[4] *Coningsby*, Bk V, ch. 2.

Waterloo and the Reform Act, which was the spiritual ancestor of
Peel's conservatism, and which traced its descent from the 'friends
of Mr. Pitt', was in no sense the standard-bearer of true Toryism or
the 'English system'. On the contrary they were a 'factitious league'
which

> had shuffled themselves into power by clinging to the skirts of a
> great minister, the last of Tory statesmen, but who, in the un-
> paralleled and confounding emergencies of his later years had
> been forced, unfortunately for England, to relinquish Toryism
> . . . Impudently usurping the name of that party of which
> nationality, and therefore universality is the essence, these
> pseudo-Tories made Exclusion the principle of their political
> constitution and Restriction the genius of their commercial code.[1]

This leads to a dissertation on recent politics. Lord Liverpool's
long rule is described as that of 'the Arch-Mediocrity' – a soubriquet
which, though largely unjustified, colours to this day the picture
that most people have of that able, hard-working, conscientious
Prime Minister. It is conceded that towards the end of his time the
Government was showing signs of 'a partial recurrence to those frank
principles of government which Mr. Pitt had revived . . .' But this
was more by accident than from any sense of principle. After the
Arch-Mediocrity's death the blunders of the Duke of Wellington
allowed power to fall into the hands of the Whigs, who in 1832 hoped
to consolidate their position for at least a generation even as they
had when they 'changed the dynasty' in 1714. Instead, they caused
'a mean and selfish revolution which emancipated neither the Crown
nor the People', although it overthrew the aristocracy. Their
immediate success in the general election was so great that it
'abrogated the Parliamentary Opposition of England which had
practically existed for more than a century and a half'. 'But no
government can be long secure without a formidable Opposition'.
The Whigs two years later are so broken and divided that Peel and
the new 'Conservative' party find themselves prematurely and
briefly in office.

In *Coningsby* Disraeli dwells not unsympathetically upon Peel's
character and attainments. He was writing in the autumn and
winter of 1843–4 at a time when he was still – at any rate in his own
estimation – on good enough terms with his official leaders to ask for
a job for his brother. The tone in *Sybil* is very different. Most of it

[1] *Coningsby*, Bk II, ch. 1.

was written after the session of 1844 and much of it during the early months of 1845. Disraeli had not finally broken with Peel even then, but he and Young England had bitterly opposed their leader over the Factory Bill and had nearly defeated him on the question of the sugar duties. In *Sybil*, Peel is the 'gentleman in Downing Street' who instructs his secretary, Mr Hoaxem, to tell precisely opposite stories to two successive delegations. 'I have no doubt you will get through the business very well, Mr. Hoaxem, particularly if you be "frank and explicit", that is the right line to take when you wish to conceal your own mind and to confuse the minds of others. Good morning!'[1] But in *Coningsby* Peel is depicted as a statesman who would have liked to escape from spurious Toryism, who escaped from Liverpool, Canning and Wellington, but was trapped by 'ceaseless intriguers'[2] into forming a premature 'Conservative' administration in 1834. Had he not done this he might have 'acceded to power as the representative of a Creed instead of being the leader of a Confederacy'. Unfortunately 'no one had arisen either in Parliament, the Universities, or the Press, to lead the public mind to the investigation of principles'.[3]

This brings Disraeli to the fifth chapter of Book ii of *Coningsby*, with its famous attack on 'Conservatism':

The Tamworth Manifesto of 1834 was an attempt to construct a party without principles: its basis therefore was necessarily latitudinarianism; and its inevitable consequence has been Political Infidelity . . . There was indeed considerable shouting about what they called Conservative principles; but the awkward question naturally arose, what will you conserve? The prerogatives of the Crown, provided they are not exercised; the independence of the House of Lords, provided it is not asserted; the Ecclesiastical estate provided it is regulated by a commission of laymen. Everything in short that is established, as long as it is a phrase and not a fact . . . Conservatism discards Prescription, shrinks from Principle, disavows Progress; having rejected all respect for Antiquity, it offers no redress for the Present, and makes no preparation for the Future.

The upshot is a situation in which neither party has any solution for the ills of the nation. The Whig–Liberal–Radical coalition has, it is true, a distinctive principle: 'they seek a specific for the evils of

[1] *Sybil*, Bk VI, ch. 1.
[2] *Coningsby*, Bk II, ch. 1.
[3] *Coningsby*, Bk II, ch. 4.

our social system in the general suffrage of the population'. But Disraeli has no faith in 'the remedial qualities of a government carried on by a neglected democracy, who for three centuries have received no education'. The Conservatives have no principle except to 'keep things as they find them as long as they can'.

> Whenever public opinion which this party never attempts to form, to educate, or to lead, falls into some violent perplexity, passion, or caprice, this party yields without a struggle to the impulse, and, when the storm has passed, attempts to obstruct and obviate the logical, and ultimately the inevitable, results of the very measures they have themselves originated, or to which they have consented . . .
> The man who enters public life at this epoch has to choose between Political infidelity and a Destructive Creed.[1]

What, then, is Disraeli's solution to this depressing dilemma? It is, of course, much easier to demolish than to build. His answer, not surprisingly, is vague and imprecise. The lines of his thought are to be seen at the end of the first of the three reflective paragraphs with which he concludes *Sybil*.

> In the selfish strife of factions, two great existences have been blotted out of the history of England, the Monarch and the Multitude; as the power of the Crown has diminished, the privileges of the People have disappeared; till at length the sceptre has become a pageant and its subject has degenerated into a serf.

Later he prays 'that we may live to see England once more possess a free Monarchy and a privileged and prosperous People'. Ten years earlier in the *Vindication* he could see hope in a Conservative victory won by Peel, but at that time he aspired to political life under the wing of Lord Lyndhurst, who, however dubious his moral character, was a pillar of the Conservative establishment. Now as an anti-establishment rebel he was not likely to see much hope in a change of heart among his leaders. At times he seems to look for a revival of the old Toryism which his imagination had created.

> Even now it is not dead but sleepeth; and in an age of political materialism, of confused purposes and perplexed intelligence, that aspires only to wealth, because it has faith in no other accomplishment, as men rifle cargoes on the verge of shipwreck, toryism will yet rise from the tomb over which Bolingbroke shed

---

[1] *Coningsby*, Bk VII, ch. 2.

his last tear, to bring back strength to the Crown, liberty to the Subject, and to announce that power has only one duty: to secure the social welfare of the PEOPLE.[1]

But it is not clear whether this was to be achieved by a new party or by Young England converting the old one. In any case the revival of monarchical power, of which there is much talk in *Coningsby*, too, seems to be Disraeli's panacea rather than an improved party system. This was quite unrealistic. Although the idea was in keeping with the romantic Stuart worship of George Smythe and his friends, it bore no relation to practical politics in the eighteen-forties.

Both novels contain scenes which are, as it were, the quintessence of their theme. Disraeli had a real sense of drama and they are not easily forgotten. In *Coningsby* it is the confrontation between the hero and his grandfather, Lord Monmouth, the new generation facing the old.

'I am sorry,' said Coningsby rather pale, but speaking with firmness, 'I am sorry that I could not support the Conservative party.'

'By ——!' exclaimed Lord Monmouth starting in his seat, 'some woman has got hold of him and made him a Whig!'

'No, my dear grandfather,' said Coningsby scarcely able to repress a smile, serious as the interview was becoming, 'nothing of the kind, I assure you. No person can be more anti-Whig.'

'I don't know what you are driving at, sir,' said Lord Monmouth in a hard, dry tone.

'I wish to be frank, sir,' said Coningsby. '. . . I have for a long time looked upon the Conservative party as a body who have betrayed their trust . . .'

'You mean giving up those Irish corporations?' said Lord Monmouth. 'Well, between ourselves, I am quite of the same opinion. But we must mount higher; we must go to '28 for the real mischief. But what is the use of lamenting the past. Peel is the only man; suited to the times and all that; at least we must say so and try to believe so; we can't go back. And it is our own fault that we have let the chief power out of the hands of our own order. It was never thought of in the time of your great-grandfather, sir. And if a commoner were for a season permitted to be the nominal Premier to do the detail, there was always a secret committee of great 1688 nobles to give him his instructions.'

'I should be very sorry to see secret committees of great 1688 nobles again,' said Coningsby.

'Then what the devil do you want to see?' said Lord Monmouth.

[1] *Sybil*, Bk IV, ch. 14.

'Political faith,' said Coningsby, 'instead of political infidelity.'

'Hem!' said Lord Monmouth.

'Before I support Conservative principles,' continued Coningsby, 'I merely wish to be informed what those principles aim to conserve . . .'

'All this is vastly fine,' said Lord Monmouth, 'but I see no means by which I can obtain my object but by supporting Peel. After all what is the end of all parties and all politics. To gain your object. I want to turn our coronet into a ducal one, and to get your grandmother's barony called out of abeyance in your favour. It is impossible that Peel can refuse me . . .'

'What we want, sir, is not to fashion new dukes and furbish up old baronies but to establish great principles which may maintain the realm and secure the happiness of the people. Let me see authority once more honoured; a solemn reverence again the habit of our lives; let me see property acknowledging, as in the old days of faith that labour is his twin brother, and that the essence of all tenure is the performance of duty . . .'

'I tell you what it is, Harry,' said Lord Monmouth very dryly, 'members of this family may think as they like but they must act as I please . . . I sent for Rigby this morning . . . You will meet him, I doubt not, like a man of sense,' added Lord Monmouth looking at Coningsby with a glance such as he had never before encountered, 'who is not prepared to sacrifice all the objects of life for the pursuit of some fantastical puerilities.'[1]

In *Sybil* the vital scene is where the hero, Egremont, brother of Lord Marney, suddenly has his eyes opened to the vast gulf which lies between his class and the brutalized industrial labourers at the bottom of the social hierarchy. The passage where this occurs is one of Disraeli's best known. Egremont has met two strangers at sunset amid the ruins of Marney Abbey. Their names are not yet revealed. The elder is Gerard, whose daughter, Sybil, Egremont is in the end to marry and who, though a factory inspector of Chartist leanings, turns out to be the rightful owner of the Mowbray estates. The younger is Morley, a Chartist agitator in love with Sybil.

'Well society may be in its infancy,' said Egremont slightly smiling; 'but, say what you will, our Queen reigns over the greatest nation that ever existed.'

'Which nation?' asked the younger stranger, 'for she reigns over two.'

The stranger paused; Egremont was silent but looked inquiringly.

[1] *Coningsby*, Bk VIII, ch. 3.

'Yes,' resumed the younger stranger after a moment's interval. 'Two nations between whom there is no intercourse and no sympathy; who are as ignorant of each other's habits, thoughts, and feelings, as if they were dwellers in different zones or inhabitants of different planets; who are formed by a different breeding, are fed by a different food, are ordered by different manners, and are not governed by the same laws.'

'You speak of – ' said Egremont hesitatingly.

'THE RICH AND THE POOR.'[1]

Amid the silence that follows the last rays of the sun fade, the evening star glitters through a vacant arch, and the voice of Sybil, who like her father belongs to 'the old faith', is heard singing in the chapel near by. The 'two nations' became a household word, perhaps the most famous of all Disraeli's inventions.

3

In *Tancred* Disraeli tries to propound his theory about the Church as 'a main remedial agency in our present state', but it cannot be said that he gets very far. Tancred is the Marquess of Montacute, adored only son of the virtuous but limited Duke and Duchess of Bellamont, and the book opens with his coming of age. To the consternation of his parents he declines to enter Parliament and declares his desire to visit the Holy Land in the hope that somehow he will receive an answer to the questions that have been silently troubling him. 'What is DUTY, and what is FAITH? What ought I to DO, and what ought I to BELIEVE?'[2]

Tancred duly surmounts the various obstacles put in his way and arrives in Palestine, but Disraeli fails to surmount the problem of what is to happen next. As Sidonia observes, 'It is no longer difficult to reach Jerusalem; the real difficulty is the one experienced by the crusaders, to know what to do when you get there.' Tancred, admittedly after an attack of brain fever, is vouchsafed a vision as he prays on Mount Sinai, but it is kinder to draw a veil over that regrettable scene: a 'mighty form' waving 'a sceptre like a palm tree', calling itself 'the Angel of Arabia', and urging Tancred to 'announce the sublime and solacing doctrine of theocratic equality'. Thereafter the book becomes chaotic. We are never told what the Church is to do or how it is function as a remedial agency.

---

[1] *Sybil*, Bk II, ch. 5.   [2] *Tancred*, Bk II, ch. 1.

Indeed, the Church is treated in a distinctly satirical spirit. There is
a caustic portrait of 'the Bishop' who tries to deter Tancred and who
is modelled on Blomfield, Bishop of London. The episcopate comes
in for as much criticism as the Venetian Constitution, in particular
the bishops made by 'the Arch-Mediocrity'.

> His test of priestly celebrity was the decent editorship of a Greek
> play. He sought for the successors of the apostles, for the
> stewards of the mysteries of Sinai and Calvary, among third rate
> hunters after syllables . . . Not a voice has been raised by these
> mitred nullities, either to warn or to vindicate; not a phrase has
> escaped from their lips or their pens, that ever influenced public
> opinion, touched the heart of nations or guided the conscience of
> a perplexed people. If they were ever heard of, it was that they
> had been pelted in a riot.[1]

Not surprisingly Tancred turns his back on a Church in so parlous
a condition. His decision to seek inspiration in the land where
Christianity began enables Disraeli to expound a series of paradoxes
on the theme of race and religion. These views were not expressed
for the first time in *Tancred*. They had been adumbrated, though
incidentally, in *Coningsby*, where the omniscient enigmatic Jewish
multi-millionaire, Sidonia, that strange fantasy fulfilment of a cross
between Baron de Rothschild and Disraeli himself, makes his
appearance and indeed instructs Coningsby in the principles of race
as well as in those of Young England. But Sidonia's famous roll of
European ministers of finance who were Jews, so often quoted by
anti-Semites, was quite incorrect. None of them was, and in his
pride at his descent Disraeli had unknowingly given both here and
elsewhere a formidable weapon to the fanatical enemies of his race.
  At the time Disraeli was writing there was a good deal of discussion going on in terms of 'race'. Gobineau had yet to write his
Inégalité des Races Humaines, but the ideas on which it was based
had been in the air for years before. Many English writers talked of
Saxon, Norman, Teuton, or Latin 'blood'. When Disraeli makes
Sidonia say, 'All is race; there is no other truth', or declare 'The fact
is, you cannot destroy a pure race of the Caucasian organisation',
his readers would not have regarded it as the nonsense we consider
it today. What Disraeli is trying to do is to vindicate his own
Jewish descent, and proclaim that the Hebrews, far from deserving
contempt, ought to be favoured above all other nations. Did not the

[1] *Tancred*, Bk II, ch. 4.

Son of Man belong to the Jewish race? Were not the Prophets and
the Apostles Jews, not to mention a long, though frequently
erroneous, list of other distinguished, if less holy, personages produced by Disraeli? He was not in any sense inventing the notion of
a hierarchy of races. He was merely turning the commonly accepted
one upside down. Sidonia is Disraeli's revenge for Fagin.

The theme gives him some splendid opportunities of puncturing
the complacency of the Western world. The English aristocracy is
'sprung from a horde of Baltic pirates who were never heard of
during the greater annals of the world'. 'How can English bishops
know anything?' asks Sidonia. 'A few centuries back they were
tattooed savages. This is the advantage which Rome has over you,
and which you can never understand. That Church was founded by
a Hebrew, and the magnetic influence still lingers.' And there is a
fine and famous passage after the author has reflected upon the
glories of the Hebrew kings and the splendour of Arabian palaces:

> And yet some flat-nosed Frank, full of bustle and puffed up with
> self-conceit (a race spawned perhaps in the morasses of some
> Northern forest hardly yet cleared) talks of Progress! Progress to
> what, and from where? Amid empires shrivelled into deserts,
> amid the wrecks of great cities, a single column or obelisk of
> which nations import for the prime ornament of their mud-built
> capitals, amid arts forgotten, commerce annihilated, fragmentary
> literatures, and populations destroyed, the European talks of
> progress, because by an ingenious application of some scientific
> acquirements, he has established a society which has mistaken
> comfort for civilisation.[1]

Most paradoxical of all is his theory of Judaism and Christianity.
Eva, who embodies the spirit of Judaism, ironically asks Tancred,
'Pray are you of those Franks who worship a Jewess; or of those
other who revile her, break her images, and blaspheme her pictures?'
She goes farther when they discuss the 'penal' condition of the Jews.
Tancred says that 'it is the punishment ordained for their rejection
and crucifixion of the Messiah'. Eva asks what is 'the essential
object of the Christian scheme', and when Tancred answers 'the
Expiation' she asks: 'Suppose the Jews had not prevailed upon the
Romans to crucify Jesus, what would have become of the Atonement?' Tancred replies that he cannot 'even consider an event that
had been preordained by the Creator of the World for countless ages.'

[1] ibid., Bk III, ch. 7.

'Ah,' said the lady, 'pre-ordained by the Creator of the World for
countless ages! Where then was the inexpiable crime of those who
fulfilled the beneficent intention? The holy race supplied the
victim and the immolators . . . Persecute us! Why if you believed
what you profess, you should kneel to us! You raise statues to the
hero who saves a country. We have saved the human race, and
you persecute us for doing it.'[1]

It is unnecessary to discuss the fallacies in Eva's thesis. There is a
better case than this for not persecuting Jews. The point is that
Disraeli seems to have believed in the argument that he puts in her
mouth, for he repeated it in *Lord George Bentinck* four years later,
and on both occasions shocked a good many people. His theological
ideas were, in reality, the rationalization of his own peculiar
psychological dilemma. It suited him to blur as far as possible the
differences between the Jewish and Christian faiths. He almost
seems at times to regard Christ's Jewishness as more important than
His divinity. To him the Jew is a proto-Christian, and Christianity
is completed Judaism. How else could a person intensely proud of
the Jewish ancestry which his less worthy enemies flung in his face,
yet at the same time a convert to the very faith of those who
sneered at him, justify both that pride and that conversion?

For all his insistence on race Disraeli was curiously hazy about
his own. 'Arabs are only Jews on horseback', he observes on one
occasion. This odd identification enables him to invoke the desert,
which seems to have fascinated him almost as much as it was to
fascinate Doughty, and T. E. Lawrence. 'The decay of a race is an
inevitable necessity,' he writes, 'unless it lives in deserts and never
mixes its blood.' Disraeli appeals to the spirit of Arabia, presumably
'the great Asian mystery', and describes the Church as 'a sacred
corporation for the promulgation and maintenance in Europe of
certain Asian principles'. Tancred's career in the Near East is
divided between his love for Eva and a strange *Hegira* in which he
and the frivolous Emir Fakredeen are to reassert the spiritual
supremacy of Asia and conquer Europe at the head of the 'races' of
'Syria' and 'Arabia'. 'A man might climb Mount Carmel,' declares
Tancred, 'and utter three words which would bring the Arabs again
to Grenada, and perhaps further.' His object is to conquer the world
'with angels at our head, in order that we may establish the happiness of man by a divine dominion, and, crushing the political

[1] ibid., Bk III, ch. 4.

atheism that is now desolating existence, utterly extinguish the grovelling tyranny of self-government'. But Fakredeen's intrigues betray him, Eva faints on the last page when Tancred avows his love, and the book ends without a conclusion.

Indeed, Disraeli himself felt the difficulty of finishing *Tancred* at all satisfactorily. The confidence that informs *Coningsby* and *Sybil* has faded. The last sentences of the three books are symbolic. Of the New Generation Disraeli asks

Will Vanity confound their fortunes, or Jealousy wither their sympathies? Or will they remain brave, single, true . . . sensible of their great position, recognise the greatness of their duties; denounce to a perplexed and disheartened world the frigid theories of a generalising age that have destroyed the individuality of man, and restore the happiness of their country by believing in their own energies, and daring to be great.

Sybil, too, ends on a magniloquent note:

We live in an age when to be young and to be indifferent can be no longer synonymous. The claims of the Future are represented by suffering millions; and the Youth of a Nation are the trustees of Posterity.

But the last words in *Tancred* are that sentence of immortal bathos: 'The Duke and Duchess of Bellamont had arrived in Jerusalem.'

4

It is not easy to disentangle the novels as novels from their 'message', although it can be done more easily now than by contemporaries. The most acute criticism of the whole trilogy came from an unexpected quarter.

Tancred contained *en passant* an amusing caricature of Monckton Milnes, who, according to Disraeli, had complained bitterly at not figuring in either *Coningsby* or *Sybil*. If this is true, he was ill advised, for the portrait of Mr Vavasour in *Tancred* was not calculated to assuage his feelings.

He liked to know everybody who was known, and to see everything which ought to be seen. He was also of opinion that everybody who was known ought to know him; and that the spectacle, however splendid or exciting, was not quite perfect without his presence. His life was a gyration of energetic curiosity, an insatiable whirl of social celebrity . . . He was everywhere and at everything; he had gone down in a diving-bell, and gone up in a balloon. As for his acquaintances he was welcomed in every land; his universal sympathies seemed omnipotent. Emperor and King, jacobin and carbonaro alike cherished him. He was the steward of Polish balls and the vindicator of Russian humanity; he dined with Louis Philippe and gave dinners to Louis Blanc.[1]

There were numerous other subtle and malicious touches in a picture which must have given a good deal of enjoyment to those who knew Milnes.

He was quick to take his revenge. He offered to review *Tancred* for the *Edinburgh,* and in the July number of 1847 there appeared, in the words of his biographer 'an analysis of Disraeli's writing so able and so ruthless that Milnes' son, the late Lord Crewe, used to attribute to this article alone Disraeli's manifest dislike of Milnes'.[2] The review is worth pausing over. The fact that it was prompted by personal irritation does not necessarily invalidate its conclusions. In fact, the seventeen pages of Milnes' article remain to this day the best statement for the prosecution against Disraeli's novels.

Milnes dealt with the whole trilogy. He comments on Disraeli's assumption that the characters in each are known to the readers of any one of them, and dryly adds:

> As there is nothing complete in the writings before us, there is no saying but that these delineations may go on till 'Coningsby' is an octogenarian at Bath, and 'Sybil' holding a salon like that of the Misses Berry.

Then he goes on to a more serious criticism – the inability of Disraeli to 'create' characters, the fact that his personalities are nearly all sketched from living persons, and intended to be known by the reader as such.

> . . . for, the moment a character is known to represent Lord —— or Mr. ——, it loses all power as a work of art. The 'historical picture' becomes 'the portrait of a gentleman'; the fidelity of the likeness is the only object of attention, not the moral fitness, the entireness, the beauty or the grandeur of the character. The great poet or novelist should mould his men and women out of the large masses of humanity, out of the manifold variety of strivers and losers, and actors and sufferers; and surely he

---

[1] ibid., Bk II, ch. 14.   [2] Pope-Hennessy, *Monckton Milnes,* 204.

degrades his function when he condescends to draw miniatures
of individuals composing the least distinctive and frequently most
vapid of all classes of the community – namely that which is conventionally called the highest.

Such portraits, Milnes argues, have not even the value of being good
likenesses, however familiar the author may be with the people concerned.

> . . . for on the one hand, if he possesses that knowledge of their
> real inner being which only friendship or great intimacy can give,
> he will be no more willing to expose those penetralia to the rude
> light of open day, than he would the profoundest struggles of his
> own heart; and on the other, if his pencil only gives the shadowy
> representation in which men of any worth appear amid the
> circumstances of ordinary life, no truth is anywise gained. There
> merely remains upon paper a superficial portrait of what the man
> appeared to superficial people, and the reality of him rests un-
> known or misinterpreted just as before . . .

Having dealt with Disraeli as a novelist, Milnes went on to
analyse the political philosophy which the trilogy appeared to
preach.

> All that we are accustomed most to admire and desiderate, all
> that we are wont to rest upon as most stable amid the fluctuating
> fortunes of the world, the progress of civilisation, the develop-
> ment of human intelligence, the coordinate extension of power
> and responsibility among the masses of mankind, the advance of
> self-reliance and self-control – all in truth for which not we alone
> but all other nations, have been yearning and fighting and pray-
> ing for the last three centuries – all that has been done by the
> Reformation, by the English and French Revolutions, by
> American Independence – is here proclaimed an entire delusion
> and failure; and we are taught that we can now only hope to
> improve our future by utterly renouncing our past.

This attack is followed by an investigation of Disraeli's 'solution'.
In *Coningsby*, Milnes points out, the story conveniently ends before
we hear any details of how Young England is to apply its philosophy
in practice. In *Sybil* there is indeed a vivid description of the evils
produced by the great extremes of wealth and poverty, and by the
agglomeration of the working masses in hideous and squalid new
towns. The evil is, however, all attributed to industry and the
aggregation of capital. Landlords are ignored, along with the whole
problem of rural poverty.

But the remedy that should apply to a busy manufacturing Manchester and an inactive agricultural Skibbereen is not disclosed; and no better means of amalgamating the alienated classes are discovered, than the alliance of two persons . . . who turn out both to belong to the upper one.

Nor is the problem solved in *Tancred*, where a young scion of a great English house ('why', Milnes observes, 'will Mr. D'Israeli be so fond of dukes?') goes on a pilgrimage to the Holy Land, is taught 'to look on Christendom as "an intellectual colony of Arabia" ', and is commanded to preach a purer theism to mankind.

It is [continues Milnes] superfluous to blame Mr. D'Israeli for not working out into the practical reality of these days a political philosophy which is in fact nothing less than an abandonment of all principles of individuality, responsibility, and self-government; and a return to the narrowest principles of loyal dependence and local patriotism . . .
. . . Such principles, or something like them, have been the basis of all the fanaticism and charlatanism that in their manifold expressions have arrested the advance of the human mind . . .

Disraeli was himself well aware that the political philosophy of his novels ran clean counter to the commonly accepted thought of his age, 'which may be popularly, though not altogether accurately described as utilitarian'.[1] He later endeavoured to meet this sort of criticism in his General Preface to the 1870 edition of his novels.

They [the novels] recognised imagination in government of nations as a quality not less important than reason. They trusted much to a popular sentiment, which rested on an heroic tradition and was sustained by the high spirit of a free aristocracy. Their economic principles were not unsound but they looked upon the health and knowledge of the multitude as not the least precious part of the wealth of nations. In asserting the doctrine of race they were entirely opposed to the equality of man, and similar abstract dogmas, which have destroyed ancient society without creating a satisfactory substitute. Resting on popular sympathies and popular privileges, they hold that no society could be durable unless it was built upon the principles of loyalty and religious reverence.
     The writer and those acting with him looked, then, upon the Anglican Church as a main machinery by which these results might be realised. There were few great things left in England and the Church was one of them . . .

[1] General Preface, xiv.

Disraeli continues, almost as if excusing himself for *Tancred,* by stating his conviction that this might have happened if an ecclesiastical statesman equal to the occasion had emerged. But little over a year after the appearance of *Coningsby* 'the secession of DR NEWMAN dealt a blow to the Church of England under which it still reels . . . It was a mistake and a misfortune.' The Anglican church might have 'found that rock of truth which Providence by the instrumentality of the Semitic race had promised to St. Peter. Instead of that the seceders took refuge in mediaeval supersititions, which are generally only the embodiments of pagan ceremonies and creeds.' Disraeli, whatever he believed when he wrote *Sybil,* had by 1870 become anything but sympathetic to Rome. The secession of Newman, then, is Disraeli's only explanation, in so far as he gives one at all, of the failure of Young England and of his own failure to provide a solution to the problems posed by his trilogy. One can but regard it as a very inadequate explanation. Milnes may have been too harsh in describing Disraeli's political principles as 'the basis of all the fanaticism and charlatanism that . . . have arrested the advance of the human mind'; but it remains true that if we take him literally Disraeli does appear to be arguing against the Parliamentary system, against self-government, against 'progress', against 'reason'; and that he is apparently substituting for them a sort of benevolent clerical monarchism supported by a conscientious aristocracy. The concept is indistinct and cloudy indeed, but unmistakably illiberal, whatever its virtues might be in improving the condition of the people. Nor is it made any less so by a racialist doctrine which, though an inversion of that usually associated with clerical absolutism, is, again if taken seriously, at best a piece of anthropological nonsense, at worst a cause of and precedent for the anti-Semitism which he most deplored.

Equally questionable is the Tory theory of history. Though not more lop-sided than some forms of the rival Whig interpretation, it does not stand up to analysis any better than the rather similar neo-Catholic version of Belloc and Chesterton, who based themselves on Disraeli, although ironically the fact did not strike them as incompatible with a marked anti-Jewish prejudice. The Tory apostolic succession is altogether too tenuous, the opinions attributed to its members, who are alleged to be extinguished by Whig historiography, are too dubious for Disraeli's theory to be acceptable. As for 'the Venetian constitution', if it ever existed at all, the period was Disraeli's own time, not the eighteenth century. The first four Hanoverians were not doges.

How seriously, then, should we take Disraeli's 'philosophy'? And how far does it affect the merits of the novels? The answer to the first question is probably 'not very'. Disraeli was writing partly to please his Young England friends, partly to assuage his own feelings as a disappointed place-seeker – the political satire is at times very bitter – but above all to puncture the balloon of early Victorian complacency, and by deliberate paradoxes to make people think. There is, after all, nothing sacrosanct about 'liberal parliamentary democracy' as practised then or now. The fact that it broke down over most of Europe during the years between the two great wars of the twentieth century, and is breaking down over much of Asia and Africa today, suggests that it is not necessarily the only solution to the problems of government and politics. In Disraeli's day there was a strong element of hypocrisy and humbug in those who advocated representative institutions as the cure of all ills, and praised the virtues of political liberty when, in the words of Carlyle, it was only too often 'for the Working Millions a liberty to die by want of food; for the Idle Thousands and Units, alas, a still more fatal liberty to live in want of work'.[1] Disraeli, though superficial in comparison, belongs to the same strand in nineteenth-century English thought as Coleridge and Carlyle, the romantic, conservative, organic thinkers who revolted against Benthamism and the legacy of eighteenth-century rationalism. The novel was the ideal form in which to air his anti-liberal anti-progressive opinions without being personally too much associated with them.

What is remarkable is not the opinions but the fact that an active Member of Parliament belonging to a political party should have put forward these vaguely anti-parliamentary views. Disraeli was not in the ordinary sense one of those Victorian 'sages' who propounded their lessons and their doctrines from the vantage-point of an agreeable detachment from practical affairs. He was a politician closely involved in the life of the House of Commons, and if the paradoxes of *Coningsby* and *Sybil* may be dismissed as effusions of a politician *manqué*, one whom hope of office had passed by, those of *Tancred* cannot, for he was on the Opposition front bench by the time it came out. Disraeli had the courage of his convictions, odd though some of those convictions were.

[1] *Past and Present*, Bk III, ch. 13.

But it remains true that the actual issues on which he fought Peel had little connexion with the philosophy of the novels. It is also a fair comment that when he became a leading political figure he never attempted at all seriously to carry out the sort of programme which he and his friends seem to have envisaged. Indeed, it would have been a vain task in the mid-nineteenth century to have solved the Condition of England question by reviving either the monarchy, the aristocracy or the Church. The extension of the franchise in 1867 and the social reforms of 1875–6 have only a superficial connexion with *Sybil*; and his flattery of Queen Victoria was more a matter of convenient management than an attempt to realize the shadowy ideas set forth in *Coningsby* of 'a free monarchy established on fundamental laws, itself the apex of a vast pile of municipal and local government, ruling an educated people, represented by a free and intellectual press'. Like all politicians of his era, Disraeli had to trim his sails to the 'liberal' wind, and the success which eventually met his efforts in 1874 was more the result of winning over the bourgeoisie than of any recurrence to the principles of Young England. Many Conservative leaders have had a hankering for Disraeli's precept, but they have usually followed Peel's practice – and so did Disraeli.

What of the merits of the novels as such? We need not share the views of the author of a *roman à thèse* in order to enjoy the novel. We can appreciate Disraeli's novels without believing that Shelburne dominated the mind of Pitt or that Charles I was the holocaust of direct taxation. *Coningsby*, *Sybil*, and indeed all Disraeli's later novels, are totally different from any other novels in the nineteenth century. For that matter there is nothing quite like them in the twentieth century either, though one might perhaps detect a faint echo in the early Evelyn Waugh.

Lord David Cecil goes so far as to say, 'Disraeli's novels, for all their brilliance, are not strictly speaking novels. They are not, that is, meant to be realistic pictures of life, but discussions on political and religious questions put into fictional form.'[1] To discuss this criticism would entail a long digression. If Disraeli's novels have any parallel at all in contemporary literature, perhaps those of Peacock come nearest. No doubt the same point can be made about them, too, but, if neither Disraeli nor Peacock wrote novels in the usual sense of the word, what they wrote was more like the novel than

[1] Lord David Cecil, *Early Victorian Novels* (1934), 290 n.

anything else. Large sections of Disraeli's books are, indeed, conversation pieces uttered by persons who are 'humours' rather than individualized characters, eg the immortal Tadpole and Taper. But in *Coningsby* he succeeded in creating – or anyway describing – two unforgettable personalities, Lord Monmouth and Rigby; and in *Sybil* he gave a highly realistic picture of life in the grim northern manufacturing towns which formed the breeding-ground of Chartism, a picture based partly on his own observations; partly on the correspondence of Feargus O'Connor obtained for him by his friend Thomas Duncombe, a Radical MP;[1] and very largely upon Part II of the Appendix to the Second Report of the Children's Employment Commission of 1842.[2] His novels were neither devoid of realism nor of characterization.

And if it is true that they are to a considerable extent conversation pieces, the severest critic must concede that the conversation is excellent, even as Disraeli's own was – witty, ironical, epigrammatic. He caught wonderfully the hard rattle of society drawing-rooms, or the languid affectation of the *jeunesse dorée*, like Alfred Mountchesney and Lord Eugène de Vere in *Sybil*, who 'had exhausted life in their 'teens, and all that remained for them was to mourn, amid the ruins of their reminiscences, over the extinction of excitement'. There is indeed an Oscar Wilde-like quality in the famous scene on the eve of Derby Day at Crockford's, with which *Sybil* opens.

> 'Nothing does me any good,' said Alfred throwing away his almost untasted peach. 'I should be quite content if something could do me harm . . .'
> 'Well for my part,' said Mr. Berners, 'I do not like your suburban dinners. You always get something you can't eat, and cursed bad wine.'
> 'I rather like bad wine,' said Mr. Mountchesney. 'One gets so bored with good wine.'

Yet there is a great gulf between Disraeli and Wilde. Disraeli's heroes, to quote Mrs Tillotson, 'all *think* – perhaps ineffectually, ignorantly, fitfully, but in their puzzled or impulsive way they do

---

[1] General Preface, xiii.

[2] Sheila M. Smith, 'Willenhall and Woodgate: Disraeli's Use of Blue Book Evidence', *Review of English Studies*, New Series, XIII, 52 (November 1962), 368–84. This careful analysis of Disraeli's indebtedness to the official report shows how very closely he followed it, sometimes to the very words. Disraeli did not admit this debt in his General Preface, though he acknowledged his obligations to Duncombe.

think about their social rights and responsibilities'. Oscar Wilde's world was the apolitical world of a revived silver forkery from the eighteen-twenties. Disraeli's was one of social stress and political bewilderment. This is what gives the novels their perennial interest, for the problems that vexed Coningsby and Egremont and Tancred are still in essence with us. Only the form has changed. Conservatives are still wondering what they should conserve. Many in recent times must have felt that only a slight variation was needed on Mr Taper's famous words, to fit their own situation – 'a sound Conservative government, I understand: Tory men and Whig measures'. And in 1966 members of the Labour party may well be thinking that an inverted version would describe theirs, too. In portraying, as he does in *Coningsby*, the conflict between political compromise and political principle, Disraeli portrays the eternal dilemma of politics. And if he does not solve it, no one else has done so either. As for *Sybil*, it is true that the two nations in our Britain are not the same or divided by the same gulf as in Disraeli's day, but although the extremes of wealth and poverty no longer exist within Britain they exist in the world as a whole and constitute one of its gravest problems. And are not Gerard's words which make the ending to Book II highly relevant today if moved from a national to a global setting?

> I speak of the annual arrival of more than three hundred thousand strangers in this island. How will you feed them? How will you clothe them? How will you house them? They have given up butcher's meat; must they give up bread . . . Why, go to your history – you're a scholar – and see the fall of the great Roman Empire – what was that? . . . What are your invasions of the barbarous nations, your Goths and Visigoths, your Lombards and Huns, to our Population Returns?

Even if we look at modern Britain there still exist profound social divisions, groups 'as ignorant of each other's habits, thoughts, and feelings, as if they were dwellers in different zones, or inhabitants of different planets'.[1] And can we be sure that the future historian of our intensely materialistic age will not echo, *mutatis mutandis* another observation in *Sybil*? 'If a spirit of rapacious covetousness, desecrating all the humanities of life has been the besetting sin of England for the last century and a half, since the passing of the

---

[1] *Sybil*, Bk II, ch. 5.

Reform Act the altar of Mammon has blazed with triple worship.'[1]

In spite of – perhaps because of – the materialism of the 1840s there arose a group, largely from generous youth, who reacted against it, seeking an ideal, a cause, something to which they could dedicate themselves and which would give a purpose to their lives. Disraeli was no longer young, but one of his most attractive traits was the sympathy with youth which he felt to the end of his career. Life to him, despite the cynicism and world-weary air which he sometimes affected, always remained the endless adventure that it was to Vivian Grey. Young England was not, in fact, destined to be the cause which inspired the youth of the time. It was too esoteric, too fanciful, too gothic, too romantic to appeal beyond a coterie. The idealism of the Victorians was to find its outlet in a renewed reinvigorated Christianity, 'godliness and good learning', and subsequently in the cause of empire, to which Disraeli late in life was to make his own contribution, though its extent is often exaggerated. Today, with the decline of belief and the vanishing of empire, with a material wealth greater and more widespread than anything in her past history and with party politics often as sterile as those of the 1840s, there are signs that Britain's new generation is again uneasily in search of soul and a role. Part of the fascination of Disraeli's trilogy is that his novels reflect the same sort of perplexity, set, of course, in a very different social structure, that is felt by many thoughtful people now who would echo Tancred: 'I am born in an age and in a country divided between infidelity on the one side and an anarchy of creeds on the other; with none competent to guide me, yet feeling that I must believe, for I hold that duty cannot exist without faith.'[2]

5

Of the three novels *Tancred* is the least successful. Some of the reasons have already been discussed. To make the discovery of religious faith the central theme of a novel or of any book it is necessary to have had some inkling of that sentiment oneself. Disraeli lacked it. He had never been through the sort of spiritual conversion which Carlyle and many other figures of the day had experienced. The result is that the worldly London scenes which constitute the first volume of the book in the original three-decker

[1] ibid., Bk II, ch. 5.   [2] *Tancred*, Bk II, ch. 1.

version are far better than the rest. Indeed, this volume contains some of Disraeli's best comedy and some of his most biting social satire: the grand chefs at the beginning; the portraits of Mr Vavasour, Mrs Guy Flouncey, Lady Bertie and Bellair; the dinner party at Sidonia's. All this is excellent, but the next two volumes trail off into a wild Oriental phantasmagoria. It would, suitably cut, make an excellent film scenario. This, indeed, is true of all three novels, above all of *Sybil*; and it is surprising that the attempt has never been made. But one becomes weary of Tancred's adventures in print. Long before the end it is clear that Disraeli has no idea what to do with his hero. Most readers finish the book with a feeling of regret that the Duke and Duchess of Bellamont did not arrive in Jerusalem a good deal earlier.

Disraeli himself liked it best of his novels. Certainly it contains many of his favourite day dreams, and it will always be read by those who are interested in its author; but as novels *Coningsby* and *Sybil* are superior. It is not easy or indeed necessary to decide between them. In many ways *Coningsby* is the better. The plot is rather more convincing, though it is not very convincing in either novel. Lord Monmouth and Rigby are characters who have no equals in *Sybil*. Rigby is supposed to be Croker, against whom Disraeli undoubtedly had a grudge. There is, in fact, no likeness at all, but it does not matter that the portrait is a libel on someone who seems to have been worthy and honourable, if rather narrow-minded. Rigby exists in his own right as the epitome of the bustling toady, the busy know-all, the efficient tool of a selfish grandee; yet not despicable if only because he is so formidable, an enemy worthy to be fought.

Monmouth is drawn from the same original as Thackeray's Lord Steyne in *Vanity Fair*, the profligate, heartless, ambitious, fabulously rich Marquess of Hertford; and is far more convincing. Lord Steyne is a mere stage villain cut out of cardboard. Lord Monmouth is seen in the round. He may be larger than life, but he lives intensely and vividly, the very quintessence of the old aristocratic order that was passing away, the arrogant grandee with his palaces, his mistresses, his minions, unscrupulous in his determination to secure a dukedom despite the loss of his rotten boroughs, hard and relentless in his fearful family feuds; but a man of polish, charm and breeding who could fascinate when he chose and who would do anything to avoid a scene. He is more real than the New Generation,

more real even than Coningsby himself, who is George Smythe, and
far more real than the rest, Lord Henry Sydney who is Manners,
Buckhurst who is Baillie-Cochrane, or Eustace Lyle who is Ambrose
Phillipps De Lisle.

Disraeli was better than any other Victorian novelist at portraying the aristocracy. To say this is not to disparage such creations as
Sir Lester Dedlock or the two Dukes of Omnium. But neither
Dickens, Thackeray nor Trollope could quite shed a sort of middle-
class uneasiness towards the nobility. It was not that they were
ignorant of the grand world. The idea that Dickens could not write
about it because he was 'not a gentleman' and had never met such
people is quite untrue. But it is true that none of them knew it as
well as Disraeli did; true, too, that none of them accepted it as
Disraeli did either. Disraeli could visit his contempt on men like
Lord Marney whose cold-hearted selfishness discredits his order or
Lord de Mowbray whose bogus pedigree conceals his descent from a
club waiter. But he felt none of the moral disapprobation which the
world of the Athenaeum felt for the world of White's. He never
doubted that there ought to be an aristocracy, and in spite of social
origins no less bourgeois than those of most other Victorian literary
men, regarded himself as meeting the aristocracy on equal if not
superior terms – a by-product of his eccentric theories about Jewry
and his erroneous belief in his own descent from its most aristocratic
branch.

Moreover by the time he came to write *Coningsby* Disraeli knew
the life of the London salons and the country houses intimately.
Politics and dandyism were more effective passports to those circles
than literature. Disraeli had yet to stay at the grandest houses of
all, but he had early been the protégé of the heir of Stowe. He and
Mary Anne were regular guests at Deepdene, the seat of the millionaire, Henry Hope, where much of *Coningsby* was written. In
London they attended the receptions given by the great political
hostesses whom Disraeli lightly and delightfully satirizes in *Sybil*.
Disraeli is always good on women, young or old. In his novels as in
life he understood them better than men, and he scarcely ever
deviates into those portraits of virtuous insipidity which mar so
many of his contemporary novelists. With regard to both sexes in
the upper class he knew what he was talking about, and when allowance is made for the epigrammatic rhetorical prose that he puts in
their mouths and the romantic extravagance with which he invests

their background his picture is probably the most authentic that we have.

The same applies to politics. Admirers of Trollope will challenge the statement, but surely in *Coningsby, Sybil,* and to a lesser degree *Endymion,* Disraeli conveys the drama and the excitement of parliamentary life – not to mention the comedy – in a way that no one else has quite achieved: the intrigues, the manoeuvres, the calculations, the rumours, the fluctuations of fortune, the agony of being out, the triumph of being in. Politics was the very fibre of his being. He loved it for its own sake and he had a wonderful eye for the amusing as well as the serious side of it. The conversation of those admirable twin political hacks, Tadpole and Taper, names that have passed into the English language, constitute some of the most entertaining passages in all fiction. It does not matter in the least whether they are accurate portraits of Bonham or other forgotten wirepullers whom Disraeli disliked. They are the vehicles of his wit and Disraeli was one of the wittiest men that ever lived.

Trollope's novels are not political at all in the sense that Disraeli's are. For one thing Trollope was not a politician. He tried and failed to get into Parliament as a Liberal and was bitterly disillusioned in the process. His profession was that of Civil Servant, and through his novels one constantly detects just below the surface that contempt, or if this is too strong a word, that bewilderment, which Civil Servants so often feel at the conduct of their ostensible masters. Trollope was concerned more with the social background of politicians than with politics as an end in itself. This does not detract from his novels. In most ways he was a far superior writer to Disraeli. But it does mean that he misses the thrills and the suspense of that strange closed world which inhabits the great gothic palace of Westminster, the absorption with victory or defeat which could make Disraeli in the 1850s describe some long-forgotten division on a matter of fleeting significance as 'an affair of Inkerman'.

It is in no way surprising that Trollope detested Disraeli and Disraeli's novels. In a well-known passage in his *Autobiography* he says

> In whatever he has written he has affected something which has been intended to strike his readers as uncommon and therefore grand. Because he has been bright and a man of genius he has carried his object as regards the young. He has struck them with astonishment and aroused in their imagination ideas of a world

more glorious, more rich, more witty, more enterprising than their own. But the glory has been the glory of pasteboard and the wealth has been the wealth of tinsel. The wit has been the wit of hairdressers, and the enterprise the enterprise of mountebanks.[1]

It is a stock criticism that Disraeli created an artificial world. But the world of high society and of politics was and is in many ways a very artificial world. Disraeli's novels would not sparkle as they do if all his diamonds had been paste. Trollope and Milnes missed the point, and despite the shrewdness of their criticisms, they never understood what it was that gives the romances their gaiety and vitality.

Coningsby is set exclusively in a background of politics and the *beau monde*. It must be admitted that Disraeli was less sure of himself in *Sybil*, where he tries to draw the contrast between the classes and the masses. The book is full of dramatic scenes which would go splendidly on the screen, but he is ill at ease in low life. Although 'the two nations' became a household word, the novel did not have the impact of Mrs Gaskell's *Mary Barton*, and not simply because of Disraeli's reputation as a society novelist or his esoteric political ideas. One never doubts that the details are correct, but he could not project himself into the lives of the poor as Mrs Gaskell did. The dialogue is too stilted and implausible. The characters are sociological case studies rather than individuals. If the descriptions of squalor are memorable it is largely because those in the Blue Books from which Disraeli lifted them are memorable, too. On quite a different level the same uncertainty in an unfamiliar field is discernible in the Eton scenes of *Coningsby*. Here again the details are correct. Disraeli had himself carefully coached by the Rev. W. G. Cookesley, a well-known Eton master. Nor had he forgotten what it was like to be a boy. The famous passage beginning 'At school friendship is a passion . . .' has a very authentic ring. Nor is the trouble to be found merely in his rococo language, although it sometimes was very odd. Who else could have referred to 'the irreclaimable and hopeless votary of Lollipop, the opium eater of school boys'? But the real difficulty is the same as in *Sybil*, an inability to enter into the unfamiliar. Sir William Fraser is surely right in saying that no Eton boys ever talked like the boys in *Coningsby*.[2]

[1] Anthony Trollope, *An Autobiography* (new edition, 1946), 230.
[2] Sir William Fraser, *Disraeli and His Day* (1891), 369.

The truth is that Disraeli lacked imagination. This may sound paradoxical. He praises the value of imagination so much that we tend to assume that he had a great deal of it himself. But imagination is not the same as day dreaming. The capacity to invent characters, to get inside them and present their development, the power to put oneself into unfamiliar scenes and situations, everything that is meant by creative imagination, these were not Disraeli's *forte*. Of course, he possessed it to some degree, or he could not have written novels at all. But compare him with Dickens, Scott, Jane Austen – or even Trollope – and one sees the difference. It comes out, too, in his creation of characters. Milnes, himself a victim, was quite right in seeing that Disraeli's were largely based on living models. Disraeli began his literary career as author of a *roman à clef*, and never quite got away from this literary genre. Even his seemingly most fantastic inventions like Sir Vavasour Firebrace in *Sybil*, the man who sought to revive the non-existent rights of baronets to sit in Parliament, were copied from life. There really was a man, Sir Richard Broun, author of *Broun's Baronetage*, who pursued this unpromising cause. He also wrote a book with the intriguing title *The Precedency of Honourable Baronetesses*. However, Milnes overstates the damage done by this practice of Disraeli. It was probably more confusing and annoying for contemporaries than it is now, when most of the originals have been forgotten and one can enjoy the copies for what they are, without worrying about their accuracy.

It is easy to list Disraeli's defects. His descriptions are conventional and unperceptive. This was largely because he was so shortsighted, and vanity forbade him to use anything but an inadequate eye-glass. His novels are hastily written, ill constructed, a series of scenes rather than a story; and what plot there is is often implausible, sometimes impossible, eg the whole business in *Sybil* about Gerard's claim to the Mowbray estates. His range was limited, and he sounds hollow and unconvincing whenever he tries to touch the deeper feelings. He could descend to astonishing bathos and commit errors of taste almost as bad as those in *Vivian Grey*.

Yet in spite of all this he lives. His prose may have been careless, indeed at times ungrammatical, and with its echo of Burke and Bolingbroke was old-fashioned perhaps for its day, but it is extremely effective. Walter Allen writes in his perceptive introduction to *Coningsby*:

It admits of no hesitations, no half-lights; it is completely sure, completely dogmatic. It is the prose of a superb lawyer presenting a case, seemingly holding nothing back, addressing the bemused inarticulate jury as one man of the world to a dozen others, flattering them by his assumption that they are men of equal sophistication and worldly wisdom, wheedling them with his wit. For above everything else Disraeli is a wit. The very structure of his sentences is witty and his epigrams invite the reader into his confidence.[1]

Disraeli was all of a piece. This was the same technique that he used in Parliament. His novels are part of his politics and his politics at times seem to be an emanation of his novels.

Just as Disraeli was at heart an optimist who enjoyed life, so his novels at their best have a gaiety, a sparkle, a cheerful vivacity which carries one over their improbabilities and occasional absurdities. In *Coningsby*, *Sybil* and the first third of *Tancred* there is rarely a dull page. They are essentially the product of an extrovert, splendid novels to read for anyone who is feeling out of sorts. They may not be very profound, they do not touch the inner depths of human character and emotions, they are often careless; but they are great fun, they deal with real problems, if not always with real people, and their vitality is attested by the fact that so many of their expressions have passed into the very language of politics, and that they are still read with pleasure long after most of their contemporaries have vanished into oblivion. Their flavour is unique.

[1] *Coningsby* (Chiltern Library edition, 1948), 17.

CHAPTER X

The Fall of Peel

1845–6

1

The summer of 1845 was one of the wettest for many years. A poor harvest was inevitable, and at the end of September an even worse disaster loomed up. A deadly potato disease, which had appeared in America the previous year and moved to Europe, reached southern England, then Ireland. This was serious enough for England, but in Ireland, where half the eight million inhabitants lived exclusively on potatoes because they could not afford bread, it was a complete catastrophe. Peel was horrified at the sinister prospect which he saw. Given the circumstances of the time, it is doubtful whether anything could have prevented the great majority of the million deaths which ultimately resulted. The root of the trouble was the poverty of the Irish peasants, so great that, even if bread had been made as cheap as it could be by complete removal of import duties on grain, it would still have been far beyond their purchasing power. The only solution was state charity, outdoor relief on a huge scale, and, apart from the ideological difficulties which this raised with any government in those days, the sheer physical task of distribution would probably have been insuperable in a country of bogs and mountains, bad roads and no railways.

Although Peel took some action on these lines – for example, the purchase of American maize, 'Peel's brimstone', which was retailed at a penny a pound – his principal remedy was to open the ports to duty-free foreign and colonial grain. Despite all that has been written in explanation and defence of his policy, it remains something of a puzzle why he thought that this could help in the immediate crisis. The mass of the Irish peasantry lived so far below the bread level that the relatively slight fall in the price, which might be expected to follow, could not have made bread a substitute for potatoes. Moreover, if Peel was convinced that total repeal was essential at once as an emergency measure, why did he bring forward a Bill which enacted not immediate abolition but the

221

gradual tapering off of import duties over a period of three years? Why did he not do what several members of his Cabinet urged – suspend the Corn Laws temporarily by Order in Council on grounds of emergency? There was provision under the existing Act for just such a step, and he would probably not only have kept his Cabinet united but also have retained the support of the party. Peel himself argued that it would be disingenuous to do this, because he did not believe that Parliament would ever consent to reimpose the duties on grain when they had once been suspended. But no one asked Peel to *guarantee* that the duties would be reimposed. 'Suspend the Corn Laws,' said Lord John Manners, 'open the ports, and leave it to the good sense of the English people to decide whether they should be closed again.'

The truth was that Peel had long been convinced on quite other grounds that the Corn Laws ought to be repealed. He had already decided to come forward at some suitable later date as an avowed free trader. For him, to continue to use the language of protectionism and talk of the suspension of the Corn Laws as a disagreeable temporary expedient, was an intolerable psychological strain. He could not pretend that he was in favour of closing the ports again as soon as the emergency was over. Yet at the same time he could not bring himself to base his case on the full economic arguments for free trade, for, if he did this, he was open to the personal charge of betraying his party and his pledges. It was only on grounds of emergency that he could justify his own action in personally piloting the repeal through the House. If the case was one to be considered in due course by 'the good sense of the English people', then there was an overwhelming argument for leaving the initiative with – indeed, forcing it upon – Russell, who had belatedly and unexpectedly announced his conversion to free trade in the middle of the crisis.

After a number of Cabinet meetings held in November, Peel resigned, unable to persuade the Duke of Buccleuch and, more important, Stanley to acquiesce in repeal. The Queen sent for Russell, who, after taking six days to make up his mind, accepted the commission, and then within forty-eight hours resigned it on a trumped-up excuse. His real reason was evidently the division in his own ranks. Peel regarded Russell's conduct with contempt. He did not attempt to dissuade him from resigning. On the contrary he accepted the Queen's commission with an alacrity which suggests that he was delighted at the prospect. 'I want,' he told her, 'no consultation, no time for reflection. I will be your Minister, happen what may. I will do without a colleague rather than leave you in this extremity.' The Queen noted that she had never seen him so excited and determined. Peel resumed office with the support of all his old Cabinet, except Buccleuch and Stanley, the latter being succeeded at the Colonial Office by Gladstone. Parliament was due to meet in a month, and Peel decided to bring forward the repeal of the Corn Laws at the first opportunity.

Disraeli was out of England when these events occurred, and he does not seem to have discerned their significance. In a letter written to Palmerston from Paris on December 14 about the King's attitude to the apparent imminence of Palmerston reassuming the Foreign Office, he observes casually '. . . if Parliament be summoned speedily, I do not think I shall be tempted to quit this agreeable residence.' Three days later, writing to Lord John Manners, he observed that Guizot had said that 'if it be a *real* famine, Sir Robert will be a great man', and went on to add his own comment,

> Now I think it is a false famine; and the question is not ripe enough for his fantastic pranks. He is so vain that he wants to figure in history as the settler of all the great questions; but a Parliamentary constitution is not favourable to such ambitions: things must be done by parties, not by persons using parties as tools – especially men without imagination or any inspiring qualities, or who, rather, offer you duplicity instead of inspiration.

Disraeli stayed on in Paris until January 16, less than a week before Parliament opened. He just missed Smythe, who arrived that very day on his return from a characteristic tour of the Continent, devoted largely to amorous intrigues. Young England was now little more than a dream. Maynooth had finally killed it and, though Smythe, like Manners, was, and remained always, deeply devoted to Disraeli, he was weak and Lord Strangford was persistent. The reshuffle of the Cabinet in December led to Aberdeen offering him the Under-secretaryship for Foreign Affairs.[1] He felt that, unless he was to break with his father irrevocably, he could not refuse. He wrote to Disraeli:

---

[1] To the immense mortification of Monckton Milnes, who expected the place for himself, and never forgave Peel. Milnes moved over soon afterwards to the Whig-Liberal camp.

Hotel Bristol

December[1] 16, 1846

Caro Dis

. . . Everything conspires to make you think me a blackguard – first of all my never writing – and Aberdeen's offer to my father, which I find in a letter here – the quadruplicate of one sent on the ninth of Jany to Venice, Florence, Rome.

I had never written to you because I had too much to say – and all maudlin and mawkish. The . . . [illegible, but evidently the name of some woman] followed me to Paris as I predicted, and here I got helplessly and damnably entangled with another woman who gave me mortification and heart burning enough – all which I wrote in a book which will now never see the light . . . at Venice I had other affairs of debauch into which I flung myself for compensation which turned out not over much; and for 3 weeks had the satisfaction of thinking the Whigs in . . . I left Venice on the 7th and here I find this letter from my father.

I have not answered yet but as after reflection I mean to accept, and as I fear us being in opposite camps may lead to a severance of sympathy – if not of friendship – I cannot *accept* without first acknowledging all I owe to you and thanking you . . .

A prudent man would be silent on the event of a passage in our lives which must irk and hurt . . . but I am not prudent and never shall forget how you found me low abused in my own esteem and that of others, morbidly debating my own powers, and how you made a man of me and set me on my legs at Manchester, and have ever been to me the kindliest and gentlest of councillors.

I am sorry to pain you – as I know I shall by thus becoming a Peelite – why I do so there are many reasons – but my object in writing this letter is only to let you know *before* I answer, what course I take: and to assure you that whatever be your feelings towards me, I shall ever feel to you as to a man of genius who succoured and solaced and strengthened me when I was deserted even by myself.

Your affectionate friend

George Smythe[2]

Disraeli's answer is unknown, but we may be sure that, however saddened at the defection, if such it can be called, of Coningsby himself, he said nothing harsh. He knew well enough the strain under which his younger friend laboured. Certainly their friendship

---

[1] Smythe distinctly writes 'December', but this must be a slip of the pen for January.

[2] Hughenden Papers, Box 144, B/XXI/S/650.

remained unimpaired, even though their paths diverged and they saw less of each other. The last letter surviving from Smythe among Disraeli's papers is dated July 2, 1852. In it he wrote,

> You were of old the Cid and Captain of my boyish fanaticism and after that I was seduced to desert you (out of domestic reasons) I could never help feeling that you were the Cid and Captain of my every sympathy.[1]

The fact that Peel's Cabinet intended to repeal the Corn Laws was well known before Parliament met on January 22 and steps had already been taken by a body known as the Anti-League to organize opposition. This, which had been founded in 1843, out of alarm at the activities of the Anti-Corn Law League and uneasiness at some of Peel's actions, was a federation of local county protectionist societies under a Central Agricultural Protection Society presided over by the Duke of Richmond.[2] It had considerable funds and used its influence at county meetings to secure declarations from Tory MPs and force them to show their hands in favour of the Corn Laws before Parliament met. A number of influential county members belonged, William Miles (Somerset), G. J. Heathcote (Rutland), Charles Newdegate (Warwickshire), Sir John Tyrell (Essex), and the only link with Young England, Augustus Stafford O'Brien (Northamptonshire). It is probably true to say that the parliamentary organization of the protectionist party was largely made possible by the Anti-League and that without some such basis Disraeli and Bentinck could never have carried on such a long struggle against the repeal of the Corn Laws.

Disraeli had no previous connexion with the agriculturists, unless we go back to the days of his intrigue with Chandos and Lyndhurst in 1836. On the contrary he and Young England tended to laugh at the more fanatical country gentlemen like Vyvyan, of whom Smythe was fond of relating ludicrous stories. Indeed, there is no evidence that Disraeli had concerted any plans with anyone when he walked into the House on January 22 – a day destined to be one of the most

[1] ibid., B/XXI/S/652.
[2] See an interesting article by Mary Lawson-Tancred, 'The Anti-League and the Corn Law Crisis of 1846', *Historical Journal*, III No. 2. (1960). Disraeli minimizes its activities in his own account in *Lord George Bentinck*, 47–48, but Miss Lawson-Tancred is probably right in explaining the omission by the fact that, at the time of writing, Disraeli was endeavouring to liquidate what remained of the Anti-League, which, by rigid insistence on protectionism, was proving something of a nuisance to him in 1849–50.

fateful in his life. But we cannot doubt that he had pondered deeply and that he came not unprepared.

What followed has often been told. Peel opened with a long and tedious speech full of details, not only about corn duties but about the price of lard and salt beef and the importation of foreign cattle, then proceeding to an account of the Cabinet meetings in November and December so involved that scarcely anyone could follow it, ending on a defiant note to the effect that he would be minister by no servile tenure and that it was not easy to 'insure the united action of an ancient monarchy, a proud aristocracy, and a reformed House of Commons'. He was received in dead silence by his party. Then came Russell with an even less intelligible speech, explaining – and it needed some explanation – his own curious conduct during the crisis, and reading copious extracts from dull documents in that thin nasal drawl which made him such an unattractive speaker. At the end of all this dreary recital the House was bored and depressed. It was generally felt that the issues of principle would be postponed for a later debate, and the impression might well have been given to the country at large that little real opposition existed to the repeal of the Corn Laws.

'The opportune in a popular assembly', wrote Disraeli, 'has some-times more success than the weightiest efforts of research and reason'. He was determined not to let Peel get away with this success on the first night. He knew that this question, to a far greater extent than any of the previous subjects on which he had baited Peel, was capable of causing a real rebellion in the Tory ranks. He jumped to his feet and delivered one of the most brilliant of all the brilliant attacks which he had launched and was to launch against Peel.

> But it was the long-constrained passion of the House that now found a vent, far more than the sallies of the speaker, that changed the frigid silence of this senate into excitement and tumult.[1]

It was a wonderful speech, and those who take the trouble to read it in *Hansard*[2] will not be bored by a single sentence; nor will they doubt that, however much Disraeli might talk of 'the opportune', he had most carefully prepared what he was going to say. The finest

---

[1] Disraeli, *Lord George Bentinck; A Political Biography* (1852), 57.
[2] *Hansard*, 3rd series, lxxxiii, 111–23.

orator in the world could not have delivered all this impromptu: the parallel with the great fleet sent out by the late Sultan under the command of an admiral who steered it straight to the enemy port declaring, 'the only reason I had for accepting the command was that I might terminate the contest by betraying my master'; the image of protection as a baby whose brains had been dashed out by its nurse, 'a person of very orderly demeanour too, not given to drink, and never showing any emotion, except of late, when kicking against protection'; the denunciation of Peel as 'no more a great statesman than the man who gets up behind a carriage is a great whip. Certainly both are disciples of progress. Perhaps both may get a good place. But how far the original momentum is indebted to their powers, and how far their guiding prudence applies the lash or regulates the reins, it is not necessary for me to notice.'

It was crude knockabout stuff in places, and much of it was unfair. Disraeli was ill advised, for example, to say that 'even' Peel's 'mouldy potatoes' and the 'reports of his vagrant professors' had failed him. But it was extremely effective. Disraeli was creating an image of Peel as a slightly pompous, priggish mediocrity who was betraying the party by which he had risen. There was just enough reality in it to appeal to the angry back benchers who felt that they were being double-crossed. They applauded with ever louder cheers each repetition – and Disraeli was a great believer in repetition – of this congenial theme. He ended with a passionate plea:

> Let men stand by the principle by which they rise, right or wrong. I make no exception. If they be wrong, they must retire to that shade of private life with which our present rulers have so often threatened us . . . Do not then because you see a great personage giving up his opinions – do not cheer him on, do not give so ready a reward to political tergiversation. Above all maintain the line of demarcation between parties, for it is only by maintaining the independence of party that you can maintain the integrity of public men, and the power and influence of Parliament itself.

By the time he sat down, amidst cheers which lasted for several minutes, it was clear that the case for protection was not going to go by default. There would be a battle and it was by no means certain that Peel would win.

2

Among those who on this memorable occasion surveyed Peel from
the Tory back benches with a baleful eye was a person whose important part in future events could not easily have been guessed at
this time. Lord George Bentinck, second son of the 4th Duke of
Portland, had been a Member of Parliament for eighteen years,
and, for three years before that, private secretary to Canning, who
was his uncle by marriage. But he seldom spoke: indeed, he remained wholly silent for his first eight years as a MP. Preferring to
use Parliament, so Disraeli says, 'rather as a club than a senate . . .
he might have been observed on more than one occasion entering
the House at a late hour, clad in a white greatcoat which softened
but did not conceal the scarlet hunting coat'. In politics he had
been a Canningite Tory, moving to the Whig side when Wellington
took office and supporting Grey's Reform Bill. In 1834 he followed
Stanley and Graham into semi-opposition, and by 1841 had become
like them an ardent supporter of Peel. But in spite of these changes
Disraeli is probably right to describe him as being at heart a Whig
of 1688, favourable to toleration and by no means averse to popular
suffrage, a supporter of the Church but an enemy of clericalism, a
firm believer in the importance of the territorial aristocracy, and
an opponent of anything that could be construed as monarchical
pretension.

Although Bentinck had taken so small a part in politics, he was
far from being an unknown person. On the contrary he was one of
the most celebrated figures on the turf, his racing stable was famous
and his successes were numerous. *Crucifix*, his best-known filly,
won in a single year, 1840, the Two Thousand Guineas, the One
Thousand Guineas, and the Oaks. Moreover, he possessed great
prestige among all reputable racing men because of his efforts to
eliminate the malpractices which marred racing at that time. His
culminating success was the exposure of the great *Running Rein*
fraud when in the 1844 Derby a four-year-old, really called *Macca-
beus*, was passed off as a three-year-old and won the race. The
worlds of sport and politics overlapped far more then than now, and
Bentinck's forceful personality was respected by many Members of
Parliament for non-Parliamentary reasons.

Bentinck had a straightforward, somewhat rigid cast of mind.
He saw life in black and white. The conduct of others was to him

either honourable, in which case he would respect it even if he disagreed, or it was not, in which case his attack would be truly ferocious. He was a man of violent temper and extreme prejudice, and he pursued his enemies with unrelenting virulence. The House of Commons was none too squeamish in those days, but the invective uttered and charges levelled by Bentinck were destined to excite disapprobation on more than one occasion. All this, however, lay in the future. At the beginning of 1846 only a few intimate friends knew that to Bentinck his former hero, Peel, had now become no better than one of the sharpers, crooks and defaulters whose villainies he had exposed on the turf. As Bentinck himself is supposed to have said, 'I keep horses in three counties, and they tell me that I shall save fifteen hundred a year by free trade. I don't care for that: what I cannot bear is being *sold*.'

Bentinck had never, apparently, even spoken to Disraeli before 1846. Ten years earlier, when Lyndhurst tried to persuade him to accept Disraeli as a parliamentary colleague, he would not even consider the idea.[1] Nor is it likely that Disraeli's mocking attacks on Peel in 1844 and 1845 pleased Bentinck at that time. Until the last moment he remained a loyal admirer of the Prime Minister. But events now brought him into close alliance with Disraeli. Conscious of his own inexperience as a speaker, he had actually contemplated briefing one of the legal members of Parliament to put his case for him, but he saw at once that Disraeli's mastery of the art of debate would solve this problem. Inevitably he could not at once become a personal friend. His first letter, on March 31, is headed 'My dear Sir' and ends 'Very sincerely yours'. In the middle of June, when their combined efforts were about to oust Peel, he becomes slightly less formal – 'My dear Disraeli' and 'Always yours most sincerely'. But it is not until December that we find 'My dear D.' and 'Yours ever'; which are as intimate a mode of superscription and signature as we find from any of Disraeli's close friends – save for one or two exceptions like George Smythe. Their friendship, once cemented, remained unimpaired until the end. Bentinck quarrelled with many people, but never with Disraeli; and no one can doubt that Disraeli's devotion to Bentinck was genuine and sincere.

Disraeli's account of their relations and of the battle over the Corn Laws is given in his famous *Lord George Bentinck* published in

[1] See above, p. 121.

December 1851. It is a most remarkable book, extremely readable, and full of often-quoted comments and descriptions. Documents have been subsequently published which show some of Disraeli's conjectures, particularly about the Cabinet crises of autumn 1845, to be incorrect, but as a vivid story of one of the great parliamentary dramas in our history it is unsurpassed. It is, moreover, extraordinarily detached. The portrait of Peel, who had died in 1850, is penetrating, not at all unsympathetic, and in many respects just. Oddly enough, as with the heroes of the novels, it is Lord George himself who fails to come to life. Disraeli depicts him as too much of a paragon, exaggerates his ability and statesmanship, and altogether underplays his own personal role, appearing merely from time to time as 'a friend who sate by Lord George Bentinck'.

This obvious distortion has caused some critics to go to the other extreme and maintain that Bentinck was a mere puppet whom Disraeli manipulated. That picture, too, is incorrect. Bentinck leaned much on Disraeli for advice and aid, but he was in no sense a puppet. Nor did he lack ability. It is true that he was not a good speaker, and his habit of never eating till after he had spoken, which was frequently at a late hour of night, did not help him, for he was often weak and exhausted before he began. But he had a great capacity for hard work and a wonderful head for figures. He used scarcely any notes. It was all very well for Monckton Milnes to observe that Bentinck 'had a marvellous memory but so had the learned pig', or for others to attribute his arithmetical skill to long experience in speedy calculation of the odds. The fact remains that a memory for statistics and the gift of quick calculation were considerable assets in these debates.

The adherence of a man like Bentinck to the protectionist cause was a notable asset. The country gentlemen of old England might applaud Disraeli, but they would not at this stage have followed him. Bentinck, younger son of a duke, wealthy in his own right, King of the Turf, grandson of one Prime Minister, nephew of another, was a very different proposition. He was the sort of man whom people instinctively regarded as a leader. It is often said that Disraeli overthrew Peel, and in a sense it is true. But it is very doubtful whether even he could have managed without Bentinck. Certainly he would have been the last person to claim otherwise.

Bentinck hitherto had been no more involved than Disraeli with the Agricultural Protection Society, or 'Anti-League', but both men were quick to see its value as an organization on which to base a third parliamentary party. The task was clearly going to be formidable. Nearly every man of proved parliamentary ability on the Conservative side was a Peelite, except Stanley. But he was a peer, and his attitude to the other protectionists was sceptical. He saw a lack among them, he said, of 'public men of public character and official habits, in the House of Commons to carry on a government'.[1] He evidently intended to see what they were going to do for themselves before he committed himself.

The Protection Society proved its value at this juncture. The managers of its central council invited all MPs who sympathized with the cause, whether members of the society or not, to attend a meeting. Lord George Bentinck's attitude was made public for the first time on this occasion. He pressed strongly for the creation of a third party with its own management and whips, and he succeeded in rallying the doubters. Plans were made to organize the coming debate, and a programme of action was drawn up. Already the Protection Society had exerted its moral influence on certain MPs who, though convinced of the necessity to repeal the Corn Laws, were persuaded by the society that they could not honourably retain their seats, but must either retire or submit themselves for re-election. Accordingly a number of by-elections pended. It was therefore important to fight a prolonged battle on Peel's motion to go into committee to consider the Corn Laws: public opinion would be heartened by signs of real resistance; and the country party might be strengthened by new recruits if the by-elections went well.

The debate began on February 9. The dissident Tories proved to be much more formidable than the Government expected. A wrecking amendment was proposed by Sir Philip Miles, a member of the Protectionist Society, and seconded by another, Sir William Heathcote. The debate was kept going for no less than twelve parliamentary nights. Disraeli spoke on the eighth (February 27), and his speech was of a more thoughtful, or as he would have said, 'philosophic', nature than his previous efforts. It throws light on his political ideas at this time, and is also notable for the first use of the expression 'the school of Manchester' in reference to Cobden,

---

[1] Lawson-Tancred, 175, quoting Lord Norreys' speech to the Oxfordshire Protection Society, January 14, 1846, in which he referred to a letter from Stanley.

Bright and their allies – a phrase which became part of the English language. Disraeli rested the case for the Corn Laws openly on the argument that of the two great branches of industry it was essential to give to the agricultural a preponderance compared with the manufacturing. England had a territorial constitution. It was upon the land that there fell 'the revenues of the Church, the administration of justice and the estate of the poor'. The 'territorial constitution' was important not because it pampered the proprietor but because it was 'the only security for self-government; and more than that the only barrier to that system of centralization which has taken root and enslaved the energies of surrounding nations'. Cobden, he declared, wanted the repeal of the Corn Laws in order to transfer power from the landed class to the manufacturers.

> My conscience assures me that I have not been slow in doing justice to the intelligence of that class; I do not envy them their wide and deserved prosperity, but I must confess my deep mortification that in an age of political regeneration when all social evils are ascribed to the operation of class interests, it should be suggested that we are to be reduced from the alleged power of one class only to sink under the avowed dominion of another . . . Instead of falling under such a thraldom . . . if we must find new forces to maintain the ancient throne and immemorial monarchy of England I for one hope that we may find that novel power in the invigorating energies of an educated and enfranchised people.[1]

The debate was wound up by Bentinck at the end of no less than three parliamentary weeks. He rose, in Disraeli's words, 'long past the noon of night', having consumed nothing during the whole day except some dry toast for breakfast, but he proceeded to address the House at immense length in a speech packed with complicated statistics.

We may well surmise that his audience felt, not so much the 'astonishment' which Disraeli claims, as exhaustion, at the recital of his interminable figures. But his final observations must have made them sit up, however weary. For Bentinck, in this respect a true eighteenth-century Whig, had no special respect for the House of Hanover, still less for the German princelings who had married into it. Prince Albert, a keen Peelite and enthusiastic free trader, had appeared on the first night of the debate to listen to Sir Robert.

[1] *Hansard*, 3rd series, lxxxiii, 1347.

Bentinck did not let this gesture go unnoticed. He proceeded to censure the Prince in what must surely be one of the longest sentences in *Hansard*.[1]

> . . . If so humble an individual as myself might be permitted to whisper a word in the ear of that illustrious and royal personage, who as he stands nearest, so is he justly dearest, to her who sits upon the throne, I would take leave to say that I cannot but think he listened to ill advice when on the first night of this great discussion he allowed himself to be seduced by the first minister of the crown to come down to this house to usher in, to give *éclat*, and as it were by reflexion from the Queen, to give semblance of the personal sanction of Her Majesty to a measure which, be it for good or for evil, a great majority of the landed aristocracy of England, of Scotland and of Ireland imagine fraught with deep injury if not ruin to them – a measure which, not confined in its operation to this great class, is calculated to grind down countless smaller interests engaged in the domestic trades and interests of the empire, transferring the profits of all these interests – English, Scotch, Irish, and Colonial – great and small alike, from Englishmen, from Scotchmen, and from Irishmen, to Americans, to Frenchmen, to Russians, to Poles, to Prussians, and to Germans.

This was strong language. The hostility of the Crown was to be one of the difficulties under which the protectionists – Disraeli not least among them – had to labour for many years after the crisis of 1846, and the attitude of Bentinck may well be a part of the explanation. He ended by declaring that the 'proud aristocracy' to which he and his friends belonged 'never have been guilty and never can be guilty of double-dealing with the farmers of England, – of swindling our opponents, deceiving our friends, or betraying our constituents'.

The division was at last taken, and the protectionist amendment was beaten by only 97 votes in a House of 581 members present. But the Government won, thanks to the help of 227 Whigs and Radicals. Only 112 Tories voted for repeal. No less than 242 of Peel's former supporters voted on the side of Bentinck.

Peel had clearly never expected such a rebellion when in December he originally undertook to remove the corn duties.[2] To be

---

[1] *Hansard*, 3rd series, lxxxiv, 348.
[2] See John Morley, *Life of W. E. Gladstone* (3 vols, 1903), i, 286, for Gladstone's account of Peel's 'glee and complacency' at the prospect and his confidence in holding the party together.

outnumbered by more than two to one in his own party was a
serious matter, however good a face he put on it. His plight was the
more perilous since his 112 supporters were by no means all convinced of the actual merits of his policy. A substantial number
voted for him solely from personal loyalty and a desire to keep him
in office. In these circumstances the hopes of the protectionists
began to rise. If they could prolong the battle, there was always a
chance that they might bring down the Government on some other
issue before the Corn Law Bill could be enacted. With a new
government, new loyalties and pressures would arise. By-elections
were going in favour of protectionists, and their prospects were
improving. Moreover, the procedure adopted by Peel gave a wide
scope for procrastination and obstruction. The motion which he
carried on February 27 was simply to go into committee of the
whole House to consider the Corn Laws. Then it would be for the
Government to propose resolutions upon which a subsequent Bill
or Bills would be founded. There would be votes on the resolutions,
votes on every stage of the Bills. Then there was the House of
Lords. Bentinck and Disraeli plunged into the struggle with enthusiasm.

It is hard to overstate the bitterness and fury which Peel's
decision to repeal the Corn Laws had provoked. Home Rule in 1886
and Munich in 1938 are the nearest parallels. Friendships were
sundered, families divided, and the feuds of politics carried into
private life to a degree quite unusual in British history. The Duke
of Newcastle severed all relations with his Peelite son, Lord Lincoln,
used his territorial influence to defeat Lincoln's election for the
county of Nottingham, and was only reconciled years later on his
death-bed. Sidney Herbert, meeting his oldest and closest friend,
Lord Malmesbury, at a party at Lady Palmerston's told him that
his conduct in leaving Peel was not worthy of a gentleman. Months
after the event passions still raged. 'Ma'am it's a damned dishonest
act,' cried the ill and ageing Melbourne to the Queen at dinner at
Windsor Castle. And in November Bentinck reporting a scandal
about Smythe wrote with relish to Disraeli:

> It is much discussed whether Smythe will be received in Society
> after such an outrage as getting an earl's daughter with child (if
> she be with child) and then casting her off and refusing to marry
> her.

This is quite a modern description of profligacy reserved for

member of Peel's moral government, the contagion of its political
bad faith spreading into private life.[1]

These violent feelings were hardly surprising. Whatever the
justification for Peel's decision, he was executing to all appearances
a complete volte-face. The cry of betrayal was bound to be raised,
and a certain unctuousness in the Prime Minister's demeanour was
not likely to diminish it.

It would be tedious to detail every stage of the contest. No new
arguments emerged. Everything that could be said on both sides
had been said. It was a battle not of persuasion but of tactics,
manoeuvre and parliamentary procedure, and in this field where he
was normally a master Peel made what turned out to be a surprising
error. With some justice he decided that the agrarian outrages
provoked by the starvation conditions of Ireland must be met by a
'coercion act', ie a measure to suspend *habeas corpus*, and to introduce military tribunals and a curfew. Had Peel brought this Bill
forward at the very beginning of the session, he would probably
have carried it without difficulty, for Parliament would usually
support a measure restoring law and order in a crisis. But members
required to be convinced that there really was a crisis, or at least
that the Government believed that there was. Yet the Bill was not
introduced until February 24, and then in the House of Lords with
no apparent sense of haste or urgency. It was not until March 30 –
and after the second reading of the Corn Law Bill – that the Irish
Coercion Bill was put down for its first reading in the lower House.

The Bill had the support of all parties in the House of Lords,
and, as the Tories were in general readier than the Whigs to subordinate constitutional niceties to the preservation of order, it seemed
likely to pass in the lower House despite Irish and Radical hostility.
When the protectionists met to discuss tactics Disraeli alone urged
them to pause before voting for the measure. Bentinck did not
agree. He and most of his followers supported the first reading on
May 1. Disraeli abstained.

The Government was in an uncomfortable position from March
30 onwards. On the Corn Law question they had been able to rely
on the Whigs, Liberals and Irish, but the Irish Bill produced an
entirely different and basically unstable balance of power. The
protectionists, it was true, supported Peel for the time being on

<hr>

[1] Hughenden Papers, Box 89, B/XX/Be/12, November 9, 1846.

coercion, but grudgingly and conditionally: they could not be relied upon. As for the Whigs, some were for it, some were against it. The Irish, O'Connell's Tail as men still called them, were, of course, its relentless opponents. Bentinck was delighted at the sight of these complicated cross-currents.

'For God's sake get quite right before you venture out,' he wrote on March 31 to Disraeli, who was ill, 'as we shall want you after Easter in earnest – just now you are not wanted and the TAIL appear to be doing our work to admiration . . .' And he ended with a fine mixture of metaphors. 'We have now fairly set them [the Government] and the Tail by the ears.'[1]

Those who are interested in the details of the parliamentary warfare which raged until Peel's fall should consult *Lord George Bentinck*, where the story is told with inimitable verve. There is, however, one episode not mentioned in that book, which deserves some reference. It occurred during the debate on the third reading of the Corn Law Bill on May 15. Disraeli spoke for three hours, and the last twenty minutes were packed with wit and invective in his best style. He described how the Peelites, like the Saxons confronting Charlemagne, 'were converted in battalions and baptised in platoons'. He acquitted Peel of any profound or long-meditated plot. On the contrary, Peel merely picked up ideas from others as he went along. 'His life has been a great appropriation clause. He is a burglar of other's intellect . . . there is no statesman who has committed political petty larceny on so great a scale.' Disraeli then gave his famous excursus, too long to quote, upon 'Popkins's plan', and he ended with a fine rhetorical flourish.

I know Sir that we appeal to a people debauched by public gambling, stimulated by an inefficient and short-sighted Minister. I know that the public mind is polluted by economic fancies – a depraved desire that the rich may become richer without the interference of industry and toil. I know Sir that all confidence in public men is lost. But Sir I have faith in the primitive and enduring elements of the English character. It may be vain now in the midnight of their intoxication to tell them that there will will be an awakening of bitterness . . . But the dark and inevitable hour will arrive . . .

The people would then 'recur to those principles which made England

---

[1] ibid., Box 89, B/XX/Be/1. Using the licence of the novelist, forbidden to the orthodox biographer, Disraeli in *Lord George Bentinck*, 158, altered the last three words to 'at loggerheads'.

great'. They would remember those who were not afraid 'to struggle for the "good old cause" – the cause with which are associated principles the most popular, sentiments the most entirely national, the cause of labour, the cause of the people, the cause of England'.[1]

Disraeli sat down to an ovation such as he had never received before. With the applause of the gentlemen of England thundering in his ears he could indeed feel that he had come a long way since his fruitless efforts on the hustings at High Wycombe. But the evening did not quite end as it had begun.

Hitherto Peel had made little effort to answer Disraeli's on-slaughts, not because he felt that they were beneath notice but because he did not know what to say. He had never in his long parliamentary career encountered an enemy quite like this. Years after Disraeli's death Morley asked Gladstone, a witness not biased in Disraeli's favour, whether the latter's famous philippics were really as effective as people claimed. 'Mr. G.', he records, 'said Disraeli's performances against Peel were quite as wonderful as report makes them. Peel altogether helpless in reply. Dealt with them with a kind of "righteous dulness".'[2]

But on this occasion, whether maddened by his tormentor's malicious wit or infuriated at the thought of this shady adventurer discoursing on 'the primitive and enduring elements of the English character', Peel attempted a personal riposte. Why, he asked, if Disraeli really believed his whole life to be one of political larceny, was he 'ready as I think he was, to unite his fortunes with mine in office'?[3]

This allusion to Disraeli's letter in 1841 was, perhaps, not much of a retort. Certainly Disraeli could have dealt with it either by a full explanation or, better still, by ignoring it. But he was foolish enough to do neither, and instead made a categorical denial of ever having sought office. Rising after Peel and asking to be allowed to make a personal statement, he began by saying, incorrectly, that Peel had accused him of 'envenomed opposition' occasioned by 'being disappointed of office'. There would, he went on, have been nothing at all dishonourable if he had solicited office. He then declared with what can only be described as reckless mendacity:

[1] *Hansard*, 3rd series, lxxxvi, 677.
[2] Morley, *Gladstone*, iii, 465, from notes which he took while on holiday with Gladstone at Biarritz in December 1891.
[3] *Hansard*, 3rd series, lxxxvi, 689.

> But I can assure the House nothing of the kind ever occurred. I
> never shall – it is totally foreign to my nature – make any appli-
> cation for any place . . . I never asked a favour of the Govern-
> ment, not even one of those mechanical things which persons are
> obliged to ask . . . and as regards myself I never directly or
> indirectly solicited office . . . It is very possible if, in 1841, I
> had been offered office, I dare say it would have been a very
> slight office, but I dare say I should have accepted it . . . But
> with respect to my being a solicitor for office it is entirely un-
> founded . . .[1]

Peel replied quite correctly that he had not suggested disappointment in office as the reason for Disraeli's opposition, but repeated
that he still remained surprised that Disraeli had been willing to
join him in 1841. He significantly ignored Disraeli's denial.

It is inconceivable that Disraeli had forgotten what he had
written to Peel. Nor is it plausible to suggest, as Miss Ramsay does
in her life of Peel,[2] that he knew his man and reckoned on Peel
being too gentlemanly to produce the letter. It is true that Disraeli
knew of Peel's refusal to read out a damaging letter from Joseph
Hume in 1830 in somewhat similar circumstances, but no one
would have dared, in the light of cool reason, to gamble upon a
repetition; even though, as events turned out, the gamble would
have come off. Disraeli had indeed denied asking for office once
before – to his constituents at Shrewsbury in 1844. He had not been
contradicted then, but that was a different matter from confronting
in person the very minister to whom he had written an almost
abject letter of solicitation. The most likely explanation is panic,
rare though such lapses were in Disraeli's life. He possibly knew that
in some circles his reputation was none too good. He may well have
been flustered, and he probably blurted out his unconvincing denial
without fully considering the risk. He certainly asked for trouble,
by not only denying that he ever solicited office, but also, and
equally untruthfully, that he had ever asked for a favour. Had he
forgotten the applications that he made to Graham and Stanley for
his brother? It is unlikely that they had.

Peel did not read out Disraeli's letter, but there is no truth in the
story apparently believed by Buckle that he was unable to find it.
Goldwin Smith in his reminiscences delares that he had first-hand
information on this point from Lord Lincoln, who had walked with

---

[1] *Hansard*, 3rd series, lxxxvi, 707–9.
[2] A. A. W. Ramsay, *Sir Robert Peel* (1928), 343–4.

Peel to the House in the morning and actually saw the letter in Peel's dispatch-case.[1] Why, then, did he miss such a splendid opportunity? We will never know for certain. Perhaps Peel, who had the hypersensitivity on points of honour of a man only half belonging to the patrician world, refrained because it would be unfair to read out a personal communication.[2] If so, it is to his credit. One cannot easily imagine Palmerston or Russell or Stanley showing a similar delicacy. Disraeli was lucky, but the general impression of his conduct seems to have been adverse. No doubt much was said in the Lobbies and the Carlton that has not survived to posterity, and people drew their own conclusions. It is not an episode on which his admirers care to dwell.

At four o'clock in the morning of Saturday, May 16, the division was taken. The third reading of the Bill was carried by ninety-eight votes. Later that morning Disraeli must have read the news in the papers that Henrietta, widow of Sir Francis Sykes, had died the previous day at Little Missenden in Buckinghamshire, the very day of his great speech in the House.

4

The Corn Law Bill now went up to the House of Lords, where it might have been expected to have an even stormier passage than in the Commons. Curiously enough, however, no comparable effort seems to have been made by the protectionists to throw it out at this stage. Stanley delivered one of his slashing orations, but there is nothing to suggest that he organized opposition. The Bill passed its second reading on May 28 by forty-seven votes. There was clearly no longer any hope of postponing, let alone rejecting, the repeal of the Corn Laws.

Bentinck and Disraeli now turned their attention to revenge. They could not stop the Bill becoming law, but they might nevertheless eject the 'Arch Traitor' from office. Not that this was easy. a vote of no confidence would certainly be lost, and the Whigs were determined to keep Peel in until the Corn Law Bill had passed its third reading in the House of Lords – a matter of at least three weeks. But Disraeli acutely perceived that there was one useful,

[1] Goldwin Smith, *Reminiscences* (1910), 177.
[2] But the explanation sometimes offered that the letter was actually marked 'Confidential' is not correct. Disraeli did not take that precaution with either of his letters, British Museum, Add. MSS, 40487, ff.286–7, 290–1, although his wife did. ibid., ff.284–5.

though by no means infallible weapon to hand, the Irish Coercion Bill – or, as Bentinck called it, 'the anti-murder Bill' – which had still to pass its second reading in the House of Commons. There were signs that Lord John Russell and most of the Whigs who had supported the first reading would for various reasons oppose the second. If in addition any considerable number of protectionists could be induced to vote against the Bill, its defeat was certain. On such an issue the Government would be bound to resign or dissolve, and Lord George had convinced himself that they would never dissolve if only because so many of them were in danger of losing their seats. The difficulty was that Bentinck and his followers, apart from Disraeli, had nearly all voted, and some of them had spoken, for the first reading.

Fortunately, however, as Disraeli was quick to remind him, Bentinck had been prudent enough to prepare a retreat. He had declared that he was only willing to support the Bill if the Government showed a genuine belief in its urgency. Now it could be argued that by postponing the second reading of the Coercion Bill for over five weeks in order to take the later stages of the Corn Law Bill the Government had shown just such a lack of urgency as would justify Bentinck in reversing his previous vote. It was not a very strong argument, but it would serve.

Although no final decision had been taken by the party before the debate began on June 8, Bentinck resolved after an hour or so to take the plunge, to speak forcibly and early, thus setting the tone for the waverers. His speech was one of the most violent and intemperate that he had yet delivered. He declared that he voted against the Bill because the Government could not be trusted to use their powers. He referred to Peel as being 'supported by none but his forty paid janissaries and some seventy other renegades'. He accused Peel of having admitted in 1829 that he had changed his mind on the Catholic question in 1825, but of having none the less in 1827 concealed his conversion and 'chased and hunted an illustrious relative of mine to death', viz Canning – merely on the ground that the latter seemed likely to forward the cause of Catholic emancipation. 'A second time,' he ended, 'has the right honourable baronet insulted the honour of parliament and of the country, and it is now time that atonement should be made to the betrayed constituencies of the empire.'[1]

[1] *Hansard*, 3rd series, lxxxvii, 183.

Bentinck's allegations about Peel and Canning involved Disraeli. On June 12 Peel replied with a lengthy vindication of his conduct in 1827. He had not changed his mind in 1825, nor had he ever said so in 1829. And he asked why Bentinck, if he had really believed in such atrocious conduct, should have been his loyal supporter for the last ten years, and should only now for the first time have revealed his belief.[1] Bentinck could not, under the rules of procedure, speak again, and so he briefed Disraeli to reply.

The difficulty was that *Hansard* seemed to confirm Peel's account. But *Hansard* was admittedly corrected and revised by speakers themselves. Disraeli discovered in the *Mirror of Parliament*, which was an unofficial, but in general reliable, organ based on newspaper accounts by reputable parliamentary supporters, the exact admission on Peel's part alleged by Bentinck. This seemed a score for Bentinck. But Peel was able to show in his reply that the only newspaper report which contained the admission was that of *The Times*; this had been adopted by the *Mirror of Parliament*, but no one else had included the sentence in question. There were other ramifications and complications, but by the time he came to write his life of Bentinck, Disraeli was satisfied that *The Times* had misinterpreted Peel's remarks and that the charge was baseless. Indeed, six months after the rumpus he advised Bentinck, who never admitted being in the wrong, to drop the matter, despite some further evidence which the latter thought he had discovered to support his case.

The debate lasted for many days while the various factions in the House of Commons intrigued, organized and calculated against the critical day when the fate of Peel's Government would be determined. It was by no means a foregone conclusion. On June 25 the Speaker was able to announce that the Lords had passed the Corn Law Bill without amendment. The division on the second reading of the Coercion Bill was taken that night. Bentinck had come nowhere near carrying with him the 242 Tories who had originally voted against the repeal of the Corn Laws. Over a hundred now supported Peel. Some eighty abstained. But more than seventy voted with Bentinck and Disraeli, and they were enough together with Whigs, Radicals and Irish to defeat the Government by seventy-three. What the Duke of Wellington called 'a blackguard combination' had beaten Peel and turned him out of office for ever.

[1] ibid., 537-9.

He announced his resignation four days later, delivering an enco-
mium of Cobden which even scandalized a disciple as ardent as
Gladstone, and a self-congratulatory peroration which jarred on
many besides the protectionists. The Queen sent for Lord John
Russell. It was to be twenty-eight years before a Conservative
Prime Minister again headed a ministry with a clear majority in the
House of Commons.

After 1832, as we can now see, there had been three possible policies
for the Conservative party to adopt. They might have become a
party of old-fashioned Protestant squirearchical reaction, resisting
all change, internal *émigrés* outside the main stream of English
political life. They might, on the other hand, have endeavoured to
compromise with the new forces in politics, ally themselves with the
industrial professional world, with the men of property in general,
in order to resist quasi-revolutionary forces such as Chartism which
the spirit of reform had conjured up. Or they might as the party of
land have sought to exploit the differences between capital and
labour, between the millocracy and the mill hands, by a programme
of factory legislation and social reform, a sort of benevolent aristocratic paternalism.

The first of these policies was that of the 'Ultras' of the 1830s, of
Chandos, the Duke of Cumberland, and in some degree of Lyndhurst. It did not prevail, for it had one huge defect: it would have
condemned the Conservatives to the status of a perpetual minority
party. Broadly speaking, Peel adopted the second. He wished to
cement an alliance of moderate men against a Whig party that
seemed to be perpetual prey to the intrigue and agitation of extremists. He was not averse from social reform, but he thought that
in the end the condition of England question would be solved by
economic prosperity, by the removal of checks on industry, rather
than by state interventionism which was in any case anathema to
accepted views on political economy. Disraeli and his friends, however, favoured the third of these alternatives; not very coherently,
it is true, nor with any clear calculation as to the specific measures
which such a policy entailed. But in a general way Young England,
Shaftesbury, Oastler, Stephens, Ferrand, and intellectuals like
Southey and Lockhart, stood for this sort of approach, a union of
discontented industrial workers with aristocratic landowners
against factious Whigs, selfish factory-owners, and dissenting shop-

keepers, with their 'anti-national' allies in Ireland and Scotland. The snag in this policy, as Disraeli would find soon enough when he reached a position of responsibility, was that it ultimately presupposed extending the franchise to the working classes. They were no use as allies if they had no votes. But to do this in the atmosphere of the 1830s and 1840s, or indeed for many years after, was politically impossible. What could be achieved in very different circumstances in 1867 would not have had a chance twenty years earlier.

The difficulty was obvious before the crisis of 1846. Peel's policy, in fact, made much better sense, but it foundered on the rock of Corn Law repeal – an issue which had no connexion at all with the ideals of Young England or the sort of popular Toryism in which Disraeli and his friends were vaguely involved. Indeed, any analysis even of the earlier issues on which Disraeli opposed Peel shows that Young Englandism had very little to do with the matter. Over the Corn Law question the protectionists had a fair case on the merits of the policy, though historians have usually ignored it. Protectionists also had a case, perhaps a stronger one, against Peel's personal conduct and against the arguments he used to defend his actions. But from the point of view of the party as a viable alternative to Liberalism, Disraeli and Bentinck were pursuing a line that was politically negative and electorally disastrous. In fact, they were going back to the first of the three alternatives that confronted the party after 1832, the policy of the ultras and the agricultural reactionaries of the 1830s. The consequence was just what might have been predicted. The Conservatives became the minority party for forty years. In wrecking Peel's career, Bentinck and Disraeli came very near to wrecking his and their party too. Between 1846 and 1886 there was to be only one Conservative administration with a clear majority behind it in the House of Commons. All the rest were short-lived minority governments existing only because of their opponents' dissensions. Disraeli was to spend a longer time in opposition than almost any statesman of comparable stature in our history.

Part II

FRONT BENCH

CHAPTER XI

The Leadership

1846–9

1

The protectionists had taken their revenge. In a famous passage which should, one feels, be read to the sound of the roll of drums Disraeli in *Lord George Bentinck* details the names of the great county members who voted against Peel, the very flower of the old 'Country party'. They were irreconcilable. Indeed, only sheer hatred of the 'Arch-Traitor' would have induced them to vote down a measure which on all other grounds they supported and approved. As a result the new Conservative party of which they formed an essential if latterly forgotten element was split for ever, anyway in the form in which it had been so laboriously and patiently reconstructed by Peel from the debris of 1832.

Moreover, the line of cleavage was of crucial significance, both for Disraeli personally and for the future of his party. Nearly all the office-holders and men of ministerial calibre followed Peel. The protectionists chiefly consisted of that class of country squires and the sons of peers who entered Parliament not as a career but as part of their status, men who no more thought of office than a Justice of the Peace thought of elevation to the Judicial Bench. There were no leaders among them in the lower House. In the Lords there was Stanley, who remained undisputed master of the whole party for the next twenty years, but in the House of Commons Disraeli had a wonderful, indeed a unique opportunity. He found himself almost the only figure on his side capable of putting up the oratorical display essential for a parliamentary leader. At a single stride he had by-passed the entire official Tory hierarchy. Two years later, with the sudden death of Bentinck, apparently still in the prime of life, his position was even further enhanced. 'By this strange event', as the Duke of Argyll says in his memoirs, 'Disraeli was soon left absolutely alone, the only piece upon the board on that side of politics that was above the level of a pawn . . . He was like a subaltern in a great battle where every superior officer was killed or wounded.'[1] The situation has no parallel in our political history. Disraeli needed genius to get where he did, but he could never have managed it without quite extraordinary luck as well.

But the very circumstances which brought him to such a position in his party rendered that position a bleak and barren heritage. The classes which governed England both before and after 1832 were basically conservative with a small 'c'. They wished to preserve the Crown and Parliament, to retain the Church of England, the Justices of the Peace, the rights of property and inheritance, with no more concession than was necessary to the forces which were transforming society. Politics largely turned on just how much concession was necessary. For the second time in sixteen years the Tory party – or rather a majority of its members – seemed to have misjudged the amount needed. The first occasion was over parliamentary reform. On that issue and on the Corn Law crisis the governing class in effect decided that the high Tory policy would provoke into reality that perennial nightmare of early nineteenth-century England, violent revolution. In other words conservatism was not best maintained by supporting the Conservative party. Hence the long lease of power for the Whigs, who, especially when combined with the Peelites, seemed to offer a safer and more prudent administration than Bentinck and after him Disraeli could hope to do even under the control of an ex-Whig grandee like Stanley. A whole generation was to elapse and many great changes to occur before the Conservative party would once again command the support of the conservative classes.

Accordingly, when Lord John Russell took office on July 5 he was better placed than the figures of his party supporters suggested. The Whigs were outnumbered by eighty or ninety, but the protectionists were determined to keep Russell in if only to keep Peel out. They sat on the Government side of the House for the last weeks of the session, which were principally notable for a series of intemperate personal charges levelled by Bentinck against some of the ex-ministers. Even Disraeli felt obliged to defend his old friend Lyndhurst against one of these. The Peelites constituted the nominal opposition, but they, too, were anxious to support Russell – in order to keep out Stanley and Bentinck.

On July 18 the protectionists in both Houses gave a great dinner at Greenwich to the two leaders. Bentinck agreed to continue as

[1] Duke of Argyll, *Autobiography*, i, 279.

leader in the House of Commons, but declared that he looked on Stanley as leader of the party as a whole. Before the prorogation, which did not occur till August 28, Disraeli accompanied Bentinck to King's Lynn to address '500 substantial squires and yeomen' at a dinner, and thence to Waltham to address a similar gathering at luncheon. His changed status in the Tory world was signalized by an invitation to stay at Belvoir Castle. The Duke of Rutland no longer regarded his son's hero as 'a designing person'. Disraeli was received, he told Mary Anne, 'by six servants bowing in rows'.

At the end of the session he repaired to Bradenham. For a week or so he felt too languid and exhausted to write even to his closest friends. A similar prostration seems to have overcome Lord George Bentinck, who had gone to Welbeck to recuperate. 'I am fast relapsing into my natural dawdling and lazy habits,' he wrote to Disraeli on September 22, 'and can with difficulty get through the leaders of even *The Times*.' And he added despondently, '. . . in face of high prices, Railway Prosperity, and Potato Famine, depend upon it we shall have an uphill game to fight.'[1] There was very little doing for the moment in the political world. It is always mortifying for prophets of doom to find that everything goes on much the same. The repeal of the Corn Laws showed no signs of ruining agriculture. Bentinck and Disraeli could only adjure their friends to wait and see, and make preparations for the next session. But Bentinck had no more intention than Disraeli of ceasing from the political struggle. To the astonishment of the sporting and fashionable world assembled at Goodwood, the news broke that he had sold his stud, and abandoned racing entirely, doing so, moreover, at a moment when his prospects had seldom seemed brighter. That someone with such a position on the Turf should have given it all up for the frail hope of reversing free trade was a remarkable example of self-sacrifice, whatever one may think of the cause for which it was made. In 1848 Bentinck's former property, the colt *Surplice*, won the Derby. The following day Disraeli met him in the library of the House of Commons researching with gloomy demeanour into the price of sugar, which was once again the subject of parliamentary dispute.

He gave [writes Disraeli] a sort of superb groan:
'All my life I have been trying for this, and for what have I sacrificed it!' he murmured.

[1] Hughenden Papers, Box 89, B/XX/Be/11.

It was in vain to offer solace.

'You do not know what the Derby is,' he moaned out.

'Yes I do; it is the blue ribbon of the turf.'

'It is the blue ribbon of the turf,' he slowly repeated, and sitting down at the table, he buried himself in a folio of statistics.[1]

Disraeli spent the autumn and early winter on *Tancred*. He also took the opportunity of the lull in politics to give careful thought to his personal affairs, for it was clear that what he would have called 'a critical conjuncture' in his career was close to hand.

It required no immodesty on Disraeli's part to see that the effective leadership of the protectionist party in the lower House was likely to fall to him sooner or later. Bentinck's early death was not predictable, but his temper and temperament were. The chances of his lasting as leader for long were not high. Yet, although Disraeli was the obvious successor, it was essential for him to obtain a certain qualification. Bentinck's position as son of a duke permitted him to be a member for a borough. If Disraeli was to lead the Country party he needed all the social prestige he could get. It was essential to represent a county. Such constituencies were in general less venal than boroughs, the process of election more dignified, and frequently superfluous, for they were often uncontested. Disraeli was already beginning to have trouble with Shrewsbury even as he had with Maidstone. Clearly the right and proper place for him now was as Knight of the Shire for his beloved county of Buckingham. But there was a snag. A county member had to be, on however modest a scale, a landowner in his own right. How was this to be accomplished?

One possibility presumably, though it does not appear to be mentioned in any of Disraeli's calculations, was to wait for his father's death, which in the course of nature could not be long distant. On any view delay would have been the more prudent course, for his money affairs were still highly embarrassed. It is true that his wife had by 1842 settled £13,000 of his debts, and was apparently willing to provide as much again. Disraeli recorded these facts in a letter to his father to be opened only in the case of his own previous death, for he was anxious that Isaac should recompense Mary Anne out of his 'patrimony'.[2] But in 1846 his debts were probably about £15,000 to £20,000, in spite of his wife's generosity,

---

[1] *Lord George Bentinck*, 539.

[2] M. & B., iii, 147.

and the size of their joint income – in reality almost all hers – which was returned for tax purposes in 1843 at £7,695.[1]

At this moment, however, there came on to the market a property admirably suited to Disraeli's requirements. Hughenden Manor, a mile north of High Wycombe, had belonged to the Norris family, whom the Disraelis had known well since their own move to Bradenham only a couple of miles away. In 1845 John Norris died and his executors put up the place and estate for sale. The house was a white, stuccoed, three-story building of simple appearance, built probably at the end of the eighteenth century. The garden and lawns sloped down to the south, cutting through woods on either side. To the east the park fell away steeply towards the little church which lay in the grounds. The place was and is most attractive. The land consisted of about seven hundred and fifty acres and the rents in 1846 were reckoned to be a shade over a pound an acre, £763 per annum.

It was in many ways an ideal property, but the sum involved – nearly £35,000[2] – far exceeded Disraeli's resources or any free money still left with Mary Anne. At this juncture Lord George Bentinck stepped in. 'We have got all that Huendon [*sic*] matter to talk over',[3] he wrote to Disraeli on December 12, just before coming down to stay for the first time at Bradenham. No doubt the whole business was thrashed out fully then. The upshot was that Bentinck and his two brothers, Lord Titchfield and Lord Henry Bentinck, agreed to put up the money to make Disraeli a country gentleman. On the strength of this promise Disraeli decided to stand for Buckinghamshire in the general election of 1847.

The complicated negotiations which followed need not detain us. Disraeli, as one would expect, was an infuriating purchaser from the point of view of the vendors, and the affair took the best part of two years before completion in September 1848, the original dates fixed being first June then Christmas 1847. The excuse given was a dispute about the valuation of timber. But in reality Disraeli was in no position to produce the money in time for June, though Isaac advanced enough to prevent the whole thing collapsing; and in the

---

[1] Dividends were £3,974, rents were £3,721. It is fair to add that the latter figure included £1,500 for the house in Grosvenor Gate, and no doubt their disposable income would have to be reduced by an even larger figure on account of various outgoings.

[2] £27,700 for the land and advowson, and £7,250 for the timber.

[3] Hughenden Papers, Box 89, B/XX/Be/16.

autumn a disastrous financial crisis made it extremely difficult for even the Bentincks to obtain credit. By the end of the year the situation looked better. Bentinck, who evidently kept a close watch, wrote on December 24, 1847:

> The Huendon correspondence is conclusive to my mind in your favour. Delay, however, is everything, Interest of money and prices of timber going down & Publick Securities going up . . . I am confident delay should be your policy.[1]

Bentinck was right: the valuation of the timber, estimated at £8,127 by the vendors and at £7,313 by Disraeli's solicitor, was fixed by an arbitrator at £7,332, and agreed deductions reduced it to £7,250, a saving of nearly £900. Disraeli, however, continued to procrastinate, and a stiff letter survives from the vendors' solicitors on August 23, 1848, ending with the sentence: 'Neither our clients nor ourselves have been treated with that courtesy which we had a right to expect.'

In the end Disraeli temporarily borrowed £19,000 from his solicitors and from the bank. He also had the advantage of his patrimony, for Isaac died early in 1848. But the basis of his credit was a loan of £25,000 from the Bentincks. This had been promised but not finally effected, when on September 21 Bentinck suddenly died – a disaster which threatened the whole arrangement for Hughenden. Lord George was not an impoverished younger son; he already had ample means and could expect on his father's death, if Disraeli is to be believed, '20 or 30 thousand *per ann*, to say nothing of his chance of being Duke of Portland, his brother Titchfield, not being married, and very ailing'. As long as Bentinck lived Disraeli was safe, but he now would depend upon the two brothers whom he scarcely knew, and perhaps upon the aged Duke.

The latter was immensely rich, indeed a millionaire many times over, with an income of £180,000, but the very rich do not necessarily throw their money about. The two brothers were in great awe of their father, who must have made relations no easier by seldom communicating with them except in writing. Lord Henry saw Disraeli in the middle of October and told him that nothing had so far been said to the Duke, but that he and Titchfield hoped that Disraeli would not object if the Duke proposed to pay off the £25,000 in return for receiving the rents and becoming the mortgagee

[1] ibid., Box 89, B/XX/Bc/45.

of the whole estate. Disraeli replied that in that case he could only
sell the estate, pay off the debt, and resign the county.[1] Lord Henry
protested that the Duke would not dream of such a thing.

> Then I went on [Disraeli writes in his letter recounting the inter-
> view to Mary Anne] to the state of my affairs, observing that it
> would be no object to them and no pleasure to me unless I
> played the high game in public life; and that I could not do that
> without being on a rock. And then I went into certain details,
> showing that I could not undertake to play the great game, unless
> your income was clear. That was all I required and ample.[2]

Lord Henry begged him to say nothing to the Duke, and promised
to see what he could personally do. 'He remained with me four
hours,' Disraeli concludes, 'and appears more devoted than even
Lord G.'

The final outcome was that Lord Titchfield and Lord Henry
Bentinck lent Disraeli the £25,000 needed and the Duke was not
involved. We do not know exactly what the terms were, but it is
reasonable to guess that at the time, though a disagreeable change
occurred later, Titchfield, like Lord Henry, had no intention of
calling in his money, and that the whole transaction was conducted
in the spirit of Lord George's wishes that it should be a political not
a business affair, a contribution from one of the great landowning
families of England to enable their class to be represented by one of
the most brilliant men of the day.

Did Disraeli remember Lord Monmouth's words to Coningsby?

> And it is our own fault that we have let the chief power out of the
> hands of our own order. It was never thought of in the time of
> your great-grandfather, sir. And if a commoner were for a season
> permitted to be a nominal Premier to do the detail, there was
> always a secret committee of great 1688 nobles to give him his
> instructions.[3]

With his capacity for half-ironical analysis he may well have seen
the parallel. There was something wonderfully appropriate in this
action by one of the greatest of all the families made by the events
of 1688. The Bentincks had been Whigs until recently, but in

---

[1] He had been elected by now.
[2] Disraeli to Mrs Disraeli, October 18, 1848, quoted, M. & B., iii, 151–2. The exact
nature of the proposal which Disraeli was rejecting is not wholly clear. Evidently it
involved some sort of contingent liability on his wife.
[3] See above, p. 199.

changing to the other side they showed a more acute political feel than the Cavendishes or Russells for the trends of the time and the interests of their order. There was no real future for the Whig aristocracy in alliance with the Liberals, Radicals and Irish, although it was to be many years before this became apparent. But the trouble for the Bentincks and others who sensed this truth was that, anyway in the House of Commons, all the clever men were on the wrong side. This was why Lord George had thought of hiring a barrister to put his case for him. Here was a far better solution: no need to brief; no need to give secret instructions; simply a matter of financing a parliamentary genius who seemed to understand the true interests of the aristocracy better than they did themselves. It was a remarkable stroke, and, if we except the possible case of Burke, one without precedent in English history.

The Disraelis finally moved into Hughenden in the winter of 1848. During the course of the negotiations much had happened both in Disraeli's private and public life. On April 21, 1847, his mother died at the age of seventy-one. It is unlikely that the loss meant much to Disraeli except in so far as it affected his father and sister. Isaac had by now been totally blind for seven years and depended entirely upon Sarah and the faithful Tita. He did not long survive his wife, dying in Tita's arms on January 19 of the following year. He was eighty-one. Disraeli felt his father's death far more acutely. In spite of Isaac's occasional complaints of neglect, especially in the days of the affair with Henrietta, father and son were deeply devoted to each other. Benjamin admired Isaac's literary talent. Isaac admired Benjamin's and took a puzzled pride in his son's political rise, although not always understanding what it was all about. In the 'seventies Lord Rowton records Disraeli saying of his father:

> . . . He never could comprehend the attacks on Peel. 'He seems a good sort of man, and the only popular one in the country,' he would say. He never realized that D., not approving Peel's policy, saw the situation, and had the boldness to make the onslaught alone, confident in the truth of Cardinal de Retz's maxim, 'Il n'y a rien dans le monde qui n'ait son moment decisif: et le chef d'œuvre de la bonne conduite est de connoitre et de prendre ce moment' (D. has just pointed out this passage to me).[1]

But affection can often exist without full understanding. Disraeli was undoubtedly fond of his father. Rowton records how in 1866

---

[1] Hughenden Papers, Box 26, A/X/B/13, December 14, 1873.

Disraeli and the younger Stanley dined together at Bellamy's and drank a bottle of champagne to celebrate the hundredth anniversary of Isaac's birth. Now in 1848 Disraeli at once set about producing editions of his collected works, and wrote the colourful but inaccurate memoir mentioned earlier. Almost all the work was done by Sarah; so Disraeli told Lord Rowton when the latter expressed some surprise at Disraeli's admission that he had recently read for the first time a chapter of a book he was supposed to have edited twenty years earlier.[1]

Disraeli was his father's heir and sole executor. It is not certain how much he inherited. For probate purposes Isaac's personal property was declared at just under £11,000 of which one-third each went to Benjamin and Sarah, and one-sixth each to Ralph and James. Benjamin as eldest son also inherited the real property, but since land in those days did not have to be declared for probate and relevant papers are missing, there seems no means of ascertaining how much it was worth. It must have been a fair amount, unless we are to suppose that Isaac had been living on capital for the latter years of his life. Whatever it came to was, no doubt, swiftly engulfed by Disraeli's debts.

Bradenham itself did not belong to Isaac; so the home was broken up, and most of his library of 25,000 books sold at Sotheby's. Sarah departed to live with friends. Ralph, who already had chambers in London, continued in his employment as a clerk in Chancery at £400 a year. James went on farming the Manor Farm at Bradenham. Tita was the great problem. He had just announced his marriage to 'Harvey', who had been old Mrs D'Israeli's maid and was now housekeeper, 'an event which we suspected,' Disraeli told Sir Philip Rose,[2] 'had taken place some years previously'. The thought of the man who had solaced the last hours of Byron and Isaac D'Israeli accepting the usual fate of the retired butler and becoming keeper of a public house or a greengrocer's shop was not to be borne. Fortunately at this moment Disraeli met Sir John Hobhouse, Byron's old friend, who happened to be President of the Board of Control; he persuaded him to appoint Tita as a messenger, and all was well for the next ten years or so. But a fresh crisis arose when the Board was abolished in 1859. Luckily the Tories were in power, and the younger Stanley at the India Office which replaced the

[1] ibid., A/X/B/21, 'Easter Day', 1873.
[2] Rose's account is in Hughenden Papers, Box 27, A/XI/A/3.

Board agreed to appoint Tita as chief messenger, 'but without the liability of having to carry messages'. In 1874 Tita died, leaving 'Harvey' a widow. Once again fortune favoured the former Braden-ham *ménage*. Disraeli was now Prime Minister, and Queen Victoria at his request conferred a civil list pension of £50 a year upon Tita's relict.

2

Parliament reassembled on January 19, 1847. It was agreed that the peculiar seating which had resulted from the split in the Tory party in the last session could not very well be continued without in-convenience. The protectionists accordingly joined the Peelites on the Opposition benches, and Disraeli and Bentinck occupied the front bench with Peel, though it was tacitly understood that neither of them would sit next to him. It was a great thing for Disraeli to be on the front bench for the first time. He symbolized his transforma-tion from brilliant rebel to grave statesman by a corresponding change in dress and speech. Both became duller. He wore a suit of impeccable black, instead of the gorgeous colours of the past, and he spoke in a more weighty manner, avoiding the extravagance, the vituperation, and the imagery of his great philippics. Of course, he could never be wholly dull: his speeches still make far better reading than those of his contemporaries, but it is only rarely that they soar again with quite the abandon of those wonderful flights which destroyed Peel.

The general election was held in June and resulted in the return of about 325 Whigs, Liberals, Radicals and Irish, prepared to support the Government, and about 330 Conservatives, of whom some 230 were protectionists, the remaining 100 being in general supporters of Peel. The situation was therefore much as it had been before, and Russell's administration seemed secure, as long as there was no reconciliation between the Peelites and the Country party.

Disraeli was elected without a contest along with a Mr Du Pré, another Tory, and a Whig from the Cavendish family, later to be created Lord Chesham. In his election address he dwelt with pride upon the political contributions of men of Buckinghamshire. 'The parliamentary constitution of England was born in the bosom of the Chiltern Hills; as today our parliamentary career is terminated among its hundreds.' He referred to Hampden, Shelburne, Grenville, Chatham, Burke and, on a slight note of anticlimax, to the Chandos clause. He ended:

'Now let the men of the North who thought that they were to govern England – let them bring a political pedigree equal to that of the county of Buckingham.'

On the practical problems of the future Disraeli's principal pledge was to give free trade a fair run – both he and Bentinck took this view – and to support 'popular principles' against 'liberal opinions', ie local self-government against centralization, factory legislation against non-intervention, Justices of the Peace against Stipendiary magistrates, the rule of the local landed proprietors against Benthamite Civil Servants from London, a national Church independent of the state against Whig Erastianism.

> I hope [he said] ever to be found on the side of the people and of the Institutions of England. It is our Institutions that have made us free, and can alone keep us so; by the bulwark which they offer to the insidious encroachments of a convenient, yet enervating system of centralization which if left unchecked will prove fatal to the national character.

The general election came not a moment too soon for the Whigs. Even in the spring signs were beginning to multiply of an imminent financial crisis. In September, to quote Disraeli, it 'burst like a typhoon'. Numerous banks closed their doors. Money could not be got for less than 60 per cent, and an autumn session had to be held to grant indemnity to the Government for having authorized – very belatedly – the Bank of England to exceed the limit laid down in Peel's act for the issue of notes in excess of bullion, and thus provide the desperately needed credit.

Bentinck surveyed the scene with a sort of gloomy relish, attributing the disaster, naturally, to the repeal of the Corn Laws. Indeed, his only regret seems to have been that the situation was not even worse. On November 14 he wrote:

> The Dukes of Sutherland and Buccleuch in the Gazette would have had a great effect and brought those dull aristocrats to their senses. I fear such small game as the Duke of Roxburgh & Lord Bellhaven and Campbell of Islay will pass with less notice than Sir John Rae Reid Irving & Company in the Gazette. My two Ducal Friends are making a terrible outcry – the Dukes of Newcastle and Richmond at having their mortgages raised to 5 per

cent: they ought to glorify themselves that they are not fore-
closed.[1]

His real dread was that the crisis might somehow result in Peel's
being sent for, but this calamity was averted and by the end of the
year the worst of the panic was over.

Meanwhile a particularly embarrassing problem arose. In the
general election Baron Lionel de Rothschild had been elected Liberal
member for the City of London, his colleague being the Prime
Minister. Rothschild was, of course, a member of the Jewish faith
and it was impossible for him to take, as the law required, the
Parliamentary oath 'on the true faith of a Christian'. Clearly an
attempt would now be made by the Liberals to remove this dis-
ability. Equally clearly the great majority of the Tory party,
particularly the county members, would feel bound, as defenders
of the established Church, to resist the admission of MPs who,
though denying the divinity of Christ, would none the less be able
to legislate on the organization, worse still the doctrine, of the
Church of England. On December 16 Russell moved that the House
should consider the removal of the civil disabilities of Her Majesty's
Jewish subjects.

Disraeli had already set forth his highly unorthodox views on
Judaism and Christianity in *Tancred*, which had been published in
March. They were there for all to read. Nevertheless they might
have been regarded as mere extravaganza from a novelist's pen and
have done him no particular harm in his party, if he had not been
determined to assert them by vote and speech in the House of
Commons. Disraeli not only regarded Christianity as the completion, the logical fulfilment of Judaism, he also considered that
the Jews were entitled to be admitted to the House because theirs
had been the faith into which our Lord and His disciples were born.
'The very reason for admitting the Jews,' he said to the House, 'is
because they can show so near an affinity to you. Where is your
Christianity if you do not believe in their Judaism?' This was quite
a different argument from the orthodox liberal thesis that no one
should be excluded from the legislature on grounds of his religious
beliefs, however false those beliefs might seem to the majority of
members.

In *Tancred* Disraeli had gone so far as to argue that Christians

---

[1] Hughenden Papers, Box 89, B/XX/Be/42.

should be positively grateful to the Jews for having prevailed on the Romans to crucify Christ. He did not quite repeat this claim to the House of Commons, but his whole approach was deeply repugnant to the other members, and this repugnance was enhanced by his curious trick – unconscious self-revelation perhaps – of referring to '*your* Christianity', and what '*you* owe to this people', as if he felt himself, in some sense, alien to both sides; which indeed he was. He ended:

> Yes it is as a Christian that I will not take upon me the awful responsibility of excluding from the Legislature those who are of the religion in the bosom of which my Lord and Saviour was born . . . It is on the religious ground on the religious principle alone that I give my vote for the proposition of the Minister; and it is to those who have objected to it on that ground that I venture to address a statement of views which I hope they will accept, not from my words, but from the eternal truths upon which they are based.

Disraeli was repeatedly interrupted throughout his speech. High Tories were prepared to meet an argument based on toleration, not one based on the view that the Jewish religion was nearly as good as Christianity. When he sat down he was received in frosty silence from both sides of the house, apart from one or two angry cries of 'Divide'.

Surprisingly Bentinck also spoke in favour of admitting the Jews, though he did not use any of Disraeli's unorthodox arguments. He had been in favour of Catholic emancipation, and had voted for removing Jewish disabilities in 1830 and in 1833 on much the same ground. He had a straightforward old-fashioned Whiggish belief in religious liberty, and he was not now going to leave Disraeli in the lurch; although he seems to have been rather hazy about his own previous attitude.

> Ld Stanley and all the Party [he wrote to Disraeli on November 3] are pressing me very hard to surrender my opinions about the Jews. Has not Lord Stanley himself voted in favour of the Jews? I confess I don't know how I have voted myself but I cannot help thinking that Lord Stanley & I both voted in favour of the Jews.[1]

Bentinck's memory was correct. Stanley had voted for the Jews in his Whig days both in 1830 and in 1833, even as Bentinck had, but

---

[1] Hughenden Papers, Box 89, B/XX/Be/40.

he probably did not feel very strongly on the matter, and saw that it would be highly inexpedient to support the Jews now that he was leader of the Country party. Nor would he have felt any objection to leaving Disraeli out on a limb: from his point of view the more Disraeli damaged his prospects of becoming leader in the House of Commons, the better. Bentinck, too, did not care greatly about the merits of the case. He was actuated above all by loyalty to Disraeli.

> This Jewish question is a terrible annoyance [he wrote to Lord John Manners]. I never saw anything like the prejudice which exists against them. For my part I don't think it matters two straws whether they are in or out of Parliament . . . I am too ignorant to enter upon any learned line connected with 'Convocations' . . . but I don't like letting Disraeli vote by himself apart from the party: otherwise I might give in to the prejudices of the multitude. I am just starting for London and I feel like a condemned felon going to Botany Bay.[1]

In spite of an attack of influenza which would have fully justified his absence from the House, Bentinck spoke and voted for Russell's motion, which was carried by a large majority, although the protectionists voted against *en masse*.

Disraeli's most captious critics must find it hard to censure his conduct over the Jewish question. He had nothing to gain and much to lose by speaking as he did. The motion was sure to be carried anyway, and it would have been easy to abstain or absent himself. His career was in the balance. A great deal depended upon his presenting to the high Tory squires with their belief in Church and State the appearance of a 'sound man'. He had just become member for Bucks, and he was about to set up as a country gentleman at Hughenden. He had a good chance of living down his erratic past and securing the leadership of the party. Of course, the balance was not wholly one-sided: there were his remarks in *Tancred* which might have been thrown back at him with some disagreeable gibes if he had seemed evasive; there was his personal friendship with Rothschild. But Rothschild was politically a Liberal: to seat him was to instal an opponent. The gibes based on *Tancred* would soon have been forgotten. The overwhelming balance of advantage from a careerist point of view lay in silence and abstention.

Disraeli never flinched for one moment on this issue. It was to occupy Parliament at regular intervals for ten years, during which

---

[1] Whibley, *Lord John Manners*, i, 283.

Jewish Emancipation Bills were repeatedly carried in the lower and rejected in the upper House. He did not often speak again, but there was no need to do so, in view of the heavy majority for emancipation. He consistently voted according to his conscience – the allegations to the contrary have no substance[1] – and in 1858 had the satisfaction as leader of giving personal support to the Bill which finally settled the matter by a compromise allowing each House to make its own rules about the form of oath. Nor was this all. In his life of Bentinck published at the end of 1851 he repeated all his most politically obnoxious arguments in favour of the Jews; and with complete irrelevance to the theme of the book, for after a chapter of twenty-five pages on the subject he thoughtfully informs the reader on the first page of the next: 'These views, however, were not those which influenced Lord George Bentinck . . .' Courage was a quality which even his bitterest enemies could not deny him.

The immediate result of the Jewish debate was Bentinck's resignation from the leadership of the protectionists. One of the Whips conveyed to him the dissatisfaction of the party, and, without waiting to ascertain how widespread it really was, he seized the opportunity. He was depressed by influenza at the time, and, though in no way acting from pique or pride, was acutely conscious of the difficulties and frustrations attending his office. He also felt with some justice that he had been outmanœuvred by the Whips. Disraeli shared this view, and Bentinck himself put his finger on a major weakness in the party organization, writing to his short-lived successor, Lord Granby, when he pointed out that the Whips had been taking orders direct from Stanley and not from the leader of the Commons.

'I cannot help giving you this friendly advice . . . to appoint your own Whippers-in; and let them take their orders from you and no one else.'[2] As we shall see, Disraeli suffered the same difficulty, and Stanley's close relations with two Whips far from well disposed to the leader in the House of Commons were to be a source of trouble for him, too.

The succession caused an acute problem. Bentinck himself wanted Disraeli and was highly indignant when he was passed over. 'None of this could have happened, had you played a generous part', he wrote furiously to Stanley on February 9, 1848, and for several

[1] See M. & B., iii, 74–78, for a conclusive refutation.
[2] Whibley, *Lord John Manners*, i, 294.

months he refused to speak to his former chief. But Stanley and the
Whips were right for the time being to take the line they did.
Disraeli's speech on the Jewish question, regarded by many Conservatives as positively blasphemous, was still ringing in their ears.
If Bentinck had been driven out on this question it was *a fortiori*
impossible for Disraeli to succeed him. Had he not been out of
Parliament, Lord John Manners might possibly have been chosen
leader. In the end the choice fell on his brother, Lord Granby, who
it is idle to pretend was other than a stick. Protectionism was his
sole remedy for all the evils of the day. Elected on February 10, a
week after the session began, he had thrown in his hand by March 4,
conscious of his own inadequacy. Many people hoped that Bentinck
would return, but he refused to budge from his new seat on the
second bench below the gangway; Disraeli by mutual consent had
remained on the front bench to avoid the appearance of a complete
split in the party. No successor to Granby could be found, and for
the rest of the session the party was without any official leader in the
lower House, Stanley doing his best to guide affairs through the
medium of the two Whips. The result was, of course, complete confusion. In April, Manners noted in his diary a conversation with
Disraeli.

> . . . he said Stanley and G. Bentinck never speak: that Beresford,
> with Stanley, manages the party, the elections etc., just as he
> pleases: that about 50 men whom he calls the Imperial Guard
> stick heartily to G.B. and himself: about as many to Beresford
> and Newdegate:[1] that Lincoln and his friends are anxious for a
> junction: that G.B. has gone so far as to say that he bears no
> personal ill-will to L.[2]

Nothing came of the overtures from Lord Lincoln. Disraeli and
Bentinck made the principal speeches for their party, but their
relations with Stanley were anything but cordial for most of the
session. 'Is there a real Stanley?' Augustus Stafford records Disraeli
saying. 'I believe it is a mere myth sung to lull Newdegate.'[3] This
acid quip suggests that no love was lost between them. However,
towards the end of July Stanley accepted, with all signs of cordiality,
a dinner invitation to Grosvenor Gate, the object of which was to
patch up the quarrel between himself and Bentinck. This act of
mediation may well have brought Disraeli closer to Stanley and it is
significant that Stanley asked him to sum up for the session. He did

[1] The two Whips.   [2] Whibley, *Manners*, i, 298.   [3] ibid., 299.

so at the end of August with characteristic imagery, ridicule and zest.

There was much indeed to satirize. The Government had been fortunate to face so feeble an Opposition, for their own performance from the autumn session onwards had been lamentably incompetent. True, it was a difficult year, all Europe resounding to the hubbub of revolution and the crash of toppling thrones, and London enduring the last great Chartist demonstration. However, this scarcely warranted Sir Charles Wood's remarkable feat, unrivalled even by our own modern fiscal experts, of introducing four budgets in six months. Disraeli's mockery was seldom better displayed than on this subject and on the suspension of the Bank Charter Act, which he compared to the liquefaction of St Januarius's blood – 'the remedy is equally efficient and equally a hoax'. Long afterwards he told Lord Rowton that this was 'the speech which made me leader'.

3

On September 21, 1848, Bentinck suddenly died of a heart attack while walking alone from Welbeck in the afternoon to visit an old friend, Lord Manvers. He had often been in poor health, but he had seemed better recently and his death came as a complete shock. Disraeli was deeply moved at the loss of his colleague, benefactor and friend. Opinions of Lord George Bentinck are various and conflicting. He was not a good parliamentarian, ponderous, rigid and clumsy. Disraeli overstated his talents. Yet he certainly was not the mediocrity depicted by his enemies. He had great tenacity, and he worked very hard. His character contained serious blemishes, bad temper, obstinacy, vindictiveness and vilification. Yet there was sincerity, loyalty, courage and honour, too. It has been said that no one is a hero to his own valet – in the days when people had valets; but this at least was not true of Bentinck. A moving letter from his servant, Gardiner, survives among Disraeli's papers. After some routine communication he continues:

> . . . But I feel I have lost the *best friend* I ever had. He never gave me an angry word in the 4 years I had the honour to serve him; and I have that pleasant feeling that all the World could not give or take away, that of having served in Life and Death, and to the Grave, one of the Noblest by Nature that ever lived.[1]

[1] Hughenden Papers, Box 89, B/XX/Be/141, October 26, 1848.

To Disraeli, despite the gulf that existed between their interests and talents, Bentinck was intensely loyal, and very grateful. The Duke of Newcastle wrote in a letter of condolence on Bentinck's death:

> . . . you were his Prime Minister, his fellow labourer and most confidential friend & I know how warmly he felt towards you, how grateful he was and how deeply be felt himself to be indebted to you in all manner of ways.[1]

Disraeli at once set about collecting material for a laudatory biography of his friend, which he described in its last sentence as 'the portraiture of an ENGLISH WORTHY'. He called him there 'one of the great personages of debate', and in a parliamentary tribute made at the beginning of the next session said, 'He has left us the legacy of heroes: the memory of his great name, and the inspiration of his great example.' But Disraeli does not seem to have been wholly convinced by his own eulogy. He told Greville privately that Bentinck's deficiencies could never have been got over, 'and, as it had been proved that he could not lead an Opposition, still less would he have been able to lead a Government'. Stanley was even more severe; speaking to Queen Victoria in 1852 he said: if alive, Bentinck 'would have made confusion worse confounded'. Gladstone's verdict was different. 'If Bentinck had lived, with his strong will and dogged industry,' he told Morley, 'there might have been a wide rally for protection, but everybody knew that Dizzy did not care a straw about it, and Derby had not force and constancy enough.'[2] But this was an opinion given in 1891, and probably coloured by dislike of Disraeli.

What was to happen to the leadership of the party in the House of Commons? The chaos that resulted from Bentinck's resignation had rendered the party useless during the session of 1848. It was vital to avoid a repetition. But Disraeli, who was now the only man capable of leading, still remained unacceptable to a large section, perhaps a majority, of the protectionists, although there was a group which at once began to intrigue in his favour. Lord Henry Bentinck was its leading spirit, the Duke of Newcastle gave his support and, among the county members, R. A. Christopher, Sir John Trollope, William Miles, George Bankes and Sir John Buller. Disraeli was not

---

[1] Hughenden Papers, Box 89, B/XX/Be/140, October 22, 1848.
[2] Morley, iii, 465.

disposed to remain an idle spectator of these interesting manœuvres, and, although in the throes of moving from Bradenham to Hughenden, made frequent visits to London in order to lobby politicians and newspaper editors.

Three people, whose decisions were vital, continued to regard him with suspicion, Stanley and the two Whips, Newdegate and Beresford.

> I have been warned repeatedly [wrote Newdegate to Stanley] not to trust Disraeli, while I see nothing in his public conduct to justify the want of confidence so many seem to feel. This I conclude is attributable to some circumstances of his earlier life with which I am not familiar, but have little doubt you are. I can scarcely help believing there must be some foundation for so general an opinion as I have alluded to, and it makes me very uneasy.[1]

The circumstances to which Newdegate alluded are easy to guess. It was a fair time since the scandal of the visit by Henrietta and Lyndhurst to Bradenham, but if Sir Philip Rose could write in 1882 that he had 'had it thrown in his teeth . . . within very recent years', how much stronger must such feelings have been in 1848. Add to this rumours of Disraeli's past conduct over *Vivian Grey*, the continued refusal of the *Quarterly Review* even to mention his name, the alleged tergiversations in his early political career, his rickety finances, the extravagancies of his novels, his views on the Jewish question, his mysterious half-foreign appearance, and the virulent abuse, much of which stuck, hurled at him by malignant journalists. No wonder Greville could write of him in 1847 that he had 'a character so disreputable that he could not be trusted'. It is not surprising that Stanley, who had personal reasons of his own for disliking Disraeli, should have tried to find someone else in place of Bentinck. His choice lighted on J. C. Herries, an elderly dug-out who had begun life as a Treasury clerk in 1798, working his way up to Chancellor of the Exchequer in Goderich's administration, and whose sole asset was that almost alone of the protectionists he had some degree of official experience.

Stanley wrote a long and elaborate letter to Disraeli from Knowsley on December 21. After observing that Disraeli's talents would always give him 'a commanding position in the House and a preponderating influence in the Party', he went on to explain that

[1] M. & B., iii, 120–1.

the party 'from whatever cause' would not give 'a general and
cheerful approval' if he were formally elected leader. He therefore
paid him 'the much higher compliment' of asking him to waive his
claim and to 'give a generous support to a Leader of abilities inferior
to your own, who might command a more general feeling in his
favour'.[1]

He wrote at the same time to Newdegate, 'I hope . . . that
Disraeli will have the good sense to acquiesce in, and aid, the
arrangement. I have never seen of late years any reason to distrust
him, and I think he will run straight, but he would not be acceptable
as leader.'[2]

Stanley reckoned without his man. Disraeli had no intention of
assisting in any such arrangement. He may have been aware of his
unpopularity in some quarters, but he knew that he had some very
active supporters, and that in ability he towered above the collection
of incoherent squires who, interspersed with one or two super-
annuated official men, occupied the benches of the protectionist
party. His reply[3] beginning, 'My dear Lord', and ending, 'Pray
believe me, my dear Lord Stanley, yours sincerely B. Disraeli' was
'cold but civil', as Greville put it.

> The office of leader of the Conservative party in the H. of C., at
> the present day, is to uphold the aristocratic settlement of this
> country. That is the only question at stake, however manifold
> may be the forms which it assumes in public discussion and how-
> ever various the knowledge and the labor which it requires. It is
> an office which, in my opinion, requires the devotion, perhaps the
> sacrifice of a life.

The man who undertook it, he went on, needed the warm personal
regard of his supporters. Had Stanley still been in the House of
Commons, Disraeli would gladly have served under his banner.
'Honor and personal feelings . . . attached me to George Bentinck
in his able but hopeless career.' But now there were no longer any
personal ties. He did not wish to sacrifice 'interesting pursuits,
health, and a happy hearth, for a political career which can bring
one little fame'. He felt that he could do more 'to uphold the cause'
in an independent position 'by acting alone and unshackled than if
I fell into the party discipline which you intimate'. He ended by
recommending 'the water cure' for Stanley's gout and congratulat-
ing him on his son's election for Lynn. It was a masterly letter.

[1] ibid., 121–4.   [2] ibid., 126.   [3] ibid., 124–6.

Stanley was too old a hand not to know what was usually involved in upholding the cause by 'acting alone and unshackled'. Nine times out of ten it meant trouble, and he could easily envisage the party dissolving into fragments if Disraeli took a different line from Herries. In any case Herries proceeded to refuse the leadership. Stanley now wrote a much more accommodating letter to Disraeli, declaring that he had no axe to grind and was prepared to act with anyone whom the party would agree on as a leader, whether Herries, Granby or Disraeli. This was on January 6, 1849, and Parliament was due to meet on February 2. Much intrigue followed and Lord Henry Bentinck even gave up hunting in order to forward Disraeli's candidature. It was now the turn of Beresford, the other Whip, to express alarm to Stanley. Early in January he said that he had discovered – rather belatedly, it would seem – 'a deep intrigue to force Disraeli on us as Leader'. He was willing to admit the latter's superiority and would not try to create disunion if the party really wanted Disraeli. But he did not mean 'to assist in an arrangement which I verily believe will bring great obloquy upon a Party, which I have joined from principle and which has its weight from character'. [1]

Stanley, however, saw that it was pointless to resist any longer. There was no possibility of finding someone whom Disraeli would accept as a second Bentinck. He was bound to be the real leader in the Commons, unless the party threw him off altogether, and this would have been madness. The most that could be done was to save the faces of the Whips and Disraeli's numerous personal enemies by an arrangement which would at least in form keep the question of the leadership open. Stanley bethought himself of a suggestion of Herries that the leadership should, as it were, be put into commission. He suggested, Disraeli told his wife on January 31, a committee of three with equal power consisting of Disraeli, Herries and Granby; 'that I should or rather must be the real leader; that this would remove all jealousies for the moment'. When Granby succeeded as Duke of Rutland, Disraeli would become titular as well as real leader. Disraeli went on: '[Stanley] was friendly and cordial. Says it is all over with the party if I retire. Refused: but at his request left it open as he has not yet even consulted Granby.'[2]

Although Disraeli never formally withdrew his refusal, he tacitly accepted this ludicrous arrangement in order to demonstrate its

[1] ibid., 315.   [2] ibid., 138.

absurdity. Herries was a mere hack. As for Granby, Disraeli's candid view, before he became leader of Young England and intimately connected with Granby's brother, Lord John Manners, is clear enough from a letter to his wife in 1841: 'Granby made a speech. The Radicals were awestruck at a future Duke & listened with open mouths to his high Castilian emptiness.'[1] Stanley did his best to make the committee a reality, and it is not true, in spite of Disraeli's own account, that he became formally leader in 1849. Stanley consulted Herries on occasions and often adjured Disraeli to do so. The Whips regarded themselves as primarily responsible to Stanley rather than to anyone else for the next two years, and it was not until the winter of 1851–2 that the committee was actually dissolved when Granby resigned. But Disraeli was the effective leader long before that, and the position of the triumvirate was aptly summarized by Aberdeen to George Smythe – 'Sièyes, Roger Ducos, and Napoleon Bonaparte'.[2]

At this inopportune moment when Disraeli was endeavouring to consolidate a reputation for solidity and soundness a spectre from his past suddenly reappeared. Robert Messer, the stockbroker's son, third member of the trio whose speculations in 1824–6 ended so disastrously, began to bombard him with dunning letters. He had, he said, been owed in 1831 as much as £1,500 and had received over the years mere trifles at irregular intervals amounting to far less than the interest on the debt. Disraeli replied by declining to communicate except through his solicitor, Mr Wright. Messer, correctly suspecting that he intended to repudiate the debt, wrote back quoting some of Disraeli's own letters to him in 1831. One is enough to show their tenor.

> I have not literally a shilling in the World . . . I have no friend in the World that I can ask to lend me five pounds – I have trespassed on my friends too much. In addition to all this I need hardly say that I have not a tradesman who is paid . . . I declare most solemnly that I have not at this moment the money wherewith to pay my journey to the metropolis . . .

After declaring that all he demanded was £12. 10s. per quarter until he could establish himself in a permanent position, Messer ended: 'From your position in Society & mode of living I feel assured you

[1] Hughenden Papers, Box 2, A/I/A/170, n.d., probably February 23, 1841.
[2] M. & B., iii, 139.

cd pay so small a sum.'[1] This was written on March 19, 1849. Before Disraeli could take any action Wright had interviewed Messer and informed him that Disraeli considered that he had no claim on him at all, and whatever he paid was out of 'pure pity' and 'extreme kindness' and was *ex gratia*. Messer wrote an indignant letter on March 23. 'I have,' he said, 'carefully preserved all your letters and memoranda which passed between us during the period of the transactions out of which my claim arises – viz. in 1825 . . . and have also my accounts in perfect order.'[2] He added that he owed to his own character as a man of honour to place the papers before some disinterested third party who could judge where the merits of the case lay. Disraeli decided to compromise. It would have been awkward for someone in the process of establishing himself as leader of his party to have letters of this sort circulated at all widely. Messer in the end alleged a debt of £1,100; Disraeli's solicitor managed to compromise it at £500 to be paid in instalments with interest over seven years, the first instalment to be followed by the return of all his letters to Messer. How far Messer was blackmailing or how far the debt was genuine there is no means of knowing.[3] Two years earlier in 1847 Disraeli had used his good offices to procure Messer a job with the railway magnate 'King' Hudson, and there was no suggestion then of a pecuniary claim in Messer's letter thanking him.[4] On the other hand, it is not likely that Disraeli would have paid unless he thought Messer had some sort of case. Disraeli's finances continued long after this to be erratic, incoherent and uncertain, but this is the last we hear of the early imprudences which cost him so much difficulty for nearly a quarter of a century.

[1] Hughenden Papers, Box 17, A/V/A/20, March 19, 1849.

[2] ibid., Box 17, A/V/A/21, March 23, 1849.

[3] In a letter to Wright, Disraeli wrote on March 25: 'Observe his date *1825*. The transactions commenced in *1823* & he has never given any account of them 'altho he received from Evans between 2 & 3000 £. Why he mentions *1825* is that that was the period *I* called on him in consequence of his being *forbidden* any longer to come to the office. I forgot that last fact (the cause of my being sent) but it is important at least for yr appreciation of all the circes.'

[4] August 20, 1847, endorsed by Disraeli, 'NB. He received from Mr. Hudson an appointment of £100 pr ann: with a certain prospect of promotion D.' Hughenden Papers, Box 17, A/V/A/18.

CHAPTER XII

The Political Scene
1846–68

1

Before we consider the career of Disraeli during his time as Derby's[1] second-in-command, it is worth glancing at the political geography which determined his actions and decisions. For the period between 1846 and 1868 has features of its own which distinguish it both from the preceding period and even more sharply from the era ushered in by the Second Reform Act. All periods of history are periods of transition, but some are more transitional than others. In a broad sense the thirty-five years between the two Reform Acts are years of change from a system in which the Crown was the dominant influence in Parliament to a system in which a mass electorate began increasingly to call the tune. The Crown had been, and the electorate was to be, a stabilizing influence in politics, in the sense that both, for diverse reasons, tended to produce governments which could control Parliament, and survive from one general election to the next. Crown patronage exercised through ministers was the basic reason which kept parties together before 1832; after 1867 it was to be the 'caucuses', those great extra-parliamentary organizations with their slogans, funds and discouragement of independent action by all but the hardiest rebel.

Neither of these factors operated effectively in the period under discussion. The twilight of royal government had begun long before 1832, with the gradual reduction of jobbery and patronage over the years. The Reform Act indirectly weakened still further the power of the executive over the legislature and, as a corollary, of the Crown over either. True, the royal eyes did not always seem aware of the gathering darkness: hence the semi-anachronistic actions of William IV, and the interventions of Queen Victoria and the Prince Consort, which make sense only if one presupposes a constitutional balance of forces already extinct.

[1] Stanley succeeded to the earldom of Derby in June 1851, and is referred to as Derby throughout this chapter.

But for a long time nothing emerged to compensate the executive for its loss of power. In the end, the place of Crown patronage was to be taken by party, and the importance of party even in the 1830s and 1840s should not be underestimated. On the contrary the provisions of the Reform Act gave a notable impetus to party organization through the need for registration of voters and many other matters. It was the era, too, of the great political clubs, the Reform and the Carlton, the effective headquarters of the two sides. Nevertheless, in a system where Parliament represented such a limited section of the population and where general elections far from being general were rather agglomerations of particular elections fought on local issues, or compromised by local bargains, party could not have the influence it was to have later. That influence depended upon the widening of the franchise and has increased with every stage in that process. For when once Parliament organized on party lines represents the whole nation also organized on party lines, politicians can no longer plausibly appeal against party discipline to a public opinion which is not expressed in Parliament at all.

But in the period between the Reform Acts this state of affairs lay well into the future. Only one in seven of the adult male population of the whole United Kingdom had the vote, in England and Wales one in five. Although the really scandalous pocket boroughs had disappeared, there still remained a large number where 'influence' in the old sense of the word had the final say. Moreover, successive general elections sharply differed from their modern counterparts in that a high proportion of seats, sometimes more than half, were not contested at all. In these circumstances the modern concept of a party programme and pledges, or the doctrine – highly dubious even today – of the 'mandate' had little significance to the average member, and still less to responsible statesmen who had to consider public opinion and national needs represented only partially, or not at all, in the House of Commons. This fact is, of course, the principal justification for Peel in 1846, and explains the paradox that, at the moment of his downfall so ingeniously encompassed by Disraeli and Bentinck, he was probably the most popular man in England.

The great difficulty, then, which every ministry from 1832 to 1868 encountered was the indiscipline of its supporters, an indiscipline which could not be countered either by the use of patronage

or by an appeal to party solidarity. Every government sooner or
later found its supporters split into warring factions. The problem
posed by Peel during the Reform Bill crisis – how is the King's
Government to be carried on? – was no mere bogy, it was real and
urgent. The difficulty could sometimes be overcome if certain conditions prevailed. One of these was the presence of a powerful figure
who dominated his fractious supporters by sheer force of personality, as Peel himself did from 1841 to 1846. Another was when
strong feelings, divided on party lines, produced a reasonable degree
of discipline; for example, the Ministerialists kept more or less
together from 1830 to 1834, and rallied again after 1835 in order to
preserve the gains of the Reform Bill; they displayed similar co-
hesion from 1846 until 1851 in order to keep out the Protectionists.
Such interludes were rare. There were six parliaments between 1841
and 1868. In only one of them did the Government which commanded the support of the House of Commons at the beginning retain
it till the dissolution: this was Palmerston's from 1859 to 1865. In
every other case the House of Commons before it was dissolved
brought about the resignation of at least one administration, sometimes two, together with numerous Cabinet crises. Today we talk –
or we did until the psephologists sniffed contemptuously at the
notion – about the floating vote in the electorate. In those days the
floating vote was to be found not so much in the electorate, for
successive elections, anyway after 1847 caused surprisingly little
change, as in the House of Commons itself. Parliament then truly
was what in legal theory it still is, a sovereign body to which Cabinets were really, not fictitiously, responsible, and which could make
and unmake governments at will.

The twenty-two years following the repeal of the Corn Laws saw
the emergence of no great issue which could stimulate party loyalty,
and of no single leader, except perhaps Palmerston after 1859, who
could inspire personal loyalty, sufficient to offset the natural
incoherence of politics. It was a period of easy-going rivalry between a number of aristocratic factions, to which the mass of the
country was content to leave government, as long as prosperity
rose, taxes fell, free trade remained sacrosanct, and British prestige
was upheld against all comers. It is often said that the 1832 Reform
Bill gave political power to 'the middle class'. That concept begs
many questions, but without discussing them here, we may safely
say that on no plausible definition of the middle classes can the

proposition be justified as it stands. Parliament could not disregard the wishes of the northern manufacturers and their ancilliaries, nor of the great commercial interests in the country: hence the Reform Act of 1832 and the fiscal revolution initiated by Peel. But the 'middle classes' were not in a position, nor did they wish, to dominate Parliament. The political influence of land was still immense. As late as 1870 four hundred peers were reckoned to own over one-sixth of the whole surface of the country. It is not surprising that Cabinet and Parliament, lower as well as upper House, were overwhelmingly aristocratic in composition.

For this was the real hey-day of that 'Venetian constitution' which, Disraeli believed, had dominated eighteenth-century England, reduced the King to a mere 'doge', and thus 'in the selfish strife of factions . . . blotted out of the history of England, the Monarch and the Multitude'. In fact, Disraeli's picture of eighteenth-century politics is a caricature, and the monarch was very far from being a doge. But it was a much truer picture of the situation in his own day. Disraeli had no real historical sense; he wrote propaganda, not history, and projected the circumstances of his own times into the past. Between 1832 and 1867 the monarch was indeed on the way to becoming a doge, although the very confusion of parties left the Crown with a residue of real power; and 'the multitude', balked of a voice in Parliament and expressing itself in the wild vagaries of Chartism, might well appear to have been blotted out, if not from history, at least from the calculations of politicians. But the power of the 'Venetian' aristocracy was immense. Examples can be multiplied. Whole counties took their political colour from their leading '*magnifico*'. Why, as Professor Gash pertinently observes, should Bedfordshire have been Whig or Buckinghamshire Tory, unless it was because the Duke of Bedford was the one and the Duke of Buckingham the other?[1] Palmerston's last Cabinet had three dukes and six peers or sons of peers. Cobden wrote to a friend in 1858:

During my experience the higher classes never stood so high in relative social and political rank compared with the other classes as at present. The middle classes have been content with the very crumbs from their table . . . Half a dozen great families meet at Walmer and dispose of the rank and file of the [Liberal] party just as I do the lambs which I am now selling for your aldermen's table.

[1] *Politics in the Age of Peel*, 185.

The political scene was characterized by another feature. Not only did general elections change the political pattern little if at all, but that pattern was itself a curiously unsatisfactory one. Of the two aristocratic groups or 'factions', on which governments might plausibly be based, neither could command unaided at any time a clear majority in the House of Commons. The Derbyite Conservatives were the larger of the two, but their numbers, though rising from about 230 in the Parliament of 1847 to '280 and more on the muster roll'[1] in 1852, sank to 260 in 1857 and never achieved a clear majority until after Derby's death. The Whigs are less easy to estimate, for they shade imperceptibly into the Liberals, and could usually count on the Radicals. But it is clear that they were a smaller party than the Conservatives.

Since neither could govern without extraneous support and since elections gave such inconclusive results, politics or the struggle for power was largely a matter of bargaining with the other groups in Parliament. Of these there were three which counted: the Peelites, the Irish and the Radicals. It was to be a fundamental difficulty for Derby and Disraeli throughout that, however much these groups might distrust the Whigs, they distrusted the Conservatives even more. The Peelites were the most hopeful converts, and after the death of Peel in 1850 and Derby's and Disraeli's abandonment of protection in 1852, there seemed no obvious difference of principle why they should not have rejoined their old party. A large number of the rank and file of the hundred or so who followed Peel in 1847 in fact did so. But the leaders would not, and it was they who counted, for they were men of ability and ministerial experience, 'men of business', precisely the reinforcement which the Conservatives so desperately needed to give their front benches a decent appearance: men like Graham, Gladstone, Dalhousie, Lincoln, Sidney Herbert, Cardwell in the House of Commons, and Aberdeen, Ellenborough, Canning in the House of Lords; all of them as Gladstone put it 'for one reason or another much above *par*', adding that there was not a 'dandy' or 'coxcomb' among them.[2] The detailed circumstances in which Derby's offers were declined will be discussed later, but it is clear from the outset that the overriding cause was not political principle but personal

---

[1] M. & B., iv, 76, quoting Disraeli to Mrs Brydges Willyams, April 13, 1857.
[2] Quoted by J. B. Conacher, 'Peel and the Peelites 1846–50', *English Historical Review*, LXXIII (1958), 431–52.

dislike for Disraeli, the man who had with relentless invective driven their beloved leader from office.

The other groups can be more speedily dismissed. The Radicals might inveigh like Cobden against the prestige of 'the higher classes', in the Liberal party, but they were not likely to do any better by supporting the Conservatives. Disraeli flirted occasionally with the idea of an alliance with Bright whom he liked, and dined with him from time to time, but nothing serious came of it. As for the Irish, although they did not always support the Whigs and were to bring down Russell in 1852 in revenge for his reckless no-popery campaign of the previous year, they were not likely to ally with the party of the Anglican establishment or with the man whom O'Connell had called 'Scorpion Stanley' and who was widely regarded as one of the deadliest enemies of Irish nationalist and Roman Catholic claims. Here again Disraeli made some tentative gestures of conciliation, particularly in 1859, when Whig foreign policy was favourable to the unification of Italy and therefore hostile to the temporal power of the Pope, but Derby quickly quashed the movement. The Irish must be counted as an element in Whig strength for most of the period, although a capricious and erratic one.

The Whigs, then, had most of the cards in their hands, but not quite all. Otherwise they would have been in office the whole time. Although the Peelites, Radicals and Irish could usually be relied on to help to turn the Conservatives out, they could not always be trusted to keep the Whigs in. The Peelites with their high-minded qualms of conscience, and Gladstone's inability to make up his mind which side he was on, were a factor almost as incalculable as the Irish. The Radicals were very far from being a homogeneous or even always a distinguishable group. There were semi-pacifist Radicals, like Cobden and Bright. There were bellicose jingo Radicals like Roebuck, whose motion brought down the Aberdeen Government in the Crimean War. Then, the Whigs had their own internal feuds. From the day that Russell under royal pressure dismissed Palmerston in 1851 until the latter's second premiership began in 1859, they were divided into two factions which constantly intrigued against one another. Palmerston soon had his revenge on Russell, thus giving Derby his first brief administration in 1852. Russell got his own back by helping to eject Palmerston in 1858 and Derby and Disraeli were in again. The two Whig leaders each had a rallying cry to appeal to the uncommitted groups and to public opinion. Russell's was a further instalment of parliamentary reform, but this never really 'took'. Palmerston's was far more effective, jingoism and gunboats, and he won. In 1859 Russell consented to serve under him. Palmerston was Prime Minister till his death in 1865. Then Russell came into his own, introduced his Reform Bill, broke his party, and let in Derby and Disraeli for the third time in 1866. But three brief minority administrations accounting for little more than four out of twenty-two years do not amount to much. The Whigs for all their factiousness and quarrels provided the normal Government of the day.

To consider the plight of the Conservative party after 1846 it is necessary to look for a moment at its past history. In the hey-day of its supremacy from 1784 to 1830 its strength had been that it was an alliance between the country squires whose support was essential for any government, and the new class of efficient administrators, official men or 'men of business' to whom the Crown was willing to entrust its patronage in Church and State in return for carrying on the King's Government; these were men like Pitt, Liverpool, Huskisson, Canning, Peel. The policy of the Tory party was the policy of the official men, but they had to take account of the interests and prejudices of the squirearchy, whose votes were just as important to them as crown patronage. In addition the Tories could rely on the Church, a substantial section of the great landed aristocracy, and a considerable support from certain business and commercial interests.

The events of 1829 to 1832 seemed to have shattered this alliance irreparably. The problems of Catholic emancipation and parliamentary reform broke the old Tory party into contending factions. The Whigs were allowed in, and by shaping the new constituencies seemed to have consolidated their power for many years to come. But thanks to the genius of Peel, the somnolence of Melbourne, and the genuine alarm caused by Whig alliances with the Irish and Radicals, the old Tory party, now called Conservative, was soon reconstructed. By 1841 Peel, the pupil of Liverpool, had effectively applied his former chief's principles in the changed circumstances of the post-Reform-Act era, and was rewarded by victory at the polls. His Cabinet was the ablest of the century, and he enjoyed the support of the country gentry, the Crown and much of the business community, too. He had achieved what would today be called a 'consensus' of moderate men of property from all classes banded against revolution but ready to accept cautious change.

But even Peel failed to surmount the Corn Law crisis. The policy of the Cabinet and the interests of the Country party were irreconcilably opposed. The party broke into two bitterly hostile sections and, with the exception of Stanley, every man of official rank and ministerial experience followed Peel. The party therefore was confronted after 1846 with a new problem. Hitherto it had been the party of the able administrator as well as of the county member with his broad acres. Its leaders were more efficient than those of the Whig party. It was less exclusive socially and offered much more of a career to the talents. Now, however, its able administrators had vanished: they were all Peelites. The party would for the first time have to depend upon the country squires, not merely for silent votes ('the finest brute-vote in creation', as Bagehot put put it), but for speeches. The county members would actually have to read Blue Books and reports, understand Board of Trade returns and, if fortune favoured them, even take office. Of course, this situation gave a wonderful opportunity to Disraeli. He would not otherwise have become leader in the House of Commons when he did. But it also meant that the actual task of leading the party was infinitely harder, and the hope of gaining office for any length of time slender in the extreme.

Of the assets which Peel had acquired or inherited in 1841, only the Church, the country squirearchy and a section of the territorial aristocracy remained. The principal commercial interests were on the side of free trade, and the Crown, the traditional ally of the party, was decisively alienated. Queen Victoria might refer to Russell and Palmerston as 'those dreadful old men', but neither she nor Prince Albert bore any love for the protectionists. Their approval was reserved for the Peelites, who like the Prince were earnest, efficient and addicted to political economy. Bentinck, aware of this *entente*, had at one time – such was his fury against the Court – contemplated moving for the repeal of the Regency Act which made the Prince Consort regent in the event of a royal minority. True, Bentinck was no longer on the stage. But Disraeli was regarded with even more aversion. 'He has not one particle of the gentleman in his composition', wrote the Prince. Derby seems to have been scarcely less disliked. The importance of court approval can easily be overestimated; there was no question in the 1850s of the monarch's prejudice having the effect that it had had half a century earlier. But the Crown was not a complete cipher, and the very confusion of politics gave it an influence at this time, which disappeared later when the Party system became more rigid after 1867. Even after that the Queen had a considerable nuisance value, as Gladstone was to experience on many occasions. Certainly at this time it was better to have the Court with you than against you. Equally certainly its goodwill was an asset which Derby and Disraeli did not possess.

To rebuild the Conservatives as an effective force in politics, a genuine alternative to the dominant Whig-Liberal party, was bound to be a difficult task, and Disraeli could not set about it as he pleased. At every step he had Derby's opinions to consider, and he had to take account of the prejudices of the party. For it was not only true that the groups and interests which he had to woo were profoundly suspicious of the Country party, it was also true that the Country party was scarcely less suspicious of its potential allies. But Disraeli had four great assets: he was immensely hard-working; he was ready to trim his sails; he had no use for lost causes; and he had already posed the question which has vexed Conservatives ever since – what will you conserve? He had not answered it completely, but he had discovered at least a negative aspect of the answer: there is no need to conserve the disabilities imposed upon you by your political adversaries.

2

In his letter to Derby about the leadership Disraeli defined the task of the Conservative leader as being 'to uphold the aristocratic settlement of this country. That is the only question at stake however manifold may be the forms which it assumes . . .' This assertion is the key to Disraeli's policy for the rest of his life. It represented his profoundest conviction and, through all the labyrinthine twists and turns of his bewildering policy, it remained to the end his guiding purpose. It is therefore important to know what he meant by 'aristocratic settlement' and why he believed in it.

He did not equate aristocracy with oligarchy: that, in Disraeli's view, was the sin of the great Whig families who, having installed themselves by what he liked to call a *coup d'état* in 1832, had preserved their power by an alliance with anti-national and basically anti-aristocratic forces such as the Irish, the 'Scotch', the dissenting shopkeepers and the Manchester manufacturers. The Whigs were a selfish clique who in their greed for power and place had betrayed the true interests of their class. They were too clever, too fond of abstract theories, too much centred on London and, despite their huge estates, insufficiently rooted in the realities of their own countryside. The aristocratic settlement which Disraeli wished to preserve was not the rule of these self-confident, casual and cosmopolitan grandees.

He had in mind, rather, the whole ordered hierarchy of rural England epitomized in his own county of Buckinghamshire. It was the world so brilliantly portrayed by Trollope, a world of careful gradations, headed by such dignitaries as the Lord Lieutenant, the county members, and the Bishop, containing its Whiggish 'magnificoes' in the form of a few great landowning peers, perhaps even a duke, but broadly and firmly based upon a wealthy Tory residential squirearchy whose substantial estates covered the country. This was the class which, in alliance with the clergy as junior partners, effectively governed a great part of England. They constituted at quarter sessions the legislature and judiciary of the county. Their capital and their keen interest in all that pertained to the land ensured the prosperity of the tenant farmers and so, at one remove, that of all the multifarious 'interests' which depended upon agriculture. They were unfashionable and cut no ice outside their own localities, but they were the solid backbone of rural England.

> You won't be amused [Disraeli wrote in April 1857 from Hughenden to Lady Londonderry] by the visits we have been paying to some of my principal supporters in the north of this county during the last few weeks: people you never heard of before, yet living with a refinement and splendour quite remarkable. Nothing more striking than some of your English gentry with châteaux, parks, and broad domains; greater men by a good deal than many German Princes, and yet utterly unknown in London society: among these one of our greatest Bucks squires, a Mr. Pauncefort Duncombe, whose home was really radiant, and contrasted very much with Woburn Abbey, which he took me over to see, larger but the most gloomy and squalid palace that you can conceive.[1]

It was the world of the Frank Greshams contrasted with that of the Dukes of Omnium. This was the order which Peel had 'betrayed';

[1] M. & B., iv, 77, quoting a letter of April 29, 1857.

and this was the society whose way of life Disraeli saw it as his task to vindicate and defend against the Whig grandees and their unholy alliance with 'the men of the North who thought that they were to govern England'.

Of course, the social structure was more complicated than this picture suggests. There were Liberal squires, and plenty of great peers were Tories, though in some cases recent converts, like Disraeli's own Duke of Buckingham or Derby himself. From the turn of the century until 1832 there had been a drift from among the ranks of the Whig families to the Tory side, largely explained by the Tories' apparent monopoly of office. But the trend was halted and perhaps even put slightly into reverse in the 1830s and 1840s. At the time of the Reform Bill, Tories had outnumbered Whigs in the House of Lords by about three to two. In the Corn Law crisis and its immediate aftermath the two parties were nearly level. In any case it would be wrong to equate the great landowning families with the whole peerage. Probably, although no reliable statistics exist, a majority of what Disraeli called 'the magnificoes' had been Whigs all along, and the number that could be counted as Tories, in the sense that they supported Derby, was actually declining during the decade following the fall of Peel.

The difference in attitude between the grand Whig or Whiggish families and the country gentlemen cannot be explained on economic grounds only, although it is true that the latter depended more exclusively upon agriculture than the former and were, therefore, more likely to be hostile to free trade. It was, rather, a difference of temperament explicable by sociological factors which would repay a closer study than can be given here. We have already discussed the fear of revolution as a cause of the repeal of the Corn Laws. This element in early Victorian politics is often forgotten, but it was very important. The great Whig noblemen with their cosmopolitan London outlook were more aware of the danger than the provincial gentry. They knew Europe and saw what was happening there. To them the Reform Bill and free trade were necessary concessions made in order to avoid a revolutionary alliance between Manchester and the mob.

The gentry tended to see the matter differently. The countryside appeared placid enough, and, even if they had been shaken for a moment by the agrarian discontent of 1830, they saw little danger fifteen or twenty years later. Chartism had been largely an urban phenomenon. The Anti-Corn Law League seemed mere agitation. The country squire was conscious that land bore a heavy burden in respect of tithes, taxation and rates. He did not of course like this burden, but he regarded protection as the *quid pro quo*. Free trade was unfair because it removed the moral basis of the tacit bargain on which the burdens upon land were founded. It was the beginning of the end of that 'territorial constitution' which had been England's greatest contribution to civilization and the true cause of her grandeur.

Why did Disraeli wish to defend the aristocratic settlement and the territorial constitution? His detractors have sometimes attributed his political philosophy to snobbery, to love of the great and grand whose names roll so sonorously from his pen in his letters to his sister. No doubt there was an element of this in his character, but it would be quite wrong to regard his attitude as simply that of a successful social climber. He believed in the aristocratic principle and the territorial constitution because he believed that they guaranteed freedom. Tithes, the poor rate and the administration of justice were burdens imposed on land, as he put it in a speech in the House in 1846.

> . . . not to gratify the pride or pamper the luxury of the proprietors of land but because in a territorial constitution you and those whom you have succeeded have found the only security for self-government, the only barrier against that centralizing system which has taken root in other countries. I have always maintained these opinions. My constituents are not landlords; they are not aristocrats; they are not great capitalists; they are the children of industry and toil, and they believe first that their material interests are involved in a system which favours native industry, by ensuring at the same time real competition, but they also believe that their political and social interests are involved in a system by which their rights and liberties have been guaranteed: and I agree with them – I have the same old-fashioned notions.

In his life of Bentinck he contrasted the British and continental systems with that of America. 'Ancient communities, like the European must be governed either by traditionary influences or by military force.' You could not transplant the American constitution – that favourite panacea of radicalism – to Europe, because conditions were not analogous. Republican democracy might flourish in the New World, but not in the Old, where dethroned dynasties, 'a confiscated aristocracy' and 'a plundered church' would appeal to the sentiments of loyalty and revenge with subversive effects which in the end could only be overcome by the sword. This was what had been happening off and on ever since 1789, and even more markedly since 1848: a mournful sequence of revolution, anarchy and military dictatorship. In *Lord George Bentinck* he writes:

> England is the only important European community that is still governed by traditional influences, and amid the shameless wreck of nations she alone has maintained her honour, her liberty, her order, her authority, and her wealth . . . But it is said that it is contrary to the spirit of the age that a great nation like England, a community of enlightened millions long accustomed to public liberty, should be governed by an aristocracy. It is not true that England is governed by an aristocracy in the common acceptation of the term. England is governed by an aristocratic principle. The aristocracy of England absorbs all aristocracies, and receives every man in every order and every class who defers to the principle of our society, which is to aspire and to excel.[1]

Disraeli believed in a territorial aristocracy partly because he was at heart a romantic, partly because he had a genuine hatred of centralization, bureaucracy and every manifestation of the Benthamite state. He felt the sort of reverence that Burke had had for the many independent corporations and institutions which, however odd and anomalous, however contrary to abstract symmetry, to what Burke called 'geometrical' theories, were the true bulwarks of English liberty. This was one of his principal arguments in favour of the Church of England, 'a majestic corporation wealthy, powerful, independent . . . broadly and deeply planted in the land . . . one of the main guarantees of our local government, and therefore one of the prime securities of our common liberties . . .' For similar reasons he opposed state interference with the ancient universities. And it was for this reason above all others that he supported the aristocratic hierarchy of the counties against the levelling spirit of the age. There was nothing incompatible with this in any of the great reform measures associated with his name: the extension of the franchise in 1867; the labour and sanitary legislation of the 1870s; the various manifestations of Tory democracy. To recognize that the masses might be supporters of a territorial constitution if the aristocracy legislated on their behalf, to perceive that the power of middle-class radicals allied with Whig magnates

---

[1] *Lord George Bentinck*, 555–7.

might be challenged by an alliance of the urban working classes and the country gentry, was indeed a stroke of imagination, but it did not contravene the fundamental tenets of Disraeli's belief.

What was more, he managed to give the impression that the aristocratic settlement was essentially English, that in upholding it he was upholding a national cause against the foreign, alien, imported theories of continental doctrinaires. The Corn Law battle is described by him in his life of Bentinck as one stage in 'the great contention between the patriotic and the cosmopolitan principle, which has hardly begun and upon which the fate of this island as a community depends'. And in 1872 he declared that beneath the superficial struggles of politics over the past forty years there had been a fundamental cleavage between a party of change animated by 'cosmopolitan' notions, and the party which sought to 'resume the national principles to which we attribute the greatness and grandeur of the country'.[1]

After the death of Palmerston, whose patriotism in foreign policy could hardly be challenged, it became possible for Disraeli to acquire the 'national' colours for his own party not only in home affairs but in the foreign field as well. Gladstone and the Liberals could be stigmatized as insufficiently mindful of 'the grandeur of the country', and the electoral advantage of the patriotic cry reaped by the renovated Conservative party – an asset which it has contrived to retain ever since. Thus devotion to the Crown, support of the territorial constitution, belief in the Empire, the assertion of England's great place in the comity of nations, together with an enlightened policy of social reform could all be combined under Disraeli's leadership in the ministry of 1874 to 1880. But all this lay far in the future. Neither Crown nor Empire nor patriotism were of much use to the Tory cause in the 1850s. Social reform was not a vote-winner when its beneficiaries had no votes. Only the aristocratic settlement remained, and its appeal was inevitably limited.

How did Disraeli see himself in the context of the territorial constitution? That an alien exotic figure of Jewish extraction should lead the country gentlemen of the English counties has often seemed paradoxical and fantastic. Indeed it was, and his acceptance can only be explained by the strange combination of circumstances already discussed. But it is not likely that Disraeli himself thought

[1] R. B. McDowell, *British Conservatism, 1832–1914* (1959), 60, quoting speech of June 24, 1872.

it so odd. He had already persuaded himself not only that the Jews were natural aristocrats with ancient lineages stretching back far beyond those of the English peerage, but that he himself belonged to its most aristocratic branch. *Tancred* is full of references to the aristocratic nature of Jewry. At the same time, with his establishment at Hughenden, Disraeli had become himself a member of the class of country gentlemen whose cause he represented, and it is important to remember that this was not such a startling transformation as is sometimes claimed. It is easy to underestimate the degree to which Isaac D'Israeli had, not by any conscious design, prepared the way.

Isaac had lived as a country gentleman at Bradenham, a considerably larger and much more beautiful house than Hughenden, for twenty years before his death. Of course, he was not a typical English squire, but he conformed to the usages of the county, as far as the tastes of an intelligent agnostic literary man allowed. He had long ago abandoned his ancestral faith, as had his wife's family. He kept up little if any connexion with his co-religionists. He was well-to-do. He preserved game. He sent his younger sons to Winchester. His daughter, but for a tragic accident, would have married into a prosperous landed family. His children were Anglicans and called him 'the governor'. What more could one ask? Apart from name and appearance there was very little to remind the world of the origins of the family at Bradenham. Benjamin did indeed attract the maximum of attention, but his brothers did not: one was a Civil Servant, the other a gentleman farmer. If Benjamin was fundamentally an urban character, it remains true that he loved the country and knew at least something about country pursuits and the sort of life that a country gentleman led. The charge of social climbing can perhaps be made against him in his younger days, although even then it was really a form of romanticism rather than the vulgar snobbery of the age. But whatever the past, by 1850 Disraeli had convinced himself that he belonged to the aristocratic order as much as any of those whom he met in the grand world of Tory politics. He had a fundamentally patrician outlook. To stay at the great country houses, the castles and palaces of the English nobility gratified him not as the social triumph of an adventurer but as the belated recognition of an equal.

CHAPTER XIII

Protection

1849–51

1

'Bentinckism is no more,' wrote Augustus Stafford to Manners when Bentinck resigned. 'Boom! boom! boom! The last echoes of its knell wailed on the last gusts of the last year.' Bentinck, too, was now no more, but it was not going to be easy for the party which he had inspired to discard the principles for which he stood. Disraeli agreed with Stafford. He was convinced that the mere reversal of free trade was a futile objective for the Conservatives to pursue. But Stanley did not see the difficulties involved in a serious attempt to re-establish protection. Himself convinced that free trade was a dangerous delusion, he failed to understand the alarm with which the graver and more 'responsible' elements of the governing class regarded the prospect of a protectionist administration. This alarm had little to do with the economic arguments for or against free trade. It was based, rather, on a conviction that, whatever the merits of the case, any attempt to re-enact the Corn Laws would provoke a revolution and thus sweep away the whole aristocratic settlement which the Court, the Peelites and the Whigs alike were no less anxious than Stanley and Disraeli to preserve. From 1846 to 1852 the emergence of a high Tory protectionist government seemed to many people scarcely less menacing than a radical Cabinet headed by Cobden and Bright.

Disraeli appreciated the problem, but by a perverse freak of temperament Stanley, so often accused by Bentinck of wavering, chose this moment to become a more rigid protectionist than he ever had been in Bentinck's lifetime. For the next four years Disraeli had to fight a long, difficult and tricky campaign to persuade the party that protection really was, as he later described it, a 'hopeless question'. He succeeded in the end, but at the cost of further inroads upon a reputation for political principle already much doubted and damaged.

A word should be said about his relations with Stanley. It was

indeed an incongruous partnership, that of a middle-class, ex-
Bohemian, debt-ridden literary man with the heir to one of the
oldest titles and greatest estates in England. On the Victorian social
and political ladder it was scarcely possible to be higher – short of
royalty – than Edward Stanley, soon to succeed his father as 14th
Earl of Derby. Dukes and marquesses were superior in rank, and
some of them, though not many, were richer. There were older
earldoms, and peerages of lesser rank that were older still, though
again not many. But as an all-rounder in sheer grandeur Stanley
would have been hard to surpass. He was, moreover, an exceedingly
clever man with a first-class if rather slapdash mind, and he was, by
universal consent, one of the finest – perhaps the finest – orators of
his generation. Beginning as a Whig he was regarded as the inevitable successor to Grey. Resigning impetuously and moving after
some years of doubt to the other side, he seemed no less inevitably
to be the heir of Peel. Now separated for a second time from the
official leadership of his party, he was the inevitable and unchallenged head of the protectionists, certain to be Prime Minister if ever
they were in a position to compose a government.

Stanley was in many ways the archetypal English statesman of
the eighteenth and nineteenth centuries, or perhaps – for, in fact,
there were very few people quite like him – it would more be
correct to say that he conformed to a pattern which, Englishmen believed to be the type of their leadership: not overkeen on office but
accepting it as a duty which went with great position; an enthusiastic sportsman, fond of shooting, a patron of the turf (though, alas,
never successful in winning the race that bore his name); devoted
to the classics, author of an excellent verse translation of the *Iliad*;
and – a final touch to the portrait – subject to attacks of gout
rivalling even those which afflicted Chatham. There was perhaps
only one quality missing, that of *gravitas*. This would not have
mattered in the eighteenth century, to which Stanley in spirit
essentially belonged. But times had changed. The world of Charles
James Fox was part of the past; Stanley, though far more respectable morally and financially than that fascinating figure, had something of his recklessness, levity and sheer love of political sport.

The accident that no proper biography has been written of him
has resulted in the notion that he was a mere figurehead, a dim
puppet manipulated by Disraeli. This idea cannot be too emphatically contradicted. He really was 'the Chief' and there was no

question of anyone disputing his authority. He dominated the party when he chose, and also the short-lived governments which he headed. Naturally, he listened to Disraeli, and he always treated him politely, though with outspoken candour if he deemed it necessary; but the distance between them, though narrowing as the years went by, was wide even to the end. Stanley wrote to 'my dear Disraeli'. Disraeli wrote at first to 'dear Lord Stanley', then to 'my dear Lord', but he did not go beyond that. It was not till the end of 1853 that he was invited to Knowsley. Stanley, though pressed from time to time with suitable deference, never visited Hughenden.

It is impossible to say exactly when the prejudice engendered in his mind by the Henry Stanley affair evaporated, but one can guess that, even after he became satisfied of Disraeli's innocence, a residue of dislike, or at least uneasiness, remained, enhanced by the great gulf in status and manner that separated the two men. But whatever his private opinion of Disraeli may have been, Stanley kept it to himself. He had few intimates, and he was not going to let slip remarks which might be repeated. He could not easily manage without Disraeli. Likewise, of course, Disraeli could not manage without him. Those who portray Stanley as keeping Disraeli out of the lead by remaining at the head of the party for nearly twenty-two years forget how shaky Disraeli's own position was for a great part of the time. The most strenuous efforts would have been made in some quarters to prevent the inheritance going to him, and they might well have been successful. It was only late in the day, the last year or so perhaps, that Disraeli was clearly seen, by most people, not least significantly by Stanley himself, as the rightful heir.

Stanley opened the session of 1849 with a prompt and uncompromising declaration in the Lords in favour of protection for agriculture. Disraeli in the lower House was from the start cautious and indeed ambiguous upon this critical point. In 1852 Derby, as Stanley had then become, told Queen Victoria that 'he did not think Mr. Disraeli had ever had a strong feeling, one way or the other, about Protection or Free Trade'.[1] 'Ever' is perhaps a strong word. Because Disraeli had come to the conclusion, even before Bentinck's death, that protection was no longer a feasible policy, it does not necessarily follow that he had always thought so, or that

[1] Memorandum by Prince Albert, November 28, 1852. A. C. Benson and Viscount Esher (ed.), *Letters of Queen Victoria*, 1837–61, ii, 492.

he had been dishonest when he trounced Peel for abandoning it.
Disraeli has often been described as a consummate actor. So in a
sense he was, but one of those actors who enter so deeply into their
role that for the time being they suspend disbelief and really live the
part which they enact. With Disraeli the line between the player
and the part is impossible to draw. There is no reason to doubt that
at the time he genuinely believed what he said. But Stanley was
certainly right in judging that Disraeli never regarded protection as
a sacrosanct dogma.

The events of the session of 1849, his first as *de facto* leader of the
Opposition in the House of Commons, seemed to confirm his
opinion that protection of agriculture was now an incubus to the
party, and that it was better to concentrate on an alternative policy.
A motion of his to go into committee to consider the state of the
nation, which was interpreted by the House as a veiled attempt to
resuscitate protection, was defeated by 140 votes. On the other
hand, a motion to consider the burdens on land was only lost by
ninety-one votes. It occasioned one of Disraeli's finer purple passages. He was arguing that agriculture and industry were comple-
mentary, not antagonistic, and that members would be ill advised
to neglect the grievances of the land and disregard 'territorial
principles'.

> Although you may for a moment flourish after their destruction,
> although your ports may be filled with shipping, your factories
> smoke on every plain, and your forges flame in every city, I see
> no reason why you should form an exception to that which the
> page of history has mournfully recorded; that you too should
> not fade like the Tyrian dye and moulder like the Venetian
> palaces.[1]

The speech was much admired. Russell praised it highly to the
Queen. Palmerston, who was his host at an evening party, warmly
congratulated him, and Lord Malmesbury told him 'that Stanley
"who never pays compliments, you know, that's not his way", said
it was one of the best things ever done'.[2] In general Disraeli seems
to have acquitted himself well during this session, and his relations
with Stanley were satisfactory, the latter telling him that in the
event of a Tory ministry 'I must be chief Minister in the Commons.

---

[1] M. & B., iii, 200.
[2] Disraeli to his sister, March 11, 1849, *Correspondence*, 221.

I confess myself that I think this a little bit too strong, and would willingly find a substitute.'[1]

Moreover, others thought not only that Disraeli was 'too strong' but that a Stanley ministry, however composed, was in the same category. Bright told Disraeli, who passed it on to his sister, that the Lords would certainly sustain the Government over the Navigation Acts ' "for though they are convinced it will destroy the commerce and navy of England, they deem such results comparative blessings compared with Stanley being Minister" '.[2] According to Greville,[3] Graham on being asked by the Queen whether Stanley really meant to beat the Government and take office, replied that he certainly did and that the consequence would be 'a struggle between the aristocracy and democracy of the country, very perilous to the former. She said she entirely agreed with this opinion.' Greville referred to the 'deplorable necessity and even degradation of taking such a pack as he [Stanley] would offer her and of dissolving Parliament at their bidding'. But he consoled himself: 'That she would struggle to avert such a calamity and appeal to all the statesmen of both parties to save her, I do not doubt.' Though Greville is not an unbiased witness, he probably reflected a widespread opinion. It is, however, unlikely that at this stage Stanley envisaged office unless he secured the leading Peelites – an achievement far less easy than he or Disraeli appreciated. A list headed 'Cabinet for 1849' survives among Disraeli's papers, and it includes most of them except Peel himself. Disraeli was put down for the India Office. Nothing came of these plans, the Government survived, and the session ended uneventfully.

At Hughenden for the autumn, Disraeli gave serious thought to future policy, more than ever convinced that protection must be dropped or at the very least put into the background in favour of some other policy. He was at this time much influenced by Henry Drummond, a successful banker and founder of the first chair of political economy at Oxford. Drummond was an eccentric high Tory of extreme views, very proud of his Jacobite origins. He wrote a pamphlet in which he stigmatized popular government as 'absolute mob rule' and described the monarchy and the hereditary aristocracy as 'emanations of Christianity'. He denounced freedom

---

[1] ibid., 223.
[2] *Correspondence*, 224, April 24, 1849.
[3] Greville, April 1, 1849.

of the Press, toleration, *laissez faire*, and equality as the great evils
of the day, and he sought salvation in a revival of royal power.
Greville described him as 'quite mad but very clever'.

Drummond suggested two points for a policy; first the familiar
one of 'equalization of taxation', ie reducing the burdens on land
by putting the rates, or part of them, on to the Consolidated Fund
to be raised by general instead of local taxes; secondly, more ingenious than convincing, the creation of a large surplus on the
budget to be used to establish a sinking fund for the liquidation of
the National Debt. The effect of this latter provision would be to
lower the rate of interest and help the landed classes by enabling
mortgagors to borrow far more cheaply. Disraeli propounded both
these plans at a speech in Aylesbury in September. He at once discovered that Stanley for all his seeming casualness had no intention
of allowing his lieutenant to commit the party to an unauthorized
policy which in his view contained grave weaknesses.

The idea of reducing the rate of interest for the mortgagor had
much to commend it from the point of view of the territorial
interest. No one who has read at all extensively in the documents
of the day can doubt that mortgages played an immense part in the
private finances of most landlords.[1] Disraeli was of all people most
conscious of the importance of the rate of interest at which one
could borrow. His whole domestic economy depended upon it. With
genuine feeling he wrote to Stanley. 'Conceive the effect on our
shattered and embarrassed aristocracy, of the interest on the debt
reduced to $2\frac{1}{2}$ or 2 per cent. With this, Californian gold, and a fixed
duty, they would be stronger than they ever were since the Conquest.'

Stanley was not convinced. How was the surplus to be raised?
Disraeli's language suggested – and certainly this was Drummond's
view – that it should be done by equalization of the land tax. But
Stanley acidly pointed out that though this might suit Bucks,
where the tax was already as high as anywhere, 'my friends in
Lancashire will not thank you for raising their tax in the first
instance from 2*d.* to 1*s.* 6*d.* in the pound'. He had received letters of
alarm from many supporters on this point. Disraeli was obliged to
make a tedious cross-country journey in order to explain away his
Aylesbury speech to an agriculturalist gathering in Essex.

---

[1] Disraeli in a letter to Manners, M. & B., iii, 238, January 1, 1850, puts the figure
of total loans on mortgage at £400 m, but does not give any authority.

No sooner was he out of this 'scrape', as he called it in a letter to Sarah, than he was in another. A slightly absurd agitation had been got up by 'Mr. G. F. Young, a shipbuilder who, with Mr. Freshfield, a retired attorney, and a mad Surrey farmer, a Mr. Foskett' wanted to organize petitions to the Queen to dissolve Parliament in the hope that a protectionist government would be returned.[1] They sent a letter to Disraeli, who had his reply privately printed and sent to Stanley among other people. It was an indiscreet document. He declared that a dissolution would result in defeat; that the agricultural constituencies should be 'prevented from running amuck against the financial system of the country'; that they could have no hope in a repeal of taxes; that a juster distribution of the burdens on land and the creation of a sinking fund supplied by import duties were the best means by which 'the Country Party might be reconstructed'; that in Bucks 'foremost in its zeal for old opinions five men could not be got together by a vague talk of recurrence to abrogated laws'.

Stanley, who was at Newmarket at the time, was much annoyed at a reply of this sort being circulated. He answered in a letter of formidable length, deprecating what seemed tantamount to a repudiation of protection. He ended with a severe reproof. 'I must regret that you have given publicity to some of the opinions contained in your letter, and, you must forgive me for adding, the tone of your observations which I fear are calculated to give needless offence.' It was a devastating letter and left Disraeli with very little to say in reply. He saw that for the moment it was no good trying to drop protection and in his next speech, on October 31 at Aylesbury, he declared his belief in protection for agriculture. Privately he was much put out by the reception which his scheme had obtained, not only from his leader but most of the party. However, he unobtrusively dropped the plan for a sinking fund which he clearly knew was not going to be accepted. Beresford told Stanley that Disraeli 'appeared at first decidedly piqued and low about the turn which matters had taken'.

He seems to have gone through a period of considerable depression that winter. On November 4 he wrote to Sarah:

I am myself not physically ill – but hipped and dispirited beyond expression – Indeed I find this life quite intolerable – & wish some

---

[1] Disraeli to Stanley, October 20, 1849, M. & B., iii, 220.

earthquake wd happen or something else of a decided nature
occur, that wd produce a great change . . . I am not at all
pleased with the Aylesbury meeting, though on the whole the
world has not taken so ill a view of it. I thought it was a shabby
concern . . . Next Wednesday we go to Chilton to stay with the
Chetwodes a couple of days; & then for one day to Lowndes
Stone: both dreadful bores, but anything is better than Hughenden. I meditate decamping privately on Monday to town.[1]

He did so, and had extensive discussions with Beresford and
others about policy. He was no more cheerful by Christmas. On
December 29 he wrote again to Sarah:

I have no news to tell you, but will send you nevertheless the
compli[nts] of the Season – I think your move[2] was very judicious;
for whether my feelings are peculiarly gloomy & uncomfortable
or not I certainly find this a most severe and unamiable Christmas. Give my best regards to your companions. I wish I were
with them.
  Yesterday I had to dine at Missenden Abbey – I went alone –
MA to whom the dinner was specially given, having been very
unwell these ten days, & confined to her room with cold & fever.
It was a most doleful visit – Dear old Carrington having prepared
what in his grandiose language might be described as a 'gorgeous
banquet' – double coups & double fish turbot & smelts, ancient
Johannisberger & many delicate wines & viands – To eat them
the Aloes, whose pretence to the county has already evaporated,
as their holding is to let, the little pair of Evetts, the male one
snuffling thro' a grace like a puritan, & a Mrs. Hobgoblin & two
Miss Hobgoblins or some name like that . . . I got off as soon as
I cd; I feel much worse to dy – a renewed cold I fancy – particularly wretched.[3]

Nor was he cheered by an invitation from Lord Exeter early in the
New Year to stay at Burghley, 'to hold a congress with Stanley &
Co.', as Disraeli put it. He was inclined to refuse, but felt in the end
that he must go, staying first at Belvoir and travelling thence with
Granby to Burghley. 'All this tho' it looks very well upon paper
seems to be rather a bore – cold & travelling, indigestion & poor
political prospects.'
  But the congress seems to have been a success. To Mary Anne,
who evidently did not go, he wrote on January 23: 'Yesterday we
had four Knights of the Garter at dinner. The D. of Richmond is

---

[1] Hughenden Papers, Box 6, A/I/B/324.
[2] From Bradenham.
[3] Hughenden Papers, Box 6, A/I/B/325.

Edward Stanley, 14th Earl of Derby
from an oil painting after Sir Francis Grant

Some of Disraeli's Cabinet

the 15th Earl of Derby (Foreign Secretary), Lord Cairns (Lord Chancellor), Sir Stafford Northcote (Chancellor of the Exchequer), Disraeli, Gathorne Hardy (Secretary for War), the Marquess of Salisbury (Secretary for India). An un-dated photograph, certainly before April 1878

very cordial & hearty. Stanley shoots too much but draws well with me & the result is altogether satisfactory.'

Thus ended Disraeli's first year as leader of the Opposition. It had not been satisfactory, and he had been foiled in his efforts to revive his party's fortunes. Indeed, his own position had been none too secure. He wrote in retrospect that his relations with Stanley 'during the whole of the year 1849 were uneasy' – a fact which he attributed to Stanley being 'in the hands of the Protection Society worked by George Frederick Young', who had also 'got hold of Beresford'. He considered that they misled Stanley about the true state of party feeling on protection. But it is equally likely that Disraeli was misled by his own optimistic assumption that others would come round as quickly as he to the view which he expressed soon afterwards to James Clay, 'Protection is not only dead but damned.'

On the merits of the dispute it is clear that in a sense both men were right. Disraeli correctly saw that the party would in the end be forced to accept free trade and would get nowhere till it did so. But Stanley, even if he had not genuinely believed in protection, would have been right to deprecate a premature volte-face. Such a policy came badly from Disraeli in view of his treatment of Peel, and in any case it is not easy for a party to discard its shibboleths, even when they have become electoral handicaps. Men cannot be expected to jettison overnight a cause dear to their hearts merely because it seems to have been repudiated by public opinion. Public opinion may change, and the first duty of a defeated party is surely to try to change it. Nor was it by any means self-evident in 1849 that protection was either dead or damned. Free trade could still be regarded as a perilous experiment, and the nation's prosperity might only be temporary. At any rate, there was plenty of room for argument.

On Disraeli's, or rather Drummond's, idea for a sinking fund, Stanley's damping criticism was fully justified. The plan was quite impracticable. Stanley understood far better what could or could not be done in Parliament. Disraeli's schemes at this time have a somewhat visionary quality, the product of the study or the library, rather than of the Cabinet room or the House of Commons. It was the same with a proposal which he made to Stanley at the end of 1849 'to introduce thirty Colonial M.P.s into St. Stephen's'.[1]

[1] M. & B., iii, 237. Disraeli to Stanley, December 28, 1849.

Admirers of Disraeli have seen in this a far-sighted anticipation of
the movement towards imperial unity at the end of the century, but
his main motive seems to have been one of party politics. 'Were it
possible,' he wrote, 'it would be a great element of future strength
to the Conservative Party.' Stanley, in reply, was dubious.[1] But
Disraeli returned to the theme two years later when he thought,
wrongly as it turned out, that the Government contemplated disfranchising some of the smaller boroughs. Why not give the seats to
colonial representatives? Once again political calculations seem to
have been the principal though not the only consideration in his
mind, 'to widen the basis and sympathies of our party'.[2] Stanley
answered him at great length[3] and disagreed on the party question.
Who would elect such MPs, he asked, and, if the same constituency
that elects their own legislatures, 'Will there not be a great risk
that the Colonial Representatives will be strongly imbued with that
Democratic spirit which is always so powerful in Colonies & which
we are desirous to check rather than encourage here?' It had all
been discussed at the time of the Reform Bill and dismissed as
impracticable and he had reflected much on the 'formidable difficulties' when Colonial Secretary. 'I have thought it only right to
lay them before you and to own that I see no solution of them.'

One is struck again and again, when reading this correspondence
between two very remarkable but very different men, by the contrast between genius and imagination on the one side and shrewd
experienced political worldliness on the other. Although Stanley
could be very offhand to some people, there is nothing cavalier
about the way he dealt with Disraeli's ideas. On the contrary, he
wrote at length and answered every argument carefully on its
merits. Disraeli casts restlessly around for something – be it a sinking fund, equalization of taxation, colonial representation, or later,
extension of the franchise, to put the party on the map. Stanley,
despite his impetuousness in debate, never forgets that ideas can
divide as well as unite, and that there are no short cuts in politics.

Disraeli has yet to undergo that most illuminating of all political
experiences, the task of taking actual responsibility for even a
minor, let alone a major, measure and carrying it through the
House of Commons. He has yet to know what it is like to be in

[1] Hughenden Papers, Box 109, B/XX/5/9, Stanley to Disraeli, January 8, 1850.
[2] M. & B., iii, 334, Disraeli to Stanley, December 9, 1851.
[3] Hughenden Papers, Box 109, B/XX/S/41, January 11, 1851.

office; to meet the numerous administrative objections and adverse precedents which the permanent officials have at their finger-tips when confronted with a novel scheme; to deal with the difficulties raised by innumerable interests, some serious, some frivolous, all requiring consideration and careful handling; to overcome the doubts of colleagues and the crochets of supporters. Stanley had experienced all this, and it had taught him the wisdom of avoiding too much detail when out of office. 'I always', he wrote in the first of these remonstrances, 'differed on this subject with poor George Bentinck, and deprecated the practice, to which he was too much inclined, of starting detailed projects in opposition.'[1]

2

The session of 1850 produced no very startling events; nor did it materially alter the position of parties. Without actually repudiating protection, Disraeli contrived to make reduction of the burdens on land the chief plank in his platform; but we hear no more about the sinking fund. There was widespread agricultural distress that year. This, of course, added vehemence to the complaints of the high protectionists, but since it was accompanied by prosperity in all other walks of life, their complaints received little attention.

Disraeli's ascendancy on the Tory benches gradually increased during this year and the next. He certainly worked hard. As he had written on one occasion, leading a party was not just a matter of asking a question at four and winding up the debate at eleven: you had to be well informed, constantly on the alert and ready to make up your mind on important matters at a moment's notice. Disraeli took all this very seriously. Beresford, staying a day or so at Hughenden the previous September, told Stanley, 'He is living very quietly and working very hard. He is reading up all the Blue Books of the past session . . . He attributes Peel's great power and effect in the House to having always had Blue Books by heart, and having thereby the appearance of a fund of greater knowledge than he really possessed.'[2] The Opposition front bench was almost entirely dependent on him. It is true that Spencer Walpole[3] was beginning to be of some assistance, and that Disraeli greatly welcomed the return to Parliament of Lord John Manners, who got in at a by-election

---

[1] M. & B., iii, 215–16.   [2] ibid., 219.
[3] Nephew and son-in-law of Spencer Perceval. Thrice Home Secretary.

that year. But he often must have felt the shortage of speakers and have asked the same question that Stanley asked once – in connexion with the Don Pacifico debate: 'Have we any others who would not do us more harm than good? If we have by all means induce them to come forward.'

Among the subjects which came up during the session was one on which Disraeli had views well in advance of most politicians, the conditions of labour. *Sybil* is evidence of his awareness, and when Ashley introduced a new Factories Bill designed to shut certain legal loopholes which had been discovered in his Ten Hours Act of 1847, Disraeli supported him. The Government, however, took over the measure and offered the compromise very reluctantly accepted by Ashley of a ten and a half hours day. Both Manners and Disraeli protested unsuccessfully, but in the full spirit of Young England on behalf of what Disraeli called 'the voice of outraged faith'.

But when the cognate question of labour conditions in the coal-mines was raised, Disraeli palpably allowed political and social considerations to override the generous sentiments of *Sybil*. Lord Londonderry, one of the greatest coal-owners in the country, described a Bill proposing inspection of mines as 'infernal', and Disraeli both spoke and voted against it in the House of Commons. His close personal friendship with that odious and overbearing figure, Frances Anne Londonderry, had recently been restored, after a temporary rift caused by her dislike of Mrs Disraeli. Londonderry himself had a foot in both Peelite and protectionist camps, and was supposed to influence Graham. Coal-owners as a class tended to belong to the landed interest and therefore to be political allies, whereas factory-owners were more often than not Liberals or Radicals. In the circumstances Disraeli's conduct was natural enough, but we would think better of him if it had been different.

The event of the session was the Don Pacifico debate caused by Palmerston's high-handed espousal of the inflated claims of a somewhat shady British subject against the government of Greece. It demonstrated for the first time Palmerston's immense hold on parliamentary and public opinion. In the House of Lords, Stanley, acting in concert with Aberdeen, carried a motion of censure. But the Government decided to stand or fall by the verdict of the Commons, and there, despite the reprobation of every leading statesman apart from his own Cabinet colleagues, Palmerston triumphantly vindicated himself with his famous *Civis Romanus* speech and won by a majority of forty-six.

Stanley expected to bring down the Government on this issue and no doubt hoped to put the Peelites in such a position that they could not decently refuse to co-operate in forming a new administration. He suspected that Disraeli was less keen than he was on bringing Palmerston to book:

> Forgive me [he wrote on June 22] if I impress upon you the great importance, on many accounts, of hitting hard and not sparing. Anything short of *guerre a l'outrance* would have the effect of reviving, in suspicious minds, old misconceptions, and expose you to misconstruction on the part of those who may look with envy at your present high position. Pray excuse me for touching on such a topic, which I can have but one motive for doing.[1]

Disraeli did not answer. Silence was often his refuge when he intended to disobey. He made exactly the sort of speech which Stanley deprecated. Gladstone, who delivered a very vigorous attack on Palmerston and virtually took over from Disraeli on this occasion, regarded the latter's speech as 'a very poor one, almost a "cross"'. And several Whigs, among them the Prime Minister, affected to regard Gladstone as the new leader of the Opposition. Disraeli's motives are by no means clear. It is possible that he did not wish to bring down the Government at that particular moment because he did not wish to take office until the protection issue had been settled. Perhaps, too, he saw that his own position might be imperilled if Stanley brought the Peelites into his Cabinet. He wrote a memorandum on the subject many years later:

> The great difficulty would have been the Leadership of the House of Commons. I was leader of 250 men and, so far as numbers were concerned, no one could compete with me; but I not only had no experience of high office, but I had positively never held even the humblest office. There was no confidential intimacy at that time between Lord Derby and myself, and I don't think he would have much hesitated in suggesting a Peelite, one of his old and even recent colleagues, as Leader, if I consented and the party generally . . . But who? I have always thought that old Goulburn was the man whom Sir Robert Peel and Lord Derby (then Stanley) would have brought forward and furbished up like an old piece of dusty furniture, under whom we might have all

---

[1] M. & B., iii, 257.

served without any great outrage of personal feelings. But I could never penetrate this.[1]

The day after the division Peel had an ultimately fatal fall from his horse. Disraeli heard the news from two strangers who rode up to him as he was returning from an afternoon drive with Mary Anne. He noted that they seemed surprised when he expressed his sorrow and alarm.

Peel, whose medical treatment appears to have been lamentably incompetent, lay in great pain for nearly four days before he died. Disraeli describes how the grand world buzzed with rumours at the possible consequences. On one of those days he attended 'a great morning fête' at Rosebank, Lady Londonderry's country cottage by the Thames, 'where to render the romantic simplicity complete Lady Londonderry, in a colossal conservatory condescended to make tea from a suite of golden pots and kettles . . . Londonderry . . . full of intrigue, showed, as usual, his cards. I missed him during the fête. He reappeared towards the end. He came up and whispered to me. It was hopeless. He had actually galloped up to London, called at Whitehall, and galloped back again, while his band was still playing and his friends still sipping ices.'[2]

Disraeli liked to believe that Peel was anxious in the last years of his life for a reconciliation. Testimony on this point is conflicting, and it is set out at length by Buckle,[3] who decides that Disraeli was probably right. But the evidence which he gives seems to contradict his conclusion. It is true that Smythe tells a story alleged to be based on Gladstone's testimony that Peel cheered Disraeli during the Don Pacifico debate. But Gladstone himself has left a memorandum in which he refers to Peel's 'extreme annoyance' at having to act with Disraeli on that occasion. Gladstone was writing forty years later, but he had a good memory and was in Peel's confidence. Smythe was not, and he was imaginative. It is inherently unlikely that Peel was ever reconciled to Disraeli, although it is pleasant if bewildering to know that Disraeli thought otherwise.

Peel's death, tragic though it was, did not at that stage come as a great loss to British politics. His refusal either to take office or to join with the Whigs or to rejoin the Tories was an important reason for the confusion that prevailed. 'Prime Ministers unattached are dangerous as great rafts would be dangerous floating unmoored in

[1] M. & B., iii, 260.   [2] ibid., 261.   [3] ibid., 261–3.

a harbour,' wrote Gladstone. '. . . The position of Sir Robert Peel in the last four years of his life was a thoroughly false one.'[1] As long as he lived it was impossible to hope for any stability in the House of Commons or to expect a strong government.

In the autumn of 1850 there occurred an event which at last shook the various groups out of their frozen postures and put an end to the peculiar circumstances which had allowed Russell's feeble Government to last so long. The Pope issued a brief dividing the country into twelve territorial bishoprics, and creating Wiseman, hitherto Vicar Apostolic of the London District, Archbishop of Westminster. Shortly afterwards Wiseman received a cardinal's hat. The papal brief was quickly followed by a pastoral letter from the new Archbishop, given out from 'the Flaminian Gate', announcing that the people of England so long severed from the See of Rome were on the point of rejoining the Holy Church. No doubt such language was both impertinent and untrue, but it hardly warranted the uproar that ensued. As for the restoration of the hierarchy, the Pope had laid proposals of this nature two years earlier before Lord Minto, the Prime Minister's father-in-law, who was travelling on a special diplomatic mission to the Italian States, and Lord Minto had made no objection. True, it turned out later that Lord Minto had not troubled to read the document, but the Pope could scarcely be blamed for that.

The spontaneous outcry which resulted from the Pope's action ought to have allayed any doubts about England being a Protestant country. But the agitation might have ebbed away without any political consequences of note if Lord John Russell had not decided to put himself at the head of outraged Protestant sentiment. Without consulting anyone, he wrote an open letter to the Bishop of Durham in which he denounced the 'aggression' of the Pope, as 'insolent and insidious . . . inconsistent with the Queen's supremacy, with the rights of our bishops and clergy, and with the spiritual independence of the nation'. Nor was he content with castigating Rome. Was there not within the Church of England a fifth column, a clique of fellow travellers, whose machinations were even more dangerous than the open hostility of the Pope? And Lord John proceeded to give the 'Puseyites' a piece of his mind. They were, he said, 'leading their flocks step by step to the very edge of

[1] Quoted, J. B. Conacher, 'Peel and the Peelites, 1846–50', *English Historical Review*, LXXIII (1958).

the precipice'. The danger to be apprehended from 'a foreign prince of no great power' was trivial 'compared to the danger within the gates from the unworthy sons of the Church of England herself'.

Russell could scarcely have done anything more damaging to his own political position. Indeed, although some people thought that it was sheer miscalculation and that political popularity was his main motive, it seems on the whole more likely that he was simply, in Disraeli's words to Stanley, 'indulging in his hereditary foible – to wit, having a shy at the Papists',[1] and that he forgot politics altogether. For the Durham letter knocked away the two props upon which his ministry depended. The Irish were furious with the man who denounced Roman Catholic ceremonies as 'the mummeries of superstition', and henceforth they refused to support the Whigs as long as Russell led the party. The Peelites were equally annoyed, for two reasons: being intelligent men of a liberal cast of mind, they deplored a revival of sectarian intolerance; and they contained among their number persons who would qualify, anyway to the low-church party, as 'Puseyites': Gladstone, Lincoln and Herbert.

Disraeli viewed the whole affair with a cynical eye. He certainly did not take the papal 'aggression' at all seriously from the religious point of view. But its political implications made an indelible impression on his mind. Hitherto, partly under the influence of Young England, he had been inclined to look at the 'old faith' with a friendly eye. In *Sybil* the heroine is an adherent, and a certain nostalgic sympathy for Rome fitted in with the romantic Tory version of history which attributes the poverty of the poor to the rapacity of the landowners who seized the great monastic estates at the time of the Reformation. But the events of 1850 convinced him that the 'old faith' was a political liability of the first order, and he never toyed with such notions again. He did not write another novel until 1869; *Lothair* gives a very unflattering picture of the Roman Church and of its English proselytizers and converts. The unpopularity of the Puseyites had no less effect upon him than that of the Pope. When he came to exercise church patronage he set his face firmly against the Tractarians, and the seeds of his attitude to the famous Bill 'to put down Ritualism' were sown at the time of the Durham letter.

The session now began and the Queen's speech contained a

[1] Derby Papers, Box 145/1.

promise to legislate against the new bishoprics. With the man-oeuvres, intrigues and details attending Russell's Ecclesiastical Titles Bill we are not here concerned. It is enough to say that the Peelites and the Irish assisted by those Radicals whose liberalism outweighted their Protestantism were the only people to speak and vote against an absurd and unenforceable measure which was carried by 438 to 95.

Before this happened Russell was reaping the first fruit of the Durham letter. On February 20, 1851, he was defeated by 100 votes to 54 on a Radical motion to equalize the county and borough franchise, the Conservatives abstaining *en masse*. He decided that this was too much to put up with, and resigned. The Queen sent for Stanley, who advised her to induce the Peelites to coalesce with Russell. But the Ecclesiastical Titles Bill, which had not yet been carried, was an insuperable bar. Russell failed, and there was nothing for it but that Stanley should try to form an administration himself.

Russell's announcement to the House after Stanley's first inter-view with the Queen provoked Disraeli into using words which further damaged his already poor reputation with the Court. Russell had said that Stanley in reply to the Queen's offer declared 'he was not *then* prepared to form a Government'. Disraeli bluntly and none too politely denied that Stanley had ever declined to form an administration – a denial greeted with cheers from the benches behind him. Russell's statement had been based partly on what the Queen told him, partly on a formal letter of advice written by Stanley to the Queen and shown by the Queen to Russell. She was seriously offended at Disraeli's speech, which seemed to cast asper-sions on her own veracity. Her correspondence is full of references to the episode, and a good deal of Stanley's time in later interviews when he really was trying to form a government was spent in explaining away a contradiction which he admitted to be 'very unfortunate'.[1]

But he stood by his lieutenant. He told the Queen that he re-gretted that Lord John had mentioned that he (Stanley) 'was not *then* prepared' to form a government, for such a statement, though true in a sense, damaged his chances of success if after all he did have to make the attempt in the end. He had not, he said,

[1] A. C. Benson and Viscount Esher (ed.), *The Letters of Queen Victoria* 1837–61 (3 vols, 1907), ii, 367.

absolutely refused, but had advised the Queen to try to make other arrangements first. The Queen said she thought the distinction 'very nice', and Prince Albert sarcastically asked him whether in these days of nice distinctions it could *now* be said that he had undertaken to form a government. Stanley, who was not the man to give way, replied that it would be better to say that he had 'attempted to undertake to form a government'.[1] The episode cannot have endeared either Disraeli or his chief to the Court.

Disraeli has left an extremely amusing account of the negotiations which followed.[2] It is characteristically inaccurate about dates and one must always bear in mind Meredith's comment of twenty years earlier – 'He could make a story out of everything.' But no doubt the general impression is correct. Stanley intended to give the Home Office to Disraeli and had already told the Queen that he must be one of the Secretaries of State. The Queen reluctantly agreed. According to Prince Albert's memorandum, she said that she had not a very good opinion of him because of his behaviour to Peel, but she would accept him.

> She must, however, make Lord Stanley responsible for his conduct, and should she have cause to be displeased with him when in office she would remind Lord Stanley of what now passed. Lord Stanley promised to be responsible, and excused his friend for his former bitterness by his desire to establish his reputation for cleverness and sharpness; nobody had gained so much by Parliamentary schooling and he had of late quite changed his tone.[3]

In the same memorandum the Prince states that Stanley proposed to offer the leadership of the House to Gladstone. Disraeli's account of the episode is more enjoyable to read, but, as it was at second hand and written down at least ten years later, it must be regarded as less reliable.

> He [Stanley] told me Her Majesty had enquired of him to whom he proposed to entrust the Leadership of the House of Commons and he had mentioned my name.
>
> The Queen said: 'I always felt that, if there were a Protectionist Government, Mr. D. must be the Leader of the House of Commons: but I do not approve of Mr. D. I do not approve of his conduct to Sir Robert Peel.'

[1] ibid., 368.
[2] M. & B., iii, 288–95.
[3] *Letters of Queen Victoria* 1837–61, ii, 365–6.

Lord Derby said: 'Madam, Mr. D. has had to make his position, and men who make their positions will say and do things which are not necessary to be said or done by those for whom positions are provided.'

'That is true,' said the Queen, 'And all I can now hope is that having attained this great position, he will be temperate. I accept Mr. Disraeli on your guarantee.'[1]

The obvious discrepancy in the two accounts is the exact position intended for Disraeli. The Prince's memorandum makes no mention of Disraeli leading the House. Disraeli says that he was quite ready to withdraw in favour of anyone whose elevation to the post would help, but that Stanley refused the offer. 'Indeed, he once said that he had no idea that the man who had brought things to this point should not reap the great reward . . . But, the truth is, the difficulty was not one which could be removed by individual sacrifice. The Protectionist party, though they were prepared (though not very willingly) to accept the Peelites in a subaltern position, made it a *sine qua non* that the Ministry should be led in both Houses by their own chiefs.'

Stanley interviewed Gladstone the day after the discussion with the Queen and the Prince and offered him any department he wished, except the Foreign Office. He did not offer him the leadership. On this point Gladstone's own account is conclusive. 'Nothing was said of the leadership of the House of Commons, but his anxiety was evident to have any occupant but one for the foreign office.'[2] Clearly Disraeli was the person to be kept out of the Foreign Office, but it looks as if Stanley had decided against offering the lead to Gladstone. In any case Gladstone would have declined it. He was not willing to serve under Stanley in any capacity while the protection question remained uncertain.

With Gladstone's refusal – and all the other Peelites followed suit – Stanley was thrown back on to forming a purely protectionist administration for which, Prince Albert noted, 'the material was certainly sad'. On later occasions Disraeli was to complain at Stanley's want of enterprise; not so, on this. 'In fact,' he writes, 'Lord Derby was full of resource, which was not his characteristic.' Lord Canning having declined the Foreign Office, he decided to write to Sir Stratford Canning, the Ambassador at Constantinople,

[1] M. & B., iii, 290–1.

[2] Morley, *Gladstone*, i, 406. Lord Canning, third son of the Prime Minister, Governor-General of India at the time of the Mutiny, was the man Stanley wanted.

and offer it to him, 'of which I greatly approved and to the D. of Northumberland the Admiralty than which nothing could be better'. He resolved also to offer Cabinet office to Henry Corry, a minor Peelite and father of Disraeli's future private secretary 'Monty', the Privy Seal to Lord Ellenborough, and, on Disraeli's advice, the Board of Control to Sir Robert Inglis. Corry refused, both Ellenborough and Inglis accepted. No name is better evidence than the latter's of the straits to which Stanley and Disraeli were reduced. Disraeli on his own showing regarded Inglis, who was the senior member for Oxford University and leader of the extreme Protestants, with amused contempt, describing him 'as a wretched speaker, an offensive voice, no power of expression, yet perpetually recalling and correcting his cumbersome and wearisome phraseology'.[1] No wonder Stanley shrugged his shoulders when the name was suggested.

At this stage everything began to go wrong. Ellenborough was dispatched to convert Goulburn. Unfortunately Goulburn converted him instead, and he withdrew his acceptance. So did Sir Robert Inglis. A general meeting was due at Stanley's house in the afternoon of February 27, and matters now looked less promising, but not hopeless. Stanley was counting on J. W. Henley, MP for Oxfordshire, and Herries to take the Board of Trade and the Exchequer respectively, but the letters offering them these posts had gone astray, and they found themselves summoned to the meeting without any warning about their own positions. Stanley made a vigorous speech, but Henley's demeanour was not encouraging.

All this time Henley, whom I believe Lord Derby did not personally know, or scarcely, sat on a chair against the dining room wall, leaning with both his hands on an ashen staff, and with the countenance of an ill-conditioned Poor Law Guardian censured for some act of harshness. His black eyebrows which met, deeply knit; his crabbed countenance doubly morose; but no thought in the face, only ill temper, perplexity, and perhaps astonishment. In the midst of this Herries was ushered, or rather tumbled into the room, exclaiming, 'What's all this?' Then there

[1] Disraeli noted in his papers an unfortunate remark of Inglis when complaining to the House that the wife of a certain prisoner was not allowed to visit him with free ingress and egress. 'He said "Things have come to a pretty pass in this country when an Englishman may not have his wife backwards and forwards." The shout of laughter in the House was electrical. Sir Robert Peel, who was naturally a hearty laugher, lost his habitual self-control and leant down his head in convulsions.'

were explanations how and why he had not received a letter, and had not been there at 12 o'clock to know that he was to be Chancellor of the Exchequer.

Herries was scarcely more helpful than Henley, though his manner was different. He was garrulous and never stopped talking about all the difficulties which Goulburn would oppose to any protectionist Chancellor of the Exchequer. Then Henley spoke and 'flatly refused to take the Board of Trade'. Disraeli, says Lord Malmesbury, did not conceal his anger at Henley's behaviour.

A general hubbub followed. Stanley took Disraeli aside and told him that it was no use going on. Disraeli demurred, but not strongly. Stanley then announced that he would throw in his hand because he could not find members in the House of Commons to support him. Disraeli's account continues:

> Beresford frantically rushed forward and took Lord Derby aside, and said there were several men waiting at the Carlton expecting to be sent for and implored Lord Derby to reconsider his course. Lord Derby inquired impatiently, 'Who was at the Carlton?' Beresford said, 'Deedes'.
>
> 'Pshaw!' exclaimed Lord Derby, 'These are not names I can put before the Queen. Well my lords and gentlemen, I am obliged to you for your kind attendance here today: but the thing is finished. Excuse my leaving you but I must write to the Queen.'
>
> We dispersed . . . 'The best thing the Country party can do,' said Malmesbury, 'is to go into the country. There is not a woman in London who will not laugh at us.'
>
> Herries who seemed annoyed that it was all over kept mumbling about not having received his summons till three o'clock: and that he remembered Governments which were weeks forming. Henley continued silent and grim. Beresford looked like a man who had lost his all at roulette, and kept declaring that he believed Deedes was a first-rate man of business.

Thus on February 27, after five days of negotiation, ended the first attempt at forming a protectionist administration. The only alternative left was for Russell to resume office. Disraeli ends his account:

> One thing was established – that every public man of experience and influence, however slight, had declined to act unless the principle of Protection were unequivocally renounced.

CHAPTER XIV

Office

1851–2

Disraeli's feelings about the fiasco described in the last chapter were less urbane at the time than his later account suggests. Stanley seems to have sensed his lieutenant's annoyance. 'I am afraid you are not satisfied with the result of our deliberation yesterday', he wrote on the morrow of his refusal to take office. 'The more I reflect on the state of the case the more I am satisfied it was inevitable, however mortifying to us as a party.'[1] But he scarcely improved matters by making a speech in the House of Lords in which he candidly attributed his failure to sheer lack of talent among his supporters. Disraeli told his sister that he did not think the speech 'by any means happy'. He feared that the upshot of the confused political situation would be Graham 'at the head of a reorganised Liberal Party & with a new Reform Bill to commence the session'. If this occurred, 'it is all up with old England, and American principles will have gained the day'.[2]

Convinced that protectionism rather than lack of ability constituted the real millstone round the party's collective neck, Disraeli was now more determined than ever to get rid of it. Oddly enough, one of his strongest allies was Stanley's son Edward, who had entered Parliament as Bentinck's successor for King's Lynn. The previous October he wrote to Disraeli deprecating another protectionist demonstration: '. . . the very turnips of Norfolk will cry out against us, as the turnip-headed inhabitants thereof have already begun to do'. He shared few of his father's tastes, preferring the Blue Book to the Stud Book and improvement of the mind to the slaughter of pheasants. He had neither the quick-wittedness nor the oratorical power of his father, but he was conscientious, hardworking and capable. He stayed at Hughenden and soon fell under the charm which Disraeli could exert over young men. It is unlikely that the elder Stanley welcomed this development, and Greville

[1] M. & B., iii, 295.
[2] Hughenden Papers, Box 6, A/I/B/341, March 8, 1851.

may have been telling the truth as well as gratifying his dislike
when he wrote two years later that Derby 'had now the mortification of seeing his son devoted to him [Disraeli]'.[1]

About this time Disraeli went through one of his periodic moods
of despondency. The party seemed so divided about protection that
he began to wonder whether the leadership was worth while. In June
he actually offered it to Thomas Baring, an independent Tory back
bencher, a highly successful financier and a man of much ability,
whom Derby[2] had tried to secure for his abortive Cabinet. Baring
took it as mere '*persiflage*', but when Disraeli assured him that he
was serious, firmly declined. At the end of the session Malmesbury
reported to Derby that Disraeli 'seemed to be very much *down* . . .
but one thing is certain – viz that he *wants* to throw over "Protection" '.

Disraeli's private affairs were giving him very nearly as much
vexation as his public life. True, his finances seemed, although
only temporarily, to be in a healthier state than they had been for
some time,[3] but Hughenden did not bring him the usual peace and
refreshment after the end of the session. A prolonged quarrel had
broken out between Mary Anne and James Disraeli, who, though he
no longer farmed at Bradenham, still lived in the neighbourhood.
The cause is not clear, but the quarrel shattered Disraeli's domestic
tranquillity. To his sister he refers to the 'absurd misunder-
standings which greatly vex me & prevent me working . . . I
have endless rows on this infernal subject'.[4] Moreover, James had
discovered another grievance; his brother ought to have had him
made a Justice of the Peace '& this obliges me to tell him the truth
viz that I did mention to the Ld. Lt. that I wished him to be made
a magistrate & had the mortification of being refused'. Lord
Carrington apparently had an absolute rule against anyone in
trade. Only thus, he said, could he keep the Radicals of Wycombe
at bay. Now that James no longer farmed the Lord Lieutenant
was ready to reconsider the matter, but James in a huff declared

---

[1] Greville, *Diary*, May 22, 1853. It is fair to say that nearly all Greville's references
to Derby are carping and disagreeable. The reason was probably, as in the case of his
feud with Bentinck, connected with the turf, on which Greville came near to ruining
himself, whereas Bentinck and Derby were very successful.

[2] He succeeded to the earldom at the end of June and will be thus described
henceforth.

[3] See below, pp. 421–4 and 754, for Disraeli's financial fortunes from 1851 to his
death.

[4] Hughenden Papers, Box 6, A/I/B/351, October 17, 1851.

that he would not accept. Disraeli continued in the same letter:

> I have asked favors for James from Ld Stanley, Sir Jas Graham, Ld J. Russell & the Ld Lt & always unsuccessfully. I regret that I moved in any of these instances – it was against my judgment but I allowed, as I too often do, feeling to guide me. The position of James is very disagreeable but he has mainly himself to blame for it, as every man has . . . I offered to give him great introductions [in Ireland or America] but he was involved by low ties. It is impossible for me to advance his social position here.

The quarrel with Mary Anne seems to have been made up early in November, but the problem of employment for James was not solved till the following year, when Derby, at Disraeli's instance, bestowed on him a County Court Treasurership worth £900 a year.

In the middle of December a political event of great significance occurred. Goaded by the Court and at last himself annoyed beyond endurance, Russell dismissed Palmerston from the Foreign Office for giving his approval to Louis Napoleon's *coup d'état*[1] without consulting either the Queen or the Prime Minister. The Foreign Secretary departed swearing vengeance. Disraeli was widely believed to have some sort of private link with Palmerston. No doubt he would have liked such a connexion, but there is no evidence of it in his papers, and on January 4, 1852, we find him writing to Derby a letter which though somewhat cryptic clearly dispels the notion.[2]

> . . . This morning brought me, however, some other letters, one from the Camarilla[3] indirectly. I received one from the same quarter about a week ago or more written in great alarm lest we were going to coalesce with Palmerston. I wrote a letter from the hint of my friend, very confidential, but to be shown to a certain person; in which I ridiculed the rumour & reprobated the factiousness of such a sudden alliance, adding we hoped we were strong enough to carry on affairs without taking in 'the discarded partner of an insolvent firm' & thought that with fair play we should not be driven to such a course. This morning I have a line from the same correspondent reminding me that six weeks ago he informed me that Palmerston was doomed (which was true; it was about Kossuth),[4] & now adding that another person (meaning

[1] The *coup d'état* took place on December 2. The Queen discovered Palmerston's action on the 13th, and Russell dismissed him on the 19th.

[2] Derby Papers, Box 145/2.

[3] Presumably the Whig Cabinet.

[4] Lajos Kossuth, one of the heroes of the Hungarian revolt in 1848–9, who had recently arrived in England as an exile.

Johnny)[1] was in 'as bad a plight'. I think you know my correspondent & the member of the Camarilla who uses him.

Derby approved:

I have no doubt [he wrote back on January 7] that both he and
Lady P. will be furious and that you will have a lively scene in
your House on the first night of the Session. I am glad, however,
that you have repudiated the idea of a coalition with Palm: and
I am sure our only course will be to side with neither of the rival
factions but leave them to fight it out among themselves.[2]

Meanwhile the protectionist controversy remained unsettled and
something of a crisis occurred at the end of 1851 over Disraeli's
own position. The situation was aggravated by the publication of
Lord George Bentinck in December. The book, though widely
praised, contained, as the high Tories were quick to see, and as
Beresford at once pointed out to Derby, a surprising omission.
Derby himself was scarcely mentioned in it, and the whole picture
was thus distorted, for Bentinck's role, though very important, had
always been subordinate to that of Derby. The latter had been
recognized as leader of the party at a very early stage, March 1846 –
a fact never stated in the book. Buckle is probably right in assuming
that Disraeli, who for the last three years had been trying to persuade Derby to play down protection, did not wish at this moment
to emphasize that he had been one of its greatest supporters. As
we saw earlier, the same reason may have prompted him to pass
very lightly over the role of the Agricultural Protection Society.
Another example is his failure to say anything about the brief
period of Granby's leadership in succession to Bentinck at the
beginning of 1848, Granby still being a member of the triumvirate
which Disraeli habitually ignored, and wished to dissolve. With
Disraeli history was not only past politics but present politics, too.

Granby was himself weary of being put in a false and slightly
absurd position. He wrote at the turn of the year a dignified letter
of resignation to Derby in which he pointed out that 'principally
from my own want of energy and ability the position I held was a
mere nominal one'.[3] He found himself made responsible for policies
of which he knew nothing. The weekly meetings which he had asked

---

[1] Lord John Russell.
[2] Hughenden Papers, Box 109, B/XX/S/42.
[3] M. & B., iii, 312–13.

for were not held. He did not complain. 'Disraeli's talents and power of speech had,' he said, 'become everywhere known and acknowledged.'

Disraeli decided in view of this letter to test party opinion both about his own position as leader and about the question of protection. His intermediary was William Miles, who canvassed many of the leading figures in the House of Commons during the first half of January. By the 19th he could report a favourable verdict on both points except from Henley, the obstructionist of a year before, and Augustus Stafford, who disapproved of the chapter on the Jews in *Lord George Bentinck*. R. A. Christopher, MP for Lincolnshire, who was one of those consulted, thought that Disraeli was being oversensitive, but Sir John Buller, MP for South Devon and a leading country gentleman, wrote to Miles on January 21:

> . . . I am not surprised at his sensitiveness, for the way in which he is spoken of by Protectionists at the Carlton must have reached his ears; add to which *I* do think that we in the House of Commons have not placed him in the position he ought *now* to fill – namely that of our *one* acknowledged leader . . .[1]

Miles strongly approved of one innovation made by Disraeli. For the first time he received at his own house on the eve of the session the principal members of the House of Commons to discuss the Queen's speech, Derby receiving the peers. Hitherto all such meetings had been held at Derby House, which, so Miles said, 'has led to the surmise that a want of confidence existed in the party towards yourself'.[2]

On February 4 Parliament reassembled, and in the speeches of explanation about the dismissal of Palmerston it was generally felt that Russell scored heavily. But on February 20 Palmerston got his own back – his 'tit for tat', as he called it – by defeating Russell on an amendment to the Government's Militia Bill. Disraeli supported Palmerston. Russell resigned in a mood of indignation at what he alleged to be a 'pre-arranged determination between Lord Palmerston and the Protectionists'. This time there could be no hesitation about Derby's taking office. He promptly accepted the Queen's commission and did not attempt to negotiate with the Peelites. But both he and Disraeli, whatever their doubts about allying with Palmerston when in opposition, were determined to try their luck

[1] ibid., 315.   [2] loc. cit.

with him now. Disraeli displayed laudable magnanimity by offering, quite without solicitation, to waive his claim to the leadership if Palmerston would accept it. 'He would not like to serve under me who [sic] he looks upon as a whipper-snapper.' Derby, declaring that he would never forget 'the generous self-sacrifice',[1] felt obliged to accept the offer.

Palmerston, however, declined; to the great relief of the Queen who had absolutely vetoed him for the Foreign Office and dreaded his presence in any capacity. Derby had decided to offer Palmerston among other choices the Chancellorship of the Exchequer, but if he refused Disraeli was to be the man. 'I had then demurred,' wrote Disraeli, 'as a branch of which I had no knowledge.' Derby's reply was characteristic: 'You know as much as Mr. Canning did. They give you the figures.' And now Derby, proceeding straight from Palmerston's house to Grosvenor Gate, formally offered the post to Disraeli, who accepted, though he frankly says in his account that it was a post 'which I didn't want'.[2]

His misgivings were shared by the world at large. The appointment was the subject of much adverse comment, public and private. Gladstone echoed the general sentiment when he wrote in a letter to his wife: 'Disraeli could not have been worse placed than at the Exchequer.'[3] Why did Derby make the choice? The Chancellorship was not at that time the obvious post from which to lead the House when the Prime Minister was a peer. Most of the recent precedents pointed to the Home or Foreign Office. Disraeli himself believed that Derby was influenced by a desire to have the leader of the House at 11 Downing Street, 'under the same official roof as himself'. Buckle suggests that the Queen's aversion to Disraeli may have been another reason, for the Sovereign did not often have to see the Chancellor of the Exchequer personally, whereas the principal Secretaries of State were given frequent audiences.

There was evidently some sort of rumour current that Disraeli was to have the Foreign Office. Lord Lyndhurst actually wrote a premature letter of congratulation upon the appointment.[4] It is

---

[1] M. & B., iii, 341–5. Disraeli's account of the formation of Derby's Government, like his account of the failure of 1851, was written some ten years later.

[2] ibid., 344.

[3] Morley, *Gladstone*, i, 416–17.

[4] Lyndhurst himself refused the Lord Chancellorship on grounds of age – he was eighty – but having no sons accepted an earldom 'which he very much desired', according to Prince Albert's memorandum (Benson and Esher, *Letters of Queen Victoria*, ii, 449), 'for the position of his daughters'.

clear, however, from Gladstone's note of the year before that Derby did not mean to offer it;[1] and even if he had wished to do so, he would probably have failed to overcome the objections of the Court. Disraeli had indeed taken a prominent part in debates on foreign policy, and he prided himself on his knowledge of European diplomacy. No doubt he would have preferred the Foreign Office, but there is nothing in his or Derby's papers to suggest that he angled for it. One thing is certain: the story repeated as late as the 1880s by Spencer Walpole in his *History*, that he sought the Exchequer because 'a strong man armed with the power of the purse must necessarily be supreme',[2] has no foundation.

The new Cabinet consisted of the following:

First Lord of the Treasury	Earl of Derby
Lord Chancellor	Lord St Leonards
Lord President	Earl of Lonsdale
Lord Privy Seal	Marquess of Salisbury
Home Secretary	Spencer Walpole
Foreign Secretary	Earl of Malmesbury
Secretary for War and Colonies	Sir John Pakington
Chancellor of the Exchequer	Benjamin Disraeli
First Lord of the Admiralty	Duke of Northumberland
President of the Board of Control[3]	J. C. Herries
President of the Board of Trade	J. W. Henley
Postmaster General	Earl of Hardwicke
First Commissioner of Works	Lord John Manners

It did not look a very convincing body. Only three had ever held office before, or were even privy councillors, Derby, Lonsdale and Herries. There were some great Tory names, the heads of the houses of Cecil, Percy and Lowther[4] all being represented, and the selection of Lord John Manners was a deliberate effort to counterbalance the refusal of Granby to join. But none of these except Manners was more than a figurehead. They gave splendid parties – 'never was a faction so feasted', wrote Disraeli in June – but they did not bring strength to the Cabinet. Of the principal office-holders in the House of Commons, Spencer Walpole, a collateral descendant of the great Sir Robert and nephew of Spencer Perceval, was perhaps the best. Disraeli thought well of him. 'He only wants an opportunity to take

[1] See above, p. 303.
[2] Spencer Walpole, *History of England*, v, 38.
[3] Responsible for what later became the India Office.
[4] Lord Salisbury, the Duke of Northumberland, Lord Lonsdale, respectively.

a position equal to any man,' he had told Derby in December.[1] But Walpole had no experience – this was his first parliament – and he did not carry much weight. Herries, who had plenty of experience, was old and timorous. Henley was no friend of Disraeli. The most undistinguished figure of all was perhaps Sir John Pakington, a country gentleman whom Derby had destined for an under-secretaryship. But Herries had declined the Colonial Office, in a temporary huff at not being given the Exchequer, and Derby could not think of a substitute. Disraeli suggested Pakington, who was announced at that very moment.

> He remained in the waiting-room while I was convincing Lord Derby that he would make a competent Secretary of State. It was, naturally, rather hard work. I don't know that Lord Derby had even a personal acquaintance with Pakington at that moment. The exigency at last conquered him, he said with an almost merry face of perplexity: 'Will you be bail for him?' 'To any amount,' I said.[2]

And Pakington was duly appointed. 'I can't help laughing', wrote Smythe in a postscript to a letter of congratulation, 'at your having disinterred Sir Roger de Coverley, to stick him in the Colonies. It is so like one of your old strokes – in fiction.'[3] In the House of Lords the most important appointment was Malmesbury to the Foreign Office. He seems to have owed his position more to a distinguished diplomatic heredity and the fact that he shot with Derby than to any obvious talent for the post.

The Cabinet goes down to history by the nickname of the 'Who? Who?' Ministry. While some unlucky peer was endeavouring to make a speech in the House of Lords, the Duke of Wellington, who was very old, and quite unfamiliar with the new ministers, kept on repeating in the penetrating voice of the deaf 'Who? Who?' as Derby tried to tell him their names. The contemporary attitude to Derby's Government, and many of its features, remind one irresistibly of the first Labour Cabinet in 1924. There was the same division of opinion in the respectable world between those who feared that it would lead to riot and commotion and those who felt that such a substantial party must be 'given a chance'. The sentiments expressed by Aberdeen, Graham and Queen Victoria are remarkably

[1] Derby Papers, Box 145/1, December 9, 1851.
[2] M. & B., iii, 345.
[3] ibid., 348.

similar to those expressed by Baldwin, Asquith and King George V. There was the same problem of a minority government, the same question about the right to a dissolution, the same sense of foreboding, the same feeling that this was a freak event contradicting the natural order of political things. The resemblance can be pressed even further: in 1852 almost as many new privy councillors had to be sworn in as when Ramsay Macdonald took office in 1924.

Meanwhile Derby and Disraeli, oblivious of these apprehensions, were proceeding with the minor appointments. The lower the office the more troublesome it sometimes was to fill.

> We have left out Emerson Tennent[1] [wrote Derby]. This will never do. I must offer him the Secretaryship of the India Board. Ossulston refuses the Treasurership in fear of the expense of an election. It will do for Claude Hamilton if not for Seaham & Tennent will be invaluable on the Charter Committee & may be dangerous if left out.[2]

And Derby was so excited that he actually signed himself 'Yours ever'. Disraeli did not agree. Henry Baillie, who had been on the Ceylon Committee and who had ruthlessly cross-examined Tennent, was also a member of the Board of Control. He replied: 'Tennent with Baillie who has treated him as a *criminal* will never do. But I trust everything to your brighter brain'.[3] In the end Tennent became Secretary to the Poor Law Board, but this was not what he wanted, and his correct placing was to cause difficulty later. However, by February 27 all the places were settled. True, there was a last-minute panic owing to an unfortunate omission. 'We have forgotten the Paymaster General', wrote Disraeli. 'The Pay Office books cannot be opened till the name is given'.[4] Lord Colchester, the Vice-President of the Board of Trade, was hastily given that sinecure post as an extra, and the new administration was at last fairly launched. Disraeli had to secure re-election, as was the rule in those days. The delay gave him a welcome break from Parliamentary duties of nearly a fortnight, during which he could learn the ropes of his new department.

While displaying in public his usual impassivity, he was privately

---

[1] Sir James Emerson Tennent (1804–69), a former Irish Whig MP, one of the very few who followed Derby when he resigned from Grey's Cabinet in 1834; Civil Secretary to the Government of Ceylon 1845–50.

[2] Hughenden Papers, Box 109, B/XX/S/49, February 25.

[3] Derby Papers, Box 145/2, February 25.

[4] ibid., February 27.

thrilled at his elevation. He told Malmesbury that he felt like a girl going to her first ball. A quarter of a century later he reflected upon the occasion in *Endymion*, referring to himself as 'a gentleman without any official experience whatever' who became leader of the House, 'which had never occurred before, except in the instance of Mr. Pitt in 1782'. It was indeed a proud moment. Many people had reached his position at his age, indeed much younger. Few if any had done so in such circumstances and against such odds.

Among his many letters of congratulation one may perhaps have made Disraeli brood for a few minutes on the past. From Paris, Count d'Orsay wrote to him on April 7:

> My dearest D'Is – I wanted to write to you all this time but I have been ill I may say for the first time of my life. Fancy me on a sofa with an atrocious lumbago for the last six weeks and obliged to write with a pencil. I cannot resist longer to congratulate you, and myself, on your present position. I say myself because for many years I said that there was no power which could prevent you to arrive at the Ministry and at the head of the House of Commons . . .[1]

The famous establishment at Gore House had succumbed to financial disaster three years earlier; the pair had fled to France in April 1849, Lady Blessington dying a few weeks later. D'Orsay went through a period of black despair, but the skies lightened after the *coup d'état* of 1851, for the new Emperor conferred on him the position of Director of Fine Arts. Alas, it was a fleeting change of fortune. His real illness was not lumbago but cancer of the spine. By August he too was dead, and one more companion of Disraeli's stormy youth had faded into the shadows of memory.

2

Two great problems needed settlement during 1852, and politicians of almost every colour were agreed on their nature, though not on their solution. One was the question of protection, the other that of the unstable balance of power in the House of Commons which had been the cause of feeble minority government ever since the fall of Peel.[2] It was also, however, generally agreed that nothing could be

[1] M. & B., iii, 167.
[2] See C. H. Stuart, 'The Formation of the Coalition Cabinet of 1852', *Royal Historical Society Transactions*, 5th Series, 4 (1954), 45–69, for an acute analysis of the political situation at this time.

done about them in the present Parliament; moreover, for various reasons, the obvious course of an immediate dissolution could be ruled out. Necessary measures such as the Militia Bill on which Russell had fallen, the Estimates, the Mutiny Act had to be carried first. Otherwise, presumably Russell would himself have asked for a dissolution. But as Disraeli wrote to the Queen, 'the question soon arose, what is "necessary"?'

Russell, who had a passion for office unsurpassed by any other statesman of the day, except Disraeli himself, was in a factious mood and ready to turn out the Government immediately. Although his brother, the Duke of Bedford, was one of the richest men in England, he himself, like Disraeli, had an uncertain financial background. Both men were much poorer than the run of Victorian statesmen and five thousand a year may have had more effect upon their conduct than upon that of their wealthy colleagues. The Peelites took a less extreme line than Russell. They held the balance and allowed it to be known to Derby that they would support the ministry on two conditions: a dissolution in the summer and a meeting of Parliament in November at which the Government must bring forward its proposals on the fiscal question. Matters proceeded on this understanding and Derby was safe for the time being.

This bargain with the Peelites had important consequences for the Chancellor of the Exchequer. Since it was accepted that any change in the fiscal system must await the election results, he could only produce an interim budget for April. His hands were further tied because income tax had been extended in 1851 by resolution of the House for one year only, pending the report of a Select Committee on the whole subject. Disraeli decided to prolong the income tax for one more year, and for the time being to make no changes at all in taxation. But under the bargain with the Peelites he would have to bring forward his proper budget as early as possible in the first session of the new Parliament, that is to say in November or December. This was an unusual and highly inconvenient time of year. Derby and Disraeli were ill advised to yield on the point. The question of free trade against protection could have been – indeed was to be – settled, quite apart from the budget, by a Resolution at the very beginning of the session. There was no real reason to anticipate the normal budget date, and Disraeli would almost certainly have fared better had he refused to do so.

Meanwhile the attitude of the Government to protection remained

ambiguous. In his opening speech as Prime Minister on February 27
Derby announced a policy which Disraeli described to his sister as
'Protection in its most odious form'. Disraeli was determined to
undo the damage as he considered it, and in his budget speech on
April 30 went out of his way to dwell on the great advantages to the
state of the nation produced by Sir Charles Wood's free-trade
budget of 1851. Privately Derby was already convinced that the
election was unlikely to give him a mandate for even the moderate
fixed duty on corn which had been the mainstay of his fiscal policy
when he took office, but he did not welcome a public abandonment
of protection. As soon as he had heard the speech he returned to
Derby House and penned a 1,400-word letter of protest. A friend of
his, Lord Monteagle,[1] he said,

> highly (and not more highly than it deserved) praised the clear-
> ness and ability of your statement but added, 'It was one of the
> strongest Free Trade speeches I ever heard' and from another
> quarter I heard the remark, 'It was the eulogy of Peel by Disraeli.'
>
> I did not like to say much to Henry Lennox[2] who came to me
> as from you to hear my opinion; and I sent him back with a very
> short and indefinite message; but I cannot deny that I feel great
> anxiety as to the consequences . . .
>
> A very short time will serve to show whether my apprehensions
> are chimerical; no one will rejoice more than I shall to find they
> are, and that you have taken a more accurate measure of the
> feelings of the party with whom we act *and must act*, than
>
> Yrs sincerely
Derby[3]

But towards the end of May, Derby himself admitted in the House
of Lords that he did not expect to obtain a strong enough majority
from the election to enable him to bring in a duty on imported grain.

The other events of the session need little discussion. A revised
Militia Bill was successfully carried with the aid of Palmerston. A
constitution for New Zealand was enacted and a number of law
reforms passed. All these measures had, of course, been prepared by
the previous Government, but it required skill, nevertheless, to
carry them against what seems to have been highly factious opposition. No doubt Peelite aid was indispensable, but the Peelites, too,

---

[1] Thomas Spring-Rice, Whig Chancellor of the Exchequer, 1835–9.
[2] See below, pp. 325–7.
[3] Hughenden Papers, Box 109, B/XX/S/54, April 30.

needed careful handling.[1] Disraeli could legitimately claim the credit
for all this. He had to do it more or less single-handed, even Walpole,
his ablest colleague in the Commons, making a serious blunder over
the Militia Bill. But Disraeli in the lower House was not such a
dictator as Derby was in the upper. Of his methods Greville wrote,
'The other members of the Cabinet have appeared as mere dummies,
and in the House of Lords Derby has never allowed any of them to
speak, taking on himself to answer for every department.'[2]

To the Court, Derby seemed to be virtually carrying on the
Government single-handed. 'In the present case,' wrote the Queen
to her uncle, the King of the Belgians, on March 23, 'our acquaintance is confined almost entirely to Lord Derby, but then *he is* the
Government. They do *nothing* without him.'[3] It is quite wrong to
think of him as in any sense a figurehead. Certainly no one thought
so at the time, least of all Disraeli. 'Lord Derby has the gout!' he
wrote to his sister on May 14. 'They say it is light; but he is in bed,
and how things are to go without him baffles my imagination.'[4]

What sort of impression did Disraeli make in his new role as
leader of the House? Greville, relying apparently on Graham, wrote
at the end of March: 'There are great complaints of Disraeli in the
House of Commons. They say he does not play his part as leader
with tact and propriety, and treats his opponents impudently and
uncourteously . . .'[5] At the end of the session Greville pays a tribute
to Disraeli's 'great ability' and the 'excellence' of his financial statement; but he prefaces this praise by observing that he was 'a perfect
will-o'-the-wisp, flitting about from one opinion to another . . .'[6]
Probably Disraeli did annoy some people by the sarcasms in which
he indulged. There is, however, no general evidence that he was
impudent or discourteous. Greville's friends were for the most part
Disraeli's political enemies, and Graham was a person whom
Disraeli particularly enjoyed baiting.

The last weeks of the session were overshadowed by the impend-

[1] They only opposed the Government once – over a proposal to divide the four
parliamentary seats taken from the disfranchised boroughs of S Albans and Sudbury
between South Lancashire and the West Riding of Yorkshire. The ground was that
the matter ought not to be dealt with by an expiring parliament, and the proposal
was heavily defeated.
[2] *Greville Memoirs*, vi, 343, July 7, 1852.
[3] *Letters of Queen Victoria*, 1837–61, ii, 467.
[4] M. & B., iii, 368.
[5] *Greville Memoirs*, vi, 337.
[6] ibid., 342.

ing general election. Disraeli was careful to consult Derby about the wording of his address to his constituents in Buckinghamshire – the nearest equivalent in those days to a party manifesto – for usage dictated that Derby as a peer should not make electioneering speeches. But Derby did not press the protectionist cause, and the only satisfaction that the landed interest could get out of the document was a vague reference to 'the possibility of greatly relieving the burdens of the community both by adjustment and reduction' and a hope that 'a Ministry formed on the principles of Conservative progress' might 'terminate for ever, by just and conciliatory measures, the misconceptions which have too long prevailed between producer and consumer, and extinguish the fatal jealousy that rankles between town and country'.

It was as well that Disraeli had thus 'squared' the Prime Minister, for no sooner was the address published than his two least friendly Cabinet colleagues, Herries and Henley, who had already raised objections to the draft, at once took umbrage. Henley wrote:

> My dear Mr. D'Israeli,
>   . . . I demur to anyone 'not the head' of the government issuing manifestoes in the name of the whole, the matter not having been submitted to the cabinet. I have said this to others and therefore say it to you.
>
> > Faithfully yrs
> > J. W. Henley

Disraeli passed this on to Derby observing: 'Henley has never acted cordially with me either in opposition or in government but I have hitherto disregarded his churlishness & treated him very kindly – wh: has however been pouring water on a sandy soil.'[1]

Then there was Herries. He, so Disraeli told Derby, 'disapproves altogether. He says we are sinking; that the flag is drooping on the staff; that we are a government of negations.' Herries wanted 'abstract protection' to be announced, 'and general protestantism asserted'.[2] After his troubles in 1851, Derby probably knew how much importance to attach to the grumbles of the two H's.

Disraeli's manifesto was not solely concerned with the question of the landed interest. The 'principles of Conservative progress' included other points: the maintenance of the colonial empire; the investigation of parliamentary reform, to be achieved 'in the spirit of our popular, though not democratic institutions'; and the

[1] Derby Papers, Box 145/2, Disraeli to Derby, June 8, 1852.   [2] ibid., June 10.

assertion that 'the Crown of England shall still be a Protestant Crown'. The latter might seem a superfluous declaration, but the shemozzle created by the 'papal aggression' and the Durham letter was far from dead. An ultra Protestant MP called Spooner had moved for an inquiry into the Maynooth Grant and much parliamentary time towards the end of the session was occupied on this unfruitful topic.

With the exception of the Peelites, none of the political groups comes out in a good light over the religious question. Derby and Disraeli were certainly not blameless, and Aberdeen seems to have finally abandoned any intention of rejoining them largely because of the way in which they exploited the religious issue. The truth was that toleration of Rome at this time, like reform of the homosexuality laws in our own day, was a matter on which most intelligent politicians agreed, but defiance of the bigotry of the masses involved political dangers which they were loath to risk. The Conservatives were no worse than the Whigs. Gladstone pointed out to Aberdeen on August 5: 'As for religious bigotry I condemn the proceedings of the present government; yet much less strongly than the unheard-of course pursued by Lord John Russell in 1850–1 . . .'[1]

On the eve of the election a tiresome difficulty arose in the Admiralty, which was headed by 'the Lord of Alnwick Castle', as Disraeli terms him in *Endymion*, with Augustus Stafford, the Parliamentary Secretary, representing the department in the lower House. The two did not get on, Stafford habitually referring to the Duke of Northumberland as 'our Doge' in his numerous letters of complaint to Disraeli. The so-called Admiralty boroughs, Devonport, Greenwich, Portsmouth, Chatham, were among the last surviving places where the government of the day might hope to win the elections by the judicious use of patronage. Stafford, being in the House of Commons, naturally paid attention to this side of things, and he considered that the Duke was too inclined to ignore it. Matters came to a head when the Duke appointed a Captain Lushington whom Stafford believed to be a Whig to the command of HMS *Albion*. Stafford begged Disraeli to intervene.

The latter forwarded the complaint to Derby. '*Audi alteram partem* is not a bad rule', replied Derby on June 2. 'Here is the case of our First Lord, and his Secretary Stafford ought to be quite sure of his facts before he asks for interference.'[2] The Duke repudiated

[1] Morley, i, 429.   [2] Hughenden Papers, Box 109, B/XX/S/61.

with some vigour the grave charge of having appointed Captain
Lushington on his merits. On the contrary he had done so because
he was told that the Captain 'was a sure Tory – otherwise Captain
Lushington is not an officer I should have appointed'.[1] But this did
not finally dispose of the matter, for it turned out that the Duke had
a Whig private secretary whose advice was, therefore, open to
suspicion, and Captain Lushington, whatever the Duke might say,
was not a Tory. At the beginning of July, Stafford wrote indignantly that, as the appointment 'will spread like wildfire thro' our
dockyard towns, you must expect it to exercise considerable
influence upon the elections there as well as elsewhere. Anything
in the way of patronage that I can do is hopeless against such a
system as this. All the old clerks in the office are laughing at us.'[2]
And Disraeli wrote to Derby on July 2:

> What is to be done about the enclosed from Stafford. It is quite
> impossible to secure a single dockyard return if this system be
> persisted in. We shall lose Devonport & Greenwich, as we have
> already lost Portsmouth. At any rate such pranks should have
> been played after the election.[3]

Derby's reply to this is not known, but the question of Admiralty
patronage was to involve the Tory ministers in a disagreeable
scandal which broke after they had been ejected from office and
which wrecked Stafford's political career. It involved a wider issue
than Captain Lushington's promotion – the whole matter of dockyard appointments. Recommendations for these had been routed to
the board through the Secretary of the Admiralty until in 1849 the
Whigs in the interests of electoral purity removed the patronage to
the Surveyor of the Navy, a permanent officer of high standing. The
Tories were not slow to point out that the Whigs, having enjoyed
the patronage for fourteen out of nineteen years since 1830, were in
a good position to adopt a high-minded attitude. By 1852 there was
scarcely a job which was not filled by a Whig supporter. Nevertheless Stafford invited trouble when at the end of April 1852 he
revoked the decision of 1849 and reassumed the dockyard recommendations for himself. He was certainly not discouraged by Derby
and Disraeli, both of whom to their dying days had an attitude to
patronage reminiscent of the era of Lord North rather than of the

[1] ibid., B/XX/S/61a.
[2] ibid., Box 143, B/XXI/S/473.
[3] Derby Papers, Box 145/2.

Trevelyan–Northcote Report,[1] but his letters hardly bear out his later claim that they pressed him against his will. The Duke of Northumberland, despite his views on the Lushington case, does appear to have had doubts: he was a lukewarm Derbyite partisan and had accepted the Admiralty as a non-party magnifico who had been himself a naval officer. The Surveyor, Sir Baldwin Walker, who, so Derby alleged to Disraeli, was 'a very mischievous influence', nearly resigned. The episode inevitably got to the ears of the Opposition. There was a Parliamentary inquiry, and long after the fall of the Government a debate in July 1853, very damaging to the unlucky Stafford and by no means pleasant for Derby and Disraeli.

Parliament was dissolved on July 1. Despite Disraeli's manifesto, the Opposition was able to make ample capital out of the shuffling attitude of the Government over free trade. Derby at no stage publicly disclaimed protection, although he privately told the Queen that a corn duty for any purpose must be regarded as out of the question even if, as he hoped, the election gave him a majority of about forty. The absence of any clear lead resulted in a wide variety of electoral pledges even from ministers, and wider still from their followers. The allegation that the Tories were protectionist in the counties, free traders in the big boroughs and fence-sitters in the small, had some truth in it. The other features of the election were the 'no popery' cry and a degree of corruption which struck contemporaries as sufficiently notorious to earn the Parliament of 1852 the nickname of 'the Bribery Parliament'. But there is no need to think that the Tories suffered unduly on that account. It was an electoral art in which they were quite capable of holding their own.

The results cannot be stated with the numerical exactitude of an election today. Contemporary estimates of Derby's supporters varied from 290 to 310. Derby himself told the Queen after the fall of his Government in December that the number who voted for the budget on that occasion, 286, verified almost to a man his calculations following the election. Whatever the precise figure, it is clear that though the Derbyites gained a few seats, it was not enough to give them a majority. The other parties consisted of about 270 Liberals whom Derby analysed into 120 Whigs and 150 Radicals, though he probably used the latter term very loosely; some thirty-five to forty Peelites, and the same number of Irish known as 'Brigaders' from the term 'Irish Brigade'. Evidently the Brigaders and

---

[1] Recommending (1853) open competition for entry to the Civil Service.

Peelites held the balance of power, but if the Peelites voted solid for Derby they could give him a bare majority, even though the Brigaders were on the other side. It was an intriguing situation, and no one could be sure of the outcome until Parliament met in November. Clearly much would depend on Disraeli's budget, and to this he proceeded to turn his mind during the next three months.

Although he was able to remain at Hughenden from the election until early October, he was fully occupied with business, and not merely that of his department. Patronage continued to give much difficulty.

For example, there was the problem of the Board of Trade; 'filled with our enemies', Disraeli said, advising Lord Malmesbury to conduct certain negotiations, which, in fact, proved abortive, for the reciprocal reduction of British and French tariffs, without its knowledge. Its officials were self-constituted guardians of free-trade dogma in the most extreme form. An opportunity of planting a friend in this hostile territory arose owing to the sudden demise of G. R. Porter, one of the secretaries, 'occasioned, I suppose', wrote Disraeli on September 5 to Derby, 'by the accession of a Protectionist Ministry'.[1] The office was 'one of real administration & must not be filled by a scarecrow'. Would it not be a neat solution to insert Sir Emerson Tennent,[2] who wanted a permanent position and whose seat was a safe Tory one? The salary was £2,000 per annum.

> He has arrived at a time of life when he can scarcely any longer dream of being Govr. Genl, leaving that future to Jocelyn and others equally qualified . . . He is perfectly qualified for the office and his seat wd be safe for a good man.
>
> In case you do not approve of this suggestion or he declines the proposition we must be prepared with a Secretary who will not disgrace us. If the worst comes to the worst there is McCulloch. He is too old but he has a European reputation & it wd at any rate be an appointment wh wd not alarm enlightened economists.

Tennent accepted. Meanwhile another bright idea had struck Disraeli. He wrote on September 10 to suggest to Derby that:

> . . . the office of the Chief of the Statistical Department, held by Fonblanque,[3] an *imbecile* as a man of business & who passes his official hours in writing libels against us, shd be suppressed & its

[1] Derby Papers, Box 145/2, Porter (b. 1792) was an able statistician.
[2] See above, p. 314. His existing post was a political one.
[3] Albany Fonblanque, 1793–1872, Radical journalist.

supervision transferred to its proper superintendent, the Commercial Secy of the Board of Trade.

It was originally a job to give office to Porter & his peculiar pursuits – but Gladstone in his evidence before the Committee on Public Salaries stated that he thought that two Secretaries to the B.O.T. were quite sufficient . . . When McGregor resigned, the Whigs preferred Porter, & quite justifiably, to the vacant post but continued the special job for the sake of providing for Fonblanque.

It wd be a delightful arrangement turning him out. We shd save 800£ per ann[m]. & when we read his abuse of us in the Examiner we wd have the satisfaction of knowing that we had done something for the distinction.[1]

Derby fully approved of this ingenious device, but thought it 'must be carefully managed; probably it would be better not to make it simultaneously with the appointment of Tennent'.[2] At this juncture a stiff letter reached Derby from the curmudgeonly Henley,[3] complaining, with some justice it would seem, that he ought to have been consulted as President of the Board of Trade about the filling of the vacancy caused by Porter's death. Much parade of hurt feelings and gentlemanly self-sacrifice ensued, Tennent offering to give up the office he had accepted. However, in the end Henley, who wanted to suppress the post altogether, surrendered, contenting himself with another disagreeable letter to Derby. 'All has concluded mildly', wrote Disraeli, '& in fact Henley's letter to you was only an exhibition of morose pique.'[4] In spite of all this trouble, Tennent's appointment was not a success; some fourteen years later we find Disraeli writing sadly to Derby: 'He has turned out to be the most inefficient & useless of our public servants: no business in him: no sound information: his dept. in a disgraceful state & himself a mere club gossip & office lounger.'[5]

One important piece of patronage seemed imminent. This was the Governor-Generalship of India, where Dalhousie had reached the end of his four-year term. His wife's health appeared so bad that he would have to retire, despite the urgent pleas of the Court of the East India Company. Disraeli's old friend Chandos, the bankrupted Duke of Buckingham, whose financial and sexual morality were

---

[1] Derby Papers, Box 145/2. Fonblanque remained in office till his death.
[2] Hughenden Papers, Box 109, B/XX/S/72, September 12.
[3] ibid., B/XX/S/73, September 14.
[4] Derby Papers, Box 145/2, September 27, 1852.
[5] ibid., Box 146/2, December 3, 1866.

PARADISE AND THE PERI

"Joy, joy for ever! My task is done –
The gates are passed, and Heaven is won!"
LALLA ROOKH *Punch*, February 28, 1874

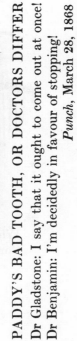

PADDY'S BAD TOOTH, OR DOCTORS DIFFER

Dr Gladstone: I say that it ought to come out at once!
Dr Benjamin: I'm decidedly in favour of stopping!
Punch, March 28, 1868

CIVIL SERVICE STORES

What can we do for you, Madam? – Royal Commission? – Select
Committee? – Papers? – Careful Consideration? – Official Inquiry?
Anything to Oblige!

Punch, March 11, 1876

alike dubious, indicated that the position would be acceptable to him. But the time had gone by when the Grenville 'connexion' could secure an important post for a man like this. Disraeli forwarded the letter to Derby, who, though none too squeamish, returned it observing:

> . . . but I have no answer to make to it. It is difficult to convey to a man without affronting him the idea that his character and habits of life would render his appointment to high office discreditable to any Government.[1]

In the end Dalhousie remained Viceroy for another four years.

Relations between Derby and Disraeli seem to have been quite good during the recess. Derby expected things to be done properly and said so when they were not. Disraeli was wise enough to avoid making excuses. 'I made a mistake from ignorance of the system on wh our business is carried on & am very sorry', he writes on one occasion. 'I will take care in future that you will not have to complain on that score.'[2] But such episodes were rare, and he soon learnt the routine of his department. He was well able to stand up to Derby if necessary. Lord Monteagle had asked Derby to obtain a pension for an ecclesiastical commissioner, the Revd R. Jones, whose job had come to an end. 'Do you think the House of Commons would listen to a special case for a retiring allowance after 17 years service?' asked Derby.[3] Disraeli did not. 'He was in receipt, I believe, of £2000 per ann^m,' he replied, '. . . his notorious Epicurean habits could alone have prevented his accumulating during seventeen years the means of independence.'[4] Mr Jones owed his position to the Archbishop and had no party claim, being 'a warm adherent of a different political connexion'. Disraeli did not mean to strain his credit in the House of Commons by supporting a job for a political opponent in order to gratify an old Whig colleague of the Prime Minister. Derby wisely did not pursue the matter.

At about this time Disraeli acquired a new friend. This was Lord Henry Lennox, MP for Chichester, whom he had persuaded Derby to make a Lord of the Treasury. Lennox, a son of the Duke of Richmond, was young, fashionable, engaging and somewhat featherheaded. His rise into favour was viewed with jealousy by the earlier

[1] Hughenden Papers, Box 109, B/XX/S/75, September 23.
[2] Derby Papers, Box 145/2.
[3] Hughenden Papers, Box 109, B/XX/S/67, August 19.
[4] Derby Papers, Box 145/2, August 23, 1852.

generation of Disraeli's admirers. Certainly he lacked the intellectual strength of Smythe or Manners, who gave Disraeli almost as much as they received. But the episode was typical. Disraeli had never had many friends of his own age. Perhaps he was inhibited by an increasing reluctance to give himself away, perhaps too by having missed the public school and university background where such relationships were most naturally formed. As a young man he had patrons, like Lyndhurst. When he grew older he had disciples, like Smythe. But friendships on equal terms were few: with Meredith, Clay, and perhaps Bulwer Lytton; it is hard to think of others. To say that Disraeli only gave his confidence to young men and old women would perhaps be an overstatement, but not an outrageous one.

Lennox was good company, entertaining, full of the latest gossip. He did not hesitate to use acid and scurrilous epithets about most of the Tory front bench, but he seems to have pleased rather than offended his chief by describing, for example, Christopher as 'that great bellowing booby', or Derby's son as 'young Morose'. His object in life was engagingly simple. Having rapidly got through the modest fortune which was the lot of younger sons even when their fathers were dukes, he was determined to restore his finances either by a good marriage or by a good place. As he wrote to Disraeli, 'there is but *one thing* left for me & that is to sell my rank and position for such a sum as will enable me to keep it up'.[1] Unfortunately his matrimonial ventures invariably foundered, whether the lady was a Spanish princess who was forbidden to marry a Protestant or the daughter of a *nouveau riche* called Macleod whom the Duke persisted in snubbing. As time went on he became less eligible. 'It is always the same thing; either the lady has too little money or I am too old', he sadly wrote to Disraeli in 1863, ending, however, on a more hopeful note. 'In this pinch a friend has suggested to me to try it on with the eldest of Sir Anthony de Rothschild's daughters.' Could Disraeli help, he wondered? If he tried, Disraeli did not succeed. Lord Henry remained a bachelor to the end.

He was no less frustrated in his endeavours to secure a place. From that point of view he was on the wrong side in politics, for the Tories were nearly always 'out'. It is easy to understand his indignation with young Stanley when in 1855 Derby for the second time declined a chance of office.

[1] Hughenden Papers, Box 102, B/XX/LX/29, n.d.

I confess that he irritated me not a little by saying 'that even if we did never come in we played a great part by controlling & checking Govt' which I told him might be very well to those who had politics *as an amusement* & the reversion of 100,000 pr. annum as a reality; but that to some younger sons it was not quite the same thing.[1]

Lord Henry's quandary was typical of his time and class. Younger sons separated by the narrow chance of birth or death from high rank and vast wealth were uneasy figures on the aristocratic scene. No one depicts their plight more cogently than Trollope in his political novels. These casualties of the system of primogeniture, debarred by social prejudice from a trade or profession, were sometimes spurred on to brilliant compensatory political careers; Lord John Russell, Lord Robert Cecil, Lord Randolph Churchill. Too often they became mere parasites living on the hope of civil, ecclesiastical or matrimonial patronage. Lennox is of interest as a type, but as a person he was never more than an intellectual flibbertigibbet. He would long ago have been forgotten had it not been for the affection which he inspired in a man of genius. 'I can only tell you that I love you',[2] wrote Disraeli on September 1, 1852, and a fortnight later, 'Even a line is pleasant from those we love.'[3] The language must be discounted as the hyperbole of the time. But it remains something of a mystery that Disraeli should have been as fond as he was of such an essentially trivial personality.

[1] Hughenden Papers, Box 102, B/XX/LX/58, Lennox to Disraeli, February 12, 1855.
[2] M. & B., iii, 387.
[3] ibid., 392.

CHAPTER XV

The Budget of 1852

'Truly it has been said', writes Morley, 'that there is something repulsive to human nature in the simple reproduction of defunct budgets. Certainly if anything can be more odious than a living tax it is a dead one.'[1] Despite this warning it is impossible to avoid some discussion of Disraeli's first essay in constructive legislation. Apart from the interim financial statement of April he only produced three budgets in the whole of his career, and that of December 1852 was by far the most controversial. The circumstances were very difficult. He was under the pressure of complicated conflicting forces which perhaps no one could have reconciled, and the blame for defeat was not his alone. Yet, although he fought with great courage, it is clear that he made serious mistakes and presented unnecessary targets. The story throws much light on his qualities and defects as a statesman.

Disraeli's problem was to satisfy the 'interests' that deemed themselves to have been damaged by free trade, and at the same time to avoid reuniting against him the whole of the opposition in the House of Commons. The principal interests were the landed, the sugar and the shipping lobbies. Long before the session opened it was clear that there could be no question of reviving protection. Yet it was no less clear that Disraeli had to do something. His shadowy promises of 'compensation' would be flung in his face by his own supporters if he did not. But what could he do without arousing the wrath of the formidable phalanx of financial panjandrums on the Opposition benches? He had to encounter such figures as Wood, Goulburn and Baring, who had introduced between them the last thirteen budgets; Russell and Graham who prided themselves upon their expertise in political economy; Cobden and Bright ever vigilant to pounce on anything that savoured even faintly of protection. Above all, there was Gladstone, disciple of Peel, determined to vindicate his master's doctrines. Already as early as July 30 he was finding, so he told Aberdeen, each successive speech of Disraeli on finance 'more quackish in its flavour than its predecessor'.[2]

[1] Morley, i, 461. [2] ibid., 429.

It was not an easy problem. The injured interests could only be satisfied by remission of taxes. This meant either cutting expenditure or imposing additional taxes on someone else. Disraeli was to find, as every new Chancellor of the Exchequer invariably finds, how narrow are the limits within which he could manœuvre. These limits may, and often do, seem in the retrospect of fifty or a hundred years absurdly conventional and unnecessary, but the self-imposed barriers of custom and habit are not less oppressive and constricting than those of the physical world. It requires an effort now to envisage rich men objecting to an income tax of $7d$ in the pound, but the problem was a real one then.

In the decade preceding Disraeli's budget, government expenditure varied between £48 m and £55 m. Rather over half of this, about £28 m, went on the service of the National Debt. The other principal item was the armed services. From 1825 to 1852 expenditure on the Army, including the Ordnance, which counted as a separate service until 1854, averaged £8¾ m, on the Navy £6½ m. Civil expenditure ran at about £5 m–6 m. When in opposition everyone talked about extravagance and the need for economy, but no one who had any experience seriously believed that substantial cuts could really be made. The service of the Debt could not be much diminished. Expenditure on the armed services tended to rise with technical innovations, and any attempt at reduction met severe opposition from the Court.

The only area where economy seemed at all feasible lay in the field of civil administration: hence the glee with which Disraeli jumped at the chance of suppressing an office, especially if it happened to be held by a political opponent. But suppression was a double-edged weapon. The Tory leaders did not wish to deprive themselves of useful patronage. The sort of conflict which followed is well illustrated by the episode of the Secretaryship of the Board of Trade described in the last chapter. In any case such economies were mere drops in the ocean. The inexorable trend of the time was for governmental expenditure to increase, as governments found themselves forced to provide the framework of an orderly and civilized society. The suppression of sinecures could do little, if anything, to offset it.

On the revenue side recent budgets had shown receipts of about £20–21 m from the Customs, £14½ m from the Excise, £6 m–7 m from the stamp duties, £4 m from a variety of direct taxes, and

£5 m–5½ m from the unpopular income tax, reimposed, after an interval of twenty-six years, by Peel in 1842. Income tax was defended as a temporary measure designed first to remove the deficit inherited from the Whigs, secondly to tide over the loss to the revenue incurred by the great tariff revisions of 1842 and 1845. These had been very successful: the remission of a large number of vexatious duties had greatly increased trade; the reduction to a low level of many others had not only increased the volume of trade but, after a year or so, actually augmented the revenue, for higher consumption outweighed the effect of lower rates. But income tax remained intensely unpopular. It had been renewed for three years in 1845 and again in 1848, but Sir Charles Wood's attempt to repeat the process in 1851 caused a parliamentary revolt: he was, as we saw, only able to renew it for one year, a period extended for one more by Disraeli's interim budget.

The fiscal experiences of the previous decade had established certain canons of financial orthodoxy. First, the national credit must never be endangered by the least hint of a deficit. Secondly, remission of duties must be made with the following considerations in mind: the good done to the consumer and to the revenue; the need to remove the last vestiges of protectionism; the need to abolish duties which cost as much to collect as they produced; and the desirability of lowering wherever possible duties on highly taxed articles of general consumption. Thirdly, the income tax, if it had to be levied at all, must be levied at a uniform rate on all types of income. It was believed by Peel and his disciples, though hotly disputed by the Radicals, that to distinguish between 'precarious' and 'realized', or, as we would say, earned and unearned income was impracticable and would wreck the whole structure of the tax. Anyone who ignored these canons did so at his peril. Disraeli characteristically disregarded almost all of them.

The exact nature of his original scheme is not known. Heavy last-minute demands for increased expenditure on the armed services caused him twice to recast his figures, first at the beginning of November, the second time only three days before introducing his budget. But during August he evidently contemplated a much more drastic plan. 'Can you *really*', wrote Stanley on August 9, 'take off half the malt tax and half the income-tax? Great will be the joy if you do, but it sounds too good to be true.'[1] It was. A war scare

[1] Hughenden Papers, Box 111, B/XX/S/560.

prompted by fear of Louis Napoleon – a fear which both Disraeli and Malmesbury rightly dismissed – swept through the Court and the Cabinet. Derby insisted on accepting the demands of the services. Disraeli's potential surplus was further reduced by the pessimistic estimates of the Treasury officials who found it difficult to calculate with certainty so early in the financial year and naturally erred on the side of caution. By the time he came to propound his budget there was no question of halving the income tax.

The malt tax, however, was another matter. For years past it had been one of the standing grievances of the agricultural party. Levied at 2s 7d per bushel, it produced in 1851 just over £5 m. To reduce it seemed the simplest way of satisfying the landed interest. The alternative which Disraeli had advocated in the past was to shift part of the burden of the Poor Rate on to the Consolidated Fund. But the difficulty here was that rate-borne expenditure which largely went on poor relief had already fallen from £6·2 m in 1848 to £4·9 m in 1851, thanks to increased prosperity in the country, and therefore the case for a further reduction had become much weaker. Moreover, the rates were mainly a tax on occupiers of land. To relieve them would not help the general public, and would look like class legislation of the worst sort. On the other hand, a reduction of the malt tax would make the growing of barley more profitable, bring new land into production, and please the whole community by lowering the price of beer. Disraeli, therefore, resolved to halve the malt tax, and also the duty on hops, the effect being to reduce the price of beer by $\frac{1}{4}d$ a quart – not, it must be admitted, a very notable contribution to the reduction of the cost of living.

Having thus dealt with the landed interest, he had to decide what to do for the shipping and sugar lobbies. He did not do much. He gave some relief to the former by reducing or abolishing certain minor but vexatious dues, and to the latter, despite contrary advice from the Customs Board, he gave the privilege of refining colonial sugar in bond.

The budget was unlikely to succeed unless Disraeli did something more to gratify the general public, or at least those with votes, as well as particular interests. Accordingly he decided to make two important changes. The first, and less controversial, was to lower the duty on tea. This was in full accord with financial orthodoxy as tending, in Gladstone's words, to stimulate 'the self-producing powers' of the revenue, and it was cordially backed by the Treasury and the

Customs Board. The tax was very high, $2s\ 2\frac{1}{4}d$ a pound, and Disraeli proposed to reduce it by stages, $6\frac{1}{4}d$ in the first year, $2d$ in the second and $1\frac{1}{2}d$ in the next four, till it fell to $1s$ after six years.

The second major change affected the income tax and was much more disputable. Originally, he intended both to reduce the total sum raised, and to make the incidence of the tax less inequitable, but he soon saw that he could not do without the full product. He had therefore to confine himself to modifying the way in which it was levied. The tax was still the same as that carried by Peel in 1842: $7d$ in the pound on all incomes over £150 p.a. in England and Scotland. Ireland was exempt, but paid higher spirit duties instead. Farmer's profits were assessed at one-half of their rental in England, one-third in Scotland. The stock criticism of the tax in Radical quarters was that it failed to distinguish between earned and unearned income. Disraeli, therefore, resolved to make a bold bid for support from that side of the House by proposing to levy tax on 'precarious' incomes at three-quarters of the rate on 'realized' incomes, ie $5\frac{1}{4}d$ instead of $7d$. He also decided to assess profits of farmers in England at one-third instead of one-half of their rental. To compensate for these losses he proposed to lower the exemption limit to £100 in the case of earned and £50 in the case of unearned income, and to extend to Ireland Schedules C and E of the income tax, ie those covering incomes derived from the Funds and from salaries.

There was much to be said on grounds of equity for distinguishing between precarious and realized incomes, and taxing the former less heavily than the latter. This has become accepted practice today, and Disraeli was ahead of his own time in putting forward such a proposal. On the other hand, it is clear that he did not examine the difficulties with enough care. He committed the serious mistake of treating the various schedules as if they could be grouped according to the distinction he wished to make. He reduced the rate on B (farm incomes), D (profits from trade, business, professions, etc.) and E (salaries), leaving A (incomes derived from land) and C (the Funds) at $7d$. But his critics were quick – and right – to point out that Schedule A also included in those days profits from businesses connected with land, such as collieries, quarries and canal companies, although these were not in principle different from the profits of a cotton manufacturer, which came under Schedule D. Conversely, Schedule D covered certain sources of income which would be more properly taxed at the full rate. For example, it included income derived from any personal or real property outside England and Scotland. The absentee Irish landlord would pay under Disraeli's scheme at $5\frac{1}{4}d$, while the Irish fund holder would pay at $7d$. Schedule D also covered income from investments in England, other than in land or government stock. Why should these pay at three-quarters of the full rate? Disraeli, so Gladstone later claimed, had never even informed the Inland Revenue Board of his intentions,[1] and it is evident that his critics, pedantic and petty though some of their arguments were, correctly guessed that he was attempting to solve a problem of immense complexity without sufficient investigation. To reverse successfully the doctrines hallowed by such authorities as Pitt and Peel required a knowledge of detail which Disraeli simply did not possess.

Finally, he had to find from some other source enough revenue to make up the deficiency caused by his reduction of the malt tax, and the tea and hop duties. He boldly – even recklessly – proposed to do this by a large increase in the house tax. The history of this highly unpopular levy was bound up with that of the even more odious window tax. From 1778 to 1834 both had featured in every budget. The exemption limit for the house tax after various changes was fixed at a rateable value of £10 in 1825. Clearly this would not be popular with the new borough electorate. Althorp, the Whig Chancellor of the Exchequer, abolished it in 1834, retaining the window tax which fell relatively more heavily upon the rich. But in 1851 Sir Charles Wood, influenced by the representations of the health reformers decided to reverse this decision; he reimposed the house tax, and abolished the window tax. He was careful, however, to put the exemption limit considerably higher than before – £20 rateable value instead of £10. The tax was levied at $6d$ in the pound on shops, inns and farmhouses, at $9d$ on all other dwellings. Disraeli decided to bring the exemption limit back to £10 and to double the rates. At one time he considered going even further and raising them to $1s$ $4d$ and $2s$ respectively, but G. A. Hamilton, the Parliamentary Secretary to the Treasury, warned him that the towns, being highly rated compared with the country, would never tolerate such a burden.

[1] Morley, i, 436, quoting some of Gladstone's fragmentary notes. In fact, some memoranda from the Inland Revenue Board do exist among Disraeli's papers. Their tenor is certainly opposed to any suggestion to vary the rates on the different schedules.

The house tax was not in itself regarded by orthodox financial opinion as undesirable, although many people felt that it ought to be levied on a graduated scale, and that the whole local rating system should be revised, if rates were to be the criterion of taxable value. But it was not a wise move politically. The class most affected by the extension to £10 houses was the very class which would also be hit by the proposal to tax incomes between £50 and £150. Any goodwill gained in that quarter by the reduction of taxes on earned income was likely to be thrown away by the lowering of the exemption limits of the income and house taxes. It is surprising that Disraeli, usually so astute in calculating the political balance, should not have seen this danger; nor for that matter the danger involved in extending the income tax to Ireland at a time when he was hoping to court the Irish vote.

The budget was discussed at a series of Cabinets held between mid-October and mid-November. Even allowing for the demands so far made by the Services, Disraeli seemed likely to end up with a comfortable surplus, but he knew that he might have trouble with some of his colleagues, and he was determined to carry Derby with him. On October 18 he asked for an interview:

> . . . I should dread going into Cabinet without further discussion . . . I will have the figures prepared for you in a clear manner. I have tried the plan on Henley who takes it very favourably & has improved it in many points, & on Walpole. I expect great *fronde* from Herries. He said to Malmesbury coming home, 'Wild work I fear on Wednesday.'[1]

Herries continued to regard Disraeli's plan as 'wild work', but he did not press his doubts and Disraeli was cordially supported by Derby. The Cabinet as a whole acquiesced in the budget. Most of them lacked the knowledge and experience to do otherwise.

The opening of Parliament took place on November 4 and the Queen's speech was delivered a week later. The Government were clearly going to run into heavy weather almost at once, for the extreme free traders led by Charles Villiers let it be known that they were dissatisfied with the ambiguousness of that part of the speech which dealt with free trade, and that they intended to move a resolution on the subject. On November 17 the terms of Villiers's resolution were announced. It declared among other things that the

[1] Derby Papers, Box 145/2.

repeal of the Corn Laws 'was a wise, just, and beneficial measure'.
The vast majority of the Tories had no intention of trying to reverse
free trade, but they were not prepared to eat all their words spoken
during and after 1846. If Villiers's motion was carried, the Government would feel forced to resign. Disraeli decided to move an
amendment. 'Our men', he wrote to Derby the same day, 'will take
anything wh: is not absolutely spitting in their faces.'[1] His amendment declared simply that free trade had improved the condition
of the working class and that the Government should adhere to it.
But Russell after some hesitation had given his imprimatur to
Villiers's motion and the prospect looked black.

Meanwhile Disraeli had been involved in an embarrassing episode
which made him look ridiculous at a moment when he needed above
all else to display a front of suitable *gravitas* to the world at large.
On November 15 it had fallen to him as leader of the House to
pronounce a suitable eulogium upon the Duke of Wellington, who
had died in September. By a curious trick of memory he used for
part of his speech words almost identical with those of a passage by
Thiers in an obituary article on Marshal St Cyr. This had first
appeared in 1829 in a French journal, but an English translation had
been published, apparently at Disraeli's own suggestion (if Smythe
is to be believed), in the *Morning Chronicle* in 1848. Some sharp-eyed
Liberal journalist spotted the resemblance, and a few days later
Disraeli to his consternation read the relevant parts of his speech
and Thiers's article printed in parallel columns in Palmerston's
newspaper, the *Globe*. There is no need to doubt that the plagiarism
was unconscious. Apart from anything else, he would never have
been such a fool as to do it on purpose. But the opportunity was too
good for his enemies to miss, and the literary world, apart from
Monckton Milnes and Lytton, who both wrote to ask if they could
help, vociferously condemned the unlucky Chancellor.

Disraeli had bigger worries than this. His amendment had been
designed to bring over the Peelites, who were known to be uneasy
about the Villiers resolution; but it failed to satisfy them. It looked
as if they would vote against it, and the Government might sink
before Disraeli could ever even launch his budget. At this stage
Gladstone intervened. Half hoping for a Conservative reunion, he
genuinely disapproved of the policy of rubbing the noses of the
protectionists in the dirt, and he considered that Russell ought to

[1] Derby Papers, Box 145/2, November 17, 1852.

have dissociated himself from the extremists. Moreover, he had an instinctive feeling that Disraeli's budget would be hasty and ill conceived. It was important, from his point of view, to oblige the Government to put forward definite proposals of some kind. If these were satisfactory the Peelites might rejoin their old party. If, as he thought much more likely, they were bad, a reputable public reason could be given for ejecting the administration and coalescing with the Whigs and Liberals.

Accordingly Gladstone and Herbert drafted a less vindictive resolution which was similar to Disraeli's own, though naturally rather more emphatic on the virtues of free trade. They took it to Palmerston, who at this particular moment stood apart from all other political groups. He cordially approved and agreed to write to Disraeli as if unprompted suggesting the compromise and offering to move it, if Disraeli was agreeable. It was a most welcome olive branch. Palmerston's speech reminding the members that they were an assembly of gentlemen and that 'we who are Gentlemen on this side of the House should remember that we are dealing with Gentlemen on the other side' carried the day. Villiers's motion was defeated by 336 to 256, and Palmerston's carried by 468 to 53, opposed only by Colonel Sibthorp and a group of ultras.

Nevertheless the debate which occupied November 23, 25 and 26 must have been unpleasant for Disraeli. He had to explain why he accepted Palmerston's resolution in spite of the party's real and his own ostensible professions of protection. He had to steer an awkward line between on the one hand giving mortal offence to his own die-hards, on the other risking the loss of Palmerston's amendment. He was, moreover, suffering from influenza and a heavy cold which made it difficult for him to speak at all. The Liberals and Radicals were hot for revenge and, although the Peelites were unwilling for the moment to let the Government be defeated, they, too, were in no mood to forgo the chance of repaying the gibes which Disraeli had showered upon them for years past. Herbert in particular assailed his personal integrity in language of extraordinary bitter-ness. Disraeli, perhaps unwisely, had tried to show at much length that he and his party had never wished to re-enact the Corn Laws. Herbert declared that he entirely acquitted the Chancellor of the Exchequer of ever having been a believer in protection: Disraeli had not, as some said, forgotten his previous beliefs; he had merely for-gotten what he once wished people to believe that he believed. He went on to make an allusion in very questionable taste to the difficulty of Jews in making converts because of the 'surgical operation' involved in the rite of circumcision. Towards the end of his speech his passion broke out. Peel, he said, would not have wished to humiliate his enemies, but if anyone did seek retribution, 'for it is not words that humiliate but deeds – if a man wants to see humiliation – which, God knows, is always a painful sight – he need but look there'. And Herbert pointed his finger at Disraeli silent, impassive and apparently unperturbed.

The Government rode out this storm, but they were soon facing the full fury of another. Some enigmatic observations from Gladstone to Derby at Lady Derby's reception a few days later made it at least clear that the Peelites' support of the compromise resolution did not necessarily mean a *rapprochement*. All would depend on the budget, and here it was only too obvious that trouble impended. The latest Service demand was for another 1,500 Marines. On November 23 Disraeli wrote in some dismay to Derby that, although he had reckoned on an extra estimate for 5,000 seamen and 2,000 artillerymen nothing had been said before about the Marines.[1] Derby's reply has not survived, but evidently he felt obliged to press for the Marines as well. This was bad enough, but on November 30 Hamilton received an even more alarming letter from Augustus Stafford.

I am afraid the Naval Estimates for 53/54 will be nearly a million more than those of last year . . . I do not see what I can cut down except the Public Works. I have my own strong notions about Dockyard Retrenchments but it is an awful subject and cannot be entered on except by a very strong Government. Your estimate was £30 per man: it is nearer £50 . . .[2]

Disraeli expostulated with the Prime Minister in a letter on the same day:

We have had no explanation from Stafford as to his letter of this day to Hamilton that the Navy Estimate for 1853/54 will be increased nearly one million. I trust that the Admiralty have not got into debt and are attempting to shuffle off this scot on future estimates. This will never do, for, if permitted, we shall never be safe.

We are pledged to the Queen as far as the seamen and Marines

[1] M. & B., iii, 407.
[2] Hughenden Papers, Box 98, B/XX/H/94.

are concerned, and we must not seem to waver; but I think you must exercise your utmost authority that there shall be retrenchment, no matter at what inconvenience, in all in which her honour and safety are not concerned . . .[1]

He added that he deeply regretted 'that on the very eve of battle I should suddenly be called on to change all my dispositions'.

Derby put his foot down over the million-pound increase. He would not, he said, permit more than £350,000 – the cost of the seamen and the Marines. But even this meant important changes. It reduced Disraeli's surplus to £100,000. This was not enough. Derby suggested that another £400,000 could be produced by spreading the reduction of malt tax, like that of the tea duty, over a period of years instead of doing it in a single step. A further possibility was to reduce tea by $4\frac{1}{4}d$ instead of $6\frac{1}{4}d$ in the first year, but on the whole Derby preferred the former course. Then there was a proposal with which Disraeli had been toying – to abolish the advertisement duty. This could not be done now, but Disraeli might make things look a bit better by estimating the loss on the malt tax at £1,400,000, instead of £1,500,000. It must be largely guesswork anyway. 'Put a good face on it,' Derby cheerfully ended, 'and we shall pull through. L'audace – l'audace – toujours l'audace.'[2]

Seldom can a Chancellor of the Exchequer have been faced with such last-minute problems of improvisation. To make matters worse Disraeli was far from well and had no help. 'I am in a forlorn condition,' he wrote to Derby, 'with a sick private secretary and not the slightest assistance.' In the end he decided against Derby's advice about the malt tax and adopted instead his alternative suggestion of reducing the duty on tea by $4\frac{1}{4}d$ instead of $6\frac{1}{4}d$ in the first year. He played about with some of his estimates ('I see you have "doctored" your figures considerably',[3] wrote Derby in approving tones), and produced a surplus of £423,000 or, as he characteristically put it in his speech, 'something less than £500,000'.

On December 3 Disraeli made his long-awaited financial statement to a packed house. He spoke for five hours. Macaulay, himself not the most terse of orators, noted, 'I could have said the whole as clearly, or more clearly in two', and anyone who bothers to read the Hansard report[4] will agree that Disraeli was inordinately long-

---

[1] M. & B., iii, 425.   [2] Hughenden Papers, Box 109, B/XX/S/81, November 30.
[3] ibid., B/XX/S/100, n.d., but probably December 4.
[4] Hansard, 3rd series, cxxiii, 836–907.

winded. His audience was very critical, some of the Whigs – notably Sir Charles Wood and Sir George Grey – openly sneering, joking and making signs to each other, in a manner that disgusted at least one observer.[1] So long a speech was a great physical strain on a man who had scarcely recovered from influenza. Towards the end he admitted to the House that he was 'quite exhausted' and when he attempted to answer one or two questions his voice was so frail as to be almost inaudible.

First reactions to the budget were not unfavourable. The general sentiment seems to have been that of Dr Johnson on hearing a woman preach, surprise that it had been done at all. But within a few days opposition began to harden. Gladstone found his worst suspicions confirmed. 'Fundamental faults of principle which it is impossible to overlook or compound with', he wrote to his wife, and again in a later letter, 'the least conservative budget I have ever known'. But the more common verdict was less extreme than this and was probably best summed up by Macaulay: 'The plan was nothing but taking money out of the pockets of people in towns and putting it into the pockets of growers of malt. I greatly doubt whether he will be able to carry it; but he has raised his reputation for practical ability.'

The debate began on December 10 and lasted for four nights. Apart from the remission of tea duties, almost every point in the budget was seriously attacked. Not always with good arguments; for example, Goulburn and Gladstone claimed that no differentiation should under any circumstances be made between earned and un-earned income, because it would be a fraud against the holder of Government securities, whose income, so it was alleged on the strength of a dubious interpretation of Pitt's Loan Act of 1801, and of certain *obiter dicta* from that great man, could never be treated less favourably than anyone else's. Disraeli had little difficulty in dealing with this somewhat esoteric charge. He was less happy when he tried to extricate himself from his muddle over the income-tax schedules. In fact, he never answered the criticism at all, and was reduced to the feeble expedient of offering to recast this part of the budget – an offer understandably ridiculed by his opponents. The reduction of the malt tax and the increased house tax came in for much attack. The former was stigmatized as a piece of sectional legislation – which, of course, it was. As for the latter, it was bound

[1] Sir William Fraser, *Disraeli and His Day* (1891), 166–7.

to be very unpopular. Disraeli's enemies had little difficulty in showing that the boons which he had conferred with one hand upon the
middle-class householder in the form of earned income relief were
neatly removed with his other when he imposed the house tax and
lowered the income-tax exemption limit. The only category of
persons who escaped this levelling process were the farmers, whose
houses were notoriously underrated, as compared with urban houses,
and who, by having their income assessments fixed at one-third of
their rental instead of a half, lost nothing by the lowering of the
exemption limit from £150 to £100.[1] Thus another example of class
legislation could be alleged.

One relatively minor item in the budget excited an immense
amount of controversy, Disraeli's proposal to wind up the Public
Works Loans Board and apply the balance of the fund to the
national income and expenditure account. The Fund consisted in
1852 of £360,000 which could be used as a revolving credit for loans
to local authorities for purposes approved by the Loan Com-
missioners. The Opposition claimed that this was a highly useful
function, and, in any case, if it was to be abolished, its balance
should be applied towards extinguishing the National Debt, since
the Fund had originally been created by borrowing. Worse still, it
was pointed out that if you took away £360,000 from Disraeli's
surplus of £423,000 there was practically nothing left. The country
was being presented, in Gladstone's words, with a proposal 'to vamp
up a surplus out of borrowed money'. Disraeli had a better case than
his enemies allowed. He had been strongly advised by Sir Charles
Trevelyan, the Permanent Secretary to the Treasury, to abolish the
Fund. 'To put a stop to this Loan Fund will be to stop *not one* but a
whole progeny of Jobs. It has been the prolific mother of Jobs,
English, Scotch and Irish' he wrote.[2] He further pointed out that
repayments had never been used before to extinguish the National
Debt, and that the only way of doing this now was to put the
balance to the Income and Expenditure account, for the law provided that one-quarter of any surplus in it must be devoted
automatically to the liquidation of the National Debt through the
operation of the Sinking Fund. There was, in fact, no other method
of putting the money to the use required by Disraeli's critics. But

---

[1] A farmer paying a rent of £300 was assessed at £100 instead of £150. He therefore
remained exempt from income tax, and probably had a house assessed at less than
£10. Those paying a higher rental gained by the earned-income relief.

[2] Hughenden Papers, Box 32, B/IV/C/2, December 13, 1852.

Sir Charles admitted that the question was highly technical. '. . . the whole system is so enveloped in obsolete forms that one cannot be surprised at almost any degree of error surviving under cover of them.'[1]

However sound Sir Charles Trevelyan's reasoning may have been, the fact remained that Disraeli's surplus had been made respectable by the appropriation of a sum which had originally been borrowed. This may have been the only legal way of using it to reduce the National Debt, but his position would have been better if he could have shown a genuine revenue surplus over and above the artificial one created by these means. Speaker after speaker dwelt on the danger which such a negligible real surplus offered to the public credit. The irony was that, if Disraeli or his officials had predicted the expenditure and income of the financial year more accurately, there would have been nothing to worry about. By April 1853 the nation's finances showed a far greater surplus than anyone dreamed of in December, but Gladstone, not Disraeli, was to be the beneficiary.

As the debate proceeded it became clear that Disraeli had his back to the wall. His supporters, Bulwer Lytton, Lord John Manners, Spencer Walpole, could not match the formidable battery of ex-chancellors who bombarded him from the Opposition benches. He received no help at all from Herries, the one financial administrator of experience on his own side, who no doubt continued jealously to regard the budget as 'wild work'. This omission did not go unnoticed. 'His studied abstinence from assenting to anything in the budget was remarkable,' said Bernal Osborne. 'When he was appealed to there had been nothing but a grave shrug and a very suspicious silence.' Henley, too, whose position as President of the Board of Trade made him a natural participant in a debate on the budget, remained equally dumb and uncooperative.

To Disraeli the prospect of defeat was most unwelcome. He thoroughly enjoyed the prestige, the deference, the sense of power which come to the holder of high office. He never even paid lip service to the convention that ministers accept their tasks reluctantly out of a sense of public duty and lay them down with a sigh of relief, returning gladly once again to country pursuits and the perusal of the classics. Politics had by now become his passion. He was prepared to try almost any expedient in order to prolong his

[1] ibid., Box 32, B/IV/C/13d, December 8, 1852.

uncertain tenure. For example, there were the Irish members. True, they were not likely to welcome the extension of the income tax to their country, but might they not be won over by concessions on a Tenant Right Bill, very dear to their hearts? Alas, Russell, as Disraeli discovered later, had outbid him by a pledge that a Whig government would not extend the income tax to Ireland.[1] In any case Derby, who had an uncanny flair for discovering Disraeli's more questionable manœuvres, and who, like other ex-Secretaries for Ireland, detested the native Irish, fired a warning shot. 'If we lose the landed gentry of Ireland, and especially of the North, we are gone', he wrote.[2] And so nothing came of this overture.

In desperation Disraeli cast about for some other device. The battle was to be joined on the resolution about the house tax and it seemed clear that the proposals, as they stood would be rejected. But what if he amended them so as to retain merely the extension of the lower limit from £20 to £10, leaving the actual rate to be determined by a later vote of the House? Might not the Radicals be placated by such a gesture? The difficulty was that, unless he adhered to his plan to double the rate of tax, he could not halve the malt tax, and any vacillation on this point was bound to enrage his own supporters.

Nevertheless at nine o'clock on December 15, the evening before the final debate and division, Disraeli sent a note to Bright at the Reform Club asking him as a matter of urgency to call. About an hour later Bright arrived and was shown up to the top of the house in Grosvenor Gate, where he found Disraeli alone at his papers in an ornate room crammed with furniture, pictures and mirrors. He stayed till half past eleven and the conversation left such an impression on his mind that he recorded it with a degree of detail and length quite exceptional in his journal. Certainly it is a queer picture which comes down to us from Bright's pen of this colloquy *à deux* late in the night before the day which was to settle the fate of the Government. Disraeli unburdened himself with remarkable candour, partly calculated, one suspects, but not wholly. 'If he could get a vote, a majority of *one* only, his honour would be saved and he would give up House Tax and Malt Tax and remodel his scheme', Bright wrote. Disraeli referred bitterly to 'those damned defences', which had wrecked his budget. He expressed, as he once

[1] Derby Papers, Box 145/3, Disraeli to Derby, April 24.
[2] Hughenden Papers, Box 109, B/XX/S/101, n.d.

had before to Bright, his anxiety to be rid of 'the old stagers and red tapists'. He added that the party would do almost anything for him: they had swallowed a great deal already and he did not see why they should not swallow the little bit more involved in a modification of the Resolution. If so, would Bright and his friends stay neutral?

Caution and an uneasy sense of still not being wholly accepted forced Disraeli to maintain a certain constraint in conversation with his Tory colleagues. To Bright he opened his mind in the way which men sometimes do to a political adversary with whom they none the less feel a certain bond of sympathy. But nothing came of the talk. Half amused, half shocked, Bright declared that he could not entertain any sort of bargain and privately noted, 'He seems unable to comprehend the morality of our political course.' Perhaps, as G. M. Trevelyan suggests, it was on this occasion that Disraeli, implicitly brushing aside such considerations as irrelevant to life in Parliament, declared, 'We came here for fame.'[1]

Even if Bright had been prepared to play, the game would have been effectively ended by Derby, who once again, through either rumour or intuition, seems to have known what Disraeli was up to. The following morning, December 16, the Chancellor received a long letter from his chief setting out with characteristic cogency and common sense the objections to a modification of the house tax at this belated stage. 'We have', he wrote, 'staked our existence on our Budget *as a whole* . . . How can we declare by concession on the house tax that we will deprive ourselves of the means of doing *anything* for that interest, to which, after all, we owe our position?' Towards the end of his letter he made an observation which sums up as well as any the line that he almost always took when Disraeli came out with some subtle plan for acquiring or preserving power. '. . . if we are to be a Government we must be so by our own friends and in spite of all combinations, and not by purchasing a short-lived existence upon the forbearance of the Radical party.' If Disraeli differed, he continued, let a Cabinet be summoned, and he (Derby) would take each opinion in turn, reserving his own to the end.[2] Disraeli quickly replied that he saw no need for a Cabinet. He fully accepted Derby's view, he said; and his only fear had been a rumour that defeat might cause Derby to retire altogether from politics. 'Personally I should then feel isolated; but as it is I would prefer

[1] G. M. Trevelyan, *The Life of John Bright* (1913), 205–7.
[2] M. & B., iii, 440–1.

being your colleague in opposition to being the colleague of any
other man as Minister.'[1]

At 10.20 that evening Disraeli rose to make what was expected
to be the final speech of the long debate before the critical division
was taken. He intended to go down fighting and to repay with
interest the attacks of his enemies, but he knew that he was on very
uncertain ground with regard to some features of the budget. It may
have been this knowledge which prompted him to have recourse, if
Gladstone is right, to Dutch courage. The latter records in his diary
that Disraeli appeared flushed and looked as if he had had too much
to drink.[2] He scarcely attempted to answer the more acute criticisms
of the budget, although, briefed by Trevelyan, he made a good
defence of his plan to abolish the Public Works Loans Fund and he
was able to point with pride to certain economies and retrenchments. Much of his speech was personal. Wood's bad manners
received a scathing indictment; after holding up one of the former
Chancellor's budgets to ridicule he went on

> The right hon. gentleman tells me – in not very polished and
> scarcely in Parliamentary language – that I do not know my
> business. He may have learned his business. The House of
> Commons is the best judge of that; I care not to be his critic.
> Yet if he has learned his business, he has still to learn some other
> things – he has to learn that petulance is not sarcasm and in-
> solence is not invective.[3]

But some of Disraeli's remarks went too far for the taste of the
House. He referred to Graham as one 'whom I will not say I greatly
respect, but rather whom I greatly regard', and mocked at Goulburn
as 'that weird Sibyl, the member for Cambridge University'. He
made an unfortunate attempt at broad humour, linking some earlier
remarks of Robert Lowe about emigration and productivity, with
the question of the possible 'productivity' in another sense of women
who might get married. Jokes of this kind were not Disraeli's *métier*,
and his efforts went down badly. He ended on a note of defiance. He
had been advised to take back his budget, but he would not, he said,
pointing at Wood 'submit to the degradation of others'. He was
faced by a coalition.

---

[1] ibid., iii, 442.
[2] Magnus, *Gladstone*, 103.
[3] *Hansard*, 3rd series, cxxiii, 1653.

The combination may be successful. A Coalition has before this been successful. But Coalitions though successful have always found this, that their triumph has been brief. This too I know, that England does not love Coalitions.[1]

He sat down a few moments later at one o'clock amidst tremendous applause from the Government benches, having driven the Opposition into a condition of apoplectic rage by his gibes, personalities and taunts. Gladstone wrote that the speech 'as a whole was grand; I think the most powerful I ever heard from him. At the same time it was disgraced by shameless personalities and otherwise.'[2] The sense of drama was heightened by a remarkable phenomenon. Although it was mid-winter a violent thunderstorm raged. Disraeli made much of his speech as if to the accompaniment of an artillery bombardment, and flashes of lightning seemed to penetrate the very chamber itself.

On ordinary form Disraeli's reply should have ended the long debate, but, to the surprise of the House, yet another member leapt to his feet. Only the day before Gladstone had written ominously to his wife, 'I am sorry to say I have a long speech fermenting within me and I feel as a loaf might in the oven.'[3] He was greeted with such a storm of shouts and catcalls – the Tories were good at hooting – that he could scarcely make himself heard. But he was no less courageous than Disraeli. He stood his ground, determined not to let the Chancellor's invective go unanswered. Amidst screams of abuse he began by censuring Disraeli's remarks about emigration and productivity. 'There were other reasons besides the reason of triviality and irrelevancy why a discussion should have been avoided tonight by the right hon. Gentleman on the subject of emigration.' At last the yells and counter-cheers died away.

> I must tell the right hon. gentleman [he went on] that whatever he has learned – and he has learned much – he has not yet learned the limits of discretion, of moderation, and forbearance, that ought to restrain the conduct and language of every member of this House, the disregard of which is an offence in the meanest among us, but is of tenfold weight when committed by the Leader of the House of Commons.[4]

He followed this by a well-reasoned indictment of the whole budget, displaying that mastery of financial detail which was to make him by far the greatest Chancellor of the Exchequer in his own, and

[1] ibid., 1666.   [2] Morley, i, 438.   [3] loc. cit.   [4] *Hansard*, loc. cit.

perhaps any other, time. Derby listening from the Peers' Gallery might murmur 'Dull!' and bury his head in his hands, but Gladstone held the House, and by the time he had finished there was little left of Disraeli's grand financial plan.

The speech was important not merely for its immediate effect. More than any other single event it made a reconciliation between the Peelites and the Derbyites impossible. It has to be read in full[1] for its wounding nature to be apparent. Gladstone was still a Conservative and his attack provoked all the bitterness of an intra-party dispute exacerbating the antagonism which invariably prevails between two rival sects each claiming to be guardians of the true faith. When he appealed to the authority of Pitt, when he declared that the budget was 'the most subversive in its tendencies and ultimate effects that I have ever known', he was striking a blow such as no Whig or Radical could strike. It was deplorable but not wholly surprising that a few days later a group of tipsy Tories actually threatened him with physical violence when he was dining quietly alone at the Carlton Club.

There is a yet deeper significance in Gladstone's speech. It is the beginning of the great parliamentary duel which for twenty-eight years was to be a feature of English public life and to dominate it for the last twelve of them. Gladstone had long disliked and distrusted Disraeli, but hitherto the latter had not reciprocated. As late as September he had commended Lord Henry Lennox for giving his vote to Gladstone at Oxford. From now onwards his attitude changed, and, although on occasions he tried to win over Gladstone to his side, he acted from motives of party expediency, not personal sympathy. As time went on the two men came more and more to embody in the eyes of the nation the opposing elements in politics and to personify according to the prejudices of the onlooker the forces of good and evil. The artist who wished to immortalize, as if upon a Greek vase, an instant of time that would illuminate the political history of the mid-Victorian era would have done well to choose the moment when Gladstone rose to answer Disraeli at one o'clock in the morning of December 17, 1852; the faces of the members, pallid in the flaring gaslight, contorted, some with anger, some with delight, arms gesticulating in hostility or applause; Gladstone on his feet, handsome, tall, still possessing the youthful good looks, the open countenance, which had charmed his

---

[1] *Hansard*, 3rd series, cxxiii, 1666–93.

contemporaries at Eton and Christ Church; Disraeli seated on the Treasury Bench, aquiline, faintly sinister, listening with seeming indifference to the eloquent rebuke of the orator. It was a scene which was not easily forgotten. It coloured the parliamentary life of a whole generation.

The division was taken at four o'clock on the morning of December 17. All the groups except the Conservatives voted against the resolution. Although the Government mustered its full strength, it was beaten by 305 votes to 286 – a narrow margin, but enough. As Disraeli, all passion spent, walked out into the wet street to return home, he observed to Sir William Fraser in the calmest of tones that it would be disagreeable weather for the journey to Osborne. Derby promptly resigned. On the 20th, the following Monday, the two leaders officially announced the news to their respective Houses. Derby in the Lords was unwontedly cross and petulant. Disraeli, however, was all sweetness and light. It had been suggested to him by Russell through Walpole that an apology for some of the personalities in his speech might not come amiss. He delivered it with urbanity, grace and good taste, and the victims of his former sarcasm replied with equal courtesy. It only remained for him to write to the Queen and the Prince thanking them for their kindness. To the latter he observed that he 'would ever remember with interest and admiration the princely mind in the princely person'. Nor did he forget less important personages. His letter to the head of the Treasury drew a most cordial reply, and from other evidence, too, there can be no doubt that Disraeli was respected and admired in the department with which he had the closest dealings.

Disraeli was unlucky over his first budget, more unlucky than most Chancellors. His financial secretary, G. A. Hamilton, wrote on October 28.

> The Chancellor of the Exchequer is undertaking a most difficult task under most disadvantageous circumstances.
> 1. He is going to make a financial statement in November, when the financial position of the country for the year is only half developed.
> 2. His statement will have virtually to comprise 2 budgets – one for the year 1853–4 – the other for 1854–5 – for his measures and calculations must take into account the whole of that period.[1]

These were serious difficulties, and if Disraeli had only been allowed

[1] Hughenden Papers, Box 31, B/IV/A/52a.

to bring his budget forward at the normal season of the year he would have had a far larger surplus to play with. There had also been the trouble about the 'damned defences', and the overwhelming pressure to do something for the landed interest. The latter constituted an insoluble dilemma. He could not please the landed interest without risking destruction in a Parliament which that interest no longer controlled. He could not resist it without risking the break-up of his party. If the method chosen had to be a reduction of the malt tax – and it is hard to see any alternative – then there would have been much to be said for repealing it entirely, thus abolishing the whole expensive and vexatious machinery of collection and giving a perceptible boon to the beer-drinker. This was indeed argued by some of his opponents. But where was the money to come from? The very people who pressed for complete remission would have been the first to protest if house tax or income tax had been increased or the tea duty left as it was. It is hard to see how Disraeli could have escaped this dilemma.

Where he courted unnecessary trouble was over the income tax and the Public Works Loans Fund. The appropriation of the balance in the latter to the income and expenditure account gave endless scope for the accusation that his surplus was in some way fraudulent or illusory, and the matter was almost impossible to explain intelligibly. More damaging still was his attempt to distinguish between earned and unearned income. As a purely political manœuvre it did not succeed; the Radicals voted against him to a man. His confusion about the schedules was a bad mistake, and he laid himself open to the legitimate charge that his reforms would create more anomalies than they abolished. Disraeli, always vague about details, had not done his homework properly. The proposed changes brought in no extra money and from that point of view were quite unnecessary. It is unlikely that any measure which he could have carried would have satisfied his supporters, but it is hard to avoid the impression that he had failed to consider the implications of some of his ideas. Gladstone, a few months later, produced the most notable budget of the century. He had the advantage of a parliamentary majority and the good luck to inherit a surplus which could have been available to his predecessor. But when every allowance is made for his good fortune, and when full account has been taken of the mistakes which he, too, made, there remains a great contrast. Gladstone's budget embodied a coherent plan. Disraeli's was a bundle of expedients.

CHAPTER XVI

Opposition Again

1852–6

1

Disraeli's year as Chancellor of the Exchequer and leader of the House made him a national figure. In its first number for 1853 the *Edinburgh Review* accorded him the honour of what would now be called a 'profile'; it was a forty-page character sketch.[1] He could not expect very favourable treatment from the intellectual organ of the Whig party, but the anonymous author at least gave him credit for becoming famous. 'What individual from February 1852 to January 1853 has most occupied the pens, tongues and ears of Englishmen?' he asked, and answered, 'The Right Honourable Benjamin Disraeli, late Chancellor of the Exchequer, is indisputably the man.' The article continued:

> His appointment to this post was one of the most startling domestic events which has occurred in our time. People seemed never tired of talking and speculating on it, with its recondite causes and its problematical results. He at once became an inexhaustible topic of animated discussion in society. His portrait was painted by one fashionable artist; his bust was taken in marble, *aere perennius,* by another; what were called likenesses of him appeared in illustrated newspapers by the dozen; and, above all, he was placed in Madame Tussaud's repository – that British Valhalla in which it is difficult for a civilian to gain a niche without being hanged. He glittered in the political horizon as a star of the first magnitude; and every glass was turned on him the more eagerly because it was impossible to discover and hazardous to predicate whether he would turn out a planet, a fixed star, a comet, or a mere vapoury exhalation, or will o' the wisp, raised by an overheated atmosphere from a rank and unwholesome soil.[2]

It does not require much further reading of the article to discover what answer the *Edinburgh Review* gave to this last question. The journal went on to quote a well-known couplet:

[1] Vol. XCVII, 420–61.
[2] ibid., 421.

The thing we know is neither rich nor rare
But wonder how the devil it got there.

The *Edinburgh Review* was not alone in paying attention to the
new celebrity. Within three years two full-scale lives of him had
appeared – *A Critical Biography* by G. M. Francis, who belied his
title by adopting a tone of unctuous praise, and *A Literary and
Political Biography Addressed to the New Generation* by T. Macknight,
evidently a fierce, if somewhat prosy, enemy. Both works are equally
valueless to the historian, save as evidence of the vigour and
diversity of the sentiments that Disraeli could inspire.

But if fame had already come to him, power was to be more
elusive. Disraeli's parliamentary career lasted for forty-four years.
During the whole of that period the Conservatives had a majority
for only eleven years, and of these Disraeli was at their head for only
six – at the end of his life. Otherwise his brief periods of office were in
caretaker administrations dependent for their precarious existence
upon the feuds of their opponents. For the next five years Disraeli
was in opposition. It was a period packed with important episodes
in British history, the Crimean War and the Indian Mutiny the
most conspicuous. But they do not require detailed attention in a
biography of Disraeli. He could do little to influence events, and
he was obliged to remain a highly critical spectator on the sidelines
for far longer than he would have liked.

The alliance which had led to the fall of Derby's Government
resulted, as Disraeli had predicted, in a coalition. Aberdeen, the
Peelite leader, though commanding only some forty votes in the
Commons, became Prime Minister and secured five more Peelite
places in the Cabinet. Russell, with a much larger following, was
passed over, mainly because the Irish members, whose support was
essential, had not forgiven him for his no-popery campaign. He was
furious at what he considered a slight. The Cabinet, composed of six
Peelites, six Whigs and one Radical, could hardly be regarded as
very representative of the forces which kept it in being. Disraeli
found himself succeeded as Chancellor of the Exchequer by Gladstone.

Naturally there was little love lost between them, and a disagreeable exchange of letters ensued on two seemingly trivial
matters; the furniture in Downing Street and the Chancellor's robe.[1]

---

[1] M. & B., iii, 476–80, gives the full text of the letters.

Hitherto, the furniture had been taken over at a valuation by the new Chancellor from his predecessor. The Government now proposed that in future it should be taken over by the Office of Works. This, so Gladstone considered, meant that Disraeli's claim for reimbursement for the money that he had paid to Sir Charles Wood should be made to the Office of Works and not to Gladstone personally. Disraeli, on the other hand, argued that new arrangements could only concern Gladstone's successor, and that, whatever was arranged for the future, Gladstone was personally responsible for paying his predecessor. Disraeli was in the right, and since the Office of Works was notorious for procrastination and red tape, the matter was not as academic as it sounds.

The robe, however, was a different affair. It was normally handed down from Chancellor to Chancellor on a similar basis of payment as that for the furniture. But Disraeli, believing it to have belonged to the younger Pitt, could not bear the thought of parting with it. Here he was undoubtedly in the wrong.

The correspondence opened with a letter from Gladstone on January 21 stating his case about the furniture and ending with a polite request to purchase the robe at an appropriate figure. On February 26, over a month later, Disraeli replied at some length, ending: 'I would suggest that your cheque for £307 16s. 6d. would as between us properly conclude the matter.' He said nothing about the robe, and he had 'the honor to remain, dear Sir, your obedient servant, B. Disraeli'. Gladstone answered on February 28 persisting in his view about the furniture and ending: 'I adverted at the close of my letter to the Official Robe but the allusion to it has perhaps escaped your attention. I remain, dear Sir, faithfully yours, W. E. Gladstone.' Disraeli now lost, or pretended to lose, his patience. He replied on March 6 in the third person, beginning: 'Mr Disraeli regrets very much that he is obliged to say that Mr Gladstone's letter repudiating his obligation to pay for the furniture of the official residence is not satisfactory', and ending: 'As Mr Gladstone seems to be in some perplexity on the subject, Mr Disraeli recommends him to consult Sir Charles Wood, who is a man of the world.' He still did not mention the robe. There followed a day later a pained letter from Gladstone, also in the third person, giving way on the question of the furniture, and ending: 'It is highly unpleasant to Mr W. E. Gladstone to address Mr Disraeli without the usual terms of courtesy, but he abstains from them only because he perceives that they are unwelcome.' But he gave up the battle over the robe. Disraeli kept it and later made it into a family heirloom. It remains on exhibit in Hughenden Manor to this day.

Disraeli did not think that the Coalition would last for long. Meanwhile he determined to repair some defects in his own party, which had in his opinion contributed to the defeat of 1852. In the first place there was the question of what would now be called 'the party machine' which had been in a parlous state ever since the great schism of 1846. How far its faults were responsible for the loss of the election is open to question. Party leaders, reluctant to believe that the electorate can reject them on their merits, are too prone to blame their defeat upon bad organization. However, there can be no doubt that changes were needed after 1852.

It so happened that the occasion was ripe for a clean sweep of the old guard. Beresford, formerly Chief Whip, and Secretary at War in the late administration, had managed the election of 1852. Disraeli never liked him, and fortunately he had come into bad odour as a result of being censured by a Committee of the House for 'reckless indifference to systematic bribery'. His successor as Whip, Forbes Mackenzie, had run into similar trouble, and was unseated for bribery at Liverpool. Disraeli was able to replace him by Sir William Joliffe, later Lord Hylton, who proved far more satisfactory. As for the party organization outside the House, he removed it from Beresford and put it under the control of his solicitor, Philip Rose. The latter, along with Markham Spofforth, a partner in the same firm, managed affairs until 1859, when Spofforth took over. The two men set up a central organization to give advice to constituencies about candidates and they re-created the system of local agents, which had collapsed with the secession of Peel's manager and agent, Bonham, at the time of the Corn Law crisis.[1] These measures, in which Disraeli took a keen personal interest, were by no means all that was needed, but they were a useful beginning.

The other great deficiency on the Conservative side was lack of press support. Disraeli as an experienced writer and journalist was particularly conscious of this. *The Times*, which had by far the biggest daily circulation (about 40,000), was in general on the Liberal side. Of the lesser lights, the *Morning Advertiser* (Liquor and Russophobia), the *Morning Chronicle* (Peelite), the *Globe*

---

[1] See H. J. Hanham, *Elections and Party Management, Politics in the time of Disraeli and Gladstone* (1959), 357.

(Palmerston), the *Daily Telegraph* and *Daily News* (both Liberal) were all in varying degrees hostile to Derby and Disraeli. On their side were only the *Morning Post* with a circulation of 2,000[1] and the *Standard* with one said to be somewhere between 2,000 and 4,000, but the former was only nominally Tory, in practice as much Palmerston's organ as was the *Globe* itself. There was also the *Morning Herald* with a circulation of over 4,000. Although undeniably a Tory paper, it maintained opinions so bigoted and 'ultra' that it was widely believed to do the cause more harm than good.

What Disraeli wanted was an organ for progressive Toryism. In this he was strongly supported by Stanley, who had been corresponding with him on the matter since 1850. Various abortive proposals were mooted. Finally it was decided to start a new weekly paper to be called the *Press*. Disraeli circularized his richer friends for financial support, explaining to one of them that he could not seek aid from the party funds, since the paper 'though Tory, is of a very progressive and enlightened design'.[2] The first number appeared on May 7, 1853. It can at least be said that Disraeli's second venture as a newspaper proprietor was more successful than his first. Among the contributors were Stanley, Augustus Stafford, Edward Kenealy (later celebrated as counsel for the plaintiff in the Tichborne case), George Smythe and Bulwer Lytton. The latter under the pen name of 'Manilius' wrote a series of 'Letters to the Whigs' which were for long attributed, owing to their extraordinary similarity of style, to Disraeli himself, until Buckle discovered some notes in Stanley's hand ascribing them to Lytton.[3]

Not that Disraeli's pen was idle. He contributed regularly, too, and we have Stanley's authority for his having written the leading articles in ten of the first eleven numbers.[4] The tone of some of these does not suggest that Disraeli's approach to political journalism was any less venomous and personal than it had been twenty years before, at the time of the *Letters of Runnymede*. Take, for example, one of Disraeli's leaders in the *Press* on Aberdeen in 1853: 'His temper, naturally morose, has become licentiously peevish. Crossed in his Cabinet, he insults the House of Lords, and plagues the most

---

[1] These and subsequent figures are taken from a letter of Stanley to Disraeli Hughenden Papers, Box 111, B/XX/S/577, November 3, 1852. They are his estimates and may not be quite correct, but they seem to be reasonably near the mark. He puts *The Times* at 35,000, when in fact it was 40,000.

[2] M. & B., iii, 491. Disraeli to Henry Hope.

[3] ibid., 496.

[4] M. & B., iii, 498.

eminent of his colleagues with the crabbed malice of a maundering witch.'[1]

Although Disraeli's part in founding the *Press* must have been widely known, he was extremely anxious to preserve secrecy about his activities as a contributor. The editor made a point of personally destroying his copy, and Disraeli himself did not disdain such stratagems as an adverse comment on one of his own speeches – 'in our opinion much too long and savouring somewhat of the Yankee school of rhetoric'. It is not difficult to see why he wished to retain his anonymity, though it is very unlikely that he deceived anyone who mattered. To be both leader of a party and at the same time not only proprietor of, but anonymous contributor to, a polemical organ well to the left of party centre, was an essentially false position, but it was not till 1858 when he was back again in office that he sold the paper. It is clear that the *Press* did not go down well with the orthodox, and it probably constituted an additional reason for the cool relations which prevailed between Disraeli and Derby during the next two or three years.

2

From the first Derby and Disraeli differed on the correct policy for the Opposition. As soon as Parliament ended, Derby repaired to Knowsley, whence Stanley reported regularly to Disraeli upon his father's attitude. On January 16 he wrote: 'The Premier observed that it was easy enough to turn out the Govt. but he seemed greatly to doubt whether it were possible to replace it.'[2] Four days later he expatiated on Derby's aversion from politics:

> The truth is – I have always told you so and I see it now more clearly than ever – the Captain does not care for office but wishes to keep things as they are and impede 'progress'. This being the case it is no use to talk to him about not having a majority in the House of Commons. The only point on which I dwell and I think you may dwell is the impossibility of keeping together the party in opposition, unless they see before them a fair prospect of getting into Downing Street . . . Your influence is more powerful than that of anyone as it ought to be. Use it . . . Malmesbury will be with us next week: he is, as you know, clear headed and liberal. May I repeat to him what you have said to me . . . ?[3]

[1] ibid., 521, quoting the *Press*, June 11, 1853.
[2] Hughenden Papers, Box 111, B/XX/S/584.
[3] ibid., Box 111, B/XX/S/585, January 20.

Disraeli entirely disagreed with Derby. He was always a fighter and he thought that the Coalition, which he later described to Derby as 'a clique of Doctrinaires existing as a Government by Court favor', could soon be defeated. Disraeli was perhaps the first statesman systematically to uphold the doctrine that it is the duty of the Opposition to oppose. Indeed, he might be said by his practice to have established the precedent on which all subsequent Opposition leaders have acted. Whatever proposal the Government put forward, whatever its merits, you could always find something wrong with it, some reason for attack. In the end, if you went on long enough, you would beat them in the House, or at the very least put yourself in position to beat them at the next general election. All this is taken for granted nowadays, but it was a new idea in Disraeli's time. Peel, for example, had done nothing of the sort in the eleven years which he spent in opposition from 1830 to 1841. He had treated Whig proposals on their merits, and after 1841 Russell had frequently reciprocated. But Disraeli's first instinct was to oppose, and, if he did not always do so, it was for reasons of expediency or because Derby overruled him. To Disraeli the object of politics was power and he never forgot it.

Derby's attitude was quite different. He was determined to avoid if he possibly could a repetition of the 'Who? Who?' ministry. The strain on him had been great, and he could not bear the thought of enduring it all over again. He was convinced that, if he was to take office at all, he would have to bring in some of those who were on the other side. Understandably he did not think that this would be best achieved by an all-out attack on the Government, and he advised against consolidating by 'an active and bitter opposition . . . the present combination between those who have no real bond of union and who must, I think, fall to pieces before long if left to themselves'.[1]

Such an attack would be all the more unfortunate, though he could not very well say so to the person concerned, if it was launched by Disraeli. Derby knew what Disraeli himself probably never fully appreciated, that the Coalition had largely come into being through sheer detestation of Disraeli. In a letter to Lord Londonderry deprecating Aberdeen's conduct, Derby wrote, 'I am afraid that personal feeling has had much to do with this step and that the course pursued is mainly to be attributed to the jealousy and hatred

[1] M. & B., iii, 483.

(the word is not too strong) felt by the Peelite party in the House of Commons towards Disraeli.'[1]

This divergence between the two leaders resulted in a poor showing on the part of the Conservative party throughout the sessions of 1853 and 1854. To a considerable degree, Disraeli went his own way. In the summer there was a serious split on the question of India. The Government brought forward a Bill which Disraeli quite rightly regarded as merely tinkering with the archaic dual control exercised by the Cabinet and the East India Company over the Governor-General of India. He thought that the time had come to vest full responsibility in a Cabinet minister responsible to Crown and Parliament, and to abolish the company altogether. A few years later, after the Indian Mutiny, Disraeli, by then in office, was able to achieve just this. But unfortunately in 1853 the reform that he proposed was also a favourite plank of the Manchester platform, and this alone made it suspect among the high Tories. Derby did not feel strongly on the merits of the case, but he wanted to keep the party together. As early as March 27 he wrote to Disraeli that Henry Lennox had told him 'that Lord Lonsdale will support the Government in legislating permanently this year for the maintenance of the East India Company which he looks upon as a good Tory body not to be quarrelled with; and that his members in the House of Commons will follow his lead'.[2] He added that the Government counted on large-scale defections among 'our men'. 'We must contrive if possible to feel their pulse before we take any irretrievable step.'

But in June, Stanley at Disraeli's suggestion put down an amendment calling for delay. Derby was seriously annoyed and on June 30 wrote a formidable letter of remonstrance,[3] but Disraeli refused to give way. He made a vigorous attack on the Bill, but he only carried 140 Conservatives into the division lobby. The Government's prestige was already high, thanks to Gladstone's great budget, which had satisfied enlightened fiscal opinion throughout the country and given Gladstone's personal reputation a notable fillip. The easy defeat of Stanley's amendment to the India Bill boosted the Cabinet's prestige even further, and they ended the session triumphant. There was widespread discontent among the Con-

---

[1] Quoted, ibid., iii, 475–6.
[2] Hughenden Papers, Box 109, B/XX/S/115.
[3] M. & B., iii, 511–12.

servatives. Malmesbury, hitherto a cordial ally of Disraeli, went over to the other side. A clique led by Lonsdale even contemplated dethroning Disraeli in favour of Pakington of all people. Other Conservatives more plausibly looked to Palmerston, rightly rumoured to be fretting under the leadership of Aberdeen, whose principles, shortly before the formation of the Cabinet, he had stigmatized as those of 'antiquated imbecility'.

It was a wretched autumn and winter. Mrs Disraeli was three times ill with influenza, and was not well again till April, her recovery being delayed by one of those prolonged periods of bitter east wind which sometimes vex the early months of the year. Disraeli caught the same malady before the winter was out. Derby, meanwhile, was laid up at Knowsley for many weeks with another of his ferocious attacks of gout. Illness and political dissension resulted in a certain lack of communication. 'My despatches from Knowsley', Disraeli told Londonderry at the end of September, 'have only taken the shape of haunches of venison.' Towards the end of October he wrote a conciliatory letter, and a month later, referring to dissension in the party, he ended a letter: 'I hope you will not be offended if I take the liberty of saying what I once said to George Bentinck in his darkest hour that "Come what will, we will stand or fall together".'

In December 1853 there occurred an event only worth notice because it had not occurred earlier. Disraeli went to Knowsley for the first time. He stayed three days from December 9 to 12. According to Malmesbury, who was also present, Derby 'seems much bored because he is obliged to talk politics with him'.[1] Disraeli described Knowsley to his wife, who could not come, as 'a wretched house'.[2] Otherwise the visit went off well enough.

One much-appreciated honour was conferred on Disraeli during 1853, an honorary DCL from Oxford University. While still Prime Minister, Derby had been elected unopposed as Chancellor, and it is the Chancellor's privilege, in his first year only, to nominate the list of degrees for Encaenia. Derby naturally included his principal lieutenant. Disraeli was received with great enthusiasm at the Sheldonian Theatre, and in the evening, when he left Christ Church hall after the gaudy, to which then, as now, the honorands were by tradition invited, the undergraduates turned out *en masse*, despite

[1] Malmesbury, *Memoirs*, I, 44.
[2] M. & B., iii, 528.

the rain, to cheer him and escort him to the gate. 'Gentlemen,' he said, 'within these classic walls I dare not presume to attempt to thank you, but, believe this, never will I forget your generous kindness.'[1]

Rather less than a year later the question of the reform of Oxford University came up in the House of Commons. It was a subject to which Gladstone had devoted much of his restless energy, and he attributed great importance to the passing of a Bill which redrew the constitution of the university. This enabled, among other changes, the creation of more professorships – Germany being the model p aised by 'progressive' opinion. Another provision of the Bill was to set up an executive commission with statutory powers of a temporary nature, to carry out various reforms. Disraeli was sceptical about professors. It was all very well in Germany, he said, where there was no other avenue to fame. In England people looked to public life. 'Though you give them £2,000 instead of £200 . . . men will look to the House of Commons, and not to professors' chairs.' What happened in Germany when for a brief moment public life became open to all? In the revolutions of 1848, the national conventions and cabinets were packed with professors. 'I should like to know what was the condition of the German universities when half their chairs were engaged in public affairs.'

As for the executive commission, it was wholly unwarranted and a blow to self-government. Why reform the constitution of the University if you were not ready to leave the reformed bodies to do their own work? It was said that anomalies had to be removed, but a greater injury was done to the country 'by outraging the principle of Prescription upon which our institutions depend than by removing a few anomalies and imperfections'. England was ruled by 'traditionary influences'.

> You may have a stronger Government than you have at present by getting rid of those traditionary influences – you may have a standing army – you may have a logical, inexorable, and vigorous system of centralized administration – you may have State education or secular education; you may have a stronger Government, but you will have a weaker people. And, Sir, among those traditionary influences, the influence of the Universities of the country has not been the least great . . . If I were asked, 'Would you have Oxford with its self-government, freedom, and indepen-

[1] M. & B., iii, 510.

dence, but yet with its anomalies and imperfections, or would you have the University free of those anomalies and imperfections, and under the control of the Government?' I would say, 'Give me Oxford, free and independent, with all its anomalies and imperfections.'[1]

To Gladstone, who believed that the Bill was the last chance of genuinely conservative reform and that, if it failed, worse things lay in the future, Disraeli's attack was no doubt very irritating. 'High fantastic trifling', writes Morley, adding that it 'helps to explain the deep disfavour with which Disraeli was regarded by his severe and strenuous opponent'. Perhaps: yet to a generation that has seen state control, through the purse, riveted upon the universities to an extent inconceivable a century ago, it may not seem quite so fantastic. Disraeli's famous affirmation that a university should be a place of 'light, liberty, and learning' has not become such a truism that we can afford to forget it a century later.

3

The long-anticipated conflict with Russia broke out at the end of March 1854. The Crimean War dominated political life for the next two years, but it needs no detailed discussion here. Disraeli had no say in its origins, its course, or its termination. His verdict on it is the verdict of history – 'a just but unnecessary war'. When it broke out he indicated a patriotic general support for the Government. 'I can answer for myself and my friends,' he declared to the House, 'that no future Wellesley, on the banks of the Danube, will have to make a bitter record of the exertions of an English Opposition to depreciate his efforts and to ridicule his talents.' This did not mean that he intended to be silent. It was one thing to give general support to a government trying to win a war which, however unnecessary, had become a *fait accompli*; quite another to condone their errors in conducting it.

Party politics were at a low ebb during 1854, and Derby was even more detached and insouciant than usual. Just before the session Disraeli complained bitterly to Malmesbury about Derby's failure to give enough dinner parties for his supporters and early in August he made a celebrated outburst to Lady Londonderry:

[1] *Hansard*, 3rd series, cxxxii, 974, April 27, 1854.

I am not myself very anxious to precipitate things. I have received from the highest quarter an intimation that, if things take *their due course*, the next, and I hope very lasting Tory government may be under a head which I never contemplated. I hardly know whether I should consider the intimation a gratifying one. I already feel, in the position which I now occupy, the want of sufficient fortune. There are a thousand things which ought to be done which are elements of power, and which I am obliged to decline doing or to do at great sacrifice. Whether it be influence with the Press, or organisation throughout the country, everyone comes to me, and everything is expected from me. Tho' so many notables and magnificoes belong to the party there was never an aggregation of human being who exercised less social influence. They seem to despise all the modes and means of managing mankind.

As for our Chief we never see him. His House is always closed, he subscribes to nothing tho' his fortune is very large; and expects nevertheless everything to be done. I have never yet been fairly backed in life. All the great persons I have known, even when what is called 'ambitious' by courtesy, have been unequal to a grand game. This has been my fate and I never felt it more keenly than at the present moment, with a confederate always at Newmarket and Doncaster, when Europe, nay the world is in the throes of immense changes and all the elements of power at home in a state of dissolution. If ever there were a time when a political chief should concentrate his mind and resources on the situation 'tis the present. There cannot be too much vigilance, too much thought, and too much daring – all seem wanting.

Alas! and Adieu!

Always y^r attached

D.[1]

The first part of the letter must mean that Disraeli either had, or thought he had, been given some sort of hint from the Court that he, and not Derby, would be offered the premiership when the next Tory ministry was formed. It seems scarcely credible, and there is no evidence in the Queen's papers to suggest that she or the Prince had any such notion in mind. Moreover, neither in February 1855 when the next occasion arose, nor in 1858, nor as late as 1866 did there appear the slightest sign that the Crown preferred Disraeli to Derby. It is true that Derby was not much liked in court circles, but that was no less true of Disraeli. Buckle suggests that the only explanation – unless Disraeli completely misunderstood something

---

[1] Lady Londonderry (ed.), *Letters of Benjamin Disraeli to Frances Anne Marchioness of Londonderry* (1938), 130.

said – was Derby's health, which might have given cause for doubt about his ability to serve again.

There is one other scrap of evidence, but its significance is questionable, since no one who has read his letters would regard Lord Henry Lennox as carrying much weight. For what it is worth, he wrote to Disraeli on October 10, 1854:

> Entre nous our Earl will never again be Prime Minister! He certainly does not gain ground with the Public & it would require only the *recurrence* of what took place at Doncaster to entail publicly some *most* unpleasant remarks which have already not been wanting in Private. Burn this letter directly . . .[1]

But he gives no authority for this categorical statement, nor is it clear what the episode was at Doncaster which caused such adverse comment. Until some further evidence appears, Disraeli's reason for writing as he did must remain a mystery.

In June the Cabinet took the critical decision to invade the Crimea, and at the beginning of September the Anglo-French armada set sail. Disraeli viewed the whole plan with misgiving. On September 4, over a fortnight before the battle of the Alma, he wrote to Mrs Brydges Willyams:[2] 'We seem to have fallen into another Walcheren Expedition, and in my opinion the Ministers ought to be impeached.' What followed confirmed his worst suspicions. The indecisive battles of the Alma, Balaclava and Inkerman were monuments alike to the courage of the troops and the inefficiency of their high command. Thereafter, the nightmare of the Crimean winter descended upon armies, encamped in the open, short of ammunition, food, and medical supplies of every kind. Before long the scandals of mismanagement began to circulate throughout London. A December session of Parliament did nothing to allay alarm. After the Christmas recess Roebuck, a prominent Radical but belonging to the jingo section of the group, gave notice of motion for a select committee to inquire into the conduct of the war. Lord John Russell promptly resigned. This inexcusable action by the leader of the House was almost certain to wreck the Government's chances of survival. Even Derby, hesitant at first, agreed that the Conservatives must join in the attack. On January 29, 1855, with Disraeli contributing a characteristic diatribe, Roebuck's

---

[1] Hughenden Papers, Box 102, B/XX/LX/48.
[2] Brydges Willyams Letters. For Mrs Brydges Willyams see below, p. 414.

motion was carried by 305 votes to 148. The figures were so astounding that for a moment the House sat silent, and then members on both sides burst, not into the usual cheers, but into peels of laughter. Thus, not much more than two years later, Disraeli found his famous dictum vindicated. England evidently did not love that particular coalition.

The Queen sent for Derby, who, instead of kissing hands at once, as Lord Ellenborough urged, asked for time in order to persuade Palmerston to serve with him. He told the Queen that 'the whole country cried out for Palmerston as the only man fit for carrying on the war with success, and he owned the necessity of having him in the Government, were it even only to satisfy the French Government'. But Palmerston refused to join Derby. The negotiations which followed concern the life of Derby rather than that of Disraeli. Like dancers executing the stately figures of a minuet or a quadrille, the Queen, the Prince and the leading statesmen of the day went through the leisurely and stylized motions which attended the formation of a government in the early Victorian era.[1] Derby declines office; the Queen consults Lord Lansdowne; Lord Lansdowne advises her to send for Lord John Russell; Lord John consults his friends (by now a fast-diminishing band); Lord John in his turn declines; the Queen again consults Lord Lansdowne; the Queen sends for Palmerston, and Palmerston does not decline.

Disraeli was furious. He could only observe, he could do nothing, and he had to accept his fate. But he never ceased to maintain, both at the time and later, that Derby had made a lamentable mistake. Gladstone, looking back, thought the same. Derby's error, he wrote, 'was palpable even gross'. This consensus on the part of two men who seldom agreed on anything has led most historians to assume that Derby must have been wrong. Yet he had a case sometimes overlooked. The demand in the country was for Palmerston. He was the Churchill of his day. Can one imagine in May 1940 a government headed by Lord Halifax whom both the King and Neville Chamberlain preferred, lasting for long if Churchill was outside it – or inside it? Derby could get no help at all from the Whigs or the Peelites. Other than Disraeli, he had scarcely anyone of ability to rely on in the House of Commons. What guarantee was there that 1852 would not be repeated all over again, and that long before he could bring the war to a successful close he would have been ejected from office?

[1] *Letters of Queen Victoria 1837–61*, iii, 102–3.

Perhaps the attempt would have been worth making, but it is unlikely that he could have converted the Conservatives into the
majority party.

Disraeli understandably was far too angry to look at the matter
in this light. If his account to Malmesbury is correct, he did not
mince his words to Derby, but 'told him some very disagreeable
truths'. Malmesbury describes him as being 'in a state of disgust
beyond all control'.[1] On February 2, Disraeli wrote a famous letter
to Lady Londonderry:

> I was so annoyed and worn out yesterday that I could not send
> you two lines to say that our chief has again bolted.
>
> This is the third time that, in the course of six years, during
> which I have had the lead of the Opposition in the House of
> Commons, I have stormed the Treasury Benches: twice, fruit-
> lessly, the third time with a tin kettle to my tail which rendered
> the race hopeless. You cannot, therefore, be surprised, that I am
> a little wearied of these barren victories, which like Alma,
> Inkerman, and Balaclava, may be glorious, but are certainly
> nothing more. What is most annoying is that this time we had
> actually the court with us – for the two court favourites, Aberdeen
> (of the Queen) was extinct, and Newcastle (of the Prince) in a
> hopeless condition; and our rivals were Johnny in disgrace, and
> Palmerston, ever detested. The last, however, seems now the
> inevitable man, and tho' he is really an imposter, utterly
> exhausted, and at the best only ginger beer and not champaign,
> and now an old painted Pantaloon, very deaf, very blind, and
> with false teeth, which would fall out of his mouth when speaking,
> if he did not hesitate and halt so in his talk – he is a name which
> the country resolves to associate with energy, wisdom, and
> eloquence, and will until he has tried and failed . . .[2]

Palmerston did not fail, and far from being ginger beer he
remained champagne for another decade. He had the perfect temperament for a Prime Minister, sanguine, vigorous and radiating
confidence. He left departmental ministers to get on with their jobs,
but he gave a lead on all the important issues. He was as unlike
Aberdeen as possible. Disraeli, despite the outburst quoted earlier,
greatly respected him. Like all good Prime Ministers Palmerston
had his quota of luck. The war began to go better. On September 8 Sebastopol at last fell. Disraeli now proceeded to wage an

[1] Malmesbury, *Memoirs of an ex-Minister* (2 vols, 1884), ii, 8.
[2] Marchioness of Londonderry (ed.), *The Letters of Benjamin Disraeli to Frances
Anne, Marchioness of Londonderry* (1938), 145–6.

all-out peace policy in the *Press*, but Russia evinced no sign of concession, and most Conservatives considered that any public move towards peace on Britain's part would defeat its own end by encouraging Russian resistance.

Derby felt particularly warm on this subject. He resented some language that Disraeli had used about shrinking from undertaking the war. 'We cannot', he went on, 'with honour or even with regard to party interests, constitute ourselves a peace Opposition merely because we have a war Ministry, and I will never consent to weaken an Administration to which I am opposed, by increasing their difficulties in carrying the country through what has become an inevitable war'.[1] Disraeli, who had a well-founded fear that nothing would satisfy Palmerston but unconditional surrender, was not convinced. 'If Lord Palmerston succeed,' he wrote to Mrs Brydges Willyams, 'the war may last as long as the Peloponnesian, or the Thirty Years War in Germany.'[2] Disraeli once again had some private source of information about the Cabinet's deliberations. It is not clear who the person was, but from time to time he seems to have passed on news of their latest plans. Disraeli loved this kind of thing. Letters signed 'X', secret messages, code names, and all the paraphernalia of melodrama ever appealed to the author of *Vivian Grey*. On November 20 he wrote to Derby at Knowsley without any superscription:

Secret & Most Confidential
. . . Palmerston is for blowing up Cronstadt having got a discoverer who builds submarine ships worked by submarine crews, & who are practising on the Thames with, they say, complete success. Except the Cabinet and the French and Russian[3] ministers I am assured that, probably, no one knew what I was despatching to you except my informant and myself. So I need not say you must exercise a strict reserve . . . My hand is too cold to write more.

You know who[4]

In the end events forced even Palmerston to abandon his policy. Napoleon III made it clear that he had had enough of the war.

[1] M. & B., iv, 21.
[2] Brydges Willyams Letters, September 4, 1854.
[3] The first part of the letter is about peace proposals and it was presumably those, not Palmerston's submarines, that the Russian minister knew about; although, given the security system of the day, it is more than likely that he knew of the latter, too.
[4] Derby Papers, Box 145/3.

After much bargaining and many delays, the Treaty of Paris was signed on March 30, 1856. Disraeli was not dissatisfied with its terms, and he had the pleasure of saying in the House that the war had been conducted so inefficiently 'that for my part, after all I have seen, I should be disposed to welcome any peace which is not disgraceful'. But this view was not accepted in Tory circles, and most of his colleagues thought that Britain had gained very little in exchange for all her losses.

4

The next two years were frustrating for Disraeli. He was at odds with most of his colleagues, and his communications with Derby dwindled to a mere trickle; only one letter has survived for the whole of 1856. He employed some of his time in composing a scheme of administrative reform for the Cabinet.[1] The Cabinet was to be reduced to ten and – a prescient touch – the Navy and Army were to come under a single Minister of War with two secretaries under him for the two Services – a sort of pre-vision of the modern Ministry of Defence. There was also to be a Minister of Education in the Cabinet. Parliamentary Secretaries for Ireland, Scotland, Justice, Police, Health and Poor Law were to be put under the Home Secretary. The Irish Lord Lieutenancy was to be abolished. Stimulated by an enthusiastic Civil Servant, Sir Richard Bromley, whom he later dropped as an importunate bore,[2] Disraeli devoted a surprising amount of energy to this unprofitable exercise. He enlisted Stanley's support, but nothing came of his plan in the end, for Derby was not sufficiently interested.

It is doubtful whether the principal objective could ever have been achieved. In that most puzzling of entities, the British Constitution, there seems to be some mysterious principle which prevents the Cabinet ever falling to ten or less. It has only happened twice, in each case under the stress of a world war. Cabinets in the nineteenth century were smaller than today, fifteen or sixteen being a normal figure, but only one fell below thirteen; and that was in 1874, when Disraeli himself made a valiant effort to convert his

---

[1] ibid 145/4, has Disraeli's memorandum together with the younger Stanley's comments.

[2] 'I should keep very shy of B.', he wrote to Pakington in 1864. 'Nothing can ever satisfy his ravenous egotism.'

theory into practice by keeping it down to twelve. Ten would have baffled even his ingenuity, and by 1878 he had been obliged to raise the number to thirteen.

He had the consolation during this frustrating period of doing a good turn to an old friend upon whom a sad family disaster had descended. Lady Jersey was one of the great ladies whose salons he attended as a young man, and, although like others of her world she did not at first approve of his marriage, friendly relations had long ago been restored. In the spring of 1855 Society was convulsed by the news that her younger son, Francis Villiers, Tory MP for Rochester, had vanished from London, leaving behind him not only huge debts but the forged signatures of many noble names to the acceptances of bills which had been circulating among the money-lenders.[1] According to Greville, his principal accomplice was 'a Mrs. Edmonds, already famous as a whore, bawd and usurer'. Some years earlier Disraeli to his great annoyance had discovered that one of his own bills had got into the hands of this shady character and had insisted upon his agent's recovering it at once.

Lord Jersey on the advice of his solicitor was at first inclined to wash his hands of the whole affair, but Disraeli urged him to try to prevent a criminal prosecution by buying up the bills, and offered to help in the matter – a task for which his past experiences made him eminently qualified. Lady Jersey, who was immensely rich in her own right, agreed to pay, and accordingly Disraeli, together with Greville, who was also a friend of the family, acted as virtual trustee in this sordid and time-consuming work.[2] When the scandal first broke the diarist noted:

> It is a very unlucky moment for such an exposure as this (besides the private grief and calamity), for there is now a run against the aristocracy and though without any just cause a case of such enormous villainy is sure to be commented on in terms calculated to heighten the prevailing and growing prejudice.[3]

Francis Villiers wrote an unintelligible letter about a conspiracy against him, and never returned to England. He died in Spain a few years later. Greville, whose comments on Disraeli had not been

---

[1] Strachey and Fulford (ed.), *Greville*, vii, 127–9, April 14, 1855. The episode is suppressed in Reeve's edition.

[2] Hughenden Papers, Box 14, contains a mass of letters on the affair and Box 27 a covering memorandum by Rose headed, 'Sacred. Lord Beaconsfield's Trusteeship'.

[3] *Greville*, vii, 128.

favourable hitherto, was much impressed at the great pains which the latter had taken.

> I have occasion to see Dis very often about F. Villiers' affairs (about which he has been wonderfully kind and serviable) and on these occasions he always enters into some political talk, and in this way we have got into a sort of intimacy such as I never thought could have taken place between us.[1]

Some £40,000 passed through their hands and in the end the creditors appear to have been satisfied. Certainly no public exposure occurred. The episode illustrates one of Disraeli's most agreeable traits, his willingness to take an infinity of trouble for the sake of gratitude and friendship.

Disraeli was exhausted at the end of the 1856 session. 'Nervous debility,' he told Mrs Brydges Willyams. He and Mary Anne decided to take the waters at Spa, and departed without telling anyone where they were until just before their return. The visit did him good, and he returned to Hughenden sufficiently invigorated to take an active part in local affairs. Disraeli never scorned local government; on the contrary, he regarded its independence as one of the most important bulwarks of the aristocratic principle – anyway in the counties. He consented to become chairman of a committee set up by the magistrates at Quarter Sessions to establish the 'new Rural Police', and was so busy that he refused all social invitations.

On November 20 the Disraelis left England again, this time for Paris. He had decided to go abroad largely to keep out of the way of the grandees of the party, with whom, from Derby downwards, he was on particularly distant terms just then. An additional reason was supplied by the Emperor, who was anxious to make some sort of contact with responsible members of the Opposition. Lord Henry Lennox acted as intermediary, and Disraeli was as anxious in 1856 as he had been in 1842, despite the change of dynasty, to encourage good relations with France. He and Mary Anne were much fêted in Paris, dining out eleven nights in succession. One of these occasions was at the Tuileries, to which, so Disraeli records, the Emperor had invited 'all the distinguished men of his clientelle'. He noted how much Girardin, Dumas, Alfred de Vigny, had changed since he last saw them.

> Meeting people after an interval of twenty years, it is like people

[1] ibid., 168, November 12, 1855.

going out of one door of a room in youth & returning immediately after thro' another as old men. I have seen such effects in some plays when there is an interval of a generation between the acts. One naturally immediately asks & feels: 'Am I so altered?' I don't think so – certainly not in feeling.[1]

He got little political change out of the Emperor, who somewhat contemptuously categorized him to Malmesbury a few weeks later as being 'like all literary men . . . ignorant of the world, talking well, but nervous when the moment of action arises'.[2] One can but echo Buckle's comment: 'A singularly inept judgment.'

There can be no doubt that Disraeli was highly unpopular at this time with a large section of the party. His position had always depended upon the indispensability of his talents. It owed little to personal affection, except among a very small group of loyal supporters like Stanley, Manners, Lennox and Hamilton. In November 1852 Derby told the Prince Consort: 'Mr. Disraeli knew that he [Lord Derby] possessed the confidence of three hundred of his supporters whilst Mr. Disraeli, if he separated himself from him, would very likely not carry five with him.'[3] If this was the case then, later events could only have made matters worse.

During 1855 and 1856 his prestige sagged heavily, thanks partly to his peace policy, partly to his disinclination to humour his followers, and partly to the line taken by the *Press*, 'which avoids ever mentioning the name of Lord Derby', so Malmesbury records, 'or of anyone except Disraeli himself, whom it praises in the most fulsome manner'.[4] At the end of 1856, Joliffe, the Chief Whip, became seriously anxious about the situation, which he discussed in December with Malmesbury, who wrote a despondent letter to Derby. The latter replied on the 15th. 'As to Disraeli's unpopularity, I see it and regret it; and especially regret that he does not see more of the party in private; but they could not do without him even if there were anyone ready and able to take his place.'[5]

If Disraeli had his defects as a leader, so, too, had Derby. He was quite as aloof as Disraeli and it could be argued that he was the last man who had a right to complain of anyone because 'he does not see

---

[1] Hughenden Papers, Box 26, A/X/A/36.

[2] Malmesbury, *Memoirs*, ii, 66.

[3] Memorandum by the Prince Consort, November 25, 1852, quoted in F. Eyck *The Prince Consort* (1959), 197.

[4] Malmesbury, *Memoirs*, ii, 45.

[5] ibid., 53–54, where the letter, an interesting one, is given in full.

more of the party in private'. There were times when Derby must
have been a sore trial to his most loyal supporters. A characteristic
letter from Lord Henry Lennox, who had been staying at the same
house (Middleton Park, Lord Jersey's seat), gives a picture of him
just before the session of 1857.

> As a leader of a Party, he is *more* hopeless than ever!! Devoted to
> Whist, Billiards, Racing, Betting, & making a fool of himself with
> either Ladies Emily Peel or Mary Yorke – Bulwer Lytton came to
> Bretby for 3 days & was in despair! Not a word could he extract
> from Derby about Public affairs: nothing but the odds & tricks;
> in despair he fell back on me; but of course I only told him as
> much as was good for him . . . I must now tell you that *Malmes-*
> *bury* wishes to be supposed to be desperate about Clementina
> Villiers!! Profitable for her, I hope you think: He comes here on
> Friday & I have told Clemmy to impress upon him that *Derby* is
> the bar to Conservative consolidation.[1]

The prospect for the new year seemed dull to a degree. To all
appearance the Government was safe, and there was no need for an
election before 1858. 'I have just sent out a circular for the meeting
of the House,' wrote Joliffe to Disraeli on January 5. 'It was difficult to know what to say to bring such People as ours to Town from
their hunting etc.'[2] But, as Disraeli liked to say, 'there is no gambling like politics.' The next couple of years were to see startling
somersaults on the parliamentary stage.

[1] Hughenden Papers, Box 102, B/XX/LX/86, January 7, 1857.
[2] ibid., Box 101, B/XX/J/42.

CHAPTER XVII

Rebuff and Recovery

1857–8

1

The session opened unpromisingly. Disraeli launched a two-pronged assault against the Government's foreign policy and the budget. He did not get very far on either front. Foreign policy is seldom a profitable field of attack: the cards are too heavily stacked in favour of the Government with its confidential information that an outsider cannot effectively controvert. The issue which Disraeli raised turned out to be something of a mare's nest; the existence of a secret treaty signed in December 1854, whereby France, with British encouragement, guaranteed the integrity of the Austrian dominions in Italy. This, so Disraeli claimed, was a flagrant contradiction of the pro-Italian policy currently pursued by Palmerston, But, in fact, it was nothing of the sort, and, although Palmerston appeared in a bad light and spoiled his own case by first denying that the treaty had ever existed, he had a good answer: the treaty was an unsuccessful but legitimate attempt to draw Austria into the war against Russia, and no one regarded it as having any validity after the war had ended. Derby, who was laid up with gout, thought so all along. 'Your treaty', he wrote on February 11, 'appears to have been what I was afraid it would turn out to be – the old arrangement limited to the war and, according to Palmerston, never executed.'[1]

Disraeli's informant was a young man by the name of Ralph Earle who was in the Foreign Service.[2] Earle was born in 1835, member of a well-known Whig family of Liverpool. He was educated at Harrow, and was appointed by Lord Clarendon as an attaché at the Paris Embassy in 1854. Disraeli had met him on his visit there a few weeks before. Earle, like Manners, Smythe and Lennox, fell under the spell which the magician could always cast over

[1] Hughenden Papers, Box 109, B/XX/S/146.
[2] See G. B. Henderson, *Crimean War Diplomacy* (1947), 267–89 for an interesting essay on Earle.

youth. He struck up an alliance with Disraeli which did neither of
them much credit, for in flagrant disregard of his duty to the service
and to his chief, Lord Cowley, he entered into an agreement,
possibly an unspoken one, to supply Disraeli with secret information
for use as ammunition against the Government. The *quid pro quo* –
again it was probably not stated in so many words – was that
Disraeli would advance Earle's career when the occasion arose. A
flood of letters from Earle signed 'X' or not signed at all poured in to
Disraeli during the next twelve months. His replies have not survived. It seems likely that he communicated with Earle via John
Bidwell, an official of Tory persuasion who had been promoted on
successive days in the last week of the Derby administration to a
second-class clerkship (December 14, 1852) and to the post of précis
writer to the Secretary of State (December 15). Bidwell later became Malmesbury's private secretary when the latter returned to
the Foreign Office in 1858. The evidence is by no means conclusive,
but Dr Henderson makes the reasonable guess that the dying Tory
ministry decided to plant a sympathizer in this important position
and that 'Disraeli had his secret service in the Foreign Office as well
as in the Paris Embassy.[1]

Disraeli's proven use of Earle and his probable if unproven use
of Bidwell cannot be defended even by the standards of the time.
The only plea which can be made in mitigation is that the concept
of a non-political Civil Service had not yet been generally accepted
and, as with the Admiralty and the Board of Trade in 1852, Derby
and Disraeli could legitimately feel uneasy because the key posts
in most departments had been filled either by Whig or Peelite
patronage. But, although it is not unknown even today for a party
which obtains power after a long interval to put its own supporters
into the governmental machine, that is a far cry from Disraeli's
system of espionage when in opposition. Earle evidently hoped that
Disraeli would have the Foreign Office in Derby's next administration. On this assumption he wrote to him on March 4, 1857, when
Palmerston's fall seemed imminent. He offered himself as Disraeli's
private secretary and went on:

Now it is difficult to believe that the present occupants of office –
to whom almost all the bureaucracy owe their appointments –

[1] ibid., 269–70. If Disraeli did use Bidwell in this way, the fact does not seem to
have made him regard the Foreign Office clerk with esteem. See below, p. 405, for his
comments on Bidwell and Malmesbury.

should retire from power without having established some relations with the permanent agents of the Govt. This seems to me
another reason for giving the great Embassies to partisans of your
administration but the reason I have alluded to this subject is on
a matter of detail. I wd. have you establish a sort of *cabinet du
ministre*' as the confidential staff of a French Minister is called.
The materials out of which you could form such a body wd. be the
parliamentary Under-Secretary and the two private Secretaries.
Now if the Embassies at Paris, Vienna & St. Petersburg were
filled by partisans, & if you substituted for their chanceries (not
of course formally) confidential private secretaries – also chosen
from among your partisans – you wd. be able to carry on any
correspondence with foreign courts without fear of its falling into
improper hands. The archives of this correspondence you wd.
carry away with you, on leaving office and no trace of it wd.
remain at our Foreign Office or at our Missions abroad . . .[1]

So much for continuity of foreign policy.

During the second Derby administration Earle acted as Disraeli's
private secretary and continued in that position for the next eight
years, replacing to some extent Henry Lennox in his chief's
affections. Lennox greatly disliked him, and the feeling was reciprocated. Each complained to Disraeli about the other's honesty and
discretion. The historian reading their letters is irresistibly reminded
of Tadpole and Taper; the same small change of politics, rumours,
gossip, false alarms, speculative combinations, subterranean intrigues, flavoured with a strong dash of personal place-hunting. In
May 1859 Earle entered the House – 'only 23 but a man in matured
thought and power of observation', Disraeli told Mrs Brydges
Willyams.[2] Under a bargain with his opponent he resigned the seat
in August, and remained out of Parliament until the election of
1865, when he was returned for Maldon in Essex.

Earle was obviously a much abler man than Lennox. He must
have had some powers of pleasing, or Disraeli, who was fastidious
about personalities, would not have employed him for so long. But
his letters do not leave a pleasant taste in the mouth. His behaviour
towards Lord Cowley was vindictive, disloyal and unpatriotic.
Although he admitted that the Ambassador was 'at least honest
and resolute', he advised Disraeli to move for the reduction of his
salary in order to drive him out of office. 'If we cannot reward

[1] ibid., 271–2, quoting from Hughenden Papers.
[2] M. & B., iv, 234.

friends, it is something, at any rate, to punish enemies.'[1] In fact, Malmesbury on becoming Foreign Secretary successfully urged Cowley to remain, and the Ambassador did not retire until 1867. This, one feels, served Earle right. It may account for the satisfaction with which he drew Disraeli's attention to a *Times* leader describing Malmesbury as 'a tenth rate mediocrity'.[2]

But the worst example of Earle's lack of patriotism was an interview with Napoleon III on April 19, 1860, which he recounted in a letter to Disraeli. He told the Emperor that he could 'safely adopt a policy of resistance to the demands [*réclamations*] of the English Cabinet'. He gave him a summary of the case which might be published by the French Government against Palmerston, and advised the Emperor to revive the Suez Canal scheme – a notorious *bête noire* of Palmerston's – in order to emphasize British dependence on French goodwill in the East. In effect he was inciting Napoleon to pursue an anti-British policy in the hope that the resulting fracas would bring down Palmerston as it had in 1858, and thus risking the danger of a serious quarrel between Britain and France and the ultimate possibility of war. The absence of clear evidence about Disraeli's attitude cannot absolve him from complicity. It is very unlikely that Earle would have written as he did unless he had good reason to expect a favourable reception. As Henderson puts it, 'the chances are that he was as deeply involved as his Private Secretary'. It is doubtful whether Earle's activities in foreign policy either then or earlier when he was still in the Paris Embassy gave his chief any real help. Disraeli's irresistible penchant for intrigue explains but cannot excuse such a correspondence.

Defeated over the alleged secret treaty, Disraeli turned to his second line of attack, an onslaught on the budget. Here he had Derby's approval, for there seemed a chance of bringing Gladstone over to the Tory side on this issue. He and the other Peelites, apart from Newcastle, the late Secretary for War, who was under a cloud because of cargoes of left boots and the like, had joined Palmerston in 1855, only to resign a fortnight later on an esoteric issue which few people understood. They had been in a detached position ever since, and it seemed possible that they would respond to a skilful bid. The Chancellor of the Exchequer, Sir George Cornewall Lewis, was a cool and scholarly intellectual who never hesitated to put

---

[1] Henderson, 273, quoting from Hughenden Papers.
[2] Hughenden Papers, Box 96, B/XX/E/50, n.d.

forward unpalatable propositions if he believed them to be true, even though it was quite unnecessary to do so. In his budget speech he made some heterodox *obiter dicta* on the desirability of having a large number of small taxes rather than a small number of large ones. His budget in content did not depart much from financial orthodoxy, but his utterances put Gladstone into a state of excitement. He told his friends that the ghost of Peel would haunt him if he did not controvert them.[1] The opportunity was too good to miss, and Derby acted as intermediary in drafting a hostile resolution, for direct dealings with Disraeli were insurmountably repugnant to Gladstone. Nevertheless a temporary pact was formed, and the two men fought together as champions of economy and the reduction of military establishments. They did not succeed. Gladstone was too violent, Disraeli too rhetorical, and the sting of their attack had been drawn by Lewis's decision to reduce income tax from 1s 4d to 7d.

The Government won by eighty votes, but a few days later it capsized in a wholly unexpected storm. Palmerston had indulged in some very high-handed conduct towards China, reminiscent of his behaviour over the Don Pacifico affair. The moral consciences of Radicals, Peelites and Conservatives were alike outraged, and Derby decided to mount a full-scale attack. Reversing for once their usual roles, Disraeli was doubtful. He remembered how successfully Palmerston had extricated himself from the earlier row. But he was overruled and for the moment Derby seemed vindicated. As they had over Don Pacifico, all the leading statesmen of the day condemned Palmerston, who was defeated in the House of Commons by 263 to 247. He soon got his own back. Accepting Disraeli's challenge to appeal to the nation, he dissolved Parliament. Gunboat diplomacy was more popular with the electorate than the House. Palmerston struck the keynote in what turned into a personal plebiscite by stigmatizing the Chinese Mandarin who governed Canton as 'an insolent barbarian'. Out of 660 members in the new House, he had some 370 very diversely assorted followers. The Manchester Radicals were routed, and the Peelites scarcely fared better.

Disraeli took the defeat philosophically. For the first time after nine contests he was personally unopposed. As for the party, he reckoned that, although its numbers had shrunk in theory from

[1] Morley, *Gladstone*, i, 560.

280 to about 260, the former figure had never been a reality.

> When the hour of battle arrived [he wrote to Mrs Brydges Willyams on April 13] we never could count on more than 220, the rest absent, or worse against us. Now we have, I am assured by Sir William Joliffe, the Chief of my Staff, 260 good men and true, fresh and not jaded by the mortifying traditions of the last Parliament . . . We shall now have a House of Commons with two parties and with definite opinions. All the sections, all the conceited individuals who were what they styled themselves 'independent', have been swept away, erased, obliterated, expunged. The state of affairs will be much more wholesome and more agreeable.[1]

On the same day he wrote to his sister:

> I don't think Palmerston's name carried a single vote. In the boroughs for a Tory Opposition we were really successful in many great seats and only lost four on the whole. As for the Counties, Protection being dead, they returned to their natural influences as was already foreseen . . . It is a great thing irrespective of the Peelites to have got rid of Deedes & Co.[2]

Disraeli was wrong about Palmerston, whose name, according to most contemporaries, carried a large number of votes. On the other hand, his analysis of the counties was probably correct. In a sense the Tories had done unnaturally well there in the 1852 election, carrying, thanks to the anti-free-trade cry, several which normally followed the lead of the local Whig magnates. There was no chance of repeating this in 1857, when all parties were agreed that free trade had come to stay. The Whig counties reverted to their old allegiances, with the result that the Tories lost no fewer than twenty-three county seats,[3] quite enough to account for their decline.

Palmerston now appeared unassailable, although in reality his majority was by no means as solid as it seemed. Russell and the dissident Whigs were biding their time, and even the jingo section of the Radicals could not be relied on to support indefinitely a Prime Minister whose views on all domestic matters was quite as conservative as Derby's. But he was safe for the time being. All eyes were fixed on events in India, where the Mutiny was running its alarming course from early May onwards, and there was no

[1] M. & B., iv, 76.
[2] Hughenden Papers, Box 6, A/I/B/367.
[3] Hughenden Papers, Box 98, B/XX/H/62, Hamilton to Disraeli, April 25, 1857.

disposition to shake the Government at such a time of crisis.

Disraeli had for some time past taken a keen interest in Indian affairs. He had been a member of the Select Committee which in 1852 inquired into the government of India. He was convinced that it was high time to abolish the East India Company, and he carried his conviction, as we saw earlier, to the point of a serious rift with Derby and the other Tory leaders in 1853. Disraeli also held strong views on another aspect of Indian policy. From 1815 onwards there had been two schools of thought on the question of Westernization. The Whigs believed that it was Britain's duty to introduce Western institutions and to 'civilize' India; Lord William Bentinck, Governor-General 1828–35, and Macaulay, the legal member of his council, were the arch-exponents of this policy, and it was reasserted in a most vigorous manner by the Peelite, Lord Dalhousie, who governed India from 1848 to 1856. The Westernizing policy also had the support of the missionaries hoping to convert the Indian masses to Christianity and their zeal was shared to a surprising degree by officers of the Indian Army.

Disraeli did not sympathize with this school of thought. He looked with alarm at Dalhousie's high-minded but doctrinaire attempt to undermine Indian customs and to dispossess the princes. He was in this respect (though not in others) on the side of men like Lord Lawrence, whose lives had been bound up with native India, and who believed that Indian traditions should be respected. The Mutiny confirmed all his misgivings, and on July 27 he made a notable speech expounding his views on the whole problem. He denounced the doctrine of 'lapse' and the annexation of Oude. We were concerned here, he argued, with a genuine revolt against British policy, not a mere protest at the violation of a taboo. 'The rise and fall of empires are not affairs of greased cartridges.'[1] English rule had been accepted because it imposed order on anarchy, and guaranteed the rights of property and religion. Latterly, however, it had created nothing but unease and anxiety in every class or caste from the princes downwards. Whatever the upshot of the hostilities, he urged the Government to announce at once that the relation between the people of India 'and their real Ruler and Sovereign, Queen Victoria, shall be drawn nearer'. Indians should be told that the Queen would respect their laws, customs and religion. 'You can only act upon the opinion of Eastern nations

[1] *Hansard*, 3rd Series, cxlvii, 475.

through their imagination.' A monarch was more likely to have this effect than a chartered company, however venerable and worthy.

The atrocities committed by the mutineers, above all the revolting brutality of Nana Sahib at Cawnpore, caused a general cry for revenge. Disraeli was perhaps unduly inclined to discount the stories of these horrors; although some were manufactured, the reality was quite bad enough. He erred in the same way twenty years later when he pooh-poohed the Bulgarian atrocities. But his scepticism had one good result: he used his influence against the public pressure for indiscriminate reprisals.

I for one protest against taking Nana Sahib as a model for the conduct of the British soldier. I protest against meeting atrocities by atrocities. I have heard things said and seen things written of late which would make me almost suppose that the religious opinions of the people of England had undergone some sudden change, and that, instead of bowing before the name of Jesus we were preparing to revive the worship of Moloch.[1]

The Mutiny, as Disraeli predicted, took much longer to suppress than Palmerston, who treated it throughout rather casually, seems to have expected. But the worst was over by the end of the year. Meanwhile during a December session of Parliament called to deal with a wholly separate issue, the suspension of the Bank Charter Act, Palmerston announced that he intended in the new year to legislate for the abolition of the East India Company. This put Disraeli in a dilemma. In principle he was in favour of such a course and had said so, but he thought that Palmerston was cheating by thus appearing to shift the blame on to the Company when, in fact, it was due to the Government's policy. All the same, he would probably have been well advised to avoid the charge of faction by letting the Bill go through. Not for the first or last time, however, he overdid the principle that an Opposition should oppose. On February 18, 1858, a hostile amendment which he supported was lost by 318 to 173; at least eighty Conservatives refused to follow him.

At this juncture a sudden and most unexpected change came over the fortunes of the Conservative party. Palmerston, who had been unbearably jaunty and self-confident for the past few months, committed one gross error and followed it by one serious misjudgement. The gross error was to appoint to the vacant post of Lord

[1] M. & B., iv, 99.

Privy Seal his wife's friend, Lord Clanricarde. The latter was a character of whom it could have been said even more truly than Derby had said of the Duke of Buckingham, 'his character and habits of life would render his appointment to high office discreditable to any Government'. Lord Clanricarde had an illegitimate son by a Mrs Handcock who died in 1853. This fact might not have mattered, had not public attention been roused by an action in the Dublin Court of Chancery, in which her relatives alleged that all her property had been bequeathed to the son, owing to the improper influence exercised by Lord Clanricarde over her daughters, who had been induced to forgo their rights. When Lord Lansdowne heard of the appointment he asked Palmerston 'if he was out of his mind'. The Queen, it need hardly be said, was scandalized. Disraeli was surprised. 'The appointment', he wrote to Lady Londonderry on January 7, '. . . has greatly injured the Government – but I hear that everything was tried and everybody sounded before it was decided on. . . . When all failed, Lady Palmerston rallied, and made a successful charge, and carried her protégé. There is nothing like female friendship – the only thing worth having.'[1] But mid-Victorian respectability was already casting its shadow before it. What would have done even in 1837 would not do twenty years later.

The Government was therefore in bad odour and its supporters much disgruntled when Palmerston was faced with a difficult problem, over which he completely misjudged public opinion. An Italian fanatic by the name of Orsini unsuccessfully attempted to blow up the Emperor in Paris with a bomb made in Birmingham. A large number of onlookers were killed, there was an uproar in France, and menacing remarks about England as a shelter for assassins were made in the addresses of congratulation presented to the Emperor upon his escape. Count Walewski, the French Foreign Minister, sent a dispatch couched in strong language asking for legislation to tighten up the law against conspiracy to murder. It did not on the face of things seem unreasonable to make the manufacture of infernal machines a felony instead of a misdemeanour, and Palmerston introduced a measure to that effect.

Disraeli voted for the first reading on February 9, but prudently declared that he was not committing himself over the later stages. The next ten days saw a strong upsurge of opinion against the Bill.

[1] *Letters to Lady Londonderry*, 171.

There was a general feeling that the Government was supinely yielding to French threats, and when Bright of all people started to condemn Palmerston for 'truckling to France', Disraeli saw that the Government might fall. Overriding Derby, who counselled caution, he used the argument that the Government had never answered Walewski's dispatch as a reason for voting against the second reading. It was not a very good point, but it sufficed. Palmerston, who displayed unusual ill temper, was defeated by 234 votes to 215, and he promptly resigned. Of the majority, only 146 were Conservatives – an indication that Disraeli was far from being in control of his own followers. His victory was due to the defalcation of some eighty Liberals, and it is probable that a great many of them were influenced as much by the Clanricarde appointment as by the actual issue on which they were voting.

2

'The Captain' did not hesitate this time. He made overtures to Lord Grey and to Gladstone. Both declined. But Derby recognizing, as he said to the Queen, that 'if he refused the Conservative party would be broken up for ever', went ahead and formed a government from his own supporters. It was not quite such a feeble affair as in 1852. Herries and the Duke of Northumberland had retired from the scene; so had Lord Lonsdale ('Lord Eskdale' in *Tancred*), 'a man with every ability, except the ability to make his powers useful to mankind'. Three new members of the Cabinet could be regarded as taking their places, though not their exact offices; Lord Ellenborough, Stanley, and – a notable acquisition – General Peel, Sir Robert's brother. Undoubtedly the Cabinet gained by this exchange, though Ellenborough was destined to be a very dubious asset. One other change took place: Lord St Leonards refused the Lord Chancellorship, and Thesiger, created Lord Chelmsford, took his place. Disraeli disliked him, and before long they were on the worst possible terms.

As in 1852, Cabinet-making was by no means an easy process. The weakness in 1858, as on the former occasion, was in the House of Commons. Derby himself could dominate the upper House, but in the Commons it was difficult to rival such figures as Gladstone, Russell, Palmerston, Graham, Cobden and Bright. Derby tried to remedy this by appointing Disraeli's old friend Bulwer Lytton to the

Colonial Office, but Lytton declared that he could not face his re-election for Herts. He was angling for a peerage, 'which I will not do for him', wrote Derby. 'If he is to be of *any* use, it must be in the H. of Commons.' Disraeli agreed. 'I . . . never contemplated that Lytton should even have been in the Cabinet, had it not been for our Chief's too gracious notice of him in 1855. . . . I think Lytton too impudent.'[1] The Colonial Office was now offered to Lord John Manners, who was much alarmed at the prospect of being ejected from his chosen haven of the Office of Works. But at the last minute Stanley, who evinced much reluctance to enter the Cabinet at all, was persuaded to take the position – to the umbrage of Lytton, who now declared that he had been misunderstood, and had only meant that he *might lose* the re-election, not that he would not attempt it. His explanation was too late, and he remained out for the time being.

The Cabinet was thus composed:

First Lord of the Treasury	Earl of Derby
Lord Chancellor	Lord Chelmsford
Lord President	Marquess of Salisbury
Lord Privy Seal	Earl of Hardwicke
Home Secretary	Spencer Walpole
Foreign Secretary	Earl of Malmesbury
Colonial Secretary	Lord Stanley
War Secretary	General Peel
Chancellor of the Exchequer	Benjamin Disraeli
First Lord of the Admiralty	Sir John Pakington
President of the Board of Control	Earl of Ellenborough
President of the Board of Trade	J. W. Henley
First Commissioner of Works	Lord John Manners

The Tory Government was in an even weaker position politically than in 1852, for it was outnumbered by something like three to two in the House, and could easily be overthrown if the Opposition could only agree. Disraeli, very conscious of this weakness, made a bold attempt to influence public opinion by trying to enlist *The Times* on his side. He wrote a private letter to Delane giving him details of Derby's interview with the Queen while the Cabinet was forming. 'I suppose this is about as imprudent a letter as was ever written, but it is written in our old spirit of camaraderie – I never forget your generous support of me

[1] M. & B., iv, 118.

in 1852.'[1] Delane was at this time a strong supporter of Palmerston
and a regular frequenter of the great parties at Palmerston's
house. He did make some friendly remarks on Disraeli personally,
but his comment on the Cabinet was scarcely what Disraeli hoped
for. The list was 'a penitential sheet', Derby's Government being,
so Delane argued, a self-inflicted punishment for the humiliation
of the Orsini affair.[2] Disraeli continued to be polite despite this
rebuff, but after enduring further attacks in May he rounded on
Delane, and everyone knew who was meant when a famous phrase
during a speech at Slough he declared that 'leading Organs are
now place-hunters of the Cabal, and the once stern guardians
of popular rights simper in the enervating atmosphere of gilded
saloons'.[3] The personal quarrel was made up in the autumn,
but the Government continued to get a bad press from *The
Times* in spite of ingratiating efforts on the part of some
ministers.

In his opening speech in the House of Lords, Derby announced
that his principal measure for 1858 would be an India Bill, for 1859
a Reform Bill. These and the budget were to be Disraeli's chief
concern. India twice almost brought the Government to a speedy
end. The trouble was the choice of Lord Ellenborough as President
of the Board of Control. He had been Governor-General from 1841
to 1844 and had the distinction of being the only one on whom the
Company used its semi-abeyant but legal right of recall. He was a
man of gigantic vanity, and no sense of proportion. While Governor-
General he had caused general ridicule by his attempt to celebrate
the end of the Afghan War: the troops were to march under a
triumphal arch through an avenue of salaaming elephants; the arch
nearly collapsed, and the elephants panicked and rushed away.
Lord Ellenborough now proceeded to draft a Bill for the government of India. It created a Secretary of State and a council of
eighteen. Half were to be Crown-appointed, but the other half were
to be chosen on a system worthy of the Abbé Sièyes: four were to be
elected by those who had either served in India for ten years or who
possessed a certain amount of stock in the Company or other
scheduled Indian investments; five were to be elected by the
constituencies of London, Manchester, Glasgow, Liverpool and
Belfast; the four in the first category must have served for ten, or

[1] *History of The Times*, ii, 1841–1884 (1939), 328.
[2] loc. cit.   [3] M. & B., iv, 151.

traded for fifteen years in India, and the five in the second category
must have been engaged in commerce with India for five years or to
have lived there for ten. Disraeli himself, as his Reform Bills were to
show, had a certain sympathy for eccentric qualifications of this
sort, but its anomalies were so obvious that the Cabinet soon had
to beat a retreat. There was something farcical in a system which
disqualified John Stuart Mill, while it qualified anyone who happened to have exported beer in a small way to India for five years.

But Lord Ellenborough's next effort was almost fatal to the
Government and wholly fatal to himself.[1] The unlucky Canning,
who had been censured by public opinion for 'clemency' in the
autumn of 1857, issued on March 14, 1858, after the capture of
Lucknow, a proclamation declaring that with a few exceptions 'the
proprietary right in the province [of Oude] is confiscated by the
British Government which will dispose of that right in such a
manner as it may seem fitting'. This apparently draconian policy
produced a revulsion when it was published in England two months
later. In fact, Canning's intention was nothing like as drastic as it
sounded. Unaware of the change of government, he explained the
real nature of his policy in a letter to Ellenborough's predecessor,
Vernon-Smith, but Vernon-Smith failed to pass it on to Ellenborough, who proceeded to draft a dispatch censuring Canning in
the severest language. He showed it to Derby, Disraeli, Pakington
and Manners, all of whom agreed, but, owing to pressure of business,
it was never formally approved by the Cabinet, nor was it shown to
the Queen, before being sent to Canning.

Thus far no great harm had been done, for if secrecy had been
preserved Canning would have had a chance of explaining in confidence exactly what he meant. But Ellenborough had an author's
vanity for a good thing. Without consulting anyone he sent copies
to Granville and Bright. On May 6 his dispatch appeared in *The
Times*. There was at once a furore. Whatever people thought of
Canning's proclamation, Ellenborough's reproof was deemed
arrogant and offensive to the highest degree. Motions of censure
were put down in both Houses. The Government would have fallen
if Ellenborough had not saved the day by resigning on May 10. In
the House of Commons immense excitement prevailed. 'I have
never seen,' wrote Sir William Fraser, 'anything approaching the personal feeling, and resentment, which was shown during

[1] Michael Maclagan, *Clemency Canning* (1962), ch. viii, gives the best account.

this debate . . . The cheering, groaning, laughing were beyond belief.'[1]

Issues of principle scarcely divided members at this time, but ill feeling was not of course lessened for that reason. Indeed, it was accentuated. Men can respect opposition based on principle more readily than opposition based solely on a desire to replace the 'ins' by the 'outs'. Disraeli secured a notable triumph in the end, for Cardwell who proposed the motion, decided to withdraw, probably for fear of a dissolution. The Government was now safe and was able to ride out the rest of the session.

The problem now was to fill the vacancy caused by Ellenborough's resignation. Inevitably Derby and Disraeli turned to Gladstone. Disraeli offered to resign the leadership in favour of Graham in order to help matters, but Graham declined. Disraeli then decided to make a personal appeal, and on May 25 wrote a remarkable letter.[2] He omitted the usual 'Dear Sir' and 'Yours . . .' signing himself simply 'B. Disraeli'.

> I think it of such paramount importance to the public interests that you should assume at this time a commanding position in the administration of affairs that I feel it a solemn duty to lay before you some facts, that you may not decide under a misapprehension.
>
> Our mutual relations have caused the great difficulty in accomplishing a result which I have always anxiously desired.
>
> Listen without prejudice to this brief narrative . . . .

Disraeli then described the various offers that he had made to give up the leadership of the House to Palmerston and Graham, in order to facilitate Gladstone's adherence, for he saw the difficulty of Gladstone serving under himself. He went on:

> Don't you think the time has come when you might deign to be magnanimous?
>
> Mr. Canning was superior to Lord Castlereagh in capacity, in eloquence, but he joined Lord C. when Lord C. was Lord Liverpool's lieutenant, when the state of the Tory party rendered it necessary. That was an enduring and, on the whole, not an unsatisfactory connection, and it certainly terminated very gloriously for Mr. Canning.
>
> I may be removed from the scene or I may wish to be removed from the scene.

[1] Fraser, *Disraeli and His Day*, 253–4.
[2] M. & B., iv, 157–8.

Every man performs his office, and there is a Power, greater than ourselves, that disposes of all this . . .

The last sentence does not sound much like Disraeli's normal tone – as Gladstone would certainly have noticed. His reply, described by Sir Philip Magnus as 'polished but cold as ice', and by Morley as expressed in 'accents of guarded reprobation', was sent on the same day.

My dear Sir
The letter you have been so kind as to address to me will enable me, I trust, to remove from your mind some impressions with which you will not be sorry to part . . .
You consider that the relations between yourself and me have proved the main difficulty in the way of certain arrangements. Will you allow me to say that I have never in my life taken a decision which turned upon them . . .
At the present moment I am awaiting counsel which at Lord Derby's wish I have sought. But the difficulties which he wishes me to find means of overcoming are broader than you may have supposed . . .
I state these points fearlessly and without reserve, for you have yourself well reminded me that there is a Power beyond us that disposes of what we are and do, and I find the limits of choice in public life to be very narrow.
I remain, my dear sir, very faithfully yours, W. E. Gladstone.[1]

Disraeli did not attempt a personal approach again. In refusing Derby's offer Gladstone made no allusion at all to Disraeli. Derby was to make one last attempt a year later to persuade his 'half-regained Eurydice', as he called him, to ascend into the light of the Conservative day, but nothing came of it.

No doubt Gladstone believed what he said when he denied any personal element in his decision to reject these offers, but it is difficult for any man to be sure that he really has discerned his own motives. Gladstone's mind must have been very evenly balanced about his choice of party. For he could not – and he knew it – abstain much longer from making some choice. Yet he himself had recently said to Graham that no worse minister than Palmerston had held office in their time. It is hard to avoid the impression that antipathy to Disraeli was the dominant element in his decision, and that during these years he was half consciously searching for an issue which could publicly justify a definitive separation from

[1] ibid., 158–9.

Disraeli. However bad Palmerston might be, he was twenty-five years older than Gladstone, whereas Disraeli was only six years Gladstone's senior. When a year later Gladstone found in the Italian problem the question of principle that he needed, he threw himself with an almost feverish enthusiasm into it, as if he had to convince himself that Derby and Disraeli were irrevocably on the wrong side, although, in fact, their attitude was by no means clear cut. The truth was that he could never have co-operated with Disraeli. He was right to choose as he did. Derby and Disraeli were pursuing a mirage

Gladstone had been given his choice between the Board of Control and the Colonial Office. Derby now decided to transfer Stanley to the former, and to offer the latter to Bulwer Lytton for the second time. He accepted, and agreed to face the necessary by-election. He was opposed by nobody except his wife, who unexpectedly appeared on the hustings to denounce him for a long list of matrimonial offences. Bulwer briskly riposted by getting a doctor to certify her, and have her locked up in a mad-house. But her friends intervened with rival doctors and she was freed. There was widespread adverse comment on an episode which, though scarcely comparable to the Clanricarde affair, was not calculated to do the Government much good. Lady Lytton was understandably in a somewhat peevish humour when released and she proceeded to enliven the post-bags of Lytton's colleagues with a series of what Disraeli called 'letters . . . of an atrocious description such as, I thought, no woman could have penned accusing you of nameless crimes, at least wh: can only be named by her . . .'[1] 'I had thought', Disraeli said, 'that you had tamed the tigress of Taunton' (where Lady Lytton lived). 'What can be the explanation? Is it possible that your agent has been so negligent or imprudent as to leave her allowance in arrear?' But it was persecution mania, not money, which was the trouble. Only the threat of legal action brought a halt to this stream of vituperation.

Lytton probably gave more trouble to Derby and Disraeli than did all their other colleagues put together and his tenure of the Colonial Office was not a happy one. He was very deaf and could therefore seldom intervene in debate, but had to wait to read *Hansard* before replying to attacks. His health was not good, he was a notable hypochondriac, and his nerves were constantly on edge, partly as

[1] Knebworth Papers, n.d.

a result of his unhappy private life. He was, moreover, a man of almost morbid vanity. But he could make an eloquent speech full of splendid phrases which read well in the Press, although his mode of delivery was almost incomprehensible to his audience, and so his opponents, too, had to read *Hansard* before answering. He added a touch of colour to a rather uninspiring Government, 'a name of European celebrity', as Earle wrote to Disraeli. There was, of course, a good deal of public merriment at the spectacle of two romantic novelists in the same Cabinet – a phenomenon unique in British history before or since.

The principal measure of the session was the India Bill, which laid down the principles on which the great sub-continent was to be governed for sixty years. Disraeli operated in close alliance with Stanley over its later stages. He had great admiration for Stanley's industry, efficiency and business-like qualities. But he did not always agree with him. There was in Stanley an element of the humdrum. Disraeli wrote once:

> When we were discussing any grave point – especially on affairs & Stanley saw nothing but difficulties he used to say, 'I know what you are going to say, I know what you are going to say.' He meant that he had no imagination and sometimes when I said so, he wd reply, 'I knew you wd say that.'[1]

There was a rumour that when the India Bill became law, Canning, who certainly had some cause to be annoyed at the Government's behaviour, would resign. Who would in that case be the first 'Viceroy'? Some people wondered whether the choice might fall on Disraeli himself. 'It is quite on the cards', Delane wrote to W. H. Russell. 'He wants the money, and the high station. They want to get rid of him here.'[2] Whether any such offer would have been made it is impossible to say. Canning did not resign, and so the world never had a chance to see the intriguing spectacle of Dizzy and Mary Anne holding the gorgeous East in fee.

Instead, the autumn of 1858 saw Disraeli engaged in more mundane occupations: the preparation of a Reform Bill, plans for his budget, and a number of problems in patronage. The budget and the Reform Bill will be discussed in the next chapter. To patronage, as we have already seen, Disraeli attached much importance. In an

---

[1] Hughenden Papers, Box 26, A/X/A/59.
[2] M. & B., iv, 177.

·ra when divisions of principle between the parties were blurred, and when party machinery was in an embryonic condition, it was indeed true that patronage was almost the only method of cementing party allegiances. He would certainly not have dissented from Earle's view: 'These questions of patronage are of the greatest importance & under present circumstances it seems to be only by attention to party claims that the Conservatives can be kept together.'[1] But on the particular matter raised by Earle, who was strongly supported by Rose and Joliffe, he did not agree. There was for once a Tory Lord Mayor of London, Sir Robert Carden. He was also MP for Gloucester. He expected a baronetcy and threatened to resign his seat, which was said to be unsafe, if he did not get it. 'The Whigs', wrote Earle,[2] 'have made so many Civic Baronets that it will be a pity if you find your only Conservative Ld Mayor to be too bad even for that dignity.'

Disraeli, however funny he might be about them in *Sybil*, believed that baronets were the backbone of the Country party, and he was not too sure that Derby with his Whiggish grandeur always remembered the fact. He promptly wrote to 'the Captain':

He [Carden] has no property and very little character, & is now ridiculous. It wd be the last blow to the order wh: you of all Ministers ought to revive and elevate. The Queen too must have had enough of civic Baronets, as the last one she has made has just gone through the insolvent court . . . As for Carden resigning his seat for Gloucester that is nonsense.[3]

Moreover, even if he did, Disraeli had a solution suggested by the Duke of Richmond through Lord Henry Lennox.[4] Did not Sir Maurice Berkeley of Berkeley Castle control Gloucester and some six seats in the neighbourhood besides? And had not the Berkeley family been engaged for years in endeavouring first to prove their right to an earldom and, after that had failed, in prosecuting a claim of unbelievable complexity to an ancient barony by virtue of their tenure of Berkeley Castle? Baronies by tenure, if allowed, were open to the gravest objection. Lennox wrote: 'I know Lord Brougham is much alarmed that he [Berkeley] could prove his claim which would be the signal to deluge the House of Lords with the lowest

1 Hughenden Papers, Box 96, B/XX/E/70, October 26, 1858.
2 ibid., Box 96, B/XX/E/69, October 25, 1858.
3 Derby Papers, Box 145/5, October 26, 1858.
4 Hughenden Papers, Box 102, B/XX/LX/117, September 23, 1858.

Parvenus who have hitherto not advanced their claims.' The solution was for Derby to create him a peer in time for him, as Lennox put it, 'to register so as to befriend Ld Derby's Govt. As you know, his Electioneering interest is unbounded.' Alas, though Derby was willing, the Queen had doubts about Sir Maurice's character. These were later allayed, but not in time for Derby. Palmerston secured a peerage for him in 1861. Carden did not get his baronetcy and lost his seat at the next election.

Although Disraeli was cautious over honours, he was less so over places. When the new Indian Council was formed he implored Stanley to appoint at least one or two deserving partisans. 'Patronage', he wrote,[1] 'is the outward and visible sign of an inward and spiritual grace, and that is Power.' If patronage were to be withheld from MPs, the House of Commons would degenerate into a mere debating club. 'I entreat you', he ended, 'to think well of this matter. An over scrupulosity in public life often leads to arrangements which are less justifiable than a course of conduct which, at first blush, might seem more coarse and obvious.' Stanley demurred. 'A suspicion of jobbery, from which we at this moment stand clear, and the Whigs, as a body, do not, would hurt us far more than we should be helped by gratifying one or two individuals.'[2]

Later in the year Disraeli had a similar battle with Sir John Pakington at the Admiralty, a department which, as in 1852, caused him much trouble with regard to patronage and estimates. It was customary in those days for at least some members of the Board of Admiralty to have seats in Parliament and support the Government, even though they were at the same time professional naval officers. This situation was becoming an anachronism by 1858, but while it still existed Disraeli was naturally anxious, if only for voting strength, to have some of the Lords of Admiralty in Parliament. He told Pakington that 'our staff in the House of Commons . . . ought not to be less than 35'.[3] But, in fact, it was only twenty-nine, and the absence of two Lords of Admiralty accounted for part of the deficiency. The difficulty was that professional naval officers were reluctant to incur the expense and trouble of finding seats, especially if it was in aid of a government which seemed likely to be short-lived. However, by means of a complicated

[1] M. & B., iv, 174. August 10, 1858.
[2] ibid., 175, August 12, 1858.
[3] ibid., 256, December 19, 1858.

arrangement with the Duke of Northumberland it seemed possible that two seats could be found, as long as the Duke's wishes were respected with regard to the appointment of the Commander-in-Chief at Portsmouth. But instead of appointing the Duke's protégé, Sir Thomas Herbert,[1] Pakington, after consulting Derby but not Disraeli, appointed Admiral Bowles. Disraeli was furious.

> I cannot refrain from expressing [he wrote to Pakington] my surprise and mortification at the course you have taken in this respect . . . Nothing is more ruinous to political connection than the fear of justly rewarding your friends and the promotion of ordinary men of opposite opinions in preference to qualified adherents. It is not becoming in any Minister to decry party who has risen by party. We should always remember that if we were not partisans we should not be Ministers.
>
> I hope my dear Pakington that you will not misconceive the spirit in which these remarks are written. I make them for the common interest and to prevent fatal consequences . . .[2]

Disraeli's anger is understandable, but Pakington had a good answer.[3] Admiral Bowles, his choice, was admittedly seventy-eight, whereas Herbert was sixty-five, but Portsmouth always went to a full Admiral, Herbert was only a Vice-Admiral, and what was more the most junior kind – a Vice-Admiral of the Blue. There was no question of passing him over, as Disraeli claimed. Moreover, 'from his defect of sight he is physically unfit for the duties of the office'. Pakington pointed out that he had consulted Derby, who concurred at the time.

> I fear he has repented his decision. I cannot say that I have. I think it was *right* & I believe it will do us more good than we should have derived from the Helstone seat or the Duke of Northumberland's pleasure.
>
> I am *very* sorry on personal grounds to have annoyed the Duke in any way . . . but in this case I blame him for having so much desired an appointment which he ought, as an old Sailor, to have known would not be a good one . . .
>
> . . . I disapprove of carrying party motives & objects into matters with which they have no legitimate connexion. And I believe that the exercise of patronage, with fairness & justice & strict regard to the *public* interest, gives more real strength to an

---

[1] Hughenden Papers, Box 107, B/XX/P/44. The name is left blank by M. & B. (iv, 257).

[2] Hughenden Papers, Box 107, B/XX/P/44, draft.

[3] ibid., B/XX/P/45, Pakington to Disraeli, December 21, 1858.

Administration than an opposite course, though it may sometimes secure a temporary object.

I cannot doubt that you concur in these principles . . .

By all later standards Pakington was in the right, despite the antiquity of his actual choice, and Disraeli in the wrong. But in this twilight era between the publication and the implementation of the Trevelyan-Northcote Report the matter was not as simple as it subsequently became. Disraeli had to manage the House of Commons. The patronage whether for places or honours was nearly all in the hands of other people, and as if Stanley and Pakington were not troublesome enough, there was the Lord Chancellor, whose views on patronage enraged Disraeli even more. Lord Henry Lennox bitterly complained on his father's behalf about Lord Chelmsford's clerical appointments in Sussex. 'My father reasons that if, as he hears, the Govt. intend to extend the County Franchise, the choice of clergy in these small parishes is most important. The three or [four] voters to be created would infallibly follow the lead of their Parson.' But neither the Duke nor Colonel Wyndham nor any of the local Tory magnates were consulted and lamentable choices were made, such as the new incumbent at the village of Merstham. 'The living', wrote Lennox, 'was given to a man who had been Curate of *our Parish* and had distinguished himself by preaching fanatical sermons against the Goodwood Races of which, as you are aware, my Father is the patron.'[1] Disraeli was to have a long score against the Lord Chancellor before he could at last get rid of him ten years later.

One agreeable event, however, did occur in the field of patronage. Disraeli was most anxious to reward Rose for his party services by a County Court Treasureship, one of the few posts which a solicitor could hold at the same time that he carried on his practice. It so happened that a Commissionership of Excise was vacant and Derby suggested that James Disraeli should be promoted, thus leaving his County Court Treasureship vacant for Rose. Quite properly, Disraeli at first declined to consider it. 'Any appointment which has the appearance even of preferring private interests and feelings to the efficiency of the public service must be avoided', he wrote. Derby did not press the matter at once, but ten days later insisted that James should have it, and that Rose should get his reward. Although gratified, Disraeli was very sensitive. Lennox, early in September, being

[1] ibid., Box 102, B/XX/LX/122, December 27, 1858.

disappointed in certain expectations of his own, was so ill-advised as to remark that his brother, Lord March, would have liked the commissionership, but had at once withdrawn on hearing that James was a candidate.[1] Disraeli wrote a long letter in reply explaining the appointment and alluding *inter alia* to Lennox's 'erroneous expectations'. It was now Lennox's turn to take umbrage.

> . . . when I consider that you have written 3 sheets to justify to *me* the appt. of *your* Brother I confess I do feel somewhat annoyed. I was perfectly aware that you had refused it for your brother & also that when pressed and accepted not a soul even among our enemies dared say a word about it.[2]

There was a *rapprochement*; but Lennox and Disraeli were never quite on the same terms again.

A more important matter was the conferment in January 1859 of a long-sought place upon Disraeli's faithful henchman, G. A. Hamilton, who was hard up and now exchanged the political office of Financial Secretary for the top permanent post in the Treasury, the previous occupant, Sir Charles Trevelyan, having accepted the governorship of Madras. There were murmurs against a post normally reserved for Civil Servants going to a MP, but Disraeli was able to reply that the governorship of Madras was usually regarded as a political plum, and so the balance was undisturbed. Disraeli was anxious to strengthen the Government with persons of official experience. The vacancy created by Hamilton's appointment gave him a chance. For some time past he had had his eye on Sir Stafford Northcote, who had been Gladstone's secretary at the Board of Trade, Derbyite MP from 1852 to 1857, when he lost his seat, and co-author of the famous report on the Civil Service. The day of the proprietary borough was not dead and Disraeli persuaded him in July to accept Lord Exeter's offer of Stamford on the promise of an official place as soon as possible. Early in the new year he was able to give Northcote Hamilton's vacant place as Financial Secretary.

Northcote was very unlike Disraeli. A conscientious, efficient, virtuous, Puseyite baronet, he belonged spiritually to the Peelites. He had indeed acted as a link between them and the Tories in 1856. In the autumn of 1855 he had made a peace speech of which Disraeli

---

[1] ibid., B/XX/LX/113, September 1858.
[2] ibid., B/XX/LX/114, September 16.

approved. This was just the sort of man who would give a respectable new look to Derbyism and the lie to the Liberal claim that the Tories were 'the stupid party'. The alliance between Disraeli and Northcote was destined to be a long and fruitful one, both for each of them and for the cause which they represented.

CHAPTER XVIII

A Second Defeat

1858–9

1

Disraeli had little chance during the 1858–9 Ministry to make his mark on the nation's financial policy. His first budget was virtually framed for him: it was too late to do much about the estimates at the end of February when he took office. The Government fell before he produced his second budget; although his plans were prepared, the actual task fell to Gladstone. Nevertheless, the preliminaries have a certain interest.

The year 1858 inaugurated a period of major expenditure on defence, which has been with us ever since. It saw the first of those great technical revolutions which have at intervals vexed the Exchequer and the Service Departments from that day to this. The Service affected was the one which was most important for British security – the Navy. For half a century the British fleet had enjoyed a long and seemingly irreducible lead in wooden ships, but suddenly at the end of the 1850s the simultaneous emergence of steam, screw, iron, and armour plate transformed the situation. *Warrior*, the first British ironclad, was not launched till 1860, although the decision to build the ship was taken by Derby's Cabinet in 1858. The extent of the revolution is shown by the fact that *Warrior* could have sunk single-handed every battleship built before the Crimean War. The result of this vast change, which was appreciated by the French earlier than by the British, was to put the navies of the world on a par with each other. Everyone had to start from scratch. A great increase in expenditure seemed imperative; the more so since there was general fear of the alleged aggressive intentions of the French Emperor.

On October 9, Disraeli, who was alarmed for his budget, wrote a long letter[1] to Derby about the service departments. He began with the War Office which had miscalculated the cost of the new

---

[1] Derby Papers, Box 145/5.

barracks at Aldershot to the tune of £85,000. 'After this parliamentary control over expenditure is a mere farce . . . There wants a commission on Sir B. Hawes, Mr Godley & Co . . .' This, however, was small beer compared with the Navy.

> I am assured on the highest authority that nothing could be worse than the condition of the Admiralty as far as the naval members are concerned. All the men that Pakington has chosen . . . are the most inefficient that could be selected. The Admiralty is governed by Sir B. Walker[1] who has neither talents, nor science – & as I believe – nor honor – but the last is suspicion, the first are facts. He has frightened the country and has lowered its tone & his only remedy is building colossal ships wh: have neither speed nor power & wh: are immensely expensive from their enormous crews . . .

Heavy frigates, Disraeli argued, were better, and more economical.

Derby entirely agreed about the barracks. 'Whoever is responsible must be brought to book', he wrote.[2] But he was not so sure about the Admiralty.

> I think you are hard in your judgment of the Board of Admiralty and Sir Baldwin Walker. I have no predilection for him, nor have I any reason for it; and I still think he acted towards us in 1852 as no man of honourable feeling would have done; but I think you underrate his professional character and that naval men generally will not concur in the opinion you express as to the comparative merits of line of Battle Ships and heavy Frigates. The points on which I look to the necessity of increased expenditure are . . . the conversion of old sailing vessels into Screw Steamers, and possibly the construction of some iron plated ships. We *must* have a naval preponderance over the French, however inconvenient the outlay may be . . .

Disraeli was not convinced. He returned to the charge at the end of November with a memorandum drafted by Earle demonstrating that Sir Baldwin Walker's calculations were based on the assumption that Britain would have to fight simultaneously all the other powers of the world united. This was as foolish, he said, as the argument recently advanced, that every single part of the coast should be fortified: 'the same frenzy which a *reductio ad absurdum*

---

[1] Surveyor of the Navy, 1848–60. Opposed Stafford over dockyard scandal. See above, 321.

[2] Hughenden Papers, Box 109, B/XX/S/182, October 12, 1858.

demolished a year ago'.[1] Disraeli then proceeded to circularize the Cabinet with an eloquent plea for economy.[2]

Derby, too, was in favour of reasonable economy, 'but not at the sacrifice of great national objects'.[3] In a later letter[4] he urged Disraeli to consider raising the money by a loan '. . . I say the larger the cost which you can prove, the better. I should look on this as a case in which our Navy had been to a great extent destroyed . . .' And he pointed out, with Knowsley doubtless in mind, that if one's mansion was destroyed by fire one would charge the capital sum by way of a loan against the estate, not attempt to pay for the whole lot out of current income. But Disraeli was against a loan in peacetime. It would never, he said wrongly, be accepted by the House of Commons.[5]

Certainly the services were not efficient, but Disraeli was unduly blinkered by considerations of his own department. He seems to have been so shaken by his experience over his first budget that he now bent over backwards to exercise the full rigour of Treasury orthodoxy. It was as if he wanted to out-Gladstone Gladstone. The result is that we find him displaying during these years, and indeed in 1866–8, too, a surprising streak of Little-Englander hostility to armaments. He failed to appreciate that in 1858–9 there really was a problem. No reductions achieved by efficient accounting and mere cutting of frills could counterbalance major expenses on renewing the Navy. Had he been at the head of affairs he would soon have seen this. As it was, the fact that Britannia continued to rule the waves owed nothing to Benjamin Disraeli.

But this time the budget was not the main issue. The fiscal question had been settled in 1852–3. The problem now was parliamentary reform. Much has been written on the subject, but in reality it is fairly simple. Disraeli had long argued that the Whigs had no divine right to a monopoly in this field and that the Conservatives were under no obligation to conserve a settlement which, made as it was by their enemies, was designed to operate – and, in

---

[1] M. & B., iv, 255.

[2] Hughenden Papers, Box 96, B/XX/E/145, n.d.

[3] ibid., Box 109, B/XX/S/182, October 12, 1858.

[4] ibid., Box 110, B/XX/S/237, n.d.

[5] ibid., B/XX/S/258, January 5, 1860, Derby to Disraeli. Referring to the events of a year before, Derby noted that Gladstone was now going to do just this, 'a course which I should have considered advisable when we were in office but was deterred from taking by your strong objections and your estimate of the opposition it would encounter in the House of Commons'.

fact, did operate – against their interests. He had maintained this general attitude ever since 1848, when in a speech on Hume's motion for household suffrage he had declared that the Country party was as much entitled as any other to 'reconstruct the estate of the Commons' when the time was ripe. He did not think that it was ripe in 1848, but three years later his attitude had somewhat changed. Although he supported Russell in opposing Locke King's annual motion to equalize the county and the borough franchise, he now declared that he had no fear of the artisan class: he was confident that they would not vote Radical, but would support the Monarchy and the Empire. Thus early Disraeli recognized a possibility which was appreciated in the Continent before it was ever accepted in England: given suitable safeguards, universal suffrage might be a conservative not a revolutionary measure.[1]

Nevertheless, he knew how difficult it would be to persuade his colleagues, and he considered that on balance it would be better to let it alone, as long as the Whigs would do the same. But in 1852 Russell himself took the initiative in abandoning 'finality'. True, his Reform Bill was immediately smothered in the collapse of his government, and his next attempt in 1854 was equally unsuccessful owing to the Crimean War. But the Whigs by thus ending the tacit pact between the two front benches had raised public expectations. The matter could not rest for ever in abeyance, and the Tories could now feel absolved from their self-denying ordinance. In the brief December session of 1857 even Palmerston, who was no lover of Reform, indicated that he intended to deal with it soon. He was defeated before he had time to do anything, but it was natural in all the circumstances that Derby should announce a Reform Bill as part of his programme for the session of 1859; he would have lost important adherents, including his own son, if he had not done so.

It would be absurd to claim that Disraeli viewed the matter other than first and foremost in the light of party expediency. The prolonged arguments of 1858–9 and 1866–7 all boil down in the end to that. Electoral geometry gave the politics of those days a complication, now removed by the general acceptance of universal suffrage and equal electoral districts. In the mid-Victorian era there was immense scope for elaborate calculations in that now vanished

[1] Malmesbury took Disraeli's view. 'He contends', wrote Stanley to Disraeli early in 1853, 'that the five pounders are democratic, the labourers conservative; therefore if we must go as low as £5 he would rather go on to universal suffrage.' ibid., Box 111, B/XX/S/588, January 28, 1853.

political dimension. It was not only a matter of the franchise. There was the question of redistributing seats; and here the Conservatives had a real grievance, for the counties, on a population basis, were heavily underrepresented compared with the boroughs; although this was a delicate argument to be used by a party which hitherto had never conceded that population had any relevance in determining the representative system. And the franchise itself gave endless opportunity for argument. Would the five-pound householder be more, or less, radical than the ten-pounder? Would the assimilation of borough and county franchises help or hinder liberalism in the counties? Was household suffrage conservative or was it revolutionary?

Although Disraeli did not exclude the idea of household suffrage, he was never at any time a believer in democracy as the word was then understood. When he defended the Reform Bill of 1859 he used words which were later often to be flung in his face by angry diehards:[1]

> I have no apprehension myself that if you had manhood suffrage tomorrow the honest brave and good natured people of England would resort to pillage, incendiarism and massacre. Who expects that? . . . Yet I have no doubt that . . . our countrymen are subject to the same political laws that affect the condition of all other communities and nations. If you establish a democracy you must in due course reap the fruits of a democracy.

And he went on to list them: great impatience at taxation combined with great increases in expenditure; 'wars entered into from passion . . . peace ignominiously sought and ignominiously obtained'; 'property less valuable . . . freedom less complete.'

Disraeli believed – and repeatedly said that he believed – in aristocracy. Where he differed from contemporaries who held the same belief was in having a very much more open mind about the best way of preserving 'the aristocratic settlement of this country'. And the openness of Disraeli's mind meant that he sometimes played with ideas that were impracticable, even foolish, and that he very often made observations totally contradicting opinions which he had propounded earlier or was to propound later. That is why judicious selectivity can make Disraeli appear a consistent democrat or an inconsistent demagogue, according to taste. The truth is that he had one real objective, but that he had a mind full

[1] M. & B., iv, 208–9, quoting Disraeli's speech, March 31, 1859.

of half-thought-out theories which sometimes emitted flashes of
brilliant intuition, but sometimes, as Baillie-Cochrane had observed,
ended in 'the mere phantasmagoria of politique legerdemain'.

Throughout November 1858 a committee of the Cabinet held
repeated meetings to draft a Reform Bill for the next session. Rose,
as manager of the party's electoral affairs, was called into close
consultation by Disraeli and Derby. Disraeli also worked closely
with Stanley, who favoured as large a measure as possible. The
committee, by substantial majorities, came down in favour of three
main proposals: to establish a £10 household franchise in the counties as well as the boroughs, together with a new £20 lodger franchise in both; to oblige the forty-shilling freeholder living in a
borough to vote in the borough and not, as the existing law stood,
in the county; to redistribute some seventy seats which were to be
taken away from the smaller boroughs and given to the larger
boroughs (18) and to the counties (52). These proposals, while not
very drastic, were too controversial to command unanimity in the
Cabinet. Henley and Walpole were the leading dissidents, and Derby
was dismayed to receive an eighty-seven-page memorandum of
protest, 'as long as a chancery brief', drafted by Walpole.

At this juncture when Cabinet solidarity was vital, Lytton for
quite separate reasons asked to resign. He was in poor health, and
did not enjoy office. He preferred Knebworth, saying, according to
Earle: 'It is so delightful to see the trees bowing to their Lord.'[1]
Lytton's conduct of affairs was far from perfect, and his departure
might in normal circumstances have been welcome. One of the
Colonial Office clerks described him to Earle as 'insolent, wild and
reckless', and added that 'he puts letters in the wrong envelopes
and sends secret and confidential documents to his clerks by mistake
for official despatches'.[2] But, whatever his deficiencies, his resignation would have been very inopportune just·then. Disraeli told him
that it would be attributed to political differences and wholly
misunderstood, and that it was easy to exaggerate ill health.
Lytton was not the man to take this lying down. He promptly replied that his pulse, normally 70, was up to 90,

> . . . and is as weak as it was strong. I have studied pathology
> eno' to know this must end if it cannot be set right; it ends but in

---

[1] Hughenden Papers, Box 96, B/XX/E/76, Earle to Disraeli, n.d., but probably
November 1858.
[2] loc. cit.

3 ways. 1st consumption to which I have so far a tendency that one lung is affected . . . 2ndly organic heart disease most probably inducing rapid termination by dropsey – 3rdly & most dreadful & in the case of nervous excitement perhaps the most probable of all – sudden paralysis . . .

As for public misunderstanding: '. . . the delicacy of my health is sufficiently stamped on my appearance & the work I have gone thro' during life may well be supposed to have told on me.'[1]

Forwarding to Derby this 'wonderful performance' which he wished to have returned, 'for it is worth keeping in the family records', Disraeli observed:

> . . . His symptoms are regularly divided under the head of (1) consumption, (2) dropsy, (3) paralysis. I have had them myself often, and five-and-twenty years ago in overwhelming degree, yet here I am writing to you . . .[2]

If it was really health, he continued, Lytton could probably be induced to stay. 'But if instead of health his wife is behind the curtain, then he will go, and the sooner the better for all concerned.' Derby thought health was genuinely the reason. 'He tells me that he is going to Malvern to try hydropathy from which he has before derived benefits (he will probably kill himself) . . . I think he has made up his mind and that you will not be able to keep him.'[3] But on New Year's Day, Disraeli could report a triumph. 'He remains . . . He expects to die before Easter but if so I have promised him a public funeral.'[4]

Meanwhile, Cabinet after Cabinet was held on the Reform Bill, but failed to produce agreement. It would be tedious to chronicle the various proposals, counter-proposals, amendments, compromises, which were put forward in order to reshape a bill which was in any case rejected by the House of Commons. In its final form it contained a number of additional franchises to those propounded by the Committee. Although documentary evidence is lacking, everything points to Disraeli as the author of such curious provisions as the clauses conferring votes on those who had an income of £10 a year from the Funds; on possessors of £60 in a savings bank; on persons receiving government pensions of £20 a year; on doctors,

---

[1] ibid., Box 104, B/XX/LY/112, December 22, 1858.
[2] M. & B., iv, 191.
[3] ibid., 192.   [4] loc. cit.

lawyers, university graduates, ministers of religion, and certain categories of schoolmasters.

The Bill, which was introduced on February 28 never had much chance of success, and got off to a bad start because *The Times* 'scooped' its contents the day before. Disraeli did his best for it in a fine opening speech. But the situation was not helped by the statements of Walpole and Henley, who both resigned, and it soon became obvious, though not apparently to Disraeli himself, that the House would reject it. The Radicals were never going to accept a Bill which did nothing for the artisan class and scarcely touched the problem of redistribution. The Whigs and Liberals were bound to oppose changes which, however much Disraeli might dress them by such euphemisms as 'lateral extension of the franchise', amounted in the end to strengthening the Conservatives at the expense of the Liberals. And, of course, everyone could have immense fun in dealing with what Bright in a famous phrase dubbed 'the fancy franchises'. A touching picture was drawn of the man who to help an indigent parent drew out £5 from his accumulated wealth in the savings bank, thereby depriving himself of the vote. Was this a proper reward for Christian charity? Financiers shook their heads gravely at money going into the savings banks at all. Was it the best form of investment, they asked? The prospect seemed ominous, but Disraeli remained sanguine and full of expedients.

Meanwhile, the Cabinet vacancies had to be filled. Lord Chandos, the son of the bankrupt Duke of Buckingham, was one of Disraeli's favourite candidates. But the trouble was that the Duke was still up to his old tricks, borrowing money which he had no intention of repaying. 'The late D of Buck^m', wrote Disraeli to Corry in 1866, 'had the talent of inspiring ruffians with enthusiasm, of charming creditors, & of taking swindlers in.'[1] With such a tiresome father, Chandos, who was bent on restoring the shattered Grenville fortunes, was most reluctant to give up his valuable position as Chairman of the Great Western Railway. He declined, and Derby fell back on Sotheron-Estcourt, a great country gentleman, and Lord Donoughmore, for the Home Office and the Board of Trade, although Disraeli was doubtful about the latter 'in case the country gentlemen require one of their order in the cabinet wh: I think they would',[2] Sotheron-Estcourt presumably being not enough by

[1] Hughenden Papers, Box 95, B/XX/D/19, September 11, 1866.
[2] Derby Papers, Box 145/6, February 23, 1859.

himself. The question of the proper representation of the hard core of the Country party in the Cabinet was always tricky.

But these subtle considerations were to be of no avail. Palmerston and Russell were already beginning to make up their old feud, and a skilfully drafted resolution was put by Russell, worded in such a way that it could be supported both by those who thought the Reform Bill did too much and by those who thought it did too little. There were good speeches on the Government side, and Lytton at last justified his selection by a really eloquent performance. 'Deaf, fantastic, modulating his voice with difficulty, sometimes painful – at first almost an object of ridicule to the superficial – Lytton occasionally reached almost the sublime, and perfectly enchained his audience'.[1] Thus Disraeli described it to Queen Victoria, to whom, as before, he continued to write the regular letter of the Leader of the House in a style unlike that of any other Leader before or since. Lytton's eloquence was in vain. Nor did a surprising intervention on the part of Gladstone, who made a vigorous if irrelevant defence of rotten boroughs and voted for the Bill, help to save the day. Russell's resolution was carried by 330 votes to 291.

2

Derby had made it as clear as he properly could that he intended to dissolve and not to resign. The Queen who was better disposed to the Tories than hitherto – largely on grounds of foreign policy – raised no difficulties this time. On April 4, Derby announced the dissolution; the elections were to begin on the 29th. Lytton, true to form, again promptly tendered his resignation; whether for fear of health or of a repetition of his wife's appearance on the hustings is not clear. Derby, who was much overwrought, regarded this as the last straw. '*Ecce iterum Crispinus*,' he wrote to Disraeli, and a day later, relapsing into the vernacular, 'What on earth is to be done with this fellow?' Disraeli evidently wrote a very stiff letter to his old friend, for it elicited a reply on April 4 which might have come out of one of Lytton's novels, beginning without any prefix: 'The letter you have sent me I would fain regard as unwritten . . .'[2] However, his feelings were quickly soothed, and he agreed to stay on.

[1] M. & B., iv, 206.
[2] Hughenden Papers, Box 104, B/XX/Ly/120.

Optimistic as ever, Disraeli thought that the Conservatives had an excellent chance of winning the election. He told Greville that with good luck they would gain sixty seats, and when Greville asked him what they would gain without good luck, he said forty. Greville was sceptical; his Whig friends put the figure at ten. In fact, it was about thirty, and Disraeli could fairly claim to have had positively bad luck, for some seats were lost by very narrow margins. It was an apathetic election and if any conclusion emerged it was the total indifference of the electorate to parliamentary reform. This was the Conservatives' best effort since Disraeli had been leader. In 1852 they had about 280, in 1857 260 – now 290, but it was still not enough.

Disraeli at once began a series of manoeuvres to strengthen his position. Even before the election was over he wrote to Palmerston asking him 'in our ancient confidence' whether he would agree to lead the Conservative party and, by bringing over some '20 or 30 gentlemen', provide the basis for a solid government? On one point, he said, he must speak 'with delicacy but without reserve' – the position of Lord Derby. 'A point of honor alone attaches him to the party post which he fills. He feels that he can never desert the Conservative party while it is in a minority, and while there is no member of it to succeed him. I have not written this with his knowledge . . . I have, however, frequently and amply brought the general views of this letter before him.'[1] Palmerston's reply was polite – he was always polite to Disraeli – but it was cool and brief. He did not, he said, regard it as necessary to go into the many reasons that made such an arrangement impossible, though he need hardly say that 'want of personal good feelings toward Lord Derby and yourself or any other members of your Government'[2] was not among them. He made no reference to 'our ancient confidence'. Disraeli's efforts to woo the Irish and the Independent Liberals were equally unsuccessful, and so was an overture, the last of many, from Derby to Gladstone.

At this juncture a latent, and for the Conservatives explosive, element began to affect the chemistry of politics. The 1850s were a decade in which foreign affairs had a quite exceptional importance in the English domestic scene. The crises of 1851, 1857 and 1858 all in some degree revolved around matters of foreign policy. In 1859

[1] M. & B., iv, 235–6.
[2] ibid., 237.

a more significant and far-reaching problem than any of them arose
to perplex British statesmen: the question of Italy. It was one of
those great ideological conflicts which from time to time polarize
English opinion. The Italian question aroused passions not unlike
those stimulated in later years by the Bulgarian atrocities, by the
Spanish Civil War and by Suez.

The question, briefly, was this: what attitude ought England to
take to the war which by the end of 1858 seemed almost certain to
break out between the Emperor of the French, supporting Pied-
montese ambitions to 'liberate' Lombardy, and the Hapsburg
monarchy, determined to retain its Italian dominions. Behind this
conflict lay the struggle for national self-determination against
dynastic rights – an issue on which all good Liberals were united,
but on which Conservatives were uncertain and hesitant, partly
because they were not well disposed towards French ambitions. In
one sense the Government owed its existence to the anti-French outburst which upset Palmerston in February 1858, and its members
were well aware of the hostility with which they were regarded in
Paris. Some Liberals, too, felt uneasy about Napoleon III and
suspected that he would never support even the best of causes
except to further some carefully calculated and crafty design of his
own. What we now know about the Emperor suggests that, far
from making careful calculations, he was influenced by obscure
intuitions, romantic dreams and theatrical phrases. But these were
perhaps just as dangerous. His character and purpose remained the
great enigma which for nearly twenty years puzzled successive
occupants of the Foreign Office.

Disraeli, however, did not think that it puzzled Malmesbury
enough, or that he was sufficiently active in enquiry. Nor did he
trust Cowley, the Ambassador in Paris. He was influenced by
Earle, who did not forgive the man whom he had injured. Characteristically, Disraeli, who was no believer in diplomatic etiquette,
sent Earle to Paris on a confidential mission at the end of the year
without consulting Malmesbury. Earle carried with him a letter
written by his chief to himself, but intended to be shown to the
Emperor. The wisdom of thus crossing lines with Malmesbury was
extremely dubious. Malmesbury had endeavoured to divert Napoleon's mind from war by a suggestion that the Emperors of Austria
and France should try in co-operation to ameliorate the government
of the Papal States, and he offered England's 'moral support and even

her material aid *eventually*'.[1] As for Lombardy, he maintained that
it was as much the rightful property of Austria as Ireland and India
were the property of England – a two-edged argument. Disraeli may
well have been more realistic than Malmesbury about the French
Emperor when he wrote in his letter to Earle:

> I have no jealousy of the external movement of France. I look
> upon the old political maxims about Spain and Italy as rococo in
> an age which has witnessed the development of America and the
> discovery of Australia. I have said this often to you: I have even
> expressed it, and in detail to the Emperor himself.
>   I contemplate the possibility of the eventual increase of his
> dominions. He is an Emperor and he must have an empire; but
> all this should be attempted with the sanction, or at least the
> sufferance of England, not in spite of her . . .[2]

On the other hand, such a message was scarcely calculated to check
imperial ambitions in Italy. It is fair, however, to say that nobody
knew the nature of a secret agreement at Plombières in the summer,
whereby the Emperor had promised Cavour to fight on the side of
Piedmont for the acquisition of Lombardy, receiving in exchange
for his help the cession of Savoy and Nice to France.

In writing an account of Earle's mission to Derby, Disraeli said
nothing about his own message to the Emperor, but he was very
critical of Malmesbury, who, he considered, wholly underestimated
the situation. The Emperor, he said:

> . . . ever since the Orsini business has been more or less fitful and
> moody and brooding over Italy . . . Having himself belonged to
> the Carbonaro Society he knows that he is never safe while they
> continue to regard him as a renegade. He is resolved, therefore, 'to
> do something for Italy . . . Sometimes he talks of placing himself
> at the head of the army of invasion, as he once talked of going to
> the Crimea. And he would do it, for, in dealing with this personage
> we must remember we are dealing with a mind as romantic as it is
> subtle.[3]

The same might have been said of Disraeli. Indeed, he analysed
Napoleon with the acumen of one who half sympathized—from the
experience of his own thoughts and dreams. The parallel between the
two men was often drawn at the time.

[1] Benson and Esher, *Letters of Queen Victoria* 1837–61, iii, 391, December 10, 1858.
[2] M. & B., iv, 218.
[3] ibid., 222–3.

All efforts for peace were in vain. The Austrian Government on the very day of the prorogation of Parliament put itself hopelessly in the wrong by launching an ultimatum which demanded the disarmament of Piedmont. Disraeli, with his tendency to attribute great historical events to the chance of personality, maintained in retrospect that there would have been no war if England had had a competent Ambassador in Vienna. Even Lord Cowley, he considered, would have been better than Lord Augustus Loftus, 'a pompous nincompoop and of all Lord Malmesbury's appointments the worst – and that's saying a good deal'. Malmesbury, he suspected, was 'the tool of his Private Secretary, Bidwell – an F.O. man, a jobber and the employed agent of the man he counselled his patron to promote.'[1] But, however deplorable these revelations about the Foreign Office in Malmesbury's day, it is unlikely that peace could have been preserved in the spring of 1859 by any action on the part of the British Government.

From now onwards the current of public opinion ran strongly against the Conservatives. The month of March had seen a great pro-Italian outburst. Neapolitan prisoners passing through London on their way to exile were fêted. Gladstone had all his memories revived of the régime which he had once declared to be 'the negation of God erected into a system of Government'. Derby and Malmesbury were regarded, like the Court, as pro-Austrian; indeed the Court seems to have thought so, too. Derby found himself for once in favour with the Queen and the Prince, although more from fear of the alternative than from any love of him. Palmerston and Russell, apart from the other numerous causes that they had given for royal resentment, were known to be violently pro-Italian. Palmerston made Italian liberation a feature of his election address; the French did not conceal their hope that he would be returned to power, and it was alleged by Malmesbury that the French Ambassador distributed money in support of Liberal candidates. A somewhat ambiguous declaration by Derby in the House of Lords just before war broke out was twisted by the Opposition into a suggestion that he might intervene on the Austrian side, although he could hardly have been more explicit in condemning Austria when hostilities began. Disraeli was never much interested in the rights of oppressed nations struggling to be free. Their cause left him cold, and for all his talk about 'race', he simply did not understand nationalism.

[1] Hughenden Papers, Box 26, A/X/A/36. For Bidwell, see p. 371, above.

But he was not the man to disregard public opinion. The election had shown how dangerous Italophile sentiment was for the Government. Now that the vital parliamentary battle impended, he pressed Derby strongly, and successfully, to resist some potentially pro-Austrian modifications of the Queen's speech suggested by the Queen herself.[1] It was too late. Already the Opposition was beginning to come together to eject the Government.

This consolidation culminated in a famous meeting held on June 6 at Willis's Rooms, when Palmerston and Russell agreed each to serve under whichever of them was sent for by the Queen. That meeting may fairly be called 'a turning-point' in English political history. It is true that if all the historians who have used this expression are right, English history would be as full of turnings as the Hampton Court maze; but there are occasions when it is legitimate. The meeting marks the real beginning of that union of Whigs, Peelites and Liberals which became the Liberal party of the later nineteenth century. The experiment had already been tried under Aberdeen; and it had ended after a bare two years in bathos and discredit. No one could have been confident in the aftermath of that fiasco that the alliance could ever be put together again.

As in 1852, Disraeli's unconscious role was by no means negligible. It may be followed in Sidney Herbert's correspondence from the Reform Bill debate onwards. 'There was a day,' wrote Graham to Herbert, 'when conduct of this kind [Disraeli's] would have been scouted as intolerable with unanimous scorn; but the House of Commons had never consented to be led by a Jew Adventurer.'[2] And a few days later Herbert wrote to Gladstone: 'Disraeli's quibblings about the date of dissolution are very disgraceful . . . But the rogue is capable of anything for a party or personal object.'[3] Then it was Gladstone's turn. If Disraeli was in opposition, he told Herbert, his force would be increased, 'and he will use it, if a judgment is to be formed from the past, with very little scruple'.[4] And Gladstone, on informing Wood that in the crisis 'a "broad bottom" Government would have pleased me best', received the reply: 'Who can be expected to join with Disraeli?'[5] One sometimes wonders

---

[1] See Disraeli's letter to Derby of June 2, M. & B., iv, 245–6, and Derby's letter of the same day to the Queen, incorporating Disraeli's phraseology verbatim, *Letters of Queen Victoria, 1837–61*, iii, 430–3.

[2] Stanmore, *Sidney Herbert*, ii, 173.

[3] ibid., 177.

[4] ibid., 185.

[5] ibid., 197.

whether Disraeli has a claim not only to be the architect of the Conservative party, but the unconscious founder of the Liberal party, too.

On June 6, a meeting of nearly three hundred Whigs, Liberals, Radicals and Peelites was held in Willis's Rooms. The reconciliation of Palmerston and Russell was symbolized, amidst some merriment, by the former, sprightly as ever at seventy-five, helping Lord John by the hand up to the dais from which they were to speak. It was decided that a major attack should be launched and that Lord Hartington should move an amendment of no confidence in the debate on the Address.

No doubt the bargain sealed the Government's fate in the long run, but it was by no means certain that it would be defeated at once. Disraeli was unintentionally responsible for this, by committing a serious and, for him, unusual blunder. Malmesbury had strongly and rightly urged that the Blue Book containing his Italian dispatches, should be laid before the House. It effectively answered Palmerston's accusation that the Government had failed to avert war because its pro-Austrian feeling prevented it from warning Austria in sufficiently categorical terms. This was one of the main charges against the ministry. Yet Disraeli did not produce the Blue Book in time for the debate, although its publication had been promised in the Queen's speech. Malmesbury maintained afterwards that twelve to fourteen members had come to him separately to assure him that if they had seen the dispatches they would not have voted for the amendment. Since it was carried by only thirteen, his complaint seems justified. Disraeli evidently knew that he was in the wrong, for he never gave any explanation. Malmesbury notes in his account of the retiring Cabinet's visit to Windsor to deliver up their seals of office: 'All my colleagues, as they were coming back in the railway carriage praised the Blue-Book on Italy, except Disraeli who never said a word.'[1] Possibly, as Buckle suggests, his mistrust of Malmesbury prejudiced him into believing that the Blue Book would do no good. Or perhaps, as Malmesbury himself believed, Disraeli simply had not read it, and was determined not to expose his ignorance.

The night before the final division Disraeli conceived one of those romantic generous ideas which dispel the notion that he was merely a self-seeking adventurer. Why not save the situation, he wrote to

[1] *Memoirs*, ii, 191.

Derby, by both of them retiring from the scene in favour of Stanley?
He would command the support of a good many Liberals and with
the Conservatives behind him could form a more stable government
than Russell or Palmerston. Nothing came of this startling proposal.
It is surprising that Disraeli should have regarded Stanley, a cautious, and slightly angular young man of thirty-three, as a suitable
prime minister. Certainly Stanley did not see himself in that role.
The division was taken the next night. Some twenty independent
members, apart from recognized supporters, voted with the Government, including Gladstone. But the alliance concluded at Willis's
Rooms was too strong. Hartington's amendment was carried by 323
votes to 310, a larger majority, so Greville says, than either side
expected. Derby resigned immediately and the Queen, after an
unsuccessful attempt to avoid an odious choice by sending for
Granville, appointed Palmerston as Prime Minister. Few people
guessed in the summer of 1859 that he was to hold office uninterrupted for over six years.

One highly individualist Tory had no doubt that Derby and
Disraeli deserved to be beaten:

> Lord Derby and Mr. Disraeli have led the Conservative party to
> adopt every measure which they opposed as Radical ten years
> ago [wrote Henry Drummond to Joliffe,[1] who forwarded this
> 'unpleasant letter' to Disraeli.] They have made that party the
> tool of their ambition & sacrificed everybody's private & public
> interest, beginning with Walpole. I do not think it creditable to
> the intelligence or to the honor of the country gentlemen of Eng-
> land to vote black to be white or white to be black at their
> bidding.

This is the eternal cry of the diehard whether of the Right or the Left –
that the way to his party's political salvation is to adhere more
rigidly than ever to the very principles on which it has suffered
defeat. All leaders hear that cry often before their careers end. Most
of them ignore it. Disraeli was no exception.

---

[1] Hughenden Papers, Box 101, B/XX/J/73.

CHAPTER XIX

Private Life

1850–65

1

Disraeli's pattern of life varied little during these years. He was devoted to Hughenden. Proud of being a country gentleman and landed proprietor, he spent as much time there as he could. It was a delightful place. Modern taste may deprecate the ornate decorations with which at Mrs Disraeli's desire the neo-Gothic architect, E. F. Lamb, 'did it up' in 1862–3, but the house possesses a charm that time has not diminished. This is due partly to the setting on a beech-wooded spur of the Chilterns, and partly to the attractive view of the hills beyond Wycombe which can be seen from the terrace on the south of the house. There on a warm afternoon Disraeli would pace up and down, or more often sit, dreamily revolving plans for parliamentary battles to come, and complacently watching the peacocks which he considered indispensable concomitants of a terrace. Sometimes in a more energetic mood he would walk through the woods accompanied by Mary Anne in a small pony cart, or stroll eastwards down the slope past the little church in the park to inspect his two swans. These, named Hero and Leander, swam on a small ornamental lake artificially formed from the little stream which flowed through the grounds and in which Disraeli occasionally caught trout.

Summer after summer when the session ended, often late in August, the Disraelis would repair to Hughenden and, unless the Conservatives were in office when cabinet meetings made it necessary to return to London in late October, they would stay there until after Christmas. Autumn sessions were rare in those days. Indeed, in that Indian summer of aristocratic rule, the life of a politician was in almost every respect more agreeable than it is today. International conferences, fact-finding trips, the endless restless bustle of the modern statesman's existence were still unknown. There was far more time for thought and reflection. Moreover, the mechanics of politics were much simpler, at all events for someone like Disraeli with a safe county seat. He did not have to waste time canvassing. There were pleasanter methods of making contact with his electorate. 'In the evening,' he writes of a visit to Mentmore, the seat of Baron Rothschild,[1] 'there was a ball attended by four hundred persons from the county of Buckingham. So I had an opportunity of seeing my constituents.'

The parliamentary struggle usually left Disraeli exhausted. He did not possess the vast reserves of energy enjoyed by his great rival. Although there was nothing surprising in this (for very few people did) it remains true that Disraeli, more than most men, needed complete rest and relaxation in order to recharge his nervous system. For days on end he would do nothing except walk round his property and read in a somewhat desultory fashion the books in his library. 'I have a passion for trees and books', he wrote in his reminiscent jottings. 'When I come down to Hughenden I pass the first week in sauntering about my park and examining all my trees, and then I saunter in the library and survey the books.'[2] He rather overdid his passion for trees. Unlike Gladstone, who loved cutting them down, Disraeli found his pleasure in planting them. Distinguished visitors were commemorated in this way to such an extent that after his lifetime the whole place was in danger of becoming choked, and a large number of trees had to be cut down.

Gradually Disraeli would recover his energy and by the middle of September would be actively writing letters, planning political moves, and entertaining visitors. Hughenden was a small house by the standards of his colleagues, but he had a constant stream of guests none the less. From September 18 to 28 in 1862 he entertained 'Lord and Lady Salisbury, Sir William and Lady Georgiana Codrington, Lord and Lady Godolphin Osborne, Lord and Lady Curzon, Lord Stanley, Lord St. Asaph, Colonel and Mrs. Fane, Baron Rothschild of Paris and many others. It's as hard work as having a playhouse or keeping an inn.'[3]

Then the Disraelis in their turn would set out on a round of visits: Alnwick, Belvoir, Burleigh, Hatfield, Knowsley, Wootton . . . Not that he greatly enjoyed them, though he made an exception for some places like Hatfield, where one was left alone and did not have to get up for breakfast. In general he complained that there was

[1] Brydges Willyams Letters, Disraeli to Mrs Brydges Willyams, February 9, 1861.
[2] M. & B., iii, 157–8.
[3] Brydges Willyams Letters, Disraeli to Mrs Brydges Willyams, September 15, 1862.

nothing to do except eat immense meals. The Christmas season was particularly odious. '. . . Nothing is so terrible', he wrote to Sarah on December 23, 1850, 'as the constant parade and pageantry of a Xmas week in a great house in the country without the slightest object of interest, yr health destroyed with the stupid excitement & your time wasted: no ease, repose, or refuge . . .'[1] Disraeli did not take the exercise which, whether in the form of shooting or riding to hounds, helped to preserve the ordinary English country gentleman from the effects of this lavish diet. But it was a duty for the defender of the aristocratic settlement to stay from time to time with some of the leading 'magnificoes', and his boredom may have been tempered by a certain satisfaction at their changed attitude towards the man they once regarded as a charlatan and an adventurer. He did not confine himself exclusively to one party. For example, in 1865 the Disraelis stayed at Lowther and Ashridge, seats of Lords Lonsdale and Brownlow, who were Conservatives, and at Woburn and Raby, whose owners, the Dukes of Bedford and Cleveland, were Whigs. It so happens that on this occasion he kept a note of his impressions.[2]

He refers to 'the silent but not scanty court of retainers' at Lowther with its 'splendid domain' but 'deplorable' exterior. At Ashridge he observes the 'sylvan beauty' of the 'vast park'. Lady Marian Alford, mother of Lord Brownlow, reminds him of Lady Blessington – 'a red and rough complexion', but 'very pretty hands which tell particularly in a large woman'. Woburn was managed by the Duke's cousin and heir, Hastings Russell, who was allowed to live there as if he owned it. The Duke preferred London. 'Let me live always among chimney pots,' he would say. 'He has two mistresses,' Disraeli wrote,[3] 'one is his nurse; the other he visits daily & dines with her. She is not faithful to him: that's not wonderful, perhaps not necessary.'

On August 31 the Disraelis went to Raby, 'a real castle . . . the general effect feudal and Plantagenet'. The future Earl of Rosebery, then Lord Dalmeny, whose mother had made her second marriage with the Duke of Cleveland, was at his stepfather's house. He was eighteen, had just left Eton and was due to go up to Christ Church in January. He described the occasion with the sharp observation

[1] Hughenden Papers, Box 6, A/I/B/377.
[2] M. & B., iv, 419–22.
[3] Hughenden Papers, Box 26, A/X/75.

of youth.[1] His mother was late, as she had been out riding, and she apologized for not being there to greet her guests. 'To which Dizzy replied with an air, "The pleasure of seeing Your Grace in your riding habit makes up for the loss of your society" – the sort of compliment, in fact, that one sees in *Coningsby*.' Dalmeny sat next to Mrs Disraeli at dinner and told her that he was going up to Oxford. She exclaimed, 'Oh yes, I love Oxford; they are all so fond of Mr. Dizzy there, they all applaud him so.' He asked her whether Disraeli had received an honorary degree. 'Yes,' she replied and added with that engaging touch of dottiness seldom absent from her utterances. 'He was made a D.T.C.L. or something of the sort.' Dalmeny's account of their conversation goes on:

> 'Do you care for politics, Mrs. Disraeli?' 'No I have no time, I have so many books and pamphlets to read and see if his name is in any of them! and I have everything to manage, and write his stupid letters. I am sorry when he is in office for then I lose him altogether, and though I have many people who call themselves my friends, yet I have no friend like him. I have not been separated from him since we have been in the country, except when I have been in the woods, and I cannot lose him' (here her voice trembled touchingly) . . .
> . . . I think this half crazy warm-hearted woman's talk is worth setting down, for she is an uncommon specimen. Parts are very touching.

Later Dalmeny went for a long walk with Disraeli in the park and was greatly impressed. The charm which Disraeli had been able to exert over younger men ever since the days of Young England had not diminished. Rosebery was to be fascinated all his life by Disraeli and by Disraeliana. He remained a Whig, but he told his sons that his first interest in politics dated from that conversation.[2] Disraeli liked him. 'Very intelligent,' he noted, '. . . and not a prig, which might be feared.'

There was another young man staying at Raby who also fell under the spell. This was Montagu Corry, second son of Henry Corry, who had been Secretary to the Admiralty in the last Tory administration. Disraeli greeted him on arrival with a friendliness that flattered him. The story[3] goes that one wet afternoon Corry was persuaded by the girls in the house party to relieve their bore-

[1] Rosebery's account is given in R. R. James, *Rosebery* (1963), 42–43.
[2] ibid., 44.
[3] Wilfrid Meynell, *The Man Disraeli*, 214–15.

dom by dancing and simultaneously singing a comic song. He reluctantly obliged, but, to his dismay, Disraeli, who had been writing letters in an adjoining room, came to the door, surveyed the scene for some minutes without a word and then vanished. Corry feared that he had been written off as an incorrigible featherhead, but that evening when they walked out of the dining-room the great man put his hand on Corry's shoulder and said, 'I think you must be my impresario.' Disraeli meant it. Within a year Corry succeeded Earle as his private secretary, and an alliance began which ended only with Disraeli's death.

These country-house visits took only a small part of his time. Most of the recess was spent at Hughenden. It would be agreeable to record that the Disraelis were popular locally, but the evidence suggests the opposite. The reason was partly the contrast with the previous owner, who was rich, spent lavishly, and under-rented the estate. Disraeli's first action was to raise the rents to an economic level. He could not afford to do otherwise, but most of the tenants left, and inevitably it was an unpopular beginning, although he seems to have got on well enough with their successors. Moreover, Mrs Disraeli, anxious to offset her husband's habitual extravagance, was apt to be mean over small matters. Sir Henry Lucy, who 'covered' her funeral for the *Daily News*, noted in his diary[1] that her parsimony had 'given mortal offence to Wycombe'. He cited as examples her having bought only six rolls for breakfast when the Prince and Princess of Teck came to stay, and an occasion when she ordered a quarter of cheese, but sent it back because Disraeli had to go unexpectedly to London. 'The smoke room at the "Falcon" ', he writes, 'was . . . full of substantial trades people and farmers belonging to High Wycombe and its neighbourhood. The dead lady up at the Manor House was the sole subject of conversation. It was sorrowful to note that there was none to say God bless her!'

It is unlikely that Disraeli was aware of this sentiment, and if his wife was, she certainly would not have cared. Both of them thoroughly enjoyed their role in the country, however incongruous it may have seemed to outside observers. Disraeli punctiliously filled the conventional duties of a squire. He attended quarter sessions at Aylesbury – 'always a busy scene in our provincial life,' he told Mrs Brydges Willyams. He had been a JP since 1836, and a Deputy Lieutenant since 1845. He served on local committees, dined with

[1] Published in *The Cornhill Magazine*, January 1912.

the Lord Lieutenant 'to meet the County as they call it', entertained
the Bishop, allowed his grounds to be used for village fêtes, addressed
agricultural meetings, and gave Bulwer Lytton advice on the price
of timber. Of course, he could never have seemed, nor would he have
wished to seem, a typical country gentleman. He wore country
clothes of too accentuated a form to carry complete conviction, and
yet he neither hunted nor preserved game. But he took a pleasure in
rural life all the deeper because so much of it was, despite his holidays at Bradenham, relatively unfamiliar. 'An estate is a little
Kingdom,' he wrote to Mrs Brydges Willyams, '& there is almost as
great a variety of interests & characters & parties & persons on these
acres as in Her Majesty's realms.'[1]

2

The recipient of that letter will always be associated with Hughenden, although she never saw it. Mrs Brydges Willyams, with whom
Disraeli came to be on such intimate terms of friendship, was an
elderly widow of Jewish origins, though like Disraeli of Christian
faith. She was the daughter of a certain Abraham Mendes da Costa
of Bath, and had some sort of relationship with the Lara family,[2]
with whom Disraeli was very indirectly connected through a step-
grandmother. She married a Colonel James Brydges Willyams of
S Columb in Cornwall. He died in 1820 aged forty-eight, before he
could come into the family property, and there were no children of
the marriage. Mrs Brydges Willyams's age is not known for certain,
but if the family tradition that she was older than her husband is
correct she must have been over eighty when she first got in touch
with Disraeli in 1851.

The circumstances in which this meeting occurred have been the
subject of much colourful mythology spread by, among others, the
historian Froude.[3] The legend is that she met Disraeli by previous
arrangement at the fountain of the Great Exhibition, asked his help
in a scarcely intelligible discourse about some litigation she was
engaged in, and gave him an envelope to take away with the details.
When he later opened it he found a bank-note for £1,000 to pay his
election expenses. Unfortunately, a memorandum by Sir Philip

[1] Brydges Willyams Letters, December 9, 1862.
[2] Roth, *Beaconsfield*, 89, points out that, despite Disraeli's belief, the Jewish Laras
had no connexion with the aristocratic Spanish house of the same name.
[3] J. A. Froude, *Lord Beaconsfield*, (1890), 180–1.

Rose[1] effectively disposes of the story. Apparently Mrs Willyams had before 1851 written one or two flattering letters alluding to their racial bond, but they were of the sort that politicians tend to acknowledge rather than encourage. Disraeli did not even acknowledge, though he ascertained that there really was such a person living at the address given, Mount Braddon, Torquay. But in 1851 he received a startling communication from her which he at once showed to Rose. In it she asked him 'as a great favour' to become one of her executors, adding 'whoever are my executors will also be my residuary legatees'. She went on to say that 'the interest they will take under my will, although not a considerable one, will at all events be substantial'. Disraeli and Rose agreed that it would be wrong to snatch at the offer. So Disraeli merely wrote a civil note to say that he would like to think about it. Then after a month or six weeks he conditionally accepted, but said that he would like to make her acquaintance when he was next in Devon. Whether he first did this in 1851 or 1853 is uncertain.

In any case the upshot is clear. She gave him a memorandum of her wishes and asked him to get Rose to act as her solicitor and make her will. Rose prudently declined, and persuaded Disraeli that in the circumstances it could give an unfortunate impression. It would be better for her to consult some local solicitor of good repute. This was done and the will duly made. The story about the Crystal Palace had this degree of substance. She did in August 1851 suggest that they might meet there, but Disraeli was out of London and the meeting never took place – a fact to which he alludes with regret more than once in their correspondence. As for the £1,000, we can safely assume that it is as legendary as the meeting by the fountain.

Although often invited, Mrs Brydges Willyams appears never to have visited either Grosvenor Gate or Hughenden. At her advanced age she probably felt that it was too much of an effort. The Disraelis, however, made an annual pilgrimage to Torquay, at times varying from early autumn to mid-December. They did not stay at Mount Braddon but at the Royal Hotel, spending the afternoons and evenings with their friend. They would drive out to see the local sights. Then there would be little dinner parties, and Disraeli would play écarté with her, making himself generally agreeable as only he knew how. For the rest of the year their friendship was conducted by correspondence. Some two hundred and fifty letters have

[1] M. & B., iii, 452–4, gives most of it.

survived. In the early years Disraeli wrote about once a month, but from 1858 onwards the correspondence becomes more copious and he averaged nearly thirty letters a year. These would be supplemented from time to time by Mrs Disraeli. Until 1857 he wrote to her without any superscription, but from then onwards 'My dearest' occurs with increasing frequency. The whole correspondence is an important source for Disraeli's social and political activities and even more important for life at Hughenden. He wished to evoke for his elderly admirer the scenes that she would never see with her own eyes, and his affection for the place glows through his letters.

> We were absent nearly a fortnight [he wrote on October 20 1858] and I find a great difference in the color of the trees – the limes all golden, the beeches ruddy brown, while the oaks and elms and pines are still dark and green, and contrast well with the brighter tints. But not a leaf has fallen; they want the first whisper of the frost and then they will go out like lamps when the dawn breaks on a long festival . . .[1]

Two years later we find him describing a fête at Hughenden.

> There are 100 school children, as many farmers and peasants with their wives; & all the county families for ten miles around – Sir George & Lady Dashwood, Colonel & Mrs. Fane, Sir Anthony & Lady Rothschild & a great assemblage of squires & clergymen. Lord Tredegar who never forgets that I made him a peer sent me a buck. They feasted in the open air & danced until sunset amid trees that were planted in the reign of Queen Anne & when Bolingbroke was Secretary of State . . .[2]

But his life was not always so active and sociable. On September 28, 1863, he writes:

> You live in the world to what I do, who never see anything but books and trees. When we left Hughenden last year we sent an architect and suite and tho' ten months have elapsed, some workmen still linger about. We have realized a romance we have been many years meditating: we have restored the house to what it was before the Civil Wars, and we have made a garden of terraces in which cavaliers might roam and saunter with their ladye loves! The only thing wanting is that you should see it; but I am going to have in due time a competent artist down, who will photograph the house, gardens, terraces, monument etc. etc., in every

[1] M. & B., iii, 469.
[2] Brydges Willyams Letters, September 16, 1860.

aspect, and these shall be sent, or, I hope *brought*, to you, for the time is approaching when we must turn our thoughts to the western ocean, the classic waves of gigantic soles and colossal prawns![1]

The latter together with other varieties of fish formed part of the regular exchange of presents which took place between Hughenden and Mount Braddon. He would pass on to her venison, grouse and black cock sent by his grand political friends from their northern moors and forests, or send her his own trout and partridges from the Hughenden estate. She would respond with turbot, soles, mullets, lobsters and prawns. 'Turbots visiting trout are patricians noticing country cousins,'[2] he wrote on one occasion, and in a moment of exuberance thanking her for a basket of prawns described them as 'the rosy colored tribute of Torbay'.[3] There was much exchange, too, of plants and flowers. 'All Hughenden sparkles with the Microfolia rose, the numerous and brilliant offspring of the colony you send from Mr. Braddon. Thus you see how races are propagated and how empires are formed.'[4] And he sent her cuttings from the Hatfield raspberry canes 'wh: Ld. Salisbury gave us about two years ago & wh: bear fruit to the end of the year – you may believe that this is no fiction for we had the pleasure of picking you a plate of raspberries this morning wh: accompanies the cuttings'.[5]

The bond between them was not only their Jewish ancestry but their alleged relationship to a particular family, the Laras, whom they both believed – erroneously – to be connected with the Spanish aristocratic house of the same name. Mrs Brydges Willyams decided in 1859 to obtain a proper coat of arms authorized by the College of Heralds. Disraeli took much pains over the matter, negotiating with the College on her behalf and even going so far as to communicate with the Spanish and Portuguese Ambassadors on the exact coats of arms borne by the Mendez da Costa and the Lara families. She was not easy to please and after three years of discussion Disraeli, showing for once a certain impatience, told her on March 20, 1862,[6] that he had done all he could. Three days later she wrote back saying that she was satisfied. She hoped that he would on her death

[1] M. & B., iii, 172.
[2] ibid., 463.
[3] ibid., iv, 355.
[4] ibid., iii, 470.
[5] Brydges Willyams Letters, November 6, 1856.
[6] loc. cit.

assume the names and arms of Lara and Mendez da Costa in addition
to that of Disraeli. Although she expressed this wish in her will, she
fortunately did not make it a condition and Disraeli decided to
leave his name as it was.

Disraeli's letters give a picture of his whole way of life, and, as
with his novels, indeed with everything he wrote, there is a sparkle,
movement, vivacity which never fail to entrance. His prose when
not rococo and ornate – and in his letters it seldom is – has the swift
quality of sunshine seen through moving leaves or on tumbling
waters. The crisp freshness is there even when he is describing events
of a character anything but sunny. During November and December
1858, 'we have spent more than a month in London in perpetual
fogs. There has been literally no day; but whether it be good fortune
or the excitement of public life I never enjoyed better health.'[1] But
usually he is writing of gay animated scenes. 'At Hatfield we dined
every day in a baronial hall in the midst of a real old English park
of the time of Queen Elizabeth, interminable avenues of lime and
chestnut, & oceans of fern six foot high; golden yew trees and glancing deer.'[2] They pay a visit to Wales, having discovered 'that a
colliery in wh: Mrs. Disraeli is interested & wh: has been represented
to us always as not being in work, has really for several years been
profitably producing without ever paying to her any royalties'.[3]
There they stay with Lord Tredegar, who was most helpful.

> Lord Tredegar is quite a Welch Prince with a flowing hospitality,
> his hall full of his neighbours, the Welch squires from their
> castles; unceasing hunting, & fishing in a thousand torrents. This
> was not much in my way but he is an unflinching supporter of
> mine with brothers & uncles in the House returned for the
> boroughs & the two counties in wh: he is paramount . . .[4]

They go to Osborne 'a Sicilian Palazzo with gardens terraces statues
and vases shining in the sun, than which nothing can be conceived
more captivating'.[5]

All through his letters there breathes the restless love of life, and
the sense of wonder and romance, which were to remain with him to
his dying day. He was not only a participant in politics but an

[1] ibid., December 11, 1858.
[2] ibid., August 3, 1855.
[3] ibid., March 20, 1861.
[4] ibid., April 11, 1861.
[5] ibid., September 7, 1858.

observer fascinated by the people and scenes that he encountered there. 'What wondrous times are these! Who cd have supposed that the United States of America would be the scene of an immense revolution. No one can foresee the results.'[1] And he added with less of his usual prescience, 'They must, however, tell immensely in favor of aristocracy.' On December 9, 1862, he wrote:

> . . . They say that the Greeks resolved to have an English King, in consequence of the refusal of Prince Alfred to be their monarch intend to elect Lord Stanley. If he accepts the charge I shall lose a powerful friend and colleague. It is a dazzling adventure for the House of Stanley, but they are not an imaginative race, and, I fancy, they will prefer Knowsley to the Parthenon and Lancashire to the Attic plain.[2]
>
> It is a privilege to live in this age of rapid and brilliant events. What an error to consider it an utilitarian age! It is one of infinite romance. Thrones tumble down and are offered, like a fairy tale, and the most powerful people in the world, male and female, a few years back, were adventurers, exiles and demireps.[3]

The letters are highly quotable. Life in London as well as at Hughenden glitters across his pages. 'It is some consolation in this refulgent summer that I live in a park even in London & that one wakes in the morning with eyes refreshed by the green shadows of stately trees.'[4] We learn of the parties they went to and those they gave, down to the list of guests and sometimes even the menus. The curious, for example, may if they wish learn that 'Tranche de Saumon à la Perigord' and 'Talmousses au Parmesan' were among the long list of dishes from which the Grand Duke of Saxe-Weimar chose when he dined with the Disraelis at Grosvenor Gate on July 26, 1862; or that on March 26 of the same year the Disraelis were invited by Mr and Mrs Samuel Gurney to mark 'the uniting of America and England by the Electric Telegraph between Ireland and Newfoundland. Tea and coffee at 9 o'clock. Conversation and Electric Correspondence from 10 to 12 o'clock.' It must have been a fascinating series of letters for a little old lady living a retired life in Torquay.

What sort of a person was the recipient? She had something of an

---

[1] ibid., December 8, 1861.

[2] In a later letter he writes, 'Had I his youth I would not hesitate, even with the earldom of Derby in the distance.'

[3] M. & B., iv, 321.

[4] Brydges Willyams Letters, July 6, 1863.

obsession about her ancestry. She was not very clever. Her letters are short and mostly full of devoted praise of 'dear Dizzi', as she calls him when writing to Mrs Disraeli. Once she ventured into a description of a dinner party which, Disraeli said, reminded him of 'Miss Austen', but this merely shows that royalty was not the only quarter where he laid it on with a trowel. Almost everyone with whom Disraeli had close dealings seems to have been an eccentric in one way or another. Mrs Brydges Willyams was no exception. She had a phobia about doctors. A mutual friend in Torquay told Mrs Disraeli:[1] 'Her theory, I believe, is that nobody need die before 100 provided they take care of themselves & *avoid* doctors.' He added: 'it is a perilous experiment I think with one as friendless as our poor friend.' This was in February 1862. She was ill again at the end of the year, not long before Disraeli's visit. The vicar of S John's, Torquay, the Reverend W. G. Parks Smith,[2] wrote to Disraeli on December 3:

> She appears, however, very uncomfortably situated in not having any friend, nor even one servant in the house in whom she can repose any confidence and consequently requested me to recommend some trustworthy person to take care of herself & the servants . . . I could obtain immediately the services of a sister of mercy but Mrs. B. Willyams wd perhaps object to have such a *lady* in the house.
> What think you?
> As Mrs. BW is very tenacious I must request you will consider this communication as strictly private and made on my own responsibility alone from the knowledge of the interest you have always taken in the poor lady's welfare . . .

Once again, however, she recovered. Three days later she was driving out in the country and the vicar wrote to tell Disraeli that there was, after all, no need to expedite his visit.

She died after a very short illness less than a year later, on November 11, 1863. Disraeli received the first warning on November 8 from a doctor who had been summoned presumably by one of the servants. He had written to her on the 5th a gossipy letter about 'the great Imperial Sphinx', and evidently did not know she was ill. He was unable to reach Torquay before her death. As she had

[1] ibid., E. W. Chetwode to Mrs Disraeli, February 28, 1862.
[2] He had flickered once before into the pages of history when Dr Phillpotts, the famous Bishop of Exeter, who regularly attended S John's, had endeavoured in a fury to tear a vase of flowers from the altar, to which it was attached by string.

promised, she left him the residue of her estate, which was sworn at just under £40,000. There were legacies which would have reduced his inheritance to about £20,000, but several of the legatees had died before Mrs Brydges Willyams. In the event the residue 'somewhat exceeded £30,000', to quote Sir Philip Rose. In her will she said that she left her money to Disraeli 'in testimony of my affection and in approbation and admiration of his efforts to vindicate the race of Israel with my views respecting which he is acquainted, and which I have no doubt he will endeavour to accomplish'. She also expressed a desire to be buried in the family vault at Hughenden church where the Disraelis expected to be buried, too. For legal reasons this proved impossible, to Disraeli's great annoyance. All three now lie together just outside the east end of the church, although at one stage Disraeli declared that he would prefer 'even Kensal Green to anything so unprotected'.

The death of Mrs Willyams deprives us of an important source on Disraeli's personal life. He was at his best when writing to female confidantes. The other personage to whom he revealed his thoughts, though far less openly than to Mrs Willyams, was his patroness and friend Lady Londonderry. But his last letter to her was in 1861. She had been in failing health for some time before her death at the beginning of 1865. His sister Sarah had died in 1859. We do not possess a similar day-to-day exposé of his comments, plans and adventures until 1873, when his well-known correspondence with Lady Bradford and Lady Chesterfield begins.

3

The legacy made a considerable difference to Disraeli's finances, which had as usual been fluctuating with erratic incalculability for the last fifteen years. The purchase of Hughenden had brought his total debts to at least £40,000, but of this some £30,000[1] was owed on mortgage to the Bentinck family under an arrangement not precisely known, though it seems clear that they had no intention

---

[1] See Sir R. Bignold, *Five Generations of the Bignold Family* (1947), 100–2. Disraeli wished to borrow money in 1851 from the Norwich Union Life Insurance Society, of which Sir Samuel Bignold (1741–1875) was Secretary. An essential condition was that no inquiry should be made or notice given to the existing mortgagees, whose charge on Hughenden was £30,000. Bignold was not willing to commit the Society, but he does appear to have lent some £2,000 from his private fortune. He was a keen Tory politician.

of embarrassing him. Disraeli, moreover, evidently repaid some of
his debts after Isaac's death, for we find him writing to Sarah on
August 1, 1851:

> . . . My time has been spent paying off my rapacious creditors
> to their great mortification. The funds, large as they were, are
> scarcely enough, but at all events I am free from any pec[uniary]
> pressure – tho' I shall be content if even with this great liquida-
> tion there is 1500 pr. ann. clear left. However years ago they sd
> Lord Jersey had no more & so I must be satisfied & no doubt as
> so many things have really turned up & always turned up when
> they were most wanted the end will be as right as we all wish – I
> think I have cause to be sanguine, & whether I have or not I feel
> so wh: is the next best thing.[1]

This happy state of affairs did not last. In 1854 Lord Titchfield,
the elder brother of Lord George and Lord Henry Bentinck, succeeded to the dukedom of Portland. Although he had joined in the
arrangement to finance the purchase of Hughenden, he probably
did so without much enthusiasm, for politically he was a Peelite.
There is little doubt that Lord George and Lord Henry had never
intended to call in the money. But in 1857 the new Duke abruptly
demanded repayment. As is the case throughout Disraeli's financial
dealings with the Bentinck family, the facts are obscure. It is not
clear why the Duke acted thus at this particular moment. He was
indeed a most eccentric man. He lived the life of a recluse, built vast
subterranean grottos at Welbeck, invariably travelled to London in
a carriage which was put on the train with the blinds drawn, and
went to extraordinary lengths to avoid speaking even to his own
servants. It was these oddities which gave such plausibility as there
was to the claims of the plaintiff in the famous Druce Portland case
after the Duke's death.

Whatever the Duke's motives, Lord Henry was in no doubt that
he meant mischief. 'I am very jealous of the course that my brother
may take with us in re Hughenden,' he wrote on April 30, '& as the
blow may be sudden it may be as well that arrangements shd be
ready for the worst – I have been quite mistaken in my man.'[2] In an
undated letter, evidently at about the same time, he urged Disraeli
to get out of the Duke's clutches '. . . for depend upon it, that in
using the dagger he will drive it to the very hilt'.[3] On May 22 he

[1] Hughenden Papers, Box 6, A/I/B/344.
[2] ibid., Box 118, B/XXI/B/373.
[3] ibid., B/XXI/B/383.

wrote again: 'It will be necessary to get hold of the Bonds and wash our Hands of my Brother without delay – any negotiation with him or arrangement of any kind is out of the question.'[1] The Bonds were two moneylenders, and with one of them, Effie, Disraeli had been involved in the dealings which for a quarter of a century inspired the unjustified suspicion of Derby.[2] He had to have recourse to them again, and since they charged 10 per cent he was soon in financial difficulties. Whether he had to borrow the whole of the money originally lent by the Bentincks, or only a part is not quite clear, but it looks as if the Duke was in a position to call in the lot and although Lord Henry was evidently well disposed, he could do nothing to help.

It is sad to record that Lord Henry's friendship did not last. He, too, had his share of the eccentricity which seems to have characterized this branch of the Bentinck family. They did everything with an intensity surpassing that of normal men. Lord Henry, when Master of the Burton, hunted with such fanaticism that he never saw Welbeck by daylight during the season except on Sundays. The Bentincks were passionate in friendship, implacable in enmity. They never forgave. On June 6, 1860, Disraeli's old friend wrote: 'Lord Henry Bentinck hopes that Mr. Disraeli will not give himself the needless trouble of calling at Claridge's Hotel tomorrow. Ld. H. will not be at home and there is no subject whatever that he has the slightest inclination to discuss with Mr. Disraeli.'[3] The cause of this breach is not clear. There exists a draft of a protest from Disraeli which ends: 'Let me at least know on what ground I am deprived of the friendship which was the pride and consolation of my life.'[4] No reply has survived; it is unlikely that there was one.

Disraeli's finances were highly unsatisfactory for the five years after 1857, and he almost certainly increased his indebtedness. There was, however, one silver lining. After his second turn as Chancellor of the Exchequer he was entitled to a pension while out of office, and from 1859 onwards he had an extra £2,000 a year. He had cheerfully written to Sarah about 'things' having 'always turned up when they were most wanted'. The extraordinary feature of his money affairs was that this really did happen again and again. The pension was one example. In the winter of 1862–3 there was an even

[1] ibid., B/XXI/B/374.
[2] See above, p. 71–3.
[3] Hughenden Papers, Box 118, B/XXI/B/376.
[4] ibid., B/XXI/B/376a.

more striking one. Andrew Montagu, a Yorkshire landowner of large estate, a bachelor and a Tory supporter, inquired of party headquarters what he could do to help the cause.[1] He was informed that one valuable form of contribution from a wealthy man would be to buy up Disraeli's debts and charge a reasonable rate of interest on them instead of the usurous figure exacted by the Bonds and their kindred. Montagu agreed to consider the idea. Rose acted as intermediary and put him in touch with Baron Lionel de Rothschild. The upshot was that in return for a mortgage on Hughenden he bought up all Disraeli's debts and charged him 3 per cent. Buckle surmises that Rothschild, too, may have given some sort of guarantee, but in the absence of evidence one can only guess. The difference that this arrangement made to Disraeli's finances was enormous. He reckoned it at £4,200 a year on one occasion, £5,000 on another. Even if we take the lower figure, his debt must have been about £60,000 on which he now had to pay only £1,800 p.a. instead of £6,000. It was to the credit of Disraeli's heart rather than his head that when he became Prime Minister he tried, at Rose's persuasion, to make Montagu a peer.[2] If he had done so and the facts had leaked out, there might have been an uproar which would have put even the Honours Scandal of 1922 into the shade. Fortunately Montagu declined.

In 1863 the death of Mrs Brydges Willyams produced a further improvement in Disraeli's finances. It is amusing to notice that Sir Philip Rose, ever resourceful in his master's interest, suggested that publicity should be given to the matter. 'I wish you would consider whether some paragraph might not be advantageously put in the newspapers alluding to the bequest and the grounds for it. These things are catching and the great probability is that the example would be followed if properly made known.'[3] Although this agreeable vista of a succession of elderly widows leaving their fortunes to Disraeli did not become a reality, he was for the time being in a better financial position than ever before. In January 1866 he reckoned their joint income at nearly £9,000 of which £4,500 was Mary Anne's.

[1] M. & B., V, 78.
[2] ibid., 79. Rose instanced Pitt's banker, Lord Carrington, but times had changed since Pitt.
[3] Hughenden Papers, Box 108, B/XX/R/18, November 16, 1863.

CHAPTER XX

Revival
1859–66

Disraeli's life for the six years following the fall of Derby's second administration was comparatively uneventful. One personal sorrow afflicted him almost at once, the death of his sister Sarah. It was a heavy blow. Of the surviving members of his family she was the only one for whom he felt any strong affection. She alone had genuinely believed in his star. Moreover, though on the best of terms with Mary Anne, she was the one person in whom he could confide his occasional tiffs and differences with his wife, and to her he revealed some secrets that he revealed to no one else, particularly with regard to his money affairs. She stayed at Hughenden in September 1859 and Mary Anne commented on her delicate appearance. Thereafter she rapidly declined, and died on December 19. 'She was . . . one of those persons who are the soul of a house and the angelic spirit of a family',[1] Disraeli told Lady Londonderry. Sir Philip Rose many years later wrote:

> . . . On the first occasion of his becoming Prime Minister I remember saying to him, 'If only your sister had been alive to witness your triumph what happiness it would have given her;' and he replied, 'Ah, poor Sa! poor Sa! we've lost our audience, we've lost our audience . . .'[2]

Because of his sister's death Disraeli did not give his usual parliamentary dinners at the beginning of the session of 1860. One observer suspected that this was not the only reason. Greville commented:

> . . . Disraeli under the pretext of a family affliction gives no dinners; but the probable cause of this is not the death of his sister which happened two months ago, but his own uncertainty as to whom he should invite and who would be disposed to own

[1] M. & B., iv, 268.
[2] ibid., i, 180. Monypenny has not transcribed it quite correctly, but the errors do not matter.

political allegiance by accepting his invitation. Such is the dis-
organised state of that party.[1]

There is no doubt that Disraeli's position was in jeopardy during
1860; he was blamed for the defeat of the previous session, and he
was suspected of disloyalty to Derby. Derby did not mean to upset
a government which was on most issues as conservative as he could
wish. 'Keeping the cripples on their legs' was how he described his
tactics. The accusation that Disraeli worked against him seems unjustified. He may have chafed, but he obeyed orders. This did not
prevent the emergence of a vociferous anti-Disraeli clique, and
Derby warned him that there was a 'Cabal' against him. The
hostility to him found expression in an acid article in the April
number of the *Quarterly Review*. It was made the more piquant by
the widespread knowledge that the anonymous author was Lord
Robert Cecil, a younger son of Disraeli's friend and former cabinet
colleague, the 2nd Marquis of Salisbury. Surveying Disraeli's career
the author wrote:

> To crush the Whigs by combining with the Radicals was the first
> and last maxim of Mr. Disraeli's tactics. He had never led the
> Conservatives to victory as Sir Robert Peel had led them to
> victory. He had never procured the triumphant assertion of any
> Conservative principle or shielded from imminent ruin any
> ancient institution. But he had been a successful leader to this
> extent, that he had made any Government while he was in
> opposition next to an impossibility. His tactics were so various,
> so flexible, so shameless – the net by which his combinations were
> gathered in was so wide – he had so admirable a knack of enticing
> into the same lobby a happy family of proud old Tories and
> foaming Radicals, martial squires jealous of their country's
> honour, and manufacturers who had written it off their books as
> an unmarketable commodity – that so long as his party backed
> him, no Government was strong enough·to hold out against his
> attacks.

These were the sentiments of Henry Drummond – strong language
from a young Tory MP. When his father remonstrated, Lord
Robert replied: 'I have merely put into print what all the country
gentlemen were saying in private.' There was an amusing sequel.
On arriving at Hatfield soon after the publication of the article,
Lord Robert was dismayed to learn that Disraeli was one of the

---

[1] Strachey and Fulford, *The Greville Memoirs*, vii, 453, January 24, 1860.

guests. He went into the garden to brood upon the best method of coping with this embarrassing situation, but coming round the turn of a path in the shrubbery he met his leader face to face. 'Ah Robert, Robert, how glad I am to see you!' Disraeli exclaimed, and cordially embraced the young man before he had time to say a word. As Lady Gwendolen Cecil puts it, 'If he had entertained any undue sense of his importance as a mutineer it must have been effectively dissipated.'[1]

Disraeli was not the man to bear malice against a Tory rebel who was only doing what he himself had done twenty years earlier. But he did resent the ingratitude with which, so it seemed to him, his services were being treated by his more experienced followers. On June 11 he wrote a long letter[2] to Sir William Miles, to whom he had written on a similar occasion in 1851 and who occupied a position analogous to that of the chairman of the 1922 Committee today. After recounting the history of his relations with the party since Bentinck's death – not quite correctly – Disraeli came to the point. 'I must resign a leadership which I unwillingly accepted, and to which it is my opinion that fourteen years of unqualified devotion have not reconciled the party.' The letter dismayed Miles, and he promptly consulted leading members of the House of Commons such as Walpole and Henley. It soon became clear that there would be general consternation if Disraeli resigned, and Miles persuaded him to withdraw the letter. There is not much evidence about Derby's attitude, but Greville's claim that he was 'violently discontented with Disraeli' seems untrue or at any rate not more than a reference to a passing mood. Their correspondence though not copious at this time is friendly enough, and Derby never hesitated to find fault directly if he had any complaint. The opposition to Disraeli was noisy rather than large, and probably did not amount to more than a dozen or so headed by George Bentinck, known as 'Big Ben', a remote cousin of Lord George and MP for Norfolk. He invariably referred to Disraeli as 'the Jew'.

If Disraeli had any hankering for an alliance of convenience with the Radicals, he suppressed it from now onwards. Throughout 1860 he behaved with impeccable conservatism: opposing the remission of the paper duties, allowing Russell's Reform Bill quietly to expire,

---

[1] Lady Gwendolen Cecil, *The Life of Robert, Marquis of Salisbury* (4 vols, 1921–32), i, 97.
[2] See M. & B., iv, 289–91, for the full text.

and generally supporting Palmerston against the left-wing Liberals. He refused to have anything to do with a proposal by Bright that the Conservatives should join with the advanced Liberals and eject the Government. He agreed with Derby in concluding an effective parliamentary truce with Palmerston for the next three years. Of course, Disraeli did not abandon the usual attacks and criticisms of debate. He and Derby regarded it as part of their duty to modify and conservatize Government measures, and in an era when the Government did not make every detail of every measure an issue of confidence, there was a good chance of carrying amendments of this kind. But the Trory leaders were determined to keep Palmerston in office.

Sometimes difficulties arose. For example, Derby and Disraeli continued, in opposition as they had in office, to differ from one another on the relative claims of defence expenditure and Treasury economy. Disraeli was fortified by Northcote, who, as a member of the Committee on Public Accounts, had discovered some 'frightful' examples of extravagance in the Navy. He decided, in spite of Derby's misgivings, to make economy the main theme of his attacks on the Government during 1862, and during one of the debates used an expression which later became famous, 'bloated armaments'. Derby had to explain in the House of Lords that his lieutenant had been referring to the whole of Europe and not to England in particular. Derby agreed, however, to an amendment to be proposed by Walpole, urging economy on the Government. But Palmerston decided to make the issue one of confidence and Walpole, alarmed lest the Government might fall, withdrew his amendment. Disraeli was much annoyed; taking advantage of the fact that the next day was Derby day, he made an acid reference to 'favourites bolting'. It was now Walpole's turn to be angry, and Derby had to smooth matters. 'My own opinion is that you were the person who had the most reason to complain,'[1] he told Disraeli, who wrote to Mrs Brydges Willyams, 'Between ourselves, as you well know, I had no desire whatever to disturb Lord Palmerston, but you cannot keep a large army in order without letting them sometimes smell gunpowder.'[2]

After 1862 Disraeli could claim with some plausibility that his fiscal views were prevailing. Gladstone, in his later Budgets, enforced economies, and his large surpluses went towards reduction of

[1] ibid., 312.   [2] loc. cit.

taxation. On one important financial matter Disraeli scored a triumph for which posterity can be grateful. Gladstone, with that fiscal pedantry which sometimes marred his judgement, pressed vehemently for the extension of income tax to charities. Disraeli successfully led the attack on this iniquitous proposal, and Gladstone had to drop it.

Throughout these years Disraeli was active in debates on foreign affairs. He kept himself very well informed as in the past on Cabinet discussions. Charles Villiers, who was President of the Poor Law Board, was his source. 'The division in the Cabinet on Tuesday week on the French Alliance was 12 to 4. Ayes Ld. Palm – Ld. John – Gladstone – M. Gibson',[1] Disraeli wrote to Derby on one occasion. On the four major issues of the period, the Risorgimento, the American Civil War, Poland, and Schleswig-Holstein, Disraeli favoured non-intervention. He strongly censured what he called the 'piratical' means by which Garibaldi had achieved Italian unity. His views pleased Pio Nono. 'Mr. Disraeli was my friend. I regret him,' he told Lord Odo Russell, and he gave his blessing to Earle when the latter on a visit to Rome revealed that he was Disraeli's private secretary. Both at this time and later Disraeli was hoping to woo the English Roman Catholic vote and he was on cordial terms with Cardinal Wiseman. He declined all invitations to meet Garibaldi when the famous hero visited London in April 1864, although Derby and the other Tory leaders seem to have felt no such misgivings.

When the American Civil War began Disraeli, like most Englishmen, expected the South to win. He privately welcomed the seeming collapse of the republic as a blow in favour of aristocracy. But he thought it unwise to take sides publicly. Palmerston, Gladstone and Russell would have done well to copy him. Many years of Anglo-American ill feeling might have been averted if they had appeared genuinely neutral in their attitude to the deadly struggle. Disraeli was right, too, though by no means fully backed in his party, on both the Polish and the Danish questions. Russell on each occasion made offers of help that he could not fulfil and excited hopes that he could not gratify. This was the policy contemptuously described by Derby as 'meddle and muddle', and it brought British prestige to almost its lowest point in the nineteenth century. The mismanagement of the Schleswig-Holstein affair was

[1] Derby Papers, Box 146/1, dated simply, 'Thurs'.

so bad that Derby and Disraeli abandoned the parliamentary truce and launched a real attack on the Government in 1864. They won in the Lords by nine votes but they were eighteen short of victory in the lower House; and so Palmerston survived.

Disraeli's *obiter dicta* on foreign affairs were not always sensible. He tended to look through spectacles tinted by the colours of lurid romance. 'At present the peace of the world has been preserved, not by statesmen but by capitalists,' he told Mrs Brydges Willyams on July 21, 1863.[1] 'For the last three months it has been a struggle between the secret societies and the European millionaires. Rothschild hitherto has won . . .' He met Bismarck at a party in London in 1862 and was much impressed when the Prussian Chancellor told him: 'I shall seize the first best pretext to declare war against Austria, dissolve the German Diet, subdue the minor States and give national unity to Germany under Prussian leadership.'[2] This indeed was an exact prediction. But in November a year later we find Disraeli writing to Earle:[3] 'Prussia, without nationality, the principle of the day, is clearly the subject for partition.' He was not the only Englishman to exaggerate the power of Napoleon III and to underestimate that of Bismarck.

Disraeli's acquiescence in Derby's general policy of keeping the Government in office won the approval of the Queen and the Prince Consort, who could never wholly rid themselves of the idea that party warfare was in some way 'factious'. The Court had not in the past looked on Disraeli with much favour. His attacks on Peel were long remembered and his first spell of office in 1852 had failed to remove this adverse impression. His second term as Chancellor of the Exchequer had been more efficacious, but it was not till the 1860s that any real cordiality appeared. Early in 1861 the Disraelis were invited to stay a couple of nights at Windsor from January 23 to 25. 'It is Mrs. Disraeli's first visit to Windsor,' he wrote to Mrs Brydges Willyams,[4] '& is considered very marked on the part of Her Majesty to the wife of the Leader of the Opposition when many Cabinet Ministers have been asked there *without* their wives.' Disraeli had a long conversation with the Prince and put as favourable a gloss as he could on the condition of the Conservative party. ' "But you have no newspapers," he exclaimed pettishly, "the

[1] M. & B., iv, 339.
[2] loc. cit.
[3] loc. cit.
[4] ibid., 382, January 19.

country is governed by newspapers! and all the Liberal journals are
in the pay of foreign Powers. So much for the liberty of the Press.
However when Parliament is sitting their influence is less." '[1]

At the end of the year occurred the premature death of the
Prince. Disraeli's public tribute to him greatly pleased the Queen,
who expressed her gratitude. There is plenty of evidence that
Disraeli genuinely admired the Prince. Three years earlier, writing
from Windsor to Mrs Willyams, he said:[2] 'Here is most agreeable
society . . . Her Majesty a most gracious hostess & perhaps better
conversation cannot be had than that afforded by the two Princes,
the Prince Consort & the Duc d'Aumale, the two most richly cultivated minds I ever met, & men too of great abilities.' After the
Prince's death Disraeli told the Saxon Minister in London, Count
Vitzthum: 'We have buried our Sovereign . . . If he had outlived
some of our "old stagers" he would have given us, while retaining
all constitutional guarantees, the blessings of absolute government.
Of us younger men who are qualified to enter the Cabinet there is
not one who would not willingly have bowed to his experience.'[3]
No doubt Disraeli sometimes went rather far. The Queen presented
him with the Prince's speeches in gratitude for his parliamentary
aid over the Albert Memorial. In thanking her he said among other
things:[4] 'The Prince is the only person whom Mr. Disraeli has ever
known who realized the Ideal', and warming to his theme ended:
'. . . the name of Albert will be accepted as the master-type of a
generation of profounder feeling and vaster range than that which
he formed and guided with benignant power.' But his admiration
for the Prince cannot be written off as a pose to please the Queen,
even if this expression of it is fairly described by Buckle as a 'somewhat hyperbolic eulogium'.

In 1863 the Disraelis scored a social victory of the first magnitude.
They were asked to the wedding of the Prince of Wales. He wrote in
triumph to Mrs Willyams:[5]

I listen hourly to the lamentations of the great ladies who are not
asked. The Duchess of Marlboro in despair! The Duchess of
Manchester who was Mistress of the Robes!!! Mme de Flahaut

[1] ibid., 295. Disraeli to Derby, January 28, 1861.
[2] Brydges Willyams Letters, April 12, 1858.
[3] C. F. Vitzthum von Eckstaedt, *St Petersburg and London, 1852–64* (2 vols, 1887),
ii, 176.
[4] M. & B., iv, 394, April 25, 1863.
[5] Brydges Willyams Letters, March 4, 1863.

only a month ago Ambassadress of France, & a host of others as eminent. None of my late colleagues are invited except Lord Derby & he would go as a matter of course as a Knight of the Garter.

But I am invited!

and what is still more marked Mrs. D too and this by the Queen's particular command . . .

Disraeli left a long memorandum[1] about the wedding which took place on March 10 – too long to be quoted here. He believed that his inclusion was due to a personal gesture of friendship on the Queen's part. He never knew that he owed the invitation to Palmerston, whose letter to the Queen explains itself:

> . . . It has been suggested to Lord Palmerston that as Mr. Disraeli has, like Lord Derby, behaved very well about the Bill for the Prince of Wales's establishment, it might be a gracious as well as a not unuseful thing if your Majesty saw fit that he, as Leader of the Conservative Party in the House of Commons might be invited to the Wedding as well as Lord Derby . . .[2]

Although sometimes cynical, Disraeli remained to the end incurably and overwhelmingly romantic in his attitude to royalty. The Queen's invitation could not have gone to a recipient who appreciated it more. He was no less gratified by the honour which he received soon afterwards of a personal audience. The Queen had accorded these only to ministers since the Prince's death, with one exception, Derby.

He went down to Windsor on April 22 and was entertained at dinner by the Prince and Princess of Wales, the Queen being busy on papers brought down by Russell, the only other guest. Disraeli told the Prince and Princess that nightingales fed on glow worms 'exactly the food which nightingales should require'. The Prince was incredulous 'and exclaimed: "Is that a fact or is it a myth?" "Quite a fact, Sir; for my woodman is my authority, for we have a great many nightingales at Hughenden and a great many glow worms." "We have got one nightingale at Sandringham," said the Prince smiling.' Disraeli breakfasted next day with Russell and the Maids of Honour.

[1] M. & B., iv, 385–91.
[2] *The Letters of Queen Victoria*, 2nd series, i, 70. February 26, 1863.

Lord John was genial, which, on the whole, he generally has been with me. For notwithstanding our fierce public struggles for long years, and the crusade which I have always preached against High Whiggism, of which he was the incarnate creation, there were really some elements of sympathy between us, being [*sic*] with all his hauteur and frigid manner, really a man of sentiment, and imagination, and culture.

Disraeli was summoned to wait for his audience in Prince Albert's special room.

In less than five minutes from my entry, an opposite door opened, and the Queen appeared.

She was still in widow's mourning and seemed stouter than when I last saw her but this was perhaps only from her dress. I bowed deeply when she entered and raised my head with unusual slowness, that I might have a moment for recovery. Her countenance was grave but serene and kind, and she said in a most musical voice: 'It is some time since we met.'

. . . She said she hoped no crisis would be brought about wantonly, for, in her forlorn condition she hardly knew what she could do. I said H.M.'s comfort was an element in all our considerations and that no action would be taken, I felt sure, unless from commanding necessity.

She said 'Lord Palmerston was grown very old.' I replied 'But his voice in debate, Madam, is as loud as ever.'

'Yes!' she exclaimed with animation. 'And his handwriting! Did you ever see such a handwriting. So very clear and strong! Nevertheless I see in him a change, a very great change. His countenance is so changed.'

Then H.M. turning from public affairs deigned to say that it had given her great pleasure to observe that I had been chosen Trustee of the British Museum in the place of the late Lord Lansdowne . . .

At last she asked after my wife, hoped she was well, and then with a graceful bow, vanished.

Already, one feels, Disraeli is investing the Queen with some strange magical quality. She *appears*. She *vanishes*. The myth of 'the Faery' is being born.

During the splendid summer of 1863 all attention was concentrated on the newly married royal couple. The Disraelis had their fill of the incessant balls, dinners and receptions, living, as Disraeli said, 'only in a glittering bustle'. Politics were at a low ebb. Everything turned on Palmerston. As Prime Minister he exactly suited the mood of the times. Seven years earlier Derby had described him as 'a Conservative Minister working with Radical tools and keeping up a show of Liberalism in his foreign policy'. This was no less true in 1863, and Palmerston knew it. He was a parliamentary tactician of consummate skill and he had in 1859 effectively neutralized all those who might make trouble. There was, moreover, a general disposition to let things drift during the Prime Minister's lifetime. After all, he could not last for ever . . . Or could he? As year followed year and the old statesman appeared sprightly and vigorous in the House, or at grand social occasions, there seemed something immortal about him.

It was true that in the autumn of 1863 when he was seventy-nine an episode occurred which for a moment made his tenure appear doubtful. Not that he showed any sign of dying. Rather the contrary, for he was threatened with citation in a case of criminal conversation, as it was called. The allegation was that he had had improper relations with a Mrs Cane. The jest went round the clubs that she was certainly Cain, but was he Abel?[1] Disraeli in his last letter to Mrs Brydges Willyams wrote: 'Lord Palmerston's almost absurd escapade . . . is probably a case of extortion founded on some slight imprudence – & it is to be hoped will evaporate.'[2] To Derby he was more frivolous:[3]

> . . . The Palmerston escapade! It should make him at least ridiculous; perhaps it may make him even more popular. How do we know the affair has not been got up to dissolve on? They want a cry.
>
> It is a little annoying for the Low Church party wh: had acknowledged him as 'the man of God' – but so was King David & he behaved even worse . . .

But Disraeli's hope expressed to Mrs Willyams turned out to be justified. The case did evaporate, and Palmerston sailed on as confidently as ever. After his victory in 1864 over the Danish question he scrambled up the stairs to the Ladies' Gallery, sc Disraeli was told, to embrace Lady Palmerston, who had been listening to the debate. 'An interesting scene, and what pluck! To mount those dreadful stairs at three o'clock in the morning and at eighty years of age! . . . It was a great moment.'[4]

[1] Hughenden Papers, Box 97, B/XX/E/298, Earle to Disraeli, November 1863.
[2] Brydges Willyams Letters, November 5, 1863.
[3] Derby Papers, Box 146/1, October 30, 1863.
[4] M. & B., iv, 405, quoting from a note left among Disraeli's papers.

The flat calm into which the ship of state had drifted was perhaps a reason why Disraeli in the early 1860s had time to assemble a number of autobiographical sketches, observations, anecdotes, character studies. It is not clear what his purpose was. If his intention was to write connected memoirs he never fulfilled it. Some of these reminiscences have been quoted here from time to time when dealing with the periods in his career to which they refer.

These years of rather uneventful opposition had at last brought Disraeli more into acceptance by the world of what would now be called 'the establishment'. The favour shown to him by the Queen was one important step. Another was his election already mentioned as a Trustee of the British Museum. But his progress had been slow. He was not elected to Grillions, a select parliamentary dining club, till 1865. Gladstone had become a member in 1840. The following year the Athenaeum made amends to Disraeli for blackballing him thirty-four years earlier, and elected him under the rule permitting every year the entry of a certain number of distinguished persons with priority over ordinary candidates. In 1868 he was elected to 'The Club', a similar institution to Grillions. Disraeli did not attend these societies more than courtesy required. He disliked men's dinner parties and went to them as a political necessity rather than a social pleasure.

On July 6, 1865, Parliament was dissolved. The ensuing election like that of 1857 was a plebiscite for Palmerston. It left the state of the parties virtually unaltered and the Conservative leaders in a state of despondency. An imprudent and much-criticized speech of Derby's comparing Roman Catholics to dogs that ought to be muzzled may have done some damage, especially as it came at a moment when Disraeli was delicately casting a fly over this particular group in the hope of winning them from their traditional Liberal allegiance. But it probably made little difference to the outcome, any more than the faults of organization which other critics found in the Tory 'machine'. Disraeli, while defending the latter to Derby, conceded that the outlook was gloomy. 'The state of Scotland alone is most serious', he wrote to Derby on July 28. 'All influence appears to have slipped away from its proprietors.'[1] Equally dismal was the scene in London, where the Liberals scored heavily. 'If Scotland and the Metropolitan districts are to be entirely and continuously arrayed against the Conservative cause, the pull of the

[1] ibid., 416.

table will be too great and no Conservative Government, unless the
basis be extended, will be possible.'[1] He offered to retire if his withdrawal would help Derby to form a coalition government with a
right-wing Whig as leader of the House of Commons. Derby firmly
refused on both personal and public grounds.

And so all seemed set for another period of somnolent opposition
when at last an event occurred which changed the whole situation.
On September 3 Disraeli passed on to Derby a rumour from his
secret source in the Cabinet that all was not well with the Prime
Minister.

> The reformers of the Cabinet, tho' obliged to postpone the con-
> sideration of details console themselves with the belief that P.
> will not be able to meet Parliament again.
>   His bladder complaint, tho' in itself not perhaps fatal, deprives
> him of his usual exercise and sleep which was his forte and carried
> him thro' everything.[2]

Six weeks later, on October 18, Palmerston died quite suddenly
two days before his eighty-first birthday. It was the end of an era.
'Our quiet days are over; no more peace for us,' Sir Charles Wood
was heard to say as he walked sadly away from the funeral.[3]
Palmerston's incongruous position as a Whig who was in many
ways more Tory than the Tories had blurred and confused the real
dividing lines in politics. His death created a new situation.

Inevitably his successor as Prime Minister was Russell, and as
leader of the House of Commons, Gladstone. At once a sharper
personal feeling became apparent. In the House of Lords, Derby
regarded Russell with a vengeful eye. He thought him far more
responsible than Palmerston for the humiliating fall of the Conservatives in 1859. In the lower House Gladstone formally became
what he had long been in reality, Disraeli's arch-opponent in the
great parliamentary duel.

On all personal grounds Disraeli regretted the passing of the old
Prime Minister. He appreciated 'characters' and Palmerston was
one. A host of stories clustered around him as they have in modern
times around Winston Churchill, some true, some merely *bien
trouvés*. Disraeli noted many in his fragmentary reminiscences. Yet
regret at the loss was tempered by recognition of an opportunity.

---

[1] loc. cit.
[2] Derby Papers, Box 146/1.
[3] Algernon West, *Recollections* (2 vols, 1899), i, 306.

Russell was certain to bring in a Reform Bill, but the Parliament of 1865 had been elected to support Palmerston, not Reform. The previous session had displayed an ominous split on the Liberal side when Robert Lowe and a group of supporters sided with Disraeli in rejecting a private member's Borough Franchise Bill. There now seemed every chance of deep division among the Government's followers if the Government itself introduced a Reform Bill.[1]

There were two possible attitudes for the Conservatives to take towards a Reform Bill. They could try to co-operate in order to make as moderate an agreed measure as possible, and thus settle the question for the next fifteen or twenty years – in effect a continuance of the party truce; or they could seize the opportunity to split the Liberals by allying themselves with the anti-Reform group which was determined to oppose any Bill however moderate on the ground that it was the slippery slope to total democracy. Derby seems to have inclined to the first course. 'From what I hear,' he wrote to Malmesbury on November 6, 'they mean to bring in a Reform Bill but one of a very mild character which we may find ourselves able to support.'[2]

Disraeli, too, appears to have toyed with this idea at one time, but he changed his mind decisively early in November, when Stanley, who had been invited to join Russell's administration – an offer that he had no intention of accepting – asked Disraeli what, if anything, he should say about the Conservative line on Reform. 'My idea', he told Disraeli, 'would be to strengthen the moderate as opposed to the thorough-going reformers.'[3] To his surprise, Disraeli counselled extreme reserve. He acquiesced, but was clearly puzzled.

Three weeks ago you and I both thought that a very small Bill passed by Conservative support would be the best solution of the difficulty; now you are against any Bill. No doubt you have good reasons for this altered view; but I don't know them and can only take it on trust that they are good.[4]

Disraeli did not believe in superfluous explanation and 'Young Morose' still ate out of his hand. It is, however, easy to guess the

---

[1] I should like to acknowledge the help I have received for the rest of this chapter and for the next from a Cambridge Ph.D. thesis soon to be published entitled *The Making of the Second Reform Bill*, which its author, Mr F. B. Smith, of Trinity College, Cambridge, and the University of Melbourne, kindly lent to me.

[2] Malmesbury, *Memoirs*, ii, 343.

[3] Hughenden Papers, Box 111, B/XX/S/724, November 4.

[4] ibid., B/XX/S/725, November 8.

way his mind was moving. His attitude to parliamentary reform was throughout these years purely opportunist. He must have seen that there was a good chance of bringing the Government down. For this purpose the last thing he wanted to do was to co-operate in a moderate Bill. On the contrary, the less moderate Russell's Bill, the greater the likelihood of his fall owing to a right-wing Liberal rebellion.

Disraeli got his way with Stanley, but his position in the party at large was precarious throughout the autumn and winter of 1865–6. Derby did little to help. He gave no lead on any of the controversies of the day, which included the case of Governor Eyre, the question of Cattle Plague compensation, and a revolt against the Malt Tax, as well as parliamentary Reform. Malmesbury, replying on October 23 to Carnarvon, who had deplored Derby's attitude, referred to 'the almost total want of communication between him and Disraeli. The latter does not court it. The former is too proud to press it.'[1] Illness and age were probably the reasons. The Conservatives were in a state of considerable unrest and matters were complicated by the attitude of the Liberal anti-Reform group, 'The Third Party', as it was called. They disliked both Derby and Disraeli, but there was just a possibility that they might serve under Stanley. Joliffe, the Chief Whip, told Derby of this plan, and Northcote in his diary records Joliffe's account of Derby's reaction. 'Ah! they think if they can get him they can float, but I don't think they will get him; and if they do, they won't float.'[2] There was not much love lost between father and son either then or later. As Northcote puts it in the same entry: 'Joliffe said the Third Party was looking to Stanley as leader and would act with Disraeli in any other capacity. They said, "Lord Derby might be disposed to sacrifice himself for the advantage of his country and his son." I said I thought him much more likely to do it for the former than the latter, to which Joliffe assented.'[3]

Although other names were mentioned from time to time, Stanley seems to have been the only serious possibility during these years as a replacement for Disraeli. But he did not aspire to be a candidate. Disraeli, who had himself suggested Stanley as an alternative Prime

[1] Sir A. Hardinge, *Life of the Fourth Earl of Carnarvon* (3 vols, 1925), i, 272.

[2] Andrew Lang, *Life, Letters and Diaries of Sir Stafford Northcote, First Earl of Iddesleigh* (2 vols, 1890), i, 241.

[3] British Museum, Add. MSS, 50,063A, February 22, 1866. The words after 'country' are omitted in Lang, i, 242.

Minister in 1859, returned to the theme in the autumn of 1865, when it seemed quite conceivable that Derby intended to retire. According to Disraeli, Stanley 'was horrified at the idea, declared that he was willing to act under Disraeli and would take the Foreign Office if desired, but would not take the Government himself'.[1] Later Disraeli, too, became convinced that Stanley had not got the qualities of a leader. Northcote reported to him on March 8 a plan of Lady Salisbury[2] that Stanley should take office under Gladstone at the head of a Conservative-Liberal alliance. Disraeli pooh-poohed the notion as

> dreams of princesses in fairyland. Lady Salisbury wants Stanley to take a leading place. It won't do. W.E.G. and S. sound very well. One is a man of transcendent ability; the other, though not of transcendent ability has considerable power. But neither of them can deal with men. S. is a mere child in such matters. The other, though more experienced, is too impetuous and wanting in judgment to succeed as a leader.[3]

Other names were occasionally canvassed. One was General Peel, Sir Robert's brother, who had once challenged Disraeli to a duel. But they were on good terms now and he had no such ambitions. As for the various more far-fetched suggestions, such as a coalition of Whigs and Tories under the Dukes of Cleveland, Devonshire, or Somerset, or under Clarendon, or even Cranborne, there was never much in them. Derby and Disraeli were in a similar position to Baldwin after the election of 1923. There was much dissatisfaction with the leadership, but no one could decide on any practical alternative.

On March 12, after numerous wrangles and last-minute changes, Gladstone, to a tepid House and an unenthusiastic Liberal party, announced the principal features of the new Bill. It dealt with the franchise only and it seemed mild enough, reducing the occupation qualification in the boroughs from £10 rating to £7 rental and in the counties from £50 rental to £14 rental. There was a provision that county leaseholders and copyholders resident in towns should vote

---

[1] Lang, *Northcote*, i, 232, Northcote's diary, February 4, 1866.

[2] The stepmother of Lord Cranborne. Her husband died in 1868 and she married Stanley, who had by then succeeded to his father's earldom, in 1870. She was fifteen years older than her second husband.

[3] British Museum, Add. MSS, 50,063A. Lang, i, 251, omits the name of Lady Salisbury.

in the counties where their tenements were situated. This partisan clause was the obverse of the equally partisan one in Disraeli's 1859 Bill requiring 40*s* freeholders resident in boroughs to vote in the borough instead of the surrounding county. There were some fancy franchises, but less elaborate than Disraeli's. It was reckoned that the Bill would enfranchise some 400,000 new voters, about half of them working class, but that the borough constituency would still retain a majority of the other classes even if all the new borough voters belonged to the working class. The Bill would give the vote to rather more than one in four of the adult male population in England and Wales, whereas hitherto it was the privilege of slightly under one in five.

The county provisions of the Bill alarmed the Conservatives, who feared that the county leaseholders in the boroughs together with the new voters in the non-borough towns and the suburbs would swamp the safe Conservative tenant farmers. The Bill also alarmed the Whig owners of small boroughs, not so much in itself as for the redistribution of seats which was bound to follow. Disraeli, who was supported by such personnages as Carnarvon and Cranborne, now made up his mind for root and branch opposition. Derby fully agreed, though owing to an attack of gout he was unable to attend the party meeting on March 16, where Disraeli made, according to Northcote, 'a capital speech, reciting the history of the Reform Bills since 1852; throwing all the blame of the present agitation upon W.E.G.; objecting principally to the county franchise proposed in the Bill . . . We must leave it to our leaders to decide in what form the opposition had better be made, having reference especially to the feelings and dispositions of our friends on the other side.'[1]

The friends on the other side, compared by Bright to the inmates of the Cave of Adullam, 'everyone that was in distress and everyone that was discontented', made most of the running, and Disraeli played a congenial part as a wire-puller behind the scene. The Cave was led by Robert Lowe, a pugnacious, quarrelsome, Wykehamist albino who sat for Lord Landsdowne's pocket borough, Calne. He hated democracy. His reasons were essentially cool symmetrical ones of intellect, a sort of Benthamism in reverse. He was also influenced by his experience of Australia and America, and perhaps by the accident of having been hit over the head during an election

[1] Lang, *Northcote*, i, 253.

riot in 1860. He had a first-class, if rather donnish, brain, and an acid, sardonic mode of speech.

Even at this stage when a temporary alliance of convenience kept them on parallel lines there was no intimacy between Disraeli and Lowe. They had nothing in common except physical short-sightedness. Lowe, so Northcote was told, 'has no dislike for Disraeli, but a good deal of contempt for him'. Disraeli had little reason to be predisposed in favour of Lowe. His brother, James, had been Lowe's fag at Winchester, and, as Disraeli noted a year or so earlier, was accustomed to say, 'No one knew what a bully was till he knew *him*.'[1] Lowe's hard doctrinaire intellectual approach was utterly alien to Disraeli's intuitive, romantic, flexible opportunism. No letter from Lowe survives among Disraeli's papers. They seem to have communicated, if at all, through the intermediary of Lord Elcho, a leading Adullamite. Later, they were to be on terms of deadly animosity.

The great parliamentary battle over Russell's Bill was dominated by Lowe and Bright. Lowe was fighting, not for the principle of aristocracy – he had no use for picturesque tradition or nostalgic sentiment – but for what would now be called 'meritocracy'. The case has seldom been better stated, nor has its answer been more splendidly made than by Bright, who supported the Bill, not for itself but as the stepping-stone to better things. Gladstone, too, made a fine contribution to a debate which for sheer intellectual quality is generally agreed to have been unrivalled in any political assembly of modern times. But Gladstone was hampered by having to defend the details of a Bill riddled with anomalies. As for Disraeli, he made some clever and amusing speeches, but in general bided his time and encouraged others.

The first crucial division was taken on the second reading when Lord Grosvenor, a dissident Whig, seconded by Stanley, moved an amendment requiring the Government to bring forward its redistribution scheme before the House decided on the changes in the franchise. In one of the most crowded houses ever known the Government only won by 318 votes to 313. Thirty-five Liberals voted with the opposition, and another six were absent. One Conservative voted with the Government. Dismayed by this rebuff, a section of the Cabinet favoured resignation, but Gladstone was strongly against it, and the Government resolved to carry on,

[1] Hughenden Papers, Box 26, A/X/B/26. Note by Corry, October 1871.

hoping to conciliate the Adullamites by agreeing to take the proposed redistribution of seats along with the proposed extension of the franchise. This was a great tactical concession to the Opposition. Any redistribution measure was bound to offer a far wider target than one confined merely to the suffrage, for it would be opposed by most of those who found their seats redistributed out of existence.

Nevertheless it required all Disraeli's skill to bring the Government down. On May 10 came the disastrous failure of the great banking house of Overend and Gurney, followed by a crash on the Stock Exchange and a rise in the bank rate to 10 per cent. Some of the Adullamites began to waver. To throw out the Government might seem factious at such a moment. Anyway, they did not really want to throw out the Government, with the consequential risk of a dissolution. They wanted Russell to shelve the Bill, but remain in office. Disraeli, therefore, had to tread a delicate path. He could not beat the Government without the help of the Adullamites, but it was difficult to persuade them to vote with him if the Government threatened to resign. He played his hand very adroitly. He was extraordinarily skilful at managing men, and his talent was needed to the full. He made one blunder, or rather his secretary Earle did. A highly technical point of parliamentary procedure was involved, but Earle displayed more conceit than knowledge when he confidently asserted that Derby, who had warned Disraeli of the error, was in the wrong.[1] Disraeli trusted much to Earle, but this episode which involved an embarrassing withdrawal may have given him doubts. Earle was not destined to remain his confidant much longer.

On June 7 a procedural amendment by Stanley was lost by twenty-seven votes. Later that evening Walpole's amendment to substitute £20 for £14 in the counties – a direct challenge – was only lost by fourteen. Five days later Ward Hunt, a Conservative county member, proposed an amendment to substitute rating value in the counties, a proposal which, since rates were always lower than rents, would have put the equivalent rental value up to £16 at least. Hunt's amendment was only lost by seven. This last episode furnished an interesting comment on Disraeli's determination to subordinate all else to defeat the Government. The conviction of the Conservative county members that they would gain from

---

[1] ibid., Box 97 B/XX/E/371, ?May 27, 1866, Earle to Disraeli. The details are too complicated and arid to be worth repeating here. 'Lord Derby is wrong on every point', he recklessly wrote.

raising the proposed county occupation franchise to £16 or £20 was largely a delusion. Dudley Baxter, partner of Philip Rose and an able statistician, who advised Derby and Disraeli on these matters, came to the conclusion after a careful analysis that the general effect of lowering the county franchise to £14 would be to strengthen the Conservatives, because the £14 to £20 occupiers would probably divide two to one in favour of the Conservatives and their enfranchisement would help to swamp the 40s freemen resident in the boroughs, who voted in the counties and were overwhelmingly Liberal.[1] But neither Derby nor Disraeli was prepared to risk a quarrel with the county members. It was too late to convince them that the amendment was unfavourable to the Conservative party. The great object was to bring down the Government, and so Baxter's memorandum was quietly disregarded.

The Conservatives were in high fettle after this near miss. They had begun the session in a minority of seventy. They were now in a minority of only seven. One more heave and the Government would either go out or drop the Bill. Disraeli felt that the next initiative would come best from the Adullamites. He and Taylor, the Chief Whip, drew up a list of possible anti-Government Liberal peers to meet at Lord Lansdowne's, and sent it to Derby, who was at last galvanized into activity. He returned it with comments and he helped to persuade likely men to turn up.[2] The meeting at Lansdowne House decided that the best manoeuvre would be to move an amendment to the borough franchise on the same lines as Hunt's for the county, ie to substitute rating value for rental. Lord Dunkellin, son of the Marquess of Clanricarde, was chosen to move it.

The case against this amendment was overwhelming because of the extraordinary anomalies and complete lack of uniformity in the assessment of rateable values. But Gladstone was very inadequately briefed, and the Cabinet could not decide whether or not to make the matter an issue of confidence. It was only at the very last moment that Gladstone, apparently on his own authority, indicated that the Government might resign, but it was too late by then to rally Adullamite waverers. The debate turned largely on the broad question of Reform. Disraeli did not speak, but he had been very active behind the scenes, using all his skill in persuasion and cajolery to win over waverers. These tactics may well have paid

[1] ibid., Box 44, B/XI/D 74, Memorandum by Baxter, June 12.
[2] ibid., Box 110, B/XX/S/345, Derby to Disraeli, June 10.

better dividends than a speech. When the division was taken the amendment was carried by 315 to 304, forty-eight Liberals voting with the Opposition. A week of chaos ensued before Russell resigned. The Queen was passionately anxious for him to remain. The Cabinet was divided, some wishing to carry on, some – Gladstone above all – to dissolve, some to resign, but the Chief Whip strongly advised against dissolution, and on June 26 Russell tendered his resignation to the Queen. Thus ended amidst a babel of intrigue and recrimination the last Whig Cabinet to govern Britain.

The week was no less eventful for the Opposition. The obvious solution to the parliamentary problem created by the fall of Russell was a broad anti-reform coalition, and this was what seems to have been generally expected.[1] Indeed, as we saw earlier, the possibility of fusion between the right-wing Whigs and the Tories had been discussed off and on ever since the death of Palmerston. But in the event nothing of the sort occurred. Why? As so often in the confused politics of the 1850s and 1860s the answer – or a large part of it – lies in the personality of Disraeli. The Third Party made it clear that they had not unseated Russell to instal Derby if this meant serving under Disraeli's lead in the House of Commons. Indeed, their preference was to keep out Derby, too. On June 22 or 23 Grosvenor told Derby through an intermediary that he could not guarantee the support of the Cave for a Tory government, and that the best answer would be a Whig Prime Minister in the Lords, such as Clarendon, with Stanley as leader of the House of Commons.[2] Elcho wrote to Disraeli on similar lines.

Disraeli was not going to tolerate this. As soon as he saw Grosvenor's letter he told Derby that the terms were 'not consistent with the honour of the Conservative party'.[3] Certainly on the face of things the Third Party was pitching its claim high, but its conditions may not have been quite so 'preposterous', to quote Buckle, as they have come to be regarded since. Many of the Adullamites seem to have genuinely believed that Derby intended to make way for a Whig Prime Minister; and although the Cave could only command one-seventh of the Conservative numbers, had not the Peelites been in much the same relation to the Whigs at the end of 1852, and

[1] Maurice Cowling, 'Disraeli, Derby and Fusion, October 1865 to July 1866', *Historical Journal*, VIII, i. (1965), 31–71, gives the most authoritative account of the crisis, and I have drawn on it freely.

[2] M. & B., iv, 439–40, Derby to Disraeli, n.d. [June 22 or 23].

[3] loc. cit.

did not they contrive to acquire the premiership together with half
the seats in the Cabinet? Moreover, although he denied it, there is at
least a possibility that Earle had given Elcho a wrong impression
of Derby's readiness to efface himself:[1] one is tempted to wonder
whether Derby or Disraeli, without making any specific promise
gave an impression to the Third Party at a time when its support
was hesitant that they would agree to some such terms as Grosvenor
and Elcho envisaged.[2]

There is no proof of this, but clearly both the Tory leaders knew
that a coalition would only be possible if they stepped down. This
was a political fact which they had discussed quite frankly on more
than one occasion. The only leading Conservative who had a chance
of being accepted as Prime Minister in a coalition was Stanley.
Whatever ideas Derby may have toyed with in the past, his action
was quite decisive now. He made no overtures to the Adullamites
while Russell's Government struggled in its death throes; they on
the contrary made overtures to him. Disraeli meanwhile urged him
to stand firm:

> The amiable and spirited Elcho has played his unconscious part
> in a long matured intrigue.
> The question is not Adullamite; it is national. You *must* take
> the Government; the honour of your house and the necessity of
> the country alike require it.
> What is counted on and intended (not by the Court) is that you
> should refuse; that a member of the late Government shall then
> be sent for, and then that an application should be made to a
> section of your party to join the Administration; which applica-
> tion will be successful, for all will be broken up.
> There is only one course with the Queen: to kiss hands.
> And the effect will be this: in twenty-four hours, all, Lans-
> downe, Granville (if you want him), Clanricarde . . . will be at
> your feet.[3]

Derby was sent for by the Queen on June 27. On the following day
he called a meeting of twenty-two of his principal supporters. They
were unanimous that he should accept the Premiership and first try
to form a government on a coalition basis. Moreover, everyone
except Lord Bath agreed that if the Adullamites refused Derby
should go ahead with a purely Conservative administration.

[1] Hughenden Papers, Box 97, B/XX/E/379, Earle to Disraeli, n.d. [June 24 or
25].
[2] Cowling, 63.
[3] M. & B., iv, 440; June 25, 1866.

Derby accepted this advice, which was indeed his own preference. He gave no opportunity to Clarendon, Granville, or any of the Whig 'possibles' to stake a claim for the premiership. Nor did he give his son a chance; their relations were distant; Derby distrusted Stanley's views on church questions, and doubted his ability to lead. These decisions killed a coalition, and must have come as a relief to Disraeli. His own position was safe now. It is doubtful whether he believed what he said about winning over the Third Party, but it may have seemed wise to appear optimistic. Derby, as Disraeli well remembered from 1855, needed encouragement: the important thing was to get him into a government-forming mood, even if he, too, knew at heart that he would make little progress with the Cave. In the end the only Liberal to join was Michael Morris, MP for a pocket borough of Lord Clanricarde. He was given permission by his patron to become Solicitor-General for Ireland.

Disraeli would have been the chief victim of fusion had it taken place under a Liberal Prime Minister or even under Stanley. If Derby had seriously aimed at fusion, he, too, would have had to jettison Disraeli. But, to his credit, he had no intention of paying that price. He told General Grey that he '*could* not throw Mr. Disraeli over in order to get [Lord Clarendon]'.[1] Undoubtedly Disraeli's own preoccupation throughout the crisis was a personal one. His fortunes were tied to Derby's success in forming a purely Tory administration – also to Derby's remaining as leader of the party. If Derby had retired at this time it was by no means certain that Disraeli would have succeeded him. These circumstances are quite enough to explain his anxiety to torpedo an anti-reform coalition. There is no contemporary evidence for the theory that his real purpose was to save the Conservatives from being tarred with the brush of reaction and to prepare the way for a Reform Bill of his own. This seems to be an *ex post facto* myth to account for a series of manoeuvres inspired by enlightened opportunism rather than a deep-laid plan.[2] Nevertheless it remains true that Disraeli's personal interests coincided on this occasion with those of his party and that any other course would have been fatal to it. At long last, after seven years of apathetic defeatism, the Conservatives had been restored to a state of vigour. The whole question of their being

[1] Royal Archives, C. 32.480. Memorandum of conversation with Lord Derby, June 29, 1866.
[2] Cowling, 70.

able to furnish a plausible alternative to Whig-Liberal rule was at stake. If Lord Bath's advice had prevailed, they might have declined into a mere appanage of the Whigs. Derby's third government, like the previous two, was to be little better than a caretaker administration while the Whigs and Liberals resolved their squabbles, but the Conservative party survived; and in the end it was the Whigs who joined them, not they the Whigs.

Disraeli got his way over the composition of the new Cabinet to a far greater extent than ever before. His strength was shown by his making Northcote's entry into the Cabinet a condition of his own. Derby demurred, but gave way. Disraeli also won on another issue. He secured the Foreign Office for Stanley. He was helped by Malmesbury's voluntary withdrawal, but Derby nevertheless had doubts, shared incidentally by the Queen, about his son's suitability. Others who could be said to be Disraeli's men and received Cabinet Office were the Duke of Buckingham, Gathorne Hardy, and – ironically, in view of later events – Carnarvon. But he was unable to secure the ejection of Chelmsford from the Woolsack, the only alternative, Cairns, being needed in the Commons. Derby, however, warned Chelmsford that he could not expect to be kept there for long.

The Cabinet, far stronger than either of its predecessors, was made up as follows:

First Lord of the Treasury	Earl of Derby
Lord Chancellor	Lord Chelmsford
Lord President	Duke of Buckingham
Lord Privy Seal	Earl of Malmesbury
Home Secretary	Spencer Walpole
Foreign Secretary	Lord Stanley
Colonial Secretary	Earl of Carnarvon
War Secretary	General Peel
Indian Secretary	Viscount Cranborne
Chancellor of the Exchequer	B. Disraeli
First Lord of the Admiralty	Sir John Pakington
President of the Board of Trade	Sir Stafford Northcote
President of the Poor Law Board	Gathorne Hardy
First Commissioner of Works	Lord John Manners
Chief Secretary for Ireland	Lord Naas

There were the usual blunders in the course of the Government's formation, especially over minor posts, and the usual hard feelings. Derby offered the Vice-Presidency of the Council to two people simultaneously,[1] and he offended Lord Stanhope, who seems to have been given reason to expect the Duke of Buckingham's post, by not only passing him over but saying nothing to him. 'It is certainly strange', wrote Northcote, 'that Lord D. should have been so awkward, but he is awkward in these matters and there is no denying it.'[2]

A few days later Disraeli, annoyed at another instance of Derby's awkwardness, delivered a rebuke, such as he would have scarcely risked a few years before. Derby had apparently turned down applications for honours with some terseness. Disraeli wrote enclosing a copy of his own form of reply, a soft answer warning applicants of the difficulties, but promising to forward the application to Derby:

> Unfortunately the very individuals who have received this sort of reply from me have received subsequently from you or by your authority answers of a very different kind which have created great discontent . . . I doubt whether the leader even of a party with a majority can ever afford to give point blank refusals to applicants for honours. I have reason to believe that Sir Robert Peel never did, altho' he had a large majority and practically was very parsimonious in the distribution of dignities.[3]

Disraeli made one important personal change. Earle, who had been back in Parliament since 1865, indicated a desire for an official position. Disraeli, although there is no sign in his papers of any cooling off, may well have felt that his private secretary, who had made two quite tiresome errors through lack of judgement, would be better placed elsewhere. He offered Earle the secretaryship of the Poor Law Board at £1,100 p.a., which was accepted with alacrity, but it would appear that Earle hoped to continue as a personal confidant of Disraeli. His hopes were to be disappointed. Disraeli had his own ideas about that role. Ignoring Earle's suggestions for a successor, he appointed the young man he had met at Raby Castle.

'Monty' Corry was the perfect choice. He was devoted to Disraeli, highly capable, and devoid of personal ambition. After Mary Anne's death he was to become even more indispensable, managing those tedious domestic matters such as engaging servants,

---

[1] British Museum, Add. MSS, 50,063A, Northcote's diary, July 4, 1866.
[2] ibid., July 8.
[3] Derby Papers, Box 146/2, Disraeli to Derby, July 16, 1866.

finding houses, etc., at which Disraeli was so hopelessly incompetent. He was gay, amusing, and very good-looking. He moved easily in society, and though relatively poor himself, was a regular guest at the great country houses. He never married – an undoubted asset in a private secretary, but he was no misogynist. On the contrary, he was what the Victorians used to call a 'gay bachelor', and he conducted numerous love affairs. Disraeli had no objection to this. 'What a Lothario Monty is', he noted in tones far from censorious. Corry under Disraeli's will was given absolute discretion in dealing with his master's papers. It is perhaps symbolic of the difference between two social worlds in Victorian England that he preserved intact the evidence of Disraeli's affair with Henrietta, against the advice of the virtuous *bourgeois*, Sir Philip Rose, who wanted it to be destroyed. To Corry such an episode was a normal part of life in the circles in which he moved.

Disraeli was soon on terms of far closer friendship with Corry than he had been at any time with Earle. It is of Corry that he is thinking in a famous passage in *Endymion*:[1] 'The relations between a Minister and his secretary are, or at least should be, among the finest that can subsist between two individuals. Except the married state, there is none in which so great a confidence is involved, in which more forbearance ought to be exercised, or more sympathy ought to exist.' T. H. S. Escott, a contemporary journalist, described Corry in 1878 as 'the social link that connected Lord Beaconsfield with a world which he surveyed as a contemptuous critic rather than inhabited as a born denizen. He gave the Prime Minister all the gossip of the clubs and all the chatter of the drawing-rooms . . .'[2] Corry did more than this. He was not only loyal, devoted and discreet, he was also, behind a manner of great charm and gaiety, extremely efficient. To quote Escott again, '. . . . in a word the model of secretaries'.

---

[1] Ch. 49.
[2] T. H. S. Escott, 'Lord Carnarvon's Resignation', *The Gentleman's Magazine*, ccxii (1878), 357–8.

CHAPTER XXI

The Second Reform Bill

1866–7

1

The first question which faced the new Government was what to do about Reform. There was clearly a good deal to be said for doing nothing. Disraeli, it is true, threw out to Derby, probably on July 21,[1] the idea of taking up Gladstone's Bill where it stood, substituting £6 and £20 rating for boroughs and counties, enfranchising the northern boroughs, disfranchising no one. 'You could carry this in the present house and rapidly. It would prevent all agitation in the recess; it would cut the ground entirely from under Gladstone: it would smash the Bath Cabal, for there would be no dangerous question ahead. Think of this.' Nothing came of this ingenious notion. Nor do the famous Hyde Park riots[2] of July 23, 24 and 25 appear to have affected either Derby or Disraeli. The session ended quietly with no promise of action.

But during the next seven weeks something made Derby change his mind. Perhaps it was the growing strength of the Reform movement in the country, the numerous orderly but determined mass meetings addressed by Bright and other popular orators. On September 16 he told Disraeli, 'I am coming reluctantly to the conclusion that we shall have to deal with the question of Reform.'[3] He suggested that they might proceed by way of resolutions in Parliament which could form the basis of a subsequent Bill. Disraeli was unconvinced, and his views were reinforced by Cranborne. Derby was not to be fobbed off. He received strong support quite independently from the Queen, and on September 27 again wrote to

---

[1] Smith, op. cit. 279. Disraeli's letter is dated July 29, which was a Sunday, and the letter begins with a reference to 'what Gladstone said yesterday'. The House did not sit on a Saturday, but on Friday, July 20, Gladstone had formally withdrawn his Bill. If this suggested dating is correct, Disraeli could not have been influenced by the Hyde Park riots, which only began on July 23.

[2] A mass meeting in favour of Reform scheduled to take place in Hyde Park on July 24 was forbidden. The crowd broke down the railings near Marble Arch and continued to demonstrate for the next two days.

[3] M. & B., iv, 453.

Disraeli. 'The Queen spoke to me about it the other day. She said she was most anxious to see it settled.'[1] Derby went on to say that he was 'not in favour of resisting all Reform, for which I believe that there is a genuine demand *now*, however it may have been excited'.

Derby had put his finger on the point. A year earlier the cause of Reform languished, but Russell's Bill and the publicity given to the debate in an age when the intelligent lower middle and upper artisan class read parliamentary reports with passionate interest, had transformed the situation. Paradoxically, no man advanced the cause more effectively than Lowe. His arguments with their disdainful dismissal of the whole working class as unfit to vote provoked a reaction which Bright exploited to the full up and down the country. Russell could have safely left Reform alone. The party which had come to power by destroying his Reform Bill could not.

At last, after yet another letter from Derby on October 9 outlining in some detail his plan for resolutions, Disraeli gave way. But it is interesting to note his reason: 'I had no idea when you first wrote to me about "resolutions" that you contemplated the possibility of not legislating the session they are passed. If we can succeed in that we shall indeed be on velvet.'[2] The correspondence effectively dispels the idea that the initiative for a Reform Bill or the original plan for the tactics in presenting it to Parliament owed much to Disraeli; and his last letter shows that he was mainly concerned to postpone legislation as long as possible.

But when once he had agreed to the idea of resolutions Disraeli was determined to snatch the maximum party advantage. Apart altogether from the general question of putting a stop to the rising mass agitation in the country, there were obvious tactical reasons for taking the initiative over Reform. The Conservatives were in office on sufferance. Their opponents when united had a majority of over seventy, and if the Conservatives merely waited upon events the Liberals would be sure to come together sooner or later on some issue, as they had done in 1852 and 1859. As long as Derby and Disraeli could take the initiative, whether they proposed resolutions or a Bill they might, if they played their cards well, keep the Opposition split.

Accordingly Disraeli gave short shrift to a proposal emanating from the Queen and Lord Grey that the whole matter should be

[1] Hughenden Papers, Box 110, B/XX/S/366.
[2] M. & B., iv, 454, October 12, 1866.

referred to a committee of the Privy Council on a non-party basis.
The Queen offered to mediate with the Liberals. 'Murmurings of
children in a dream', wrote Disraeli to Derby on October 21. 'The
royal project of gracious interposition with our rivals is a mere
phantom. It pleases the vanity of a court deprived of substantial
power . . .' Disraeli often used language that exalted the role of
the Crown, but not when it was inconvenient. An agreed non-party
solution was the last thing he wanted, for nothing would be more
fatal to Conservative prospects of retaining power. 'Our future,'
he continues in the same letter, 'and in some degree the future
of the country, depends on the course we shall chalk out for
ourselves.'[1]

Derby and the rest of the Cabinet evidently agreed, and nothing
came of the Queen's proposal. Before the introduction of the 1859
Bill, a special Cabinet committee had been set up to consider the
matter, and the subject was fully discussed by ministers in great
detail after the Committee reported. No such procedure was adopted
this time. Disraeli told Derby that it was unnecessary, as 'there is so
much previous knowledge now on the main subject'. It was true
that, thanks to the network of Tory agents who reported to him and
the statistical researches of Dudley Baxter, Disraeli did have a great
deal of information, though, as we shall see, not enough. But his
main motive was to avoid trouble with Cranborne, Carnarvon and
General Peel, the members of the Cabinet known to be the most
cautious over Reform.

On November 8 Derby and Disraeli presented the resolutions to
the Cabinet in a provisional form, and according to Carnarvon
pushed them through, largely because, although no one liked them,
the Opposition was 'so fragmentary and uncombined'. The resolutions were very widely drawn. The only specific points were that the
occupation franchise should be based on rating, that fancy franchises would be inserted, that no one class should have predominance, and that a Royal Commission should be set up to inquire
into borough boundaries and 'obtain such further information as
may be the ground for well-considered legislation'.[2] Throughout the
winter Disraeli and Derby were principally concerned to procrastinate. They were anxious to take the initiative away from the

[1] Derby Papers, Box 146/2. Disraeli wrote in similar language a day later to
Northcote, who was staying at Balmoral (M. & B., iv, 455).
[2] Hughenden Papers, Box 110, B/XX/S/374. Note in Derby's hand of 'Resolutions provisionally adopted November 8'.

Liberals, but they wanted to postpone legislation. The Royal Commission was vital for this purpose, as long as it could be provided with some plausible subject for investigation sufficiently complicated and indigestible to cause delay. To find such a topic was none too easy and it is in this context that Derby wrote his famous letter to Disraeli, 'Of all possible hares to start I do not know a better than the extension to household suffrage, *coupled with plurality of voting.*'[1]

But pressure for some immediate action was increasing before and after Christmas. The Reform demonstrations were more formidable than ever and Disraeli, though still adhering to a policy of delay, took the precaution of issuing in January his collected speeches on parliamentary reform under the nominal editorship of Monty Corry. It was as well to be prepared for all eventualities, and to stake in advance the Conservative claim to deal with the matter. At the Cabinet meetings during January Derby's 'hare' was discussed, and apparent agreement was reached on incorporating it in one of the resolutions. Plural voting, based on rateable value as in the parochial elections, could be made to produce something like 360,000 votes to counter-balance the four to five-hundred thousand who would get the vote under household suffrage. Both Cranborne and Carnarvon expressed some misgivings lest the counter-balance might all too easily disappear, but Disraeli, suiting his arguments to each of them separately, managed to persuade them.

Meanwhile Reform, though the most important, was by no means the only theme to engage Disraeli's attention. Foreign affairs was one. The events leading to the Luxemburg crisis in April 1867 were the subject of much correspondence between Disraeli and Stanley, and between Disraeli and the Queen. It is of interest only in so far as it foreshadows, however dimly, the conflict of opinion which was to arise ten years later over Stanley's handling of the Eastern question. Already we can discern faintly but unmistakably the future pattern; Disraeli and the Queen in favour of a positive policy, and Stanley supporting minimal intervention. Disraeli had attacked Palmerstonianism in the election of 1865, and his differences with Stanley must be seen in that framework. Neither wanted to copy

[1] ibid., B/XX/S/380, December 22. 'Plurality' meant that a voter could exercise several votes, according to his various qualifications. It was already a recognized principle in local government elections where the elector cast a number of votes according to the rateable value of his property. 'Duality' simply put the upper limit at two, however many headings under which the elector qualified.

Palmerston, but Disraeli began to think that the reaction was being overdone.

In general Disraeli was all for a policy which saved expenditure on arms, and as in 1852 and 1858, he soon found himself up against his old *bête noire*, the Admiralty. 'The maladministration, not to to say, malversation, of the Admiralty', he wrote to Derby on August 20, 1866,[1] 'has struck deep into the public mind and is at this moment, the predominant feeling of the nation. If dealt with vigorously it will divert attention from Parliamentary Reform . . .' Mr Laird, MP for Birkenhead, had told him that much of the trouble was caused by retaining excessive stores. The dockyards employed 18,000 men and had about £5m worth of stores. Laird, a great shipbuilder, employed 4,000, but, as soon as the value of his stores exceeded £60,000, waste began. If he had followed the Admiralty's practice he would have had over £1m worth of stores.[2] The other trouble was 'the vast sums which they have vainly expended in cobbling up old wooden ships' instead of building iron ones. Disraeli would not, he said, communicate with Pakington himself, but he begged Derby to assert his authority. All extraordinary motion in the great departments should come from you . . . A First Lord is surrounded by the criminals, and it requires intellectual grasp, and a peremptory firmness to deal with them.'

It is hard to say how effective Derby's efforts were, but he certainly wrote to Pakington. A month later Disraeli is again lamenting 'the fecklessness and absurdity of the administrative scheme of the Department. Power is exercised there by individuals who have no responsibility. If something is proposed Sir A. Milne will resign, I am told, or Sir John Hay if the proposition is not insisted on. Fancy a Secretary of the Treasury or an U. Sec. of State threatening to resign because he does not approve of his Chief's policy. The Admiralty should be remodelled on the general scheme, a Sec. of State with Under-Secretaries.'[3] And on February 2nd he writes: 'The Admiralty is beyond the control of a Chancellor of the Exchequer, or any other subordinate Minister. It is the Prime Minister who alone can deal with that department . . . It is useless to attempt to reason with them. The whole system of administration is palsied by their mutinous spirit.'[4] Disraeli did succeed to the

[1] M. & B., iv, 474.
[2] Derby Papers, Box 146/2, Disraeli to Derby, August 20, 1866.
[3] ibid., Disraeli to Derby, September 30, 1866.
[4] M. & B., iv, 478.

extent of obliging Pakington to do without a second supplementary estimate, and he managed to produce a surplus of £1,200,000 for the 1867 budget.

Disraeli's fiscal activities followed orthodox Treasury lines, and he was constantly on the look-out for economies. This inevitably made him regard certain matters in somewhat of a Little Englander spirit. For example, although he conceded the temporary need, he was strongly opposed to the maintenance of British forces in Canada any longer than required by the Fenian alarm. Colonies that claimed to govern themselves should defend themselves. He also favoured withdrawal from West Africa. He wrote to Derby:

> It can never be our pretence or our policy to defend the Canadian frontier against the U.S. . . . Power and influence we should exercise in Asia; consequently in Eastern Europe, consequently also in Western Europe; but what is the use of these colonial deadweights which *we do not govern?* . . . Leave the Canadians to defend themselves; recall the African squadron; give up the settlements on the west coast of Africa; and we shall make a saving which will at the same time enable us to build ships and have a good budget.[1]

Disraeli's imperialism was a later development, and essentially concerned with India, which appealed to something in his imagination in a sense that the 'colonies' did not.

Disraeli suffered one serious political loss during the autumn. The Attorney-General, Cairns, for whom he had a high opinion, and who had only missed the Woolsack because Derby was anxious to have his services in the House of Commons, asked to be appointed to a vacant Lord Justiceship. His reason was health. Possibly he may have expected Derby to get rid of Chelmsford and make him Lord Chancellor. If so, he was disappointed. Disraeli's feelings are expressed in a letter to Corry:[2]

> . . . I don't want to ask anything of the Lord Chancellor as I have always snubbed him and I believe he knows that I recommended Lord Derby not to reappoint him and if Cairns had had the spirit of a louse he would not have been reappointed.
>
> Only think of Cairns asking for the Lord Justiceship! It is a great blow for the party and mainly for myself. For he was my right hand in debate and with him I was not afraid to encounter Gladstone and Roundell Palmer. Now I have got them both without the slightest assistance.

[1] ibid., 476, October 17, 1866.   [2] Hughenden Papers, Box 95, B/XX/D/23.

2

The process whereby the 1867 Reform Bill was launched constitutes one of the oddest histories of confusion, cross-purposes and muddle in British political history. To begin with, there was no intention to bring in a Bill at all during 1867. Whatever Disraeli may have persuaded himself to believe later, the Cabinet at no time even discussed a Bill before Parliament opened on February 5. The plan at this stage was Derby's original one – resolutions, a Royal Commission, and leisurely legislation some time in 1868. But the drafting even of the resolutions in their final form for presentation to the House had been left amazingly late. They were due to be introduced on February 11. It was not till the 6th that the Cabinet attempted for the first time to formulate the actual wording of Derby's resolution about household suffrage and plurality of votes.

Some of the leading ministers were separately consulted in advance, and no one dissented at the meeting. But the next day General Peel, who either had not been consulted or had changed his mind, wrote to Derby to say that he could not remain if household suffrage was mentioned in the resolutions. To avoid a break-up at the start of the session Derby and Disraeli gave way, the latter acting as go-between. 'You will find him very placable,' Disraeli told the Prime Minister, 'except on the phrase "household suffrage", when his eye lights up with insanity.'[1] Accordingly, on February 9 the Cabinet agreed to omit household suffrage while leaving in plurality of voting.

Two days later Disraeli introduced the resolutions. The full debate was fixed for a fortnight later, February 25, but it was clear on the 11th that they were not going to have a good reception. The following day, in answer to a question from Lord Robert Montagu, Disraeli made what was either a blunder or a Machiavellian manoeuvre. He pledged the Government to bring in an immediate Bill. No doubt there were sound tactical reasons for doing so. Much pressure for legislation was piling up from all directions, including the Conservative back benches, and if the Government confined itself to resolutions, Gladstone and the Liberals were likely to bring in a Bill of their own. But Disraeli undoubtedly acted without authority from the Cabinet.[2] Not surprisingly his volte-face aroused

[1] M. & B., iv, 492, Disraeli to Derby, February 7, 1867.
[2] Lady Gwendolen Cecil, *Salisbury*, i, 224–5, quoting a memorandum by Cranborne and Carnarvon.

acute suspicion among those ministers who mistrusted the whole
Reform policy; and General Peel again threatened to resign.

Having committed himself, Disraeli now had to think up a Bill.
He saw Cranborne on February 15 and suggested a Bill based on
household suffrage in the boroughs counter-balanced by plural
voting, no one to have more than four votes altogether; but plurality
was to be based, not on rateable values as in parochial elections,
which had been the earlier suggestion, but on fancy franchises, such
as payment of 20*s* in direct taxation, possession of £50 in the savings
bank, and some sort of educational test. Cranborne was uneasy at
this change, realizing that it would be much less easy to defend
the extra votes if they ceased to be based on a well-established
principle in local government. But he agreed, subject to a £5 lower
limit (rating) for the borough occupier.[1]

The matter was discussed the next day in Cabinet, and a Bill on
these lines was agreed with one important modification; the maximum number of votes exercised by any one elector was cut from
four to two. The £5 limit did not satisfy Peel, who declared himself
opposed to any reduction in the borough franchise. Nevertheless, he
was persuaded by the Queen to remain for the time being. Derby
and Disraeli regarded the £5 limit solely as a concession to Peel. If
he was equally hostile to any reduction they saw no point in keeping
it, and so inhibiting themselves from outbidding the Liberals.
Accordingly 'to the extreme surprise'[2] of Cranborne and Carnarvon,
who had now drawn closely together, the Cabinet on February 19
dropped the £5 limit. Disraeli promised to produce statistics to
show the resulting balance of classes in the boroughs in time for a
final Cabinet on Saturday, February 23.

For the next three days Baxter and Corry worked frantically on
the figures. The difficulty of framing a Bill so belatedly and the
inadequacy of mid-Victorian statistical information were now all
too obvious. The fancy franchises offered insuperable problems.
Savings banks' records did not distinguish between the sexes. The
figures of direct taxation had to be taken from a return of 1861.
The educational qualifications included 'Ministers of Registered
Chapels', although there was no Act under which all chapels were
registered. But Baxter did his best and the result was most alarming. The working class on the assumption of a straightforward

---

[1] ibid., 229–30.
[2] loc. cit.

change from a £10 to a simple rate-paying suffrage would be in a majority of 335,000, or more than two to one. He recommended reversion to £5 coupled with plurality, not duality, of voting.[1] But Disraeli was convinced that it was too late to change. He had reason to believe that a rating suffrage was not as alarming as many people thought because a large number even of £10 householders refused to pay rates and thus disqualified themselves. He received suggestions to this effect from several sources and passed some of them on to Derby.[2] It seemed more than likely that a great many borough occupiers would fail to register, and there were various ways of making it difficult for them.

The important thing now was to prevent Cranborne and Carnarvon from finding out too much about Baxter's statistics. Derby accordingly opened proceedings in Cabinet on the 23rd by saying that he was in a hurry as he had another engagement.[3] Disraeli rattled out some of the figures, and the meeting closed with virtually no discussion. All seemed well, but the two leaders had reckoned without Cranborne, whose suspicions were now thoroughly aroused. He made his own calculations, working hard for the whole weekend, and discovered that even on the figures as presented, the fancy franchises would amount to a substantial number only in big boroughs where the Liberals anyway had an overwhelming majority. He consulted Carnarvon and Peel, and on Sunday night posted a letter to Derby which was tantamount to resignation.[4] Peel and Carnarvon made it clear that they would go with him.

Derby read the letter with consternation early next morning. 'The enclosed just received is utter ruin', he wrote to Disraeli at 8.45 am. 'What on earth are we to do?' Disraeli was not feeling well and had decided to stay in bed for the morning. 'This is stabbing in the back', he replied. 'I will come to you as soon as possible . . . It seems like treachery.'[5] It was indeed an embarrassing situation, although the two leaders had no right to blame Cranborne after the way in which they had tried to 'bounce' the Cabinet on Saturday. At 2.30 Derby was going to address a party meeting at Downing Street. At 4.30 Disraeli was due to explain the Reform proposals to the House. There was great difficulty in summoning ministers for an

---

[1] Hughenden Papers, Box 44, B/XI/E/5, n.d., memorandum by Baxter.
[2] M. & B., iv, 490; Hughenden Papers, Box 45, B/XI/G.
[3] Hardinge, *Carnarvon*, i, 345–6.
[4] M. & B., iv, 499–500.
[5] loc. cit.

emergency Cabinet. After frantic last-minute consultations the Cabinet decided, rather than lose the three ministers, to put forward a limited Bill, £6 rating franchise in the boroughs, £20 in the counties, fancy franchises but no plurality. This was agreed only ten minutes before the party meeting – a fact revealed later, for his own purposes, by Pakington. Hence the name of the 'Ten Minutes Bill' by which the measure received a dubious immortality. None of the Cabinet liked it.

Disraeli ate no luncheon that afternoon. He drank a single glass of wine at Downing Street,[1] and then went down to propound to a packed and expectant House the Cabinet's plan for Reform. He wished the House first to pass the resolutions and then to deal with the Bill. While he explained the details of the Ten Minutes Bill in a bored and unconvinced manner, indignation mounted among his audience. When he finished there was an uproar. He was probably by no means displeased.

During the next few days demand for a Bill based on household suffrage gathered momentum at the Carlton Club among Conservative back benchers. On February 26 Disraeli withdrew the resolutions and, barely anticipating Gladstone, undertook to bring in a reconsidered Bill. On the same day S. R. Graves, MP for Liverpool, John Laird for Birkenhead, Sir George Goldney for Chippenham and Colonel Jervis for Harwich represented to Disraeli the case for household suffrage.[2] He did not conceal his sympathy, and a meeting of 150 members at the Carlton Club was called by Laird for Thursday, February 28. Although no formal vote was taken, the great majority favoured household suffrage safeguarded by three years' residence, personal payment of rates and plurality. A minority headed by Disraeli's old enemies, Beresford Hope, who was Cranborne's brother-in-law, James Lowther and George Bentinck ('Big Ben') wanted the Ten Minutes Bill, but they were overborne.[3]

The Adullamites, too, had a meeting and plumped for household suffrage and plurality. Horsman gave notice of a Bill on these lines and Disraeli was delighted. 'The thing gets riper every hour', he told Derby, 'tho' I don't think it would have been so ripe, if we had originally proposed it – I must confess that.'[4] He evidently felt that Derby needed stiffening. The previous day he wrote twice to him

[1] T. E. Kebbel, *Lord Beaconsfield* (1888), 12.
[2] M. & B., iv, 503.
[3] ibid., 507–8.
[4] Derby Papers, Box 146/3, February 28, 1867.

warning him against any attempt at a deal with Gladstone or with the Whigs,[1] and on the same day as he wrote the letter quoted he also reassured Derby about the working classes.

> . . . What are called the 'working classes' in the small boroughs are those who are under the patronage of the Upper classes and depend on them for employment and existence. In great towns the 'working classes' are powerful trades formed into Unions and the employers are dependent on them.[2]

The point was that the Liberals would win anyway in the big boroughs, but the Conservatives would still be safe in the small.

Derby and Disraeli now felt strong enough to force the issue in Cabinet. On Saturday, March 2, they carried a proposal to revert to the earlier measure and drop the Ten Minutes Bill. The three ministers at once resigned. Peel would have, and Carnarvon might have, acceded to Derby's appeal to stay, but Cranborne was adamant, and they had pledged themselves to act with him. Lord John Manners describes the final scene:

> At last Lord Derby seeing it was useless to persevere, said, rising, 'This is the end of the Conservative Party.' Then as Cranborne was leaving the table, Peel said 'Lord Cranborne, do you hear what Lord Derby says?' But Cranborne took no notice, and the die was cast.[3]

Of course, it was not the end of the Conservative party. A day or so later Derby met Lady Cranborne on the crowded staircase at an evening reception. 'Is Robert still doing his sums?' the Prime Minister acidly inquired. 'Yes,' she answered, 'and he has reached rather a curious result; take three from fifteen and nothing remains.'[4] It was a good repartee, but no one is indispensable in politics. The vacant places were filled by a reshuffle, the Duke of Buckingham taking Carnarvon's place, Northcote Cranborne's and Pakington Peel's. Two dukes were brought into the Cabinet, Marlborough as Lord President, Richmond to the Board of Trade, while Henry Corry replaced Pakington as First Lord of the Admiralty.

Cranborne came to believe that Derby and Disraeli had secretly decided to bring in household suffrage with or without safeguards

---

[1] M. & B., iv, 506–7.
[2] Derby Papers, Box 146/3, February 28, 1867.
[3] Whibley, *Lord John Manners*, ii, 126, quoting Manners's journal.
[4] Lady Gwendolen Cecil, *Salisbury*, i, 237.

ever since summer 1866, perhaps even since 1859. This was not true, though some later remarks of both leaders give it plausibility. Certainly Disraeli had been through gyrations so extraordinary that a sinister explanation might well seem called for. Household suffrage with plurality of votes based on rating was proposed on February 6, only to be dropped on February 9. Procedure by resolutions and a Bill in the next session was proposed on February 11, procedure by resolutions and a Bill in the same session on February 12. On February 15 Disraeli suggested household suffrage, this time with plurality of voting based on fancy franchises. Next day the Cabinet agreed to a £5 limit with duality instead of plurality. On February 19 the £5 limit went and household suffrage returned. On February 25 under the Ten Minutes Bill a £6 limit was proposed and duality was dropped. On February 26 the resolutions were withdrawn. Finally on March 2 household suffrage was reinstated for the fourth time, and duality revived. Strange though these numerous changes may appear, they were the result of muddle, confusion, lack of forethought, inadequate statistics and Cabinet dissensions, rather than of a Machiavellian plan prepared by Derby and Disraeli. But Cranborne can be pardoned for suspecting the worst, especially as he had never really trusted Disraeli. From now onwards he became very bitter. It was perhaps fortunate for Disraeli that Cranborne had neither the inclination, temperament nor skill at managing men required to lead a rebellion against Disraeli such as Disraeli had led against Peel.

On March 4 Disraeli announced the withdrawal of the Ten Minutes Bill, and stated that a fresh measure based on personal payment of rates and dual voting would be introduced in a fortnight's time. He did not then appreciate the difficulties involved in personal payment. The object of his restriction was to keep down numbers by excluding not only lodgers but also the large number of householders who 'compounded' for their rates, that is to say, paid them through their landlord and so did not themselves appear on the rate book which was the basis of the electoral register. These were reckoned to constitute some two-thirds of all borough occupiers. The difficulty was that compounders above the £10 limit had to some extent been enfranchised already by an Act passed in 1851 at the instance of Disraeli's one-time boon companion in exploring the dissipations of the Near East, James Clay. Under this Act compounders who were prepared to apply each year to have their names entered in the rate book could get themselves on to the register. The new Bill would have disfranchised them. So Baxter, who was drafting it, tried to meet the difficulty by allowing the compounder to qualify if he paid the full rate to the landlord along with his rent. But the essence of compounding was that in return for the advantage of collecting from the landlord rather than a multiplicity of small occupiers the local authorities allowed rebates of anything up to 25 per cent. Compounders who wanted to vote would therefore in effect be fined the amount of the rebate. Nor was this all. The practice of compounding varied widely according to whether or not the local authority had chosen to come under the Small Tenements Act, which was a permissive measure. Vestries could thus in effect disfranchise a large section of occupiers by adopting the Act. This abuse was not new, but it would now affect far more people.

There were other difficulties in the Bill. The fancy franchises were unsatisfactory, even from a purely party angle. For example, the provision giving the vote to those who paid 20s in income tax enfranchised in practice only those whose incomes exceeded £120 p.a. These were the very best-paid artisans and successful small shopkeepers, who were supposed to vote Liberal. It excluded a large category of dependent and deferential lower-middle-class people, clerks in banks, solicitors' offices, and the like, who were reckoned to be Conservative.[1] The dual vote was a further complication. The Cabinet nearly broke up on the subject, and Disraeli, convinced the House would never accept it, secretly meant to drop it at the first opportunity.

Another oddity was the distinction made between occupiers above and below £10. The former were governed by the old law, that is to say they needed one year's residence, and could qualify in respect of occupying any 'building' or part thereof. But those below £10 under the new Bill had to have two years' residence, could only qualify in respect of a dwelling house and moreover had to occupy the whole of it.

The county franchise caused less difficulty. It was a straightforward reduction from £50 to £15.

As time went on Disraeli, prodded by Derby, began to be seriously worried about the drafting of the Bill. The truth was that

[1] Hughenden Papers, Box 47, B/XI/J/213, Ward Hunt to Disraeli, March 31, 1867.

Baxter was not up to the task. At the last minute Disraeli decided to consult Thring, the Home Office legal draftsman. He declared that Baxter's Bill was riddled with legal defects. Baxter at once took umbrage and refused to speak to Thring. Matters had thus reached an impasse on Thursday, March 14, and the Bill was due to be printed in draft for the Cabinet meeting two days later. 'It was painful,' wrote Disraeli to Derby, 'but decision was absolutely necessary. I decided for Thring. He will sit up all night . . .'[1] Thring did, and the Bill was ready in time. Baxter resigned in a rage.[2]

Derby and Disraeli took the then unusual step of summoning a party meeting on the 15th and expounding the Bill to their supporters before presenting it to the House three days later. Derby declared that he would recommend a dissolution if beaten on any major issue – a threat which did much to keep the waverers from wavering. The innovation of a party meeting was a great success. It made members feel that they were being kept in the picture, that their advice was appreciated and that their leaders trusted them. If Peel had pursued the same course over the Corn Laws he might have fared better.

The Bill that was to emerge at the end of the session bore little resemblance to the one introduced by Disraeli. What began as a limited addition to the borough franchise, hedged with careful safeguards, ended as simple household suffrage. It was a far more sweeping measure than the Bill rejected by the House a year earlier, and indeed more sweeping than anyone envisaged when Disraeli first expounded it on March 18. The explanation of this paradox is, of course, partly the changed climate of parliamentary opinion caused by the mass agitations which imparted an urgency to the Reform question, lacking in the previous year. But it is not the whole explanation. Even Bright whose views were relatively advanced would have been satisfied with a milder measure than the one which ultimately became law. The transformation of the Bill is explicable only by the determination of Derby and Disraeli to avoid a repetition of the humiliation imposed on them by Russell in 1859, and therefore to stay in office and pass a Bill of *some* sort, come what might. Since they were in a minority, this inevitably meant that the Bill would be shaped by others. Disraeli freely admitted that he

[1] M. & B., iv, 518.
[2] Hughenden Papers, Box 47, B/XI/J/89, Baxter to Disraeli, March 14.

depended upon the co-operation of the House, and that apart from rating suffrage and personal payment he was prepared to consider amendments to almost every clause of the Bill.

But there was a proviso which he did not publicly admit at first, although he came very near to doing so later. Whatever amendments he might accept from other members of the House, he had no intention of submitting to any suggestions from Gladstone. Disraeli was influenced partly by personal dislike, but there was another element in his calculations. He sensed that the mass of the Conservative party, buoyant with the knowledge that they at last had the political initiative, would follow him wherever he led them, as long as he could continue to make them feel that they were winning. But they would never think that they were winning if he was forced to amend the Bill at Gladstone's behest. The result was perhaps the strangest paradox of all. Gladstone's amendments, which would have prevented the indiscriminate enfranchisement of the borough occupiers, were rejected, while Radical amendments which greatly extended it went through with scarcely a debate. And all this was done by a Conservative Government which on principle and past practice had been prepared to concede only the minimum 'safe' increase in the number of voters. Disraeli was assisted in bringing off this remarkable manoeuvre by the general Conservative hatred of Gladstone and by the desire of a large block of members on both sides to get the question settled and done with. He was helped, too, by the ignorance of most MPs when discussing the technicalities of rating law, a dry, tedious and excessively complicated matter which bored the House. Disraeli was himself by no means an expert, but he knew a good deal and he knew what to avoid saying. Gladstone, who really did understand the subject, tended to explain it at such length that he soon lost the attention of his audience.

Although it was natural that Disraeli should be suspected of planning the final form of the Bill all along, most of the evidence is against that theory. He did, indeed, give it some colour by declaring later that he had been 'educating' his party, but this was a piece of retrospective boasting. He even on one occasion said that the Cabinet had been in favour of household suffrage since 1859, a statement at once challenged by Henley, and quite untrue. Disraeli contrived to put up, as most politicians do, a façade of consistency, but, in fact, he lived from crisis to crisis, improvising, guessing, responding to the mood of the moment. There is nothing to suggest that he was

other than satisfied on public grounds with the original Bill; but it is
true that he did not greatly care about its details, and he had convinced himself that even a very wide rating suffrage would in practice be innocuous because a high proportion of electors would not
take the necessary steps to qualify. Disraeli wanted to pass a Bill,
do down Gladstone and Russell, and stay in power. This was
Derby's attitude, too. There is no reason to think, as many people
did at the time, that Derby was persuaded or manipulated by
Disraeli. The younger man had indeed become more of an equal
partner than he had ever been before, and, as the main parliamentary battle had to be fought in the lower House, he was more prominent, and often felt obliged to take decisions on the spur of the
moment without consulting anyone. But Derby seems to have fully
approved the lines on which Disraeli conducted a masterly retreat,
disguising it all the while as a series of brilliant victories.

Disraeli could not have managed so successfully but for the
tactics of the Radicals headed by James Clay, who knew his Disraeli
well, and entered into secret correspondence with him on March 24,
soon after the introduction of the Bill.[1] Clay believed and had told
his fellow Liberals as early as February 26 that the best way of
widening the suffrage was to let a Conservative Bill go through on
its second reading; then to move a series of amendments in the
committee stage, so worded that they could be plausibly regarded
as details, and the Government would not lose face if it refused to
make them issues of confidence.[2] He was actually referring to the
Ten Minutes Bill, which had not then (February 26) been withdrawn, but the same tactics were applied to the wider measure. He
was convinced that the Radical cause would thus gain far more than
by joining with Gladstone in an attempt to throw out the Government, with the probable consequence of a dissolution which almost
everyone wished to avoid.

The attitude of Clay and his friends explains another strange
feature of the parliamentary history of the Bill. On its introduction
Gladstone made a devastating analysis. The Bill would enfranchise,
not 240,000 as Disraeli claimed, but only 140,00. He pointed out its
numerous anomalies, listing ten major defects. He wanted to abolish
the restrictions, personal payment, dual vote, etc., but to raise the

[1] ibid., Box 122, B/XXI/C/248.
[2] A. I. Dasent, *John Thadeus Delane, Editor of 'The Times'* (2 vols, 1908), ii, 191.
Letter from Bernal Osborne to Delane describing Clay's speech on February 26 to a
party meeting.

rating level to £5. This would confine the vote to the upper artisan class. He rightly saw that Disraeli's restrictions would probably disappear in committee and, like the majority of moderate reformers, he was against enfranchising any substantial section of 'the residuum', the name given to the impoverished masses reputed to be venal, improvident and irresponsible. Yet Gladstone was quite unable to carry his party with him to oppose the second reading of the bill. Disraeli, who had made a wonderfully clever reply to Gladstone's first onslaught, made an even better one in the debate on the second reading. He skilfully widened the gap between the Radicals and the Liberal leader. He presented Gladstone as a dictator endeavouring to force a series of wrecking amendments. He alleged that Gladstone was guilty of inconsistency in trying simultaneously to remove the restrictions of the Bill while inserting his own restriction in the form of a £5 rating level. At the end of a speech generally agreed by all those who heard it to have been 'the speech of the session', the House accepted the second reading without a division, and went into committee.

Gladstone now made a last effort to remould the Bill. He first tried to reinsert a fixed minimum rating value, but he was defeated by a rebellion on the part of Clay and his friends, known to history as the 'Tea Room Revolt', for the rebels met in the tea room of the House of Commons. Foiled in this attempt, Gladstone tried to revise the minimum by indirect methods. He proposed an amendment removing the requirement of personal payment of rates, believing that if this disappeared the House would be bound to bring back a £5 or similar minimum, for there would be no other way of excluding the 'residuum'. It was an ingenious proposal which had a chance of catching votes from both sides, the Radicals because it apparently extended the franchise, the Adullamites and the Cranborne 'Cave' because it prepared the way for resuscitating the £5 limit.

Derby was laid up with gout and Disraeli, who was temporarily in charge of the Government, at once saw the danger of this manoeuvre. He announced in a letter to his followers, which he took care to put in *The Times*, that the Government would give up the Bill if Gladstone's amendment was carried, and he hinted at a dissolution. When he wound up he made yet another of his well-judged attacks on Gladstone. The amendment was 'a declaration of war' and a 'party attack' dictated by 'a candidate for power' who forgot that he 'has had his innings'. Disraeli was at once vigorous, persuasive, amusing and conciliatory. At 2 am on April 13 the division was taken. The Government won by twenty-one votes. No fewer than forty-five Liberals paired or voted against the amendment, among them nineteen Adullamites and nine Radicals of the 'Tea Room Revolt'. Gladstone's manoeuvre had failed. Moreover, he persuaded only seven Tory dissidents, headed by Cranborne, into his lobby. The rest, including General Peel, could not swallow their dislike of the amendment and refused to support it even for the sake of bringing down Disraeli.

The division must be counted as a decisive step in Disraeli's career. He had already during previous debates acquired a personal hold over his party such as he never enjoyed before. He now consolidated it. There was thunderous applause in the House and, on the way to Grosvenor Gate, Disraeli looked in for a moment at the Carlton Club, where an excited crowd was eating and drinking in the large dining-room. Sir Mathew Ridley amidst cheers proposed a toast: 'Here's to the man who rode the race, who took the time, who kept the time, and who did the trick.' And the enthusiastic members implored him to stay to supper with them. But Disraeli detached himself and returned home. Mary Anne was up and waiting for him with a pie from Fortnum and Mason's and a bottle of champagne. He ate half the pie and drank all the champagne, and it was then that he paid his famous compliment to her: 'Why, my dear, you are more like a mistress than a wife.'[1]

3

Disraeli could retire for the Easter recess with a sense of satisfaction at the events of the last two months. Only one episode marred his contentment. Among the Tory rebels was none other than Earle. He had taken strong though irrational umbrage at the way in which Corry had displaced him in Disraeli's confidence, although it is difficult to see why. By accepting minor office he was bound to be in quite a different position. It has been surmised that his dissatisfaction came to a head because Disraeli refused him some request for promotion,[2] and this may well have been so. The three Cabinet ministers resigned on March 4, and that would have been the natural occasion for Earle to go if he genuinely disapproved of the Reform

---

[1] T. E. Kebbel, *Lord Beaconsfield and Other Tory Memories* (1907), 40.
[2] G. B. Henderson, *Crimean War Diplomacy*, 285.

Bill. In fact, he resigned on March 20, an interval long enough for him to have given up any hope of promotion as a result of the ministerial reshuffle.

He was foolish enough to make an attack on Disraeli in the House, but he was a feeble speaker and his performance excited general contempt.[1] It certainly did Disraeli no harm. He was very angry nevertheless. No doubt he had some cause, but his capacity for forgetting inconvenient facts is seldom shown better than in his letter to Lord Beauchamp on the subject of 'the treason of Earle' – a fine instance of the pot and the kettle in view of the way he had encouraged Earle's treatment of Cowley.

> I have known him for ten years and tho' warned from the first by the Cowleys, whom he treated as he has treated me, I utterly disregarded their intimations and ascribed them all to prejudice and misapprehension.
> I have worked for his welfare more earnestly than for my own, and do not believe that I ever, even in the most trying times, gave him a hasty or unkind word. I loaded him with favours and among them introduced him to you. I am ashamed at my want of discrimination.[2]

Some time later Sir William Fraser met Earle at a party. Earle told him: 'Disraeli and I have quarrelled and, as you know, the quarrel is absolutely hopeless; it can never be made up under any circumstances.' Earle added surprisingly: 'I know everything that occurred. It was not Disraeli's Bill: it was Lord Derby's.'[3] On that enigmatic note he fades from history. He did not seek re-election in 1868, and went into business, becoming an agent for Baron Hirsch in the Turkish railway negotiations out of which the Baron reputedly made a million pounds. He gave Earle £10,000 as a commission. Evidently Disraeli's former secretary had a certain business flair, for when he died in 1879 at the early age of forty-four he left £40,000.[4] He had continued to take an interest in politics and for a time kept up a correspondence with Cranborne, whom he no doubt reckoned as a sympathetic audience for his acid comments on his old chief.[5] In 1878 there appeared a series of venomous articles attacking Disraeli in the *Fortnightly Review*. These were widely

[1] See Fraser, *Disraeli and His Day*, 364.
[2] M. & B., iv, 528, April 18.
[3] Fraser, 365.
[4] Henderson, 288.
[5] Salisbury Papers.

attributed to Earle, but he denied any connexion with them in a letter to *The Times*.[1] After his death his papers were destroyed. Disraeli would not have regretted the fact, if he had known it. The story of his relations with Earle is not one of the more commendable passages in his life.

Disraeli had achieved his first objective in the Reform battle. He had defeated Gladstone, who contemplated retiring to the back benches. 'A smash, perhaps, without example', Gladstone noted after the division on April 13. He knew that he had been outwitted and decided that his only course was to intervene henceforth as little as possible. Disraeli was in a much better position now to carry his Bill, but the question of what would be in it remained open. As Stanley wrote, 'I think our Bill, or at least a Bill, is safe'. He was replying to a letter in the same slightly cynical vein from Disraeli, who was considering the question of the lodger franchise, a proposal which he had rejected as coming from Gladstone. 'I wish', he told Stanley, '. . . you would get up an anti-lodger speech or a speech either way; as I think our debates want a little variety . . .'[2]

Nothing sums up better Disraeli's attitude to the numerous amendments which were to be forced on him in committee. He was mildly against the lodger and the compounder, and mildly in favour of two years' residence, the dual vote and fancy franchises. But his preferences were not strong enough to prevent him from acquiescing in the disappearance of what he favoured and the insertion of what he opposed, provided that the suggestion did not emanate from Gladstone. The great thing was to go on winning. If an amendment seemed likely to be carried against him he must either declare it not to be a matter of confidence and accept it quickly enough to escape trouble from his back benchers, or cover up defeat by some face-saving formula. And all the while he had to keep the Liberal party divided, and isolate Gladstone from both the Radicals and the Adullamites.

To pilot the measure, however battered and bruised, to the harbour of the statute book required parliamentary talent of a very high order. Disraeli had to do it almost single-handed, although Gathorne Hardy, one of the ablest of his younger colleagues, was a considerable help to him. But Disraeli did not lean much on other ministers. 'General Grey entirely agrees with your Majesty that Mr.

[1] Henderson, 289.
[2] M. & B., iv, 535–6.

Disraeli is evidently the directing mind of the Ministry', wrote the
Royal Private Secretary on May 7.[1] He was usually alone in his
private room in the House, except for Corry, and Lambert, a Civil
Servant of the Poor Law Board and a statistician, who replaced
Baxter in the indispensable task of calculating the effect of the
numerous amendments.[2] He also frequently consulted Thring on
legal points. But in the House he acted largely on his own authority
and seldom sought advice from his colleagues. Very often he had no
time to do so, for emergencies frequently arose requiring a quick
decision. Throughout the session he remained calm, courteous,
urbane, and to all appearances completely in control of the business.
He spoke relatively little, but he was always there, always on the
alert. He never relaxed, even on days when the House grew intolerably stuffy in that hot summer, and members drowsed or slipped
away, bored by interminable discussion about the Compounding
Acts.

As soon as Parliament resumed after the Easter recess, the
Radicals moved in to the attack. Their first amendment to cut down
two years' residence to one was carried on May 2 by eighty-one
votes. Disraeli accepted defeat, declaring that it was not a vital issue
and that he was happy to defer to the opinion of the House. Next
came an amendment moved by a Radical, J. T. Hibbert, to allow
compounders to qualify by paying, not the full but the composite, ie
reduced rate, to the local authority. Disraeli considered that this cut
across his principle of direct rating, and moved a counter-amendment,
which would in practice almost certainly have been either legally
meaningless or administratively unworkable.[3] It was carried on
May 9 by over sixty votes, but fortunately it was not destined to
become law.

In May, W. M. Torrens, another independent Radical, moved the
insertion of a lodger franchise. This had always been a great bone of
contention. Lodgers were regarded by good Conservatives as dangerous, though it is hard to see why. Torrens wanted lodgers at a
£10 rental to be enfranchised. Disraeli argued for £15. Bright
suggested a compromise, £10 *rating* value of the unfurnished lodging.
This would in practice be nearer Disraeli's figure than Torrens's. So
the former quickly agreed, and he also contrived to stiffen the

[1] *The Letters of Queen Victoria*, 2nd series, i, 424–5.
[2] W. White, *Inner Life of the House of Commons*, 76–77; M. & B., iv, 547.
[3] Smith, 404.

residence qualification. Lambert advised him that the lodger franchise thus restricted would make very little difference.[1] He was right. By 1869 only 12,000 lodgers were registered, over two-thirds of them in Westminster and Marylebone. Manchester had twenty-eight, and Birmingham only one.

On May 17 Grosvenor Hodgkinson, MP for Newark, moved the amendment which has put his name in the history books. He proposed to solve 'the difficulty of the compound householder's vote by the bold and simple expedient of abolishing the compound householder'.[2] Hodgkinson's amendment repealed the Small Tenement Acts, and declared that henceforth no one except the actual occupier could 'be rated to parochial rates in respect of premises occupied by him within the limits of a Parliamentary borough', ie every ratepayer would now pay rates personally. To the astonishment of most people, including a large number of his own by now bemused supporters, Disraeli accepted it. He knew that it would potentially enfranchise some half-million occupiers and, although there were reasons to think that the number actually enfranchised would not be so great, the increase was bound to disturb the numerous Conservatives who reckoned on the exclusion of the compounders. Yet Disraeli faced a genuine dilemma. He had always said that the essence of his proposed franchise was personal payment of rates. Hodgkinson's amendment left this principle intact. Moreover, there was another amendment in the offing, very similar and, in fact, more practicable, but sponsored by Childers, a mouthpiece of Gladstone. To let that go through would never do. Disraeli in a thin House of less than a hundred, without consulting a single colleague, agreed to abolish the compounder.

The sensation was immense. It was soon after 9 pm, and the news quickly spread. Members crowding in after dinner could scarcely believe their ears, and Disraeli acted only just in time to prevent a major debate. Nevertheless he was uneasy about the consequences and he wrote a long self-exculpatory letter to Gathorne Hardy.[3] His main plea was that Gladstone had attempted a '*coup*', and that he thought 'we might take a step which would destroy the present agitation and extinguish Gladstone & Co.' Hardy assented in slightly chilly tones. The amendment totally disrupted the whole landlord-tenant system and proved quite unworkable, but it was typical of

[1] Hughenden Papers, Box 48, B/XI/L. Memorandum of July 19, 1867.
[2] Lady Gwendolen Cecil, *Salisbury*, i, 268.   [3] M. & B., iv, 540-1.

the general attitude of the House that few members understood the difficulties. If Disraeli had appreciated these, which constituted by far the best argument against Hodgkinson, he might possibly have resisted.

The truth was that from the moment of his decision to rest the Bill on personal payment and rely on the exclusion of the compounders to preserve a 'respectable' household suffrage electorate, Disraeli was in a false position. The exclusion of compounders as such was indefensible. On the other hand, to exclude the poorest, and therefore, least responsible, most dependent and most corruptible householders was, by the standards of the day, perfectly reasonable. In practice the vast majority of such householders were compounders, but not all compounders were such householders. In reality the only way of excluding 'the residuum' was Gladstone's and Russell's, a fixed lower level. But this had become politically impossible as soon as Disraeli decided to use household suffrage as a shibboleth to appeal over Gladstone's head to the Radicals. In Gladstone's words, 'the Government, it must be admitted, bowled us over by the force of the phrase'.[1] The Government was now reaping the inescapable harvest of this manoeuvre. Disraeli appears to have managed the Cabinet somehow. Derby was ill off and on throughout this time. It is not known whether he approved of Disraeli's surrender to Hodgkinson, but there was little that he or any other minister could do about it.

The enfranchisement of compounders and lodgers meant that the fancy franchises became superfluous. Almost everyone who qualified under them was either a lodger or a householder. The dual vote never had much chance and it had vanished even sooner than the fancy franchises. The county clauses were less contentious. Disraeli accepted £12 as a compromise between £15 in the bill and £10 pressed by Locke King who had been fighting for fifteen years to secure that figure, but he was able to block a Radical attempt to abolish that well-known abuse, the creation of non-resident faggot-voters.[2]

During the later stages of the Bill, John Stuart Mill took advantage of his brief and incongruous interlude in the House to introduce female suffrage. Disraeli was by no means unfriendly to the idea,

[1] Morley, *Gladstone*, ii, 225.
[2] Voters artificially created by the minute splitting–up of property to give a bare qualification for the franchise.

anyway in principle. Indeed, few people would have gained more than he by votes for women. But he did not regard the proposal as practical politics and neither spoke nor voted on the motion, which was easily defeated by 196 to 73.

Before the Reform Bill had finished its course in the House of Commons, Disraeli introduced a Redistribution Bill. The guiding principle behind this was to keep the counties as rural as possible and to prevent their being swamped by the voters in the suburban areas which sprawled outside the boundaries of the expanding boroughs. At the same time new county seats were to be created, and unrepresented towns in the counties given seats of their own. The object was to limit as far as possible the effect of the lowered borough franchise by ensuring that the new and supposedly Liberal voters would vote in places which were either already Liberal or might be neutralized by the creation of extra Tory seats. Disraeli had to accept various amendments, but substantially he got his way. The Boundary Commission was packed with Conservative country gentlemen. No less than 700,000 people were transferred from counties to boroughs; and this was done in spite of substantial revision in 1868 by a Select Committee which Disraeli opposed. The Commission's original proposals were much more drastic.

Throughout the debates on the two Bills, Disraeli was the object of bitter attacks, particularly from Lowe, Cranborne and General Peel. The Redistribution Bill, said the latter, had taught him that nothing had so little vitality as 'a vital point', nothing was more insecure than a 'security', and nothing so elastic as the conscience of a Cabinet minister. On the third reading of the Suffrage Bill, Cranborne declared that its success had been 'purchased at the cost of a political betrayal which has no parallel in our Parliamentary annals'. Disraeli's conduct, said Lowe, 'may fail or not; it may lead to the retention or the loss of office; but it merits alike the contempt of all honest men and the execration of posterity'. Disraeli treated these diatribes with calm indifference. He could afford to. 'A majority is better than the best repartee', is supposed to be one of his sayings. He had his majority. The Bill was safe. He ridiculed Lowe's classical allusions with a phrase that stuck, 'the production of some inspired schoolboy'. But he did not forgive Lowe any more than Lowe ever forgave him. Nine years later he was to take a remorseless revenge on his old enemy, who had by then added more fuel to Disraeli's smouldering hatred.

The later history of the Bill is of less importance. Derby maintained complete control in the House of Lords, displaying an
authority over that body unrivalled since the death of the Duke of
Wellington. The only amendments carried there went through when
he was absent owing to gout. All of these, bar one, were rejected in
the House of Commons. That one was the minority vote[1] in three
member constituencies, an odd quirk in Britain's electoral history,
and disliked by Disraeli, despite its Conservative sponsorship. It is
principally memorable for inspiring the creation of the Birmingham
Caucus.

Both Disraeli and Derby suffered from that most common malady
of politicians, which only politicians can explain, the determination
to claim that they had never yielded to circumstances and had been
actuated by consistent policy throughout. This was quite untrue,
and laid them open to the charge of deliberate deception, surely
worse than mere inconsistency. Disraeli declared that household
suffrage had been his objective all along, and Derby made a haughty
and seemingly cynical speech in which he frankly admitted that he
was determined as soon as he took office for the third time not
to be 'made a mere stop-gap', and 'to convert if possible an existing
minority into a practical majority' by carrying a Reform Bill. He
described the Bill later as 'a leap in the dark' – probably the truest
epithet of all; and he never really denied Granville's charge of
having said to a friend that his object was 'to dish the Whigs'.

These utterances by the two leaders gave further ammunition to
their enemies. In the autumn both the *Edinburgh Review*, the organ
of the Whigs, and the *Quarterly Review*, the mouthpiece of high Tory
sentiment, launched vigorous attacks.

The article in the *Quarterly Review* was by Cranborne, written
with his characteristic hard, cold, melancholy clarity of style, like
the blue of a northern sky as the light begins to fade. He did not
spare the two leaders. Those who sought for a parallel to such a
betrayal would, he said, find no precedent in our parliamentary
history.

Neither the recklessness of Charles Fox, nor the venality of Henry
Fox, nor the cynicism of Walpole will furnish them with a case in
point. They will have to go back to a time when the last revolu-

---

[1] Each voter had two votes, the hope being that the Liberals would use up their
votes on their two most popular candidates, and the Conservatives might thus secure
one seat in such normally Liberal areas as Birmingham, Sheffield, Leeds, etc.

tion was preparing – to the days when Sunderland directed the councils and accepted the favours of James while he was negotiating the invasion of William.[1]

Disraeli got his own back on the two journals in November when he addressed a great Conservative banquet at Edinburgh. No man, he said, admired the Reviews more than himself. But they were like first-class post houses which carried on a roaring trade in the era of the stage coach.

> Then there comes some revolution or progress which no person can ever have contemplated. They find things are altered. They do not understand them, and instead of that intense competition and mutual vindictiveness which before distinguished them, they suddenly agree. The boots of the 'Blue Boar' and the chambermaid of the 'Red Lion' embrace and are quite in accord in this – in denouncing the infamy of railroads.[2]

Thus Disraeli claimed that Conservative policy was the policy of true progress, a claim which his successors have not ceased to reiterate from that day to this.

The 1867 Reform Bill is usually regarded as one of Disraeli's major achievements. So in a sense it was, but the picture of what happened has often been distorted. The most popular version, propagated by the Liberals and even today generally accepted, is that Disraeli enfranchised the householder at Gladstone's behest, in order to keep office; that the working-class householder having received the vote from Disraeli said, 'Thank you, Mr. Gladstone'; and accordingly voted him into power in 1868.

This theory, though correct on Disraeli's motives, leaves some facts unexplained. Gladstone was throughout in favour of a more restrictive Bill. His own amendments were invariably defeated, and he fades into the background during the later stages of the debate. If Disraeli had acted at Gladstone's behest, he would never have retained power. As for the gratitude of the working-class householders, much depends on the definition of 'working class'. But the compounders of whom so much was said did not get on to the register in time for the 1868 election. In fact, Hodgkinson's famous amendment was shattered on the rocks of landlord and local authority opposition, as well as that of the tenants. In 1869 Goschen carried a Bill which simply allowed compounders to register as voters, and

[1] Quoted in Cecil, *Salisbury*, i, 280.
[2] M. & B., iv, 557.

thus abolished the last semblance of 'personal payment'. This may explain an increase of nearly 190,000 in the borough electorate of 1874 compared with that of 1868.[1] And in 1874 the voters did not thank Mr Gladstone. The Conservatives won their first clear victory for thirty-three years.

But if the Liberal myth dissolves on examination, so, too, does a scarcely less widely held Conservative one. It is often believed that Disraeli, infinitely more discerning than the dull squires who followed him, had long perceived that household suffrage would enfranchise a class basically more Conservative than the electorate created in 1832; that he aimed throughout at this objective, carrying Derby with him and educating the rest of his party in the process; that the Conservative break-through in 1874 and their predominance in the last quarter of the nineteenth century was the result of Disraeli's vision of the new social forces at work.

This theory is scarcely more defensible than the Gladstonian one. Disraeli had indeed always claimed that the Conservatives were entitled to change an electoral system which seemed unfairly weighted against them. But he was never a Tory democrat, and, whatever he and Derby may have said in the first euphoria of victory, it was certainly not true that either of them had been planning to enfranchise the artisan householder as a safe Conservative. If they had, Disraeli would surely not have devoted so much care to neutralizing the effect of household suffrage by redrawing the county and borough boundaries. His and Derby's previous essays in Reform had not amounted to much more than gerrymandering disguised by the euphemism of 'lateral reform of the franchise'. They had the wide franchise of 1867 forced on them as the price of staying in power. All the evidence of his contemporary papers suggests that Disraeli saw the electorate in traditional terms of rural voters being Conservative, urban voters Liberal; and that he thought of politics as a matter of 'management' and 'influence' in the old-fashioned sense, not mass persuasion of a new class. He was sixty-three when the Bill went through. Political life had been like that ever since he first sought the suffrages of High Wycombe thirty-five years earlier. It would have been strange if he had suddenly seen it differently.

---

[1] It was 1,210,000 in 1868, 1,399,745 in 1874 – a rise of over 15 per cent. The potential increase as a result of Goschen's Act was much larger, but apathy and ignorance probably explain why more Compounders did not bother to register.

It is probably true that the Reform Bill did in the end enfranchise a class which for a number of reasons tended to vote Conservative rather than Liberal. It is also true that Disraeli, more than any other statesman of his day, had the imagination to adapt himself to this new situation and to discern, dimly and hesitantly perhaps, what the artisan class wanted from Parliament. Imperialism and social reform were policies which certainly appealed to them – or to a large section of them – and Disraeli seems to have sensed this in his curiously intuitive way, although even here it is important not to overstate the case. But there is nothing – or very little – to suggest that he had any such awareness in 1867. The importance of that period in his life is quite different. In the course of two years from the summer of 1865 he transformed his position in the Conservative party. It was his sparkling success in the session of 1867 which made him, as he had by no means been before, Derby's inevitable successor. In this respect as a stage in his career the session of 1867 can only be compared to that of 1846. For, whatever Cranborne and his exiguous 'Cave' might say – and they said much very acidly – the party as a whole was dazzled by his sheer parliamentary skill. They loved the sense of victory which he gave them; it was a feeling they had not had for years, some of them never before. And they were with a few exceptions so delighted to see the question settled over the heads of the official opposition that they blinded themselves to the magnitude of the concessions made to the Radicals. It was like a moonlight steeplechase. In negotiating their fences few of them saw where they were going, nor much cared so long as they got there first.

No one could exploit this mood more effectively than Disraeli. For him, too, it was an exciting sport, a race requiring steady hands, good nerves and plenty of courage. He was a master at disguising retreat as advance. Of Disraeli at this time it could be said as Lord Beaverbrook wrote of Lloyd George: 'He did not seem to care which way he travelled providing he was in the driver's seat.'[1] For what he did in 1867 he deserves to go down to history as a politician of genius, a superb improviser, a parliamentarian of unrivalled skill, but not as a far-sighted statesman, a Tory democrat or the educator of his party.

[1] Beaverbrook, *Decline and Fall of Lloyd George*, 140.

Part III

TOP OF THE GREASY POLE

CHAPTER XXII

Prime Minister
1868

1

The English Reform Bill received the royal assent on August 15, and the long session ended six days later. Disraeli retired with a more than usual sense of relief to Hughenden. There was as yet no question of a general election. A new register had first to be compiled, and it was necessary to pass Reform Bills for Scotland and Ireland. No election seemed feasible before 1869. But Disraeli did not have long to relax at Hughenden. King Theodore of Abyssinia in a fit of rage at some real or imagined slight had seized all the British subjects he could lay his hands on, and incarcerated them in chains at his mountain fortress and capital, Magdala. This could not be tolerated. Stanley sent an ultimatum – war unless the prisoners were returned within three months. It was clear by early September that they were not going to be released. Preparations were at once made for an expedition from India under the command of Sir Robert Napier. An autumn session of Parliament would be necessary in order to vote supplies.

Meanwhile Disraeli had accepted an invitation to attend a great Conservative banquet in Edinburgh. It was his first visit to Scotland since the unfortunate affair of the *Representative* forty-two years earlier. Disraeli cannot be classed among the British statesmen who had any great affection for the northern kingdom. Indeed, the very word 'British' was one that he never used, invariably preferring 'England' and 'English', to the annoyance of patriotic Scotsmen. Apart from disagreeable associations with a youthful failure, Scotland suffered in Disraeli's esteem because of her overwhelming Liberal majority. A year earlier he wrote to Corry:[1]

> See Hamilton about the Aberdeen University and tell him that I do not wish the settlement wh: I made in 1859 to be departed from.
> The Scotch shall have no favors from me until they return

[1] Hughenden Papers, Box 95, B/XX/D/18, October 8, 1866.

more Tory members to the H. of C., and of all parts of Scotland
the most odious are the Universities. They have always been our
bitterest and most insulting foes. Of course I have not said this
to the D of R. [Duke of Richmond].

But Disraeli decided none the less to accept the invitation, and,
although some notable Scottish Tories such as the Duke of Buccleuch were unenthusiastic, the banquet was a great success. It was
presided over by Sir William Stirling-Maxwell, the historian and
bibliographer, whom Disraeli was able to make a Knight of the
Thistle in 1876 – in those days a very rare honour for a commoner.
The banquet was the occasion when he made the entertaining comparison of the *Quarterly* and *Edinburgh Reviews*, quoted in the
last chapter. One passage towards the end of the speech is worth
quoting:[1]

> In a progressive country change is constant; and the great
> question is not whether you should resist change which is in-
> evitable, but whether that change should be carried out in
> deference to the manners, the customs, the laws, and the tradi-
> tions of a people, or whether it should be carried out in deference
> to abstract principles, and arbitrary and general doctrines. The
> one is a national system; the other, to give it an epithet, a noble
> epithet – which it may perhaps deserve – is a philosophic system.
> Both have great advantages: the national party is supported by
> the fervour of patriotism; the philosophical party has a singular
> exemption from the force of prejudice.
> Now, my lords and gentlemen, I have always considered that
> the Tory party was the national party of England. It is not
> formed of a combination of oligarchs and philosophers who prac-
> tise on the sectarian prejudices of a portion of the people. It is
> formed of all classes from the highest to the most homely, and it
> upholds a series of institutions that are in theory, and ought to be
> in practice, an embodiment of the national requirements and the
> security of the national rights. Whenever the Tory party de-
> generates into an oligarchy it becomes unpopular; whenever the
> national institutions do not fulfil their original intention, the Tory
> party becomes odious; but when the people are led by their
> natural leaders, and when, by their united influence, the national
> institutions fulfil their original intention, the Tory party is
> triumphant, and then under Providence will secure the prosperity
> and the power of the country.

Disraeli seems to have enjoyed his visit. The University of Edin-

[1] M. & B., iv, 557.

burgh conferred an honorary degree upon him, and thus perhaps softened his harsh verdict on Scottish universities. And he had a very successful open meeting in the Music Hall at which he made a great impression on an audience of working men.

'I fancied, indeed, till last night that north of the border I was not loved,' he told Sir John Skelton, who records the story in his *Table Talk of Shirley*, 'but last night made amends for much. We were so delighted with our reception, Mrs. Disraeli and I, that after we got home we actually danced a jig (or was it a hornpipe?) in our bedroom.' Skelton was fascinated by the Disraelis. She seemed to him like one of the witches in Macbeth. 'And the potent wizard himself, with his olive complexion and coal black eyes, and the mighty dome of his forehead (no Christian temple, be sure), is unlike any living creature one has met . . . The face is more like a mask than ever and the division between him and mere mortals more marked. I would as soon have thought of sitting down at table with Hamlet, or Lear, or the Wandering Jew.' But Skelton was far from thinking that Disraeli was an alien, or indifferent to England. 'England is the Israel of his imagination, and he will be the Imperial Minister before he dies – if he get the chance.'[1]

The autumn session opened on November 19. Disraeli had to take charge of all the preliminary business, for Derby was laid up from early September onwards with the worst attack of gout that he had ever suffered, although he just managed to attend Parliament. On the eve of the session Disraeli himself had to ask Stanley to take his place at the usual House of Commons dinner because Mrs Disraeli was seriously ill. Her collapse occasioned one of the rare relaxations of mutual hostility between Gladstone and Disraeli. The Liberal leader made a generous and kindly reference in the House to her health, to which Disraeli replied with tears in his eyes, following up his response with a cordial letter. Gladstone answered in the same vein. He was genuinely fond of Mrs Disraeli, and, so she told Kebbel,[2] would on occasions come round to Grosvenor Gate after a debate in order to show that there was no ill will. This helped to soften the acerbity of the great political duel. The real hatred which prevailed between the two rivals dates from after her death. Perhaps if she had lived it would have been less acute. Mrs Gladstone's influence was quite the reverse. She fanned the flames. Disraeli, on

[1] ibid., 558–9.
[2] ibid., 570.

the other hand, invariably treated her with an elaborate courtesy
which no doubt only made her dislike him the more. Mary Anne
recovered after a time, but her illness can probably be seen in
retrospect as the first sign of the cancer from which she was to die
five years later. She was never quite the same again.

Soon after the beginning of the session Disraeli, too, collapsed.
He was stricken by an attack of gout. The two of them would communicate by letter from their respective bedrooms. 'Being on my
back, pardon the pencil', Disraeli wrote. 'You have sent me the most
amusing and charming letter I ever had. It beats Horace Walpole
and Mme de Sévigné.' Her letters have not survived, but she faithfully preserved his in a packet inscribed 'Notes from dear Dizzy
during our illness when we could not leave our rooms'.

It was an awkward time at which to be ill. Before taking to his
bed, Disraeli had managed to obtain, despite Lowe's opposition, the
necessary vote of credit – £2m – for the Abyssinian campaign, but
there were many other vexatious problems. On December 12 the
Irish American secret society known as the Fenian Brotherhood
endeavoured to rescue some prisoners from Clerkenwell jail by
exploding a barrel of gunpowder outside the wall. No one was
rescued, but there were twelve deaths and a hundred and twenty
casualties. Since Scotland Yard had received a detailed warning of
the exact time, place and technique of the outrage it is not surprising that the Government should have been dismayed at such
negligence. This episode was followed by a rumour which turned out
to be a hoax that a Danish brigantine had left New York with a
crew of Irish assassins bent on murdering the Queen. All these
matters necessitated long letters to Knowsley, where Derby had
returned as soon as the short session ended.

Then on top of it all came another naval scare. Formidable
memoranda were emitted by the Admiralty all tending to show that
the French had more ironclads than Britain, and that a Franco-
Russian combination would be overwhelming. It was alleged that
whereas Britain had 31 afloat and 8 under construction, the figures
for France were 35 and 11, for Russia 25 and 4. Therefore a large
increase must be made in the naval estimates. Disraeli would not
accept it. If the Admiralty wanted more ironclads they could build
them out of money saved by cutting their expenditure on small
unarmoured wooden ships scattered all over the world.[1] 'This is the

---

[1] M. & B., iv, 578–9. Disraeli to Derby, January 28, 1868.

keystone of the position. We spend an enormous sum annually for building and repairing these ships for their three-yearly reliefs. Why?' Derby, who had been stricken in mid-January with another acute attack of gout, was more inclined to take the Admiralty seriously. 'I must confess that for the last few years the comparison of the relative strength of the British navy with that of the two other navies of the world has not been of a satisfactory nature.'[1] But he agreed that it was impossible to increase the estimates.

The Fenians and the Navy were by no means the only problems that vexed Disraeli during this hectic winter. There was the question of creating a Ministry of Education which caused much argument and lengthy correspondence. There was a knotty problem about the forthcoming Corrupt Practices at Elections Bill. The Government intended to transfer jurisdiction over disputed elections from the House of Commons to the judges of the High Court, but the latter violently objected. 'In short the Judges have struck', Disraeli wrote to Derby on February 6. Another troublesome matter connected with the judiciary came up at the same time. Disraeli wanted a vacant judgeship to be filled by a Conservative MP. Lord Chelmsford took a haughty line, snubbed him sharply, and declared that he would tolerate no interference with his right to appoint as he saw fit. This was the last of a long series of episodes in which Disraeli considered that the Lord Chancellor had been singularly unhelpful in matters of patronage.

It was now beginning to be clear that Derby could not continue much longer as Prime Minister. He was naturally reluctant to retire. He was not as old as either Palmerston or Russell had been at the end of their active political careers. The party was in a very delicate position. Derby was well aware that his name carried more weight in the country than that of any other Conservative, and he was anxious not to leave his colleagues in the lurch. In spite of his latest attack he had hoped to see out the session of 1868, but in the middle of February he received medical advice which he could not ignore. He was told that there was no prospect of recovery while he remained in office. Before informing the Queen he at once wrote to Disraeli and asked him whether he was ready to take over.[2] In fact, although Derby did not know, the Queen had already sounded Disraeli through General Grey, her secretary, when he was staying

[1] Derby Papers, Box 195, Letter Book 1.
[2] M. & B., iv, 584.

at Osborne towards the end of January, and had made it clear that
she regarded him as Derby's successor. He wrote to Derby on
February 20:[1]

> My dearest Lord – I have not sufficient command of myself at
> this moment to express what I feel about what has happened,
> and, after all, has happened so rapidly and so unexpectedly.
>   All I will say is that I never contemplated nor desired it. I was
> entirely content with my position, and all I aspired to was that,
> after a Government of tolerable length, and at least fair repute,
> my retirement from public affairs should have accompanied your
> own; satisfied that I had enjoyed my opportunity in life, and
> proud that I had been long confidentially connected with one of
> the most eminent men of my time, and for whom I entertain
> profound respect and affection. I will not shrink from the situa-
> tion, but I do not underrate its gravity, and mainly count, when
> you are convalescent, on your guidance and support . . .

On receiving this Derby at once informed the Queen that he intended to resign and advised her to appoint Disraeli. 'He and he only
could command the cordial support *en masse* of his present colleagues.'[2] Derby was perhaps somewhat exceeding his strict
constitutional role. The Queen had not consulted him and the usage,
though not always observed, is for an outgoing Prime Minister to
give such advice only if asked. But the point is of no great importance. Although the Cranborne 'Cave' was bitterly hostile, and
although a few Tories may have looked to one of the grand territorial
houses, for example to Derby's heir or even to the Duke of Richmond, the great majority recognized that any other choice would
be absurd. There was no great enthusiasm for Disraeli, and Derby's
departure was widely regretted, but there was no serious opposition.

A curious hiatus now ensued. Derby did not formally resign
when he wrote to the Queen. He wished to have time to deliver the
seals in person, and he was particularly anxious to recommend
certain peerages. In these rather awkward circumstances Disraeli
behaved with exemplary forbearance, and refused to give the
slightest semblance of grasping for office. The problem was resolved
by the Queen, who politely but unambiguously requested Derby to
resign at once. And so at last Disraeli's career after so many vicissitudes was crowned by the highest office in the land. He was himself
struck, and so was the world, by the odd change of fortune that

[1] ibid, 585.
[2] *The Letters of Queen Victoria*, 2nd Series, i, 497, February 21, 1868.

made Grey who had beaten him for High Wycombe thirty-six years earlier the bearer of the message from the Queen. On February 25 Stanley announced the news in the House of Commons. On February 26 the Queen wrote to her daughter, the Crown Princess of Prussia:

> . . . Mr. Disraeli is Prime Minister! A proud thing for a Man "risen from the people" to have obtained! And I must say – really most loyally; it is his real talent, his good temper and the way in wh. he managed the Reform Bill last year – wh. have brought this about . . .[1]

On February 27 Disraeli went down to Osborne and formally kissed hands. 'Yes,' he said to friends who congratulated him, 'I have climbed to the top of the greasy pole.'[2]

At the end of March the Disraelis gave a great reception to celebrate the event. They borrowed the Foreign Office from Stanley, Disraeli commenting, as he made the request, that Mary Anne thought Downing Street 'so dingy and decaying'. The weather was as atrocious as only an English spring can provide – snow, sleet, bitter cold; but a vast concourse thronged the rooms – the Prince and Princess of Wales, dukes and their duchesses, ambassadors and bishops, most of society, everyone who was anyone in Tory politics, and prominent Liberals, too, the Gladstones among them. It was a scene from *Coningsby* or *Endymion*, and few of the guests ever forgot it. Bishop Wilberforce, who was there, wrote in his diary: 'Dizzy in his glory leading about the Princess of Wales; the Prince of Wales, Mrs. Dizzy – she looking very ill and haggard. The impenetrable man low. All looks to me as if England's "Mene, Mene" were written on our walls.'[3]

2

A new Prime Minister automatically has all the political posts at his disposal. Disraeli did not contemplate a major reshuffle and his colleagues were asked to remain in office with one exception, Lord Chelmsford. He had always disliked the Lord Chancellor, who was a poor debater, no asset in council, and seventy-five years of age. Derby himself had told Chelmsford that he would have to make way

[1] Royal Archives, Kronberg Letters, February 26, 1868.
[2] Fraser, *Disraeli and His Day*, 52.
[3] Reginald Wilberforce, *Life of the Right Reverend Samuel Wilberforce, D.D.* (3 vols, 1881), iii, 242.

some time for Cairns, but he had intended to soften the blow by giving him the Lord Presidency or some other sinecure office when a vacancy arose.[1] Disraeli had no intention of waiting for that. It was necessary to strengthen the Government in the House of Lords at once, and no doubt he was not uninfluenced by the frequent disputes over patronage mentioned earlier. His letter to Chelmsford was courteous, but clear. He regretted that he could not continue him in office, referred to Derby's proviso, and asked what consolatory honour would be acceptable in the circumstances.[2]

Chelmsford was furious, gave out – quite untruly – that the letter was brutal, aired his grievance in the Press, and appealed to Derby, who tried to pour oil on the waters, but had to confirm Disraeli's reference to his own intentions.[3] No agreement could be reached about the honour. The Queen at Disraeli's instance offered the GCB. Chelmsford refused and demanded an earldom, a prize awarded only to Chancellors of exceptional distinction or length of service. 'It seems impossible that your Majesty can entertain such preposterous claims',[4] Disraeli wrote to the Queen. So Chelmsford went into retirement and a huff, attributing his 'dismissal' to Disraeli's love of a job, muttering angrily that some people became 'dizzy' with promotion, and contrasting the late and current ministries as the Derby and the 'Hoax'.

Apart from this the change of government went smoothly. Walpole, who had been a reluctant minister without portfolio ever since the fiasco of the Hyde Park meeting the previous May, took the occasion to retire. There was no need to replace him. It was necessary, however, to appoint a new Chancellor of the Exchequer, for Disraeli wisely did not accept Derby's advice to combine it with the Premiership. The problem was a tricky one. Northcote, the obvious candidate, could not leave the India Office while the Abyssinian campaign was still unfinished. In the end Disraeli promoted Ward Hunt, the Financial Secretary to the Treasury, a country gentleman and member for Northamptonshire, who weighed twenty-one stone. 'He is more than six feet four inches in stature,' Disraeli told the Queen,[5] 'but does not look so tall from his proportionate breadth; like St. Peter's no one is aware of his dimen-

---

[1] Derby Papers, Box 195/1, February 27, 1868, Derby to Chelmsford (copy).
[2] M. & B., iv, 594 (?February 27), 1868.
[3] Derby Papers, loc. cit.
[4] *The Letters of Queen Victoria,* 2nd Series, i, 509, March 2, 1868.
[5] ibid., 507 February 26, 1868.

sions. But he has the sagacity of the elephant as well as the form.'
Derby wrote: 'Hunt's promotion is a rapid one but I think he will
justify your selection.'[1] Derby's own place as leader in the House of
Lords was taken by Malmesbury. Disraeli would have preferred the
Duke of Marlborough, but the latter told him that Malmesbury had
so often acted as Derby's deputy that he could not be passed over.

On one matter Disraeli showed a certain insensitivity. He invited
Cranborne through Sir Stafford Northcote to rejoin the Cabinet.
The reply was an uncompromising negative.

Disraeli's Cabinet was as follows:

First Lord of the Treasury	B. Disraeli
Lord Chancellor	Lord Cairns
Lord President	Duke of Marlborough
Lord Privy Seal	Earl of Malmesbury
Home Secretary	Gathorne Hardy
Foreign Secretary	Lord Stanley
Colonial Secretary	Duke of Buckingham
War Secretary	Sir John Pakington
Indian Secretary	Sir Stafford Northcote
Chancellor of the Exchequer	G. Ward Hunt
First Lord of the Admiralty	H. J. Lowry Corry
President of the Board of Trade	Duke of Richmond
First Commissioner of Works	Lord John Manners
Chief Secretary for Ireland	Earl of Mayo

Disraeli's behaviour towards his former chief was a model of
conduct in such circumstances. In spite of occasional differences and
at least one major disappointment, he was deeply attached to
Derby. He wrote on February 27:[2] '. . . I consider myself, and shall
always consider myself, only your deputy . . . I shall never take
any step of importance in public life without apprising you of it
before it is decided on, and without at least seeking the counsel
which I trust will never be refused.' Derby's reply[3] was equally
generous. 'I cannot accept for you the position that you are willing
to accept for yourself, of being considered my deputy. You have
fairly and most honourably won your way to the highest round of
the political ladder, and long may you continue to retain your
position.' Derby went on to say that he would if asked always gladly
give his frank opinion. 'But I shall not be so unreasonable as to

[1] Derby Papers, Box 195/1 (copy), February 28, 1868.
[2] M. & B., iv, 590.
[3] loc. cit., February 28, 1868.

expect that it shall always be adopted, or be surprised, still less affronted, if upon any ground you find yourself unable to act upon it.' Disraeli was true to his word and for the rest of his premiership consulted Derby on most major issues and on the principal lay and clerical appointments. Derby never hesitated to give his advice and never took umbrage if it was not accepted. The correspondence makes an agreeable close to their long partnership.

Disraeli from the first moment of taking office laid the foundations of a relationship with the Queen, to which there is no parallel in her long reign. He intuitively guessed that, for all the stiffness of her demeanour and the severe court etiquette which surrounded her, she would respond to a personal approach, the more so now that her husband was dead. He was to achieve his full measure of success in his second term of office, but he went a long way during his first. It would probably be wrong to see in his flattery and compliments a deliberate pose consciously assumed for political purposes. It was part of his nature to treat women like this, and he was a genuine romantic, even a sentimentalist, in his attitude to the throne. But he was also aware of the advantage to be gained from friendship with a sovereign whose constitutional powers, however diminished and ill defined, were sufficient for her goodwill to make a difference.

Anyone who knew Disraeli might have guessed that he would try to woo the Queen in this way. Historians have, however, been perhaps unduly puzzled by his success. They underestimate the degree to which monarchs all down history have from time to time craved for someone who would cut through the formal, grave, hierarchical protocol which constitutes their normally necessary defence against familiarity or impertinence. The history of court jesters, doctors and other familiars shows this well enough. The divinity that hedges a king can be too much of a strain. Disraeli by-passed all the ordinary barriers. If it is permissible to draw a parallel which would scarcely have pleased him, he played a role in the Queen's life not entirely dissimilar to that of John Brown.

The Queen was at once struck by Disraeli's charm. 'The present Man will do well,' she wrote to her eldest daughter on February 29, 'and will be particularly loyal and anxious to please me in every way. He is vy. peculiar, but vy. clever and sensible and vy. conciliatory.'[1] On March 4 she wrote again. 'He is full of poetry, romance &

---

[1] Royal Archives, Kronberg Letters.

chivalry. When he knelt down to kiss my hand wh. he took in both his – he said: "In loving loyalty & faith." '[1] Disraeli's first letter to the Queen after she had appointed him set the tone for their future correspondence:

> . . . He can only offer devotion.
>
> It will be his delight and duty to render the transaction of affairs as easy to your Majesty as possible, and in smaller matters he hopes he may succeed in this; but he ventures to trust that, in the great affairs of state, your Majesty will deign not to withhold from him the benefit of your Majesty's guidance.
>
> Your Majesty's life has been passed in constant communion with great men, and the knowledge and management of important transactions. Even if your Majesty were not gifted with those great abilities, which all must now acknowledge, this rare and choice experience must give your Majesty an advantage in judgement, which few living persons, and probably no living Prince, can rival.
>
> He whom your Majesty has so highly preferred presumes to trust to your Majesty's condescension in this behalf . . .'[2]

He recurred to the same theme on March 9 when suggesting the Duke of Atholl for the vacant Thistle resulting from Lord Rosebery's death:[3]

> Yr Majesty is a much better judge of these matters than himself; and indeed there are very few public matters on wh., he feels more and more every day, yr Majesty is not much more competent to advise than be advised.[4]

Not only did Disraeli lay it on, as he himself is said to have admitted, 'with a trowel', but he wrote letters which must have been far more entertaining than anything which the Queen received from any of her other ministers. The pen of the novelist can be discerned again and again. The correspondence abounds with witty comments and vivid portraits. His picture of Ward Hunt was quoted earlier. Here is the Duke of Northumberland, one of whose letters Disraeli forwarded to the Queen, 'as he thinks it is interesting to yr Majesty to be acquainted with the character and feelings of yr Majesty's principal subjects'.[5]

[1] ibid.
[2] *The Letters of Queen Victoria*, 2nd Series, i, 505, February 26, 1868.
[3] The 4th Earl; grandfather of the Prime Minister.
[4] Royal Archives, A.37.9.
[5] ibid., A.37.16, April 30, 1868.

The Duke of Northumberland is very unpopular and has the reputation of being the proudest man in yr Majesty's dominions. He *is* proud, but he is more shy; and suffering under a morbid feeling that he has never been appreciated. The Duke has talents – and has thought a great deal and has passed the greater and more important part of his life with people of highly cultivated taste and of even learning, but of very fantastic opinions, mainly the late **Mr.** Drummond of Surrey whose daughter he married and who inherits all her father's tastes, much of his knowledge and his freakish mind. He is devoted to her . . .[1]

And here is the Duke of Portland:

. . . [Mr Disraeli] mentions to your Majesty that the Duke of Portland, one of the most powerful subjects of yr Majesty, had withdrawn his adhesion from the Liberal party and transferred it to yr Majesty's Government in consequence of the Church question.

Mr Disraeli encloses a very characteristic letter from His Grace wh: leaves no doubt on this head. It is addressed to a perfect stranger to the Duke, Sir James Fergusson, whom His Grace always violently opposed in Ayrshire.

The offer of a dwelling in Caithness-shire and all the conditions illustrate the character of one of the most singular species in Yr Majesty's dominions: the Bentinck.[2]

The truth of the last observation Disraeli could have amply confirmed from his own dealings with the very same duke. The Queen was evidently enchanted by the style in which he wrote. 'She declares', wrote Lady Augusta Stanley to Lord Clarendon, 'that she never had such letters in her life, which is probably true, and she never before knew *everything*.'[3] Soon presents were being exchanged. It was like Mrs Brydges Willyams again. She sent him spring flowers. 'Mr Disraeli is passionately fond of flowers,' wrote Mary Anne, adding, one suspects, not wholly unprompted, 'and their lustre and perfume were enhanced by the condescending hand which had showered upon him all the treasures of spring.'[4] He sent her the collected edition of his novels,[5] and she responded with *Leaves*

---

[1] loc. cit.

[2] ibid., A.37.42, July 13, 1868. The letter from the Duke is unfortunately not there.

[3] Sir H. Maxwell, *Life and Letters of . . . Fourth Earl of Clarendon* (2 vols, 1913), ii, 346.

[4] M. & B., V, 48, to Princess Christian.

[5] Mr Disraeli with his humble duty to Yr Majesty:
Your Majesty once deigned to·say Yr Majesty would not refuse to accept some volumes wh: he once wrote.

from the Journal of Our Life in the Highlands. Did he really say, 'We authors, Ma'am'? The story has never been authenticated, but it deserves to be true. In September, Disraeli had his first experience of staying at Balmoral. He seems to have been in luck, for the weather was not as cold as usual, and he was comparatively comfortable. His letters to his wife, who did not go with him, give a pleasant picture of life there. But he commented in a letter to Bishop Wilberforce on the difficulty of conducting affairs of state six hundred miles from London, and he only went once again, in 1874, thereafter excusing himself on grounds of work.

The contrast between Disraeli's success and Gladstone's failure to manage the Queen is one of the commonplaces of history. It was not solely a matter of personality, for Gladstone's policies were in any case displeasing to her. But personality did affect her attitude, and the difference is well illustrated by the way in which the two men approached the great royal problem of the day, how to find suitable employment for the Prince of Wales. It was clearly essential to obtain the Queen's goodwill. An obvious possible occupation was for him to cement the crumbling loyalty of Ireland, a country in which, as Disraeli told the Queen, the Sovereign had only passed twenty-one days in two centuries. Taking the occasion of an invitation by the Irish Government to the Prince to attend the Punchestown races, Disraeli suggested that he might make a longer visit later in the year and 'hunt for example with the Kildare and Meath . . . This would in a certain degree combine the fulfilment of public duty with pastime, a combination which befits a princely life.' Disraeli, although he did not say so, envisaged this as the first step to a more permanent association, but the Queen strongly objected. He promptly dropped the whole plan, and said nothing more.

Three years later Gladstone took up a similar proposal with all the intensity and persistence at his command. He wished to reconstruct the Government of Ireland so that the Prince could be permanent viceroy. Not surprisingly, the Queen was adamant in opposition, and, although Gladstone pressed the matter far beyond the bounds of tact or constitutional propriety, he had to give way – but

---

The edition is not worthy of Yr Majesty, but it is the only complete one now to be obtained; & it is humbly offered, not, as he hopes, from the vanity of an author, but that he should not appear indifferent, or insensible, to the condescension that was graciously expressed.

only after causing serious offence which affected his relations with the Queen for the rest of his life.

3

Disraeli was well aware of the weakness of his political position. His Government was a caretaker administration dependent upon the goodwill or divisions of the Opposition. He could not hope to do more than mark time till the general election, but there are powers which even a minority Prime Minister possesses, and Disraeli savoured some of them. Few things could have given him greater pleasure than to advise the Queen on March 26 to confer the Lord Lieutenancy of his county upon the son of his old patron and friend, Chandos of the Chandos clause:[1]

> . . . The Duke of Buckingham has still the largest estate in the county. Mr. Disraeli remembers more than twenty years ago in the dark troubles of His Grace's youth telling him that he had a mission to fulfil; & that was to build up again the fortunes of an ancient house.
>
> With a steady exercise of some virtues, with the continuous application of a not inconsiderable intelligence & in no slight degree by your Majesty's favor & considerate sympathy, the Duke has succeeded in this noble enterprize.
>
> Mr. Disraeli believes that he is meeting Yr Majesty's views in recommending the Duke of Buckingham to Yr Majesty's favor for the high office of Ld. Lt. for the County of Bucks, now vacant.
>
> Having in his youth, & days of great obscurity, received Kindnesses from the House of Grenville he shd. feel grateful to fortune if by Yr Majesty's permission he was authorized to make a communication in this spirit to the Duke of Buckingham.
>
> The flag waves again over Stowe, wh: no one ever expected; & if Yr Majesty confers on the Duke the great honor of being Yr Majesty's representative in his county, the honors of the Grenville family will after great vicissitudes & searching trials be restored.

The Opposition did not object to a minority Prime Minister conferring Lord Lieutenancies which were purely honorific appointments. But they were very angry when both the Governor-Generalship of Canada and the Viceroyalty in India fell vacant during his

---

[1] Royal Archives, A.37.12. The Queen cordially agreed. '. . . No one bore his great misfortunes more nobly, or more truly deserves reinstitution in the ancient family seat than the Duke . . .'

brief ministry. Disraeli offered Canada first to Mayo and then Manners, both of whom refused. In the end he had to make a non-political appointment, Sir John Young, ex-Governor of New South Wales. For the Viceroyalty he chose Mayo, and there were Liberal threats, not in the end implemented, to exercise the right of recall, if they won the election. Disraeli told the Queen; and it would appear that her disapproval operated against such a drastic course. Mayo's career as Viceroy, though tragically cut short by assassination, was a success.

The biography of a Prime Minister is not a history of his times. The activities of the session of 1868 need only a brief mention. Hampered by being outnumbered in the House, Disraeli had to do the best he could. This handicap was at its worst over the Irish and Scottish Reform Bills, where Opposition amendments played much the same part as they did with the English Bill. Another setback was the report of the Select Committee on the decisions of the Boundary Commission. The Committee was headed by Walpole, who seems to have become quite detached from his former colleagues; it went some way, though not the whole, towards undoing the skilful gerrymandering of the Commission which had been packed with Tory squires. In other spheres the Government's legislation was more successful, although it was naturally of the comparatively non-partisan nature, which all governments carry when public opinion and the Civil Service are ready. The judges withdrew their objection to the Corrupt Practices Bill, and it goes down to history as the first effective attack on electoral bribery. Bills were carried to improve the public schools, the railways and the Scottish legal system. Public executions were abolished. The first measure of nationalization was carried when the Government passed a Bill empowering the Post Office to buy up all the telegraph companies. Perhaps Disraeli's most far-reaching action was to appoint a strong Royal Commission on the Sanitary Laws, headed by Sir Charles Adderley. This was to have important consequences later.

Disraeli was able to report one resounding success in foreign affairs. Napier's expedition resulted in the release of King Theodore's prisoners, the capture of Magdala, the suicide of the King, and the orderly withdrawal of the British forces without the addition of a barren and superfluous territory to the Empire. The cost, it is true, turned out later to be nearly double the estimate,[1]

[1] £9m instead of £5m.

and Disraeli's colourful rhetoric about the standard of S George being hoisted on the mountains of Rasselas caused a certain amount of laughter, but on the whole the episode redounded to the Government's credit.

All these matters were, however, relatively unimportant compared with the question of the Irish Church which was brought forward by Gladstone and dominated both the Parliamentary session and the ensuing election. Disraeli had undoubtedly scored off Gladstone during the Reform Bill struggle of the previous year. His brilliant parliamentary conjuring tricks had reduced his old enemy to an angry smouldering silence. A favourite Tory riddle was to ask why Gladstone was like a telescope; the answer being, because Disraeli draws him out, sees through him, and shuts him up. But Gladstone never remained silent for very long. At Christmas 1867, Russell had retired from the party leadership. Gladstone was certain to be the next Liberal Prime Minister. He now leapt into the fray with a programme which united his own party and threw his enemies into confusion.

Both sides were concerned during 1868 to do something about Ireland. The Fenian outrages were responsible for this sudden solicitude, and a melancholy example among many others of the efficacy of violence in calling the attention of the English to the grievances of their subject peoples. The key to the Irish problem, as Disraeli had recognized in the past, was the unsatisfactory system of land tenure, but neither Conservatives nor Liberals fastened on this in 1868. Both parties saw the problem as essentially a religious one which was indeed partly true. But they differed in their remedies. Derby and Disraeli, as they had in 1858–9, sought to revive the schemes of Pitt and Castlereagh. Aware of the doubtful position of the Irish Church, they wished to bring in a plan of concurrent endowment of both Roman Catholicism and Presbyterianism, to level up not down, and as a first step to grant a charter and financial support to a Roman Catholic university in Dublin. The snag in this proposal was the extreme reluctance of the English Protestant taxpayer to produce the necessary money.

But that stage was never reached. At first the plan seemed to go reasonably well. Disraeli kept in close and cordial contact with Manning, the newly appointed Archbishop of Westminster. He gained the impression that Manning was not only in favour of the scheme himself but able to carry the Irish hierarchy with him. On

March 10 a private member's motion on the state of Ireland gave
Lord Mayo, then still Irish Secretary, an opportunity to propound
the plan for a new university. It was well received by Liberal and
Roman Catholic spokesmen in the House, and the proposals were
duly forwarded to the representatives of the hierarchy. Meanwhile
the debate continued for another three days, and on the last of
them, March 16, Gladstone exploded a mine under the Government's feet. He declared his conviction that the Anglican Establishment in Ireland should be swept away altogether, and his
intention to bring forward resolutions in that sense at the first
opportunity. The effect of this pronouncement was felt at once.
Manning ceased all further communication with Disraeli. His last
letter is dated the very day of Gladstone's declaration. The hierarchy affixed such impossible conditions to acceptance of the
university scheme that they ensured its abandonment. Disraeli
considered that Manning had led him up the garden path, and he
was not mollified by a lame letter of explanation nine months later
when he was about to quit office. But literary statesmen have a
means of getting their own back denied to their less articulate
brethren. The character of Cardinal Grandison in *Lothair* was
Disraeli's revenge.

Although Gladstone's move turned out to be a brilliant success,
it would be unfair to attribute political opportunism to him. On the
contrary, it was by no means self-evident that disestablishment of
the Irish Church, however popular in Ireland, would be an effective
rallying cry for the Liberals in England. It might well have raised
the no-popery agitation which had in the past so often been disastrous to those who attempted to do something for Ireland. The truth
was that Gladstone had for a long time past been brooding spas-
modically over the Irish problem. At the back of his mind ever since
the Maynooth Act there was the inchoate belief that the Anglican
Establishment in Ireland had become an indefensible anomaly and
that its removal was the essential first step towards the reconciliation of the Irish to English rule. Critics could indeed point to his
perhaps unfortunate declaration, made as late as 1865, that the
question of the Irish Church was 'remote and apparently out of all
bearing on the practical politics of the day'. But he could reply that
a great deal had happened since then: Fenianism demonstrated
beyond doubt the intense discontent prevailing in Ireland; it was
essential to act, and to act quickly.

The attack put Disraeli into an embarrassing position. There were, it is true, strong arguments against Gladstone. Disestablishment could be argued to be contrary to the terms of the Act of Union and the Coronation Oath. Was it not also a perilous precedent for the Church of England? Disendowment which was demanded as an essential accompaniment raised grave questions about the rights of property. But the Irish Church was not a popular cause. Nothing could get round the fact that, although endowed on the scale needed to look after the whole population of Ireland, it actually ministered to little over one-eighth – and that eighth the wealthiest section of the country. The Cabinet was divided. Gathorne Hardy, who led the High Church group, favoured all-out resistance, and Derby's weight, considerable even though he was no longer Prime Minister, was thrown on the same side. Stanley and Pakington, on the other hand, believed disestablishment to be inevitable and wished to concentrate on securing the best possible terms. There was a third element, the Low Churchmen, headed by Cairns, who though hostile to disestablishment were, from hatred of Rome, scarcely less hostile to Disraeli's alternative of concurrent endowment.

As a result of these divisions it was difficult for the Government to take any clear stand on principle. Gladstone's resolutions were laid on the table of the House on March 23 and the motion to go into committee on them was taken a week later. The Cabinet decided to meet it with a temporizing amendment urging the expediency of leaving the question to a new Parliament, but the amendment which was moved by Stanley admitted that 'considerable modifications' might be necessary in the Church of Ireland. Derby was dismayed, and protested that this gave the whole game away. Stanley's speech dismayed him even more, and indeed the whole party. 'Anything so disheartening . . . never was heard', wrote Hardy.[1] It is difficult to see why Disraeli chose as principal speaker someone who notoriously did not believe in the case that he was supposed to be making, and Cranborne seemed to have some justification when later in the debate he accused Disraeli of preparing for surrender just as he had over the franchise.

Cranborne's speech was very bitter. He declared that he would as soon predict which way a weathercock would be pointing as prophesy Disraeli's attitude to the great questions before Parlia-

[1] Gathorne Hardy, *A Memoir*, i, 265.

ment. The offer made earlier by Disraeli had probably, as Lady Gwendolen Cecil surmises,[1] incensed rather than mollified the recipient. But Disraeli was patient, and did not believe in unnecessary trouble. He had seen the political wheel come round too often to despair of even so seemingly implacable a foe as Cranborne. In a calm reply he merely said that he thought Cranborne's invective lacked finish in spite of the study which had been given to it, and devoted most of his speech to Lowe, who had also attacked him with much venom. 'When the bark is heard on this side of this house the rt. hon. member for Calne emerges, I will not say from his cave, but perhaps from a more cynical habitation. He joins immediately in the chorus of reciprocal malignity and "hails with horrid melody the moon".'

It was Cranborne's last speech in the House of Commons. A few days later he succeeded his father as 3rd Marquess of Salisbury. His sentiments towards Disraeli emerge clearly enough from a letter which he wrote to a Mr Gaussen in reply to a request to take his father's place as a supporter of the Hertfordshire Conservative Registration Society. It is perhaps the most incisive statement of the views of the anti-Disraeli 'Cave', made by the most formidable intellectual figure that the Conservative party has ever produced:[2]

> Your letter is a very painful one to me as it imposes upon me the necessity of coming to a decision on questions in respect to which I should have preferred to remain wholly inactive . . .
>
> As far as I can judge the one object for which they [the Conservative party] are striving heartily is the premiership of Mr. Disraeli. If I had a firm confidence in his principles or his honesty, or even if he were identified by birth or property with the Conservative classes in the country – I might in the absence of any definite professions work to maintain him in power. But he is an adventurer: & as I have too good cause to know, he is without principles and honesty.
>
> You will say that I am giving great prominence to a question of mere personal esteem. It is true: But in this matter the personal question is the whole question. Mr. Disraeli's great talent and singular power of intrigue make him practically master of the movements of his party. It was shown as clearly as possible last year. The conversion of the Cabinet and the party to household suffrage was a feat which showed that there was nothing strong enough in either to resist his will. For all practical purposes Mr.

[1] Cecil, i, 291.
[2] Salisbury Papers, draft, May 11, 1868.

Disraeli for the time being at least is the Conservative Party . . .
The worst alternative that can happen is his continuance in
power. He is under a temptation to Radical measures to which no
other Minister is subject: because he can only remain in power by
bringing stragglers from his adversary's army – & the stragglers
are the men of extreme opinions. He can forward Radical changes
in a way that no other Minister could do – because he alone can
silence & paralyze the forces of Conservatism. And in an age of
singularly reckless statesmen he is I think beyond question the
one who is least restrained by fear or scruple.

Disraeli managed to avoid any serious charge of being lukewarm
about the Church. He could fairly defend delaying tactics if only
on the ground that it was wrong to take so contentious a subject
in an expiring Parliament elected on an unreformed franchise. But
he made a vigorous plea for the Establishment on its merits, too.
The union of Church and State was a symbol that Government
recognized 'its responsibility to the Divine Power'. If the Irish
Church was disestablished it would be the thin end of the wedge for
England, Scotland and Wales. Finally he beat the Protestant drum
in terms reminiscent of Russell's Durham letter. 'High Church
Ritualists and Irish followers of the Pope have long been in secret
combination and are now in open confederacy.' Cairns considered his
speech 'magnificent', but Hardy thought it 'obscure, flippant and
imprudent'. Whoever was correct, the speech was certainly not
successful. On April 4 Gladstone, rallying the Liberal party to vote
together as they had not done since Palmerston's death, won the
day by sixty votes.

Disraeli was in an awkward situation. It was morally certain that
the resolutions would be carried after the Easter recess. In modern
conditions, if such a thing as a minority government could exist at
all – which is most unlikely – the Prime Minister when defeated
would presumably dissolve at once. But to dissolve in May 1868 on
the old register would have been most unpopular. On the other
hand, to carry on for several months against a reunited hostile
majority would be embarrassing, humiliating, perhaps impossible.
There would certainly be strong pressure from the Cabinet to
resign rather than attempt to do so. But Disraeli could not bear the
prospect of having the tables thus turned on him by Gladstone and
ceding the Premiership less than three months after he had gained
it. Moreover, he hated to lose the initiative, and in those days it was
widely believed with some plausibility that the party which was

actually in office at the time had an advantage at a general election. Accordingly he decided, with the support of Derby and the Queen, who was, as Hardy put it, 'very anti-Gladstonian', to stick it out.

The difficulty was the Cabinet, but he managed on April 22 to secure what in the light of later recriminations must have been a very provisional assent to his plan. As soon as Gladstone carried the first resolution, at 2.30 am on May 1 by sixty-five votes, Disraeli moved the adjournment of the House, and without convening another Cabinet tendered formal advice to the Queen that she should dissolve 'as soon as the public interests will permit and that an earnest endeavour should be made by the Government that such appeal should be made to the new constituency'.[1] The Queen replied that 'she cannot hesitate, as she has already verbally informed him, to sanction the dissolution of Parliament under the circumstances stated by him, in order that the opinion of the country may be deliberately expressed on the important question [of the Irish Church] . . .'[2]

The game was now in Disraeli's hands. His exchange of letters with the Queen, though clearly indicating that an appeal to the country should if possible be delayed, did not preclude a penal dissolution at once on the old register. With this threat to back him up he could safely challenge a vote of censure. Gladstone and the leading Liberals were very angry and a series of accusations and counter-accusations followed Disraeli's announcement. But he mollified the critics by affording Gladstone every facility to carry through the House of Commons the other resolutions, and a Bill, promptly rejected by the peers, to suspend the Crown's Irish Church patronage. Gladstone dared not risk a vote of censure, and passions were to some extent quieted when Disraeli was able to announce that the new register would be ready in November – much sooner than anyone expected. His Cabinet colleagues were far from pleased that he had failed to consult them before seeing the Queen. Disraeli was technically in the wrong, but he had some reason to believe that they would have gone back on their previous resolution, and he did not mean to risk it. In the end Stanley, Hardy and the Dukes of Richmond and Marlborough, who were the strongest supporters of resignation, decided to remain. Nevertheless Disraeli must have been wearing his rose-coloured spectacles when he wrote to the Queen on May 8:[3]

[1] M. & B., v, 32.   [2] loc. cit.   [3] Royal Archives, A.37.23.

> . . . At no time have the unity & even the enthusiasm of the
> Tory party been so marked as at this moment . . . Since the
> commencement of the great struggle, the Cabinet has never been
> more serene & united. The Duke of Marlborough seemed a little
> bilious when Mr. Disraeli returned from Osborne & so ultimately,
> acting on Yr Majesty's sanction Mr. Disraeli announced to His
> Grace that Yr Majesty had been pleased to confer on him the
> blue ribbon.
>
> Mr. Disraeli does not anticipate further complications about
> the Irish Church: indeed the rabid rage of Mr. Bright yesterday
> indicated a consciousness of failure . . .

The last sentence refers to a speech of Bright's which brought to
an end what Buckle calls 'the unconventional but undoubted
friendship which had existed between him and Disraeli for twenty
years'. More than one critic thought that Disraeli had made rather
too much use of the Queen's name when announcing to the House
his policy over dissolution, with an implication that it was the
personal preference of the Queen which decided him to retain office.
But Bright went far beyond this criticism. Enraged by a sneer of
Disraeli's about the Liberals quarrelling over 'the plunder' of the
Irish Church, he described the Prime Minister as talking 'with a
mixture of pompousness and sometimes of servility', and insinuated
that he had 'the Sovereign in the front of a great struggle' and was
'guilty of a very high crime and a great misdemeanour against his
Sovereign and against his country'. There is a conflict of testimony
about whether Disraeli 'lost his temper and shook his fist' at Bright –
Lord Ronald Gower's version; or 'replied in the most gentlemanlike
manner' – Lord Malmesbury's account. Perhaps he did both. At all
events he gave as good as he got. 'I defy the hon. member for Birmingham notwithstanding his stale invective to come down to the
House and substantiate any charge of the kind which he has only
presumed to insinuate.' Bright did not pursue the matter.

Disraeli was safe for the rest of the session. Gladstone was himself
not unwilling to remain in opposition for the time being. In any
case he had little choice. He could afford to wait. Everything turned
on the general election, and it was widely expected that the Liberals
and their allies would win it, just as they had won every election
since 1841.

CHAPTER XXIII

A Setback
1868–74

1

The 1860s were a decade in which religion played a predominant part in politics. This is indeed true of much of nineteenth-century history, although the fact is only now beginning to be noticed by historians. The Church of England in 1868 faced, as it had for many years, the danger of dissension from within and assault from without. By tradition its defender was the Conservative party. But Disraeli was perhaps the least suited by temperament and background of all contemporary statesmen to deal with the problem. An agnostic home, education at a Unitarian establishment, his refusal to go to Oxford, his highly individual, if not eccentric, religious opinions, made it hard for him to identify himself convincingly with the Anglican cause, still harder for others to do so. This was not because he was himself in any sense a non-believer as Isaac had been. On the contrary he not only worshipped regularly at Hughenden and took the Sacrament at Easter, but he really did believe in Christianity of a somewhat peculiar sort. The accusation of crypto-Judaism made by Gladstone and others does not stand investigation; Disraeli was surprisingly ignorant of Jewish observances, and seems to have had very vague notions about the content of Judaism. Otherwise he would scarcely have argued that 'Christianity is completed Judaism' and deplored the fact that 'millions of Jews should persist in believing only part of their religion'.

On the other hand, his Christianity did not fit into any ordinary category. Here, too, he was curiously hazy. It is probably hopeless to extract a coherent body of doctrine from his observations on religion. He believed different things at different times and failed to see their inconsistency. Dr Roth, whose analysis of this subject is by far the most penetrating so far attempted,[1] concludes that in his enthusiasm for the Jewish race and his anxiety to draw parallels between the two religions he disregarded the differences. He no

[1] Cecil Roth, *Beaconsfield*, Ch. vi.

doubt believed in the Virgin Birth, the Divinity of Christ and the Resurrection, but not with strong conviction, or an appreciation of how fundamental these doctrines are for Christian faith. And Dr Roth points out, as indeed did contemporary critics, that his Jewish sympathies led him close to some very queer notions indeed. For example, in *Lord George Bentinck*: 'If the Jews had not prevailed upon the Romans to crucify our Lord what would become of the atonement? . . . Can that be a crime which secured for all mankind eternal joy?' This is perilously like the ancient heresy of Gnosticism. But even if these oddities were disregarded it cannot have been easy to take Disraeli very seriously as defender of the faith. There was his flippancy. 'I am the blank page between the Old and the New Testament,' he is supposed to have said on one occasion to Queen Victoria, and to a Broad Church divine, 'Remember, Mr Dean – no dogma, no Dean.' Then the very arguments that he used on their side, for example that the Church was an essential part of local government, must have made the devout shudder.

It is Disraeli's eccentricity in religious matters, his cynicism half affected half real, his ignorance of matters which were such a familiar part of the background of most educated Englishmen, that make him an apparently incongruous figure in Victorian England. It is in this sense, rather than in the more normally accepted social sense, that Disraeli really was regarded as an outsider by the Victorian governing class – or rather by a particular section of it. The qualification is important. There was another section, often forgotten, to whom he was by no means unacceptable.

For the ruling class, the *élite*, the Establishment – or whatever one wishes to call it – in nineteenth-century England consisted of at least two distinct but overlapping circles. There was the traditional aristocracy with their country cousins, the squirearchy. They were rich, grand, tolerant, often eccentric, not infrequently dissipated. They belonged to monosyllabic clubs; they usually kept racehorses, sometimes kept mistresses. The Regency bucks, the dandies of the 1830s, the 'heavy swells' who clustered round the Prince of Wales, constitute a lineal succession of a certain type among them. They were not all of them mere fribbles. There were conscientious men devoted to public duty among them, just as there had been in the eighteenth century, to which tradition so many of them belonged. Then there was another circle, the hard-working, serious-minded, gravely religious, or gravely agnostic upper

middle class, often educated at the same schools and universities as the aristocracy, but somehow in attitude and outlook
indefinably different. They provided some ministers and MPs, and
the majority of judges, divines, Civil Servants and dons. Of course,
no hard and fast line should be drawn. There were pious aristocrats
like Shaftesbury and Sidney Herbert. There were roué members of
the upper *bourgeoisie* like Lyndhurst. Many people belonged to both
worlds or had a foot in both. Gladstone married into a great Whig
family. Salisbury married the daughter of a judge.

Disraeli had nothing in common with this second circle, the one
which was perhaps most characteristic and influential in mid-
Victorian England and the one that counted most in Church affairs.
But he got along excellently with the first. His rise was essentially
a social rise, a conquest of London society upon which he had made
an impression for good or ill seldom forgotten. The aristocracy has
always been tolerant of individual oddities. It has been prepared to
put up with entertainers, buffoons, jesters and freaks as long as they
give good value. Actors, writers, artists and wits have never found
it difficult to do what Disraeli unkindly described the editor of *The
Times* as doing – 'simper in the enervating atmosphere of gilded
saloons'. Disraeli certainly did not simper, but he was instinctively
at home in the great houses and, as we saw earlier, he had convinced
himself of his own intrinsically patrician status – queer though this
may seem. He prided himself on being a man of the world, cool,
sardonic, urbane. It was the enthusiasm of Gladstone and his other-
worldly indifference to the London drawing-rooms which annoyed
Disraeli at times almost as much as his politics.

The moral and intellectual problems which vexed the graver
portion of the Victorian governing class were of no interest to
Disraeli. He was a very clever man, but, like Derby, he was not an
intellectual. The spiritual worries of the Tractarians, the theological
difficulties discussed in *Essays and Reviews*, the questions of eco-
nomics and politics which exercised Bagehot or Mill, constituted a
language which he simply did not understand, or, if he did, refused
to take seriously. He could feel for the wretchedness of the poor.
The contrast between the two nations appealed to his Byronic sense
of drama, and he tried, within limits, to do something about it. But
he could not feel for the moral anxieties of the prosperous intelligentsia. 'My Lord, I am on the side of the Angels.' Thus to an
audience of dons and undergraduates at the Sheldonian Theatre in

1863 did he dismiss the whole controversy about Darwin's *Origin of Species*. The intellectuals detested him almost to a man. Who but Disraeli could have brought Freeman and Froude to denounce him from the same political platform?

This lack of *rapport* with the more serious-minded element in the contemporary ruling class was a real handicap to Disraeli in dealing with the Church question. He convinced himself, relying on his memory of the Papal Aggression in 1851, that the attack on the Irish Church would rouse Protestant feeling all over England. He turned out to be wrong, but the miscalculation was not unreasonable, and he is to be judged less by that than by the way in which he exploited the situation as it appeared to him. He decided that it was essential to galvanize the Church of England into electoral activity, and that this could best be achieved by judicious use of Church patronage.

The Church could be roughly divided into three parties – High, Low and Broad. The last were anathema to Disraeli, for they were usually Liberals, but he had to face the difficulty that the Queen, carrying on the tradition of the Prince Consort, tended to favour them long after she had fallen out of sympathy with the Liberal party. Disraeli was no less hostile to the High Church men, not because they had any particular political affiliation, but because he believed that their extreme ritualistic wing had thoroughly alarmed public opinion on account of its alleged 'romanizing' objectives, and that the Protestant feeling which he hoped to mobilize would not rally behind a Church in which they had too strong a voice. He denied any bias against the High Church party as a whole in an open letter to a clerical correspondent which he somewhat unconvincingly dated 'Maundy Thursday', in order to show sympathy. Just as he overdid his country clothes, so he sometimes overdid his ecclesiasticism. Privately he had no intention of promoting High Churchmen unless it was unavoidable. 'I don't know who is for them,' he wrote to Stanley, 'except some University dons, some youthful priests, and some women; a great many perhaps of the latter. But *they* have not votes yet.' He decided accordingly that his best move would be to strengthen the Low Church or Evangelical party. They were violently anti-papal and theirs was the predominant tone in the threatened Church of Ireland. Disraeli had completely reversed his old policy of placating the Roman Catholics. Since his dealings with Manning he regarded them as irreconcilable.

It so happened that his brief premiership brought a shoal of ecclesiastical patronage, five sees including Canterbury and London, four deaneries, including S Paul's, and several canonries. Disraeli had never moved in ecclesiastical or academic circles, and knew little of the personalities involved. His only important contact was Wilberforce, the Bishop of Oxford, in whose diocese he lived, and with whom he had for many years been on terms of friendship. But the Bishop was High, and, Disraeli told the Queen, is 'a prelate who, tho' Mr. Disraeli's diocesan, he is bound to see as absolutely in this country more odious than Laud'. Wilberforce, Gathorne Hardy, and an old friend, Lord Beauchamp, tried to persuade Disraeli towards High Church appointments, but he preferred for most of the while to take advice from Cairns, who was on the opposite side. It must be said from the outset that Disraeli was influenced exclusively by political and electoral calculations. If he failed to get his way on all occasions, it was chiefly because he lacked sufficient knowledge to argue successfully for his own choice to the Queen. Dean Wellesley, her trusted adviser on these matters, wrote in 1875 a note for her, which would have been just as applicable in 1868:

. . . . Mr. D'Israeli's letters confirm the Dean in the notion that he will never wittingly propose to your Majesty for high preferment a clergyman of the Liberal party. He regards the Church as the great State-engine of the Conservatives and that [sic] any appointments with regard to its future reformation will weaken him politically with his followers . . . The Dean has always foreseen that there would be greater difficulty with Mr. D'I than even with Mr. Gladstone ecclesiastically – Because whatever Mr. G's own opinions he was obliged as leader of the Liberals to promote Temple, Kingsley, Fraser and many other such, and he understood who were the distinguished men in each party much better . . .[1]

This was Disraeli's problem: he simply did not know enough. 'Ecclesiastical affairs rage here. Send me Crockford's directory; I must be armed', he wrote from Balmoral to Monty Corry,[2] and to Derby 'You can't fight for a person you don't know'.[3]

Parliament was prorogued on July 31, and the election announced for mid-November. On August 14 Disraeli struck his first blow for the Protestant cause by proposing Canon McNeile of Liverpool for

[1] Royal Archives, D.6.12, January 30, 1875.
[2] M. & B., v, 58.
[3] ibid., 69.

the Deanery of Ripon. The Canon, who was seventy-three and a famous Evangelical preacher, had been involved in frequent ecclesiastical controversy. He was one of the best-known enemies of Rome in the country. The Queen assented to the appointment with reluctance. Disraeli replied that he had considered the matter carefully, that there was no hope of conciliating the Roman Catholics, and that even the High Church party would welcome the appointment if only because it was not a bishopric.[1] He followed this up two days later with a letter stating his whole position.

Affairs at this moment ripen so rapidly in England that he must lay before yr Majesty the result of his reflexions on a mass of data, that for amount and authenticity was probably never before possessed by a Minister. He receives every day regular reports and casual communications from every part of the United Kingdom. He confines himself to England and here there is no sort of doubt that the great feature of national opinion is an utter repudiation by all classes of the High Church party. It is not only general but universal. It is not only the inhabitants of the towns but every farmer is against them and a very large proportion of the gentry and all the professional classes.

If the Irish Church fall it will be owing entirely to the High Church party and the prejudice wh. they have raised against ecclesiastical institutions. One of the most remarkable circumstances at this moment is the almost universal report by the agents that the new County Constituency of £12 qualification turns out highly Conservative, tho' universally opposed to the High Church.

Mr. Disraeli speaks on this subject entirely without prejudice. The bias of his mind from education being brought up in a fear of fanaticism being certainly towards the High Church . . .

But Mr. Disraeli has no doubt from all that he observes and all that reaches him that it [the election] will be a great Protestant struggle – & that if the Government of the country temperately but firmly and unequivocally enlist that Protestant feeling on the side of existing authority the institutions of this country will be greatly strengthened and the means of governing proportionately facilitated.

But if not thus guided and even consciously controlled the Protestant feeling will take a destructive instead of Conservative form and those who may have the honor and happiness of being Yr Majesty's servants must prepare themselves to meet embarrassments and difficulties of no ordinary character.[2]

[1] *The Letters of Queen Victoria*, 2nd Series, August 19, 1868.
[2] Royal Archives, A.37.49, August 21, 1868.

The Queen gave way over McNeile, but when Disraeli proposed Canon Champneys, 'an insignificant Low Churchman', as the Queen called him, for the See of Peterborough she riposted with a counter-suggestion: Dr Magee, Dean of Cork, a moderate Evangelical, and one of the greatest preachers of his day. It is an example of Disraeli's ignorance that he appears to have known little about a man who was, even from the purely political point of view which Disraeli held, a far more satisfactory appointment. He wisely accepted the Queen's proposal. Magee admittedly had no love for Disraeli, but he made one of the finest of all the speeches in the House of Lords against Irish disestablishment. The Deanery of S Paul's, which was also vacant, Disraeli was able to confer on an old ally, Dr Mansel, the Regius Professor of Ecclesiastical History at Oxford. He had published a witty lampoon on University reform, had been a valued contributor to the *Press* and was a cordial enemy of Professor Goldwin Smith, who had attacked Disraeli many years earlier in the *Morning Chronicle*.

The appointment of McNeile caused such indignation in circles by no means High that Disraeli began to wonder whether he had gone too far. The Dean of Chichester, Hook, published a letter declaring that he would oppose Lord Henry Lennox, the sitting MP for that borough. Disraeli was very indignant. 'If we act in the spirit of the Dean of Chichester,' he wrote to Wilberforce, from Balmoral, 'we may all live to see the great Church of England subside into an Episcopalian sect. I will struggle against this with my utmost energy.' Nevertheless he decided rather late in the day to bestow his patronage in a slightly less one-sided fashion. Leighton, the Warden of All Souls, became, despite his friendship with Wilberforce, a Canon of Westminster, Gregory, also a High Churchman, Canon of S Paul's, and Bright, another moderate High Churchman, succeeded Mansel at Oxford.

On the eve of the election the most important of all pieces of ecclesiastical preferment became unexpectedly vacant. The Archbishop of Canterbury, Longley, died. The Queen, who was a shrewd tactician, got in the first word by suggesting Dr Tait, Bishop of London, as the new primate. Tait, a Liberal, a Broad Churchman, and a contributor to *Essays and Reviews*, was precisely the sort of person whom Disraeli was most anxious to avoid. He riposted with Dr Ellicott, Bishop of Gloucester, who was learned but lacked presence. Dean Wellesley told the Queen that she could 'fairly begin by positively declining the Bishop of Gloucester. He is an amiable insignificant man talking constantly and irrelevantly . . .'[1] Derby when appealed to by Disraeli rather confirmed this verdict: 'He has a foolish voice and manner which make him appear weaker than I believe he really is.' As Disraeli did not personally know the Bishop, he decided to look elsewhere. Meanwhile he told the Queen that he found Tait 'as an Ecclesiastical statesman, obscure in purpose, fitful and inconsistent in action, and evidently, though earnest and conscientious, a prey to constantly conflicting convictions'. Worse still, 'there is in his idiosyncracy a strange fund of enthusiasm, a quality which ought never to be possessed by an Archbishop of Canterbury, or a Prime Minister of England'. Warming to the theme he went on: 'The Bishop of London sympathises with everything that is earnest; but what is earnest is not always true; on the contrary error is often more earnest than truth.'[2] But he struggled in vain. There were difficulties of one sort or another about all his alternative names. In the end he gave way. The Queen had outmanoeuvred him.

There was a general expectation that Wilberforce would succeed to the vacant see of London, but Disraeli aroused the resentment of the High Church party and the animosity of the Bishop by passing him over and appointing instead Jackson, the Bishop of Lincoln, a reputable but far less eminent figure. Wilberforce was a man of great energy, as conspicuous in the social as in the intellectual world. He knew everyone. He would have made an excellent Bishop of London. Disraeli was probably wrong not to appoint him. He much exaggerated Wilberforce's unpopularity, although it was unlucky that at this of all moments the Bishop's only daughter should have gone over to Rome. As for the comparison with Laud, it was a travesty. Dean Wellesley took a juster view, though not wholly flattering to the Bishop. 'Laud was a bigot, even to the point of self-sacrifice,' he wrote to the Queen, 'but there is a want of moral strength in Wilberforce which prevents him being really dangerous in the Church whilst his brilliant and popular talents prevent him being hated in the country.'[3]

Wilberforce was angry. He might legitimately have counted on Disraeli's friendship and esteem – for Disraeli undoubtedly admired his talents – to carry him to London or even Canterbury. He became

---

[1] *The Letters of Queen Victoria*, 2nd Series, i, 545.
[2] ibid., 549–50.
[3] Royal Archives, D.1.89, n.d., but almost certainly September 11 or 12, 1868.

henceforth a strong Gladstonian and his diary and letters abound
with pejorative references to the Conservative leader. Probably
these opinions got back to Disraeli, but he might have recognized
that Wilberforce would hardly have been human if he had felt no
grievance, and it was perhaps a little unkind to put him, too, along
with Manning and Goldwin Smith, in the less flattering section of
the portrait gallery in *Lothair*.

It is questionable whether Disraeli's distribution of Church patronage did him any good in the general election. The Evangelicals were
no doubt active on his side, but their efforts were probably neutralized by the apathy or hostility of the moderate High Churchmen who
anyway lacked enthusiasm for the ultra Low Church of Ireland.
The Queen and her advisers come much better out of the story than
her Prime Minister. It is, moreover, interesting to see how little the
myth that the Queen ate out of his hand corresponds to reality. On
the contrary she got her own way on some of the most important
decisions. She understood Church affairs, knew who was who, and
was not influenced by partisan considerations. None of these things
can be said of Disraeli, and his methods did not even have the
justification of success.

Dean Wellesley told the Queen in the memorandum already
quoted:

> Every allowance is to be made for the critical position in which
> the Ministry is placed as to Church appointments on the eve of a
> general election principally turning on a religious subject. But
> Mr. D'I makes this mistake. The people of this country will un-
> doubtedly not tolerate Ritualism but it is equally certain that
> they will not put it down through the instrumentality of the
> Puritanical party. Strongly as he defends his reason for throwing
> the poor Deanery [Ripon] as a [? sop] to millions of fanatics, he
> will not gain by it more votes than he will lose, mainly from the
> moderate party.[1]

Events showed that the Dean was on this occasion a sounder judge
of the electoral situation than Disraeli.

Disraeli's opinion of his prospects at the election fluctuated. In
April he told Lord John Manners that 'it was very doubtful whether
we should have a majority in the new Parliament', but in September

[1] ibid., September 10, 1868. The Dean's memorandum is a commentary for the
Queen on Disraeli's letter in defence of McNeile's appointment. M. & B., v, 62–64,
gives the version taken from a draft at Hughenden.

he forwarded to the Queen a more sanguine estimate from the party committee in charge of the elections. In the existing house the rival strengths were: Liberals 364;[1] Conservatives 294.[2] The committee predicted that the new House would give the Conservatives a tiny majority: 330[3] against a Liberal score of 328. A month later Disraeli sent the Queen a less optimistic estimate based on the calculations of 'Mr. Sudlow of Manchester, a very eminent solicitor & reputed to have the most accurate & extensive electioneering knowledge in England'. Mr Sudlow thought that the party would do very well in Lancashire, but that the Conservatives would not win more than 320 seats altogether. Disraeli told the Queen that the new county constituency was reckoned to be Conservative and that the boroughs were less certain, 'but that the Conservative feeling is more predominant in the humbler portion of the Householders & that generally speaking there appears to be nothing to dread from this franchise if their natural leaders do not desert them'.[4] Yet in spite of those remarks Disraeli made little attempt to appeal specifically to the class that Derby and he had enfranchised. The administration's record in social reform had been respectable. His failure to exploit it suggests that he was either less aware of the needs of that class or more apprehensive of the danger to party unity in meeting them than is generally believed. It is true that in a speech at Aylesbury he touched on education and defended government expenditure to improve the condition of the people against Liberal charges of extravagance, but by then most of the results were in. His election address was almost wholly negative, and there was no sign of 'Tory radicalism' in his campaign or that of his colleagues.

Apart from success in Lancashire, the Conservative predictions were wrong. The extent of the Liberal victory came as a surprise even to detached observers. In the new House the Conservatives fell to 274, the figures in England and Wales being 227, Scotland 7, Ireland 40.[5] The Liberals rose to 384, the corresponding figures being 266, 53 and 65. Only in Lancashire was there any considerable eddy against the Liberal tide. There even Gladstone lost his seat and

---

[1] England and Wales, 265; Scotland, 43; Ireland, 56.
[2] England and Wales, 235; Scotland, 10; Ireland, 49.
[3] England and Wales, 266; Scotland, 13; Ireland, 51.
[4] Disraeli to the Queen, October 28, 1868, Royal Archives, A.37.62.
[5] They only won 25 out of 114 seats for boroughs of over 50,000, and only 4 out of 25 London seats. The corresponding figures in 1865 had been 22 out of 100, and nil.

his celebrated oratorical campaign, however effective nationally, made no impression locally. A combination of the Derby influence, and intense anti-Irish sentiment resulted in substantial Conservative gains.[1] Disraeli's election address, based on the threat to the Irish Church, probably helped there, but not elsewhere, and it alienated or neutralized two groups traditionally Tory, the English Roman Catholics and the Wesleyan Methodists. The cry of no-popery and 'the Church in danger' had been useful weapons in the past, but Disraeli's reliance on them is one more illustration of the danger of politicians remembering too much political history.

It is fair to say that the ground was not of his choosing. He could not evade the challenge, and even if Stanley was correct in telling him that two-thirds of the party favoured compromise, Disraeli could not afford to risk the fury of the one-third that regarded the Church as sacrosanct. Nevertheless he undoubtedly handled some matters badly. Common sense would have suggested that for an election fought on the Irish Church it would be prudent to have a figure of weight as Irish Secretary – or at any rate one who knew something about Ireland. Mayo was such a person, but on his appointment to India a substitute had to be found. Disraeli seems to have been mainly concerned with humouring the Viceroy, the Duke of Abercorn. After trying Manners, who refused, his choice lighted on Colonel Wilson-Patten, later Lord Winmarleigh, the Chancellor of the Duchy of Lancaster and an old-fashioned country gentleman. He knew nothing of Ireland, suffered from poor health, did not want the job, and only took it on condition that he had as little work as possible. Nor was Disraeli very helpful when Patten asked him what to say to his constituents about Irish policy. 'All you have to tell them [is] that the question will receive the most deliberate consideration of H.M. Govt., & that they will be prepared to advise that course wh. they think most conducive to the public interest.'[2]

But although he made mistakes it is unlikely that anything would have saved the day for Disraeli. Gladstone had the advantage and he made good use of it. If the picture seemed black at the time to most Conservatives, there were nevertheless some gleams of light which can now be seen as precursors of their recovery in 1874. In

[1] The 28 Lancashire seats had been evenly divided in 1865. In 1868 the total number was 34 of which the Conservatives won 21. In 1874 they won 26.

[2] H. J. Hanham, *Elections and Party Management; Politics in the Time of Disraeli and Gladstone* (1959), 297.

Westminster and Middlesex Conservative candidates were victorious, W. H. Smith ousting John Stuart Mill in the former, and Lord George Hamilton defeating Henry Labouchere in the latter. It was the first symptom of the swing away from Liberalism which was to be so marked in the middle-class constituencies at the next election. In the English counties the Conservatives actually gained, and in England as a whole held their ground. The Liberal gains were in the Celtic fringe, but this might not always be a reliable foundation. Moreover, in an age when territorial influence still counted it was some consolation that many of the great Whig peers, alarmed at Gladstone's attack on the Irish Church with all that it implied to the rights of property, refused to help the Liberal party. It is true that this reluctance had its counterpart on the Conservative side, where, for example, the Duke of Northumberland, Lord Salisbury and others had been alienated by the Reform Act, but the vagaries of individual magnates mattered less to a party that could rely on the support of the landed class as a whole.

Ever since 1832 powerful elements in the country, which were conservative with a small 'c', had been divided about the wisdom of supporting Conservatism with a big 'C'. Now there were signs that this division was ending. The death of Palmerston had already begun to have its effect. W. H. Smith, who had stood as a Palmerstonian Liberal in 1865, may be regarded as a personal embodiment of a change that was to be accelerated by Gladstone's radical programme during the next six years.

If Disraeli saw these trends at all he gave no sign. He was busy with more immediate problems. The Liberal victory was so decisive that he resolved to resign without meeting Parliament. His action set a precedent, and incidentally marked the first stage in the slow decline of the House of Commons from a sovereign body which made and unmade governments to its position today. Before Disraeli left office he took a surprising step which occasioned a good deal of criticism. He asked the Queen to confer a peerage, not on himself, for he wished to stay leader of the party in the lower House, but on his wife. He cited the precedent of the elder Pitt, whose wife was made Baroness Chatham, pointed out that 'Mrs. Disraeli has a fortune of her own adequate to any position in which your Majesty might deign to put her', and requested the Queen to create her Viscountess Beaconsfield.[1]

[1] M. & B., v, 99.

The Queen was by no means happy at this proposal. She consulted General Grey, who replied, 'This is indeed, as your Majesty says, very embarrassing.' The General felt – and so did the Queen – that 'it would not be a kindness to Mrs. Disraeli to subject her to what would be made the subject of endless ridicule'. Nevertheless to refuse Disraeli was even more awkward. 'On the whole though with much doubt and diffidence General Grey is inclined to think your Majesty will be better pleased to comply with his wishes than to refuse them and would therefore venture to advise your Majesty to follow the dictates of your Majesty's own kind heart.'[1] The Queen consented in a charming letter which gave no hint of her doubts.[2] So Mary Anne became a peeress. From that moment onwards she subscribed herself to Disraeli as 'your devoted Beaconsfield', and within a week she was using coroneted writing paper.

At the time it was no doubt easy to laugh. Today the gesture seems appropriate. Disraeli was fully entitled to a peerage, but it did not suit him to leave the House of Commons. His debt to his wife was immense. She was old and most unlikely to live till he was again in power, if indeed he ever would be. He already knew that she was suffering from cancer. The peerage was a symbol of defiance, triumph – and gratitude.

2

Disraeli was now sixty-four. It was nearly thirty years since the Conservatives had won a majority in the House of Commons, and the latest election seemed to have decisively confirmed the position of the Liberals as the dominant party. In the circumstances he might well have been inclined to give up. He had held the highest office in the land. What hope was there of holding it again – or if he did of being anything more than head of a minority government existing on sufferance while the Liberals patched up some internal squabble? But Disraeli possessed a tenacity, determination and patience not often to be found in politics. Moreover, he loved the great game. To him it was the very breath of life. And after all, strange and unpredictable changes could take place. Who foresaw the fall of Peel? Disraeli himself had described that government as a Walpole administration. He decided to carry on, although he must

[1] *The Letters of Queen Victoria*, 2nd Series, i, 557–8.
[2] M. & B., v, 100.

have been well aware of the discontent in the party and the blow to his prestige resulting from the loss of the first election held on his own new franchise.

But he knew that it would be hopeless to do much for the moment while Gladstone was in the full flood of his activity at the head of a triumphant majority. He was the more convinced of the need for caution, since the session of 1869 was bound to be mainly concerned with the Irish Church – an issue which divided his own party and united the Liberals. There is therefore little to say about Disraeli's political career during 1869. The most notable event of the year was the death of Derby. Worn out by gout, he went into a gradual decline precipitated by his doctor's overprescription of opium to ease the pain. He died on October 23. Disraeli sincerely mourned him. Their relations remained unclouded to the end, although they had to agree to differ about the Irish Church, for which Derby fought a last-ditch struggle in the House of Lords, with a speech that was both memorable, dramatic and pathetic.

Disraeli kept very quiet during this and the next two sessions. Such measures as the Education Bill, the Irish Land Bill, the abolition of Purchase in the Army and the reform of the Civil Service did not lend themselves to attack. His whole position was shaky and a symptom was his difficulty over the leadership in the House of Lords. Malmesbury resigned the post after the election, and a section actually favoured Salisbury as his successor. This should have been out of the question. It was meant to make Disraeli's position impossible, for the two were not even on speaking terms. To his credit Salisbury refused to be considered. Accordingly Cairns was elected, but one session was enough for him and he resigned at the end of 1869. The obvious choice now seemed to be Stanley, who had succeeded as 15th Earl of Derby a few weeks earlier. He was unanimously elected, but after considering the matter for a day declined the honour. Salisbury was again suggested, but, since he had recently made a thinly disguised attack on Disraeli in the *Quarterly Review* as a 'mere political gamester', nothing came of the proposal. Instead the Duke of Richmond, an amiable but ineffective nonentity, was chosen and remained leader until 1876, when Disraeli himself entered the upper House. These repeated efforts to put forward Salisbury were a clear sign of the resentment felt towards Disraeli in powerful quarters.

The leisure brought by defeat turned Disraeli's attention to literature. He had written nothing since *Lord George Bentinck* in 1851 and no novel since *Tancred* in 1847. At first sight it seems surprising that he should have waited so long, for he had been out of office for most of the time. But the fluidity of politics during the past twenty years made the task of an opposition leader almost as heavy as that of a minister. Now, however, it was clear that there could be no chance of ejecting the Government for a considerable time to come. An offer from a publisher of £10,000 for a novel may have finally decided him, although he refused it. Early in 1869 he settled down to write *Lothair*, preserving such secrecy that even Corry only heard of it for the first time in an advertisement early in 1870.

Lothair, dedicated to the Duc d'Aumale, was published in May of that year. The incident which seems to have been the seed of the plot was the success of the Roman Church in capturing at the end of 1868 the young Marquess of Bute, to whom Lothair, with his fabulous wealth greatly increased by a long minority, bears a shadowy resemblance. The story begins with the preliminaries of Lothair's coming of age, and its theme is the efforts made by the Church of England, the Church of Rome, and the secret nationalist revolutionary societies of Europe to gain him and his money for their cause. The Church of England has on her side not only 'the Bishop', who thinly disguises Wilberforce, but 'the Duke', who is so grand that he is never named, and one of his lovely daughters, Lady Corisande. For Rome there is Cardinal Grandison (Manning), who before being converted to Rome had been appointed one of Lothair's guardians, and the St Jerome family with a beautiful niece, Miss Arundell. For the revolutionary cause we have the mysterious and romantic Theodora, an Italian lady ten years older than Lothair. A large part of the book is devoted to the intrigues to win him over. The struggle between Romanism and revolutionary nationalism for Lothair mirrors the great European struggle between these forces, concentrated at this particular moment on the struggle for Rome itself.

Eventually Theodora converts him to her cause. Lothair fights by her side during Garibaldi's abortive campaign in 1867. She is killed at Viterbo and with her dying breath extracts a promise from him never to be received into the Roman faith. He is then badly wounded at the battle of Mentana and left for dead, but an Italian woman finds him and an ambulance brings him unconscious to the

Palazzo Agostino in Rome, which belongs to the St Jeromes. There Miss Arundell nurses him back to health. Now comes the central crisis of the book. The subtle Monsignori, who are familiars at the Palazzo, weave an ingenious plot to persuade Lothair when at last he recovers consciousness that he was fighting not for the revolutionary but the papal side, that he has been the subject of a miracle; the Italian woman was the Virgin herself, and it is his duty to be received at once into the Church of Rome. Cardinal Grandison, who turns up again, lends his authority to this pious fraud, and the scene in which he explains to Lothair why he must not rely on his own memory of what happened is one of the best pieces of comedy Disraeli ever wrote. Fortunately, just as he is about to succumb, Lothair is rescued by an English doctor who sends him to Sicily for his health. Thence, although still surrounded by priests, he manages to escape in a fishing-boat to Malta just in time to issue a formal denial of his conversion which the Cardinal had prematurely given to the Press. The rest of the story is less interesting. He goes to Greece and Jerusalem, then returns to London, where he finds everything just as it was, the Cardinal moving silently through the gilded saloons as if nothing had ever happened. Miss Arundell takes the veil, Lothair marries Lady Corisande and his Protestantism is inviolate.

Lothair is perhaps the best of all Disraeli's novels. *Coningsby* is the nearest rival, but it is too much of a novel-with-a-purpose to come off quite so successfully. In *Lothair*, too, we are spared the Dis-Rothschildishness which can be tiresome elsewhere. Disraeli depicts with a touch of satire, so subtle that perhaps its objects did not recognize it, the grand social world in which he had been a familiar though slightly mocking traveller for over thirty years. The wit and humour are splendid. The conversation sparkles and there is a good thing on nearly every page. The characters, too, are excellent. There is the Duke, who has only one misfortune; he has no home, because duty compels him to divide the year into short periods spent at each of his numerous palaces. There is Lord St Aldegonde, the radical heir to another dukedom. He is opposed to all ranks, except dukes, who are a necessity, and favours the equal division of all property, except land, which is the mainstay of liberty. It would be quite wrong to treat *Lothair* as a gaudy romance of the peerage. Disraeli saw that the aristocracy, having lost much of their political power but having preserved all their prestige and multiplied their wealth, were in danger of losing the sense of duty which alone prevented them from degenerating into a useless caste. Of course, this perception is never explicitly stated, but it is always there beneath the glitter. Froude in his life of Disraeli devoted a brilliant chapter to *Lothair*. He concluded:

> . . . the true value of the book is the perfect representation of patrician society in England in the year which was then passing over; the full appreciation of all that was good and noble in it; yet the recognition, also, that it was a society without a purpose, and with no claim to endurance. It was then in its most brilliant period, like the full bloom of a flower which opens only to fade.[1]

The novel, published on May 2 in three volumes, was at once an immense success with the public. A novel by an ex-Prime Minister was a unique event. Indeed, there has only been one since, also by Disraeli. The fashionable world was entranced. Everyone who was anyone had to read *Lothair*. Its popularity was so great that the name christened a ship, a new scent, a song and a street, while Baron Rothschild named his famous filly which was to win the Cesarewitch, Corisande. 'On Monday Mr. Mudie's house was I am told in a state of siege', wrote Thomas Longman the publisher. Any danger of flagging sales was removed by the publication at just the right moment of a furious letter from Cornell University by Professor Goldwin Smith, who had at one time held the Regius Chair of History at Oxford. He thought, probably rightly, that he was 'the Oxford Professor', appearing in Chapter XXIV, who 'like sedentary men of extreme opinions . . . was a social parasite' – and a good many other unflattering things, too. 'The stingless insults of a coward', wrote the Professor in a rage. Disraeli was delighted. He was getting his own back for the anonymous abuse heaped on him by Goldwin Smith some twenty years earlier in the *Morning Chronicle*. 'This is hardly the person to inveigh against personalities . . .' he wrote to an American friend, 'I have sometimes brushed him off as I would a mosquito, but am always too much occupied to bear him, or any other insect, any ill will'.[2]

Financially Disraeli did well. *Lothair*, exclusive of American sales, had brought him over £6,000 by 1876. The American sales probably amounted to another £1,500. The popularity of the book stimulated interest in the earlier novels, and in the autumn of 1870 he brought

---

[1] Froude, *Beaconsfield*, 231. [2] M. & B., v, 166.

out a collected edition in ten volumes. He had received £1,000 in royalties for this when in 1877 Longmans offered him £2,100 for the copyright. If these sums are added up one can safely say that Disraeli earned directly and indirectly from the publication of *Lothair* at least £10,600 over the next seven years. He was so encouraged by his success that he began another novel, but it was still uncompleted when Gladstone fell in 1874.

The reviewers were less kind to *Lothair* than the public. Press notices were almost uniformly bad, apart from *The Times*, and the *Pall Mall Gazette*. However, Disraeli had answered his enemies in advance. 'You know who the critics are?' he makes Mr Phoebus say. 'The men who have failed in literature and art'. He recurred to the same theme at greater length in the General Preface to the collected edition of the novels. The verdict of contemporary critics is far from being always wrong; it accords more frequently with that of posterity than is often recognized, but on this occasion it has not stood the test of time. *Lothair*, in spite of much careless prose, especially in the early chapters, is perhaps the best-constructed work from his pen.

Buckle comments on the marked absence of congratulatory letters from Disraeli's political colleagues. Monckton Milnes summed up the opinion of the political world before the book appeared: 'His wisest friends think it must be a mistake and his enemies hope that it will be his ruin.' After it had come out, his friends probably could not decide what to make of it, and took refuge in silence. The book did him no good politically. It seemed a frivolous, if puzzling, production from a statesman, and the reissue of the other novels, especially *Tancred* and *Vivian Grey*, could only draw attention to attitudes which most of his friends would have preferred forgotten.

Disraeli's political stock slumped steadily during the first three sessions of the new Parliament. He was often ill and often absent. The theory has been advanced that he still could not escape from the role, which had been his for so long, of wire-puller and *eminence grise* to Lord Derby, and that Derby's retirement left him uncertain and lacking a leader. If so, his attitude ought to have changed after Derby's death. Perhaps even then Disraeli could not quite bring himself to come forward as the personal embodiment of the Tory party. It is easy to forget Derby's immense prestige, and the sense of anticlimax which Disraeli's succession produced in that deferential era. One must remember too that his brief premiership had

been a failure by the only test that matters in politics. The party's
fortunes were almost at their lowest ebb since 1832. He may well
have felt a temporary lack of confidence and wondered what to do
next. Whatever the reason for Disraeli's inactivity, there was
much discontent among his colleagues. Manners and Northcote
were apparently the only dissentients at a meeting at Lord Exeter's
seat, Burghley, on February 1, 1872, when it was agreed that the
new Lord Derby would be a more effective leader.[1] The Chief Whip
declared that his name alone would be worth forty or fifty seats.
No one had the nerve to convey these doubts to Disraeli, nor did
Derby give the slightest encouragement. But Disraeli knew that
there was trouble afoot. The newspapers were full of it, and the
rival merits of the two leaders were the subject of much public discussion.

Accordingly he decided to assert himself. He began with a brisk
and quite unwarranted rap on the ducal knuckles of the leader of the
House of Lords for insufficient co-operation. He then opened the
session with a vigorous speech in which he declared that the
Government had lived in 'a blaze of apology' for the last six months;
but on the most important immediate issue, the *Alabama* arbitration, he did all he could to strengthen its hand against what he
called 'wild and preposterous' claims. Privately, he was sure that
Gladstone had mismanaged the affair, but he considered it unpatriotic to say so just then. Earlier, in connexion with the Franco-
Prussian war and the Russian repudiation of the Black Sea clauses
of the Treaty of Paris, Disraeli had made no bones about his opinion
that Gladstone, partly through excessive naval and military economies, partly through mistaken internationalism, was letting down
British prestige.

Immediately after this there occurred one of those seemingly
inexplicable gusts of public opinion which now and then by some
freak of political weather come down from a calm sky to ruffle the
hitherto still political waters. On February 27, along with all the
leading statesmen of the day, Disraeli attended the thanksgiving
service at S Paul's for the recovery of the Prince of Wales from
typhoid fever. The London crowd had a good opportunity to
demonstrate their feelings about each person. Gladstone was
received in silence with occasional hoots, but Disraeli was applauded

[1] Others present were Hardy, Cairns, Pakington, Ward Hunt, the Duke of Marlborough and Gerard Noel, the Chief Whip.

to the echo. Later that morning Sir William Fraser saw him in the morning-room of the Carlton Club ostensibly listening to another member, but staring into vacancy, immovable as a statue. 'I have heard it said by one who spoke to Napoleon I . . . that his face was as of one who looks into another world: that is the only description I can give of Disraeli's look at the moment I speak of.' In the afternoon Fraser asked the member what Disraeli was talking about. He replied that it was some county business. 'I said, "I will tell you what he was thinking about: he was thinking that he will be Prime Minister again." '[1] Fraser, though sometimes silly, was often a shrewd observer.

Disraeli seldom made public speeches to great mass audiences, but he did so twice during 1872. The first was at Manchester on April 3 at the Free Trade Hall. The previous day had been marked by a great parade of the Conservative Associations of Lancashire, some two hundred and fifty passing before him and Mary Anne, who came in spite of her fast failing health. It was a most encouraging demonstration. In his speech Disraeli announced that 'the programme of the Conservative party is to maintain the Constitution of the country'. He spoke for three hours and a quarter, sustaining himself with 'white brandy', indistinguishable to the observer from the water taken with it. He is said to have consumed two bottles by the end.[2] He was principally concerned to show that powerful Radical forces were determined to destroy the Church and the House of Lords, that even the Crown was menaced – it was the high-water mark of English republicanism just then – and that Gladstone had never clearly repudiated these left-wing supporters. He also attacked the Government for a feeble foreign policy, for neglect of the Navy and for menacing England with a standing army. The latter charge was a travesty of the Cardwell reforms, but the Government's record over the Services was not impeccable. One of the newest ships, *Captain*, had recently turned turtle in a storm, and army manoeuvres had been somewhat feebly cancelled because of wet weather. Posterity has fastened not so much on these matters as Disraeli's observations about the need for health legislation and the well-known jest – '*Sanitas sanitatum, omnia sanitas*'. But, in fact, he touched on that theme only briefly, giving it not more than five minutes or so. His most famous passage was a memorable and much-quoted denunciation of the Cabinet:

[1] Fraser, *Disraeli and His Day*, 376.   [2] M. & B., v, 187.

As time advanced it was not difficult to perceive that extravagance was being substituted for energy by the Government. The unnatural stimulus was subsiding. Their paroxysms ended in prostration. Some took refuge in melancholy, and their eminent chief alternated between a menace and a sigh. As I sat opposite the Treasury Bench the Ministers reminded me of one of those marine landscapes not very uncommon on the coasts of South America. You behold a range of exhausted volcanoes. Not a flame flickers on a single pallid crest. But the situation is still dangerous. There are occasional earthquakes, and ever and anon the dark rumbling of the sea.

There was now no question who commanded the Conservative party, and as if to clinch the matter Disraeli followed up the Manchester speech with a shorter, but equally striking, oration at the Crystal Palace on June 24. He recurred to a familiar theme, that the Liberals were the party of 'Continental' or 'cosmopolitan' ideas and that the Conservatives were the 'national' party. The Reform Act of 1867 was founded on the belief that the working classes of England were Conservative in the 'purest and loftiest' sense. By this he meant, he said, that they

> are proud of belonging to a great country, and wish to maintain its greatness – that they are proud of belonging to an Imperial country, and are resolved to maintain, if they can, their empire – that they believe on the whole that the greatness and the empire of England are to be attributed to the ancient institutions of the land.

Disraeli said something, though tantalizingly little, about his concept of empire. It was chiefly an attack on the alleged Liberal efforts to disrupt it. He was in favour of self-government, but thought that it 'ought to have been accompanied by an Imperial tariff . . . and by the institution of some representative council in the metropolis'. There should, too, have been 'a military code' defining home and colonial responsibilities and enabling England to call on colonial aid in war if need be. Disraeli here foreshadowed the imperial policy of Joseph Chamberlain and others at the turn of the century, but his ideas seem to have been thrown out more or less casually and without any special appreciation of their significance. He barely mentioned India.

In the same speech he again dwelt on the improvement of the condition of the people, housing, health, 'air, light and water', and he referred with pride to the Conservative record over the Factory Laws. He made a good deal of the Liberal member's remark that this was a 'policy of sewage'. The people of England would be idiots, he said, 'if . . . they should not have long perceived that the time had arrived when social and not political improvement is the object which they ought to pursue'. Disraeli was adumbrating here the social legislation which was to be such a conspicuous part of his Government's activities in 1875–6, but, like the imperial theme, it occupied relatively little of his time. The Manchester and Crystal Palace speeches are often cited as the major contribution of Disraeli to a new concept of progressive conservatism. Their importance should not be underestimated. It is nevertheless a fact that in the forty-five pages which they take up in Kebbel's edition of his speeches, the subject of empire occupies slightly under two and that of social reform just over three.

Meanwhile domestic sorrows were darkening Disraeli's life. At the end of 1868 his brother James died. Since his wife's death some years earlier he had been living with a Mrs Bassett by whom he was supposed to have had two daughters. He left her a legacy of £4,000, and the residue of his estate to Disraeli. There is more than one hint in Disraeli's papers that James's mode of life was 'irregular', including an illiterate threatening letter from someone who claimed that she had been dismissed from the service of Mrs Augusta Leigh because of her 'acquaintance' with James, who now refused to answer her letters. She said she would put it all in the papers. 'He is fond of the aristocrace [sic] a scandal in High Life I would wonder how it would affect Mrs. Disraeli to hear of it a delicate high minded woman . . . Sir will you not induce him to keep his promise as a gentleman.'[1] Whether Disraeli said anything is unknown. The few letters from his brother which survive for this period concern the more congenial subject of claret. Mrs Bassett married a poor farmer in Cornwall who got through the legacy. There is a rather pathetic letter to Disraeli much later from one of her daughters appealing for help, and saying that she had only just learned who her father was.[2]

The residue inherited by Disraeli, who was the sole executor, amounted to £5,300. Ralph was much hurt at being left out altogether without even a mention. He seems to have been offended with Disraeli, too. He wrote a stiff letter agreeing to come to the

[1] Hughenden Papers, Box 8, A/I/D/39, n.d.
[2] ibid., A/I/D/38, n.d.

funeral, 'tho' you cannot be surprised that under all the circumstances my being present at Hughenden must be most distasteful to me'. He ended: 'Certainly my Brothers have not been to me "Brothers not only in name but in spirit", as is written in a certain Political Biography'.[1]

A far graver loss lay ahead. Mary Anne had been growing palpably frailer during the three years since Disraeli's resignation. According to the obituary notice in *The Times*, she had known for some while past that she suffered from cancer of the stomach, but was determined to conceal it from Disraeli, little realizing that he, too, knew the truth, but was equally determined to keep his knowledge from her. She had insisted on accompanying him to Manchester in April, but the strain was too much and she was seriously ill afterwards. Nevertheless she rallied, and, encouraged by her doctor, Sir William Gull, made an effort to move in society. She continued to attend receptions and parties, despite being taken ill suddenly in the middle of a court function on May 9; and, after a brief interlude at Hughenden for Whitsun, she returned to Grosvenor Gate with every intention of seeing out the season. But on July 17, at a reception to meet the Duchess of Cambridge, she collapsed, and had to be taken away at once. She never went out in society again.

She was in her eightieth year, and had always been likely to predecease a husband twelve years younger. Disraeli must at least have contemplated the possibility, but now that it became imminent reality he was heartbroken. His letters to his friends at this time make pathetic reading.

> We have not been separated for thirty three years [he wrote to Cairns] and during all that time, in her society, I have never had a moment of dullness. It tears my heart to see such a spirit suffer, and suffer so much! May you, my dear Cairns, never experience my present feelings . . .

She was too ill for their usual move to Hughenden at the end of the session. So Disraeli took her for long drives in the, to him, new world of London suburbia. Even this he invested with the touch of romance always ready at his summons. He made some notes for a letter, apparently never sent, to the Queen.

[1] ibid., Box 9, A/I/E/77, December 26, 1868. The allusion is to *Lord George Bentinck*, 587. 'Followed to his tomb by those brothers who if not consoled, might at this moment be sustained by the remembrance that to him they had ever been brothers not only in name but spirit . . .'

What miles of villas! and of all sorts of architecture! What beautiful churches! What gorgeous palaces of Geneva.

One day we came upon a real feudal castle, with a donjon keep high in the air. It turned out to be the new City prison in the Camden Road, but it deserves a visit; I mean externally . . .[1]

He reckoned that they covered 228 miles in August and September.

At the end of September she rallied, and Disraeli was at last able to take her to Hughenden. But from then onwards the downward path was inexorable. In vain Disraeli's rich friends sent her the most appetizing and recherché compositions of their chefs. She could not eat, and the illness gained on her. She was well enough to receive some visitors at the end of November, Rosebery and Manners for two days, and then Sir William Harcourt and Lord Ronald Gower. Harcourt sent her some Trinity audit ale as a present after he left, and Disraeli told him later that it was almost the last thing which passed her lips before she died. That year winter came on early, cold and dark. On December 6 she was found to have congestion of the lungs. She refused to go to bed, and died in her chair on December 15, after a week of acute illness and mental delusions. The funeral was private, attended only by Disraeli, Corry, Rose, her doctor, and farm tenants and household staff. She was buried outside the east end of Hughenden church. It was a wild wet day. After the coffin had been lowered into the grave, Disraeli stood gazing down at it for fully ten minutes, bare-headed in the pouring rain and bitter wind.

Letters of condolence poured in upon him; from the Queen, the Prince of Wales, Gladstone, and a host of friends, colleagues, political supporters and political opponents. Many came, too, from perfect strangers. Disraeli's grief was intense, and his situation was the sadder, for he had almost at once to set about moving from Grosvenor Gate. For the next year he had to use a suite in Edward's Hotel as his London base. Moreover, her death meant the loss of an income of £5,000 a year and the danger of a return to his old days of financial insecurity, although he was helped to some extent by the generosity of Andrew Montagu[2] who reduced the interest on his mortgage from 3 per cent to 2.

Some of Disraeli's colleagues feared that the blow would induce him to quit political life entirely, but he had no intention of doing

[1] M. & B., v, 225.
[2] See above, 424.

this. He had now quite re-established his control over the party, and the great game was a distraction from his sorrows. In the middle of January he summoned Hardy and Cairns to Hughenden to discuss tactics, and made it clear that he meant to speak and lead, although he asked Hardy, whom he treated at this time as his deputy, to give the usual parliamentary dinner. By February he was up in London, dining quietly from time to time with friends, for 'hotel life in the evening is a cave of despair'.

The political prospect was at last beginning to brighten. Disraeli's famous simile of the exhausted volcanoes was no mere gibe. Gladstone had begun with a great burst of reforming energy. It is fair to claim that from 1869 to 1872 he created much of the institutional framework of Britain as we know it today, and if the Judicature Act of 1873 is thrown in, the claim becomes even stronger. But, for the past year, the Government had been vexed by that combination of accidents, scandals and blunders which so often for no apparent reason seem to beset an energetic administration in its later stages. Gladstone's use of the royal prerogative to by-pass the Lords' opposition to Cardwell's army reforms and his high-handed action over the Collier and Ewelme cases early in 1872 caused many moderate Liberals to wonder about his judgement.[1] The session of 1873 had barely begun when he ran into renewed trouble and Disraeli was faced with a tactical decision of the first importance.

Having dealt with the questions of religion and land, Gladstone sought to crown his work for Ireland by doing what Disraeli had failed to do, to establish a Roman Catholic university at Dublin. The Bill satisfied neither Catholics nor Protestants, and it would seem that on the attitude of the former, Gladstone, like Disraeli, was misled by Manning. Disraeli made great play of the fact that, in order to avoid controversial subjects, the new university was to teach neither theology, modern history, nor moral philosophy, and that any teacher who offended the religious beliefs of his students could be dismissed. The Government threatened to make the second reading an issue of confidence. Disraeli refused to be intimidated, and on March 12 an unusual alliance of Conservatives and Irish Catholics defeated the measure by 287 to 284. After some hesitation,

[1] Magnus, *Gladstone*, 222. The first was a judicial appointment and the second a piece of clerical patronage. In both cases Gladstone evaded the disqualifications imposed by statute upon his appointees, by methods of smart legalism which created a storm in Parliament. He narrowly escaped defeat on each occasion.

the Cabinet decided to resign. The Queen at once invited Disraeli to form a government.

But Disraeli had had enough of minority governments, and he refused to take office. The Queen then, through her secretary, Colonel Ponsonby, asked him whether he would accept on the understanding that he could dissolve Parliament. This was a more difficult offer to decline, but Disraeli did so none the less. On the surface the argument between Gladstone and Disraeli, who dispatched lengthy memoranda aimed at each other[1] to the Queen, was a constitutional one. Gladstone said that a party which had defeated the Government on an issue of confidence had a duty to take office. Disraeli replied that this was not so when the vote resulted from an accidental alliance between two groups with nothing in common except their distaste for a very bad Bill which ought never to have been made an issue of confidence. Behind these considerations, however, there lay important tactical calculations. Disraeli believed that the tide was turning in his favour. In 1871 the Liberals had lost six by-elections and in 1872 seven, without any gains to offset them.[2] But he was convinced that the movement had not gone far enough for a dissolution in the early part of 1873 to produce a decisive result. Moreover, he believed, or at any rate argued – that the Conservatives could not dissolve at once. The formation of a new ministry, the ministerial re-elections, the necessary time to acquire official information, the passing of the estimates and the Mutiny Act would take at least two months. During that period they would be at the mercy of the Liberal majority, and their standing in the country would inevitably decline.

Ponsonby, who was of a Whiggish outlook, had never held any close discussion with Disraeli before. He did not know quite what to make of the Conservative leader, as his note of their interview at Edward's Hotel well shows.

> . . . there was something in his over-civil expressions about the Queen or 'my dear Colonel' which made me think he was playing with me, and I felt once or twice a difficulty in not laughing; but when he developed the reasons for his policy he rose and stood much more upright than I had ever seen him, spoke in a most

[1] See Morley, *Gladstone*, ii, 446–56, and Appendix, 652–3, and M. & B., v, 208–17, for the relevant documents.

[2] Their net loss in 1869 had been two, in 1870 one.

frank and straightforward manner, and with a sharpness and decision which was different from his early words. Yet probably he had measured the length of my foot, and had been more sincere and honest in his message to the Queen than when he made me to believe in his frank exposition of policy.

He was far easier to speak to than Gladstone, who forces you into his groove, while Disraeli apparently follows yours and is genial almost too genial in his sentiments . . .[1]

Disraeli, who was backed by Hardy, Richmond, Northcote, Cairns and Ward Hunt got his way. Gladstone had to reassume office in a far weaker position than before. It was a masterly piece of restraint on Disraeli's part and a contrast with the readiness to profit by adventitious Radical alliances, which that he had sometimes shown when Derby was leader. It is impossible to say for certain what result a dissolution would have had. The most authoritative modern account suggests that Disraeli was right and that the consequence would probably have been a Conservative or Liberal majority of about ten. 'By waiting and allowing Liberal divisions to become deeper the Conservative position was immensely strengthened.'[2] Gladstone would not have done well at a general election in the opening of 1873, but it was his last chance of preventing a heavy defeat. There is little doubt that Lord Kimberley, the Colonial Secretary, was right when he noted in his diary, 'I regret for my part that we did not dissolve.'[3] Although Disraeli was criticized with some justice for having given away too much in an overelaborate speech of explanation to the House, his own standing in the party was enhanced by the episode as a whole. It was a conclusive answer to the charge of snatching for office.

The session which had started so badly for the Government continued as it had begun. It terminated with a series of scandals connected with the posts and telegraphs, and as soon as the recess arrived Gladstone, who was privately very angry at what had happened, reshuffled the ministry. Among other changes he moved Lowe, the Chancellor of the Exchequer, to the Home Office and took on the Chancellorship himself. This raised a major legal conundrum. Was he obliged to submit himself for re-election? It was no mere academic point, for his seat at Greenwich was regarded as unsafe. Gladstone had been advised by the law officers that he need

---

[1] M. & B., v, 211–12.
[2] Hanham, *Elections and Party Management*, 221.
[3] *Camden Miscellany*, 3rd Series, xxi, 37.

not vacate, but other lawyers took a different view. The dispute rumbled on for the rest of the year.

Meanwhile Disraeli was beginning to find new interests in his personal life to distract him from the sorrow of his bereavement. Mary Anne in a valedictory letter written many years earlier urged him to remarry after her death.

> My own dear Husband – If I should depart this life before you, leave orders that we may be buried in the same grave at whatever distance you may die from England. God bless you my dearest, kindest. You have been a perfect husband to me. Be put by my side in the same grave. And now farewell, my dear Dizzy. Do not live alone dearest. Someone I earnestly hope you may find as attached to you as your own devoted MARY ANNE.[1]

Disraeli was not destined to take this step, although there is some reason to believe that encouraging hints were given by more than one lady of distinction, and it is certain that at least one did not content herself with a hint. Disraeli had long been acquainted with the dowager Lady Cardigan, widow of the Crimean hero and owner of Deene. Although very rich, she was not well regarded in society. As Miss Adeline de Horsey she had openly lived with the Earl during the last few months of the life of his first wife. They married as soon as she died, but this did not reconcile the social world, and Lord Cardigan's brother-in-law described Deene as 'an infamous house'. After the Earl's death she became more and more eccentric, among other things having herself rowed in the bay at Cowes, reclining in the stern of a gig, playing the guitar.

According to her own account, she first met Disraeli in 1846 at Lady Palmerston's, when she was seventeen. Early in 1873 she began a correspondence with him, of which, apart from one draft letter at Hughenden, only her side survives. She twice offered to be his private secretary and her tone became rapidly warmer. Finally in June, possibly in reply to a letter from him in which he said that he 'wd fain hope you will not misinterpret my suggestion that at present it wd be better that we shd not meet',[2] she went a step

---

[1] M. & B., v, 232, June 6, 1856.

[2] Hughenden Papers, Box 13, A/IV/K/24a. It is not absolutely clear whether this draft letter which survives at Hughenden is the cause of, or a reply to, Lady Cardigan's offer of marriage. Monypenny to Lord Knollys, December 1, 1909, Royal Archives, x, 33, 343. See Joan Wake, *The Brudenells of Deene* (1953), 448–56, for these and other letters of Lady Cardigan. Miss Wake states that none of Disraeli's letters have survived at Deene.

further. She had had, she said, '12 offers of marriage since Lord Cardigan's death', but she had long decided upon the 'union which would to me secure happiness comfort & the realization of my most ambitious hopes'. All their '*real* friends', she continued, would regard as 'most excellent in a moral political sensible & practical view' the alliance of 'the greatest man we have in genius & intellect with the wealthiest relict of the staunchest Conservative Peer that ever lived'.[1]

This must have been embarrassing. There was a break in the correspondence for a couple of months, but on August 26 she wrote to tell him of her forthcoming marriage to the Comte de Lancastre, and later asked him to destroy the letter of June. Perhaps it is as well that he did not. She subsequently claimed that it was he who had asked her to marry him, and that she had refused him. She even stated in a book of reminiscences that she had consulted the Prince of Wales on the matter one day when hunting with the Belvoir, but King Edward VII, as he was by then, had no recollection of the episode.[2] Her letters to Disraeli did not cease. She endeavoured to get him to persuade the Court to receive her, but Queen Victoria, who already disapproved of her, was even more annoyed at her habit of calling herself Countess of Cardigan and Lancastre, the Queen's own incognito being Countess of Lancaster. Lady Cardigan, growing ever odder, outlived her second husband and all her generation. She died in 1916. A union with Disraeli would not, one suspects, have been a success.

In the summer of 1873 he began the last of those strange romances which coloured every stage of his life. At the age of sixty-eight he fell head over heels in love with Lady Bradford, who was fifty-four and a grandmother. His letters to her and her sister, Lady Chesterfield, whom he regarded with affection rather than passion, are one of the great sources for his biography, indeed for the history of the times until his death.[3] He had known them for many years. They were daughters of Lord Forester, the Shropshire magnate, through whose influence Disraeli had secured the nomination to Shrewsbury in 1841. Another sister who died young had married Lord

[1] ibid., A/IV/K/24, n.d., but certainly June 1873.
[2] ibid., Box 301, Lord Knollys to W. F. Monypenny, November 29, 1909.
[3] He wrote 1,100 to Lady Bradford and 500 to Lady Chesterfield. See Lord Zetland, *The Letters of Disraeli to Lady Bradford and Lady Chesterfield*, 2 vols (1929), and M. & B., v and vi, for copious quotations.

Carrington's son, and it was at Wycombe Abbey in the 1830s that Disraeli first met Selina Forester, as Lady Bradford was then. The two sisters now took pity on him in his solitude, and a visit that summer to Bretby, Lady Chesterfield's country house, at which Lady Bradford was also present, began this new chapter in his life. He could not consider marriage to the one he really loved, for Lord Bradford, a well-known sporting peer and a minor office-holder in the last Tory administration, was very much alive. But Lady Chesterfield, who was seventeen years older than her sister, had lost her husband in 1866, and Disraeli actually proposed to her, though chiefly with the idea that he would thus see more of Lady Bradford. It is hardly surprising that he was refused. But he continued to be a welcome guest at Bretby.

His relations with Lady Bradford were far more tempestuous. It is difficult to avoid the impression that, although flattered at his attention, and delighted to be 'in the know', she never really cared for him much. She may well have found his ardour somewhat embarrassing, and indeed when we read of him sending two or three letters a day to her from Downing Street and, as Buckle puts it, traversing 'in his private life the whole gamut of half-requited love – passionate devotion, rebuff, despair, resignation, renewed hope, reconciliation, ecstacy', it seems incredible that this is a septuagenarian Prime Minister writing to a happily married woman in her mid-fifties.

These turbulent emotions lay ahead. In the autumn of 1873 Disraeli was filled with the sense of happy anticipation of a fresh and delightful relationship. So much did he feel the renewal of youth that at Weston, Lord Bradford's seat, he actually agreed to go cub-hunting, although he had only ridden a horse twice in the last twenty-five years, and never hunted at Hughenden. Perhaps he remembered the day long ago when he rode Henrietta's 'Arabian mare' on a run of thirty miles. The repetition was unwise. He was so exhausted on dismounting that he nearly collapsed.

Politically things were going well. During November he had a great reception in Scotland. He had been elected two years earlier as Lord Rector of Glasgow University, but his wife's illness prevented him from going up for his installation and address. Now he repaired the omission and also made a much-applauded political speech. There seemed almost a hope that at last the Scots might take his advice to 'leave off . . . munching the remainder biscuit of an effete Liberalism'. There was one minor setback. Although the Liberals lost seven by-elections in 1873, they managed to win back Bath, and some people considered that Disraeli's letter to the Tory candidate had done more harm than good. It was certainly vigorous. The Government for nearly five years 'have harrassed every trade, worried every profession, and assailed or menaced every class, institution, and species of property in the country'. This condition of 'civil warfare' had only been varied by jobbery and errors. But the country had decided 'to close this career of plundering and blundering'. Disraeli was unrepentant. He believed in hard hitting, and defended his letter with vigour. Moreover, no permanent ill effects could be alleged. Early in the new year the Conservatives gained a seat at Stroud and lowered the Liberal majority at Newcastle-upon-Tyne from 4,000 to 1,000.

Disraeli surveyed the political developments with pleasure but no sense of urgency. A general election seemed inconceivable before the summer and could be delayed until 1875. He moved restlessly from country house to country house, Ashridge and Blenheim in early December; Hardy's house, Hempsted Park, in the middle of the month for a party conclave, for he was unable to face a gathering at Hughenden; then to Trentham, whither the Duchess of Sutherland had invited him to escape a lonely Christmas; and after that to Lord Alington's at Crichel, where he knew Lady Bradford would be staying, to Heron Court, Malmesbury's seat, and to Bretby. The chief political topic of the hour was whether Gladstone was still entitled to his seat in Parliament and everyone looked forward to an exciting dispute on this subtle constitutional question as soon as the new session began.

CHAPTER XXIV

Power

1874–6

1

Disraeli went up to London on Friday, January 23, staying as usual at Edwards's Hotel. He intended to make further inquiries about a house and to return to Hughenden after the week-end, for the opening of the session was still a fortnight off. But he abruptly changed his plans when to his astonishment on Saturday morning he read in *The Times* that there was to be an immediate dissolution. Three columns of the paper were filled with Gladstone's election address, whose principal theme was an undertaking to abolish income tax. Although the time and place, a week-end and a London hotel, were anything but convenient, Disraeli was determined, with the aid of such colleagues as he could muster, to reply at once. Cairns was his chief assistant and between them they got out his answer in time for Monday's papers.

Disraeli described Gladstone's address as 'a prolix narrative', and declared that the Conservatives also had always been in favour of abolishing income tax. He did not say much about social reform or the Empire, although he devoted a good deal of space to the alleged iniquities of the Government's policy over the Straits of Malacca – an issue on which they had, so he claimed, been insufficiently careful of British interests. Neither of the two manifestoes sounds particularly inspiring today, and it is hard to avoid the impression that both leaders had forgotten how much smaller a proportion of the electorate by then paid income tax. Disraeli's main theme was essentially negative – a straightforward conservative attack, as in the Manchester and Crystal Palace speeches, upon 'incessant and harrassing legislation' and the dangerous opinions of the advanced Liberals. He conceded that the Prime Minister 'is not certainly at present opposed to our national institutions or the integrity of our empire', but he claimed that many of his supporters were hostile to the monarchy, the House of Lords, the Church of England, and the Union with Ireland.

This rather negative line probably accorded better with the public mood than a more constructive declaration of policy. Often after a period of strenuous reform a moment arrives quite suddenly when the British people tires of being improved. The winter of 1873-4 was just such an occasion. Gladstone's administration, though bearing the same party label as Palmerston's ten years earlier, was entirely different in policy and outlook. It was the first avowed and vigorous reformist Government since Grey's, and its legislation had annoyed almost as many groups and interests as the Whigs had managed to offend between 1830 and 1834. In fact, Disraeli found himself playing the role of Peel in the 1830s, a rallying-point for the forces of property disturbed at excessive innovation though ready to accept the need for cautious piecemeal reform. The more Disraeli's career is examined the clearer it becomes that Palmerston's death marks the real dividing line in his political life. It brought to an end the sort of conservative liberalism which had been such an obstacle to the Conservative party ever since 1846. It gave Gladstone his opportunity to imprint his own stamp upon the Liberal party, and Disraeli the chance to assume not only the Peelite mantle in home policy but the Palmerstonian mantle in foreign affairs. In this respect the apparently disproportionate fuss which he made about the Straits of Malacca had a significance at the time which some historians have overlooked. Disraeli was determined to beat the patriotic drum, and he was right in gauging the impatience of the voters with the Little Englander and internationalist tone which seemed to sound so often in the speeches of leading Liberals.

Some degree of Conservative reaction was to be expected in 1874, but the extent of it, which surprised almost everyone, is explicable by three principal reasons. First there was the timing of the election. Gladstone could scarcely have chosen a worse moment to dissolve, and indeed took his own followers completely by surprise. Naturally people assumed that the question of his own seat had something to do with the decision, for a general election did at least solve that problem. In fact, this was not what influenced him. His choice was governed by an undisclosed split in the Cabinet. Although he had a large budget surplus, it was not enough for the abolition of income tax. His plan was opposed by the service ministers, who declared that they could not consent to the necessary reductions in their estimates unless the Government received a clear mandate from the electorate. Therefore, if he was to carry out his scheme he had to dissolve at once.

A second element in the Conservative victory requires further analysis by psephological historians. The borough electorate had increased by some 15 per cent, or 190,000 persons, since 1868. A large part of this increase must have been from among the compounders enfranchised by Goschen's Act in 1869. These tended to be the poorer householders. If Disraeli's advisers were correct when they told him in 1868 that 'the Conservative feeling is more predominant in the humbler portion of the householders', this addition to the electorate may well have contributed to his success at the polls six years later.

A third factor operating against the Liberals was the great improvement which under Disraeli's auspices had been made to the Conservative party's organization.[1] He brought to an end after the 1868 election the unsatisfactory system whereby Spofforth of Rose, Norton & Co. had acted as Principal Agent. The firm was no longer charged with electoral work, and Rose was consoled with a baronetcy as soon as Disraeli got back into office. The new Principal Agent was John Gorst, an able young barrister who had lost his seat at the general election. He was told by Disraeli that his first task was as far as possible to ensure that every constituency was contested by a candidate chosen in advance. Some measure of his success is shown by the fact that in Scotland, the worst area for the Conservative cause, he raised the number of contested constituencies from twenty-one out of fifty-six to thirty-seven, and that over Britain as a whole more seats were fought in 1874 than ever before.

Gorst, moreover, virtually created the Conservative Central Office, which, with an equally able man as Secretary, Major Keith-Falconer, was performing by 1874 nearly all the tasks that it does today. The two also renovated an already existing institution – the National Union of Conservative and Constitutional Working Men's Associations. At Disraeli's instigation the expression 'Working Men's' was dropped as being unsuitable to a party which sought to minimize class conflict. The National Union was administered from the Central Office, Gorst and Keith-Falconer acting as joint secretaries. Its local associations flourished greatly in Lancashire, where there was a brand of popular Conservatism unique at that time.

[1] M. & B., v, 184–5; and see Hanham, *Elections and Election Management*, 114–15, and 358–68, for a full account of the organizational changes made at this time.

Disraeli had suffered one loss since 1868; Lord Neville to whom he deputed general supervision of the party machine had succeeded to the earldom of Abergavenny and retired from active management, although he remained a much valued counsellor. He had no exact successor and Disraeli now dealt direct with the Chief Whip[1] and Gorst. He differed from Gladstone in treating them as independent powers and refused to subordinate the Principal Agent to the Whip – a practice which he later abandoned with, according to Gorst, disastrous results.

The Conservative coffers were well filled by the time of the election. Here, too, they were better placed than the Liberals. It is, however, of interest to notice that the main source of funds, even after Disraeli's day, continued to be the landed proprietors, especially some of the great magnates. There is nothing to substantiate the claim sometimes made that from 1871 onwards the liquor trade was a major or even an important contributor.[2]

For the moment the Conservative organization was better than that of the Liberals, but in spite of these pointers to success Gorst was cautious in prediction. In fact, his estimate was very similar to that made by his predecessors in 1868 – Conservatives 328, Liberals 325 – and equally wrong though in the opposite direction. On February 6, by which time the borough elections had shown a strong swing to the Conservatives, Gorst predicted a majority of twenty-seven. When the counties polled it was clear that they had won a great victory. In England they had a majority of over 110. In Scotland they raised their numbers from 7 to 19. In Ireland the Liberals were shattered by the emergence of the new Home Rule party which took most of its gains from them, leaving the Conservatives more or less intact. Disraeli, who had a contest himself for the first time since 1852, much to his annoyance because of the expense, came head of the poll in Buckinghamshire. The final figures for the whole country were, Conservatives 350, Liberals 245, Home Rulers 57.

Gladstone was astounded and chagrined at the result. With his penchant for seeing politics in terms of moral black and white he put down his defeat to the animosity inspired by his Licensing Act among the liquor trade. He told his brother that he had been 'borne

[1] The Chief Whips during Disraeli's leadership were Colonel Taylor, 1859–68 and 1873–4, The Hon. Gerard Noel, 1868–73, Sir William Hart-Dyke, 1874–80, Rowland Winn, 1880–5.

[2] Hanham, 225.

down in a torrent of gin and beer', and Queen Victoria that 'the most powerful operative cause has been the combined and costly action of the Publicans except in the North where from their more masculine character the people are not so easily manageable'.[1] Although the Bill may have cost him some votes, there seems little reason to suppose that it was the chief reason for his defeat. The latest historian of these years finds no evidence of a systematic attack by the licensed victuallers on the Government.[2]

For a moment Gladstone contemplated meeting Parliament in the hope that he might somehow be able to dispose of his £5 m surplus before his hated rival could get at it. 'Is it not disgusting,' Mrs Gladstone wrote to her son Herbert, 'after all Papa's labour and patriotism and years of work to think of handing over his nest-egg to that Jew?'[3] But there was no way out. In the end Gladstone followed Disraeli's precedent and resigned without waiting for defeat in the House.

On February 17 the Queen sent for Disraeli. He was well prepared. At the last moment he had discovered a suitable house, No. 2 Whitehall Gardens, and so was able to conduct in reasonable comfort the negotiations for forming a Cabinet. The colleagues whom he most closely consulted were Cairns, Derby, Northcote and Hardy. It was plain sailing but for one rather angular cape that had to be rounded. Lord Salisbury's trenchant mind and eloquent voice would not only be a valuable asset if he was in the Cabinet; they might be a serious danger if he was not. Lady Derby[4] conducted the negotiations. Disraeli awaited their outcome with anxiety. After some hesitation Salisbury, who was pressed by such normally anti-Disraeli figures as Carnarvon, Sir William Heathcote, and the Duke of Northumberland, gave way. His accession drew the sting from the party's Right.

Disraeli could now go ahead. He was determined to have a small Cabinet. He did not manage to achieve the target of ten which he had laid down many years before as the theoretical optimum. But his Cabinet of twelve, six peers and six commoners, was the smallest since 1832. On the whole the appointments were obvious. The six

[1] Royal Archives, C.33.23, February 9.
[2] Hanham, *Elections and Party Management*, 1867–85, 223–6, effectively rebuts Sir Robert Ensor's theory in his *England, 1870–1914*, 21–22, that the liquor trade was a major element in Tory strength from the 1874 election onwards.
[3] Georgina Battiscombe, *Mrs. Gladstone*, 158.
[4] Salisbury's stepmother.

peers with one exception, the Duke of Richmond, went back to positions that they had held during 1866–8. The Duke became Lord President with the leadership of the House of Lords. He would have liked the War Office, but Disraeli intended to have the great spending departments in the House of Commons. The previous tenants were not available. Monty Corry's father was dead, and Pakington, to Disraeli's relief, had lost his seat. The War Office in the aftermath of the Cardwell reforms was likely to be the less easy of the two, and Disraeli gave it to Hardy, who had been Home Secretary in 1868. The Admiralty went to Ward Hunt. The new Chancellor of the Exchequer was, of course, Northcote, who would have been Disraeli's first choice in 1868.

This left one important vacancy, the Home Office, and for that, after considering Hicks Beach, Disraeli made his most sensational choice, Richard Cross, a completely new man who had never held office before.[1] Cross was a friend of Derby, and a power in Lancashire. He possessed deep knowledge of local government, and turned out to be a great Home Secretary. Whether or not Disraeli, who had met him once at Manchester, perceived this flair one cannot say. He probably realized that Cross was at least competent, and for the rest wished to please Lancashire and Derby. Lord John Manners, removed from his familiar niche of First Commissioner of Works to that of Postmaster-General, completed the Cabinet, which was composed as follows:

First Lord of the Treasury	B. Disraeli
Lord Chancellor	Lord Cairns
Lord President of the Council (and Leader of the House of Lords)	Duke of Richmond
Lord Privy Seal	Earl of Malmesbury
Home Secretary	R. A. Cross
Foreign Secretary	Earl of Derby
Colonial Secretary	Earl of Carnarvon
War Secretary	Gathorne Hardy
Indian Secretary	Marquis of Salisbury

[1] Disraeli seems to have had difficulty in making up his mind about filling the three key posts for home affairs. His first draft gave Beach the Home Office, Cross the Board of Trade, and Sclater Booth the Local Government Board. He then switched Cross to the Home Office, Beach to Local Government, and Booth to the Board of Trade. His final version kept Cross at the Home Office, removed Beach to the Irish Secretaryship, returned Booth to the Local Government Board, and brought in Adderley, one of his worst appointments, to the Board of Trade.

Chancellor of the Exchequer	Sir Stafford Northcote
First Lord of the Admiralty	G. W. Hunt
Postmaster-General	Lord John Manners

There were only three members of Disraeli's former Cabinet left out: the Duke of Marlborough who did not wish for office and declined the Viceroyalty of Ireland, Pakington and Wilson-Patten. The two latter were consoled with peerages. Of ministers outside the Cabinet there were at least three, W. H. Smith, Financial Secretary to the Treasury, Sir Michael Hicks Beach, Irish Secretary, and Lord George Hamilton, Under-Secretary for India, who were destined to make their mark later. Another able man was Viscount Sandon, MP for Liverpool, who held the important post of Vice-President of the Committee of Council on Education, ie in effect Minister of Education. There was one minister who was far from able, but was nevertheless most offended at being excluded from the Cabinet, Disraeli's now middle-aged protégé, Lord Henry Lennox. He did not refuse the post offered, First Commissioner of Works, but his conversation henceforth was full of disloyal spite. He was a failure in his job and caused Disraeli much worry. But in general the Tory administration of 1874 was a strong one and until the disruption caused by the Eastern question very harmonious. It had a professional touch that was a far cry from the 'Who? Who?' ministry of 1852, and the contrast is the measure of the change that had come over the Conservative party in the past two decades. Queen Victoria was delighted and was able to reassure her daughter, the Crown Princess of Prussia, 'You will see that instead of being a Govt. of Dukes as you imagine it will only contain 1 & he a very sensible, honest & highly respected one. The others are all distinguished & able men not at all retrograde.'[1] It was the first Tory Government since Peel's day which could in point of talent stand up to the Liberals. Moreover, it pleased all the diverse elements in the party. Salisbury and Carnarvon were pledges to the High Church and the Right. Derby stood for Erastian liberal-conservatism; the presence of the appropriately monosyllabic Cross and Smith showed that neither Lancashire, suburbia nor the middle class had been forgotten. Evangelicalism was represented by Cairns, the Peelite tradition by Northcote, and the last enchantments of Young England by Lord John Manners, sole survivor, other than Disraeli himself, from the Cabinet of 1852.

[1] Royal Archives, Kronberg Letters, February 21, 1874.

More troublesome than forming the Cabinet was the choice of the Household. Yet it probably gave Disraeli more pleasure. Here was the world of *Coningsby* and *Sybil*. To parcel out these semi-honorific positions among the great Tory families and to gratify the hosts, or rather the hostesses, of the stately homes where he was wont to stay, was indeed a triumph, in spite of the numerous snags. For example, he at once offered the Mastership of the Horse to Bradford, but received a refusal. Then he suggested the Duke of Beaufort to the Queen, but she objected on grounds of his disreputable private life. His next suggestion was the Duke of Marlborough, 'who does not ride', Ponsonby dryly noted, but the non-equestrian Duke also declined. Finally he returned to Lord Bradford, who now accepted. Then there was difficulty over Lords Beauchamp and Bath, whose High Church tendencies alarmed the Queen. Had not Lord Beauchamp signed a dissenting report for the Ritual Commission on the perilous subject of 'Lights as an accessory to the Holy Communion'? But she gave way eventually. In the end it was all settled, the throne was surrounded with a suitable galaxy of high-born nobility, and the political aid of the great Tory magnates was appropriately rewarded.

Exhausted by writing dozens of letters, not least by those in which he tried to mollify disappointed place-hunters, Disraeli repaired to Brighton for a brief holiday. But he cut it short on learning that both the beloved sisters were going to be in London for a day or so. To his intense chagrin they did not stay for long. 'Constant separations! Will they never cease?' he wrote to Lady Bradford.[1] 'I am certain there is no greater misfortune than to have a heart that will not grow old.' Lady Bradford evidently rebuked him for some of the expressions that he used. 'Your view of correspondence, apparently, is that it should be confined to facts and not admit feelings. Mine is the reverse', he replied,[2] and ended bitterly: 'I awake from a dream of baffled sympathy and pour forth my feelings, however precious, like water from a golden goblet on the sand.' But within two days all was well again. The Bradfords had promised to spend Whitsun at Hughenden.

These little dramas were repeated again and again. There would be periods of sunshine. Then Disraeli would cause offence by an exuberant letter, and Selina would rap him over the knuckles, or worse still say nothing, even in reply to telegrams. This led to cruel

---

[1] Zetland, i, 57, March 13, 1874.   [2] ibid., 59, March 17, 1874.

disappointments. 'While I was working at some Despatches last night in my room in the House of Commons Monty knocked and came in triumphant with a telegram . . . His countenance was radiant with my anticipated pleasure. Alas! it was from the Mayor of Norwich I fell in a clear heaven like a bird shot in full wing.'[1] His passion led him into actions which even he could not excuse. He even opened a letter from her to Corry. 'Dearest M. She did not write to me & I opened hers to yourself!!! It is heinous: I cannot defend or palliate my act. But you may always open hers to myself. D.'[2] This emotional seesaw was perpetually in process all through the years of his Premiership. It was distracting and time-consuming, but perhaps it helped to give him that zest for life which despite all his illnesses and setbacks never left him while there was breath in his body.

For the next six years the attention of Britain and, for much of the time, Europe, too, was centred upon Disraeli. He found this by no means a disagreeable sensation and never failed to play up to the part in which the turn of electoral fortune had cast him. In Parliament and in public he was an impressive, almost elaborately ceremonious figure, very conscious of the dignity of his great office. In Cabinet he was patient, formal and slightly remote. He did not talk much, but all accounts agree that he dominated discussion. He was not dictatorial. On the contrary he went to great lengths to conciliate refractory or difficult colleagues. He did not fuss or harass departmental ministers. He believed in leaving them alone to get on with their work, but he was always available for consultation and he became more accessible to back benchers, especially the younger ones, than he had ever been in his middle years. He was never rigid about methods or details for which he cared little. What made him emphatically a strong Prime Minister was that he seldom relinquished his purpose, or failed to get his way when he had decided on a policy. Of course, he did not always have a policy, but this was not a sign of inability to persuade or direct his Cabinet, rather of ill health, weariness and old age. 'Power! It has come to me too late,' he was heard to murmur at the apogee of his success after the Congress of Berlin. 'There were days when, on waking, I felt I could move dynasties and governments; but that has passed away.'[3]

---

[1] ibid., 83, May 12, 1874.
[2] Hughenden Papers, Box 95, B/XX/D/252, n.d.   [3] M. & B., v, 299.

Yet, although old age and illness were part of the explanation, it is true to say that Disraeli never possessed the drive, energy or application which were the qualities of Pitt, Peel, Palmerston, or Gladstone. Of course, no Prime Minister ought to work too hard and become too enmeshed in minutiae, but it is impossible to direct affairs without some knowledge of detail as well as broad principles, for they are inseparable, especially in the field of domestic legislation. Disraeli probably went too far to the opposite extreme. He had given very little thought to what his Government would actually do if he won a general election. Cross was sadly disappointed at the Prime Minister's lack of initiative when the Cabinet first met to decide upon the measures for the first session:

> From all his speeches I had quite expected that his mind was full of legislative schemes, but such did not prove to be the case; on the contrary he had to entirely rely on the suggestions of his colleagues, and, as they themselves had only just come into office, and that suddenly, there was some difficulty in framing the Queen's speech.[1]

This procedure seems to have continued throughout Disraeli's Premiership, though naturally with experience ministers had more suggestions to make. During the early autumn heads of departments would be asked for their suggestions for legislation in the next session. These would be discussed in the November Cabinets and strung together by Corry to constitute the draft of the Queen's speech. Disraeli reconciled differences, settled disputes, decided priorities; but he did not initiate nor did he try to understand the details of the measures proposed. 'He detests details . . . He does no work . . . M. Corry is in fact Prime Minister,' declared Carnarvon in a burst of irritation.[2] This was an extreme view, but Cross confirms it to some extent. 'Disraeli's mind was either above or below (whichever way you like to put it) mere questions of detail.'[3] Neither Carnarvon nor Cross were in possession of Disraeli's full confidence, though Cross soon came to have it, but their evidence cannot be disregarded. In the field of foreign policy Disraeli's attitude was quite different and far more active. He followed it with keen interest, and, as his doubts about Derby grew, he intervened

---

[1] Viscount Cross, *A Political History* (printed for private circulation, 1903), 25.
[2] Hardinge, *Carnarvon*, ii, 78.
[3] Cross, *A Political History*, 44.

continuously and personally to an extent which has no parallel in the case of the other great departments.

Like most Prime Ministers, Disraeli treated with special confidence and trust a small inner ring of his colleagues.

The inner Cabinet consisted of Cairns, Derby, Northcote and Hardy. Later Salisbury replaced Derby, but at first he and Carnarvon were inevitably on terms of polite formality with Disraeli rather than intimate friendship. Cairns was the man whose judgement Disraeli most respected. Hardy was the man upon whose oratory he most relied. With Derby his relations were complicated and ambivalent. He had a personal friendship with him of longer standing than with any of his colleagues except Manners. Together in the old days they had often discussed how to rejuvenate the party and cajole 'the Captain'. But their intimacy seems to have lessened as time went on. Perhaps the public discussion in 1871–2 of Disraeli's supersession may have contributed. On February 8, 1874, while the election results were coming in we find Salisbury writing his wife, after dining with the Derbys: 'I gathered that they had not quite given up the idea of his having the first place.'[1] It is hard to see how they could have expected this, unless Disraeli voluntarily retired, but if they did, it may account for a certain constraint. Derby with his cool humdrum attitude was worlds apart from Disraeli. Oddly enough his demeanour and outlook were in many ways less patrician than Disraeli's. He spoke, according to Disraeli, 'a sort of Lancashire patois'.[2] His opinions on the franchise, on Church questions, indeed many other topics, were those of a middle-class Liberal rather than a Tory aristocrat. Later the Eastern question was to drive the two men far apart. Northcote in a memorandum on the Cabinet's foreign policy left among his papers wrote:

> How he [Lord Derby] stood with Lord Beaconsfield was very difficult to say. They had long been personal friends and respected each other's merits, though each in turn would say sharp things of the other. Lord Beaconsfield had great influence over him and often brought him to do what he very much disliked.[3]

Northcote's own relations with Disraeli were most cordial, but essentially those of a subordinate rather than a colleague. He

---

[1] Cecil, Salisbury, ii, 44.
[2] Hughenden Papers, Box 26, A/X/A.
[3] British Museum, Add. MSS, 50063A, f. 306.

always addressed the Prime Minister as 'Dear Mr. Disraeli', whereas, except for Cross from whom such an address was natural in the circumstances, the others wrote 'Dear Disraeli', or if on really close terms, like Derby and Manners, 'My dear D.' Northcote was a born second-in-command. It was unlucky that later events were to give him the reasonable expectation, though never fulfilled, of rising to the top. He was loyal, popular, good-tempered, efficient, conscientious, but he lacked the vital spark.

Disraeli controlled both Houses and dominated his ministerial colleagues. There remained one element in the constitutional balance capable of obstructing him, if only to a limited degree – the Crown. But he soon established relations with Queen Victoria even closer and more cordial than in 1868. The progressive stages of his movement into the confidence of the Faery, as he called her in an ironic romantic allusion to Spenser's *Faerie Queene*, have often been chronicled. Long before the end of his Premiership he had broken through the strict etiquette which surrounded her. She did not cavil when against all the rules he proposed her toast as Empress of India at her own dinner-table. She allowed him to write to her in the first person – a privilege which he wisely reserved for special occasions. She invited him to be seated during his audiences, only enjoining him to keep the secret. Naturally he did not, and an exultant letter promptly whizzed from his pen to Lady Bradford. At an early stage he also broke through the normal channels of communication with the Queen. He remained on excellent terms with Ponsonby, whose impartiality he genuinely respected; but still Ponsonby was a Whig. There might be advantages in putting his opinions to the Queen directly or by another route, usually Lady Ely, one of the Ladies of the Bedchamber to whom Corry wrote regularly on his master's behalf.

The Queen's political sympathies after five years of Liberal ascendancy were very definitely on Disraeli's side. With a few exceptions Gladstone's programme of legislation seemed to her inimical to the prestige of the Crown. She was nervous, too, of his impetuousness and his incalculability; and his hold over the forces of militant democracy had perturbed her still further. She regarded the election of 1874 as a wholesome sign that the nation had recovered its senses. 'Since 46 under the gt. good & wise Sir R. Peel there has not been a Conservative Majority!!'[1] she wrote to her

[1] Royal Archives, Kronberg Letters.

eldest daughter on February 10. 'It shows a healthy state of the country.' It is wrong to suppose that the Queen's disapproval of Gladstone dates only from the Bulgarian atrocity agitation of 1876. That indeed aggravated it, and turned it into fear, even hatred. But her feelings about Gladstone earlier are shown well enough in another letter to the Crown Princess of Prussia on February 24:[1]

> Ld Palmerston was quite right when he said to me 'Mr. Gladstone is a very dangerous man'. And so vy. arrogant, tyrannical & obstinate with no knowledge of the World or human nature. Papa felt this strongly. Then he was a fanatic in religion – All this & much want of égard towards my feelings (tho' since I was so ill that was better) led to make him a vy dangerous & unsatisfactory Premier. He was a bad Leader of the H. of Commons.

There could be no complaint about lack of *égard* for her feelings on Disraeli's part. He was genuinely considerate and made things as easy for her as he could. His letters were admirably summed up by Ponsonby writing on one occasion to the Queen: 'Mr. Disraeli has a wonderful talent for writing in an amusing tone while seizing the points of an argument.'[2] Gone were the dismal days when the Queen received a memorandum of such length and complexity from Gladstone that she had to get a précis made by Sir Theodore Martin. To his wife, Ponsonby, who was never at ease with Disraeli, made a less-flattering comment on the new Prime Minister: '. . . it seems to me that he communicates nothing except boundless professions of love and loyalty and if called on to write more says he is ill.'[3] Ponsonby thought that Disraeli's letters of sympathy were written with his tongue in his cheek, but he shrewdly added: 'Are not her woes told in the same manner?'

The language which Disraeli used to the Queen does indeed sound artificial, absurd, and at times perilously near to bathos. He would, he once said, have thought himself like Proserpine in Hades, if the gift of primroses from Osborne 'did not remind him that there might yet be spring & tho' Proserpine be absent there is happily for him a Queen to whom he is devoted at Windsor.'[4] On another occasion he mentions some plans of his 'to yr Majesty in secrecy . . . but in life one must have for one's secret thoughts a sacred deposi-

[1] ibid.
[2] ibid., D.4.67, June 20, 1874.
[3] Arthur Ponsonby, *Henry Ponsonby; his Life from his Letters* (1942), 245.
[4] Royal Archives, B.61.2, May 2, 1879.

tory & Lord Beaconsfield ever presses to seek that in his Sovereign Mistress'.[1] And when she inquired after his health at a moment when the Government had just won an unexpected victory at a by-election, he replied:

> No doubt political success is a skilful physician but there is a sanitary talisman more efficacious even than that – & that is the condescending sympathy of a beloved Sovereign whose Kindness is always as graceful as it is gracious.[2]

This sort of thing invites censure from austere critics, but it was not meant for publication, and if the Queen liked it, and Disraeli chose to please her, there seems no reason to cavil.

Two criticisms of a more serious kind need to be considered. Did Disraeli exercise undue personal influence over the Queen, and – a closely connected question – did he encourage her in unconstitutional notions about her own power? On the first point it is by no means the case that the influence was all in one direction. Sir Thomas Biddulph, the Keeper of the Queen's Privy Purse, thought 'that Dizzy is a perfect slave to the Queen', so Ponsonby wrote to his wife.[3] At the height of the Eastern crisis in a letter to Salisbury, Derby wrote: 'I know what the pressure of the court is on our Chief.'[4] And rather earlier Salisbury had written on the same theme to Carnarvon: 'Balmoral is becoming a serious nuisance.'[5] Of course, far more often than not, Disraeli persuaded the Queen to do what he wanted, but he could never be sure of success, and on two important measures, the Public Worship Regulation Bill of 1874 and the Royal Titles Bill of 1876, especially the latter, the Queen pressed him into action which he might not otherwise have taken. During the Eastern crisis she almost threatened abdication, 'the greatest power the Sovereign possessed – nothing could stand against it for the position of a Minister who forced it on would be untenable', so Gladstone once said.[6] Disraeli might well have wondered whether he had conjured up something more formidable than he had bargained for. When the Eastern question was at its height he had to remind the Queen, who was ·violently pro-Turk

[1] ibid., B.61.15, June 9, 1879.
[2] ibid., B.63.27, February 8, 1880.
[3] Ponsonby, 245.
[4] See below, 636.
[5] Salisbury Papers, Salisbury to Carnarvon, May 27, 1877.
[6] Ponsonby, 187.

and seemed to be reproaching him for weakness, that he was not her Grand Vizier.

But he cannot be acquitted of having himself made such a reminder necessary. 'Is there not just a risk,' wrote Derby on May 4, 1874, 'of encouraging her in too large ideas of her personal power, and too great indifference to what the public expects? I only ask; it is for you to judge.'[1] It was perhaps not improper, in spite of Gladstone's disapprobation, to keep the Queen informed of Cabinet discussions and the names of dissentients. 'In a Cabinet of twelve persons there are seven parties,' Disraeli wrote on one occasion, and he then analysed them at length.[2] There were precedents for this frankness. More doubtful but not clearly unconstitutional was Disraeli's habit of enlisting the Queen in overpersuading obstinate or recalcitrant ministers. 'In what frame of mind will the Queen find Sir Stafford Northcote?' she asked on November 12, 1877.[3] 'It would be as well to intimate . . . that our military and naval preparations shd be adequate for emergencies,' replied Disraeli the same day,[4] and on November 28: 'Lord Beaconsfield . . . was pleased with the Chancellor of the Exchequer's tone & perceived that a "Faery Queen" had waved her magic wand over him.'[5]

Yet there certainly were occasions when his language, if taken literally, attributed powers to the Queen that were anachronistic even then. When a newly appointed law officer had allowed his promotion to leak out before the Queen's formal assent had been given, 'Mr Disraeli is determined to put down this loose habit & make yr Majesty's subjects understand where the Constitution has placed the Government of the Country.'[6] During the Eastern crisis, when the Queen threatened 'to lay down the thorny crown' and seemed to be implying that the Cabinet had not fulfilled their promises to her he wrote: '. . . your Majesty has the clear constitutional right to dismiss them.'[7] This was nonsense, and both Disraeli and the Queen must have known it, even if they were prepared to suspend disbelief for the moment. The truth is that Disraeli's language should not be taken literally. It was part of an elaborate comedy of manners in which he was author, actor and

[1] M. & B., vi, 414.
[2] ibid., vi, 194.
[3] Royal Archives, B.53.43.
[4] ibid., B.53.44.
[5] ibid., B.53.53.
[6] ibid., A.50.1, November 19, 1875.
[7] M. & B., vi, 246.

spectator, with the Queen cast in the other principal role, while Whiggish figures like Derby and Ponsonby observed dryly and dubiously from the wings. To analyse all this in terms of Bagehot is to take it far too seriously. There was little danger of the actors stepping suddenly into real life. The Queen had no more intention of abdicating than Disraeli had of being dismissed.

2

Parliament met on March 19. The Liberal party was in a state of disarray. Gladstone, much put out at his defeat, wished to resign the leadership at once. 'I deeply desired', he wrote many years later, 'an interval between Parliament and the grave.'[1] He was dissuaded from immediate action, but he was determined to retire before the next session. Meanwhile he announced that he would attend only occasionally. With a united Cabinet, a friendly monarch, a majority in both the Houses of Parliament, and the Opposition in chaos, Disraeli was in a position to carry whatever programme he wished. There was, as we have already seen, only one snag – he had not got one. Having at last obtained power he had curiously little idea what to do with it. The suddenness of the election is part but not the whole of the explanation. It is doubtful whether a longer period of waiting would have resulted in his working out a policy for immediate legislation. Although he had on occasions piloted complicated measures through the House, for example the Reform Bill of 1867, he never really had a legislative mind. Ideas, impressions, tone – these he was a master at suggesting. They are his great contributions to the Conservative Party. For concrete legislative achievements we must look elsewhere.

The immediate question was the budget. In this, like all Prime Ministers, Disraeli took a keen interest, and discussed it at length with Northcote. They decided that Gladstone's panacea was impracticable. Income tax could be reduced, but not abolished. A penny off the income tax, abolition of the sugar duties, substantial aid to the rates for expenditure on lunatics and policemen, these were the main features of Northcote's first budget. It was a compromise that pleased some and not others. The farmers were angry that the Malt Tax still remained. The landed gentry were delighted at rate relief – a measure for which the Country party had agitated

[1] Morley, ii, 498.

ever since the repeal of the Corn Laws. The abolition of the sugar duties pleased the free traders, and the reduction of income tax was, as Disraeli predicted, 'a golden bridge for all anti-income tax men in our own ranks. They will grumble, but they will support us.' Northcote had no difficulty in carrying the House of Commons. Even Gladstone was not very censorious.

Otherwise little else was planned by the Cabinet, apart from a Royal Commission on the Trade Union legislation which had been badly botched by the Liberals, a new Factory Act and a Licensing Act to amend Bruce's unpopular measure.[1] These together with the budget and routine matters were expected to provide sufficient occupation for the session. But Parliament, like nature, abhors a vacuum. The Archbishop of Canterbury stepped in where the Cabinet hesitated to tread. The session of 1874 was to be dominated by an ecclesiastical storm which no one had predicted a few months earlier.

With the concurrence of the Bishops, Tait had drafted a Bill designed to expedite and cheapen the legal process of enforcing discipline on recalcitrant clergy. The Bill was primarily aimed at the extreme Ritualists, but the danger was that it might be used by fanatical evangelicals against moderate High Churchmen, and there was also the opposite possibility, viz. action by the High against the Low. Although the Queen was enthusiastic, and the Archbishop pressed strongly, Disraeli would have been glad to leave the matter alone, for a Cabinet which contained Cairns on the one hand and Salisbury on the other could never be united on such a prickly topic. He was, however, prepared to do his best behind the scenes, and, without any public appearance, he succeeded in getting the Bill greatly improved in the House of Lords, where it was introduced.

When it came down to the House of Commons, however, still as a Private Member's Bill, Gladstone descended from Hawarden like a thunder clap and moved six portentous resolutions defining the whole position of the Church of England, and fiercely attacking what he called 'a Bill to put down Ritualism'. This was too much for Disraeli, who suspected that Gladstone was not likely to have

---

[1] The popularity of Cross who introduced both measures is attested by the following jingle:

> 'For he's a jolly good fellow,
> Whatever the Rads may think;
> For he has shortened the hours of work
> And lengthened the hours of drink.'

much support and who now came into the open denouncing 'Mass in masquerade', as he called the Ritualist practices. He won easily. Gladstone withdrew his resolutions, and the Bill was carried with one important amendment which resulted in something of a brush between Salisbury and Disraeli. The former urged the peers not to be intimidated by a 'blustering majority'. Disraeli in reply referred to his colleague as 'a great master of flouts and jeers'. Happily no offence was taken. As for the Bill, although its passage pleased the Queen and strengthened her affection for her Prime Minister, it proved difficult to enforce and caused far more harm than good. Moreover, the High Church party henceforth regarded Disraeli as a sworn foe, and part of their bitter hostility to him over the Eastern question stemmed from this episode.

Disraeli had planned to visit Ireland that autumn, but as early as April his health was beginning to show the premonitory symptoms of the illness which later prevented him. He had more than one attack of gout during the session, but nothing serious, and he was not inhibited from attending during the season a succession of dinner parties, routs and balls, especially if there was a chance of seeing Lady Bradford. In September he paid his second and last visit to Balmoral. Ponsonby found him 'clever and bright in sparkling repartee but indolent and worn out . . . he shot little arrows into the general discourse pungent and lively and then sat perfectly silent as if it were too much trouble to talk'.[1] He caught a chill there and was treated by Sir William Jenner for incipient bronchitis. 'This morning the Queen paid me a visit in my bedchamber. What do you think of that?' he wrote to Lady Bradford. Although he soon recovered, and went from Balmoral to Bretby, he was ill again, this time with gout. The Irish visit, which involved three non-political speeches and a multitude of further engagements in less than a fortnight, was beginning to cause him much perplexity. On September 15 Derby wrote a long letter to dissuade him from going. 'First you are overdoing yourself . . .' and then what was he to say? 'Every question in Ireland whether of the past present or future is a party question . . . You cannot be decently civil to Catholics without offending Protestants and *vice versa* . . .'[2] The attack of gout now made the visit impossible that year. The chance did not come again, and Disraeli, whose political life was so largely spent on Irish disputes, never set foot upon Ireland.

[1] Ponsonby, 244.   [2] M. & B., v, 346–7.

He recovered sufficiently to attend the autumn Cabinets and make the traditional Guildhall speech, but he was far from well, and when the Cabinets were over was persuaded by his doctor to spend some weeks at Bournemouth. He did not relish the experience and his letters to the sisters abound with jeremiads. Monty Corry could only stay with him for a day. The weather was bitter. The hotel, although a son of Baron Rothschild had taken a suite in it, turned out to be atrocious; the Rothschild indeed lived on hampers from Gunnersbury, and his father kindly offered to provide them for Disraeli, too. But even this had its difficulties. What with turkeys from Bretby as well, and twenty pheasants from the Prince of Wales, he had so much food that he was obliged to dispense with hotel meals; and as he was not drinking wine he could not 'order their choice and costly vintages. This would have been the use of Monty.' Now he would infallibly be 'denounced as a screw'. True the Lord Chancellor offered to put him up in his new house near Bournemouth, but driving past it one day Disraeli observed that it appeared to be still unfinished. 'Any fires would have been the first lit in his steaming walls. What an Irish invitation, to be the guest of a man whose house is not yet built.'[1]

However, in spite of these vicissitudes his health did improve, and he was in a much better state for the January Cabinet meetings before the new session. While still at Bournemouth he performed an imaginative gesture in advising the Queen to recognize the importance of literature by conferring a GCB and a pension on Carlyle, and a baronetcy on Tennyson. In the former case he was certainly being magnanimous, for Carlyle had in the past denounced him in very strong terms. It is, however, fair to add that Derby, who suggested the idea, did so partly because 'it would be a really good political investment', since Carlyle was 'for whatever reason very vehement against Gladstone'. Both men refused the offers; although Carlyle was softened for the time being, and, so Lady Derby said, 'scarcely knew how to be grateful enough'. But the curmudgeonly old prophet could not keep it up for long. Two years later we find him referring to Disraeli as 'a cursed old Jew, not worth his weight in cold bacon'.[2]

The session of 1875, thanks partly to Gladstone's formal retirement and replacement by Hartington, was the easiest of Disraeli's

[1] Zetland, i, 179.
[2] M. & B., v, 358.

ministry. It was also the most constructive, for the major measures of social reform associated with his period in office were passed then. The list is impressive: two important Trade Union Acts; the Public Health Act which consolidated a multitude of earlier measures; the Artisans Dwellings Act empowering local authorities to replace slums by adequate houses; an Agricultural Holdings Act which met, though only partially, some of the tenants' grievances; an Act to safeguard the funds of Friendly Societies; a Factory Act to protect women and children against exploitation – there had already been one in the previous session to establish the principle of the ten-hour day; and finally the Sale of Food and Drugs Act which remained the principal measure on that subject until 1928. No other session was quite as productive, although the Rivers Pollution, Merchant Shipping and Education Acts of 1876 were important, and so, too, was the Factory Act of 1878 based on the report of a Royal Commission set up two years earlier.

Whether we look at these measures from the point of view of Disraeli's career or of the history of the Conservative party, it is important to see them in the right perspective. They certainly represented a substantial effort to redeem electoral pledges, and taken together constitute the biggest instalment of social reform passed by any one government in the nineteenth century. But it is an exaggeration to regard them as the product of a fundamentally different political philosophy from that of the Liberals, or to see in them the fulfilment of some concept of paternalistic Tory democracy which had been adumbrated by Disraeli in opposition to Peel during the 1840s and now at last had reached fruition. The forces of property, commercial and industrial as well as landed, were by 1874 too deeply rooted in the Conservative party to make it politically possible for the party to pursue the idea of an aristocratic anti-middle class alliance with the working masses even if it had wished to do so. As a result of the Act of 1867 it was electorally necessary to make some concessions to working-class demands, and it may be that the Conservatives after 1874 were more ready to do this than the Liberals after 1868, because those demands had become more articulate. But it would be straining the evidence to go beyond that.

There is nothing discreditable in the way in which the Conservative party arrived at these measures. Governments usually act in just such an empirical hand-to-mouth fashion. But it is wrong to present their legislation as if it marked a substantial shift from *laissez faire* to state intervention. On the contrary Cross and other spokesmen were at pains to disavow anything that savoured even remotely of collectivism, except in the case of the Factory Acts and health legislation which were recognized by both parties to involve special considerations. In other spheres one is struck by the cautious attitude behind the Conservative social reforms. Disraeli made a positive virtue of permissive as opposed to compulsory legislation. 'Permissive legislation is the characteristic of a free people,' he declared in June 1875.[1] In general he was probably right, and compulsion is always unpopular in England, but the defects of this approach in some fields are shown by the history of the Artisans Dwellings Act of 1875, rightly acclaimed as the first attempt at encouraging slum clearance. Six years later only ten of the eighty-seven English and Welsh towns to which it applied had made any attempt to implement its provisions. But it is doubtful whether the temper of the times would have allowed anything more *dirigiste*. The Merchant Shipping Act is another good illustration of this reluctance.

One has to allow not only for the individualist self-help creed which prevailed almost as much in the Conservative as in the Liberal party, though no doubt the extreme doctrinaires, eg Henry Fawcett, were to be found in the latter. It is also important to allow for the unwillingness of both parties to spend taxpayers' or ratepayers' money. Historians have been slow to recognize the strength of this inhibition, although it has been a potent factor ever since (except perhaps during the two world wars). The Conservatives, based heavily on the counties and small boroughs, where landowners perpetually complained at rising rates, felt particularly sensitive about proposals, such as educational reform, which increased that burden. Indeed, the Education Act of 1876 can be interpreted largely as an attempt to prevent the incursion of rate-aided 'boards' into the counties, and at the same time to preserve as far as possible the position of the voluntary denominational schools. Conservatives were equally reluctant to spend the taxpayer's money. Extravagance was a stock accusation made by Liberal 'economists' against Conservative budgets, and after 1876, when declining prosperity began to reduce the yield of existing taxes, the Chancellor of the Exchequer dug in his toes more firmly than ever against any increase in government expenditure.

[1] *Hansard*, 3rd Series, ccxxv, 525.

In these circumstances it is not surprising that much the most successful of the Conservative social reforms were the two measures introduced by Cross in June 1875 to deal with the labour question: the Employers and Workmen Bill, which, superseding the old Master and Servant Act, made breaches of contract normally no longer liable to criminal prosecution; and the Conspiracy and Protection of Property Bill which changed the law of conspiracy in favour of the trade unions and legalized peaceful picketing. The two Acts satisfactorily settled the position of labour for a generation. Since they involved neither interventionism nor public expenditure, and since they gave the unions almost everything which they wanted and had been denied by the Liberals, it is not surprising that the party was jubilant. Disraeli, who took a keener interest in these than any of Cross's other measures, told Lady Chesterfield that the legislation 'will gain and retain for the Conservatives the lasting affection of the working classes'.[1]

The social-reform measures of the Conservative Government were of varying quality and efficacy, but it would be safe to say that on balance they did a great deal more good than harm. It would be wrong to pitch Disraeli's claims too high as author of this valuable legislation. Some of it was already in the Civil Service pipeline, some flowed naturally from the publication of official inquiries, some was of the codifying nature which would probably have been passed by any government then, and much of it was due to the hard work of Cross, whose role in this Cabinet can only be compared with that of Neville Chamberlain in Baldwin's.[2] Disraeli had emphasized that social rather than political reform would be the Conservative policy. There was, too, his famous quip about *sanitas sanitatum*. Moreover, he took a close interest in the trade-union question, going to the trouble to procure an opinion from Hardy in 1873 on the legal aspect, and backing Cross successfully against the rest of the Cabinet when the Home Secretary wisely insisted on going far beyond the recommendations of the Royal Commission of 1874. He certainly sympathized with social reform. *Sybil* testifies to his

[1] Zetland, i, 260, June 29, 1875.

[2] Cross was responsible for the Artisans' Dwellings Act, Licensing and Factory Acts, the legislation about Trade Unions and also an important Explosives Act. The Public Health, Sale of Food and Drugs, and Rivers Pollution Acts, though often attributed to him, were the work of Sclater Booth, President of the Local Government Board. Sandon was responsible for the Education Act, Adderley for the unsatisfactory Merchant Shipping Act, and the Chancellor of the Exchequer for the Friendly Societies Act.

genuine dismay at working-class conditions in the north a generation earlier. 'The palace is not safe when the cottage is not happy,'
he said in a speech in Lady Londonderry's grounds in 1848. He had
given sporadic support to various Factory Bills for most of his
political life. The measures of 1875 did not threaten the interests of
the landed classes. They were quite compatible with the sceptical
but empirical attitude of most businessmen and employers to state
intervention. The strongest exponents of *laissez faire* were to be
found on the Liberal not the Tory benches.

But social reform was not the principal or even a leading secondary preoccupation of Disraeli. He took little interest in the details.
'I believe that Mr Secy. X is working on a Dwellings Bill', he wrote
vaguely to Salisbury before the November Cabinets of 1874. His
letters to Cross contain scarcely anything about that or kindred
subjects and he seldom spoke in the parliamentary debates on them.
True, he told Lady Bradford that these reforms were 'a policy
round which the country can rally', and at the end of the 1875
session wrote to the Queen: 'Since Mr. Disraeli has been in Parliament he does not remember a Royal Speech which contained the
announcement of so many important & truly popular measures
having been carried.'[1] Yet he seems to have forgotten all this by
the general election of 1880, when a certain amount of boasting over
the Government's achievements would have been legitimate, and
he said nothing about it in his manifesto.[2] Nevertheless if Prime
Ministers are blamed when matters go wrong, even though their
personal responsibility is remote, it seems only just that the converse should apply. The social measures passed in 1874–80 did
something to make the lot of the urban masses less unhappy, less
precarious and less unhealthy. Disraeli was at the head of the
administration that brought this about, and he encouraged the
policy even if he did not concern himself with its details. He deserves
his share of the credit.

Social-reform legislation was the most important feature of the
last reasonably smooth session in Disraeli's Premiership. True, it
was not entirely smooth. There were awkward questions of parliamentary privilege in connexion with Dr Kenealy, the excitable
counsel for the Tichborne claimant, and John Mitchel, an Irish

[1] Royal Archives, A.49.33, August 5, 1875.
[2] Oddly enough, Cross in his own election address also scarcely mentioned the
subject.

felon. Disraeli does not seem to have shown himself at his best in coping with either. At any rate, he came in for a good deal of criticism, not merely from the Opposition. Then there was trouble over a Liberal resolution on compulsory education, Conservative attendance being low owing to 'casual and social causes; principally Ascot races, always perilous to the Tories'. Disraeli told the Queen, adding that 'he kept the wires of the telegraph vibrating alternately with menaces and entreaties' in order to get the truants back in time for the division.[1] Finally there was a crisis over the Merchant Shipping Bill. An incompetent President of the Board of Trade, Sir Charles Adderley, at odds with his officials, had to steer a tricky course between the enthusiasm of Samuel Plimsoll and the interests of the shipowners. In the end the Bill had to be shelved till the next session. This provoked a notable tantrum on the part of Plimsoll. He danced with rage on the floor of the House and shook his fist at Disraeli, thus raising another problem of privilege. Disraeli had every intention of moving Adderley after this fiasco, but he somehow did not manage to do so until 1878. Asquith is supposed to have said that a good Prime Minister must be a good butcher. On that test Disraeli was a bad Prime Minister; he was kind-hearted and he never found it easy to get rid of failures.

In place of the Merchant Shipping Bill, Disraeli substituted an Agricultural Holdings Bill which was intended to remove some of the grievances of tenants against landlords. This was a delicate matter for a Conservative Cabinet to deal with. Disraeli justified it in a letter to the Queen. He admitted that there was 'no immediate clamor' and continued:

'Tenant Right' is a perilous subject. In various forms it has harassed many parts of Europe since the great Peace of '15. It is used by the party of disturbance in Europe & in this country to effect their ulterior objects in changing the tenure of land, on wh: in England the monarchical & aristocratic institutions mainly depend.

The advocates of Tenant Right would *compel* its adoption. The compulsory principle is so odious in this country that there would be no great fear if the Tenant Right Cry was only combined with the principle of compulsion – but unfortunately there is much in the relations between Landlord & Tenant in this country, wh: is unsatisfactory & anomalous; more in theory no doubt than in practice but still existing, & connected with the cry of Tenant

[1] M. & B., v, 380–1, June 11, 1875.

Right. These circumstances give it a popular & powerful character & influence. The object of the measure of Yr Majesty's Government is to take advantage of these tranquil times, get rid of those anomalies & circumstances of apparent injustice, & leave the cry of Tenant Right combined only with the odious condition of Compulsion.[1]

During the session Disraeli did not neglect the social duties of his office. He gave a series of grand dinner parties and was himself, as in the season of 1874, a regular guest at dinners, receptions and balls. It was an odd feature of the rules of precedence in those days that the Prime Minister went in behind all the peers and bishops, even those whom he had made. As a result he was sometimes badly placed. On one occasion, Disraeli recorded with horror, he was actually sandwiched between two *men*. But these hazards did not deter him, especially if there was even an off-chance of seeing Selina. During Whitsun and the autumn recess Disraeli repaired as of old to Hughenden, enjoying, at least for a time, absolute solitude and repose. 'I have been here nearly a week,' he wrote to Lady Bradford on May 19,[2] 'and have not interchanged a syllable with any human being. My personal attendant,[3] tho' sedulous, and sometimes I believe, even honest, is of a sullen and supercilious temperament and never unnecessarily opens his mouth. This I think a recommendation . . .' In October he described his days at Hughenden to the same correspondent; how he rose at 7.30, went through his mail, sauntered on the terrace after breakfast inspecting the peacocks, worked in his 'little room (my cabinet)' till '*dejeuner*' at one o'clock, and after that in the library, where 'I like to watch the sunbeams on the bindings of the books'.[4] Thus we can envisage the old statesman getting through his red boxes, sometimes indulging in day dreams, and constantly, pen in hand, writing the endless stream of letters which has made posterity fancy, perhaps delusorily, that of all the great political figures in history he is the one it knows best.

There was one matter which gave him some annoyance at his country retreat. The church, which was much dilapidated, had been restored partly at Disraeli's own expense, and the vicar, the Reverend Henry Blagden, who was High, made the ceremony of reopening it something of a demonstration. 'The sacerdotal pro-

---

[1] Royal Archives, A.49.27, July 23.
[2] M. & B., v, 378.
[3] His German valet, Baum.
[4] M. & B., v, 404–5.

cession was tremendous,' Disraeli told Lady Bradford. '. . . certainly nearer a 100 than 50 clergymen in surplices and parti-colored scarves . . . Everything was intoned.' He added: 'I was obliged to bring in a Protestant sentiment by way of protest', and in his speech at the luncheon that followed he expressed his hope that henceforth at Hughenden it would be possible to 'combine the "beauty of holiness" with the pure Protestant faith of the Church of England'.

During the autumn he was much vexed by difficulties connected with the Navy, which was so often the bane of his political life. The Admiralty issued instructions about fugitive slaves which, Disraeli, unlike Derby, Ward Hunt and the law officers, at once saw were certain to raise an anti-slavery uproar. He promptly had them cancelled. Then two battleships collided in the Irish Channel and one of them, *Vanguard*, sank. Nor was this the whole catalogue of disasters; the Queen's yacht with the Queen on board ran down a private schooner, the *Mistletoe*, in the Solent and three lives were lost. 'Water I trust will not prove fatal to the Government', wrote Disraeli to Salisbury. 'Between Plimsoll, the *Vanguard*, and the Admiralty Instruction and Minute we seem to be in a leaky state.'[1] The affair of the *Mistletoe* caused endless correspondence. The public took sides, and the queen was much distressed when following the coroner's verdict the Admiralty censured Captain Welch who commanded her yacht. Disraeli promised to keep it out of the Press, but he did – and could have done – nothing. Matters were not eased by the personality of the First Lord. 'I fear Hunt has got into some terrible scrape with H.M. about Welch,' Disraeli told Salisbury. 'Our friend has the art of doing disagreeable things in a disagreeable manner, 'tis pity.'[2]

Much the most important episode in the recess was the purchase of the Suez Canal shares. This will be discussed in the next chapter, but other matters connected with the east are worthy of note. The winter of 1875–6 was the occasion of the Prince of Wales's visit to India. It was entirely his own idea prompted by love of sight-seeing and desire to consolidate the Crown's prestige. Writing from 'that temple of the winds', as he called Windsor Castle, Disraeli said in a letter to Salisbury on March 30:

. . . It seems that our young Hal kept it a secret from his wife &

[1] M. & B., v, 433, October 15.　　[2] Salisbury Papers, December 29, 1875.

induced his mother to give her assent on the representation that it was entirely approved by Her Ministers.

The Wife insists on going! When reminded of her children she says 'the husband has the first claim'.

The mother says nothing will induce her to consent to the Princess going & blames herself bitterly for having rashly sanctioned the scheme without obtaining on the subject my opinion & that of my colleagues . . .[1]

Disraeli persuaded the Queen, who had become very hostile to the whole idea, to leave the management in his hands. The Prince's visit could not now be cancelled, but there were genuine objections to Princess Alexandra going, for the correct treatment of Western wives at the courts of the Indian Princes who were to be visited caused grave problems of protocol and propriety. Moreover, Derby, among a long list of reasons for keeping the Princess at home, added a final one that could not very well be avowed: '. . . and lastly, "Hal" is sure to get into scrapes with women whether she goes or not, and they will be considered more excusable in her absence. . . .'[2]

Foiled in her efforts to go to India, the Princess now made the modest request to be allowed to visit Denmark with her children. The Queen objected to this, too, and maintained, on the strength of an opinion given by the judges in the reign of George II, that she had the right to prevent the children from leaving the country. Disraeli consulted Cairns, who thought the precedent a bad one, and that in any case the Queen ought not to exercise the right even if it existed. 'To force the Prs to live in seclusion as she must do for 6 months in England is a serious matter.'[3] In the end the Queen gave way. As for the Prince's visit to India, it was a success in spite of her forebodings. Of course, there were many more troubles to overcome, not the least of them being money. The House of Commons, aware of the Queen's great wealth, was always stingy about paying for any sort of royal progress. The Prince's cause was espoused by Lord Randolph Churchill in the House of Commons, not very successfully if Disraeli is to be believed: '. . . he had prepared a Marlboro House manifesto, and utterly broke down, destroying a rather rising reputation.'[4] Disraeli himself, however,

[1] Sir Philip Magnus, *King Edward the Seventh* (1964), 132.

[2] Hughenden Papers, Box 112, B/XX/S/1109, March 31, 1875.

[3] Hughenden Papers, Box 91, B/XX/Ca/160, Cairns to Disraeli, September 19, 1875.

[4] M. & B., v, 429–30, to Lady Bradford, July 17, 1875.

agreed that the Prince must not go in a 'mesquin' fashion. In the end enough money, but no more than enough, was voted. It required several letters from Disraeli, beginning 'Sir and dear Prince', his somewhat eccentric mode of address, to smooth over the situation.

During that autumn it fell to Disraeli for the second time in his career to appoint a Viceroy of India. He had no use for Lord North-brook, the incumbent whom he had inherited from Gladstone. The last straw was when the Viceroy refused to use secret service money '*on moral grounds*', as Disraeli indignantly wrote to the Queen. Fortunately his son had got himself entangled with an undesirable lady in Simla, and Northbrook decided to disentangle him by resigning and returning home. But the vacancy, though welcome, proved difficult to fill. Disraeli, who believed in rewarding friends, began by trying two of his Young England supporters, but Manners refused and so did Lord Powis, another disciple of those distant days. Disraeli then offered the post to Carnarvon, but he had just lost his wife, and he declined. Finally Disraeli's choice fell on the second Lord Lytton, Bulwer's son, then British Minister in Lisbon. Lytton, who wrote bad poetry under the pseudonym of 'Owen Meredith' and inherited some of his father's worst failings, proved in many ways to be a disastrous appointment, though much can be forgiven to a man whose character is an archetypal illustration of the consequences of a broken home. But Disraeli with his views about the need to appeal to an Oriental people through their imagination seems to have regarded poetry as a qualification. And as always he invested the appointment with that sense of drama and romance ever present in his mind. On January 20, 1876, Lytton back from Lisbon came to see him.

> He told me his first remembrance of me was calling on me at a little school he was at – at Twickenham, and I 'tipped him'. It was the first tip he ever had; and now I have tipped him again and put a crown on his head! It's like meeting the first character of a play in the last scene.[1]

The year that had just begun was to be an unhappy one for Disraeli. His health deteriorated, temporarily as it turned out, but long enough for him to have to quit the House of Commons. His leadership came in for much criticism; and half-way through the

---

[1] ibid., 437, to Lady Bradford, January 20, 1876.

year the Eastern crisis with its dangers and complications loomed over the political horizon. It is true that matters did not go too badly at first. Disraeli induced the Queen to open Parliament in person, although he himself narrowly escaped being trampled underfoot by the rush of members to see the novel spectacle. Moreover, he had no difficulty in defeating the opponents of the Suez Canal purchase, who were made to look carping and little-minded. But from then onwards his passage became choppy. The Government survived an adverse motion on the Slave Circular by only forty-five votes, there was a tiresome debate on the affair of the *Mistletoe*, and one of the major measures of the session, the Royal Titles Bill, ran into unexpectedly fierce opposition.

This Bill, like the Public Worship Regulation Bill of 1874, was a case of Disraeli's yielding to the Queen. Not that he disapproved of the contents, for he was all in favour of her becoming Empress of India; but the timing was inconvenient and he would have postponed it if he could. He did not wish, however, to cross his 'Royal Mistress', who had set her heart on the idea. 'The Empress-Queen demands her Imperial Crown,' he told Cairns on January 7,[1] and on January 11 he counselled Salisbury to put the announcement in the Queen's speech after the paragraph referring to the Prince's Indian visit. 'What might have been looked upon as an ebullition of individual vanity may bear the semblance of deep and organised policy.'[2] Proposals to adopt the imperial title for India had been in the air ever since the Mutiny. The plan can only be understood if the traumatic nature of that disaster is remembered. It caused lasting apprehension about the stability of British rule. Furthermore, since the days of the Mutiny a new threat exercised those of nervous disposition, the advance of Russia in Central Asia. The Tsar was an Emperor. Basically the Royal Titles Bill, like the Prince's visit, was a counter-blast to the threat of Russian invasion or subversion in India, a measure designed to reaffirm and symbolize British power. Whether it made any difference to the average Indian is very doubtful. At the most it may have given some satisfaction to the Princely class which Salisbury in a later letter described to Disraeli as 'the only one over whom we can hope to establish any useful influence.' He continued in reference to a proposal by Lytton to establish an Indian peerage:

[1] ibid., 457.
[2] ibid., 458.

The masses are no use, the literary class which we have unwisely warmed into life before its time is of its nature *frondeur*. Whether the aristocracy themselves are very powerful may be doubted . . . but . . . their goodwill & co-operation, if we can obtain it, will at all events serve to hide to the eyes of our own people & perhaps of the growing literary class in India the nakedness of the sword upon which we really rely.[1]

Disraeli fully agreed with him and with Lytton's proposals, although nothing came of them.

The usefulness of the change of title may have been open to argument, but it is hard to see what positive damage could have ensued. The hostility excited both in London society and in the Liberal Press, quarters seldom in harmony, is surprising. It is true that Disraeli had made a serious blunder by failing to inform the Opposition in advance, as was the normal convention with regard to such legislation. He also forgot to tell the Prince of Wales, who, returning from his tour, was understandably cross when he learned for the first time from the newspapers that he would one day be Emperor of India. The Queen took the blame for both these omissions, but the first of them certainly made Disraeli's conduct of affairs more difficult. The struggle in both Houses was prolonged and exhausting, though in the end victorious. It bore heavily on Disraeli, who was far from well, but he could console himself when it was all over with two reflections. He had earned the lasting gratitude of 'the Faery', and, a curious by-product of the battle, he had taken final vengeance on Lowe.

Disraeli's old enemy had dealt some effective blows at the Suez Canal purchase, but he surpassed all bounds of prudence when he delivered a venomous attack on both the Queen and the Prime Minister during April in a public speech at East Retford, where he claimed that at least two Prime Ministers had resisted the pressure of the Queen to change her Indian title. 'More pliant persons have now been found and I have no doubt the thing will be done.' Disraeli seized the opportunity. Gladstone at once denied having been one of the Prime Ministers concerned, and the Queen allowed Disraeli to quote her statement that she had never made such approaches. He asked permission of the House to use her name in debate, and in a brilliant oration of withering invective proceeded to destroy Lowe, who was obliged to make an abject recantation. His public life was

[1] Hughenden Papers, Box 92, B/XX/Ce/77, June 7, 1876.

terminated. He never held office or the respect of the House again. 'He is in the mud and there I leave him,' Disraeli wrote to Lady Chesterfield. He did not usually bear malice against his enemies, even those whom he had worsted. Lowe was an exception. Shortly before his death Disraeli was asked by a friend whether there was anybody in London with whom he would refuse to shake hands. He paused to think. 'Only one,' he replied, 'Robert Lowe.'

During the whole of spring and summer of that year Disraeli's letters abound with complaints about his health. He was afflicted by bronchitis, asthma and gout; and his condition seems to have been made worse rather than better by some of the medical advice that he received, for example Sir William Gull 'ordering me . . . to drink port wine, wh: I have not done for ten years, and wh: has nearly killed me'.[1] Although illness was largely responsible for his deficiencies in leadership the fact did not prevent hostile comment. Sir William Heathcote, a high Tory and former MP for Oxford University, wrote a revealing letter to Salisbury:

> The aspect of the Govt. in the House of Commons distresses me most seriously and I can hardly imagine how you are to keep the machine going if you are not somehow relieved of the incubus of your present Chief.
>
> Cold and lukewarm in all that might serve the Church or Religious Education and thus (to place it on its lowest ground) real conservatism, he is earnest only in sensational clap trap in which he is continually compromising himself by contradictory utterances . . .
>
> In the ordinary conduct of business Disraeli shows himself at every turn quite incompenent to guide the House . . .[2]

Heathcote's views on 'real conservatism' can perhaps be discounted, but his opinion of Disraeli as a leader is confirmed by others. In a biographical study which, though it does less than justice to Disraeli's first two years as Prime Minister, rings true about his third, Bagehot writes:

> In 1867 he made a minority achieve wonderful things but in 1876 when he had the best majority – the most numerous and obedient – since Mr. Pitt, he did nothing with it. So far from being able to pass great enactments, he could not even despatch ordinary business at decent hours. The gravest and sincerest of Tory

[1] M. & B., v, 495, to Lady Bradford, July 3, 1876.
[2] Salisbury Papers, April 15, 1876.

members – men who hardly murmur at anything – have been heard to complain that it *was* hard that after voting so well and doing so little, they should be kept up so very late. The Session just closed will be known in Parliamentary annals as one of the least effective or memorable on record, and yet one of the most fatiguing.[1]

Whether or not Disraeli was aware of these murmurings, he certainly felt that the personal strain on him of another session would be too much. The alternatives were either to resign, or to retain the Premiership but go to the House of Lords. The Queen spontaneously suggested the latter course to him at the beginning of June. But Disraeli in reply expressed – how sincerely it is hard to say – a strong preference for resignation. Moreover, according to his own account given to Hardy, he actually sounded Derby as to whether the latter would be willing to succeed him.[2] He seems to have envisaged at that time, though he did not say this to Hardy, a combination of Derby as Prime Minister and Hardy as Leader of the House of Commons. But Derby put a stopper on all these plans by a categorical refusal to take over; he also indicated that Hardy would not be his choice as leader, although his principal reason for declining was a conviction that he could not manage the Queen or lead the party on Church questions. Finally he said that he would not serve under anyone else.

Disraeli thus had no option but to stay on. It may well be that he expected this outcome, and he must have been aware of the reluctance with which the Queen would have accepted Derby. He wrote to all his colleagues asking them their frank opinion on his leading them from the House of Lords, and of course they all urged him to do so. As Buckle writes, 'It is difficult to believe that Disraeli did not foresee and desire the issue of the crisis.'[3] The problem now was who should lead the House of Commons. Here Disraeli changed his mind, plumping on second thoughts for Northcote. He was influenced by the fact that Hardy was quick-tempered and so not altogether popular in some quarters, whereas Northcote was universally liked. He considered, too, that Hardy's uxorious tendency to dine at home kept him from being in his place in the House as regularly as he should; and Disraeli had stern standards in this respect. Also there was the problem of what would happen if Disraeli's

---

[1] *Biographical Studies* (2nd edition, 1889), 366–7.
[2] Gathorne Hardy, ii, 4, July 12, 1876.
[3] M. & B., v, 496.

own health really did collapse and Derby was forced to become Prime Minister. Hardy took his disappointment manfully and magnanimously, but stipulated that he, too, should go to the Lords at the first convenient moment. Later Disraeli came to believe that he had made a mistake. The unexpected return of Gladstone to the fray put a premium on fiery and combative leadership. Northcote could contribute much but not that, and he was particularly inhibited by having been at one time Gladstone's private secretary. Hardy would have made a more effective showing.

Late on Friday, August 11, Disraeli made his last speech in the House of Commons, a reply to the Opposition's allegation of neglecting the Bulgarian atrocities. No one except a few Cabinet colleagues realized that he would never be seen there again except as a visitor. At the end of the debate he strolled down to the bar of the House and stood apparently in a reverie, gazing back. Then he retraced his steps and after exchanging some conversation with Lord George Hamilton, took his usual exit behind the Speaker's chair. An observer noticed earlier in the evening that there were tears in his eyes. Next day the news that the Queen had created him Earl of Beaconsfield[1] appeared in all the papers. One can well believe Disraeli's sincerity when he told the Speaker that the change had cost him a 'pang'. He had lived for the House of Commons for nearly forty years. It had been the scene of his vicissitudes and triumphs. In the end he had acquired a mastery over it which only Gladstone could rival. Whatever his deficiencies in the last year, his departure left it a poorer and a duller place. As long as he was in the House there was drama, mystery, romance, excitement. All these were to come again, but, for the moment, life seemed suddenly more drab and humdrum, especially to the younger men who had been fascinated by this extraordinary and unorthodox leader with his inimitable turn of phrase, his far-ranging sweep of vision, his sardonic contempt for hypocrisy and cant. Out of the many letters that he received, one passage from an opponent, Sir William Harcourt, must have particularly pleased him. 'To the imagination of the younger generation your life will always have a special fascination. For them you have enlarged the horizon of the possibilities of the future.'[2] It would not be a bad epitaph.

---

[1] I shall continue, however, to call him by the name by which he will always be known to posterity.

[2] M. & B., v, 498.

Disraeli was a great Parliamentarian and a superb actor, two characters often though not always conjoined. Until ill health undermined his concentration and energy his skill was universally admired; not only skill but courage, the quality for which after his death Gladstone sincerely praised him in his valedictory address. He needed all the courage at his command. For long years he stood alone, trying to answer most of the great orators of the day ranged against him on the opposite benches. His tongue-tied colleagues in the early days of his leadership could give him little support, save their goodwill. But he never faltered, never surrendered, never failed in resource, eloquence and ingenuity. In an age of amateurs he was, along with Gladstone, Palmerston, perhaps Graham, but few others, a professional politician, always in his place, always alert, a master of the rules of procedure and debate. The House of Commons was his life, and he loved it. In the end it came to respect, and even, though with exceptions, to love him.

He could always command its attention. His voice was full, clear, without the slightest trace of a provincial or – despite his alien appearance – a foreign accent. His pronunciation was very precise, giving full weight to every syllable of words which most Englishmen tend to slur or telescope. 'Bus-i-ness', he would say, or 'Parl-i-a-ment'. He told Sir William Fraser that he regretted one physical deficiency. Short-sighted even as a young man, he was so myopic from his middle age onwards that he could not see the expressions on the faces of the back benchers, and so found it hard to gauge the effect of his words. He did not make many gestures. He always began slowly, deliberately and quietly. When he was going to score some special hit, his unconscious signal to the *cognoscenti* was a slight nervous cough and the production of a white handkerchief from his left pocket, which he would pass to his right hand, sniff at for a moment, and return again to the same pocket with his left hand, holding it there until a new subject for his wit, eloquence or indignation came up.[1]

Disraeli's approach to his audience was essentially practical, and seemingly commonsensical. He addressed them as a sophisticated man of the world addressing an assembly of like-minded persons. He did not, after his first few years as leader, go in much for the rather baroque eloquence which had been his technique in his attacks on Peel. This cool worldly tone was not enough to make him

[1] Fraser, *Disraeli and his Day*, 401–2.

stand out in contrast to the Liberal leadership as long as that position was held by Palmerston. But Palmerston's death gave him a chance not only to assume a distinctive policy but also to emphasize a distinctive style, the antithesis of Gladstone, who was himself in so many ways the antithesis of Palmerston. Although we tend to think of this great duel as dominating the whole mid-Victorian era from 1850 to 1880, in fact the direct confrontation of the two men as leaders of their respective parties in the House of Commons lasted little over eight years. Gladstone only became leader in the session of 1866 and virtually abdicated after the election of 1874, though he did not formally retire till the next year. When he returned in full spate after the Bulgarian atrocities Disraeli had moved to the House of Lords.

Disraeli never made the mistake of trying to beat Gladstone at his own game. The torrential flood of words, the convoluted sentences with their parentheses within parentheses, the lofty moral appeals, the ingenious quasi-theological arguments, the fierce denunciations, were addressed to an opponent lolling with his legs crossed, his hat tilted forward, and his eyes half closed. When Gladstone or for that matter any other opponent became really indignant Disraeli would move round in a westerly direction, put his eyeglass slowly to his eye, gaze at the clock over the entrance door, and then relapse again 'into simulated sleep'.[1] But his attention never relaxed. Once when Gladstone paused as if losing the thread of his argument Disraeli quickly said across the table as though to help, 'Your last word was "Revolution".'[2] The many examples of his wit are too well known to quote here. One can well believe that he was missed by opponents as well as by friends and that the House of Commons seemed a different place without him.

In the House of Lords, that 'dullest assembly in the world', as Lord Salisbury called it, he at once acquired an ascendancy unrivalled since that of the 14th Earl of Derby. Although the House had a Conservative majority, it had latterly by no means always obeyed the orders of the Conservative Cabinet. An example was the drastic amendments made to the Judicature Act in 1875. There was no more of this after Disraeli took his seat. He had declared with the sublime confidence of youth nearly fifty years earlier in *The Young Duke* that whereas his style in the Commons was going to be

[1] loc. cit.
[2] ibid., 393.

that of *Don Juan*, in the Lords it would be based on *Paradise Lost*. In fact, it was much the same in both, and equally effective. Observers noticed that he at once adapted himself to the new forms and, unlike most ex-MPs accustomed to addressing the Speaker as 'Sir', never failed to begin 'My Lords'. Yet although he enjoyed being an earl – with his beliefs how could he have failed to do so? – he missed the vigour and warmth of the popular assembly. When a friend asked him how he found his new surroundings he replied, 'I am dead; dead but in the Elysian fields.'

CHAPTER XXV

Foreign Affairs
1875–6

1

'Look at Lord Roehampton,' Disraeli makes Lady Montfort say to Endymion. 'He is the man. He does not care a rush whether the revenue increases or declines. He is thinking of real politics: foreign affairs; maintaining our power in Europe.' Disraeli meant what he said; he always regarded foreign policy as the most important and fascinating task of the statesman. Yet a lifetime of political experiences had so far given him little opportunity to show what he could do in that field. In the days of the elder Derby he had sometimes tried to interfere, but without responsibility, and hence without success. He had criticized Malmesbury in private, Palmerston, Clarendon, Russell and Granville in public, but his criticisms were those of an amateur rather than an expert. The ten months of his first premiership and the first year of his second gave him no particular opportunity. It was not until 1875, when the Eastern question became important, that he had his chance. Thereafter foreign affairs dominated Cabinet and Parliament until the dénouement at the Congress of Berlin three years later.

Although Disraeli's alien origins gave him a certain air of cosmopolitanism, and he was not averse to encouraging this impression, he had, in fact, little knowledge of foreign countries. Since his tour of the Mediterranean in 1830–1 he had only been abroad four times, on a honeymoon in Baden and Munich and on three visits to Paris, in 1842, 1845 and 1856. He could scarcely speak French at all, and of other foreign languages he was almost wholly ignorant. These defects are by no means fatal to one who aspires to conduct foreign policy. It can be argued that too much knowledge of other countries is a positive disadvantage; but in Disraeli's case there is little evidence of a compensating flair for diagnosing the trends of the time, or discerning the future course of events. A man who could see European politics principally as a struggle between the millionaires and the secret societies, between the Rothschilds and the

Carbonari, was out of touch with the realities of his day. Moreover, he was curiously ignorant of geography. How, otherwise, could he have blithely written to the Queen at one stage during the Eastern crisis: 'the Empress of India should order her armies to clear Central Asia of the Muscovites and drive them into the Caspian Sea'?[1] Today we can but rub our eyes and charitably assume that it was the author of *Tancred* speaking, not the Prime Minister of England.

When Disraeli took office in 1874 it is doubtful whether he had any clear ideas on foreign policy other than doing something – it did not much matter what – to reassert Britain's power in Europe. He had been highly critical of Gladstone's allegedly inactive attitude during the last six years. Failure to mediate in the Franco-Prussian war, to prevent the Russian denunciation of the Black Sea clauses, or to modify the results of the *Alabama* arbitration, all were cited as instances of Britain's isolation and general decline; and as leader of the Opposition Disraeli naturally had made the most of them. He was, therefore, in the mood to seize the first chance which came his way of demonstrating that the tone of British policy had changed.

An opportunity arose in the early summer of 1875. The great new feature of the diplomatic scene since Disraeli had last been in power was the decline of France and the domination of Europe by the Dreikaiserbund, the League of the Three Emperors. This was a Conservative alliance between what were oddly described as the Northern Courts, Berlin, St Petersburg and Vienna. When Disraeli first became conscious of politics as a young man in the 1820s, Europe had been dominated by a superficially similar confederacy. His hero, Canning, had made a great name by reversing Castle-reagh's policy of collaboration with the Holy Alliance and asserting an independent role for Britain. Conditioned by the memories of youth, Disraeli set his sights on the disruption of the Dreikaiser-bund.

The war scare of May enabled him to show that Britain's voice would henceforth be heard in Europe. Disraeli persuaded Derby to associate Britain with the protest made by the Russian Chancellor, Prince Gorchakov, at the apparent intention of the German Government to launch a preventive war against France. There is to this day an element of mystery about Bismarck's real plans, but if he did meditate such action – and this is by no means certain – he quickly went into reverse. He was greatly irritated at Gorchakov's

[1] M. & B., vi, 155.

THE EASTERN QUESTION

A Turkey and the Balkans, 1876
B The Treaty of San Stefano
C Congress of Berlin, 1878

well-publicized claim that Russia had preserved the peace, and there began a personal feud which had its repercussions at the Congress of Berlin. As for Derby's intervention, Bismarck seems to have been more surprised than affronted. He thanked him officially and told Count Münster that, if Britain had shown in 1870 a fraction of the effort exerted in 1875, the Franco-Prussian war would have been averted.[1]

Disraeli's restless imagination was stimulated by the affair. He saw it not merely as a matter of preserving the peace but of separating Russia from Germany, perhaps even securing in the former a continental ally. He was in no way a Russophobe at this time. 'My own impression', he wrote to Derby on May 6, 'is that we should construct some concerted movement to preserve the peace of Europe like Pam did when he baffled France and expelled the Egyptians from Syria. There might be an alliance between Russia and ourself for this special purpose; and other powers, as Austria and perhaps Italy might be invited to accede . . .'[2] Some days later in answer to a congratulatory letter from the Prime Minister, Derby replied: 'We have been lucky in our foreign policy. What we did involved no risk and cost no trouble while it has given the appearance of doing more than we really did to bring about the result.'[3] This prosaic outlook corresponded to reality, but it was symptomatic of the gulf which even then existed between the Foreign Secretary and his chief.

Derby has been described as 'the most isolationist foreign secretary that Great Britain has even known'.[4] He was isolationist largely because he found Britain isolated and he had a deep aversion from positive action of any sort. Mr Southgate in his book, *The Passing of the Whigs, 1832–1886*, points out that British Foreign Secretaries during the nineteenth century can be more readily classified by temperament than by party. They divide into 'activists', Canning, Palmerston, Russell, and 'passivists', Aberdeen, Granville, Malmesbury.[5] Derby was one of the latter. He favoured prudence, caution, the minimum of intervention, and the minimum public emphasis upon such intervention as he did undertake. Disraeli, an 'activist' if ever there was one, came only slowly and reluctantly to

---

[1] R. W. Seton-Watson, *Disraeli, Gladstone and the Eastern Question* (1935), 14 n.
[2] M. & B., v, 422.
[3] ibid., 424. Derby to Disraeli, May 20, 1875.
[4] A. J. P. Taylor, *The Struggle for the Mastery in Europe, 1848–1918* (1954), 233.
[5] Donald Southgate, *The Passing of the Whigs, 1832–1886* (1962), 266.

recognize the profound difference which separated him from his former pupil. The Queen, also an 'activist', saw it far sooner than he. But his letters to her even at this stage betray a certain uneasiness. His emphasis on Derby's good qualities and anxiety to defend him sound at times as if Disraeli was unconsciously trying to convince himself as well as the Queen that Derby was really sound at heart after all. His mixed feelings are entirely creditable, and can be explained by his complicated psychological and social relationship with the Stanley family for two generations, but excess of loyalty was destined to land him in many a difficult dilemma before the final unhappy parting of the ways three years later.

In the summer of 1875 the Eastern question, dormant since the Crimean War, burst into life again. During July a rebellion broke out in the remote and desolate province of Herzegovina, which has been described as Turkey's equivalent of the North-West Frontier. It spread to Bosnia and all efforts to extinguish it met with failure. In October the Sultan Abdul Aziz, insanely extravagant and in the words of the Russian Ambassador at Constantinople, '*en proie à une véritable fièvre de chemin de fer*', suspended half the payment on his Government's debt largely incurred by expenditure on uneconomic railway projects. Six months later he suspended the other half. About 30 per cent of the debt was in British hands, and there was consternation in the City. The sick man of Europe whose demise had been so often erroneously predicted that people had almost ceased to believe in it now seemed on the verge of death at last. Disraeli wrote to Lady Bradford: 'I really believe "the Eastern Question", that has haunted Europe for a century and which I thought the Crimean War had adjourned for half another will fall to my lot to encounter – dare I say to settle.'[1]

What was the Eastern question? Many volumes have been written on this complicated subject, but the essence of it as far as Britain was concerned can be summed up shortly. In 1875 the Turks, governed by rulers who had the spiritual authority of the popes, combined all too often with the moral outlook of the more deplorable Roman emperors, were still in possession of a vast polyglot dominion covering most of the Middle East and stretching far into Europe. The whole of modern Bulgaria and Albania together with much of modern Yugoslavia and Greece still remained under

[1] M. & B., vi, 14, November 3, 1875.

Turkish rule. The cruelty and corruption of the régime were tempered only by incompetence. It was at its worst in Europe, for the Christian subjects of the Sultan were treated as inferior citizens fit only for exploitation. The Sultanate survived because of the dissensions of the great powers. Militarily Turkey no longer counted, and for over a hundred years had lost almost every European war in which she fought unaided.

The powers principally concerned were Russia, Britain, and Austria-Hungary. France had at one time pursued an active Eastern policy, but the defeat of 1870 had forced her into the background. The main conflict lay between Russia and Britain. Austria-Hungary, a multi-racial empire, like Turkey threatened by Slav nationalism, watched from the sidelines, preferring the preservation of Turkey, but determined to seize a share of the spoils if Turkey collapsed. The Orthodox Christians, mostly Slav, groaning under Turkish misrule, naturally looked towards Russia. Although successive Tsars instinctively mistrusted the spirit of nationalism, and panslavism was not encouraged officially, the appeal made to religious and nationalist sentiment by the oppressed Balkan peoples could not be disregarded. The autocrat of all the Russias, whether Peter the Great, Alexander II, Lenin or Stalin, has never been able to ignore public opinion entirely. Moreover, the disruption of the Turkish Empire in Europe seemed likely to open the way to Russian expansion southwards, in particular to the reconquest of Bessarabia. The cession of this province to Rumania under the Treaty of Paris was regarded by Alexander II as the last surviving 'humiliation' of the Crimean War.

Any moves which seemed likely to break up the Turkish Empire were certain to be resisted in Britain. It had become a well-established article of British diplomatic faith that Turkey must be propped up for as long as possible. This belief stemmed basically from mistrust of Russian intentions towards India. Russia was the one great power which could in theory either march overland to India direct, or achieve the same object indirectly by cutting the British route to India. Britain's great deterrent, the Royal Navy, was powerless against this threat.

It is hard to escape the conclusion that both dangers were exaggerated. It is true that during the 1860s there fell to Russian arms in central Asia a number of effete Oriental kingdoms whose names echo with the romance of vanished half-legendary empires:

Chimkent, Turkestan, Samarkand, Bokhara. But the distance to India still remained vast. Whatever some of the wilder Russian expansionists might say or write, the Russian Government never even contemplated such an improbable conquest. As for cutting the route to India, this was an equally chimerical menace. Perhaps it had some semblance of plausibility at the time of the Crimean War, when the overland route via Syria and the Euphrates valley to the Persian Gulf still retained its importance. But since 1869 the only route to India that mattered went through the Suez Canal. Egypt, though nominally under Turkish suzerainty, was, in fact, independent. Port Said is nearly a thousand miles away from Constantinople by sea, and a good deal more overland.

By the 1870s an occasional voice of protest could be heard even in the Conservative party against the dogma that Constantinople was the 'Key to India'. Salisbury, for example, regarded the 'old Crimean policy' of preserving Turkey's territorial integrity as quite futile. He was equally sceptical about the alleged Russian threat via central Asia and he observed that much of the trouble came from British statesmen using maps on too small a scale. It must be admitted that Disraeli was an offender in this respect. How otherwise can one account for his apparently genuine belief that if the Russians were in Constantinople they could threaten the Suez Canal? In October 1876 Lord Barrington made a note of an interview with Disraeli. Why, he asked the Prime Minister, should Britain not follow the advice of those who wanted her to forget about Constantinople and secure the route to India by annexing Egypt?

> . . . But the answer is obvious [said Lord B.]. If the Russians had Constantinople, they could at any time march their Army through Syria to the mouth of the Nile, and then what would be the use of our holding Egypt. Not even the command of the sea could help us under such circumstances. People who talk in this manner must be utterly ignorant of geography. Our strength is on the sea. Constantinople is the Key of India, and not Egypt and the Suez Canal . . .[1]

It cannot be said that the danger was non-existent, but it was certainly remote by the 'seventies. Disraeli was himself showing ignorance of geography, an ignorance the more surprising since he had actually visited the places concerned. The truth was that the

[1] ibid., 84, October 23, 1876.

British obsession with the Eastern question stemmed from ancient habit rather than clear thought. The preservation of Turkish integrity had perhaps at one time been a sensible method of safeguarding a vital British interest, but statesmen continued to advocate the same course of action long after the strategic realities behind it had changed, and after they had themselves almost forgotten what these were. As so often, Salisbury injects a note of melancholy realism into the discussion.

> The commonest error in politics [he wrote to Lytton] is sticking to the carcasses of dead policies. When a mast falls overboard you do not try to save a rope here and a spar there in memory of their former utility; you cut away the hamper altogether. And it should be the same with a policy. But it is not so. We cling to the shred of an old policy after it has been torn to pieces; and to the shadow of the shred after the rag itself has been torn away.[1]

Apart from its dubious value for Britain there was another cause for doubting the wisdom of the old Crimean policy. During the past twenty years the task had become much more difficult if only because British public opinion was beginning to rebel. Turkey had promised a whole series of reforms in 1856, but it was notorious that scarcely a single one had been implemented. Turkish misrule was not only disgraceful – it had always been that – but publicly and flagrantly disgraceful. English Turcophiles were finding it harder and harder to convince their compatriots that the Balkan outcry was artificially fomented by Russian intrigue. They were slightly more successful with the argument that surrender to the agitation would bring Russian hegemony in the Balkan peninsula. But, in fact, both arguments were unsound. The reality of Turkish oppression is attested by overwhelming impartial evidence, and the Slav nationalities far from being tools of Russia only looked to the Tsar as an ally against the Turks. Having once got rid of the Sultan they soon acquired a hearty detestation of their former protector. Gladstone and Salisbury were right in prophesying that the liberated Slav nations would be a more effective bulwark against Russian expansion than ever the Sick Man of Europe had been.

Disraeli, predictably, did not share this belief. He instinctively lacked sympathy with small nations struggling to be free. Nationalism, the strongest political impulse of his day passed him

---

[1] Cecil, *Salisbury*, ii, 145, May 25, 1877.

by, and what he saw of it he disliked. Basically this hostility
stemmed from his fundamental creed, the necessity to uphold 'the
aristocratic settlement'. Nationalism in his time was essentially a
radical force. There were exceptions, Poland and Germany for
example; but in most cases national self-determination was tied up
with the struggle for land reform and the expropriation of landlords
with a different language and religion from those of their peasant
tenants.

Britain's parallel to the Balkans was Ireland, and Disraeli saw it.
'Fancy autonomy for Bosnia with a mixed population,' he wrote to
Lady Bradford, 'autonomy for Ireland would be less absurd.'[1] On
another occasion he wondered 'whether in the advice which we are
asked to give Turkey we are not committing ourselves to principles
which are, or which may be soon, matter of controversy in our own
country: for instance, the apportionment of local taxation to local
purposes and the right of the peasantry to the soil'.[2]

Disraeli's tour of the Middle East in 1830–1 was a doubtful asset.
It had lasted long enough for him to plume himself on his local
knowledge, and it had occurred long enough ago for that knowledge
to be largely irrelevant. In the days of the Sultan Mahmud there did
seem a possibility of Turkey being reformed from within. Forty-five
years had elapsed since then, but the régime far from improving had
actually deteriorated. Like many foreign visitors, Disraeli preferred
the Turks to their Christian subjects. This is understandable. People
who are ill treated do not become any the nicer for the experience.
Oppressors are often more pleasant to meet than the oppressed. 'I
find the habits of this calm and luxurious people entirely agree with
my own preconceived opinions of propriety and enjoyment,' Disraeli
had written to his sister, 'and I detest the Greeks more than ever.'
We saw how he volunteered to join the Grand Vizier's army in suppressing the Albanian revolt, and how after meeting that functionary he expatiated on 'the delight of being made much of by a man
who was daily decapitating half the province'.[3] Disraeli would have
had to have undergone a change indeed if he was to be stirred by
the moral indignation which Turkish misgovernment inspired in
Gladstone. This is not to say that Disraeli consistently pursued a
policy of maintaining Turkish independence. On the contrary, he

[1] M. & B., vi, 13.
[2] ibid., vi, 19.
[3] See above, 65.

often contemplated partition as a possible solution; but it was partition by, and in the interests of, the great powers, not for the sake of oppressed Christians.

The Eastern question did not at first cause any great controversy in Parliament or the Press. Disraeli was not anxious to intervene at all. He assented reluctantly in August to a proposal made by Andrassy, the Austro-Hungarian Foreign Minister, in concert with the Russian and German ambassadors for joint mediation by the consuls of the six great powers in Bosnia and its neighbourhood; he suspected that any such move would be basically anti-Turkish; he preferred to let the combatants fight it out, and he disliked the way in which the Dreikaiserbund had taken the initiative.

> There is no balance [he wrote to Lady Bradford on September 6] and unless we go out of our way to act with the three Northern Powers, they can act without us which is not agreeable for a State like England. Nor do I see as I have told you before any prospect of the revival of France as a military puissance. She is more likely to be partitioned than to conquer Europe again.
>
> When I entered political life there were three Great Powers in danger – the Grand Signior of the Ottomans, the Pope of Rome, and the Lord Mayor of London. The last will survive a long time: but the fall of France has destroyed the Pope, and will, ultimately drive the Turk from Europe.[1]

At this stage and indeed for a considerable time to come Disraeli's main interest in the Eastern question was to discover some means of asserting British independence against the Northern Courts in as striking a manner as possible. He hinted at this by no means obscurely in his Guildhall speech in November, when he declared that England had interests as 'considerable' as those of the three powers, and that she intended to maintain them. The hint was not taken. At the end of the year, the consular commission having proved totally useless, Andrassy, again consulting only Berlin and St Petersburg, put forward a joint note demanding various reforms. The other three powers were asked to adhere. Disraeli, in spite of Derby's willingness to agree, was most reluctant to identify England with the demands. He disliked following Andrassy's lead and he disliked the actual proposals. But once again he had to give way; this time because the Turks themselves asked England to join, and 'we can't be more Turkish than the Sultan'. In reality the Turks had

---

[1] M. & B., vi, 13.

no intention of implementing the note: they used it simply to gain time in preparation for dealing with Serbia and Montenegro, which they regarded as the instigators of the revolt.

The concrete result of eight months of proposals and promises was meagre. The Turks had made only one concession. They allowed the bell of an Orthodox Church to be rung in Sarajevo. It was a very small one and sounded more like a clock striking than a bell ringing.[1]

2

Although frustrated in his efforts to make a splash over the Turkish question during 1875, Disraeli was able that autumn to bring off the sensational *coup* with which his name will always be associated, the purchase of the Khedive's interest in the Suez Canal Company. In doing so he displayed many of his highest qualities, boldness, flair, intuition and above all a sense of opportunity. It is doubtful whether any of his contemporaries would have acted with such speed and vigour.

The Suez Canal, which had been opened in 1869, cut the distance from Britain to India by several weeks and some thousands of miles. In 1875 four-fifths of its traffic was British. It is true that even more British ships continued to use the Cape route, and also true that the Canal carried only about one-tenth of the total British import-export trade in the world. But the signs for the future were there for all to read. Moreover, its strategic importance was even greater than its commercial. In the event of another Indian Mutiny, or an invasion by Russia, the Suez Canal could carry reinforcements far more quickly than the old Cape route. As Cairns put it in a letter to Disraeli after the purchase, India had become a wholly different empire. 'It is now the *Canal and India*; there is no such thing now to us as India alone. India is any number of cyphers; but the Canal is the unit that makes these cyphers valuable.'[2]

At this time the country which had by far the greatest stake both in Egypt and the Canal Company was France. Most of the Egyptian bonds were in French hands. So were all the founders' shares and 56 per cent of the ordinary shares of the Suez Canal Company. The

---

[1] Sumner, *Russia and the Balkans*, 155, quoting a dispatch of April 7, 1876, from the British Consul.

[2] Hughenden Papers, Box 91, B/XX/Ca/168, January 29, 1876. Before the purchase Cairns seems to have been against it.

remainder of the ordinary shares belonged to the Khedive, who had, however, mortgaged them until 1895. It seemed all too likely that if the Khedive, whose financial profligacy was only surpassed by that of his nominal suzerain, the Sultan, finally went bankrupt, the French Government would seize the chance of intervening, and would be in a position to threaten a vital British interest.

From the start of his Premiership Disraeli had been interested in the affairs of the Canal Company. It was running at a loss and de Lesseps tried to raise the shipping dues. His action was in the end condemned by an international commission as a breach of the terms of the company's concession. Even so he only gave way to a threat of military action by the Khedive. Since the trouble had been caused by financial difficulties, Disraeli investigated the possibility of buying de Lesseps out. He employed the backstairs methods to which he was addicted and sent Baron Rothschild's son to Paris on a secret personal mission of inquiry. Nothing came of it. De Lesseps, who was at that time backed by the French Government, refused to sell.

Now a fresh opportunity presented itself. The Sultan's bankruptcy in October precipitated the long-expected financial ruin of the Khedive, whose last remaining asset was the 176,602 ordinary shares which he held out of a total of 400,000 in the Suez Canal Company. Early in November he began secret negotiations with two competing French syndicates for the sale of these, in order to raise the sum needed to pay the next instalment on the Egyptian debt, between £3m and £4m. The news was communicated to Frederick Greenwood, editor of the *Pall Mall Gazette*, by the financier Henry Oppenheim, and it was passed on by Greenwood to Derby at the Foreign Office on November 15 with the strong advice that the British Government should step in to prevent the company's becoming wholly French owned. Derby's instinct, as always when faced with a novel and unprecedented proposal, was to say no. But Disraeli, who may have had the news of the Khedive's negotiations independently through the Rothschilds, persuaded him and, two days later, the Cabinet that 'the thing must be done', as he put it to the Queen. Most of his colleagues, including Cairns, Derby and Northcote, were against him. So the decision was a personal victory for the Prime Minister.

It was a matter of some urgency. One of the French syndicates already had an option to purchase the shares, which expired on

November 19. Fortunately the intrigues of the rival syndicate had prevented the option-holders from raising the money in Paris. But, although the Khedive was informed on the 17th that the British Government was ready to buy his shares and although he indicated his approval, he reopened negotiations with the original syndicate next day, this time on the basis of mortgage, not sale; but a mortgage on such onerous terms that it was most unlikely ever to be redeemed. There was great difficulty in raising the money in Paris, for at this time viewed purely as a commercial proposition the Suez Canal seemed a very doubtful asset. De Lesseps implored the French Government to intervene. But the situation had changed since 1874. British help at Berlin over the war scare in the summer had not been forgotten. The Duc Decazes, the Foreign Minister, inquired of Derby what the British reaction would be, and Derby was unusually categorical in his reply: the Cabinet, he said, 'would certainly be opposed to these shares falling into the hands of another French company'. Accordingly the French Government declined to intervene, the French syndicate failed to raise the money, and the Khedive agreed on November 23 to sell his shares to the British Government for £4m. Three days later the shares were deposited in the British Consulate at Cairo.

Before the matter could be settled the Government had to produce the money, and since Parliament was not sitting it could only be done by loan. Monty Corry is responsible for a colourful version of what happened: how he waited outside the Cabinet door for a prearranged signal; how Disraeli opened it for a moment uttering simply 'Yes'; how he sped to New Court and told Baron Rothschild that the Prime Minister wanted £4m. 'When?' 'Tomorrow.' 'What is your security?' 'The British Government.' 'You shall have it.' And as a further touch of authenticity we are told that Rothschild ate, and ejected the skin of, a muscatel grape before asking his second question. It is a pity to tarnish what Sir Winston Churchill has called 'these gleaming toys' of history. No one can say that this account is actually untrue, but Corry like his chief was fond of good stories, and they grew no less good with time.

What is certain is that the Rothschilds lent the money. They charged a commission of $2\frac{1}{2}$ per cent, ie £100,000. The Treasury was disturbed at the amount, and it became one of the principal objects of criticism in the ensuing debate in the House of Commons. Disraeli's old enemy Lowe was particularly sharp on this point, and

for once that disagreeable and cantankerous figure seems to have
had some justification. £2m had to be provided on December 1,
£1m on December 16, £1m on January 5. Parliament voted the
money on February 20. The average rate of interest works out at
about 13 per cent p.a. Rothschild himself justified the size of the
commission, on the ground that only he could have effected the loan
sufficiently secretly to avoid grave disturbance of the money
markets; whereas the Bank of England, to which, so critics argued,
the Government ought to have applied, had uncertain powers and
in any case could not have acted secretly.[1] He also maintained that,
although the risk of Parliament refusing to ratify was remote, there
were other more serious risks: the Khedive might have insisted on
payment in gold sovereigns; the Rothschilds might have lost
valuable clients if there had been a sudden call for a loan while the
money was tied up; unforeseen events might have caused a rise in
the price of money. These are cogent arguments, but the fact
remains that they were charging on a short-term loan to the
strongest financial power in the world something like the rate at
which the Khedive had to borrow in the last years before his
financial collapse.

Disraeli was not the man to worry about this aspect of the affair.
He was cock-a-hoop at bringing off a *coup* worthy of Sidonia, and
on November 24 he wrote in triumph to Queen Victoria:[2]

> . . . It is just settled; you have it, Madam. The French Govern-
> ment has been out-generaled. They tried too much, offering loans
> at an usurious rate, and with conditions which would have virtually
> given them the government of Egypt.
>   The Khedive, in despair and disgust, offered your Majesty's
> Government to purchase his shares outright. He never would
> listen to such a proposition before.
>   Four millions sterling! and almost immediately. There was only
> one firm that could do it – Rothschilds. They behaved admirably;
> advanced the money at a low rate, and the entire interest of the
> Khedive is now yours, Madam . . .

To Lady Bradford he wrote on the same day even more exuberantly.[3]

> . . . We have had all the gamblers, capitalists, financiers of the

---

[1] ibid., Box 94, B/XX/Co/114. Memorandum by Corry of conversation with Baron
Rothschild, February 19, 1876. Partly quoted, M. & B., vi, 448.
[2] M. & B., v, 448–9.
[3] ibid., 449–50.

world organized and platooned in bands of plunderers, arrayed against us, and secret emissaries in every corner, and have baffled them all, and have never been suspected. The day before yesterday, Lesseps, whose company has the remaining shares, backed by the French whose agent he was, made a great offer. Had it succeeded, the whole of the Suez Canal would have belonged to France and they might have shut it up . . . The Fairy is in ecstacies . . .

It can be seen from the foregoing account of what actually happened that Disraeli was once again displaying that 'perfect disregard for facts' which his warmest admirers can scarcely deny. The French Government had not been outgeneralled by him; nor had de Lesseps, for if the French syndicate could have raised the money there is every reason to suppose that the Khedive, who does not seem to have been at all 'in despair and disgust' at the terms, would have closed with them. De Lesseps was not the 'agent' of the French Government. On the contrary, he was rebuffed, for reasons connected with the general international situation. As for the claim that the French 'might have shut up' the Suez Canal but for Britain's purchase of the shares, it rested on a misconception which has had a very long life, and was by no means extinct as late as the crisis of 1956.

Disraeli was confusing the ownership of the Canal Company with the ownership of the Canal itself. The proprietors of the company had no right whatever to shut up the canal or to make any discrimination between countries. Freedom of passage was assured by the Khedive's declaration in the concession of 1866 subsequently ratified by a Firman of the Sultan that the Canal would be perpetually open as a neutral passage for all merchant ships on payment of dues to the Canal Company. Legally, no doubt, the Firman might have been revoked, but this depended on the Khedive and the Sultan. Later the position was made as secure as it could be under international law by the signature in 1888 of the perpetual maritime convention which governs the legal status of the Canal today. It holds good, whoever owns the company's shares, whether a French syndicate or, as now, the Egyptian Government. In any case, Disraeli, despite his own conviction to the contrary, did not acquire a controlling interest. Not only was the Khedive's holding less than half the total, but his shares, having been mortgaged in 1871, had no voting rights at all until 1895, and even then only carried ten votes – the maximum allowed under the company's articles to any shareholder.[1]

To say all this is not to decry the purchase. High-handed action by the French proprietors was less likely when over 44 per cent of the shares were owned by the government which had by far the greatest interest in the shipping that used the canal. Nor would the French be so well placed to put pressure on the Khedive as they would if they had owned all the shares. It was argued that Britain could wait till her rights were actually threatened, and then send the fleet to Port Said. To this Disraeli had a good answer suggested to him by Cairns, who in the same letter quoted above wrote:

> It is said – yes, but you cd always have the Canal by war: & even now you must have war all the same.
>
> In the first place there is a large territory *between* peace & war; i.e. negotiation, compromise, influence, pressure etc.; & in this wide territory we shall now be armed with a leverage we never had before.
>
> Then if our rights have to be maintained, of course they must be retained in the last resort by war; & war, *mechanically*, is always the same whatever be the cause. But in our former condition it must have been war to destroy or take possession of the property of others; now it will be war to defend our own property. Is there no *moral* difference?[2]

There was much common sense in the argument. Whatever Gladstone might say, there was a real practical advantage in preventing France from having the exclusive control of a company whose bargaining power with the Khedive was bound to be formidable. There was, moreover, a further advantage in the purchase, though this was not apparent at the time or in Disraeli's life. It turned out to be an excellent investment. Until 1895 the British Government merely received the Khedive's mortgage payments – about £200,000 p.a. But in that year when the shares came out of pawn the first dividend was received and amounted to £690,000. By 1901 it was £880,000. In 1898 the market value of shares which had cost £4m was over £24m and rising at the rate of about £2m a year. Shortly before 1914 they were valued at over £40m.

Disraeli's *coup* was widely heralded as a new departure in foreign policy. Particularly in Liberal circles it was expected to foreshadow a British occupation of Egypt; Cairo would replace Constantinople

---

[1] That the purchase gave no commensurate control on the board is shown by the fact that Britain in 1876 only secured three seats out of twenty-four.

[2] Hughenden Papers, Box 91, B/XX/Ca/168.

as the key to India, and the odious task of bolstering up Turkey would be abandoned. Right-wing Liberals, like Hartington and Goschen, welcomed what they believed to be imminent, while Tory diehards uttered warnings against abandoning the old Crimean policy. Britain did in the end both occupy Egypt and give up the effort to defend Turkey, but no such intention existed in Disraeli's mind at the time. Historians who have seen in his action a deeply matured plan which came to fruition later are in error. Although there would have been much to be said for such a change of policy, all the evidence points to Disraeli's determination to adhere to the traditional course. It was months after the Suez purchase that he disclaimed to Barrington any intention to substitute the annexation of Egypt for the integrity of Turkey, and throughout his period in office he consistently refused to be drawn by Bismarck into the Egyptian imbroglio.

His objective was rather to forestall France and prevent a French occupation than to take any step towards seizing Egypt for Britain. No doubt with his capacity to dramatize events he wished it to be believed, even believed himself, that he had done much more and that somehow the Canal had actually fallen into British hands. The facts cannot sustain this fantasy. Derby stated them more correctly in a speech at Edinburgh, to the annoyance of the Queen, who considered that he had 'tried to pour as much cold water as he could on the great success'. We were acting, he said, simply to prevent a great highway filled with our shipping coming under the exclusive control 'of the foreign shareholders of a foreign company'. But it was Disraeli's more colourful version that got the ear of Europe and of posterity. And so a new historical myth came into being half consciously fabricated by the most potent myth-maker in British history.

3

There were few developments in the Eastern question during the early months of 1876. Disraeli's time was occupied with making the Queen Empress of India, and with general domestic business. But in May, Turkey once again came into the headlines with the murder of the French and German Consuls at Salonika by pro-Moslem rioters. The Northern Courts decided to address yet another note of protest and exhortation to the Sultan, and once again invited

Britain, France and Italy to sign without previous consultation. Disraeli was determined to refuse.

The Berlin Memorandum, as the document is called, arrived in London during the weekend, at 5 pm on Saturday, May 13, and owing to a Foreign Office blunder did not get to Disraeli till 1 pm on Sunday. Both the timing and the delay annoyed him. He gave Derby a very sharp rap over the knuckles, but it is an exaggeration to suppose that he rejected the memorandum from ill temper. He had long wanted to have a hit at the Dreikaiserbund, and to make an emphatic assertion of British independence. He was concerned more with this than with buttressing Turkey, although it is also true that he regarded the proposed measures as either impracticable or 'a scheme which must end very soon in the disintegration of Turkey'. He carried the Cabinet with him after speaking in a manner of 'unusual solemnity', according to Northcote. The leaders of the Opposition made no objection. Gladstone did, indeed, protest later, but when he spoke on July 31 it was with knowledge of the Bulgarian atrocities which put a new complexion on matters. One important personage had misgivings. The Queen, so Ponsonby wrote on her behalf, 'fears our refusal to join the other countries may have a serious effect and may encourage the Porte to refuse to listen to advice and to look to us for support in their difficulties'.[1]

Some of the ablest professional diplomats shared these doubts. Lord Odo Russell warned Derby of 'the serious consequences' of rejecting the memorandum, and appears to have been greatly surprised at the decision. To Disraeli's anger he had expressed in Berlin his confidence that the British Government would accept the note. 'An unheard-of step', Disraeli called it when he saw Lord Odo's letter. Lord Stratford de Redcliffe, whose experience of Turkey was unrivalled, also considered the decision to be unwise, and so did Lord Hammond, the Permanent Under-Secretary at the Foreign Office from 1854 to 1873. But they were old and retired, and were not in contact with Disraeli.

These criticisms have been endorsed by most historians and their force seems incontestable. It is true that the immediate sequence of events appeared to justify Disraeli's decision. There was a revolution in Constantinople on the very day that the Memorandum was to be presented, May 30. Abdul Aziz was deposed and found dead in highly suspicious circumstances soon afterwards. He was succeeded

[1] Royal Archives, H.7.155, May 16, 1876.

by his nephew Murad V, a feeble-minded youth who had a taste for poetry and an even stronger taste for champagne laced with brandy. Effective power was in the hands of the 'liberal' minister, Midhat Pasha, who promptly announced a comprehensive but specious programme of reforms. It was impossible not to give the new régime a chance, and so the Berlin Memorandum became for practical purposes a dead letter from the start. The revolution seemed to lend at least *ex post facto* justification to Disraeli's decision, but the Queen had put her finger on the real criticism when she feared that the Turks would be emboldened by British abstention to ignore the necessity for genuine reform.

This had always been the difficulty. Successive Turkish governments believed that, whatever Britain might say, she would be compelled by her own vital interests to support Turkey in the last resort, and that this consideration would override any Turkish maltreatment of the Christians. If Britain had associated herself with the other powers or, failing that, had produced a constructive alternative, then there might have been some chance of averting the crisis by convincing the Turks that they must reform or perish. Disraeli's coolness towards the Andrassy note and his rejection of the Berlin Memorandum merely confirmed the wishful thinking of the Porte. He further confirmed it by sending warships to Besika Bay just outside the Dardanelles. Their ostensible purpose was to intervene if there was a repetition in Constantinople of the massacre in Salonika, but inevitably their presence was interpreted by the Turks as a sign of British support such as preceded the Crimean War.

The confusion in Constantinople, the failure of the great powers to achieve any reforms, together with the news not yet fully available in the West of Turkish atrocities in Bulgaria combined to induce a mood of mingled hope and desperation among the Serbs. At the end of June, Serbia and Montenegro declared war on Turkey, despite official warnings both from Vienna and St Petersburg. Meanwhile Disraeli seems to have had some *arrière pensées* about the rejection of the Berlin Memorandum. On June 9 he delivered a speech surprisingly conciliatory in its tone towards Russia. That evening at dinner with Baron Rothschild he made an overture to Count Shuvalov, the Russian Ambassador, and repeated it the next day. We only have Shuvalov's account,[1] for the matter is not mentioned

[1] Seton-Watson, *Disraeli, Gladstone and the Eastern Question*, 40–42, quoting Shuvalov to Gorchakov, June 11, 1876.

in Disraeli's papers, but there is no reason to doubt its accuracy.
Disraeli declared that his Cabinet did not 'distrust a Great Power
which is governed by wise men and on conservative principles'; that
Russia was 'wrong to hold back Serbia and Montenegro'; and that
war was inevitable, because the rebels were fighting for independence which the Turks would never concede. He hoped Britain and
Russia would consult together. 'We think blood-letting to be
necessary.' If the Christians win 'we shall only have to register
accomplished facts: if Turkey crushes the Christians and the re-
pression becomes tyrannous, it will be the turn of all the Great
Powers to interpose in the name of humanity'.

Nothing came of this. Shuvalov was puzzled and regarded it,
probably rightly, as an indication that Disraeli was uneasy about
Britain's isolation. A fortnight later Disraeli veered yet again and
Shuvalov could get little out of him except a denial that Britain
meant to annex Egypt. The Ambassador in his report to Gorchakov
described British policy as 'hesitating, tortuous but not warlike . . .
The British Government *wishes an agreement with someone but cannot
find anyone.*' There were objections to Andrassy, to Bismarck and to
France. Only Russia remained, but the age-old mistrust divided the
two countries. 'Thus it is not a bellicose *élan*,' continued Shuvalov,
'but fear of us which prompts British armaments and naval
demonstrations. It may be positively asserted that no one here
wants war, but it is a question whether Mr. Disraeli's policy is not
unconsciously leading up to it.'[1] The episode is chiefly of interest in
showing how undecided Disraeli was at this stage about the best
course to pursue. It is hard to avoid the conclusion that he was waiting on events rather than seeking a solution to the problem of
Turkey-in-Europe.

Disraeli was far from well at this time, and in addition to bad
health he had to endure a particularly exhausting session – his last
in the House of Commons. He was evidently feeling the strain. This
probably explains not only the vacillations of his foreign policy but
also the erratic and irascible nature of his personal judgements. It
may have been correct to dismiss Sir Andrew Buchanan the
Ambassador in Vienna as a 'hopeless mediocrity'[2] and Lord
Augustus Loftus at St Petersburg as 'not only absurd; he is mischievous'[3] (Lord Granville, too, thought him 'wanting in tact and

---

[1] ibid., 43, Shuvalov to the Tsar, July 2.   [2] M. & B., vi, 49.
[3] *The Letters of Queen Victoria*, 2nd Series, ii, 478.

a great bore'), but it was surely wrong to describe Lord Odo Russell, one of the outstanding diplomats of the day as 'the Russian courtier, Odo'.[1] Another instance of a judgement wildly off the mark was his opinion of Sir Henry Elliot at Constantinople as unduly pro-Russian. Elliot's fault was the opposite, excessive Turcophilism. And, if Disraeli could write of Layard when the latter was at Madrid that he was 'prejudiced and passionate, and always – I will not say, misleads, but certainly misinforms us',[2] why promote him to take Elliot's far more important place at Constantinople? For that matter, if Loftus was really as hopeless as Disraeli said, it is difficult to see why he was retained at St Petersburg. The British diplomatic service was open to criticism, especially the Foreign Office itself, but Disraeli's letters suggest that he was taking a view which was, to say the least, unbalanced.

His opinions of foreign diplomats were equally unflattering. Count Munster 'is suspicious and stupid', Beust 'fantastical and dreamy', Waddington 'feeble and sly', Shuvalov 'does not know the A.B.C. of his business' – the last a singular comment on a man who was probably the most able ambassador Russia ever sent to London. Disraeli's letters abound in picturesque invective; it should be read as the ebullition of illness and irritation, not as a considered judgement, let alone a fair one, on the persons concerned.

The diplomatic situation in July was that the three Northern Courts and Britain were from their different standpoints adopting temporarily, with varying degrees of willingness, a 'hands-off Turkey' policy. Serbia and Montenegro had commenced hostilities. The Bosnian revolt flourished. In Constantinople chaos and revolution had been succeeded by a bogus 'liberal' régime promising reforms which, as anyone who knew Turkey realized, were most unlikely to be fulfilled. A further element in the situation totally unknown in London even to Count Beust was the signature of a secret agreement at Reichstadt between Russia and Austria-Hungary concerting their arrangements for the various eventualities which might arise in the course of the war.

In Britain the Eastern question had not impinged to any great degree upon public opinion, and the Government's policy, or lack of it, commanded until the end of June an uninterested assent. But

[1] M. & B., vi, 112.
[2] ibid., v, 417.

then news from Turkey, which was to transform the whole situation, began to reach Britain.

On June 23 the *Daily News* published a terrifying account of the barbarities committed by Turkish irregular troops upon the Bulgarian peasantry as reprisals for a widespread revolt which had broken out in the spring. It was alleged that some 25,000 men, women and children had been slaughtered. Grisly details were given of accompanying outrages, arson, sodomy, rape, torture and other atrocious acts. To a generation that has known the cold-blooded extermination of six million Jews in Germany and unnumbered millions of political prisoners in the labour camps of Siberia, this may seem small beer. But in the civilized atmosphere of the nineteenth century the reaction was profound. It ought to have been clear at once that this was not a matter which could be shrugged aside. Yet that was precisely what Disraeli tried to do when questioned in the House of Commons three days later.

Disraeli was instinctively sceptical about atrocity stories. He had taken the same line at the time of the Indian Mutiny. He had no cause to love the *Daily News*, which was a Liberal organ and very hostile to him personally. Moreover, his Turcophil bias which cannot be denied made him reluctant in any case to believe the truth of the reports. Another difficulty was the character of Sir Henry Elliot. The Ambassador was strongly pro-Turk, and suffered from poor health throughout 1876. Prejudice inclined him to accept Turkish assurances and illness to refrain from pursuing the allegations of the newspaper correspondents. Elliot was, of course, aware that terrible things had happened in Bulgaria. He had reported to London part of what had been passed on to him by the British Consuls, and he had protested to the Porte against the employment of irregular troops. But he undoubtedly toned down some reports and suppressed others.

The *Daily News* described massacres on a scale altogether more horrible than was suggested by any of the official accounts that reached London, and, although the paper exaggerated and was incorrect in many details, it was much nearer to the truth than Disraeli or Elliot conceded. The Turks had indeed not massacred 25,000 Bulgars, but the best evidence is that they did slaughter some 12,000 and in circumstances of peculiar horror. The combination of prejudice and poor information which hampered Disraeli was shortly to land him in a most awkward predicament.

On June 26, when the matter was first raised in the House, he dismissed the stories in the *Daily News* as untrue, and designed 'to create a cry against the Government'. On July 10, answering further questions, he admitted that 'proceedings of an atrocious character' had occurred in Bulgaria, but he denied that torture had been practised. Oriental people, he said, 'seldom resort to torture but generally terminate their connexion with culprits in a more expeditious manner'. The House took this as a joke; to Disraeli's annoyance, for he was merely using one of those typically orotund phrases to which he had latterly become addicted. For years to come he was accused from platform and pulpit of having made a heartless jest about the Bulgarian massacres.

Even more annoying was his discovery soon afterwards that the Foreign Office had been in possession for nearly a fortnight of a dispatch from the British Consul at Rustchuk, which suggested that, even on a cautious interpretation of current rumours, there was a strong case for detailed inquiry. Disraeli was very angry. 'I must again complain of the management of your office', he wrote to Derby on July 14. 'It is impossible to represent the F.O. in the House of Commons in these critical times without sufficient information.'[1] And on August 7, referring to the same episode, he wrote: 'The F.O. misled me in the first replies which I gave on their voucher and had I seen that despatch of Consul Reade which never reached me, I would never have made those answers and what is more should have pressed it on you to follow up Reade's revelations.'[2] By now aware of Elliot's deficiencies, too, he concluded: 'It is a very awkward business and I fear a great exposure of our diplomatic system abroad and at home.'

Disraeli's strictures seem in this instance to have been fully justified, but he suffered from a defect, endemic among politicians, the greatest reluctance to admit publicly that he had been in the wrong, even when the fault lay with his subordinates. On July 31, when he had had ample time to peruse Consul Reade's dispatch, he was unwise enough to refer to some of its evidence as 'coffee-house babble' – another phrase which stuck. The information available to him on July 10 had warranted playing down the atrocities. No such defence can be offered for the line that he took three weeks later. The debate that day was notable for Gladstone's first intervention

[1] M. & B., vi, 44.
[2] ibid., 46.

on the Eastern question. Forgetting for the moment both Granville and the Duke of Argyll, he claimed a special voice as the only active survivor of the Crimean Cabinet. He criticized the rejection of the Berlin Memorandum and affirmed the right of the great powers to enforce reforms. In the light of later events it is interesting to notice that he did not dwell much upon the Bulgarian atrocities, merely pleading for a genuine, not a sham, inquiry into the facts. In reply Disraeli refused to 'enter the politics of the Crimean War', and defended both the rejection of the Berlin Memorandum and the sending of the fleet to Besika Bay.

The last debate of the session took place on August 11. In the interval a preliminary report had arrived from Walter Baring, who had been sent out by the British Government to investigate the atrocities. This left no doubt that an appalling massacre had occurred. Disraeli tried to do his best with the argument that the *Daily News* had doubled the true number slaughtered, but most people considered 12,000 to be quite bad enough. This was Disraeli's last speech in the House of Commons. He ended it appropriately on the imperial note. We were ready to do our duty if Turkey's incompetence had been definitively established, but this was not the case yet. We did not uphold Turkey 'from blind superstition, and from a want of sympathy with the highest aspirations of humanity . . . What our duty is at this critical moment is to maintain the empire of England.' Privately he admitted to Derby that the debate had been 'very damaging' for the Government.

The end of the session came as a relief to Disraeli. The country was in something of an uproar over the atrocities. He realized that the Cabinet had not come too well out of the affair, and he hoped that it would now blow over. Personally he seems to have felt little of the indignation which the massacres inspired in most Englishmen of whatever political colour. He continued to refer to the 'atrocities' in inverted commas, as if he did not really believe in their existence, and he regarded the episode as a tiresome hindrance to his foreign policy, rather than a fearful crime against humanity. 'Had it not been for those unhappy "atrocities",' he wrote to Salisbury on September 3, 'we should have settled a peace very honourable to England and satisfactory to Europe.'[1] The only silver lining that he saw was the possibility of England being better placed to dictate terms to the Porte. Derby, however, was genuinely shocked at the

[1] ibid., 52.

conduct of the Turks and on September 5 issued a categorical warning that 'in the extreme case of Russia declaring war against Turkey HMG would find it practically impossible to interfere in defence of the Ottoman Empire'.

Both Derby and Disraeli were well aware of this danger. The Turks contrary to general expectation had won battle after battle against the Serbs, and were in the mood to impose peace terms so outrageous that Russia would be almost compelled to intervene. Unless a moderate peace could be arranged, England would be faced with an irreconcilable conflict between her treaty obligations and indignant public opinion. Matters were further complicated by a second revolution in Constantinople at the end of August. The alcoholic and now insane Murad V was deposed, and succeeded by his half-brother Abdul Hamid, destined to be one of the worst tyrants in Turkish history, but greeted with singularly misplaced enthusiasm in Turcophil quarters. Disraeli was deceived, too. 'He has got the Commons Blue Book translated for him,' he wrote to Salisbury, 'and Forster's speech on "atrocities". He has only one wife . . . a Roxalana. Will he be a Solyman the Great?'[1]

But it would be wrong at this stage to picture Disraeli as having made up his mind in favour of preserving the territorial integrity of Turkey. He was not as pro-Turk as is sometimes supposed. 'All the Turks may be in the Propontis as far as I am concerned',[2] he told Derby, adding, improbably, that he had said the same thing to the Turkish Ambassador after the rejection of the Berlin Memorandum. If Derby's efforts at peace-making failed, as seemed likely, then Disraeli anticipated a joint invasion by Russia and Austria-Hungary in the following spring. He was not unduly perturbed at the prospect. England should take a lead in the resultant partition and snatch what she could out of it in terms of prestige and of weakening the alliance between the Northern Courts. 'Constantinople with an adequate district should be neutralized and made a free port, in the custody and guardianship of England as the Ionian Isles were', he wrote to Derby on September 4, and he speculated upon Bismarck's policy in such circumstances. 'Does he want "compensation"? Is it to be in Austrian or even Russian Germany? . . . Or would he desire as a remote and maritime Power to place himself on the level of England and share with us the guardianship of the Hellespont

[1] ibid., 72–73.
[2] ibid., 53.

and the Symplegades, like the *garnison confédératif* of Mainz and other places after the peace of 1815?'[1] Clearly at this time Disraeli was chiefly thinking, as he had all along, how to assert England's position as a great power and how to exploit the potential differences within the Dreikaiserbund.

As usual, he spent the beginning of the recess at Hughenden. He was, however, given little respite from work. In a letter to Lady Bradford on September 2 he described his mode of life.[2] He was called at seven o'clock and the post together with the Government bag was brought to him. He was lucky if he could be in his study by nine o'clock for work. At eleven o'clock a second post arrived and all the newspapers 'which I must inspect or at least glance at – and then my letters! It is the post that, if you write, brings one from you. It generally rewards me and supports me for the whole day – but not always.' At one o'clock came the messenger with the red boxes, and Disraeli had 'to work immensely hard to get him off by half past 3, in time for the London post. It is absolutely necessary that I should have half an hour for luncheon, which is my real and almost only meal – on which I live.' Then, as often as not, there would be one or two cipher telegrams which he had to decipher personally – a lengthy and tedious task. This could, of course, have been avoided, but Disraeli disliked having any secretary in the house except Corry, who was on leave, 'in some wild archipelago in Scotland'.

> I prefer decyphering the telegrams myself to having a strange secretary here [he wrote to Lady Chesterfield]. What should I do with him when he was not decyphering? I should have to amuse him and eat with him and drink with him and talk with him, or else his feelings would be hurt! I think it would quite finish me.[3]

Thus the time passed busily but not unpleasantly. The old statesman could feel that from Hughenden he was manipulating the pieces on the European chessboard, that he and Derby, between whom complete trust still prevailed, were the arbiters of English foreign policy. The atrocity uproar was no doubt awkward, but with any luck it would blow itself out during the long autumn recess. Then calmer counsels would prevail, and the true interests of Britain could be maintained.

[1] loc. cit.
[2] Zetland, ii, 70.
[3] ibid., 71.

Disraeli reckoned without his old enemy. On September 6 the post brought a disagreeable surprise in the form of a complimentary copy of one of the most famous political pamphlets ever written, Gladstone's burning attack entitled *The Bulgarian Horrors and the Question of the East.*

CHAPTER XXVI

Divided Counsels

1876–7

1

Gladstone wrote the pamphlet in three days while in bed with lumbago. The sensation was tremendous: 40,000 copies were sold in a week, 200,000 by the end of the month. His arguments have often been summarized and his famous peroration often quoted; though, in fact, by giving the impression that Gladstone wanted the whole Turkish population, not simply the apparatus of government, to be evicted from Europe his grand finale spoiled his own case.

> Let the Turks now carry away their abuses in the only possible way, namely by carrying off themselves. Their Zaptiehs and their Mudirs, their Bimbashis and their Yuzbachis, their Kaimakams and their Pashas, one and all, bag and baggage shall, I hope, clear out from the province they have desolated and profaned . . . There is not a criminal in an European gaol, there is not a cannibal in the South Sea Islands whose indignation would not arise and overboil at the recital of that which has been done . . . If it be allowable that the executive power of Turkey should renew at this great crisis, by permission or authority of Europe, the charter of its existence in Bulgaria, then there is not on record since the beginnings of political society a protest than man has lodged against intolerable misgovernment or a stroke that he has dealt at loathsome tyranny, that ought not henceforth to be branded as a crime.

Why did Gladstone intervene at this particular moment? The suggestion that he acted prematurely and should have awaited the appearance of Baring's full report has no justification. On August 29 the *Daily News* published a preliminary report by the American Consul General Schuyler, which, coming from a source of unimpeachable detachment, gave Gladstone ample evidence on which to base his pamphlet. Nor was it a case of political opportunism in any ordinary sense of the word. His action did, it is true, bring about by a series of almost inevitable steps his resumption in 1880 of the leadership of the Liberal party. Hartington's mistress, the German-born Duchess of Manchester, anxious for her lover's prospect of the Premiership, told Disraeli some weeks earlier at the end of the session: 'That gentleman is only waiting to come to the fore with all his hypocritical retirement.'[1] And it is certainly true that for a man who had resigned as leader in 1875 because he 'deeply desired an interval between Parliament and the grave', Gladstone had been surprisingly active. But, although his latest move only confirmed the Duchess, along with most of the upper class, in their belief, Gladstone was not a hypocrite. He certainly had no intention of ousting Granville and Hartington, even if he was not very considerate in his treatment of them. Nor can the timing of his intervention be explained by the imminence of a by-election for the Buckinghamshire county seat made vacant by Disraeli's peerage. The home counties were the least 'atrocitarian' constituencies in the country, and the Rothschilds, hitherto pillars of Buckinghamshire Liberalism, seceded, approving, like most of English Jewry, of the Government's Turkish policy.

The truth is that Gladstone was swept into the main current belatedly, reluctantly and scarcely knowing where he was going. The idea that he had long been watching for the appropriate occasion and that his action was a superb example of 'right timing' has been effectively demolished; likewise Buckle's picture of him stalking Disraeli, like an 'old hunter, once more sniffing the scent' and seizing his opportunity.[2] On the contrary Gladstone was slow to act, and his pamphlet came out long after the agitation had been gaining momentum. As the leading authority puts it, the episode was 'less a case of Gladstone exciting popular passion than of popular passion exciting Gladstone'.[3] Gladstone had retired from the leadership of the Liberal party because the defeat of 1874 seemed to him a clear sign that he had lost that understanding with the virtuous masses, which since the 'sixties had been the inspiration of his political life. Suddenly, and surprisingly late in the day, he saw that the atrocity agitation might recover it for him. This was what he meant when he wrote that 'the game was afoot and the question still alive' – words which Morley omitted[4] – or even more significantly on August 29 to Granville: 'Good ends can rarely be attained in politics without

[1] M. & B., vi, 60.
[2] R. T. Shannon, *Gladstone and the Bulgarian Agitation, 1876* (1963), 110–12. The book is a brilliant and illuminating analysis of the whole subject.
[3] loc. cit.
[4] ibid., 100.

passion: and there is now, the first time for a good many years, a virtuous passion.'[1] For Gladstone politics was a moral crusade based on the highest instincts of British democracy; or it was nothing. In the sense that he saw an opportunity of taking part in just such a moral crusade, he might be described as an opportunist, but not in any other sense.

Gladstone wholly lacked Disraeli's acute, though sporadic, comprehension of the material needs of the working class. Bread and butter politics were of no interest to him, and the intervals between his crusades – Ireland, Bulgaria, Ireland again – were devoted, if in opposition, to theology, if in office, to Scrooge-like exercises in Treasury economy. But this ignorance of the masses did not preclude an extraordinary faith in their inherent goodness, in their capacity for righteous wrath, which he contrasted with the selfishness of the classes. And it really was true that at this era of their history, the British masses were susceptible to gusts of outward-looking moral indignation unparalleled before or since, or in any other country. Victorian religious and ethical sensitivity was at its apogee. That Disraeli of all people should have been Prime Minister at this particular moment seems indeed an irony of history.

It is hard to believe that Gladstone's intervention, reluctant and belated as it was, did not owe something to this very fact. He had been greatly disconcerted by his defeat in 1874 at the hands of a man who might well have been dismissed as a spent force in politics, although Gladstone himself never made that error. Disraeli's rise to power had come late in the day, but it was all the more spectacular when it did occur. That Gladstone distrusted, indeed, despite protestations, detested his rival is obvious enough. It is less obvious but no less true that he genuinely dreaded what Disraeli might do in an hour of triumph. He had never forgotten the 'diabolical cleverness' with which he had been outmanoeuvred in the session of 1867, when commanding ostensibly a majority of seventy. Disraeli, he once wrote 'is a man who is *never beaten*. Every reverse, every defeat is to him only an admonition to wait and catch his opportunity of retrieving and more than retrieving his position.'[2] Some of Gladstone's suspicions were absurd; that Disraeli was mainly influenced by Judaic sympathies; that what he hated was Christian liberty; that

[1] Agatha Ramm, *The Political Correspondence of Mr. Gladstone and Lord Granville, 1876–86* (2 vols, 1962), i, 3.

[2] G. W. E. Russell, *Malcolm MacColl, Memoirs and Correspondence* (1914), 248, quoting Gladstone to MacColl, August 11, 1877.

he intended to seize Egypt 'so he may become Duke of Memphis yet'. But it is true that strange ideas were revolving in Disraeli's head; dreams perhaps, but then who has ever had more extraordinary skill, or luck, in turning dreams into the semblance of reality?

Later in the year, at the instigation of the Duke of Argyll, Gladstone read *Tancred* for the first time. Was the Royal Titles Bill some shadowy realization of Fakredeen's advice to Tancred to persuade the Queen 'to collect a great fleet . . . stow away all her treasure, bullion and gold plate . . . and transfer the seat of her empire to Delhi'? . . . Perhaps the novel suggested even more alarming possibilities. Gladstone was aware that Disraeli flattered Queen Victoria and encouraged her to hold ideas of questionable constitutional propriety. Now he read how Tancred was urged to 'magnetise the Queen'; how he could not help succeeding, 'especially if you talk to her as you talk to me, and say such fine things in such a beautiful voice'. Could Disraeli be doing just this? If Gladstone had seen even a fraction of the correspondence between the Prime Minister and his Sovereign he would have been alarmed indeed.

Whatever Gladstone's conscious and unconscious motives may have been for intervention, it inevitably brought out all the pride and obstinacy of which Disraeli was capable. It is hard to avoid the impression that even before this his scepticism about the atrocities was partly conditioned by dislike of those who made a fuss about them, 'this Hudibrastic crew of High Ritualists, Dissenting ministers, and "the great Liberal party" ', as he described them to Derby.[1] He was determined not to seem to yield to popular pressure. It was for this reason that he refused to accept even the Queen's advice to make some concession to the humanitarians by condemning the atrocities in public. He considered that he had done enough in Parliament, and after the end of the session he remained silent, apart from a letter to *The Times* on September 7 repudiating the idea that he had intended to jest when he had referred to massacre rather than torture as being the custom of an Oriental people. 'I hope the misplaced laughter of another is no proof of the levity of your humble servant.'

His obduracy was now intensified. It was galling enough to be told by anyone that the British nation 'must teach its Government almost as it would a lisping child what to say'. But to be told so by

[1] M. & B., vi, 53, September 6, 1876.

Gladstone was more than he could bear. He regarded the pamphlet with contempt. 'Vindictive and ill-written – that of course. Indeed in that respect of all the Bulgarian horrors perhaps the greatest.'[1] Gladstone followed up with a passionate oration delivered in pouring rain to a vast audience at Blackheath. Disraeli decided to strike back in an eve-of-poll speech to his late constituents at Aylesbury on September 20.

It was perhaps not one of his more statesman-like performances. He declared that there was a danger lest the noble sentiments of the British people might be exploited by 'designing politicians . . . for the furtherance of sinister ends'. Such conduct 'in the general havoc and ruin which it may bring about . . . may, I think, be fairly described as worse than any of those Bulgarian atrocities which now occupy attention'. After this hit at Gladstone he went on to one of his favourite themes and proceeded to talk what can only be described as nonsense about 'secret societies'. Peace would have been restored in the Balkans but for Serbia. 'Serbia declared war on Turkey, that is to say the secret societies of Europe declared war on Turkey.'[2] Presumably Disraeli believed in this farrago, but it can only be regarded by the historian as a sign of his complete failure to understand the realities of Slav nationalism and Turkish misrule.

The by-election was widely regarded as a test case for the Government. To lose a seat vacated by the Prime Minister would have been a disaster indeed. In the event all was well. T. F. Fremantle, the Conservative candidate, beat the Liberal, a brother of Lord Carrington, by 200 votes. 'The election,' Disraeli told the Queen, 'was too close, but considering all things was a great victory – a defeat would have been a serious blow. The struggle has been most costly, the contest having lasted a month; and Lord Carrington's command to win being carte-blanche.'[3] In fact, the Conservatives were fairly safe in a home-county election. Granville lamented to Gladstone 'the complete absence of country gentlemen

---

[1] ibid., 60, to Derby, September 8. Oddly enough, he expressed a modified view to Lady Bradford, the next day (Zetland, ii, 73), 'apparently not so ill-written as is his custom'.

[2] Baring's full report, though reluctantly corroborating the atrocities, on a superficial reading gave a certain colour to this conspiratorial theory. Disraeli's decision to delay publication till the day before his speech was not accidental. Shannon, 129.

[3] Royal Archives, H.9.150, September 23, 1876. To Lady Chesterfield a fortnight earlier Disraeli complained that the Carringtons were 'introducing bribery into County Elections – a thing quite unheard of here!' Zetland, ii, 72.

on C's side',[1] and Disraeli's agent eleven days before the poll reckoned that victory was certain.[2]

Gladstone's decision to lead the atrocity campaign injected a bitterness into British politics unequalled since the Corn Law debates. The uncertain floating elements in public opinion crystallized at once around the two old rivals. Henceforth it became almost impossible for even intelligent men to consider the Eastern question rationally or disinterestedly. The country was divided into 'Turks' and 'Russians', like the Blues and the Greens of Byzantium. Reason vanished and passion prevailed. Oddly enough there was something very un-English about both the leaders; Gladstone with his torrential flood of earnest moral indignation, and Disraeli with his elaborately phrased sarcasm. Behind the scenes on both sides there were English voices of moderation, Derby, Salisbury, Hartington, Granville; but they had little effect for the moment.

Generalizations about the social and religious forces supporting the two rivals are subject to many exceptions and should be made with caution.[3] Broadly speaking the strength of the atrocitarians lay in the north of England, in the south-west and in Wales. They were relatively weak in Scotland and counted for nothing in Ireland. This geographical distribution was obviously connected with nonconformity which saw an analogue of its own grievances. As Palmerston once said of the Christian subjects of the Sultan, they were the 'nonconformists of Turkey', and throughout the agitation leading nonconformists were among its most prominent figures. Irish silence can be explained by the silence of the Vatican, a result of the traditional Papal antagonism to the Greek Orthodox Church. The few English Catholics who protested were, as one would expect, 'old Catholics' mostly from grand families, unfriendly towards Manning and ultramontanism. In Scotland liberalism was already so deeply entrenched as to be the current orthodoxy. There was nothing much to protest about. Bulgaria rang no bell.

The Church of England was in general anti-atrocitarian. The exception, though not monopolizing that position, was the High Church party, enemies of the Establishment from within even as the nonconformists were from without. The evangelicals were strongly pro-Disraeli, and they constituted the great majority of the inferior

[1] Ramm, op. cit., i, 2, August 26, 1876.

[2] Hanham, *Elections and Party Management*, 17, quoting Hughenden Papers, J. K. Fowler to Disraeli, September 10, 1876.

[3] Shannon, op. cit., 147–238, is the best modern account.

clergy. On the episcopal bench the division followed lines of patronage. The 'Derby-Dizzy' bishops supported the Government, Gladstone's appointees were inclined to the other side. Tait, though no lover of Disraeli, supported his policy on general Erastian principles and anxiety to preserve the unity of the Church. Magee, Bishop of Peterborough, doubted on September 18 whether the whole history of democracy, 'rife as it is with instances of passionate injustice supplies a grosser one than the cry against the Ministry of the last three weeks'.[1]

The intelligentsia were too readily dismissed by Disraeli as enemies. The older generation undoubtedly opposed him, but the younger intellectuals, the supporters of empire, efficiency and no nonsense were on his side. Already liberal imperialism was casting its shadow before it. Whereas Carlyle, Ruskin, Freeman, Froude, Browning, Trollope, Darwin, Spencer – an incongruous mixture, no doubt – supported the agitation, Fitzjames Stephen, Jowett, Hyndman, Matthew Arnold, regarded it as a tiresome irrelevance. So, for somewhat different reasons, did Karl Marx.

The struggle between the 'Bulgarians' and the 'Turks' is often presented as one between the metropolis and the provinces. This is an oversimplification. There was plenty of atrocitarianism in London, and large areas of the provinces were pro-Government. But it is true that London society, 'the upper ten thousand', condemned by Gladstone, was overwhelmingly behind Disraeli. Of course, there were exceptions and – what particularly annoyed him – Conservative exceptions; like Lord Bath, or worse still Lord Bute, Disraeli's own Lothair, who as a Tory and a Catholic convert ought on any count to have been sound. But, in general, clubland, the aristocracy, the gentry and the City were on his side. So, too, was the rough world of what would once have been called the London mob. The London Press was on the whole favourable to the Government. Apart from the *Daily News*, Disraeli's consistent foe, the morning papers either vacillated or came down in his favour. A notable capture was the *Daily Telegraph*, owned by the Jewish family of Levy-Lawson. English Jewry tended to be pro-Turk for obvious reasons. Disraeli's enemies often attributed his own attitude to his ancestry, and an unpleasant streak of anti-Semitism colours many of the religious and radical writers who attacked him. Freeman was

---

[1] J. C. Macdonell, *The Life and Correspondence of William Connor Magee* (2 vols, 1896), ii, 49.

the worst. T. P. O'Connor, Froude and Goldwin Smith contributed their share, and the *Church Times* described him as the 'Jew Premier'.[1]

Last but not least in an era when royalty still counted for something in politics, the Court was emphatically anti-atrocitarian. The known views of the Queen affected the whole outlook of London society. Queen Victoria's attitude, shared by all her family except the unpopular Duke of Edinburgh who had married a Russian princess, was unequivocally pro-Turk. The Queen had only recently become converted to this view. She had queried the wisdom of rejecting the Berlin Memorandum, and she had expressed genuine indignation at the Bulgarian atrocities, constantly prodding Derby on the subject. But Gladstone's activities appear to have aroused such indignation in her that, by a process of reaction illogical but not unnatural, she supported the Turks if only because Gladstone denounced them. Disraeli behaved in much the same way. What infuriated the Queen and the Prime Minister was Gladstone's claim that *realpolitik* should give way to a moral crusade and that the higher interests of humanity should prevail over 'the permanent and important interests of England', as Disraeli termed them in his speech at Aylesbury.

The almost pathological animus of the Queen against Gladstone, which lasted until his dying day, dates from this period. She had indeed never liked him. He was 'tiresome', 'obstinate', 'tyrannical' and 'tactless'. These are unflattering adjectives, but they are nothing compared with the language she now began to use in her letters to her favourite child the Crown Princess of Prussia, which are perhaps the best evidence of her spontaneous reaction to events. On September 19 she describes his behaviour as 'most reprehensible and mischievous . . . shameful and unjustifiable'.[2] A week later she refers to 'the disgraceful conduct of that mischief maker and firebrand, Mr. Gladstone'.[3] By February 1877 he has become 'that half madman', and henceforth she evidently regarded insanity as the only explanation of Gladstone's policy.

It has sometimes been suggested that Disraeli stimulated the Queen's hostility to Gladstone. He certainly had no reason to discourage it, but a close examination of his letters to her reveals only

[1] Shannon, 201.
[2] Kronberg Letters, September 19, 1876.
[3] ibid., September 26.

two mild instances of even an innuendo against his rival. He could not resist a slightly malicious hint in 1874, apropos of Lord Ripon's conversion to Rome, that it had been caused by reading articles in the *Contemporary Review*, 'a new periodical under the influence and patronage of Mr. Gladstone'.[1] And in 1878, referring to something Gladstone had published in the *North American Review*, he wrote: 'Lord Palmerston's "dangerous man" has at length verified that statesman's prophecy of his ultimate insanity.'[2] Disraeli may have said things in audience, which he never committed to paper. But it seems unlikely. The truth was that he had no need to do so.

To his friends Disraeli expressed himself without inhibition. He detested Gladstone at this time. He wrote to Derby in words often quoted:

> Posterity will do justice to that unprincipled maniac Gladstone – extraordinary mixture of envy, vindictiveness, hypocrisy, and superstition; and with one commanding characteristic – whether Prime Minister, or Leader of Opposition, whether preaching, praying, speechifying or scribbling – never a gentleman![3]

The word 'Tartuffe' appears frequently in his letters to Lady Bradford and Lady Chesterfield, Mrs Gladstone even figuring on occasion as 'Mrs. T'. At times Disraeli followed the Queen's lead in describing Gladstone as insane, but the verdict which most probably represents his true opinion is to be found in a letter to Lady Bradford on October 3, a year later.

> What you say about Gladstone is most just. What restlessness! What vanity! And what unhappiness must be his! Easy to say he is mad. It looks like it. My theory about him is unchanged: a ceaseless Tartuffe from the beginning. That sort of man does not get mad at 70.[4]

Gladstone always denied that he actually hated Disraeli and added that he did not believe Disraeli hated him. He was wrong in the latter belief, although it is to his credit. Moreover, it is hard to believe that he was correct about his own feelings. Sir Philip Magnus writes in his brilliant biography: '. . . those who knew him best were agreed that at that time his sentiment towards his rival

[1] Royal Archives, D.5.61, September 19, 1874.
[2] ibid., B.58.63, September 19, 1878.
[3] M. & B., vi, 67.
[4] ibid., 181.

became that of black hatred.'[1] Disraeli, Gladstone told Hartington, 'has never wanted courage but his daring is elastic and capable of any extension with the servility of the times'. Lord Acton, who knew Gladstone well, endeavoured to remonstrate with him five years later for proposing a public monument to a man whom, he said, Gladstone had regarded as 'the worst and most immoral Minister since Castlereagh'. Nearly twenty years later Gladstone delivered to his close friend Lord Rendel what was perhaps his final judgement on his long-deceased rival: 'In past times the Tory party had principles by which it would and did stand for bad and for good. All this Dizzy destroyed.'[2]

If the two rivals felt like this about each other, it is easy to imagine how violent were the passions of their supporters then and later. Perhaps the nadir of bad taste was achieved by the historian Edward Freeman, who after Disraeli's Guildhall speech in November referred in print to 'the Jew in his drunken insolence', and a year later, when the Queen lunched at Hughenden, described her as 'going ostentatiously to eat with Disraeli in his ghetto'. But professors did not have the monopoly of offensiveness. Dukes could be as bad, and one of them, the Duke of Sutherland, in January 1878, publicly stated that 'Russia's principal agents were Mr. Gladstone and General Ignatyev'. Few political issues have raised such venomous feelings. Munich and Suez are the nearest equivalents in recent times, but on neither occasion did even the most vehement partisans use language like this in public.

2

Disraeli's attitude to the Eastern question had been erratic and changeable for the past eighteen months. It is hard to discern any consistent thread other than a general determination to assert Britain's prestige and to disrupt the Dreikaiserbund. But from October 1876 onwards his opinions hardened. The more Turcophobe Gladstone became, the more Russophobe was Disraeli. Whereas at one time he talked of partition as the solution, and indeed was to consider it again for a moment after the collapse of the Constantinople Conference, his normal attitude henceforth was to support the independence and territorial integrity of Turkey, in fact the old

[1] Magnus, *Gladstone*, 244.
[2] Lord Rendel, *Personal Papers* (1931), 100.

Crimean policy. It was in October 1876 that he had the conversation with Lord Barrington mentioned earlier, in which he declared that Constantinople, not Egypt, was the key to India.

If we accept this thesis – and a very big 'if' is needed – then Disraeli's policy had a certain logic, given two premises. The first was that Russia aimed at the destruction of Turkey and the seizure of the Straits, the second that she would only be deterred if convinced that Britain, as in 1854, would fight rather than allow it. The Crimean war was the great bugbear of official diplomatic thinking at this time. Over the past twenty years its causes had been endlessly discussed. The widely accepted opinion was that if only Aberdeen had proclaimed from the outset Britain's readiness to go to war rather than give way, then the Tsar would never have taken the steps which made war inevitable. In other words, the preservation not only of Britain's interests but of peace itself depended on the credibility of the British threat to intervene on the side of Turkey.

The maddening feature of the atrocity agitation from Disraeli's point of view was that it undermined that credibility at the very moment when the collapse of Serbia and the appalling abuses of Turkish rule were providing Russia with ample excuse for invading Turkey under the cover of a crusade on behalf of the oppressed Slav Christians. Both Disraeli and the Queen were convinced that such an invasion would end in a Russian occupation of Constantinople, but it was very doubtful whether British public opinion would now permit any intervention on the side of Turkey. More important, it was certain that the Russian Government would never believe in the possibility of such intervention as long as the atrocity campaign raged in Britain.

In his great work, *Disraeli, Gladstone and the Eastern Question*, Professor R. W. Seton-Watson made some cogent criticisms of Disraeli's attitude. Many of them are justified, but he was less than fair to the Prime Minister when he suggested that Disraeli wanted war and positively sought to pick a quarrel with Russia.[1] Disraeli was no warmonger, any more than Churchill was in the nineteen-

---

[1] p. 563. It was first published in 1935, reprinted 1962. This book and B. H. Sumner's authoritative study of the Eastern question as seen from the Russian standpoint, *Russia and the Balkans, 1870–1880* (1937), have to be studied as well as Buckle's chapters in order to obtain a balanced picture of Disraeli's role. It is fair to remember, when reading Professor Seton-Watson's highly critical account, that he was a Scottish Gladstonian Liberal, and a passionate believer in Balkan nationalism.

thirties, but he was determined not to go down to history as a second Aberdeen. He believed that in the circumstances peace could be preserved only by the threat of war, and, after hostilities had broken out between Russia and Turkey in May 1877, that Britain's vital interests could be maintained only by a similar threat. A threat un-backed by real force is useless, and naturally he discussed in much detail, though sometimes with wild eccentricity, the actual military and naval steps that might be taken. He certainly felt no moral objection to an alliance with Turkey – and here he differed not only from Gladstone but from at least half of his own Cabinet – but he did not want war for its own sake.

It is impossible to pass judgement on Disraeli's policy without deciding how accurately he estimated Russian intentions. In other words, were his premises correct? Did Russia really aim at the con-quest of Constantinople? The answer depends in its turn on what one means by 'Russia'. Professor Seton-Watson, who secured the secret correspondence[1] between Tsar Alexander II, his Chancellor, Prince Gorchakov, and his Ambassador in London, Count Shuvalov, makes a strong case for the basically pacific and limited objectives of Russian foreign policy throughout the crisis. 'We are now looking into the Tsar's own cards,' he writes on one occasion, 'and it is difficult to believe that even the most confirmed Russophobe in the British cabinet of those days could have failed to be reassured if it had been possible for him to do the same.'[2] But, of course, it was not possible, and in any case, however pacific the advice given by Gorchakov and Shuvalov, there was another Russia besides the cosmopolitan French-speaking officialdom of St Petersburg – a Russia which had vaster aims, more sweeping ambitions, and was not without influence in the highest quarters; the Russia of Moscow and the Panslavs.

The Tsar usually listened to Gorchakov while in St Petersburg, but he often vacillated, taking colour from his surroundings. For example, in Livadia – a sort of inverted Balmoral on the Black Sea – where he was surrounded by Panslav influences, he tended to become altogether more expansionist and nationalistic in outlook.

[1] These documents covering the period 1875 to January 1878 were published in the *Slavonic Review* (8 vols, 1924), iii–vi. Professor Seton-Watson's transcripts covering January to May 1878 are in the British Museum. None of this very important material was available to Buckle.

[2] Seton-Watson, 127, referring to Gorchakov's instructions to Ignatyev in November 1876.

In the Russian foreign service Panslavism[1] was represented by
General Ignatyev, who occupied the key position of the Constantinople Embassy. He frankly aimed at the overthrow of Turkish
power in the Balkans and at Russian seizure of the Straits. He was
clever, unscrupulous, amusing, ingratiating and dangerous. Years of
intrigue in Constantinople had made him almost more Oriental than
the Turks whom he outmanoeuvred, and his nickname among the
diplomatic corps in the city was 'Menteur Pasha'. One of his most
intimate friends was Fadeyev, a soldier and adventurer who in 1875
accepted an invitation from the Khedive to reconstruct the Egyptian
Army. His purpose, but not the Khedive's, was to use it against the
Sultan in conjunction with a Slav uprising in the Balkans. As author
of *Opinion on the Eastern Question* he was one of the best-known
exponents of extreme Turcophobe Panslavism.

These manifestations did not escape the attention of the anti-
Russian party in Britain, and even if the assurances of Gorchakov
and Shuvalov were regarded as genuine, which, as we can now see,
in fact, they were, there was no certainty that their advice would
prevail with the Tsar; nor even if it did was there any guarantee
that the Tsar himself would not be committed by semi-mutinous
Panslav proconsuls into actions far beyond his original intentions.
The classic instance of this, fresh in men's minds, was the annexation
of Khiva in 1873 by Kaufmann, the Governor-General of Turkestan,
despite categorical promises conveyed via Shuvalov to the British
Government. It was followed by the massacre of the Yomud Turco-
mans – an atrocity so frequently cited by the Russophobes during
1876 that Gladstone, in conjunction with his ally, Mme Novikov,
endeavoured not very successfully to refute it in the November
number of the *Contemporary Review*. It was, therefore, by no means
unreasonable for Disraeli to feel hesitation in trusting the effective-
ness of Shuvalov's promises, whether or not he considered that the
Ambassador was personally honest, and whether or not he believed
that he correctly conveyed the sentiments of the Chancellor and the
Tsar.

For the moment it was clearly useless to threaten British intervention on the Turkish side. Derby, therefore, worked with much
energy towards securing a Turkish-Serbian armistice. Protracted

---

[1] For an authoritative analysis of Panslavism see Sumner, 56–80. It is perhaps
significant by contrast that Panslavism only rates a single reference in Seton-
Watson's index.

manoeuvring ensued, but was brought to an abrupt end by an ultimatum from the Tsar on October 31, which the Sultan had no
option but to accept. Derby now proposed a conference of the six
great powers to consider the future of Turkey. This was to be held
at Constantinople in the second half of December, each country
having two representatives. The bases for discussion were the
territorial integrity of Turkey; local or administrative autonomy for
Bosnia, Herzegovina and Bulgaria; *status quo* for Serbia and Montenegro; and no special concessions to any of the great powers. For a
fleeting moment Disraeli contemplated going himself, but he soon
saw that this would not be appropriate, and readily fell in with
Derby's suggestion that Salisbury should be the man.

No better choice could have been made. Salisbury was anything
but 'Turkish'. Gladstone told Mme Novikov that it was 'the best
thing the Government has yet done in the Eastern Question' and
that Salisbury 'has no Disraelite prejudices, keeps a conscience and
has plenty of manhood and character'. At the same time, as
Secretary for India he was not likely to be 'Russian' either. His
appointment was welcomed by all shades of opinion. Salisbury, who
anticipated correctly 'seasickness, much French and failure',
accepted with reluctance; but the experience was to be a turning-
point in his own career. The Prince of Wales sensibly advised him to
meet the principal statesmen of Europe on his way out. Lord
Tenterden, the permanent head of the Foreign Office, a true bureau-
crat, advised him not to. Disraeli was emphatically on the Prince's
side. He told Salisbury, 'You should personally know the men who
are governing the world . . . don't concede your own convictions on
the subject to Tenterdenism – which is a dusty affair and not suited
to the times and things we have to grapple with.'[1] It must be
admitted that Disraeli was himself singularly ignorant of the
characters of most European statesmen, but his advice, which
Salisbury accepted, was excellent.

Salisbury was due to leave for his tour of the European capitals
on November 20. Meanwhile events occurred which seemed to bring
war appreciably nearer. Lord Augustus Loftus reported from
Livadia that the Tsar, though ridiculing any idea of Russian ambitions towards Constantinople, let alone India, was emphatic that
Russia would not put up with further Turkish procrastination. If
necessary she would act alone to enforce reforms. Disraeli decided to

[1] Cecil, *Salisbury*, ii, 95.

reply at the Lord Mayor's banquet. Accordingly on November 9, 'in a heated hall full of gas and aldermen and trumpeters and after sitting for hours talking slip slop to a defunct Lady Mayoress',[1] he made a speech on the Eastern question. He declared that the object of the conference was to combine real reforms with the territorial integrity of Turkey and he went out of his way to be polite to Russia, but he ended on a note of defiance, describing as 'inexhaustible' Britain's resources for a righteous war. 'She is not a country that when she enters into a campaign has to ask herself whether she can support a second or third campaign. She enters into a campaign which she will not terminate till right is done.'[2]

'The provocation offered by Disraeli', wrote Gladstone rather extravagantly, 'is almost incredible', adding: 'Some new lights about his Judaic feeling in which he is both consistent and conscientious have come in upon me.' Two days later what seemed like a reply came from the Tsar, who normally never uttered in public on political matters. Breaking his journey from Livadia to St Petersburg at Moscow, he made a speech in which he expanded his earlier words to Loftus. If the conference failed he would act alone to enforce reform on Turkey, and he ended to the delight of the Panslavs, 'May God help us to fulfil our sacred mission.' In fact, his intervention was a coincidence. There had been no time for the Guildhall speech to reach him, but naturally to the whole of Europe it seemed as if war was becoming imminent. It seemed even more imminent when on November 14 the mobilization of six army corps was announced from St Petersburg.

The practical steps which Britain might take in the event of a Russo-Turkish war had been in Disraeli's mind for some time, and his papers in the autumn of 1876 are full of military plans. The first appreciation which he had from the War Office calculated that an expeditionary force of 46,000 was enough to hold Gallipoli and the lines north of Constantinople.[3] If the Turks were induced to appeal to Britain for such aid, Disraeli believed that it could be sent without declaring war on Russia, and that preparations need not attract undue public attention. At the same time his mind was moving towards more grandiose plans. He feared, he told Salisbury, that if Russia was not checked, 'the Holy Alliance will be revived in

[1] M. & B., vi, 90, to Lady Bradford, November 8.
[2] ibid., 92.
[3] ibid., 103–6, for Disraeli to Salisbury, November 29, December 1.

aggravated form and force. Germany will have Holland; and France, Belgium, and England will be in a position I trust I shall never live to witness.' But if Britain acted as he suggested and furthermore occupied some Black Sea equivalent of Malta or Gibraltar – Varna, Batoum or Sinope were possibilities – the situation might yet be saved.[1] This latter proposal was grotesquely impracticable as it stood, but it was probably the origin of the Cyprus Convention which was certainly intended to give Britain what Disraeli called a *place d'armes*, though not in the Black Sea, from which to resist Russian designs on Turkey.

Disraeli's military plans were speedily torpedoed by a fresh appreciation from the War Office. 'The "Intelligence Dept." must change its name', he wrote crossly to Corry. 'It is the department of Ignorance.' The War Office now put its minimum claim up from 46,000 to 75,000 men. It also demanded more and heavier guns and 'a railway for stores and telegraph lines from Malta to Crete etc.; in short a very big business in which the present state of affairs hardly justifies us in embarking'.[2] In the end all that he could do was to send out Colonel Home of the Sappers to report on the situation, and as a precaution to suspend temporarily with the full consent of the makers the dispatch of eight huge guns weighing 100 tons each, ordered by the Italian Government from Armstrong and Company. 'There is no gun in existence that can stand against them,' Derby minuted to Salisbury, 'and none can be made under two years.'[3]

Meanwhile the anti-Turk party was far from idle. On December 8 a 'National Convention on the Eastern Question' opened at the S James's Hall, Piccadilly, with a double meeting under the chairmanship of the Duke of Westminster and Lord Shaftesbury. 'This intolerable assembly', as Disraeli called it, was attended by Gladstone, who made a special journey from Hawarden to address it. His own speech was comparatively moderate, but other orators uttered very extreme sentiments. Freeman referred to 'the brag' which went forth 'from amid the clatter of wine cups' at the Guildhall, and asked whether the Government would 'fight to uphold the integrity and independence of Sodom'.[4] The Queen was horrified at these remarks and, so Disraeli told Lady Bradford, thought 'the

[1] loc. cit.

[2] ibid., 106, Disraeli to Corry, December 13.

[3] Hughenden Papers, Box 113, B/XX/S/1191a, and ibid., c, for Disraeli's memorandum, December 3, 1876.

[4] See Seton-Watson, 112–13, for further specimens.

Attorney-General should be set at these men; it can't be constitutional'.[1] At the end of the meeting Gladstone conspicuously escorted
Madame Novikov from the platform, an episode which caused a
storm of controversy. That evening, according to a story which
reached Lord Cairns, he dined with Mrs Thistlethwayte, a high-class
courtesan whom he had rescued. Among those present was Shuvalov,
who congratulated him on his 'grand triumph'. 'Could not the *World*
or some such paper,' asked the Lord Chancellor, 'be got to publish
this?'[2]

The detailed history of the Conference of Constantinople belongs
to the life of Salisbury. The biographer of Disraeli needs to decide
only one point. Was he responsible for its failure? That failure was
immediately caused by the refusal of the Turkish Government to
accept even the watered-down programme of reforms which were
finally agreed by the representatives of the six powers. The charge
levelled against Disraeli is that he allowed or encouraged the Turks
to believe that the Turcophil Elliot was a truer spokesman of the
Cabinet than Salisbury, and hence to believe that in the last resort
they could rely on British military assistance if their obduracy provoked a Russian declaration of war. It is not, of course, claimed that
Disraeli made any categorical promise. It is rather a matter of the
general atmosphere created by his attitude.

The original instructions given by the Cabinet to Salisbury on
November 20 excluded any coercive or enforcing action against the
Porte, but on November 27 these were modified in the sense that a
temporary occupation of Turkey was not ruled out if the Porte
rejected all proposals for reform.[3] The new version in its turn seems
to have been amended by a private letter on December 1 from
Disraeli to Salisbury,[4] which evidently did not have the authority of
the Cabinet. Disraeli put an important gloss on the instructions of
November 27. Salisbury was to say that England would not exclude
occupation, but only on condition that Turkey acquiesced; if so,
Russia and Austria-Hungary were to be kept out and he was to
manoeuvre the Porte into asking for an English occupation. This
was a drastic modification and in the course of the next three weeks
Disraeli went even further. He decided that there should be no
occupation by anyone, even England. His notes for the Cabinet

[1] M. & B., vi, 107, December 16.
[2] Hughenden Papers, Box 113, B/XX/Ca/198, Cairns to Disraeli, December 16.
[3] Sumner, 239.
[4] M. & B., vi, 104–6.

meeting on December 22 which confirmed his decision contain the words:

> Principle – not to coerce the Porte or to sanction coercion by others, but to use every means of friendly influence and persuasion.
> Russian system – always to induce England to join in coercion of the Porte.
> Mr. Canning's experience and its consequences.[1]

Disraeli often harked back to Canning. His argument here presumably was that Canning's policy of joint Anglo-Russian pressure on Turkey to make concessions on the Greek question had after Canning's death led indirectly to the crushing defeat of the Turks by Nicholas I and the Treaty of Adrianople in which Britain had no say whatever and which vastly increased Russian influence all over the Near East. It was a doubtful parallel to the situation prevailing in 1876.

Two other considerations seem to have influenced him. First there was the National Convention with its almost hysterical attacks on Elliot and its plea for active intervention on behalf of the Bulgars. Nothing was better calculated to make Disraeli back Elliot and refuse to coerce Turkey. Opposition leaders who really want to influence the Government should think twice whether their tirades may not produce the exact contrary of the effect intended. Under a parliamentary system the Government has its majority and excessive protest may merely harden its determination to go its own way. This was the second occasion on which Gladstone unconsciously drove his enemy in the very direction that the Liberals most deplored. Disraeli was quite determined not to give the slightest appearance of trimming his sails to the Gladstonian hurricane.

The other element in his mind was an increasing uneasiness about Salisbury. It is difficult to avoid the impression that in agreeing to Derby's choice of a representative Disraeli did not fully appreciate the extent to which Salisbury's views – and Derby's, too – differed from his own. Both were much more shocked than he had been by the atrocities. Both, though from standpoints far apart, were determined not to get pulled into fighting for Turkey against Russia. Salisbury earlier had made plain to the Prime Minister his dissent from 'the pure Palmerston tradition',[2] but perhaps the fact had not

[1] ibid., 109.
[2] ibid., 71, Salisbury to Disraeli, September 23, 1876.

fully impinged. Now that he read Salisbury's reports from the scene of action he saw how wide the gulf was. Disraeli's new opinion appears in a letter to Derby written later. 'Sal. seems most prejudiced and not to be aware that his principal object in being sent to Const. is to keep the Russians out of Turkey, not to create an ideal existence for Turkish Xtians. He is more Russian than Ignatyev: *plus Arabe que l'Arabie!*'[1]

Salisbury did indeed get on surprisingly well with Ignatyev, who amused him and who was unlike anyone he had ever met before. He savoured with the relish of a connoisseur both Ignatyev's duplicity and his aplomb when found out. But Ignatyev did not influence his judgement to any substantial degree. Salisbury shrewdly perceived from the start that if the Turks assented to any reforms they would only do so under duress. He saw, too, that as long as Elliot was there he could never convince them that he, Salisbury, spoke for the British Government. His task was made even more difficult by various unofficial Turcophils present in Constantinople, the worst being H. A. Butler-Johnstone, MP for Canterbury, who claimed, with no justification, as far as can be seen, that he was Disraeli's secret emissary. And apart from all these difficulties how could Salisbury hope to convince the Turks of Britain's determination to abandon them if they refused to reform, when all the while Colonel Home and other officers were busy surveying the country for a suitable landing-place for a British expeditionary force? Salisbury did his best. He tried to have Elliot sent home. Disraeli checkmated him neatly, if somewhat disingenuously, by telegraphing that Ignatyev had pressed Shuvalov to urge the same course on Derby. 'If this gets out – and everything does get out at Constantinople – and Elliot withdraws, we shall be turned out the first day of the session by our own men.' In fact, all Ignatyev had done was to inform Shuvalov that Elliot undermined Salisbury with the Turks. This perfectly true statement fell a good deal short of advice to remove Elliot. When he later learned from Lady Derby of the use made of it by Disraeli Shuvalov was most indignant.[2]

No doubt Disraeli ought to have removed Elliot. Nevertheless it is probable – and Salisbury himself came to believe so – that nothing would have had any difference. Contemporary diplomats and subsequent historians are too inclined to treat the Turks as

[1] ibid., 111, December 28, 1876.
[2] Seton-Watson, 132–3.

passive figures capable of being manipulated in any direction if only
the correct method was adopted. In fact, they were seething with
rage, intensely hostile to the conference, and from the start determined to refuse all concession. The fury of the mob in Constantinople would probably have caused the fall of any government which
surrendered to the Christian powers. The atmosphere of religious
fanaticism and outraged nationalism prevailing in the capital at the
time should not be discounted.

3

The conference broke up on January 20, and to mark their dis-
pleasure the six powers agreed to withdraw all their delegates from
Constantinople, including the ambassadors. The problem of what
to do next was by no means clear. The Turks had engaged in their
usual practice of proclaiming a constitution, this time on the day the
conference opened. There was, therefore, an excuse for doing nothing
and giving the new régime 'a chance'. No one who knew Turkey
believed that anything would come of this, and the Turcophils
received a disagreeable setback when Midhat Pasha, the liberal
Grand Vizier, was kidnapped by the Sultan and deported to Brin-
disi, his place being taken by a ferocious reactionary, Edem Pasha.
In Russia a strong party regarded war as now inevitable. The Tsar
still hesitated. He decided that it was essential to do a deal with
Austria-Hungary in order to assure the latter's neutrality if war
came. The negotiations were tough and were not brought to a successful conclusion until March 18. Meanwhile Ignatyev, who had
returned to St Petersburg, persuaded the Tsar to authorize a draft
protocol for signature by the six powers embodying the minimum
requirements to be demanded from the Porte.

Disraeli, who was ill off and on for most of the year, seems to have
pursued no very clear policy during the months which passed
between the collapse of the conference and the outbreak of war. He
suggested an overture to Vienna, but received an evasive answer.
Andrassy's negotiations with Russia were a closely guarded secret
not revealed until 1919, and Disraeli often during the next year
placed false hopes upon a *rapprochement* with Austria-Hungary, the
Continental power which in some respects seemed to have the
greatest interest in checking Russia and preserving Turkey. In view
of this extreme secrecy – Andrassy concealed the agreement even

from his own Ambassador in London – Disraeli cannot perhaps be blamed, but it is interesting to notice that at an early stage Salisbury guessed that Russia had 'squared Vienna'.[1] In the House of Lords, Disraeli vigorously and effectively defended the Government's line at the Conference. He was polite to Russia. There were two policies open to Europe; the Russian, 'deserving of all respect', involved the setting up of autonomous tributary states, but, on the historical analogy of the similar states which existed in the centuries before 1454, was there not a danger that Constantinople would in the end fall? Then there was the British policy which favoured territorial integrity, but 'administrative autonomy', ie 'institutions which would secure to the Christian subjects of the Porte some control over their local affairs and some security against the excesses of arbitrary power'. Russia had given up her policy and accepted that of Britain 'very cordially'. Only Serbia had prevented peace.

The Turcophobes were beginning to lose some ground at this time even in the Liberal party. Granville and Hartington were frankly uneasy at Gladstone's extreme views, and Hartington was strongly against the publication of *Lessons in Massacre*, Gladstone's second pamphlet on Bulgarian horrors. His opposition did not stop Gladstone, but the pamphlet, compared with its predecessor, can only be described as a flop. It sold a mere 7,000 copies. Disraeli's pro-Turk sentiment often waxed and waned with the rising or falling success of Gladstone's agitation. At the end of February he made an overture to Shuvalov of a surprisingly conciliatory nature.[2] He was worried at the time lest Germany might attack France, reduce her to a second-class power and so leave England isolated. He assured Shuvalov that he had no hostile feelings towards Russia, but one must not precipitate the fall of 'the Ottoman Empire whose days are numbered'. A chance must be given for reform. He intended a reply to the Russian protocol such as would be not merely 'a golden bridge . . . but *a bridge of diamonds and rubies*'. When Shuvalov urged that Turkey would only reform under coercion, and that unless Britain agreed to this, she would have to allow isolated action by Russia [ie war], Disraeli to his surprise did not protest, but sympathized with the Russian difficulties. 'I want peace and hope we shall soon drink a glass of wine to celebrate its conclusion. But when all is over we shall have to agree upon a pacific solution for

[1] Cecil, *Salisbury*, ii, 131, March 12.
[2] Seton-Watson, 159–60.

the moment of the sick man's death.' Like Shuvalov, the historian can but be puzzled at this curious conversation so different from Disraeli's usual attitude.

It prompted the Tsar and Gorchakov to take the unwise step of sending Ignatyev with his draft protocol on a personal visit to the European capitals including London. Shuvalov was horrified and warned Gorchakov that it would be like Elliot visiting Russia, but the Chancellor pooh-poohed these objections. Shuvalov and Ignatyev were notorious enemies and represented extreme opposite views on Russian policy. Ignatyev, taking advantage of a rash invitation from Salisbury, stayed at Hatfield. He made the worst impression on almost everyone, trying to intrigue at Salisbury's own dinner-table with Hartington and Forster, who promptly told their host. He was nothing if not outspoken. When Lady John Manners asked him whether he felt well after his journey he replied: 'I always feel well. My conscience is clear because I defend the Christians and so my wife and I are always gay.'[1] He and his wife dined with Disraeli, whose account of the occasion dwells on diamonds rather than diplomacy. Mme Ignatyev's 'paled' before those of Lady Londonderry, who 'staggered under the jewels of the 3 united families of Stewart Vane and Londonderry'.[2] After dinner they all attended a concert at Lady Dudley's house. Gladstone was there and was introduced to Ignatyev, who talked so much that even Gladstone could not get a word in. At last the Russian ceased, but was called away by Mme Ignatyev just as Gladstone was about to speak. 'His glance was demoniacal,' Disraeli gleefully told Ponsonby for the benefit of the Queen.[3]

Ignatyev's visit did nothing to improve the situation, and Shuvalov had to pick up the pieces after he had gone. But after much discussion the Cabinet decided, largely at Salisbury's insistence, to sign the London Protocol, as the document came to be called. It seemed scarcely credible that the Turks would reject what was now a most conciliatory and innocuous agreement which would probably have been quite ineffective. Once again everyone reckoned without the Turks. Their armies were much stronger after a six-month armistice, and they may have thought that Russia's finances, which were chaotic, and her military organization, which was

---

[1] Hughenden Papers, Box 106, B/XX/M/211, Lady John Manners to Disraeli, n.d.
[2] Zetland, ii, 109–10.
[3] Royal Archives, H.12.197, March 22, Ponsonby to the Queen.

deplorable, would cause her to withdraw. Another factor probably played its part. The same Cabinet meeting which decided to accept the London Protocol also agreed on the nomination of H. A. Layard, famous for his excavations at Nineveh thirty years before, as Elliot's successor at Constantinople. He was a most forceful personality, a keen Turcophile, and incidentally the nephew of Disraeli's former patroness, Mrs Austen.

That Elliot should need replacement had been a matter of sharp controversy. Disraeli and Derby had intended to keep him and had decided to do so without reference to the Cabinet, as indeed was their right.[1] But a hostile motion was put down in the House by W. E. Forster and the Cabinet could no longer be kept out of the business. Salisbury raised a heated protest against the continuation of Elliot. The Queen, on the other hand, urged Disraeli to stick to his guns 'or we shall never be able to do what we think right as regards foreign missions & *Parlt.* & not the *Sovereign* will be their *Masters*!!'[2] Salisbury was backed by most of the Cabinet, influenced by the Chief Whip, who declared that 'we could not rely on our own men' if the appointment was not countermanded. Three months earlier the Government was alleged to be in danger if Elliot was removed from his Embassy. Now it appeared to be no less in jeopardy if he was not. Derby caused consternation by declaring that, since he had already given a promise to the Ambassador, he would have to resign if overruled. But Disraeli got round this difficulty by personally explaining the situation to Elliot. The latter, for all his defects, was a man of honour and saved the faces of those concerned by formally requesting a different embassy.

The new Ambassador was not only a violent pro-Turk but well known to be such. It is a reasonable assumption that this was Disraeli's chief reason for choosing him, for if his previous judgement on Layard was anything more than an expression of bad temper he had no high opinion of his conduct as a diplomatist at Madrid. The choice effectively neutralized the British signature of the London Protocol. On April 9 the Turkish Government formally rejected it. On April 24 Russia declared war on Turkey.

The Russians claimed from the outset that they were fighting

---

[1] ibid., H.12.209, March 31, Disraeli to the Queen. This gives a full account on which the rest of this paragraph is based. M. & B., vi, 135, misleads in saying without qualification, 'Beaconsfield insisted that Elliot could not go back.' He certainly did not do so at first.

[2] ibid., H.12.207, March 29.

solely to enforce the London Protocol. They had no mandate from the other signatories to do so, but it was not possible for Disraeli, however suspicious of Russia's ulterior motives, to go to war against the enforcement of a document which his own Government had signed. Nor would public opinion have tolerated such action. The Cabinet was therefore united on a policy of neutrality for the time being, and there was general support for Derby's note to Russia of May 6 defining the British position. It possibly fell short of what Disraeli wanted, but he was taken ill at the relevant Cabinet meeting on May 1 and had to leave before the final decision. Derby's note warned Russia that Britain would regard her vital interests as jeopardized by military action which threatened any of the following areas: the Persian Gulf, Egypt, the Suez Canal, Constantinople or the Straits. The plan which Disraeli had been pressing at earlier meetings for a British occupation of the Dardanelles was shelved. The Derby note, despite the vicissitudes of war, the complicated divisions in the Cabinet, and the shifts in public opinion remained, as Disraeli called it, 'the diapaison of our diplomacy'[1] for the next nine months.

The parliamentary opposition was for the moment in disarray. Hartington, more perturbed than ever at Gladstone's excitability, tried to steer a middle course. He feared that his old leader's policy would divide the Liberal party, many of whom felt that, however deplorable Disraeli's Turcophilism might be, Gladstone was in danger of appearing as an uncritical supporter of Russia, and this very fact would play into Disraeli's hands. Gladstone put down five formidable anti-Government resolutions to be debated in the House on May 7, but Granville and Hartington threatened to 'move the previous question', and Gladstone decided to propose only the first two which were the least controversial. He made a speech described later by Balfour as 'unequalled', but he was defeated by 354 to 223, a good deal more than the Government's normal majority.

The division in the Opposition was thus plain for all to see. Far less obvious but no less sharp were the divisions which had already begun to plague the Cabinet. From an early stage Carnarvon had been profoundly suspicious of Disraeli; even more so than his closest friend Salisbury. 'I see pretty plainly . . . that Lord B. contemplates & as far as it depends on him, intends us to take part in the war and on behalf of Turkey', he wrote to Salisbury, then in Constantinople,

[1] M. & B., vi, 135.

on Christmas Day, 1876.[1] '. . . I may do him wrong but his mind is full of strange projects and I feel uneasy as to what he intends and what he may be able to do before there is time or knowledge enough to stop him.' He went on to say: 'I hardly understand Derby's mental position. I think he is uneasy and so far as he is concerned inclined to wait upon events . . . My impression is that he is entirely in Disraeli's hands.' Carnarvon, as we shall see, was quite wrong on this point. At the end of March his anxiety about Disraeli's plans was increased by a visit to Windsor. He wrote an alarmed, indeed alarmist, letter to Salisbury, anticipating that Disraeli would try to dismiss them both.[2] 'The ground has been completely undermined here . . . She is ready for war – says that rather than submit to Russian insult she would lay down her crown . . . Unlike Derby he [Disraeli] has plenty of courage and I am not sure that it is not all things considered the best game for him to play.' And Carnarvon sadly ended: 'It is strange to go through the same suspicions, intrigues, open struggle as we did ten years ago: and together.' Their experience of the Reform struggle in 1867 strongly influenced the two men – and very naturally. Salisbury was, however, the cooler and more cautious. He wrote back at length pointing out the unlikelihood of Carnarvon's fears being realized; and indeed there is nothing to suggest that either Disraeli or the Queen contemplated dismissing the two peers.

Carnarvon, who was very High Church, was probably the most Turcophobe of the Conservative ministers. His ultimate resignation suggests that he regarded war against Russia on the Turkish side as inadmissible under any circumstances. He was a clever man, as even the Queen conceded, but he had the angularity which sometimes accompanies a clever independent mind. He was small in stature and his nickname 'Twitters' suggests a certain lack of impressiveness in his demeanour. He never carried the weight in council of his friend Salisbury. Disraeli was irritated by him, especially when he declared that 'for his part the amelioration of the Xtian subjects of the Porte is the chief object that he presents to himself'.[3] 'This is disgraceful', the Queen minuted to Ponsonby.[4] Salisbury, too, was deeply suspicious of Disraeli, but unlike Carnarvon he could envisage a situation in which war or the threat of war against

[1] Salisbury Papers.
[2] ibid., March 25.
[3] Royal Archives, Dr.H.12.192, Disraeli to the Queen, March 21, 1876.
[4] ibid., H.12.193, n.d.

Russia was the lesser of two evils. Perhaps in the last resort he attributed more importance than Carnarvon to holding the party together. Hence their ultimate divergence when the crisis came in January 1878. But in May, Salisbury was far from thinking that the threat of war was necessary. His advice throughout the next few months was on the side of moderation.

The opposition group in the Cabinet came to be known as 'the three Lords'. The third was Derby, who, in spite of Carnarvon's opinion, was very far from being 'in Disraeli's hands'. Derby's role in the Eastern question is one of much controversy and its final elucidation must await the day when a biography of him comes to be written. But the facts that have been published by Professor Seton-Watson from Shuvalov's papers, together with those that appear here for the first time from the Royal Archives and from Disraeli's letters, are enough to reveal a situation of the most extraordinary nature.

Derby surely must be the only Foreign Secretary in British history to reveal the innermost secrets of the Cabinet to the ambassador of a foreign power in order to frustrate the presumed intentions of his own Prime Minister. The strong criticisms made by the Queen, Disraeli and Salisbury against Derby's 'indiscretion', as they called it, were suppressed by both Buckle and Lady Gwendolen Cecil. Neither biographer was aware that Derby and Lady Derby communicated the secrets of the Cabinet to Shuvalov not from carelessness but in the deliberate hope of preserving the peace. The Queen and Disraeli, too, had no idea of this explanation, which indeed only saw the light of day with the publication of the Shuvalov correspondence in 1924. To them the leakage of secrets could be explained only by indiscretion and Derby's obstructionism by the oddities of his personal character. Derby *was* an odd character, odder than is generally realized, if some of the rumours about him are true, but it is clear that his obstructionism was not mere apathy and that his indiscretion was deliberate. No one could have been more un-English than Shuvalov or more English than Derby, but a certain aristocratic freemasonry still existed in Europe. This was probably the last occasion in the age of nationalism when two grandees, each equally contemptuous of the chauvinism in their respective countries, could co-operate so closely in trying to preserve peace.

Shuvalov was a strong opponent of Panslavism and of all popular movements. He was anxious to avert a war, above all because of the radical and revolutionary currents which war would set flowing in Russia. In character he was about as unlike the phlegmatic somewhat bovine Derby as any man could be. He was vivacious, entertaining, universally liked, an agreeable rattle at every party. He was fond of wine, perhaps too fond. Disraeli, for example, saw cause for comment when at dinner he found him 'calm and not at all claret-y'.[1] He was also fond of women and had the reputation of being a notable amorist. Everyone knew what was meant if they called in the afternoon and were told 'Count Shuvalov is out driving in his carriage'. Yet in spite of these frivolities he was one of the most capable ambassadors ever sent by Russia to the Court of S James's. He sized up the unfamiliar and complicated politics of London with extraordinary speed. So deeply absorbed did he become that he ended by deploring in a letter, to be seen by the Tsar of all people, the unconstitutional behaviour of the Queen and the Royal Princes in meddling with affairs of state.

It took Disraeli a long time to realize how far removed Derby was from his own point of view. The first sign of dissatisfaction comes in a letter to the Queen on April 17. 'So much timidity, so much false religionism that [Lord Beaconsfield] has the utmost difficult task to achieve that ever fell to his lot . . . This morning a torturing hour with Lord Derby who was for doing nothing and this afternoon with Lord Salisbury who evidently is thinking more of raising the Cross on the cupola of St. Sophia than of the power of England.'[2]

The procrastination and sloth of which the Queen and the Prime Minister so regularly complained were not caused solely by temperament. They were also part of Derby's defence mechanism against a policy of which he disapproved. His standpoint differed from that of the other two 'lords'. The religious sympathies which operated with Carnarvon and to some extent, though not as much as Disraeli claimed, with Salisbury, had no effect on him. He told Disraeli that he had no objection to an alliance with Turkey if it promoted British interests.[3] Nor does he appear to have doubted, as Salisbury did, the ultimate British interest in preserving the Straits and Constantinople from Russia. The principal spring of action, or rather inaction, seems in his case to have been a firm conviction that intervention was unnecessary, because the Russian Government

---

[1] M. & B., vi, 34, Disraeli to Derby, June 24, 1876.
[2] Royal Archives, H.13.24.
[3] M. & B., vi, 152, Disraeli to the Queen, July 12, 1877.

meant what it said, viz. that the object of the war was to secure the necessary reforms for the Christians, not the total disruption of the Turkish empire. It followed that the real danger of war lay in belli-cose pronouncements by the British Government likely to provoke the Tsar into doing the very things which Britain least wanted him to do. And it followed further that, the more the Tsar and his advisers were aware of the divisions in the Cabinet and the lack of support for Disraeli, the better the chances of peace. Of course, to Disraeli and the Queen, who were convinced that only a tough ulti-matum could stop the Tsar from seizing Constantinople, the precise opposite seemed true. To them Derby's conduct appeared baffling, sluggish and incompetent.

During the first three months of the war Russian arms carried all before them, and the alarm of the English Russophobes, headed by the Queen, became little short of hysterical. Shuvalov, who was in St Petersburg for most of May, brought back a conciliatory, though not unambiguous, answer to the Derby note. But the good effect of this was neutralized by the Tsar, who had gone to his military head-quarters and, chameleonlike as ever, took colour from his Panslav entourage. He promptly reversed a promise which he had made not to insist on autonomy for southern as well as northern Bulgaria, thus supplying the Russophobes in Britain with another instance of Russian shiftiness.[1]

The breach between Disraeli and Derby now began to widen, although Disraeli did all he could to bridge it. The Cabinet was in a state of chaos and it would be an interminable task to analyse the shades of opinion varying as they did almost from day to day. Derby put his foot down against all action that implied war. The Queen's indignation knew no bounds. When she reminded him of the Crimean War he replied: 'In this country feeling is much divided; but Lord Derby believes that a war not forced upon us by necessity and self defence would be unpopular even now, and far more so when once entered upon. Lord Derby well remembers the Crimean War; and has never seen so near an approach to a really revolu-tionary condition of public feeling as after the first failures and disasters of that struggle.'[2] The Queen passed the letter to Disraeli, who 'returns Lord Derby's deplorable epistle'.[3] But on June 17

[1] Sumner, 316.
[2] *The Letters of Queen Victoria*, 2nd Series, June 11, 1877.
[3] Royal Archives, H.14.83, June 14, 1877.

Disraeli made a last effort to enlist Derby's aid. He referred to 'the sacerdotal convictions' of Lord Salisbury, who was evidently 'acting as he has done throughout under the influence and counsel of Lyddon' [*sic*].[1] Would Derby at least support a vote of credit for the armed forces? Derby's answer was cool and unhelpful. The Queen commented, 'Warning after warning arrives and he seems to take it all without saying a word!! Such a Foreign Minister the Queen really never remembers!'[2] She suggested that Lord Lyons would be a suitable replacement. This was not possible, and anyway two months later Lord Lyons proved himself just as bad. His opinion 'astonishes the Queen, as he was all for England's maintaining her position and not falling into a miserable cotton-spinning milk and water, peace-at-any-price policy which the Queen will not submit to'.[3]

Disraeli did not see the problem in such black-and-white terms as these, and for reasons of personal affection and party management he was very reluctant to get rid of Derby. But he was, as we saw, suspicious of Russian intentions and, although he did not seek war, he believed that the British Government must be in a position to threaten war. Yet the Queen's language was so extreme as to be embarrassing. He had to remind her that he was not her Grand Vizier and that for the time being the Cabinet was committed to neutrality, however lamentable this might be. It was impossible in such circumstances for Britain to prevent the Russians from capturing Constantinople. The most we could do was to occupy the Dardanelles 'as a material guarantee'.[4] Even that step could be taken only if the Sultan consented, and he would not do so unless England became his ally – an impossible condition given the state of English opinion. When the Queen, now at her most excitable, seemed to imply that Disraeli was going back on promises that he had made to her, he riposted with a hint that he 'errs perhaps in being too communicative to your Majesty in often imparting plans to your Majesty which are in embryo . . . but it relieves his mind, and often assists his judgement to converse and confer with your Majesty without the slightest reserve . . .'[5] The Queen at once surrendered. She was '*greatly grieved* that *he* thinks she meant *him* by what is said. How could he think so? She meant his *Colleagues* . . .'[6]

---

[1] M. & B., vi, 145, Canon Liddon of St Paul's.   [2] ibid., 147, June 25, 1877.
[3] Royal Archives, B.53.2. September 22, the Queen to Disraeli.
[4] M. & B., vi, 152, Disraeli to the Queen, July 16, 1877.
[5] ibid., 154, July 22.
[6] Royal Archives, B.52.12, July 23.

Nor was there any doubt which of those colleagues she chiefly meant. On August 1 her suspicions of Derby and Lady Derby came into the open. Disraeli had induced the Cabinet on July 21 to agree that Britain would declare war if Russia occupied Constantinople without promising an early withdrawal. The Queen thought that Layard should be informed and was indignant at Derby sending a telegram to the Ambassador re-emphasizing British neutrality. She asked for 'some *secret* information as to what has led to all this'. Had the situation even been made clear to the Tsar?

> In the letter the Queen wrote to Lord Beaconsfield the night Lord Salisbury was here (the 25th) she *urged so strongly* (& Ld. S. agreed) the *importance* of the CZAR knowing that we *will not let him have Constantinople*! Ld. Derby and his wife most likely say the *reverse right and left* and RUSSIA GOES ON! It maddens the Queen to feel that all our efforts are being destroyed by the Minister who ought to carry them out. The Queen must say she can't stand it! . . .[1]

This is the first sign that the 'indiscretions' of Lord and Lady Derby had become known in the highest quarters. As the war tension increased the alliance between the Derbys and Shuvalov became closer, and Disraeli's relations with his old friend and protégé grew more and more remote. As early as June he had established a private link with Layard unknown to the Foreign Secretary. For the moment the whole diplomatic situation became less tense because of the unexpected resistance put up by Osman Pasha, the Turkish Commander at Plevna. The Russian forces were halted in two battles on July 20 and 30, and early in September a third defeat seemed to endanger the communications of all the troops that had crossed the Danube. The Turcophils were cock-a-hoop. The threat to Constantinople suddenly receded. It looked as if the war would come to the halt conventionally imposed by winter, and would be renewed in a second campaigning season in the following spring.

Disraeli pressed the Cabinet on August 15 just before the recess to inform Russia that England would not remain neutral in the event of a second campaign. No decision was reached, as so often; but this did not inhibit Disraeli from sending in strictest secrecy an emissary to the Tsar to inform him that the Cabinet was absolutely

---

[1] ibid., B.52.17, August 1, 1877.

united in its determination to go to war if there was a second campaign. Colonel Wellesley, the British military attaché in Russia since 1871 and son-in-law of Disraeli's *bête noire* Lord Augustus Loftus, was selected for this delicate task. Only the Queen knew about it. The rest of the Cabinet, including Derby, from whom Wellesley conveyed a formal official message, were kept entirely in the dark. This surprising transaction is no less strange than Derby's dealings with Shuvalov. Mistrust between colleagues could scarcely go further. The Tsar received Wellesley, who was a personal friend, with civility. He must have been aware from Shuvalov that there was another side to the boasted unity of the Cabinet, but if he took the threat seriously it probably had the opposite effect to what Disraeli desired: it gave him every inducement to finish the war as soon as he could without the need for a second campaign.

CHAPTER XXVII

The Congress of Berlin
1878

1

The session of 1877 was uneventful as far as domestic affairs were concerned. Indeed, the only episode of political interest in Disraeli's life was an attempt by some Opposition back benchers to press a charge of personal jobbery against him. The allegation was that he had appointed T. D. Pigott, a clerk at the War Office, to the post of Comptroller of the Stationery Office because his father, a clergyman, had been a political supporter and Disraeli's appointee as Vicar of Hughenden. It was true that the older Pigott had been the incumbent of that living. But he had been chosen by the previous patron, he was a Whig supporter, he quarrelled with Disraeli about a right of way, he reproved him once for 'Sunday travelling' (receiving a sharp snub for his pains), and he left Hughenden in a general aura of ill will. Disraeli's appointment of Sir Digby Pigott, as he later became, was open to some criticism in that a Select Committee had recently recommended that the post should in future go to a person retired from business, or, as Disraeli put it, 'from whom business had retired'. But it was not a 'job'. A snap motion of censure was carried in the House of Commons, thanks to the negligence of the Whips. Disraeli had to defend himself in the House of Lords. He had a conclusive answer, and the occasion provided him with a splendid opportunity of play acting. When he entered the House he appeared old, bent, worn out, weary, half guilty. As he spoke he gradually became alive, and the expression of horror and astonishment with which he uttered the word 'job' was unforgettable. By the time he had finished, his audience, frosty at first, was wholly on his side, and he himself appeared to be twenty years younger. The motion of censure in the House of Commons was quickly rescinded with apologies and without a division.[1]

Disraeli had one important Cabinet post to fill at this time. On July 29 Ward Hunt died at Hamburg from fatty degeneration of

[1] M. & B., vi, 163–7.

the heart. He had been by no means an ideal minister, though no doubt poor health accounted for much. Disraeli, whose opinion of successive Tory First Lords of the Admiralty ever since 1852 had been very unfavourable, was determined to choose a really efficient man, and after offering the post first to Lord Sandon, he resolved to promote W. H. Smith, the great bookstall proprietor, from the position of Secretary of the Treasury, where he had done very well. 'He is purely a man of the middle class,' he wrote to the Queen, 'and the appointment would no doubt be popular.'[1] The Queen demurred slightly in her reply. 'She *fears* it may *not please* the Navy in which Service so many of the *highest rank* serve and who claim to be equal to the Army – if a man of the Middle Class is placed above them in that very high post . . .'[2] She suggested Manners or Hicks Beach instead.

Disraeli pointed out in reply that Childers and Goschen in the previous government were socially no higher than Smith and nothing like as rich.[3] Hicks Beach would be satisfactory, but was wanted where he was. No one appreciated Manners as much as Disraeli – 'his friend of more than forty years. But the appointment would not be approved – nay, it would be condemned; which would be painful as well as injurious.' Smith made the same excellent impression on the House as Cross, and had acquired its complete confidence. Moreover, Smith sat for Westminster and there was a standing grievance that the Cabinet ministers in the House of Commons were none of them borough members. 'Hitherto this has been a necessity, as all the leading ability of the Tory party has generally speaking been contributed by the Counties.' Finally 'the Admiralty requires a strong man and Mr. Smith is such.' Faced by this barrage of arguments, which she admitted were 'unanswerable', the Queen gave way. 'But he must not "lord it" over the Navy (which almost every First Lord does) and be·a little modest and not *act* the Lord High Admiral which is offensive to the Service . . .'[4] W. H. Smith turned out to be one of Disraeli's most successful appointments and he became a notable source of strength in the Cabinet.

Disraeli spent the last fortnight of August and the whole of September at Hughenden. He continued to be in a low state of

[1] Royal Archives, E.53.37, August 3, 1877.
[2] ibid., E.53.38, August 4.
[3] ibid., E.53.43, August 6.
[4] ibid., E.53.44, August 7, 1877.

health, and he badly needed rest. But he got no better. Bronchitis was eased, merely to be replaced by asthma which 'destroys my nights and makes me consequently shattered by day'. He decided to see whether three weeks at Brighton would bring an improvement. Before departing he summoned a Cabinet meeting. The Queen had indeed been pressing him to do so earlier, but Disraeli did not agree:[1] 'The system of having a great many Cabinets till its members have agreed on some policy is a bad one. Every day there are fresh difficulties. A mind like the Chancellor of the Exchequer's, for example, would make a fresh difficulty every day.' But the continued failure of the Russians to take Plevna had given him an idea. Why not propose British mediation, terms to be a settlement of Bulgaria on the lines of the London Protocol and the cession of Bessarabia to Russia. If the Turks agreed and Russia refused, then Britain would inform the Sultan and the Tsar that she would abandon neutrality and give Turkey material aid if Constantinople were menaced. Disraeli wrote beforehand to Derby, pressing him to put forward this proposal. 'I am not prepared to support the proposal which you suggest, still less to put it forward,' replied the Foreign Secretary. And on October 5 at the Cabinet, in spite of Disraeli's ambiguously optimistic account to the Queen the plan was evidently shelved.[2]

The visit to Brighton was not a success. For one thing Corry was taking a well-deserved holiday from his secretarial duties on grounds of health. 'It comes at a moment of great public anxiety for I have no substitute for him', Disraeli grumbled to Lady Bradford.[3] '. . . Whenever Monty leaves me having convinced himself that nothing can happen for a while the most pressing business immediately prevails . . .'[4] Disraeli was apt to be an exacting master. He liked the other two secretaries: 'faithful, able, and gentlemen; but I can't live with them'. Then there were the lion-hunters who thrust unwanted invitations on him, but he had a means of dealing with these. He sent their cards to London to be answered by Algernon Turnor. 'I hope this will sicken them.'[5] And finally Disraeli's health did not improve. He broke his holiday for a three-day visit to the Duke of Bedford at Woburn, where 'I sleep in a golden bed with a

[1] ibid., B.53.3, September 24.
[2] Contrast M. & B., vi, 183 (Disraeli to the Queen) with Cecil, *Salisbury*, ii, 161 (Salisbury to Lady Salisbury).
[3] M. & B., vi, 187, October 11.   [4] loc. cit., October 13.
[5] M. & B., vi, 190, October 25.

golden ceiling'.[1] Lord Lyons and Lord Odo Russell were also of the party. Disraeli had long talks with them both, but found them, so he told the Queen, 'absolutely cowed by Prince Bismarck'.[2] Disraeli seldom failed to include in his letters those pen portraits which delighted the Queen. 'The Duke of Bedford is a strange man', he wrote. 'He enjoys his power and prosperity, and yet seems to hold a lower opinion of human nature than any man Lord Beaconsfield was ever acquainted with. He is a joyous cynic . . . Lord Beaconsfield has seen Lord Derby, a cynic also but not a joyous one . . .'

Disraeli was in a state of acute depression at the end of October. 'I am very ill . . .' he told Lady Bradford on October 23. 'If I could only face the scene which would occur at headquarters if I resigned, I would do so at once; but I never could bear scenes and have no pluck for the occasion.'[3] And two days later he wrote: 'I can't lead a House of Parlt. even H of L without a voice witht health. And Lord Mayor's Day when my words may govern the world, what am I to do? If it were not for the Fairy I would at once retire but I await her return before I broach it.' It is never easy to know how seriously Disraeli meant remarks of this sort. But a fortunate chance altered the situation very soon after. He had been pressed by Cairns and others to try a new physician, Dr Kidd, who had a large practice in bronchial and similar cases. On November 1 he was examined by the new doctor, who reported that there was 'no organic deficiency' and managed to make Disraeli well enough for the Guildhall speech. Kidd was a homoeopath and so was not *persona grata* with his professional colleagues, but he undoubtedly managed to effect a real improvement in his patient's health.

According to Kidd,[4] Disraeli was suffering from Bright's disease, bronchitis and asthma, and his condition was aggravated by the remedies of previous physicians, who had prescribed ipecacuanha for asthma, and 'steel [probably some medicine containing iron] and port wine' to cure his 'debility'. The ipecacuanha merely made him feel sick; the 'steel' and port gave him a headache and accentuated his tendency towards gout. He suffered badly from insomnia owing to coughing at night, and this brought on depression and a general inability to work or concentrate.

[1] ibid., 188, October 17.
[2] ibid., 188–9, October 18.
[3] ibid., 190.
[4] Joseph Kidd, 'The Last Illness of Lord Beaconsfield', *The Nineteenth Century*, 26 (July 1889), 65–71.

Dr Kidd at once stopped the ipecacuanha and the 'steel', substituting potassium iodide. This is still used today and would certainly have been an improvement. He also wisely forbade port and prescribed instead 'the finest Château Lafite' – a change which suited Disraeli, who disliked port but was devoted to claret. Another prudent measure was to insist on a light dinner 'without pastry pudding or fruit'. 'A mild course of arsenic' to clear the bronchial tubes would not, however, meet with modern approval. It probably did more harm than good. Nor would a doctor today try to encourage perspiration before going to bed.[1] Dr Kidd attached much importance to this. The most that can be said is that it may have helped Disraeli to sleep. To aid his digestion – although this seems to have been his own idea, not Kidd's – he had a concordat with his cook that when he dined alone there should be ten minutes between each course, during which he would read one of the classics. The upshot of these changes in his regimen seems to have been highly beneficial. Nausea disappeared, he recovered his appetite for breakfast and lunch, he slept well, and felt more cheerful and vigorous than for a long while past. But any deviation from his routine was liable to be disturbing. For example, it is not surprising that the round of festivities at the Congress of Berlin made it necessary to summon Kidd urgently.

Disraeli was a co-operative patient, but a shrewd observer of doctors – a class of whom he had had much experience. Dr Kidd confirms that basically Disraeli had a tough and hardy constitution, but Kidd regretted his inability to persuade him to take exercise. 'My grandfather lived to ninety years,' Disraeli said to him on one occasion. 'He took much open-air exercise. My father lived to eighty, yet he never took any.'[2] He could only be induced to go for a walk if he had an amusing companion, and even then sauntered so slowly that as exercise it was useless.

Disraeli needed all the improvement in health that he could obtain, for the impasse to which Plevna had brought the Russo-Turkish war was showing ominous signs of ending in defeat for the Turks. Even while Disraeli was at Woburn news came through of a great Russian victory on the Transcaucasian front, and it was clear that Osman could not hold indefinitely against the reinforcements

[1] I am obliged to my colleague, Dr P. B. C. Matthews, M.D., for his comments on Dr Kidd's treatment.
[2] Kidd, 66.

arriving on the Balkan front. But the Cabinet seemed more hopelessly divided than ever. It was two days after he saw Dr Kidd that
Disraeli furnished the Queen with the analysis mentioned earlier,
which began: 'In a Cabinet of twelve members there are seven
parties or policies as to the course which should be pursued.'[1]

On December 9 Plevna fell, and it was clear that there would now
be no question of a second campaign. The struggle between the war
and peace parties in the Cabinet became acute. Disraeli pressed for
an early summoning of Parliament, a vote of credit for the forces
and British mediation between the belligerents. The Cabinet hesitated, Derby strongly opposing the proposal. On December 15 the
Queen, who had only once before been the guest of one of her Prime
Ministers (Melbourne), published her support of Disraeli to the
world by the most unusual step of lunching with him at Hughenden,
thus occasioning Freeman's deplorable comment quoted above.[2] She
was accompanied by Princess Beatrice, and each of them planted a
tree in the grounds. She chose by ill chance an unfortunate day, the
anniversary of Mary Anne's death, and when she discovered it too
late her contrition was heartfelt. Two days later Disraeli partially
won the battle in the Cabinet. 'The three recusant peers surrendered', he told the Queen. The Cabinet agreed to his proposals, but
only provisionally.

At about the same time the trouble over Derby's communications
with Shuvalov came to a head. Colonel Wellesley had for some
months past been reporting on the remarkably detailed information
about Cabinet discussions regularly passed on by the Ambassador
at St Petersburg. The favour shown by the Foreign Secretary to the
Russian Ambassador was so marked that it had created comment in
society, and those who were aware of the leakages could not fail to
put two and two together. Both the Queen and Disraeli were even
more disturbed than they had been in the summer. All Disraeli's
efforts would be nullified if the Tsar, in possession of secret information which he ought never to have had, reckoned on Cabinet dissensions paralysing British action when it came to the point.

The Queen wrote to Disraeli on the matter.[3] She principally
blamed Lady Derby, and he considered reading her letter to the
Cabinet, but decided to consult Salisbury, who was Lady Derby's
stepson – an additional complication in an affair difficult enough

---

[1] M. & B., vi, 193–5, November 3.   [2] See 607.
[3] Hughenden Papers, Box 80, B/XIX/B/971, December 7, 1877.

already. He advised Disraeli to approach Derby first. Disraeli replied to the Queen: 'Lord Salisbury said Lord Derby would bow to any suggestion made by his Sovereign but that he might be seriously offended if such delicate matters touching himself were brought forward to be discussed by Mr. Smith, Mr. Cross, etc. etc.'[1] Derby raised the question himself 'very formally' and 'Lord Salisbury as the husband of the only other wife who could interfere in such matters expressed himself without reserve'.

Disraeli's letter to the Queen does not tell us what Derby said, but presumably he gave some sort of assurances about Shuvalov. Whatever he said or did, the matter was not finished with, for about three weeks later the Queen charged Dean Wellesley (significantly not Ponsonby, whom she regarded as too Gladstonian) to write to Lady Derby. The Dean did so and told the Queen that 'as she [Lady Derby] has taken in good part the very stringent advice the Dean has ventured to give her as to the exclusiveness and familiarity which have marked her receptions of the Russian Ambassador and which (even if there was nothing more) would in themselves give occasion for the spreading of rumours against her, the Dean feels assured that there will be an end of any intelligence abroad that might be traded to that source'.[2] In fact, Lady Derby did not take the advice in good part at all, and wrote to the Dean in a very hurt tone.[3] Returning her letter to the Queen, who had sent it on to him, Disraeli replied: 'The letter of the Lady is not satisfactory; but then it could not be. The step taken afforded the only means of arresting the evil, if that be possible.'[4]

Disraeli's misgivings about Derby were heartily reciprocated. Sensing perhaps that Salisbury was no longer the reliable ally that he had been, Derby wrote to him on December 23 a letter of appeal. In this the full measure of his suspicion of Disraeli comes out very clearly.

. . . It is difficult to give a definite reason for suspicions however strongly one may entertain them; but I know our chief of old, and from various things that have dropped from him I am fully convinced – not indeed that he wants a war – but that he has made up his mind to large military preparations, to an extremely warlike speech, to an agitation in favour of armed intervention

[1] Royal Archives, B.54.7, Disraeli to the Queen, December 8, 1877.
[2] ibid., H.18.57, December 29, 1877.
[3] ibid., H.18.69, December 29, 1877.
[4] ibid., B.54.42, January 3, 1878.

(recollect that he said in Cabinet: 'The country is asleep and I want to wake it up'), and if possible to an expedition that shall occupy Constantinople or Gallipoli.

Now I am not inclined to any of these things, and I believe others among us are not so either, but if we don't take care, we shall find ourselves, as you said last year about the vote of credit, 'on a slippery incline' . . .

I have no feeling towards the Premier but one of personal friendship and good will and would make any personal sacrifices to help him out of a difficulty, but his views are different from mine where such matters are concerned, not in detail but in principle. He believes thoroughly in 'prestige' as all foreigners do, and would think it (quite sincerely) in the interests of the country to spend 200 millions on a war if the result was to make foreign States think more highly of us as a military power. These ideas are intelligible but they are not mine nor yours and their being sincerely held does not make them less dangerous. We are in real danger and it is impossible to be too careful. I write without any more specific object than that of a general warning: *but I know what the pressure of the court is on our Chief. I am convinced that the Queen has satisfied herself that she will have her way (it is not disguised that she wishes for a war): and the conviction is universal among the diplomatists that the Premier will leave no stone unturned to accomplish their purpose.*

The first thing is to see that nothing shall be done without the Cabinet being consulted. That I can ensure as far as diplomatic business is concerned . . .[1]

Salisbury was the key to the political situation. Everything depended on the way he went. A day later Disraeli, too, appealed to him.

If every resolution of every council is regularly reported by Count S. it seems inevitable that our very endeavours to secure peace will land us in the reverse.

I have endeavoured to arrest this evil by some remarks I made in Cabinet and I have been told that Lady Salisbury with the wise courage which distinguishes her has socially expressed her sentiments to the great culprit. But more decisive means are requisite.

We must put an end to all this gossip about war and peace parties in the Cabinet and we must come to decisions which may be, and will be, betrayed but which may convince Russia that we are agreed and determined. You and I must go together into the depth of the affair and settle what we are prepared to do. I dare

[1] Salisbury Papers. All except the sentences in italics appears in Cecil, *Salisbury*, ii, 170–1.

say we shall not differ when we talk the matter over as becomes public men with so great a responsibility . . .[1]

Salisbury was sympathetic on the leakages, but he did not commit himself to Disraeli or to Derby, although his mind was for a number of reasons moving more and more against the latter. He saw that the now headlong Russian advance had created a situation in which Britain might have to threaten, or even go to, war for reasons other than Disraeli's alleged bellicosity. It was no longer a matter of bolstering up a Turkey morally condemned by the whole of Europe. Turkey's prewar 'territorial integrity' had gone for ever by now. It was a question of Russian designs on the Straits, and of the right of the Concert of Europe to have a say in the final settlement.

As the Russian advance continued, passions reached new heights in England. This was the time when the Duke of Sutherland called Gladstone a Russian agent and Freeman called Hughenden a ghetto. It was the time of the famous music-hall song, and night after night the numbers swelled of those who did not want to fight, but by jingo if they did . . . Gladstone was hooted in the street and 'patriotic' ruffians broke the windows of his house. Carnarvon made an imprudent speech on January 2 to the effect that a repetition of the Crimean War would be 'insane'. He received a cutting reprimand from Disraeli in Cabinet and a rebuke from the Queen. He consulted Salisbury, who advised him not to resign 'on account of a rude phrase by a man whose insolence is proverbial'. He also wrote to Derby propounding various courses as ninepins to be knocked down, one of which was to announce that he stood by his views and would remain 'in the Cabinet contregré malgré to carry them'.[2] Derby to his surprise advised him to do precisely this. Carnarvon stayed.

On January 20 the Queen offered Disraeli the Garter. He declined, feeling the moment inopportune, but wrote a letter which she described as 'beautiful'. As for the Russians, the Queen went on, 'Oh if the Queen were a man, she would like to go and give those horrid Russians whose word one cannot trust such a beating.' Parliament had opened on January 17. At a series of Cabinet meetings on the 21st, 22nd and 23rd Disraeli carried three proposals: to begin negotiations with Vienna; to give public notice of the request

[1] Salisbury Papers. The italicized portion is omitted by both Buckle and Lady Gwendolen Cecil.
[2] ibid., January 4, 1878.

for a £6m vote of credit (the Cabinet's previous decision was provisional and private); to send Admiral Hornby's ironclads through the Dardanelles. Carnarvon at once resigned – on the second and third proposals. So did Derby, but on the third only. Disraeli secured the Queen's consent to Salisbury as his successor. There followed the often-told comedy of errors about the fleet. The order had to be revoked when it was revealed that a ciphering error had given the wrong impression that Russia intended to exclude the question of the Straits from any subsequent European Congress. The revocation made it possible, though not necessary, to bring Derby back into the Cabinet. Great pressure was put on Disraeli to do so. It was said that the whole of Lancashire would be lost and even the vote of credit jeopardized if Derby went. Disraeli gave way. The Queen, whose glee at the resignations of both 'Lords' was immense, received a bitter blow. It required all Disraeli's tact and a letter in the first person beginning 'Madam and Most Beloved Sovereign' to mollify her.

Disraeli had made a serious error in surrendering to this electoral alarmism. Derby returned with the sole object of doing what he earlier advised Carnarvon to do. His object was to prevent 'mischief'. The truth was that the strain of events had produced something little short of a nervous breakdown; he was drinking heavily and he seems to have relapsed into a state of paralysed apathy. In effect foreign policy passed out of his hands. Control fell into the hands of a committee of three, Disraeli, Cairns and Salisbury. Derby signed papers in a curiously detached way almost as if he was a clerk in the Foreign Office with no final responsibility. Yet all the while his resignation with its allegedly portentous consequences hung like a thunder cloud over the Cabinet. This was an impossible situation. No wonder that the very colleagues who had agitated for his recall now began to wish him away, to the point of personal rudeness.

On January 31 an armistice was signed at Adrianople, together with the preliminary bases of peace. These were at once ambiguous and elastic. Lord Tenterden was stirred into sending a formal memorandum to the Cabinet of the most foreboding nature. Even Derby seemed less irresolute than usual, and when a rumour, untrue as it happens, reached London that the Russians were cheating over the armistice and had crossed the demarcation lines, the Cabinet at last took the decision to send the fleet to Constantinople. The Sultan now panicked, fearing that this would precipitate the Russian seizure of the city. But the Cabinet decided to disregard his plea. Salisbury was one of the strongest supporters of the decision. On February 15 Hornby's six ironclads anchored at the island of Prinkipo within sight of the city. The atmosphere in London was one of excitement and mounting war hysteria.

> *Confusion générale, totale, absolue* [wrote Shuvalov to Gorchakov on February 14] . . . *La Reine et ses princes interviennent sans cesse dans les affaires publiques; ils crient bien haut que si l'humiliation de l'Angleterre devait durer quelques jours de plus, ils pendraient Lord Derby au premier arbre de Hyde Park. Les clubs signent des pétitions pour que le Comte soit renvoyé de son poste; l'on se croirait vraiment à Constantinople!*[1]

For the next ten weeks an Anglo-Russian war seemed likely to break out at any moment. The Cabinet was now at last ready to face the realities of the situation. The vote of credit was carried. Preparations were made for an expeditionary force. Lord Napier of Magdala was appointed as commander, with Sir Garnet Wolseley as his chief of staff. How far did this belatedly tough policy succeed in preventing Russia from seizing the Straits? There is no simple answer. As far as the Dardanelles were concerned it undoubtedly did succeed. Derby warned Shuvalov on February 12 that if the Russians entered the Bulair lines or occupied Gallipoli war would follow. Hornby was instructed to resist such a move by force. On February 21 Gorchakov agreed to refrain as long as Britain did so, too.

The situation regarding Constantinople was different. Hornby was told not to open fire if the Russians entered the city, and the words *casus belli* were at no stage used in communications with Shuvalov. He was simply informed that Britain would break off diplomatic relations if the Russians occupied the city without the Sultan's permission. The Tsar, who considered war inevitable now and distrusted English perfidy, was anxious to seize the city, but, with that curious indecisiveness to which he was almost as prone as Derby, he never gave his brother, the Grand Duke Nicholas, who commanded the army, a direct order.[2] Yet even so it is surprising that the Grand Duke failed to take this last crucial step when he

---

[1] Sumner, 380, quoting Seton-Watson transcripts in the British Museum.
[2] ibid., 374–98.

knew the Tsar's wishes and was urged on by Ignatyev and the whole Panslav party. The explanation seems to lie in events in London. On March 27, in reply to Gorchakov's refusal to allow all the terms of the treaty to be open to revision by the forthcoming congress, Disraeli carried further drastic measures in the Cabinet. It was decided to move troops from India to the Mediterranean and use them to seize a *place d'armes*, either Cyprus or Alexandretta. It was also decided to call up the reserves in England. This second step was the only one publicly announced, but it was quite enough to show that British threats were not bluff. Derby now at last resigned, and Salisbury took his place – a clear indication of a firmer policy.

To the Tsar at St Petersburg these developments rendered it more important, not less, to occupy Constantinople. But this was not the reaction of the Grand Duke. He was now convinced that the course pressed on him would cause a complete breach with England, and that in such circumstances the Turks would resist. He believed that the forces at his disposal were not strong enough to defeat a Turkish army of 100,000 men. He refused to act without orders, and these never came. On April 1 the Tsar decided to remove his brother from command, ill health being the excuse. It was not until April 27 that his successor Totleben arrived at San Stefano. By then tension had slackened. The threat of hostilities with Austria-Hungary as well as England loomed large. The war fever at St Petersburg began to abate. On May 9 Totleben dealt a final blow to the war party by reporting to the Tsar in favour of a purely defensive policy. The report was accepted, and the danger of war at once receded. In this somewhat fortuitous manner the military preparations on which Disraeli insisted may be said to have done the trick, not by intimidating the Tsar, but by frightening his brother.

Derby's resignation led to a complete breach with Disraeli. At first all was smooth: generous and polite letters exchanged; an offer of the Garter declined but appreciated. Yet in the end all parties concerned, including Disraeli, behaved badly. Disraeli caused Derby much umbrage by promoting his brother Frederick to Cabinet rank in the ensuing reshuffle – a very palpable move to secure some residue of the Stanley influence in Lancashire. Derby, moreover, was annoyed because the public assumed naturally enough that he had resigned on account of the call-up of the reserve, which seemed a poor reason; whereas, in fact, he felt far more strongly about the other and still secret measures. On April 8

Disraeli made ill-advised and unfair remarks in the House of Lords, which implied that Derby had resigned on a triviality. Derby riposted by hinting at darker causes. No further letters passed between them from that day on. Three months later Derby revealed, as he had permission to do, the decision to seize Cyprus or Alexandretta with an Indian expeditionary force. Since this had in the event proved unnecessary and delicate negotiations concerning the peaceful transfer of Cyprus were still going on with Turkey, the revelation was embarrassing. In the House of Lords, Salisbury compared Derby to Titus Oates and denied, quite incorrectly, that the decision had ever been taken. The Queen wrote a stiff letter which Derby wrongly believed to have been prompted by Disraeli. No *rapprochement* was now possible. Derby resigned from the Conservative party just before the election of 1880 and supported Gladstone. It was a sad end to a personal and political friendship of over thirty years.

2

The Treaty of San Stefano imposed by Ignatyev on the Turks at the pistol point was wholly unacceptable in London. It included a big Bulgaria in the most odious form stretching south of the Balkans to the Aegean Sea and west as far as the Albanian frontier. This provision was as offensive to Austria-Hungary as it was to Britain, and it enraged the numerous non-Bulgar Slav peoples, many of whom would be incorporated into this grandiose new creation. The Asiatic clauses of the treaty were equally disagreeable to the British Government. The Russo-Turkish frontier in Asia Minor was advanced some fifty miles south-west along the Black Sea coast, and nearly a hundred miles in places inland. The Russians acquired Batum, Ardahan, Kars and Bayazid, and they controlled a vital section of the important Trebizond–Erzerum–Tabriz caravan route.

There was only one consolation: the Russian Government conceded at the end of January – they could scarcely do otherwise – that the great powers had a right to be consulted on such modifications of the 1856 and 1871 treaties as were of 'general European interest', and early in March agreement in principle was reached to hold a congress, or conference, at some time in the future. Andrassy proposed Vienna as the *venue*. Gorchakov would only accept Berlin, and, in spite of the Queen's violent protests, Berlin was chosen. But what was meant by 'general European interest'? It had been Gorchakov's apparent determination to reserve the right to exclude whatever Russia saw fit, which prompted Disraeli to propose the measures that finally drove Derby out of the Cabinet. The British Government could not concede unilateral reservation by Russia of *any* of the clauses of the treaty. The prospect of a congress receded into the indefinite future. On April 1 Salisbury issued his famous 'circular' setting out the reasons why Britain could not enter one on Gorchakov's terms, and also why she objected to the Treaty of San Stefano.

The change at the Foreign Office made an immense difference to Disraeli's life. The atmosphere of sullen fog was rapidly dissipated by a mind as sharp and bracing as an east wind. Whereas policy had drifted aimlessly with the ebb and flow of torpid uncertain tides, now it was borne upon a swift current heading for a definite destination. Instead of the confusion and inaction which, in so far as they did not spring from Derby's congenital defects, were symptoms of a fundamental antipathy to the Prime Minister's opinions, clarity, speed and energy characterized the new Foreign Secretary, perhaps the cleverest man to hold that office during the nineteenth century. Disraeli greatly admired his incisive style of writing, his quickness of apprehension, his grasp of detail. Above all he admired his courage – the quality he himself possessed in so pre-eminent a degree. Shortly before his death he said to Salisbury's daughter and biographer, Lady Gwendolen Cecil: 'You will find as you grow older that courage is the rarest of all qualities to be found in public men. Your father is the only man of real courage that it has ever been my lot to work with.'[1]

Salisbury reciprocated this admiration. He could never be an intimate friend of Disraeli, but he found quite suddenly that he no longer distrusted him. He respected Disraeli's lack of hesitation, his readiness to take responsibility, his refusal to shirk the big issues, and he admired the indomitable pluck with which the old statesman overcame age and illness. Moreover, he was touched by Disraeli's gratitude and obvious dependence on him. Salisbury was in the very prime of life. Disraeli was approaching the twilight. He could not be expected to display the energy, the mastery of detail, the command of facts, which are needed in the conduct of diplomacy. Salisbury could and did, and he was determined not to let his chief down.

[1] Cecil, *Salisbury*, ii, 205.

There were other bonds: a common dislike of humbug; the same love of a mordant phrase or a vivid metaphor. It was a most fruitful alliance.

Detailed diplomacy during the next two months was conducted by Salisbury rather than by Disraeli, although Disraeli kept in the closest touch with the Foreign Secretary and conferred with him alone before every Cabinet meeting. Feeling the load lifted to some extent from his shoulders, he began to enjoy dinner parties again, pleading to the Queen, always solicitous for his health, that it was essential because of Corry's absence. 'Lord Beaconsfield assures your Majesty that he is prudent in his social movements . . . There is a certain tact in the management of even great affairs which only can be acquired by feeling the pulse of society. Mr. Corry, who went everywhere, used to perform this office for him, but now he is alone!'[1] Corry's illness prevented Disraeli from carrying out a plan to take a house in Richmond or Wimbledon for the Easter holiday in order to be nearer to London than Hughenden and yet have some country air. Hopeless as always in dealing with domestic affairs, he decided to stay at Hatfield for a few days instead. He thus got to know the Cecil family with some intimacy for the first time. But the country air was not a success: 'A north east blast with a sprinkling of hail', he told Lady Bradford.

Disraeli was determined to force drastic amendments to the Treaty of San Stefano. Accordingly there was no slackening in war preparations, which were pressed on with ostentatious lack of concealment. On April 17 he announced that 7,000 Indian troops had been ordered to Malta – a move which was denounced as unconstitutional by the Opposition, but which impressed St Petersburg. A number of separate influences were now converging to make the Russians less obstinate than hitherto. Throughout April Ignatyev's star was on the wane. Moderate opinion began to see the Treaty of San Stefano not as a triumph of Panslav policy but as the reckless seizure of a position which Russia could not relinquish without humiliation, but could not in the long run hold without a war against England and possibly Austria-Hungary, too. Even Ignatyev saw that some kind of agreement must be reached with one of those powers, but his total failure to secure an accommodation with Andrassy was another stage in his downfall. He faced, too, the unremitting hostility of Gorchakov and the Ministry of Foreign

[1] M. & B., vi, 282.

Affairs. At the end of May he faded from the scene, and departed into angry retirement on his estates at Kiev.

Meanwhile at St Petersburg confusion grew more confounded. Gorchakov was ill and took to his bed, but he was not ill enough to give up responsibility. The Tsar vacillated hopelessly. All initiative ceased. But there was one man who had clear views about what should be done. Shuvalov regarded the Treaty of San Stefano as a disastrous error, and he was convinced by the resignation of Derby, which he deplored, and by the war preparations in London that the British Government really would fight in the last resort. He now seized the strategic opportunity created by the anarchy at St Petersburg to come forward with a policy of his own for an accommodation with England before the Congress met. If he were successful might he not snatch the coveted reversion of the Chancellorship from Ignatyev? He persuaded the Tsar and for several months he was the dictator of Russian foreign policy. Then he, too, was toppled from power and like Ignatyev disappeared into the shadows.

Disraeli and Salisbury considered that the two worst features of San Stefano were the big Bulgaria and Russia's Asiatic gains. In the complicated negotiations with Shuvalov which began on April 29 and ended in the Anglo-Russian Conventions signed at the end of May, Salisbury was concerned above all to reverse or neutralize these. It became clear very early that although the Bulgarian settlement might be drastically changed, there were two things which the Tsar would never surrender, Bessarabia and his acquisition of Batum and Kars. The former was a matter of indifference to Britain. The latter was not, for it was feared to be a jumping off ground for Russian penetration either into Asia Minor or south-east towards the Persian Gulf. On the other hand, it might be possible to neutralize this danger if Britain had a base at the eastern end of the Mediterranean from which she could extend her own military and political influence into Anatolia. Therefore, while negotiating very stiffly with Shuvalov over Transcaucasia, Disraeli and Salisbury pursued at the same time in the utmost secrecy the negotiations with the Sultan which culminated in the Cyprus Convention. If these were successful they would give way on Batum and Kars. If not they would resist to the end. It was not until May 26 that the Sultan, in return for a defensive alliance with England, agreed to the cession of Cyprus and to safeguards for his Christian subjects in Asia Minor, and it was only then that Salisbury could bring the negotiations with Shuvalov to a satisfactory conclusion.

The Anglo-Russian Conventions are described by the leading historian on the subject as 'a very notable success for British diplomacy'.[1] Shuvalov gave way to all the important demands of Salisbury as regards Bulgaria. It was to be divided into two parts, the Balkan range being the boundary. The northern part was to be an autonomous principality, the southern was to remain, with stringent safeguards, subject to Turkish rule, and its access to the Aegean was to be cut off. The precise line of the Balkan frontier and the precise military rights of the Sultan in southern Bulgaria were left for the Congress, as also was the question of the Straits, the degree of European participation in organizing the two Bulgarias, and the length of Russian occupation. In Asia, Salisbury agreed to the cession of Batum and Kars in return for a Russian promise to acquire no more territory in Asiatic Turkey. But he did succeed in moving the Russians out of Bayazid, so that they no longer bestrode The Trebizond–Tabriz caravan route. Nothing was said about the Cyprus Convention. At the same time what Andrassy called 'a general agreement as between gentlemen' was made with Austria-Hungary. The western frontier of north Bulgaria was not to extend beyond the Morava River. England would undertake to support the annexation of Bosnia, but Salisbury preferred not to commit himself about Herzegovina.

Bismarck, informed of all these preliminary arrangements, now agreed to the fixing of a definite date for the Congress. Important matters were still left open, and it is a myth to suggest that the Congress was a mere façade registering decisions already taken in secret between the principal powers concerned. But there seemed a sufficient measure of agreement for Bismarck to run the remote risk that the Congress might fail, and he was determined to use all his own strength and prestige to see that it did not. The first meeting of the Congress of Berlin was fixed to take place at two o'clock on June 13.

3

There could be no question who would represent England. When it had been merely a matter of a conference the Cabinet had selected Lord Lyons, but at a full-scale congress attended by the

[1] Sumner, 495.

imperial chancellors of the Northern Courts Disraeli and Salisbury were bound to be the English plenipotentiaries. Disraeli was seventy-three, by no means robust even before he left, and towards the end of the Congress he was in a state of semi-collapse. But he was determined to go, and he politely brushed aside the Queen's anxiety about his health. He travelled with the utmost leisure, taking four days on the journey, stopping first at Calais, then at Brussels, where he dined with the King of the Belgians, and finally at Cologne, before arriving at the Kaiserhof Hotel in Berlin at eight o'clock on June 11. He was therefore fresh and well able to cope with an unexpected request to call on Bismarck that same evening. The preliminary meeting did not go too well. 'Not unsatisfactory', Disraeli describes it to the Queen, which can be translated a good deal less favourably. But this state of affairs soon ended. Bismarck and Disraeli came to respect each other, and none of the many anecdotes about the Congress is better known than Bismarck's famous words: '*Der alte Jude, das ist der Mann.*'

In many respects the alliance could have been predicted. Both men prided themselves on *realpolitik*, and had a sovereign contempt for anything that smacked of cant, especially religious cant, which they were all too ready to suspect in any humanitarian movement. Both were quite indifferent to the claims of the Balkan Slavs, regarding them either as hostile pieces in a great game of diplomatic chess or as tiresome disturbers of the European balance of power. Bismarck, like Disraeli, had been a Byronic romantic in the past, and thought in those terms still. Both men loved sweeping phrases, high-flown generalities, cynical asides. They were impatient of detail, bored by the humdrum. They shared the same broad views on policy: at home the preservation of an aristocratic settlement, Junker supremacy in Prussia, the ascendancy of the landed class in England; abroad the bold assertion of those national interests of which they seemed to be the incarnation in their respective countries. Bismarck admired Disraeli's courage, power of decision and refusal to be bogged down in details. In contrast he disliked Salisbury, who had the ungrateful task of negotiating on all the secondary matters, and who lacked the pliability and *bonhomie* to make his obduracy acceptable. There was another bond between Disraeli and Bismarck: neither of them could abide Gladstone.

Disraeli was from the start 'the lion of the Congress', as Sumner calls him. Everyone wanted to see him and talk to him. His extra-

ordinary career and mysterious origins fascinated the whole of the
cosmopolitan world assembled at Berlin. Stories of the long-vanished
romance of his youth were revived again and *Henrietta Temple*
became the rage in the fashionable world. Disraeli's vitality was
astounding. The social life at Berlin, to judge from his own account,
would alone have been enough to exhaust most men. Bismarck and
the Crown Princess fêted him incessantly, and every delegation gave
grand parties. There were receptions and dinners night after night.
Disraeli scarcely missed a single one. He was indefatigable in making
the acquaintance of every person who mattered, and he never
relaxed for a moment in his struggle for British interests. Then
there were the long and tiring meetings of the Congress itself and,
although it is true that most of the really tedious work fell on Salisbury, Disraeli's presence was essential. His was the personality that
alone could enforce British claims. Yet in spite of all this he found
time to write lengthy accounts of each day to Queen Victoria in his
most scintillating vein, packed with vivid pictures, incisive pen
portraits and amusing stories. Nor, it need scarcely be said, did his
correspondence with Lady Bradford and Lady Chesterfield ever
flag.

The Russian plenipotentiaries were Gorchakov and Shuvalov.
The former, vain, semi-senile and addicted to making absurd scenes,
was a very dubious asset to his own side. But Disraeli hated to
quarrel with him. Long ago he had been Lady Londonderry's lover.
Later she had told him that Disraeli would one day be Prime
Minister, and she hoped that they would be friends.[1] Shuvalov,
however, made up for some of his master's deficiencies, for he was
the ablest and best tempered of all the diplomats present. 'Schou
fights a difficult and losing battle with marvellous talent and
temper', wrote Disraeli to Lady Bradford. 'He is a first rate parliamentary debater, never takes a note, and yet in his reply never
misses a point.' His battle was made no easier by the malignant
jealousy of Gorchakov, who denounced him incessantly behind his
back to St Petersburg. In the circumstances the Russian delegation
was severely handicapped. It had to contend not only with Britain
but with Austria-Hungary, represented by Andrassy and a formidable team of assistants. Andrassy was perhaps the most successful
of the plenipotentiaries, and in the end secured nearly all Vienna's
objectives with the minimum of demonstration or fuss.

[1] Zetland, ii, 174–5, Disraeli to Lady Bradford, June 26, 1878.

The literature on the Berlin Congress is immense. We are concerned here only with Disraeli's role. He concentrated primarily on three matters left open by the Anglo-Russian Conventions: first that the Sultan should have full military rights in the southern of the two Bulgarias; secondly that the Balkan frontier should be so drawn that the Turks controlled the vital passes; thirdly that the province should be called Eastern Roumelia, not Southern Bulgaria, so as to strike a blow at any subsequent moves for unification. Disraeli caused a great sensation by making his opening address to the Congress in English, not French – thus offending the Russians. According to a well-known story, he was persuaded into doing so by Lord Odo Russell. The Ambassador, acutely conscious of the Prime Minister's atrocious French accent, urged him not to disappoint the delegates who were looking forward to hearing a master of the English language. But this explanation is unhappily by no means certain.[1] Whatever Disraeli's motive – it was probably sheer ignorance of French – his action set a note of British intransigence from the start.

Intransigence sometimes pays. Disraeli got his way over Bulgaria in almost all essentials. He did so by allowing it to be known that he would break up the Congress if the Russians resisted. But the other well-known story, that they only came to heel because he told Corry to order a special train, and that Bismarck alarmed at the prospect of a total collapse put pressure on them to give way, seems to be a myth. Disraeli may have ordered, or said he would order, the train. Bismarck undoubtedly did do all he could to avert a breach. But these events occurred on June 21, whereas the Tsar's instructions to yield were sent by special messenger from St Petersburg on the 20th. It was probably Disraeli's strong language earlier to Shuvalov, reported no doubt to the Tsar, which determined the nature of the instructions.

Disraeli succeeded over Bulgaria, but not over a secondary matter which he also strongly pressed. This was the question of Batum. Under the Anglo-Russian Conventions, England promised not to make a *casus belli* of Batum. Unfortunately the Foreign Office, true to form as regards security, surpassed all previous efforts by allowing the leakage of the text of the Conventions. It appeared in the *Globe* on June 14 owing to the scandalous laxity of the

[1] Lord Odo undoubtedly did make such representations, but it is quite likely that Disraeli had already made up his mind.

Foreign Office in employing as a copyist a temporary and underpaid clerk who sold it to the Press. This was highly embarrassing, because the Cyprus Convention which was to be the British compensation for the cession of Batum could not yet be announced. The jingo party in England, already half convinced that Disraeli and Salisbury would give too much away, was up in arms at once. Accordingly Disraeli and Salisbury tried to limit the damage by at least securing that Batum should not become a naval base. The Russians agreed that Batum should be 'a free port', but this was not enough. Salisbury wanted to add the words '*exclusivement commerciel*', but Gorchakov, catching Disraeli when he was ill, managed to get his agreement to the word '*essentiellement*' instead of '*exclusivement*'. Eight years later the Russians turned Batum into a fortified base, arguing that this was not prohibited by the new wording. Gorchakov also tricked Disraeli over the precise frontier by some jiggery-pokery with maps -- a favourite manoeuvre in Russian diplomacy. But this was not really of great importance and by now the Cyprus Convention had been announced. It placated the jingoes at home, although it made a bad impression on some of the delegations at Berlin, especially the Russians. Bismarck, however, was delighted. 'This is progress,' he said, and Disraeli commented to the Queen, 'Evidently his idea of progress is seizing something.'[1] Cyprus was a sensational stroke, and Disraeli was again the focus of all attention.

The Treaty of Berlin was formally signed at four o'clock on July 13. Disraeli had been seriously ill during the later stages of the congress, and Dr Kidd had to be sent for. He was able to put his patient on his feet to attend the final act of formal ratification, and Disraeli added his own signature to the document. But he was too exhausted to attend the farewell banquet that night. He set out with Salisbury on the return journey to England next day. To the cheering crowd which, thanks partly to some organization by Lord Henry Lennox, greeted them as they drove to Downing Street he declared that he had brought back 'peace with honour'. The Queen offered him the Garter, a dukedom, and the settlement of a peerage on his brother or nephew. He declined everything except the Garter and made it a condition that Salisbury should receive the same honour. It was a triumphant moment. 'High and low', wrote the Queen, 'are delighted, excepting Mr. Gladstone who is frantic . . .'[2]

[1] M. & B., vi, 332.
[2] ibid., 347.

Disraeli was in no mood to care about Gladstone. When the latter denounced the Cyprus Convention as an 'insane covenant' and an 'act of duplicity', Disraeli in a speech at a public banquet described Gladstone as 'a sophistical rhetorician inebriated with the exuberance of his own verbosity and gifted with an egotistical imagination that can at all times command an interminable and inconsistent series of arguments to malign an opponent and glorify himself'. Not perhaps a very felicitous choice of epithets, but the provocation was considerable. Disraeli made some remarks of the same tenor a few days later in the House of Lords and declared that Gladstone had described him as 'devilish'. Gladstone, by now very excited, imprudently asked him to supply a list of the personal epithets which he was alleged to have used together with the occasions. Disraeli replied in the third person that he was busy and that the research would take some time. Meanwhile he instanced one or two of Gladstone's speeches, but he conceded that the word 'devilish' which he had attributed to Gladstone was used by 'one of Mr. Gladstone's friends, kindly enquiring of Mr. Gladstone how they were "to get rid of this Mephistopheles": but as Mr. Gladstone proceeded to explain the mode, probably the Birmingham Caucus, Lord Beaconsfield may perhaps be excused for assuming that Mr. Gladstone sanctioned the propriety of the scarcely complimentary appellation'.[1]

Disraeli was now at the height of his fame and fortune. The Treaty of Berlin was regarded throughout the country as a major victory for British diplomacy. The old Jew was indeed the man. But achievements of this sort cannot be judged simply by popular applause. What sort of balance sheet can be drawn eighty years later?

There will probably never be any agreement about the rights and wrongs of English policy during the Eastern crisis even when it is viewed in the longer perspective of history. On the debit side it can be said that the Berlin settlement deprived the Sultan of far more territory than the British Government would have considered tolerable when the crisis began: that Balkan nationalism was to be a more effective barrier to Russian advance than the Sick Man of Europe could be; in particular that the apprehensions felt at the creation of a Big Bulgaria were falsified less than ten years later by the anti-Russian attitude which the country then adopted. Then,

[1] ibid., 356–8.

there are wider questions. Was it really necessary to bolster up Turkey in order to protect the route to India? Was the disruption of the *Dreikaiserbund* – Disraeli's other defence – worth all the trouble? Could any supposed British interest outweigh the moral issues raised by the atrocities? What was the justification for annexing Cyprus, a possession destined to cause nothing but difficulty in the long run?

Yet there are powerful points on the credit side, too. Russian troops almost certainly would have entered Constantinople but for British threats, even though these threats contained a large element of bluff. For good or ill Russia is not in Constantinople yet. A Big Bulgaria with frontiers comprising a polyglot population in which the Bulgars were a minority would have given far more scope for Russian penetration than the Bulgaria created at Berlin. Cyprus made sense as a naval base when Britain had none east of Malta, and as a *point d'appui* for the British military consuls in Asia Minor to whom Salisbury attached genuine importance and who were perhaps the only hope of enforcing some degree of reform in Asiatic Turkey. But the occupation of Alexandria in 1882 changed the situation; there was now no need for a naval base and no one bothered to deepen the harbour at Famagusta for ironclads – an omission which was to be embarrassing nearly eighty years later when the Suez expedition was being planned. As for the military consuls, Gladstone recalled them after his victory in 1880, thus extinguishing the last flicker of hope that Turkey might reform. These developments were not predictable in 1878, and in any case they still left one item on the credit side: there was at least that much less of the world governed by the unspeakable Turk, a fact which ought logically to have pleased the 'atrocitarians'; but somehow it did not.

Disraeli's fear about the route to India was widely held, though it may have been unwarranted. Certainly Constantinople was a long way from the Suez Canal. Yet, improbable though the menace now seems, the fact remains that armies had in the past made the journey, notably Mehemet Ali's over forty years earlier, though in the reverse direction. It was hard to predict quite what the consequences of a complete disruption of the Ottoman Empire at the hands of Russia would be. Salisbury, most sceptical of all the Cabinet in regard to the Indian argument, was convinced that Britain must prevent the fall of Constantinople, at the cost of war if

necessary. Although the Tsar, Gorchakov and Shuvalov now appear
from their published correspondence to have had moderate aims, it
was impossible for Disraeli to see into their hands, and if he had,
how could he have been sure that some sudden gust of Panslav
enthusiasm would not have blown the cards out of the window. It is
hard to believe that the Russian army, once in Constantinople,
would ever have retired save under duress, which in spite of Disraeli's confidence Britain was in no position to apply. Disraeli's
ignorance of military matters was an asset when it came to bluff,
for he genuinely believed what he said, and being convinced he
sounded convincing. It might have been disastrous if there had
been a real war.

As for the aim of disrupting the *Dreikaiserbund*, it must be judged
in the light of what one considers to be the general aims of British
policy. To isolationists it no doubt seemed pointless. But Disraeli
was emphatically not an isolationist, and statesmen must to some
extent, though not exclusively, be judged by their own intentions.
He believed that Britain was not only a great power but a great
European power. It was by no means an unreasonable objective in
the aftermath of French defeat to endeavour to shake the alliance
between the three 'Northern Courts' which seemed bent on excluding all the other powers from an effective say in the affairs of
Europe. The *Dreikaiserbund* never did recover from the Eastern
crisis while Disraeli was in office, and its later revival after Gladstone put 'Beaconsfieldism' into reverse took a different and less
stable form. It is true that Disraeli's strong emphasis on this aspect
of his policy was in some measure retrospective, but there is plenty
of evidence to show that it played a part, if not the major part, in
his calculations all along.

Disraeli's policy was not always consistent. Foreign policy
seldom is. He took opportunities as they came. He sometimes contradicted himself. He sometimes veered with changing winds. But
on the whole one can say of British policy over the Eastern question
that it was more fully the personal responsibility of the Prime
Minister than any of the other policies associated with his régime.
Some of these, like the successful measures of social reform, had his
benevolent support, but were essentially the work of his colleagues.
Others like the Bill 'to put down Ritualism' and the Imperial Title
Bill were forced on him by the Queen. Others again, such as the
disastrous Afghan and South African wars, were the result of dis-

obedience or impetuosity by men on the spot whom he had to defend. But there is no doubt that foreign policy, from the Suez Canal purchase to the Berlin Congress and beyond, was essentially Disraeli's. He can neither be denied the credit nor escape the blame.

Whichever view is taken of the merits of that policy, it is hard to dispute the skill with which he steered his way through the uproar of the Gladstonian hurricane, between the Scylla of the 'three Lords' and the charybdis of the Queen and the war party. It should not be forgotten that as well as the pro-Russians there was an extremist pro-Turk right-wing group which regarded him as too soft. 'What are you waiting for, Lord Beaconsfield?' cried an indignant lady of fashion at the height of the crisis during a banquet. 'At this moment for the potatoes, madam,' he calmly replied. But, although he could put people like that in their places it was not so easy when the Queen herself seemed to be threatening abdication unless he declared war on Russia. Disraeli did not want war. He wished to preserve as much of Turkey as he could, stop the Russians entering Constantinople, break up the *Dreikaiserbund*, if possible without war, though he did not flinch at war if there was no alternative. He succeeded in his object, despite the divisions of the Cabinet, despite the opposition of Derby, who was not only Foreign Secretary but one of the most powerful figures in the Conservative party, despite the deep divisions in the country, despite Gladstone and despite his own bad health.

Of course he made mistakes, the worst being total failure to feel and therefore comprehend the indignation caused by the Bulgarian atrocities. Refusal to make any concession to the humanitarians was a disadvantage even from his own point of view. It meant that anything like a national consensus was unobtainable, and by stimulating the fury of the Opposition he put unnecessary difficulties in the way of his own chosen course. No wonder Cairns could write to Cross: 'I wish D. had a touch even of the slightest sentiment.'[1] This attitude was honest, a part of his dislike of humbug and hypocrisy, but it seemed heartless, and in some quarters it was never forgiven.

None the less, judged by the criteria of tactical skill and achievement of objectives, Disraeli's foreign policy was an undoubted success. As for the Berlin settlement, of course it was not perfect.

[1] Cross, *A Political History*, 38.

No treaty ever is. But it was followed by almost as long a period of peace between the European great powers as the interval separating the Crimean War from the Congress of Vienna. As one of the two principal plenipotentiaries at Berlin Disraeli must share with Bismarck some part of the credit.

CHAPTER XXVIII

Afghans and Zulus
1878–9

1

For the moment Disraeli possessed a prestige unsurpassed by any statesman of his time. After his death Gladstone in a generous tribute selected the return from Berlin as the apogee of his rival's career, and applied to him the lines of Virgil:

> *Aspice ut insignis spoliis Marcellus opimis*
> *Ingreditur, victorque viros supereminet omnes.*

Two years earlier Bagehot had said of Disraeli '. . . though he charmed Parliament he never did anything more. He had no influence with the country.' The comment, doubtfully true even then, certainly could not have been made in the summer of 1878. His fame had spread far and wide throughout the land. He was a national figure, the hero of the hour.

Ought he to have taken his opportunity and held a general election? The idea was discussed in Cabinet on August 10, but rejected. The usage of those days was that Parliament, unless some special reason could be adduced to the contrary, should last into its sixth year and preferably until the completion of its sixth session. But the Parliament of 1874 was only four and a half years old, and the Government's majority on all issues of importance remained unimpaired. A dissolution would have been hard to justify, the Chief Whip was against it, and there seemed no reason to think that the party's standing in the country would decline. The general verdict has been that Disraeli missed a golden chance of renewing the Conservatives' mandate for another six years, but Professor Hanham, whose study is the most recent, argues otherwise.[1] While agreeing that a dissolution in 1878 would have been more favourable than in 1880, he doubts whether the Conservatives would have secured an overall majority of more than three or four at the earlier date, and they might even have been in a minority against Liberals

---

[1] *Elections and Electioneering*, 227–9.

and Home Rulers combined. Unemployment had been rising steadily, and the municipal elections that year did not go well for the Conservatives. It is true that by-elections honours were even, three losses and three gains, which was a rather better result than in the preceding four years, when losses outnumbered gains by ten to six. It seems on balance unlikely that Disraeli missed any great opportunity by postponing the election.[1]

What cannot be doubted is that from then onwards his fortunes began to fail and nothing went well for the Government. To a deepening agricultural and industrial depression were added two serious mishaps abroad, which, the Opposition could argue, stemmed from an over-ambitious imperial policy, the disaster at Isandhlwana and the massacre of Kabul. Disraeli's personal responsibility for these setbacks was minimal, but luck has always been as much an ingredient of a statesman's success as skill. During the last year and a half of his administration Disraeli and his colleagues undeniably lacked luck.

The Cabinet did not lack talent. It had largely been reconstructed in the last two years and consisted now of the following:

First Lord of the Treasury	Earl of Beaconsfield*
Lord Chancellor	Earl Cairns*
Lord President of the Council	Duke of Richmond*
Lord Privy Seal	Duke of Northumberland
Home Secretary	R. A. Cross*
Foreign Secretary	Marquis of Salisbury
Colonial Secretary	Sir Michael Hicks Beach
War Secretary	Col. the Hon. F. A. Stanley
Indian Secretary	Viscount Cranbrook (Gathorne Hardy)
Chancellor of the Exchequer	Sir Stafford Northcote*
First Lord of the Admiralty	W. H. Smith
President of the Board of Trade	Viscount Sandon
Postmaster-General	Lord John Manners*

An Asterisk denotes those who held the same office in 1874.

In effect, Derby, Carnarvon, Malmesbury and Ward Hunt had been replaced, though not always in the exact office, by F. A. Stanley, Hicks Beach, Northumberland and W. H. Smith; and one

---

[1] The notion that he did so in order not to gain an unfair partisan advantage from an issue of foreign policy is too naïve to be taken seriously, although Gathorne Hardy (*Memoir*, ii, 78) seems to have believed it. Disraeli was made of sterner stuff than that.

extra post, the Board of Trade, had been brought into the Cabinet, held by Sandon who was competent, in place of Adderley, created Lord Norton, who was not.[1] With two exceptions these changes left the Government stronger, or at any rate no weaker, than it was before. The exceptions were the elevation of Hardy to the Lords, which further weakened the front bench in the House of Commons, and the appointment of the Duke of Northumberland as Lord Privy Seal. That office had given Disraeli much anxiety since Malmesbury's resignation in 1876. For more than eighteen months he doubled it with his own post in order to preserve the balance of six peers and six commoners, but the Queen feared that too prolonged tenure by him might make the economists demand its suppression. The problem would have been easier if it had not been assumed that the Lord Privy Seal must be in the Lords. Eventually Carnarvon's resignation released a place for a peer. The choice of the Duke, who was quite undistinguished, caused some amusement, and was attributed – perhaps rightly – to the Prime Minister's romantic penchant for the great noble houses.

The difficulties which beset Disraeli over India were not solely due to bad luck. He must bear the responsibility of choosing, admittedly after trying many others first, the Viceroy whose disobedience led indirectly to disaster. The fact was that Lytton's startling elevation from Minister in Lisbon to Viceroy of India went to his head. It is true that he had some virtues. Like Disraeli he was commendably free from any racial prejudice, and he severely punished its worst manifestations in India. He introduced many valuable reforms. He was undoubtedly both clever and industrious. The notion that he was a lazy poetaster, launching witticisms to his parasites, was quite incorrect. He certainly caused much offence at the Viceregal Court by his reckless repartee, but this was quite compatible with hard work. Nor is it true to say that he was a mere yes man to the Prime Minister – another common Liberal charge. On the contrary, it would have been better for all concerned if he had been less rather than more independent of London.

But he was curiously unbalanced in judgement. For example, he stirred even Derby to remonstrance by circulating in the autumn of 1877 a pamphlet denouncing the Government for seeking an alliance with Russia. Since England was then on the verge of war

[1] As a result the Cabinet numbered thirteen instead of the twelve to which Disraeli had for long tried to limit it.

with Russia, his apprehensions seem to have been superfluous. 'This production is either the result of insanity or intrigue,' wrote Derby. 'In the latter point of view I fail to see what he has to get by it: in the former the look out for India is unpleasant.'[1] Disraeli on this occasion issued a rebuke, but in general until the Afghan imbroglio disillusioned him he defended Lytton with vigour both to his colleagues and the Queen. He could forgive a great deal in a man whom he believed to have 'imagination'. 'We wanted', he told Salisbury, 'a man of ambition, imagination, some vanity and much will – and we have got him.'[2] Salisbury let this pass at the time, but in a later letter was sceptical. He feared, he said, that Cranbrook trusted Lytton too much. 'He does not realise sufficiently the gaudy and theatrical ambition which is the Viceroy's leading passion.'[3]

The problem of India at this time was Afghanistan, a problem that was itself the by-product of a greater, indeed the one that underlay the whole Eastern crisis, the threat of Russia's advance in central Asia. It was from Afghanistan that from time immemorial northern conquerors had invaded India. If this mysterious, mountainous, half-savage land fell into the control of an enemy power, it could be a threat to the whole stability of British rule. As early as the 1830s Russian agents established themselves at Kabul, and the first Afghan War (1839–42) was successfully fought in order to oust them. For a long time after that Russia was quiescent. In 1857 a treaty was signed by Lord Dalhousie with the Amir Dost Mohammed, and there was no attempt from the Afghans to interfere with the course of the Indian Mutiny. Yet even this apparently successful piece of diplomacy did not go uncriticized. The great John Lawrence viewed it with misgiving as liable to embroil the Government of India in the dark and bloodthirsty convolutions of Afghan politics. In 1863 Dost Mohammed died and a fierce wâr of succession ensued. Lawrence, now Viceroy, firmly declined to intervene, and confined himself to recognizing the victor, who, of course, felt no particular gratitude for the gesture.

From the period of the Mutiny or even earlier there had been two opposed schools of thought about the north-west frontier: the advocates of the 'Forward Policy', such as Lords Dalhousie and

[1] Hughenden Papers, Box 113, B/XX/S/1343, October 9, 1877.
[2] M. & B., vi, 379, April 1, 1877.
[3] Salisbury Papers, Salisbury to Disraeli, October 10, 1878, copy.

Canning, believed that India would not be secure unless Afghan
foreign policy was conducted on advice from Simla; on the other
hand, Lawrence and the supporters of 'Masterly Inactivity', as
it came to be known, regarded the Indus rather than the Hindu
Kush as the natural frontier of India, and considered that the barbarous tribes beyond should be left alone unless they showed some
signs of attempting to cross it. Lawrence, the only Indian civilian
since Warren Hastings to rise to the Viceroyalty, had an immense
prestige with the whole Indian administration, and his doctrine
became the accepted orthodoxy, especially in Liberal circles. Nor
was it in practice challenged by the Conservatives in 1866–8; Lord
Mayo, their own nominee as Lawrence's successor in 1869, made no
new departure. He received the victorious Amir Sher Ali, but gave
him neither the treaty, subsidy, nor dynastic pledge which he
sought.

It was not likely that Disraeli, once in possession of untrammelled
power, would be content with a policy of masterly inactivity. As
soon as he returned to office in 1874 he began to chafe at the attitude
of Lord Northbrook, the Viceroy whom Gladstone had appointed
after the murder of Mayo in 1872. Moreover, the situation had
changed. It could be argued that Lawrence's policy was safe and
economical only while there was no major hostile power pressing
upon the farther frontier of Afghanistan, but that the Russian
advance in central Asia made this no longer true. As early as 1870
General Kaufman, the Russian Governor of Turkestan, had entered
into friendly negotiations with Sher Ali. The Amir understandably
wished to know where he stood with Britain. Once again he asked
for a treaty of assistance in case of Russian attack. Even the
cautious Northbrook would have agreed to this, but the Duke of
Argyll, in one of his last dispatches as Gladstone's Indian Secretary,
refused.

Although the actual moment chosen by Northbrook to resign was
inconvenient, both Disraeli and Salisbury welcomed the chance of
getting in their own man. Lytton was left in no doubt that masterly
inactivity had ceased to be the official policy; his first task would be
to persuade the Amir to receive a permanent British mission from
which it would be possible to send information and countermine the
Russians. For two years he made little progress. Sher Ali was
suspicious and Lytton dared not quarrel with him as long as there
was any chance of an Anglo-Russian war, for one of the principal

plans in such a campaign was an invasion of Asiatic Russia by a British Indian army marching through Afghanistan.[1] This scheme, sufficiently crackbrained on the most favourable assumptions, stood no chance at all unless the Amir was ready to help in supplying food, etc., for the troops. But the Amir, convinced that the army massed on his frontier was aimed not at Russia but himself, refused to co-operate.

At last in July 1878 the Viceroy's opportunity came. A Russian mission under General Stolietov arrived in Kabul despite a formal protest from Sher Ali, and was received by him with full honours. Lytton was determined to compel the Amir to receive a British mission, and not only that, to dismiss the Russians, too. The Russians had repeatedly disclaimed any desire to incorporate Afghanistan into their sphere of interest. Moreover, the Congress of Berlin had ended any danger of a general Anglo-Russian war, and hence any need to be tender towards the Amir's susceptibilities. Lytton asked for authority from London at the end of July to send a mission. Authority was given on August 3, but the Viceroy was clearly told that the route should be through Kandahar and not via the Khyber Pass. Lytton, however, was determined to take the second route and made his preparations accordingly, throughout August and with much publicity. In London there was considerable discussion whether to treat the matter as a purely Indian affair or at the same time to send a diplomatic protest to St Petersburg.[2] At first it was decided to make no representations through the Foreign Office and Cranbrook gave Lytton the impression that this course had been agreed. A few days later Cranbrook changed his mind and pressed the reluctant Salisbury, who regarded such protests as futile, to send a dispatch to St Petersburg. It went on August 19. It is a moot point whether the ministers concerned, Disraeli, Salisbury, and Cranbrook, intended to await an answer before finally authorizing Lytton to send his mission. A month later the first two maintained that they did, and subsequently Cranbrook agreed with them. But if so Cranbrook seems to have acted with remarkable negligence at the time, for he never even told Lytton that the dispatch had been sent, let alone that the mission was not to go before it had been ans-

[1] ibid., Lytton to Salisbury, October 28, November 8, November 30, 1876, May 21, 1877, July 13, 1878.
[2] See for a full discussion of this and other aspects of the origins of the Second Afghan War, Maurice Cowling, 'Lytton, the Cabinet and the Russians, August to November, 1878', *English Historical Review*, lxxvi (1961), 60–79.

wered.[1] Cranbrook was inattentive and slightly lazy, and his heart was no longer in politics. From mid-August he was on holiday in Scotland, and, although he 'managed to get some Afghan reading done'[2] on Sir John Fowler's yacht, he was away from his files and more interested in deer-stalking than in India. Nevertheless it seems extraordinary that he should not have mentioned such an important proviso in his letters to the Viceroy, and one cannot help wondering whether all three ministers were not being wise after the event.

For, whether or not Cranbrook was keeping Lytton properly informed, it seems clear that Disraeli, along with Salisbury and Cranbrook, did not appreciate the nature of the Viceroy's plans until very late in the day. The telegrams which Lytton sent during July and August were vague and sketchy; it was not until September 9 that the full details of his instructions to the head of the mission, General Sir Neville Chamberlain, arrived in London. Then for the first time Disraeli realized that Lytton intended to make Sher Ali's dismissal of General Stolietov's mission a prior condition of sending his own and reopening Anglo-Afghan negotiations. This was a very different matter from merely sending a British mission, and only justifiable on the ground that a major confrontation with Russia was necessary. To Lytton in India, Stolietov's presence at Kabul might seem to warrant such a trial of strength. To Disraeli and Salisbury the issue was not so simple. The decision to send Stolietov had obviously been taken many weeks before he arrived. Might not his presence be a carry-over from an earlier state of affairs, a riposte to the British gesture of bringing Indian troops to the Mediterranean? Was not the decision to protest to St Petersburg – anyway in retrospect, whatever was thought at the time – intended to secure an answer to just this question? Disraeli expressed his alarm at Lytton's ignorance of the negotiations with Russia.[3] The three ministers agreed that Lytton must postpone the dispatch of the mission until the Foreign Office had received an answer.

But Lytton felt himself too far committed to withdraw. He expected Ali to accept the mission; he believed that the Government at heart wanted him to go ahead and was only inhibited by 'that deformed and abortive offspring of perennial political fornication', as he elegantly described the British Constitution in a letter to

---

[1] ibid., 66.
[2] Gathorne Hardy, ii, 81.
[3] M. & B., vi, 380–1, quoting Disraeli to Cranbrook, September 12, 13 and 17, 1878.

Cranbrook.[1] On September 13 Lytton received from London clear orders not to act until a reply had arrived to the dispatch to St Petersburg. This was the first that he had heard of Salisbury's diplomatic protest. On September 16 he telegraphed Chamberlain to delay for five days. On the 21st, although he still had no authority from the India Office, he ordered Chamberlain to enter Afghanistan. It was an act of double disobedience, for the Khyber Pass route was the one chosen, but Lytton was probably right in thinking that no one would have minded if it had come off. Alas, it did not. The General was turned back at the frontier, a rebuff which made war virtually inevitable, given the considerations of Oriental prestige and 'face' which then prevailed. Disraeli was very angry. 'When V-Roys and Comms-in-Chief disobey orders, they ought to be sure of success in their mutiny', he wrote to Cranbrook. 'Lytton by disobeying orders had only secured insult and failure.'[2] The Amir's 'insolent reply', as Lytton called it, arrived in London on October 19 and Disraeli was clear that Lytton must be supported. Even Salisbury, who felt far more bitter against the Viceroy, agreed. The Cabinet decided to send a final ultimatum, carefully worded to strengthen the *casus belli* and at Lytton's request expiring on November 20.[3]

In the interval Disraeli made his annual oration at the Lord Mayor's dinner. The speech with its keynote sentence – 'The fate of England is in the hands of England' – was a bold justification of the whole policy that culminated at Berlin and a vigorous onslaught against those who declared that British power was on the wane and that 'ours will be the lot of Genoa and Venice and Holland'. But to the consternation of his colleagues Disraeli made a reference to India's north-west frontier as 'a haphazard and not a scientific frontier', and hinted that steps would soon be taken to 'terminate all this inconvenience'. The Opposition was not slow to accuse the Government of planning war against the Afghans in order to rectify the frontier – a charge which was untrue, but stuck none the less.

The Amir made no answer to Lytton's ultimatum, which was sent on November 2. With its expiry hostilities became inevitable, and Disraeli effectively defended his policy at the necessary autumn session of Parliament on December 11. Fortunately the campaign

[1] Quoted, Cowling, 70.
[2] M. & B., vi, 382.
[3] ibid., 386–8, quoting Disraeli's account of the meeting to the Queen.

went well, thanks largely to the brilliant operations of the column commanded by General Roberts. Sher Ali fled to Turkestan, leaving the country in charge of his son, Yakub Khan, whom he had imprisoned for the last five years. The latter, though in reality both weak and shifty, seemed well disposed to Britain. A treaty was signed in May 1879 after months of negotiation, and a mission was installed at Kabul under Sir Louis gavagnari, an officer as gallant as he was gullible. There was no reaction from Russia. Lytton's policy seemed for the moment to have been vindicated, and Disraeli gave no hint to the Viceroy that his disobedience had caused such disapproval.

Posterity has correctly judged the Second Afghan War as unnecessary. There is no evidence that Russia harboured any deep-laid plans. The Cabinet was right in regarding Lytton's instructions to the Chamberlain mission as altogether too high-handed. The blame can be varyingly apportioned between Cranbrook's slackness and Lytton's 'gaudy vanity'. Apart from the initial error of appointing the Viceroy, Disraeli cannot be held seriously responsible. Perhaps, as with the communications which were passing at roughly the same time between Hicks Beach and Frere in South Africa, he ought to have made sure that the men on the spot were fully apprised of the limits within which the Government expected them to work. But this would have required much interference, whereas Disraeli believed in leaving departmental ministers to get on with their job. We must remember, too, that the Congress of Berlin had only ended in the middle of July and that a younger man than the Prime Minister might well have been exhausted by the experience. The truth was that, in an era of slow communications and an ill co-ordinated governmental machine, it was not at all easy to control those high officers of state whom an unkind person once described as 'prancing proconsuls'. It was traditional to give them a large measure of independence, and the many instances where this policy paid off should be set against the few which ended in trouble.

2

It would be an error to imagine that after the Congress of Berlin the Eastern question went into cold storage. Of course, Disraeli and Salisbury would have liked it to have done so; indeed, in the immediate aftermath they talked as if it had. The more trouble there was in enforcing the settlement with the concomitant danger of renewed hostilities, the easier it would be for the Opposition to belittle their success. As Disraeli observed to both Cranbrook and Salisbury in a slightly different context, the Government would be popular while the country believed that it had secured 'Peace with Honor . . . but if they find there is no peace they will be apt to conclude there is also no honour'.[1] Unfortunately the Congress had left some very awkward problems behind. The two that most affected England were first the question of Russian evacuation of the Balkans, second the reform of Turkish rule in Asia Minor, which was a corollary of the Cyprus Convention.[2]

The second was never solved. Even before Salisbury left office he had almost given it up as hopeless. In the summer of 1879 the Sultan dismissed Khaireddin, the 'liberal' Grand Vizier and with him went the last remnants of Layard's influence in Constantinople. Whatever faint chance there was of reform finally evaporated with the Liberal victory in 1880, when Gladstone, by recalling the British military consuls installed in Anatolia, removed the only appeal that might have influenced Abdul Hamid. But this was not the most urgent problem. More pressing by far was the need to get the Russians out of both Bulgarias. They were given nine months' grace under the treaty, and were due to depart by May 3, 1879. It was clear from the outset that it would be no easy task to induce them to go peacefully. It is impossible to describe here the details of what followed. In any case they belong to Salisbury's rather than Disraeli's life. The important point is that throughout the winter of 1878 and nearly the whole of 1879 there seemed at least a possibility of renewed hostilities with Russia. Although the evacuation at last began on May 3 – it should have finished by then – this did not end the danger, and Anglo-Russian relations, largely because of unwarranted suspicions on both sides, remained very bad for the rest of the year. The British Army, as always, except during the two mass wars of the twentieth century, was extremely thin on the ground. The last thing that Disraeli wanted was a remote campaign which would draw troops away from Europe and weaken his ability to threaten Russia. The Afghan War, though unwelcome, was not too bad, for it was fought by the Indian Army on the spot and could

[1] ibid., 381, Disraeli to Cranbrook, September 17, 1878. The same phrase is used in a letter to Salisbury.

[2] W. N. Medlicott, *The Congress of Berlin and After* (1938), gives the most authoritative account of diplomatic negotiations, 1878–80.

be regarded as a hit at Russia anyway. But when yet another diso-bedient proconsul landed Britain in yet another war, this time as distant from the main stream of events as could well be imagined and when, to cap everything, it opened with a major disaster, Disraeli's sang-froid deserted him. If he behaved in a manner which for him was quite abnormally unjust and undignified, pardonable irritation must be the only excuse.

The war which so gravely disturbed Disraeli's calculations broke out in South Africa.[1] It was the first occasion when the troubles of this unhappy land seriously impinged upon English politics, the beginning of a long series which has not ended yet. On the whole, Disraeli had taken little interest in the colonies. His much quoted remark that they were 'millstones round our neck' may perhaps be discounted as an outburst of petulance, but it remains true that, apart from some compressed and prescient observations in the Crystal Palace speech, he said very little about them. When he entered office in 1874 he was quite content to leave colonial policy to Carnarvon, just as he left social reform to Cross. Carnarvon had a high reputation in these matters. It was under his auspices that the federation of Canada had been achieved in the previous Conserva-tive administration. Unfortunately, as so often occurs with states-men, he took this successful measure as a precedent for solving a problem superficially similar but actually quite different. If federation worked in Canada, he argued, why should it not work in South Africa, where there also existed two sets of white colonists with different languages and nationalities?

The important difference was that the colonists in Canada wanted federation, whereas only a small minority of the English, and virtually none of the Boers favoured it in South Africa. It is true that the objective case for South African federation was extremely strong. There seemed no other satisfactory way of presenting a firm front to the ever-present menace of a Kaffir war. But the Boer republics did not owe even a nominal allegiance to the British Crown; and Cape Colony, which did, disliked the idea of sharing the expense of native policy with less affluent neighbours. It must be remembered that the gold and diamond discoveries, destined to make the Transvaal one of the richest countries in the world, still lay in the future. However, Carnarvon plunged in with doctrinaire

[1] The best account of Isandhlwana, its antecedents and aftermath is Sir Reginald Coupland's *Zulu Battle Piece* (1948).

enthusiasm. He indited an unanswerable dispatch which merely annoyed the colonists. He sent out his friend, the historian Froude, who, on two successive visits in 1874–5 preached federation with all the cocksure confidence of the academic mind, but gain no converts and merely misled the Colonial Secretary. Then Carnarvon summoned a conference in London which was cut by most of the people who mattered. Disraeli, though in principle favouring federation, was far from pleased with Froude's mission. Monty Corry echoed his master's voice, if somewhat ungrammatically, when he wrote to Ponsonby a good deal later on May 13, 1878:

> Ld B. is extremely dissatisfied with all that has taken or is taking place at the Cape. The troubles commenced by Lord Carnarvon who, he says, lived mainly in a coterie of editors of Liberal papers who praised him and drank his claret, sending Mr Froude – a desultory and theoretical littérateur who wrote more rot on the reign of Elizabeth than Gibbon required for all the Decline and Fall – to reform the Cape, which ended naturally in a Kaffir War . . .[1]

By then much had happened. In 1876 the Boers of the Transvaal had suffered a humiliating defeat at the hands of Chief Secocoeni of the Bapedi. Yet this tribe was less formidable than Cetewayo's Zulus, who remained by far the greatest threat, though holding their hand for the moment, thanks to the influence which Sir Theophilus Shepstone, Secretary for Native Affairs in Natal, had acquired with them and their King. Convinced that the Boers would now welcome British protection, Carnarvon resolved that federation should begin from the Transvaal instead of the Cape, and sent back Shepstone, who had been in London for the conference, with orders to annex the republic at the first plausible opportunity. At the same time he appointed Sir Bartle Frere to the post of Governor of the Cape Colony and High Commissioner for South Africa. Sir Bartle was one of the leading proconsuls of the day, ex-Governor of Bombay, member of the India Council, and a staunch advocate of 'forward' policies. He would not at this stage of his career have accepted an ordinary governorship. His brief was to create a South African federation and to act as its first Governor-General. He expected a free hand in achieving this aim. He arrived in April 1877, just when Shepstone announced from Pretoria the annexation of the Transvaal. There was no resistance, but no enthusiasm. The Boers

[1] M. & B., vi, 419–20.

accepted in sullen silence, and the chance of reconciling them soon evaporated. Treasury stinginess and prolonged delay in settling the constitution denied them both the material benefits and the political liberty which might have made annexation tolerable.

Frere soon saw that federation was not practicable for the moment. Feeling against it was too strong both in the Cape and the Transvaal. His immediate concern was with the native question. Trouble seemed impending from every direction for many reasons. There was a disastrous drought in 1877 and 1878, which inevitably set the tribes on the move to conquer new lands either from each other or the colonists. In August, Frere was involved in the ninth Kaffir War, which ultimately in June 1878 resulted in the pacification of Griqualand. It may be noted in passing that Disraeli was singularly unlucky over the weather in the last years of his administration. While lack of rain contributed to the Zulu War which so greatly damaged his prestige abroad, excess of it, summer after summer, produced the series of bad harvests which aggravated the general economic depression at home. The drought was not the only danger in South Africa. Until Shepstone annexed the Transvaal the Zulus had been looking forward to a war against the Boers, whom they detested with every reason. Now, however, an attack on the Boers meant war with the English, towards whom Cetewayo was on the whole quite well disposed. Why in that case, it might be asked, go to war at all? The answer is that the whole social structure of the Zulu state was geared to that purpose. Cetewayo had revived the traditional system whereby the youth of the nation was conscripted into strictly celibate regiments confined to great military homesteads in the area of the royal *Kraal*. Marriage was rigidly forbidden until the young warrior had washed his assegai in blood, as the saying went. The strongest of human instincts, therefore, was allied with natural bloodthirstiness in a determination to fight someone somewhere.

At an early stage Frere became convinced that South Africa could not be secure until British paramountcy had been asserted over all the tribes from sea to sea south of the Portuguese colonies, and in particular that the Zulu system must be destroyed before it destroyed the colonists. But the last thing that the Cabinet wanted at the height of the Eastern crisis was a war in South Africa. Probably neither Disraeli nor his colleagues, except Carnarvon, appreciated the significance of appointing Frere, an exponent of expansionism if ever there was one, at precisely the moment when the Government was least ready to take the risks involved. Even Carnarvon, who was less anti-Russian than any of the Cabinet, vetoed hostilities. 'A native war', he told Shepstone in January 1878, '*is just now impossible and you must avoid it.*'[1] Soon afterwards Carnarvon resigned on the Eastern question. The new Colonial Secretary, Hicks Beach, was a strong anti-Russian, and had no particular knowledge of or interest in his predecessor's South African plans. The High Commissioner ought to have realized that his own position was bound to be weakened by the change.

But Frere continued to take the line that Britain 'must be master up to the Portuguese frontier',[2] as he said in a dispatch to Hicks Beach on August 10. Yet, although he issued several warnings about the need to subordinate the Zulus to a British protectorate and although a preventive war was undoubtedly the logical implication of much that he said, he never explicitly stated what his plans were until far too late. In London throughout the summer Hicks Beach appeared to agree with all Frere's objectives, but he either ignored or failed to see that they could hardly be achieved without war. If Frere deserves blame for not spelling out his own true intentions, the Cabinet is no less to blame for never asking him categorically to do so. A further difficulty was slowness of communication. There was no cable to Cape Town, the nearest point for telegrams being S Vincent in the Cape Verde Islands, to which they had to be sent by steamer. The fastest telegram on record took sixteen days to reach London. Letters took at least three weeks, often a month. Gradually the gulf between the Colonial Office and the High Commissioner widened. By the autumn it had become unbridgeable.

Disraeli had paid little attention to the South African situation, but in September the imminence of war with Afghanistan caused him to sit up and take notice. On September 28 he wrote to Lady Bradford

> . . . if anything annoys me more than another, it is our Cape affairs, where every day brings forth a new blunder of Twitters.[3]

The man he swore by was Sir T. Shepstone, whom he looked upon as heaven-born for the object in view. We sent him out entirely for Twitters' sake, and he has managed to quarrel with

---

[1] C. W. De Kiewiet, *The Imperial Factor in South Africa* (1937), 217.
[2] J. Martineau, *Life of Sir Bartle Frere* (2 vols, 1895), ii, 259.
[3] Carnarvon's nickname.

Eng., Dutch, and Zulus; and now he is obliged to be recalled, but not before he has brought on, I fear, a new war. Froude was bad enough and has cost us a million; this will be worse. So much for Twitters . . .[1]

Disraeli's apprehensions were correct. A visit to Pietermaritzburg at the end of September convinced Frere that, unless he broke the Zulu military power, peace in South Africa could never be secured. On September 30 he sent a dispatch to Hicks Beach asking for reinforcements, and at last specifically stated: '. . . the peace of South Africa for many years to come seems to me to depend on your taking steps to put a final end to Zulu pretensions.' The Cabinet was dismayed at this prospect. An Afghan war now seemed certain, and Anglo-Russian relations were as bad as ever. Hicks Beach accordingly refused to send reinforcements and informed Frere of the Cabinet's belief that 'by meeting the Zulus in a spirit of forbearance and reasonable compromise, it will be possible to avoid the very serious evil of a war with Cetewayo'. Frere received this advice on November 4th with consternation. He realized now for the first time the extent of the divergence between him and the Colonial Office, but the fact did not deter him from pressing on with preparations for war.

On November 7 Hicks Beach sent a letter specifically forbidding war. It did not reach Pietermaritzburg till December 13, but a telegraphed summary arrived on November 30. On December 11 Frere issued an ultimatum to Cetewayo, which was certain to, and intended to, start a war. It demanded abolition of the ban on marriage in the Zulu army and a British veto on mobilization, conditions Cetewayo was bound to refuse. Meanwhile the Cabinet had changed its mind on reinforcements, hearing that the request was backed by Lord Chelmsford, son of Disraeli's former *bête noire*, commanding in Natal. On November 20 it was decided to send them, but on strict condition that they were used for defensive purposes only. Frere was in no hurry to tell the Cabinet about the ultimatum. He did not send the text for another five days, and it arrived in London on January 2, nine days before the ultimatum expired.

The war was, therefore, emphatically Frere's war. Whether or not he was right depends upon something which will never now be known for certain, the exact intentions of Cetewayo; but there can be no question that Frere consciously disobeyed instructions. Like

[1] Zetland, ii, 189.

Lytton, he would have been forgiven if he had been successful. Unhappily he was not, and the war opened with a major diaster. On January 22, 1879, a Zulu *impi* or army of 20,000 men, moving with extraordinary speed and secrecy, utterly destroyed the force of some 1,200 men, defending Chelmsford's temporary base camp at Isandhlwana. No proper *laager* had been formed, and no trenches dug, despite the warnings given by none other than Paul Kruger, the future President of the Transvaal. It is fair to add that scarcely anyone realized how far and fast a Zulu *impi* could travel without a sign of activity under the very noses of British scouts, and that the camp was only a temporary one, to be moved as soon as Chelmsford and the advance guard of his column had reconnoitred their route.[1] The news of the disaster reached London on February 12.

Whatever the excuses, the fact of defeat was undoubted. Disraeli, who reasonably believed that success alone could warrant insubordination, was at first almost prostrated by the blow, and when he recovered became extremely angry. Chelmsford at once requested further reinforcements and could not be refused, but Disraeli considered that his whole foreign policy was thrown into jeopardy by this inopportune call on British reserves, while the cost was all too likely to damage the national finances, already in an unsatisfactory state because of the economic and agricultural depression. Disraeli's health suffered a relapse, probably psychosomatic, and he was sunk in a mood of depression and irritation for several weeks. Nor was he consoled by any quick reversal of fortune. Once bitten, Chelmsford proceeded with extreme caution, and the campaign seemed to be bogged down in a morass of sloth and indecision. Moreover, there was at least one further reverse, militarily insignificant, but looming large in the public eye.

Among those who went out with the reinforcements was Louis Napoleon's son, the Prince Imperial, who had been trained at Woolwich and was keen to volunteer for some fighting. With the aid of the Duke of Cambridge the matter was arranged over Disraeli's head by the Queen and the Empress Eugenie. He did not approve.

I am quite mystified about that little abortion, the Prince Imperial [he wrote to Salisbury on February 28]. I thought we had agreed not to sanction his adventure? Instead of that he has royal audiences previous to departure, is reported to be a future

[1] See Coupland, *Zulu Battle Piece*, 64–67, for discussion of this question.

staff officer and is attended to the station by Whiskerandos[1] himself, the very general who was to conquer Constantinople.

I have to go to Windsor tomorrow after the Cabinet and as I have not seen our Royal Mistress for three months shall have to touch on every point. What am I to say on this? H.M. knows my little sympathy with the Buonapartes . . .[2]

Salisbury agreed, but it was too late to do anything. Neither of them could have foreseen what happened. On June 1 the Prince on a reconnaissance with a few companions was surprised by a volley from an ambush just as they were about to saddle up for the ride home. No one was hit, but the Prince was unable to mount his badly frightened horse. The others rode off, apparently not realizing what had happened. When they found that he was missing they returned, only to discover his body speared to death by Zulu assegais. The Queen was greatly distressed at the news, which indeed caused a further slump in the Government's prestige. There were complications, too, about the funeral, which was celebrated with a degree of pomp considered excessive by Disraeli in view of the fact that the Prince was only a pretender to the French throne, indeed one of several. 'Nothing cd be more injudicious than the whole affair,' he told Lady Chesterfield.

The defeat of Isandhlwana caused an outcry in England for the supersession of both Frere and Chelmsford. There was something to be said for bowing to the storm and recalling them at the earliest moment. There was more to be said, as an alternative, for backing them to the full and allowing them to redeem their blunder, if such it was. But there was nothing to be said for what Disraeli actually did. He persuaded the Cabinet to leave Frere in charge for the moment, but to send a dispatch which sharply reprimanded him and yet said at the same time that they had 'no desire to withdraw in the present crisis of affairs the confidence hitherto reposed in you'. As the dispatch was published, it is surprising that Frere did not resign. This double-faced document gave Sir William Harcourt an enjoyable opening in the House of Commons. He read out an imaginary letter from Hicks Beach. 'Dear Sir Bartle Frere. I cannot think you are right. Indeed I think you are very wrong; but after all you know a great deal better than I do. I hope you won't do what you are going to do; but if you do I hope it will turn out well.'

---

[1] Presumably Lord Napier.
[2] Salisbury Papers, February 28, 1879.

The lack of progress in the campaign brought about renewed pressure on Disraeli in April, and he was greatly annoyed by Sir Bartle Frere's cool vindication of himself in his dispatches home. 'Sir B.F. who ought to be impeached writes always as if he were quite unconscious of having done anything wrong', he told Lady Chesterfield on June 28. Before then he had taken another step against Frere and Chelmsford. On May 28 a telegram was sent to Chelmsford informing him that Sir Garnet Wolseley was coming out as High Commissioner and Commander-in-Chief in Natal, Transvaal and Zululand with plenary powers, civil and military. Chelmsford was to subordinate his plans to the new Commander-in-Chief, and Frere's territory would henceforth be confined to Cape Colony, where there was nothing of any importance to do. It is certain that Disraeli meant to recall Chelmsford and probable that he expected Frere to resign, but once again that tough proconsul stayed on from a strong sense of duty, although it would have been better to leave after such a rebuff. The telegram arrived too late to stop Chelmsford from implementing his own plans to conquer Zululand. At last success attended his efforts, and on July 4 at Ulundi he finally crushed the power of Cetewayo, ignoring the orders sent to him by Wolseley two days earlier. Wiser than Frere, he resigned immediately afterwards.

Disraeli's treatment of Frere and Chelmsford caused one of his few serious differences with Queen Victoria. She considered that insufficient allowance had been made for their difficulties and that the Government ought not to supersede them in the middle of the campaign. Moreover, she strongly disapproved of the choice of Sir Garnet Wolseley, who as a Liberal and a supporter of Cardwell's reforms, was anathema to her cousin the Duke of Cambridge. 'The Horse Guards are furious, the Princes all raging, and every mediocrity as jealous as if we had prevented him from conquering the world', wrote Disraeli to Lady Chesterfield on the day of the decision, and three days later;

> They all complain of the hurried way in wh. the affair was managed. I dare say. If there had not been a little hurry he never wd have gone. They wd have got up some little conspiracy wh wd have arrested everything.[1]

Disraeli was under no delusions about Wolseley. Writing to the

[1] M. & B., vi, 433-4.

Queen at the end of August, he calmly remarked: 'It is quite true that Wolseley is an egotist and a braggart. So was Nelson.'[1] In general no man was a stauncher adherent than Disraeli of the practice of making political appointments in every sphere, but he admired Wolseley and there was no plausible 'Conservative' soldier available, Lord Napier being too old, and Roberts being in India. He was adamant with the Queen, who at last said that she 'would sanction the proposal submitted if her warnings are disregarded but she would *not approve* it'.[2]

This was not the end of his difficulties with his royal mistress. When Chelmsford returned to England the popular view which the Queen so often personified was that Ulundi had obliterated Isandhlwana, and that he should be given a victor's honours. She pressed Disraeli to invite him to Hughenden at the end of August. Disraeli regarded this as the last straw and riposted with what Ponsonby described to the Queen as 'a tremendous indictment'. Disraeli wrote *inter alia:*

> He mixes up Lord Chelmsford in no small degree with the policy of the unhappily precipitated Zulu War, the evil consequences of which to this country have been incalculable. Had it not taken place your Majesty would be Dictatress of Europe; the Sultan would be in military possession of the line of the Balkans; the Egyptian trouble would never have occurred; and the Grecian question would have been settled in unison with our views.
>
> Lord Beaconsfield charges Lord Chelmsford with having invaded Zululand 'avec un coeur léger', with no adequate knowledge of the country he was attacking, and no precaution or preparation. A dreadful disaster occurred in consequence, and then Lord Chelmsford became panic-struck; appealed to yr Majesty's Govt. practically for reinforcements, and found himself at the head of 20,000 of yr Majesty's troops in order to reduce a country not larger than Yorkshire . . . and had he not been furtively apprised by telegraph that he was about to be superseded, Lord Chelmsford would probably never have advanced to Ulundi. His retreat from that post was his last and crowning mistake, and the allegation that he was instructed to do so by Sir G. Wolseley has been investigated by Lord Beaconsfield and found to be without foundation.'[3]

Ponsonby minuted to the Queen that he did not himself agree with

[1] ibid., 435.
[2] ibid., 431, May 26, 1879.
[3] ibid., 459.

this tirade. 'But Lord Beaconsfield could not have written this had his mind not been convinced of what he says; and his words therefore deserve all attention.' He persuaded her to tone down her counterblast and omit an accusation that Wolseley had sent home 'all the best officers he can in order to curry favour with the Press and the H. of C.'[1] Even so, she wrote a very strong letter.[2] But although the correspondence was prolonged she made no impression on Disraeli. He probably exaggerated the harm done by the Zulu War and he was certainly harsh to Chelmsford, who was in a sense less to blame than Frere. But Chelmsford was there and Frere was not. Ponsonby commented to the Queen:

> Lord Beaconsfield has always been impatient of ill success and this Zulu War has interfered so seriously with his European action that it is not surprising that he should be so bitter about it. But he makes no allowance for the difficulty of South African campaigns and rather unfairly attributes every disaster to the shortcomings of the General.[3]

Disraeli invited Redvers Buller and Sir Evelyn Wood, two other prominent soldiers in the campaign, to Hughenden, but he refused to ask Chelmsford. The most that he would accord was a formal interview at Downing Street.

His anger with Chelmsford is understandable and no doubt Ponsonby was right about the reason. Nevertheless Disraeli's dealings with Frere and Chelmsford constitute one of the least creditable episodes in his Premiership. He ought in the summer of 1878 to have examined the correspondence between Hicks Beach and Frere more closely, and as Prime Minister he must share some responsibility for the fatal ambiguity of the Government's attitude. Much worse, when once the disaster of Isandhlwana had occurred he pushed the Cabinet into a double-faced treatment of both the High Commissioner and the Commander-in-Chief, which seems on any view indefensible. He should either have sacked them or backed them. On this rare occasion of divergence from her favourite Prime Minister the Queen was in the right.

[1] Royal Archives, B.61.39, Ponsonby to the Queen, September 1.
[2] M. & B., vi, 460.
[3] Royal Archives, loc. cit.

3

Scarcely had the evil consequences of the Zulu War begun to die away than a fresh disaster occurred in the field of 'forward policy'. On September 3 Sir Louis Cavagnari and his entire staff were slaughtered by mutinous Afghan soldiers in Kabul. He appears to have had no inkling of trouble, although there had been some suspicious episodes, and the tragedy came as a complete shock to all concerned. The complicity of the Amir was never proved, but on the most favourable view he had shown himself weak, cowardly and unfit to rule. A punitive war was the only answer, and for the second time Roberts conducted a brilliant mountain campaign against the Afghan forces. Disraeli strongly backed Lytton in this new crisis and his attitude was in sharp contrast with his treatment of Frere. The Opposition made the Viceroy a personal target of attack and declared that all the trouble stemmed from his abandonment of Lawrence's masterly inactivity. Disraeli hit back with vigour and at the Guildhall speech that autumn pronounced a notable panegyric on Lytton. Earlier and in private he was not quite so enthusiastic. Lytton had sent to London an acid commentary in which he cut to pieces the principal officers in the Indian Army except Roberts, and said that one of them, Sir Sam Browne, deserved a court martial. 'And these are the men whom only a few months or weeks ago he commended for all these distinctions', Disraeli wrote to Salisbury on September 9. 'I begin to think he ought to be tried by court martial himself; but I have confidence still in his energy and resource.'[1] Fortunately for Lytton there was no Isandhlwana in the Afghan hills. Roberts entered Kabul in triumph on October 13, having crushed all resistance.

The Third Afghan War finally determined the Liberals to make the Government's foreign and imperial policy their main object of attack. Yet Disraeli's foreign policy since the Congress of Berlin had been by no means unsuccessful. Regarding the destruction of the League of the Three Emperors as one of the principal achievements of Berlin, he had striven hard ever since to prevent its revival. Bismarck was anxious to bring Russia back into the conservative alliance, but the essential prerequisite, an Austro-Russian *rapprochement*, was twice prevented by British diplomacy. The most

[1] M. & B., vi, 481.

authoritative historian of the period regards the years 1878–80 as a struggle, none the less real for being largely concealed, between Disraeli and Bismarck for the leadership in Europe.[1] Disraeli certainly believed that if England was to be a great power she must act as if she was one and show herself to the world in that role. Such diplomacy presupposed a degree of intervention and assertiveness that was bound to be detested by the Little Englander element now in the ascendancy in the Liberal party. Moreover, events forced Disraeli and Salisbury to take the lead, quite apart from the question of the *Dreikaiserbund*. For the burden of forcing Russia to comply with the Berlin treaty fell on Britain; Bismarck was not going to offend Russia more than he could help, and although there was for most purposes an informal Anglo-Austrian front, Andrassy, who had refused a formal British alliance at the height of the crisis, had no intention now of pulling Salisbury's chestnuts out of the fire. There remained the threat of British warships steaming into the Black Sea, where the Russians had no fleet, and thus defending Turkey by threatening the Ukraine. This was the basis of British foreign policy while the Conservatives remained in office, and it was on the whole effective. By August 1, 1879, not a Russian soldier remained in the Balkan peninsula.

Late in September, Bismarck made a curious *démarche* to Disraeli which has produced much historical speculation, since the evidence is both incomplete and contradictory. Count Münster, the Ambassador, came to stay at Hughenden on September 26, bearing with him, according to Disraeli's account, the secret offer of an alliance with Germany and Austria-Hungary. Münster apparently went so far as to assert categorically that 'Russia is preparing to attack Austria' – a statement which Bismarck may or may not have believed, but which was certainly untrue. Disraeli, who forwarded long memoranda of the discussion both to the Queen[2] and Salisbury, replied cautiously, if his version is correct, and while encouraging further discussion indicated that the difficulty would be relations with France. The conversation, which lasted for an hour before dinner and was resumed afterwards, ended on a note of goodwill, but with no commitments. Münster's own account to Bismarck[3] differs on some important points. According to him, the proposal

[1] See Professor Medlicott's essay in *Studies in History and Historiography* (1961), ed. A. O. Sarkissian, 242–50.
[2] M. & B., vi, 486–8.
[3] *Grosse Politik*, iv, 7.

for an alliance came from Disraeli, and when Münster asked what England would do if Germany was involved in war with Russia because of her support for England and Austria in the Balkans he replied, 'We will in that case keep France quiet.' On this Bismarck crossly commented, 'Is that all?'[1] – though it is difficult to see what more he could have expected.

Both Disraeli and Münster, whose letters were to be seen by their respective Sovereigns, may have had reason to attribute the initiative to the other.[2] The Queen was not going to approve of England asking for an alliance with Germany, and the Emperor, who in his old-fashioned way still hankered after the traditional dynastic friendship with Russia, was unlikely to welcome an anti-Russian move by Bismarck. Each monarch would find an approach from the other country less unacceptable. A further difficulty in elucidating the story is that Münster's instructions from the Chancellor on this point were verbal and no written record remains. It is therefore far from clear what Bismarck really wanted. Whatever it was, he soon dropped it. His own negotiations for a military alliance with Austria-Hungary, which were going on simultaneously, came to a successful conclusion on October 7. Moreover, during the second half of September he entered into friendly discussions with Saburov, the Russian Ambassador in Berlin, which may have persuaded him that the danger of Russian hostility was unreal. Münster said no more about the alliance and when Salisbury raised it with him at Hatfield he gave the impression that there was less interest on Bismarck's part.

No more was heard of a proposal elevated by some historians into one of the 'lost opportunities' of an Anglo-German *rapprochement* which might have prevented the First World War. This is very unlikely. Certainly no one of weight in England thought at the time that any particular opportunity had been lost, and Salisbury went out of his way to welcome the Austro-German alliance, calling it in a speech at Manchester 'Glad tidings of great joy', to the scandal of Liberal pietists. Both Münster and Disraeli agree in their versions that the question of Anglo-French relations was crucial. Disraeli all his life appreciated the importance of keeping in with France. It was particularly important just then, for early in the year the Khedive of Egypt finally declined into total bankruptcy, and Layard in June

[1] ibid., 12.
[2] Medlicott, *The Congress of Berlin and After*, 386–7.

after much cajolery induced the Sultan to depose him in favour of his son Tewfik. It was vital for Britain to be on good terms with the French, who held the majority of Egyptian bonds, and to act in concert with the French Government in rehabilitating Egyptian finance. One of Disraeli's many counts against Frere and Chelmsford was that the Zulu War had weakened his hand at precisely the moment when he wanted to be in a strong bargaining position with the French. In fact, friendly relations did prevail and, in Disraeli's time at least, dual control worked reasonably well. To have jeopardized good relations with France for the sake of Bismarck's ambiguous proposals would not have made sense.

Although Bismarck had secured an Austro-German alliance, he was still far from achieving a revived *Dreikaiserbund*. Disraeli's policy was successful. Haymerle, who succeeded Andrassy, continued to favour the Anglo-Austrian front against Russia. Bismarck's position as arbiter of Europe depended on the dissolution of this entente, but it remained intact until the end of Disraeli's premiership, and the initiative stayed with Britain and Austria-Hungary discreetly supported by France and Italy. Both Russia, and to some extent Germany, remained isolated. But soon after his resignation in April 1880 Disraeli wrote to Queen Victoria:

> The Diplomatic World has not recovered from its astonishment at the fall of the late English Ministry and is quite perplexed by it. What I fear myself is the revival of the Kaiser-Bund. The paramount fact of the Congress [of Berlin] was breaking up that Alliance. This was one of those vast results that do not appear in treaties or protocols, and can perhaps never be publickly mentioned, but which are more important than all that is signed or sealed . . .[1]

His fears were justified. In so far as Gladstone's Government had any clear foreign policy it was based on a vague and virtuous resolve to reverse 'Beaconsfieldism' in all its forms. There was no attempt to preserve the accord with Vienna. By September, Haymerle had agreed to join a resuscitated League of the Three Emperors. Among other pledges the new alliance agreed to insist upon Turkey's refusing to allow the entry of warships into the Straits. Britain's only effective means of bringing pressure on Russia disappeared, and since Gladstone had withdrawn the military consuls from Anatolia her only means of bringing pressure on the Sultan evaporated, too.

[1] Royal Archives, B.64.3, Disraeli to Queen Victoria, June 14, 1880.

Britain no longer had the principal say in the Near East; and in Europe generally the initiative moved from the British Prime minister to the German Chancellor. 'Beaconsfieldism' was indeed dead.

Logically Bismarck should have welcomed the result of a general election which substituted a man who played into his hands for a man who thwarted him. In fact, he disliked Gladstone for temperamental reasons almost as much as Disraeli did, and always retained a respect for 'the old Jew' mingled with friendly amazement at his ability and sheer effrontery. When *Endymion* was published at the end of 1880 Bismark read without offence the portrait of himself as Count Ferrol, and was moved to reminisce among friends about his former rival. 'It was easy to transact business with him: in a quarter of an hour you knew exactly how you stood with him; the limits to which he was prepared to go were clearly defined, and a rapid summary soon concluded matters . . . I must say that in spite of his fantastic novel-writing he is a capable statesman . . .'

CHAPTER XXIX

Society and Patronage

1868–80

The troubles that beset the last two years of his administration did not prevent Disraeli from enjoying his post as Prime Minister. For one thing, his health, though far from good, was better than it had been. Dr Kidd was a sensible diagnostician and his belief in homoeo-pathy was not a disadvantage. One of the tenets of that school is to give medicines and drugs only in very minute quantities. At a time when physicians were all too liable to prescribe a positively deleteri-ous remedy, this at least limited the harm that could be done. Disraeli remained prone to both bronchitis and gout, and was always liable to catch a cold leading to bronchial trouble after country-house visits in the late autumn or winter. It is easy to forget how much even the rich were prepared to endure in the way of chilly living-rooms, icy bedrooms and draughty corridors only a century ago, and as Disraeli never took any exercise if he could help it, he suffered particularly from this discomfort. The Queen, who seems to have been wholly impervious to cold, was one of the worst hostesses in this respect. 'That castle of the winds' was Disraeli's description of Windsor, and, if he was right, it was a breach of etiquette even to blow one's nose during an audience. Fortunately he was safer at Hughenden, where he had installed a primitive form of central heating a few years earlier, and the house was tolerably warm.

Despite the misgivings of the Queen, who, apart from anything else, disapproved of London society on moral grounds, and all the more strongly because it revolved round the Prince of Wales, Disraeli attended the dinners and receptions of the beau-monde with the assiduity of a man of half his age. Prime Ministers of England have seldom been fashionable figures, although they have often been rich and sometimes grand. In the nineteenth century Disraeli, along with Rosebery and perhaps Melbourne, was an exception. He was not only at the top of the political pyramid, he was very close to the top of the social pyramid, too. He was sought by every great hostess. He knew exactly who was who in that restricted world, their incomes, their love affairs, their past or impending scandals. He was not infrequently called upon to arbitrate in delicate social matters, and he managed to avert more than one social disaster. It is odd to think of this gaunt wheezing figure, the pallor of his lined face accentuated rather than relieved by the rouge which, like Palmerston in old age, he regularly applied, dining night after night during the season amidst the glitter of the great London houses, listening impassively to the gay rattle of duchesses and the social gossip of men-about-town. And, although from our more austere and egalitarian standpoint we may tend to dismiss such conduct as mere frivolity, it is worth remembering that on one occasion in very recent times a Prime Minister might have averted a major scandal if he had been slightly more in touch with the modern equivalent of Disraeli's social world. Gossip may be reprehensible, but it can sometimes put even a statesman on his guard.

From Disraeli's published letters to the Forester sisters, to Queen Victoria and to others, a vivid picture emerges of him, his tastes and the circles in which he moved as seen through his eyes. One is struck at once by the sheer pleasure in society which his great position gave him. Of course, he grumbled about the food at one dinner party, the wine at another, the company at a third, the cold rooms at a fourth. Although his own table was notoriously bad, and had been so even in Mary Anne's time, he was a critical gourmet when it came to other people's hospitality. His comment at one establishment when the champagne arrived is well known, 'Thank God for something warm', and his letters abound with similar acid observations. But his complaints, which were largely designed to elicit sympathy, somewhat unforthcoming, from Lady Bradford, seldom resulted in any interruption in his social round of receptions and dinner parties during the season and country-house visits after it was over.

Other functions which he seldom missed were weddings. Here he was like Asquith, whose assiduity in this respect was the subject of a slightly carping comment by Lloyd George. Disraeli regularly attended these occasions, and it was very appropriate that he should have been a central figure at the grandest wedding of the decade, that of Lord Rosebery to Miss Hannah Rothschild, the greatest heiress of the day, with a fortune of two million pounds. On March 20, 1878, at the height of the Eastern crisis, only a week before Derby's resignation, he gave away the bride, who was married in the fashionable Christ Church, Down Street. 'The Premier', wrote the *Morning Post*, 'acted the heavy father *à ravir*.'[1]

If at times we feel surprised at the amount of leisure which Disraeli seemed to have, it is necessary to remember first the very different tempo of political life in those days, and secondly the fact, true in a sense even now, that the Prime Minister has no departmental office to tie him to a particular routine. The heads of the Foreign or Home Office, or the service departments, were far busier. His job was then, and is now, very much what he chooses to make it, within certain limits, of course. Disraeli, as we saw earlier, was not an energetic Prime Minister, and he expected his three private secretaries, Corry, Algernon Turnor and James Daly, to do a great deal of his work for him. What strained his strength and patience most was the only major departmental matter in which he felt he had to interfere, foreign policy while Derby was Foreign Secretary. When Salisbury took over, life became far easier and he could enjoy the pleasures of society.

There was, however, one aspect of a Prime Minister's duties which could not be delegated and which Disraeli would not have wished to delegate. It happened to be one in which his friends in society were particularly interested.

Like all Prime Ministers, Disraeli spent a great deal of his time on patronage. He regarded it as an important element in party management. There were two aspects of it, places and honours. Honours, of course, have always been and still are bestowed in part as rewards for political services, but by the 1870s there was a change in the climate of opinion regarding places. For some time past it had been felt that ecclesiastical preferment should not be dictated solely by political partisanship or personal connexions. A similar change was affecting civil patronage. Meritocracy was beginning to be the shibboleth. In 1870 Gladstone made the Order-in-Council which introduced competitive examination into the Civil Service.

Disraeli had no sympathy whatever with these trends, and was, as might have been expected of one who would probably have been a very bad examinee himself, sceptical about the new tests of merit. 'I want a man of the world and of breeding, culture and station to be Chief of the Civil Service Commission, 'he wrote, 'so that if any

---

[1] R. R. James, *Rosebery*, 86.

absurd or pedantic schemes of qualification are put before him he may integrate and modify them and infuse a necessary element of common sense.' On one occasion the Queen was anxious for a Mr Maude to get into the Treasury. Disraeli told her that it was difficult, 'the late Ministry having established open competition for places in the Treasury. Mr Disraeli thinks this an unwise step. Posts in the Treasury and Foreign Office require so much trust in their holders that some social experience is requisite of those who hold them. There should be a moral security for their honour and trustworthiness.' Luckily in this particular case a loophole in the Order-in-Council 'enables him to accomplish Your Majesty's wishes'.[1]

The truth is that Disraeli's attitude to patronage had not altered since his words to Stanley in 1858. It was 'the outward and visible sign of an inward and spiritual grace, and that is Power'. This point of view was, perhaps, to be expected in the leader of a minority party. The Tories had been in office so little since 1846 that they were inevitably all the hungrier for its fruits when they did get in, resembling in this respect the Republicans after Eisenhower's victory in 1952 or the Labour party in 1964. Moreover, Disraeli's whole official experience had been under Derby, whose essentially eighteenth-century outlook on matters of this sort was singularly impervious to the wind of change. Last but not least, Disraeli was devoid of that perverse rectitude which consists in refusing to reward friends for fear of what may be said by foes. He liked rewarding his friends.

Naturally he could not openly reverse the measures of previous governments, but there still remained an area of uncertainty where the criteria for appointments were matters of custom or usage not yet definitively established. Here he did not hesitate to use his discretion in quite the opposite sense to his predecessors. For example, of a dozen posts which were in the gift of the First Lord of the Treasury, and which under Gladstone had virtually become the perquisites of permanent Civil Servants, Disraeli bestowed ten as partisan rewards.[2] His attitude was summed up in his words in 1877 to Sir William Stephenson, the retiring Chairman of the Inland Revenue Board: 'These appointments [on the Board] should be considered not as official promotions but as political prizes.' When

[1] Royal Archives, A.47.84, Disraeli to the Queen, December 18, 1874.
[2] Hanham, 'Political Patronage at the Treasury, 1870–1912', *Historical Journal* (1960–1), iii, 77.

Sir Algernon West, who hoped for the Deputy Chairmanship, reported this to Gladstone, his comment was an unusually terse, 'Damn him' – maintained by West to be one of the only two occasions on which Gladstone ever used this expletive.[1] But one should add that in this instance Disraeli played fair by the Civil Service, appointing Charles Herries, the Deputy Chairman and a son of J. C. Herries, to the Chairmanship and, after an agonizing interval, West to the place vacated by Herries. However, he was firm in filling West's place with a straight political choice: Walter Northcote, son of Sir Stafford. A typical appointment as Commissioner of Inland Revenue was that of the Hon. Charles Keith Falconer in 1874, a former soldier and currently Secretary to the Conservative Central Office. Disraeli discreetly recommended him to the Queen, saying that since he had left her service, 'his labors in favor of constitutional principles both by his pen and his organising power have been of an eminent character and entitle him to general confidence and respect'.[2] Altogether Disraeli looked after four ex-ministers and three party officials in this way. Moreover, to Gladstone's great indignation he created in 1875 the post of First Civil Service Commissioner at £2,000 p.a., and gave it to Lord Hampton, the former Sir John Pakington, who was hard up and needed the money.

One of the most surprising charges made against Disraeli is Sir William Fraser's allegation that he displayed ingratitude towards old friends in these matters. Buckle rightly expresses astonishment at this criticism, and indeed, if Disraeli's use of patronage deserves censure it would be for the opposite reason: he was too lavish in rewarding people whose chief, though doubtless not their only, merit was their claim on his friendship or gratitude. We have seen how he procured a pension for 'Tita's' relict, omitting incidentally to mention to the Queen that Tita had been his father's factotum for so many years. He also obtained a pension for the widow of his cousin, Captain Basevi, and on a more exalted plane one for Lord John Manners, who suffered from the impecuniosity endemic in those days among the younger sons of millionaire dukes. He did his best for another victim, Lord Henry Lennox, who had been obliged to resign the post of First Commissioner of Works owing to a financial scandal. Disraeli offered him numerous positions which he foolishly refused.

[1] Algernon West, *Recollections*, ii, 78.
[2] Royal Archives, A.47.11, Disraeli to the Queen, March 24, 1874.

The list of Disraeli's efforts to reward friends and relations could be extended almost indefinitely. He caused something of a scandal by making his friend Lord Rosslyn, who was a society figure and man of pleasure, High Commissioner of the Church of Scotland. But when Lord Rosslyn angled for the Thistle Disraeli jibbed. He took much trouble over his brothers, and his successful effort, after the most complicated negotiations, to obtain for Ralph in 1875 the post of Clerk Assistant in the House of Lords elicited a letter of genuine gratitude from that touchy and ungracious figure. He offered the Viceroyalty of India to two people who had little obvious claim except that of sentiment: Lord Powis, a former Young Englander, who declined, and Lord Lytton, who accepted. He conferred a peerage on Baillie-Cochrane, another Young Englander, but long estranged from Disraeli and very unpopular. He made Lord Exmouth, with whom he had had financial dealings thirty years earlier, a Lord in Waiting. He offered a peerage to Andrew Montagu, who only refused because his heir was a natural son. He made Philip Rose a baronet. He offered numerous posts, including that of Clerk of Parliament, to Monty Corry, whose loyalty made him decline them all.

Nor was his sense of gratitude restricted to the lay field. He secured the Deanery of Ripon for the Reverend Sydney Turner, an unimportant clergyman whom he had earlier pressed on the Queen in vain for a canonry of Westminster which she was determined to give to the Reverend Mr Duckworth, Prince Leopold's former Governor.[1] Dean Wellesley was puzzled at this persistence.[2] He would have been less puzzled had he appreciated that Sydney Turner's father, Sharon Turner, had been a great friend of Isaac d'Israeli and was responsible for insisting upon the d'Israeli children being baptized when Isaac quarrelled with the Sephardic synagogue of Bevis Marks.[3]

Disraeli also obtained promotion for another clergyman of no special eminence, the Reverend and Honourable Orlando Forester. He was a brother of Lady Chesterfield and Lady Bradford. 'Dearest Lady C, Don't be later than five o'clock. There is a vacant canonry at York. You shall give it to Orlando. Yours ever D.'[4] To the Queen he wrote in a graver vein:

[1] *Letters of Queen Victoria*, 2nd Series, ii, 374–7.
[2] Royal Archives, D.6.12, Wellesley to Queen Victoria, January 30, 1875.
[3] See above, 11.
[4] Zetland, i, 115, July 8, 1874.

Mr Forester . . . is one of the most sincerely pious and benevolent beings that ever existed. Mr Disraeli has known him from his first curacy in Buckinghamshire before Your Majesty's happy accession.

Mr Forester is a man of science as well as of theology and literature.

His Church opinions are Evangelical, perhaps it should be said extremely Evangelical but his native high breeding guards him from the slightest approach to fanaticism.

Mr Forester is extremely pronounced against the Sacerdotal party and it is daily becoming more difficult to find men of his rank and culture actively adverse to Ritualism.[1]

The Queen, who disliked the Evangelicals as much as she disliked the Ritualists, evidently had doubts about this recommendation. She asked Ponsonby to consult Dean Wellesley, who replied that there was no objection to the appointment, although 'Mr Forester is a quiet clergyman quite undistinguished'. He suggested that when she gave her approval she 'might possibly hint that in selecting men of good family for those Cathedral dignitaries, it would be well if Mr Disraeli could choose men of distinction and eminence'.[2] The Queen was too outspoken to confine herself to a mere 'hint'. She passed on the Dean's views more or less verbatim, adding: '. . . it is very *important* that merit and true *liberal* broad views should be the recommendation. It is by such appointments alone that one can hope to strengthen the very tottering fabric of the Established Church. The extreme Evangelical School do the Established Church as much harm as the High Church.'[3]

It is fair to say that in general Disraeli was a good deal more cautious about ecclesiastical patronage than he had been in 1868, when the battle over the Irish Church was imminent. He did not place such emphasis on the Low Church party, and tried to hold a more even balance between the various factions, for example recommending Canon Lightfoot to the See of Durham as a recognition of 'that powerful party of the Anglican Church, which Lord Beaconsfield would describe as the "right centre": those who, though High Churchmen, firmly resist, or hitherto have resisted the deleterious designs of Canon Lyddon [*sic*] and the Dean of S Pauls,[4] who wish to terminate the connection between the Crown and the Church, and

[1] Royal Archives D.85, July 8, 1874.
[2] ibid., D.5.3, Ponsonby to the Queen, July 10, 1874.
[3] *The Letters of Queen Victoria*, 2nd Series, ii, 342.
[4] Dean Church.

ultimately, unite with the Greek Church.'[1] Nevertheless, Disraeli almost invariably thought of clerical patronage in political terms, and it was after a year of his second Premiership that Dean Wellesley made the observation quoted in an earlier chapter: 'He regards the Church as a great State-engine of the Conservatives.'

In one field Disraeli found it hard to bring in politics – surprisingly, that of legal appointments. 'Unfortunately,' he told the Queen, 'the promising lawyers are on the Opposition side of the House of Commons, several of them by no means opposed to Conservative views, but unhappily not anticipating the result of the last General Election.'[2] This was one of the penalties of being the minority party. Disraeli was making a virtue of necessity when he wrote to the Queen advising the appointment of Lord Moncrieff as a Scottish Lord of Appeal, although a Liberal. 'Lord Beaconsfield could not allow for a moment that in the high administration of justice such a consideration should prevail.'

Honours were recognized by everyone to be a legitimate source of oil for the political wheels. Disraeli was, perhaps, more candid than Gladstone in admitting this when he submitted recommendations to the Queen, but his motives were not basically different. He was less lavish than Gladstone, although more so than Palmerston. In the six years of Palmerston's last administration fifteen peerages were created. In Gladstone's first ministry, which lasted barely more than five years, the figure was thirty-seven. Disraeli, who was in office for slightly over six years, made twenty-two new peers, of whom one was a royal duke. Gladstone's second administration, which again only just exceeded five years, saw the creation of twenty-eight peers.[3]

Disraeli's programme of honours at the end of 1875 may be regarded as typical. He advised four peerages: R. Ormsby Gore, MP for Shropshire; M. G. Sturt, MP for Dorset; John Tollemache, who owned property in Suffolk and Cheshire; and Sir Robert Gerard, the scion of an old Lancashire Roman Catholic family. The last three had £45,000 to £60,000 p.a. each, and the first possessed

---

[1] M. & B., vi, 407, Disraeli to the Queen, January 27, 1879.

[2] Royal Archives, A.49.31, Disraeli to the Queen, July 30, 1875.

[3] These figures exclude eldest sons called up in their fathers' lifetime, and, of course, promotions within the existing peerage. Between 1830 and 1874 there had been 163 Liberal creations of peerages and 39 Conservative. As the Conservatives had been in office for only ten out of forty-four years, this seems fair enough, but, not surprisingly, few Conservatives regarded it in that light. The corresponding figures for baronetcies were 201 and 48.

large estates, though not as large as these. Disraeli proposed the
Earl of Abergavenny for a marquisate. He had £70,000 p.a. and as
Lord Neville, before his accession to the earldom in 1870, he had
been one of the ablest managers of the Conservative party. An
English peerage was to be conferred on the Earl of Erne, the richest
of those whom Disraeli was wont to call 'the mere Irish Peers'.
Finally, Lord Wharncliffe, who had restored his family fortunes by
a combination of hard work and good luck in the matter of mineral
resources on his property, was recommended for an earldom.

After that came the list of baronets, which included representatives of Scotland, Manchester, Staffordshire, Bedford, Surrey,
Lancashire and Devon.

The Queen agreed to these honours. Disraeli was pleased and
wrote in reply:

> The programme he placed before Your Majesty had been deeply
> considered; it consists in a great degree of representative men,
> and carried into effect by Your Majesty's favor, it will gratify
> large bodies of Your Majesty's subjects.
>   Notably both Protestants and Catholics; the landed interest
> especially: the three Kingdoms all recognized, while Manchester
> is not forgotten.
>   It will greatly strengthen Your Majesty's ministers and inspirit
> their friends.[1]

All seemed well, and the peerages went through without a hitch.
The baronetcies, however, caused difficulties. Disraeli had to withdraw the name of the Scottish representative

> who wants to be a peer and unreasonably. [His] main claim for
> that distinction is his having given half a million to the Scotch
> Church. As Mr. Disraeli is informed, [he] is not particularly de-
> voted to the Scotch Church, or any other Church, and if in this
> age of vast and rapidly formed fortunes it is to be understood
> that anyone who gives half a million to a public purpose should
> have a claim on the exercise of Your Majesty's highest preroga-
> tive, the House of Lords will soon be more numerous than the
> House of Commons.[2]

This turned out to be a correct prophecy. Disraeli had to look
elsewhere, but it was no good. 'Mr. Disraeli failed in finding a
Scotchman of sufficient importance to fill the post . . . Almost all

---

[1] Royal Archives, A.50.12, Disraeli to the Queen, November 28, 1875.
[2] ibid., A.50.22, Disraeli to the Queen, January 21, 1876.

Scotchmen, at least Conservative Scotchmen, are Baronets. That title abounds in Scotia.'[1]

The Queen was much more accommodating towards Disraeli than towards Gladstone, who often had to argue at length for his recommendations. The reason was not solely personal. The Queen welcomed Disraeli's relative frugality in the matter of honours, and frugality was by no means easy. No one who reads the correspondence of a Prime Minister for the first time can fail to be surprised at the importunacy of applicants for places and honours, and the frankness with which they canvass their claims. There is a vast number of such letters among the Hughenden Papers. One taken at random out of hundreds may be quoted. It is dated April 22, 1868, from a Mr Mackinnon of Aryse Park, Kent, whose lack of verbal fertility does not obscure his meaning.

> Dear Sir – In the course of my life I have entertained a great respect and kind feeling towards you. I have been desired by Lord Derby to address you when any object was desired by me. I am very desirous to have a Peerage conferred on me. My income is upwards of twenty thousand a year. The conferring of such an honour will bind me to you for life – Always faithfully yours W. A. Mackinnon.[2]

And he followed this up three months later with the assurance that 'I can command fifty votes in Kent and a good many in Lancashire'.[3] Evidently they were not enough: Mr Mackinnon remained a commoner.

During his first Premiership Disraeli was continually being told of promises or alleged promises made by Lord Derby. They were mostly the emanation of wishful thinking. One applicant was prepared to go back even farther. When Disraeli in 1868 made the Marquess of Abercorn a duke[4] he received a letter from the young Marquess of Ormonde, who said that Lord Liverpool had promised to revive the dukedom which his family had once possessed. He had taken the first step and promoted his grandfather from earl to marquess in 1825, but the Prime Minister's unfortunate 'seizure' had forestalled the second step. The family then decided not to press their claim, unless a new dukedom was created. Now it had

[1] ibid., A.50.23, Disraeli to the Queen, January 28, 1876.
[2] Hughenden Papers, Box 148, C/I/A/54a.
[3] ibid., C/I/A/68, July 31, 1868.
[4] The last non-royal creation of a duke except one, Westminster made by Gladstone in 1874.

been. Disraeli, however, saw no reason to act in the matter.

Another quaint and unsuccessful request came from the Marquess of Queensberry's mother-in-law. She was, she said, anxious to guard against the 'machinations' of his father-in-law (her husband), who was a Liberal. Queensberry was a Scottish peerage. Could Disraeli give him a United Kingdom peerage so that he could sit in the House of Lords and remain 'a good man and true'? 'He is very young: only 23: with good abilities and good principles but suffering from the overwhelming weight of high rank and nothing to do.'[1]

The fuss made over hereditary titles may seem absurd in a more democratic age, but there are, when all is said and done, more harmful ways of recompensing supporters. Disraeli summed up the matter well in a letter to the Queen on the subject of Earl Beauchamp, who wanted to be a marquess and refused to be fobbed off with a GCB.[2] Beauchamp had been Lord Steward of the Household and had apparently offended the Queen by peremptory dealings with some of the royal servants.[3] Disraeli agreed to relieve him of his office, but Beauchamp was reluctant to go unless some recognition of his services was conferred on him. The Queen was not willing to agree to the marquisate. Disraeli in reply admitted that Lord Beauchamp was 'a disagreeable man'. But he had 'conducted for four years the business of the Home Office in the House of Lords with sustained ability'. Moreover

> . . . he is a great partisan, fought at the last election his own county and several boroughs in his county. It is impossible to throw such men over if you wish to keep a political party together. Such men must be rewarded and if they have fancies for Marquisates, it is better that they should be Marquesses than Cabinet Ministers.[4]

But presumably Disraeli did not press the matter. At all events Lord Beauchamp did not become a marquess. Happily any hard feelings had died away two years later, for, in what Disraeli rather unkindly described to Lady Bradford as 'a letter of menacing hospitality', Beauchamp offered to put him up in his town house after the fall of the Government in 1880.

In addition to these hereditary titles such honours as the Garter

---

[1] Hughenden Papers, Box 148, C/5/A/76, August 31, 1868.
[2] ibid., Box 83/B/XIX/C/528, Disraeli to the Queen, April 10, 1878 (copy).
[3] ibid., Box 101, B/XX/Ln/84, Beauchamp to Disraeli, May 15, 1878.
[4] ibid., Box 83, B/XIX/C/533, April 12, 1878 (copy).

and the Thistle were important counters in the political game, and in those days were bestowed on purely partisan lines. It is only recently that they have reverted to the personal gift of the Sovereign. For example, in 1868 Disraeli refused to recommend the Garter for the Duke of Northumberland. The Duke wanted the Garter badly, but insisted on sitting on the cross benches. Disraeli was not prepared to accept such terms. But dukes frequently seemed perverse. The Duke of Norfolk quixotically refused the Garter in 1878 because he was going to join the Conservative party. The Duke of Portland refused it for no reason at all – at any rate none that he would avow. Possibly he remembered calling in his loan to Disraeli nearly twenty years earlier, or perhaps it was sheer eccentricity.

Then there was the Thistle. A vacancy occurred in 1876. Should it go to the Duke of Hamilton, who had fought valiantly for the Royal Titles Bill against Lord Shaftesbury's 'malignant motion', or should it go to Sir William Stirling-Maxwell, 'the most eminent man in Scotland', with a European reputation, 'high social position and vast fortune'?[1] It is scarcely necessary to add that he was also a redoubtable partisan and, with a gap from 1868 to 1874, had been Conservative Member for Perth since 1852. Disraeli plumped for Sir William, thereby, as we saw earlier, setting a new precedent in conferring that honour upon a commoner.

Just over a year later Sir William died, thus causing vacancies for the Thistle and both the Parliamentary representation and Lord Lieutenancy of Perthshire. This required delicate handling. Lord Lieutenancies were important counters, too, and it so happened that another one was vacant, Wiltshire. Disraeli advised giving the Thistle to the Duke of Hamilton, 'provided he fulfils the condition which is requisite'; and, he added in a letter to Lady Bradford, he 'must manage to go to Court – which he never yet has done'. He recommended the Duke of Athole as Lord Lieutenant, but there was no hurry in the matter. Perthshire was not a safe seat and the active efforts of all the local Conservative magnates were needed. 'It is as well that the Perthshire election should be decided before the Ld. Lieutenant is named, as the appointment of the Duke of Athole might cool the ardor of the Earl of Mansfield.' For differing reasons delay over Wiltshire would be a good thing, too. The position was passionately sought by Lord Bath. But 'Considering his very offensive conduct during the agitation of last year and his banquets

[1] Royal Archives, A.51.10, Disraeli to the Queen, November 8, 1876.

to Messrs. Liddon, Gladstone and Freeman Ld. Beaconsfield thinks it shd not be hastily bestowed on Lord Bath. Even if ultimately accorded to him, he ought to be kept in a period of "dread suspense".'[1]

There was one Lord Lieutenancy which had much more than an honorific status, that of Ireland. Disraeli had a serious problem on his hands when in 1876 the Duke of Abercorn resigned. Disraeli favoured the Duke of Marlborough, 'because he is quite at a loss to fix on any other suitable Peer'. He reviewed the various possibilities in a letter to the Queen:

> Lord Brownlow will not go; Lord Bradford will not go; Lord Beauchamp, who might have done (tho he wd have been a quarrelsome Viceroy) has now lost his wife, a necessary appendage for such a post.
>   Tho' the D. of Marlboro' is not rich for a Duke, he is rich enough for the office. Of late the Duke has been parting with his outlying properties (notably in Bucks where he sold the Waddesdon Estate last year to Ferdinand de Rothschild for £240,000) and has been putting his house in order and Mr. Disraeli has been informed that His Grace has his Oxfordshire estate now quite clear. That is an affair of 22,000 acres and brings in a revenue of £35000 pr annum, at least. Lord Skelmersdale has not capacity for the office and his fortune tho' adequate for a Baron is only half that of the D. of Marlboro's – about £20,000 pr annum.[2]

The Duke of Marlborough had refused the position when Disraeli offered it to him in 1874. To fill it in proper style cost £40,000 p.a., and the salary was only half that figure. Now he decided to accept for a reason which leads one naturally to consider another time-consuming, though to Disraeli far from disagreeable, aspect of his life as Prime Minister, the problems of royalty. Throughout the early months of 1876 society had been humming with one of the juiciest scandals for years. This was the famous Aylesford affair, which caused a resounding quarrel between the Duke's younger son, Lord Randolph Churchill, and the Prince of Wales.

The story is told in Sir Philip Magnus's biography of the Prince.[3] We are concerned here only with Disraeli's part. Briefly the facts were that Lady Aylesford, wife of one of the Prince's boon com-

---

[1] Royal Archives, A.62.1, Disraeli to the Queen, January 20, 1878. Lord Lieutenancies were important in England not only as honours for those chosen but because of their patronage in recommending the appointment of JPs.

[2] Royal Archives, A.50.56, Disraeli to the Queen, August 7, 1876.

[3] Sir Philip Magnus, *King Edward the Seventh* (1964), 143–50.

panions, had fallen passionately in love with Lord Blandford, the
Duke's elder son and heir. While the Prince was in India accompanied by Aylesford, Blandford, who was himself married, proposed
to elope with her. Aylesford declared his intention to institute
divorce proceedings, and hurried back to England ahead of the
Prince. Lord Randolph Churchill, rushing impetuously to his
brother's rescue, convinced himself that the Prince had it in his
power to stop Lord Aylesford and only abstained from doing so
because the two were engaged in a conspiracy to throw Lady Aylesford into Blandford's arms. Obtaining from Blandford a packet of
letters written at an earlier stage to Lady Aylesford by the Prince
himself and couched in indiscreet language, Lord Randolph now
tried to blackmail the Prince into bringing pressure on Aylesford.
Moreover, the Prince still being out of the country, he called on
Princess Alexandra at Marlborough House and told her that he had
letters whose publication would guarantee that the Prince 'would
never sit on the throne of England'.

The Prince was furious, issued a challenge to a duel, and meanwhile charged Lord Hardwicke to put the whole matter before
Disraeli, who was now drawn, by no means reluctantly, into an
affair more reminiscent of the Regency than the last quarter of the
nineteenth century.

He summoned Churchill, who was obdurate, but the combined
pressure of the Prime Minister and Lord Hardwicke was effective on
Aylesford, who withdrew the divorce proceedings. Public scandal
was thus averted, but the Prince was, not unnaturally, determined
to get his own back. The Churchills were socially ostracized. They
departed on a tour of America, but were pursued by letters informing them that the Prince would accept nothing less than an apology
drawn up by the Lord Chancellor and approved by Disraeli and
Hartington. Lord Randolph signed, deliberately choosing the
anniversary of Saratoga for the date and adding in a postscript
that 'as a gentleman' he had to accept the word of the Lord Chancellor for the drafting of the document. This action was not calculated to placate the Prince, who let it be known that he would refuse
to go to any house which received the Randolph Churchills. In these
circumstances the Duke of Marlborough, like an inverted Lord
Lundy, resolved to go out and govern Ireland, taking his erring son
with him as his private secretary.

It is hard to avoid the impression that Disraeli rather enjoyed this discreditable affair. It was a far call from his youthful obscurity that he should not only be Prime Minister of England, but – by no means a concomitant of that position – a social arbiter as well; settling disputes between the heir to the throne and a ducal house. According to Sir Philip Magnus, the slight hint of irony which was discernible in his attitude irked the Prince. Certainly the Prince, though far more sympathetic towards Conservative than Liberal policies, was less at ease socially with Disraeli than with Gladstone.[1] He was not the only person to be disconcerted at the elaborate manner of the Prime Minister and to wonder, perhaps only half consciously, just what sardonic reflections might be flowing behind that cryptic countenance.

The quarrel between the Prince and Lord Randolph was not made up until after Disraeli's death and at a time when Lord Randolph had become famous. But Disraeli was not a bad prophet. In July 1880 he told Sir Stafford Northcote that he thought the Prince had been very unfair, for it had been understood that the apology would end the matter, 'but the Prince having got his apology still kept up the grievance; but nothing, said the Chief, will help Randolph into favour again so much as success in Parliament; the Prince is always taken by success'.[2]

The Aylesford affair was the most serious of royal problems during Disraeli's Premiership, but it was far from being the only one. Another less grave, but scarcely less tiresome, was the episode in March 1877 of the Duke of Edinburgh and Prince Alexander of Battenberg.[3] Prince Alfred, Duke of Edinburgh, was the Queen's second son and, though a competent naval officer, seems to have been by far the least agreeable of the royal princes. He was, moreover, married to the Tsar's only daughter and was naturally inclined to sympathize with the Russian point of view during the Eastern crisis. In such circumstances it was scarcely sensible to give him command of *Sultan*, one of the ships in Admiral Hornby's squadron destined for Constantinople. The situation was made all the more delicate because one of *Sultan*'s junior officers was Prince Louis of Battenberg, whose brother, Prince Alexander, was not only ADC to the Commander-in-Chief of the Russian armies, the Grand Duke Nicholas, but the Russian candidate for the throne of the Big

[1] Magnus, 147.
[2] *British Museum*, Add. MSS, 50063A, Northcote's diary, July 12, 1880.
[3] Viscount Chilston, *W. H. Smith* (1965), 112–14.

Bulgaria which the Tsar hoped to carve out of Turkey-in-Europe. In these circumstances it was, to say the least, unwise of Prince Alfred to ask Prince Alexander to dinner on board his ship.

The Queen was furious when she heard the news, and, although the episode later appeared slightly less grave when it was learnt that Prince Alexander had tactfully worn German, not Russian, uniform, she was determined to have her son officially rapped over the knuckles. Admiral Hornby seemed the obvious person to do this, but unluckily it turned out that the Admiral had himself gone to the ill-fated dinner on board *Sultan*. On March 16 Disraeli wrote to the Queen: 'The more Lord Beaconsfield attempts to deal with the business of the Duke of Edinburgh the greater become the difficulties. Indeed it costs Ld Beaconsfield more trouble than the Eastern question itself.'[1]

Meanwhile the Queen had written to her son informing him that a letter of reprimand was on its way.[2] No letter arrived and the Prince threatened to demand a Court of Inquiry. Matters were further complicated because of the danger that the Prince might return home – a contingency which greatly alarmed the Queen, who regarded him as a bad influence on her youngest son, the Duke of Connaught. Disraeli conducted a lengthy three-cornered correspondence throughout the summer with the Queen and W. H. Smith. '*The Gentleman must not* come home', he wrote to Smith on one occasion. 'You don't know him.'[3] Smith showed great patience, tact and good sense. There were many other difficulties, the root of the problem being the Queen's inability to allow her son to be treated as an ordinary naval officer, which resulted in a continual crossing of wires. She was most annoyed with the unfortunate Hornby and at first refused to give him the KCB for his services in the Straits. It required the combined efforts of Disraeli and Smith to overcome her reluctance. 'Ld B thanks yr M. for yr M's Kindness', wrote Disraeli on August 6. 'It is magnanimous but for the best.'[4]

It was typical of Disraeli's tact that, although acting as an umpire in these and other delicate matters he remained on excellent terms with all the parties concerned. Lord Randolph never ceased to admire the old statesman to whose mantle he later aspired. The Edinburghs invited Disraeli to a house-warming party at Clarence

[1] Royal Archives, B.57.11.
[2] Quoted by Viscount Chilston, *W. H. Smith* (1965), 114.
[3] op. cit., 113.
[4] Royal Archives, B.58.54.

House, where, apart from Dr Quinn, the first homoeopath in England and as a famous wit much in demand, he was the only non-royalty present. Whatever slight uneasiness the Prince of Wales may at times have felt did not affect his conduct. Disraeli often stayed at Sandringham, not wholly to the liking of the Queen, who surveyed any intimacy between her Prime Minister and her heir with a dubious eye. In fact, Disraeli did not greatly enjoy going there, especially after the Congress of Berlin, for the King of Greece, who was Princess Alexandra's brother, had a chronic grievance about the frontier settlement. 'The Greek question is becoming a serious and painful question under that roof,' Disraeli wrote to the Queen on April 4, 1879, '. . . and its [the Greek] Govt evidently counts on the support of influences which in their nature are not responsible . . .'[1] And he managed on this occasion to excuse himself.

At the end of 1879 the Prince intimated that he would like to stay *en garçon* at Hughenden for a night, and on Disraeli's request nominated as co-guests Lord Salisbury and Sir William Hart-Dyke, the Chief Whip, from the world of politics, Lord Rosslyn and Bernal Osborne from that of fashion. The task of preserving the Prince from boredom was one that taxed the united efforts of the English and Continental *haute monde* for over forty years. Disraeli anticipated the visit with some apprehension; the more so since it was to occur in mid-January, he could only accommodate a small house party, and there were no ladies. But all went off well, although Disraeli had to make up a four of whist with his august guest – he hated cards except with one or other of the beloved sisters – and there was a snowstorm the next morning. Rosslyn and Osborne played the part of court jesters; 'expressed and elicited many a flashing phrase', as Disraeli told the Queen, or, as he put it to Lady Bradford, 'the dinner was like a pantomime where there are two clowns, and both capital ones'.

[1] ibid., B.60.45, Disraeli to the Queen, April 4, 1879.

CHAPTER XXX

The Fall of 'Beaconsfieldism'

1879–80

1

One can admire Disraeli's triumph over old age, bereavement and bad health, but in terms of politics his vitality was only relative. It was remarkable that he carried on at all, but there is no doubt that, anyway after Berlin, he lacked the power to galvanize a tired administration. The session of 1879 was the least productive in his ministry. The newly found obstructionist technique of the Parnellites is part, but not all of the explanation. Ministers were losing the initiative; it is hard to avoid the impression that during the last eighteen months of his Premiership Disraeli waited upon, rather than shaped, events. And events could scarcely have gone worse.

The troubles in India and Africa have already been described. Far more serious was something which lay outside governmental control altogether, as its scope was then understood: the halting of the great period of economic expansion which had begun in the 1840s and continued without a serious check ever since. The reasons for this change are the subject of much controversy, but the fact is beyond dispute, and first became obvious in 1876. During that year the slump which had hitherto affected particular regions started to become general. The consequences can be seen in trade-union statistics of unemployment: 4·7 per cent in 1877, 6·8 in 1878, 11·4 in 1879, which was one of the worst years in the second half of the nineteenth century. There was a spate of bankruptcies, and the failure of the City of Glasgow Bank in 1878 was only the most sensational of a series of commercial disasters.

Even graver and, as it turned out, more far-reaching developments occurred in agriculture. The repeal of the Corn Laws had hitherto produced none of the consequences predicted by the pessimists. For thirty years English farming had flourished as never before and with it the landed class which Disraeli had so valiantly defended, regarding all others in comparison as 'leather and prunella'. Now that long ascendancy came to an end. The situation

was aggravated by four wet summers running, with their inevitable
bad harvests, but the real trouble lay deeper. The ending of the
American Civil War, the consequential opening up of the great
plains of the west, new agricultural machinery, and the fall in
freight rates caused by the change from sail to steam, all combined
to hit English and European grain prices like a typhoon. In 1877
English wheat averaged 56s 9d a quarter. The following year it had
fallen to 46s 5d and dropped steadily thereafter. The farmer, moreover, no longer had his old consolation that a bad harvest would at
least mean higher prices. Cheap imported grain made the consequences of a rainy summer doubly disastrous. This alarming
economic change affected all the countries of Europe and, with the
exception of Belgium, all reacted in the same way: they raised
tariffs on imported foodstuffs, and, since their manufacturers soon
demanded similar protection, free trade became a dead letter within
a few years. But in Britain no such action followed.

It is a major question in assessing Disraeli's career to decide why
this was. On the face of things it might have seemed little short of
providential that the man who had so bitterly opposed the repeal of
the Corn Laws should be Prime Minister thirty years later when
events were belatedly vindicating everything he had said. It has
often, and not surprisingly, been made a reproach to Disraeli that
he did nothing at all. He was certainly aware of the problem. His
own experience as a landlord at Hughenden would have convinced
him, quite apart from the jeremiads of his grand friends and the
well-publicized distress up and down the whole country. There was a
great deal of agitation either for reciprocity or for the simple re-
imposition of the Corn Laws. But Disraeli believed it to be politically
hopeless; he said so quite frankly in the House of Lords on March 28
and again on April 29. It was all very well quoting 'rusty phrases of
mine forty years ago'. The issue had been settled and could not be
reopened. He was probably right. Agriculture was now only one of
many English industries, and although it still employed more men
than any other, it no longer determined the prosperity of the whole
nation. The fall in prices had, moreover, an obverse side. However
unwelcome to the farmer and landlord, it was a boon to the consumer. The urban working classes at a time of industrial depression
and rising unemployment would have reacted bitterly against protection, which was bound to deprive them of their one consolation,
cheap food. Any widespread working-class hostility would be fatal

at a general election. Disraeli's own Reform Act of 1867 had killed whatever chance there was – and it was not much – of resuscitating the Corn Laws.

The natural time to have dissolved Parliament according to the normal usage of the day would have been after the sixth session, which could if necessary be curtailed; that is to say some time in the summer or autumn of 1879. But, for reasons which are not at all clear, Disraeli let the moment slip by. It was a mistake for which he was to pay dearly. An election in, say, the early summer of 1879 would probably have resulted in defeat, but nothing like the disaster of 1880. By July the Liberal machine was fully geared for battle, and the autumn municipal elections showed a significant further swing away from the Conservatives. In the counties rising discontent at the failure of the Government to assist agriculture caused a substantial element of the normally most loyal Tory class to move from Conservatism to the newly founded Farmers' Alliance which put up its own candidates at the election of 1880. Finally, the delay gave the Liberal party managers the chance to organize one of the most successful demonstrations in British electoral history, Gladstone's first Midlothian campaign.

The decision to run Gladstone as candidate for this Scottish county seat was the result of careful thought and much detailed planning. It was a marginal constituency won back for the Tories in 1874 by Lord Dalkeith, son and heir to the Duke of Buccleuch, who was the greatest proprietor in the Lowlands, where he possessed nearly half a million acres. Although Buccleuch owned relatively little in Midlothian, the family was popular and their enormous wealth a great asset. Nevertheless a secret canvass convinced W. P. Adam, the Liberal Chief Whip, at the beginning of 1879, that a small Liberal majority existed among the still very limited electorate, under 3,000 all told. Accordingly in January a 'Requisition' bound in the most expensive leather was sent from the Liberals of Midlothian urging Gladstone to be their candidate at the next election. The GOM accepted, and the two parties at once entered into a desperate struggle fought in terms reminiscent of the eighteenth century, with such devices as the creation of 'faggot votes' and the intimidation of tenants who, whether from sheer conservatism or from a well-founded fear of corruption, seemed to behave as if the Ballot Act had never been passed. The Conservatives had no monopoly in these matters. The young Lord Rosebery, another great local landowner, though not as rich as the Duke of Buccleuch, was quite rich enough. He exerted all his 'influence' in favour of Gladstone, and as far as the actual electors of Midlothian were concerned the battle was largely an old-fashioned contest between two great Scottish noblemen using the old-fashioned but still effective weapons of a previous era.

This silent struggle was very necessary if Gladstone was to win the seat, but it was not what made Midlothian famous. That was Gladstone's decision to speak during the late autumn at a series of mass meetings and demonstrations arranged on a hitherto unparalleled scale. They were largely organized by Rosebery, who had once attended a Democrat convention in New York and who applied with notable success transatlantic techniques to Scottish electioneering. Gladstone made Disraeli's foreign and imperial policies the principal objects of attack, in particular the continuing campaign for Kabul. A single much-quoted sentence gives the keynote of his oratory. 'Remember that the sanctity of life in the hill villages of Afghanistan, among the winter snows, is as inviolable in the eye of Almighty God as can be your own.' His 'progress', which lasted from November 24 to December 8, drew vast crowds and great enthusiasm. How far this tour, and his second in 1880 on the eve of the general election, were responsible for the nation-wide Conservative defeat remains a moot point. It is, however, clear that his oratory had less effect on the electors of Midlothian than did the activities of Rosebery and the local Liberal manager. Most of the vote which was to put Gladstone in by a narrow margin for Midlothian had been secured before the campaigns began.

Disraeli, whether genuinely or otherwise, dismissed these rhetorical ebullitions as of no importance. 'I have not read a single line', he told Lady Bradford on November 28, '. . . what a waste of powder and shot! Because all this was planned on the wild assumption that Parliament was going to be dissolved, whereas, as Sir George Bowyer, apparently from authority has just informed the world, Parliament will probably not be dissolved till the year after next.' The question of dissolution was, in fact, still undecided. Although it is very unlikely that Disraeli ever seriously considered delaying till February 1881, the latest date permissible under the Septennial Act, he was in no hurry to go to the country yet, and he evidently envisaged another full session. The immediate electoral prospect certainly seemed black. True, there was no particular reason for it to become any less so, but politicians tend to be Micawbers.

This lack of urgency may have been why Disraeli made no effort to answer in kind Gladstone's massive indictment of the Government's record. It was probably not his only reason. The Conservative tradition was against 'stump oratory' until Lord Randolph Churchill put an end to such false modesty. Disraeli was better in Parliament than mass meetings, and, although peers were not inhibited from platform speaking except in the course of an actual election campaign, he probably felt the practice to be beneath his dignity. Moreover, it was an odious winter of frost, snow, fog and fearful storms, one of which produced the Tay Bridge disaster; no weather for an elderly asthmatic invalid who found it hard enough to go up from Buckinghamshire for the November Cabinets, let alone orate to the nation. Perhaps, too, having survived Gladstone's onslaughts at the time of the Bulgarian atrocities, Disraeli and his colleagues did not take Midlothian very seriously. If so, they made an error. It was all very well for Disraeli to talk privately of 'Gladstone's rhodomontade and rigmarole'. The absence of any reply inevitably caused the public to conclude that no effective reply could be made.

Accordingly Disraeli and his colleagues spent much of the winter preparing legislation for the next session. Sir Stafford Northcote believed that he could produce a budget that would not increase taxation. Disraeli regarded this as a vote-winner. Moreover, the Cabinet had up its sleeve an amended Corrupt Practices Act, removing the prohibition on payment by candidates for the conveyance of voters to the polls in boroughs. Since the existing Act already allowed such payments in the counties, and since the ban was habitually evaded in the boroughs, there was a good argument on common-sense grounds for assimilating the practices, but inevitably the Opposition would be likely to protest at its partisan implications. The only two other measures of importance both emanated from Cross. One was a relatively uncontentious Bill dealing with Scottish law. It can be regarded as a belated effort to acquit the Government of the stock Liberal charge that it neglected Scotland. The other, and as it turned out much more controversial, measure was a Bill to buy out the eight private water companies supplying the London area and replace them by a single public authority.

Disraeli's immediate preoccupation after Christmas was the visit of the Prince of Wales to Hughenden. With that behind him he went up to London and plunged into a whirl of Cabinet meetings and dinner parties, including one at Stafford House – 'a worse dinner I never saw and poisonous claret. He must have sent round to some neighbouring estaminet at 5 francs a head and Gladstone liquour.'[1] The result was a 'feverish attack' which laid him up for nearly two weeks. As chance would have it a large number of his colleagues were incapacitated at the same time. Salisbury was too ill to leave Hatfield, Lord John Manners injured himself hunting, Sir Stafford Northcote took to his bed with influenza, and a London pea-souper induced asthma in the Lord Chancellor, who fled to Bournemouth, only to find the fog there even worse.[2] Disraeli was barely able to attend for the opening of Parliament performed in person by the Queen on February 5, and deputed the task of carrying the sword of state to the Duke of Richmond.

The Queen, who was much disturbed at the possibility of Irish obstruction making the session impossible, mooted the idea of a dissolution. She wondered whether she ought to use her influence to facilitate an agreement with 'some of the sensible and reasonable and not violent men on the other side to put a stop to what is clearly a determination to force the disruption of the British empire'.[3] In reply Disraeli said: 'There are no "sensible and reasonable and not violent men" in the ranks of the opposition on whom your Majesty might now act.' The nominal leaders had no authority and the rest 'under the . . . inspiration of Mr. Gladstone, who avoids the responsibility of his position, are animated by an avidity for office such as Lord Beaconsfield after more than forty years experience cannot recall'. He also pointed to the awkwardness of dropping promised legislation, and difficulties about supplies and the Mutiny Act.[4] On the following day, February 14, he reported to the Queen that the Cabinet was unanimously opposed to an immediate dissolution unless some unexpected crisis blew up.

But on that very day news came through which was to produce a complete volte-face. Already in the New Year there had been apparent signs of a change in the electoral climate. A by-election at Liverpool where the Liberals confidently expected to gain a seat resulted in the Conservatives holding it by 2,200 votes. Admittedly this was less than the general election figure of 3,500, but in all the

[1] Zetland, ii, 260, Disraeli to Lady Bradford, January 19.
[2] ibid., 261, January 29.
[3] M. & B., vi, 511, the Queen to Disraeli, February 12.
[4] loc. cit., Disraeli to the Queen, February 13.

circumstances it seemed a good result, although Gladstone shrewdly pointed out that on the true comparison, that between the proportion of voters supporting the Government in 1874 and 1880, the figures looked less favourable to the Conservatives. The number who voted had gone up from 37,000 to 50,000 and therefore in order to equal their performance at the general election the Conservatives should have won by 4,700.[1]

But there now followed a by-election which the Liberals could not laugh off. This was at Southwark, a Liberal stronghold which the Conservative candidate, Edward Clarke, QC, managed to gain. True, the Liberal vote was split and so a Conservative victory was not unexpected. But the significant feature was that Clarke, who was a very good candidate, did not get in on a mere plurality but polled rather more than the combined vote of his opponents, obtaining 7,683 against the official Liberal's 6,830 and the dissident Radical's 799. Cross recalls how the telegram with the news arrived in the middle of the Cabinet meeting and how Disraeli struck his hand upon the table in a gesture of triumph.[2] The Queen was no less delighted. She had just sent a valentine for which Disraeli had thanked her in characteristic terms. His 'life of anxiety and toil', he said, 'has its romance when he remembers that he labours for the most gracious of beings'. The Queen followed up her gift with a telegram of glee: 'I am greatly rejoiced at the great victory at Southwark. It shows what the feeling of the country is.'[3]

But did it? That was the question. Certainly it caused consternation among the Liberals. 'Liverpool except upon the surface was bearable enough,' wrote Gladstone to Granville, 'Southwark is a disgrace as well as a defeat.'[4] Granville could only offer the consolation that the official Liberal 'was a lamentable candidate . . . I doubt it being much of a test'. But he conceded that it was 'a great moral blow'.[5] The Conservative party managers thought it was also a straw in the wind. On March 6 the Cabinet reconsidered the

[1] Gladstone to Granville, February 10, 1880. A. Ramm, *The Political Correspondence of Mr. Gladstone and Lord Granville, 1876–86*, i, 112. A modern psephologist would say that the by-election indicated a 2.5 per cent swing to the Liberals. The swing at the ensuing general election, in so far as it can be calculated at all, seems to have been about 5 per cent. See below, 712.

[2] Cross, *A Political History*, 63.

[3] Royal Archives, B.63.5, draft.

[4] Ramm, 113.

[5] ibid., 115.

question of dissolution. The peers abstained from pushing their views on what was regarded as essentially a House of Commons matter, but the Commons ministers, with the exceptions of Beach and Manners, were in favour of an early election, and were supported by the Whips and the Central Office. Northcote and Cross, normally cautious enough, were particularly enthusiastic.[1] Disraeli backed them and the Cabinet decided to dissolve as soon as possible.

The Southwark by-election was undoubtedly the chief reason for this ill-starred decision, but Cross's Water Bill was a contributory factor. Hence the jest that the Conservatives 'came in on beer and went out on water'. For the Bill, which was never actually debated, had a very bad reception from Press and public on its introduction in the House at the beginning of March. It was said that the sum offered to compensate the companies, £33m, was grossly excessive and that a leakage of confidential information had been the cause of the great recent rise in the value of the companies' shares. The charges were unfounded, and when after twenty-three years of highly unsatisfactory conditions, including more than one water famine, the companies were at last municipalized by the LCC in 1903, the price that had to be paid was £47m. But there is no doubt that the dissolution saved the Cabinet from the awkward dilemma of either trying to carry a very unpopular Bill or dropping it with inevitable loss of face.

The announcement of the dissolution on March 8 caused general surprise, for the Queen had opened Parliament in person and it was assumed that this precluded an early election. Disraeli's supporters were as much taken aback as the Opposition, and with more serious consequences; the Conservative party machine had become extremely rusty, whereas the Liberals' was in excellent working order. Disraeli had made the same mistake as Gladstone in 1874, springing an election on to an ill-prepared party at very short notice.

Although there may be argument about the reasons, there is no doubt about the fact that the Conservative organization was in a bad way. Gorst, who in 1877 had resigned from the Central Office in a huff, warned Disraeli that the party was heading for a fall. He attributed the trouble to the new Chief Whip, Sir William Hart Dyke's, managing elections at the Treasury. 'I always thought this a most unwise policy on the part of the late government and since we have been in office experience has justified that opinion. Instead of

[1] M. & B., vi, 523, quoting memo. by Lord Barrington.

the management being vested in my office under Sir W. Dyke's control I have been consulted intermittently, in certain elections only, and at certain stages only of the elections: money has been spent against my advice and without my knowledge.'[1] Gorst had a grievance. He had failed to get into Parliament in 1874, and when he did return a year later he was discontented at what he considered the inadequate offer of the secretaryship of the Board of Trade. He refused, but made the mistake of not seeking an interview with Disraeli. Later Disraeli reproached him saying, according to Gorst's son,[2] 'Why did you not come and ask me for something. I have always been accustomed to people pestering me for appointments, and I could not understand your keeping away. You have been very badly treated and I am extremely sorry for it.' These mollifying remarks removed any resentment felt by Gorst towards his chief, but not his hostility to the rest of the Tory hierarchy. Dyke frequently refers to his 'crotchets', and Gorst was indeed a prickly man. But it seems likely that his criticisms were well founded.

Perhaps the situation would not have been so bad if Dyke himself had not fallen ill at the end of 1879 from overwork. Gorst's successor Skene was weak, there was no clear chain of responsibility; and the conduct of the election fell into commission between the assistant whips, who acted without co-ordination. Nor was there any proper supervision of the election fund, which was managed, rather surprisingly, by the Serjeant-at-Arms to the House of Lords. Disraeli must bear some of the blame, but he had become out of touch with electoral matters since he went to the House of Lords, and he may have expected Northcote as leader to the Commons to take the same share that he himself had taken under Derby in fostering party organization and morale. If so, he misjudged his man. Northcote had his virtues, but the capacity to rejuvenate a weary party was not one of them.

At about this time a curious chance gave Disraeli the chance to do something to show his gratitude towards the family that had in a sense made his political fortune. The eccentric 5th Duke of Portland, who had thwarted him by refusing the Garter, died in December 1879, having long outlived his younger brothers. The dukedom and a large part of his vast estates passed to a cousin, a young officer of

[1] March 3, 1877, quoted by Hanham, 362.
[2] H. Gorst, *The Fourth Party* (1906), 34.

twenty-two in the Coldstream Guards. Both his parents were dead, but his stepmother Mrs Cavendish-Bentinck, of whom he was very fond, was still alive. It occurred to Disraeli that he might give pleasure to the family by making her a peeress in her own right with special remainder to the heirs male of her deceased husband. He secured the Queen's somewhat hesitant assent, arguing that it was not intended on general social grounds as a precedent for step-mothers of dukes, but rather because 'it would add greatly to the strength of your Majesty's present government'. He wisely did not say how, confessing instead, 'as he has no secrets from your Majesty . . . that he is himself much interested in the question'.[1]

The Duke then received an invitation to Hughenden and he would often describe the strange experience that followed. He was accompanied on the train by Corry and driven through the foggy winter evening from High Wycombe station to the house. The three of them dined alone with no other guests. Disraeli wore the blue sash of the Garter and scarcely uttered a word throughout the meal. It must have been an alarming ordeal for a young man, however great the position he had inherited. It must have been even more frighten-ing when, at the end of dinner, after the dessert was on the table and the servants had left, Disraeli unexpectedly rose to his feet and commencing with a bow and the words 'My Lord Duke' made a brief oration in his grandest manner, expressing his obligation to the Duke's family and his intention to recommend a peerage for Mrs Bentinck. The Duke remembered to the end of his life – and would often describe – the sudden flicker of animation crossing Disraeli's parchment countenance when almost hissing the phrase, he said, 'I come from a race which never forgives an injury' – and then the shutter of impassivity came down – 'nor forgets a benefit.' When the speech was over the young Duke began to stammer out his thanks, but Disraeli cutting him short with a gesture excused him-self on the grounds of work and left him with Corry. On April 23 Mrs Bentinck's peerage was gazetted in the resignation honours as Baroness Bolsover. When she died in 1892 the title passed to the dukedom, where it still remains – a silent reminder surviving in the books of the peerage that Disraeli was able to repay something of the debt of gratitude which he had owed to the shade of Lord George Bentinck for over thirty years.

[1] *The Letters of Queen Victoria*, 2nd Series, iii, 69, February 8, 1880.

2

Parliament was to be formally dissolved on March 24, and the first borough elections were to begin a week later. Meanwhile on March 9 Disraeli's election manifesto appeared. It took the form of an open letter to the Duke of Marlborough in his capacity as Viceroy of Ireland, and its burden was the imminent danger of Irish separatism. Apart from one famous phrase – 'men of light and leading' – it was a singularly uninspiring document, and abounded with obscure clumsy sentences, including one that was wholly ungrammatical. The content was no more satisfactory than the form. Oracular warnings about Home Rule couched in terms of 'muffled grandiloquence', as Garvin puts it, rang no bell for an electorate quite unprepared for this political theme. It alienated Irish voters in England who were urged by the Home Rule Confederation to 'vote against Benjamin Disraeli as you would against the mortal enemy of your country and your race'. Yet it failed to arouse any compensating rally of unionist sentiment which saw no particular danger in a Liberal party officially just as much committed to the Union as the Conservatives.

Disraeli's manifesto may be looked at in two ways. He was, of course, right in the long run. The Liberals did espouse Home Rule and ruined themselves politically in the process, but this happened five years after he had departed from the scene. In the long run, as Keynes once observed, we are all dead. At the time the manifesto seemed an attempt to distract public attention by stirring up racial prejudice. Irish immigrants created as much of a social problem then as black immigrants did eighty years later. Gladstone, ironically in the light of later events, described Disraeli's warnings as 'baseless' and 'terrifying insinuations' whose 'true purpose is to hide from view the acts of the ministry and their effect upon the character and condition of the country'.

And on the subject of that effect he was eloquent indeed. Undeterred by a forged telegram sent in Lord Rosebery's name by Lord Claud Hamilton urging him to withdraw from the Midlothian contest,[1] he undertook a second whirlwind campaign which occupied the whole of the last fortnight in March. Already in his election address he had denounced the Government for having

neglected legislation, aggravated the public distress by continual

[1] R. R. James, *Rosebery*, 103 n.

shocks to confidence . . . endangered the prerogative by gross misuse . . . weakened the empire by needless wars . . . dishonoured it in the eyes of Europe by filching the island of Cyprus from Porte . . . aggrandised Russia, lured Turkey on to her dismemberment if not her ruin, replaced the Christian population of Macedonia under a degrading yoke, and loaded India with the costs and dangers of an unjustifiable war . . . From day to day, under a Ministry called, as if in mockery, conservative, the nation is perplexed with fear of change.

In Midlothian he presented the struggle as one between the classes and the masses.

We cannot make our appeal to the aristocracy, excepting that which must never be forgotten, the distinguished and enlightened minority of that body [he was again staying at Dalmeny] . . . With that exception in all the classes of which I speak I am sorry to say we cannot reckon upon what is called the landed interest, we cannot reckon upon the clergy of the established Church either in England or Scotland . . . We cannot reckon upon the wealth of the country, nor upon the rank of the country . . . But, gentlemen, above all these and behind all these there is something greater than these – there is the nation itself. This great trial is now proceeding before the nation. The nation is a power hard to rouse, but when roused, harder still and more hopeless to resist.

His energy was immense. 'Travelled forty miles and delivered three speeches of forty-five minutes each, at Juniper Green, Colinton, and Mid Calder,' he noted in his diary of March 20, adding, 'Enthusiasm unabated . . . Corrected and despatched proofs of *Religion, Achaian and Semitic*'.[1] The next day, a Sunday, he went for a seven-mile walk with Lord Rosebery, and the day after that delivered four more speeches in Edinburgh and various parts of the constituency. It was a wonderful performance for a man of seventy-one, the more effective because, as in 1879, it was never answered.

Indeed the Conservatives gave two further handles to their opponents. The first was by using the fag-end of the old Parliament to push through the Corrupt Practices Act.[2] This measure has been described by the leading historian of the subject as 'the only piece of reactionary electoral legislation of the century',[3] and although as

[1] Morley, *Gladstone*, ii, 609.
[2] See above, 701, for details.
[3] Cornelius O'Leary, *The Elimination of Corrupt Practices in British Elections, 1868–1911* (1962), 118.

right, cartoon of Disraeli
by 'Vincent', undated, in
the possession of the author

left, by Ape (Carlo Pellegrini)
in *Vanity Fair*, 1878

MOSE IN EGITTO
Punch, December 11, 1875

A BAD EXAMPLE

Dr Punch: What's all this? You, the two head boys of the school, throwing mud! *You ought to be ashamed of yourselves!*
Punch, August 10, 1878

we saw earlier there were quite good arguments for it, the fact remains that the richer party was bound to have a further advantage if borough as well as county candidates were allowed to convey voters to the polls at their own expense. Gladstone declared that it would 'again legalize one of the worst systems of electoral corruption'. The London cab interest replied with posters urging the electorate to 'vote for Gladstonkoff, Commander-in-Chief of the Russian forces in Great Britain'.[1]

The other handle given to the Liberals was Sir Stafford Northcote's budget. Disraeli had pinned his hopes to some extent on the assurances of the Chancellor that there would be no additional taxation. Northcote fulfilled that promise, but only by raiding his Sinking Fund to provide terminable annuities in order to pay off by 1885 an accumulated deficit of £8m. This was a large sum by contemporary standards and, although it could be explained as the result of the Zulu War, the excuse merely provided another reason for condemning the Government's imperial policy. As for the raid on the Sinking Fund, critics shook their heads at the impropriety of treating a sacrosanct fund as if it were so much cash in hand. Northcote himself seemed uneasy about it and his budget speech was delivered with unusual hesitation and lack of conviction.

Apart from all these difficulties the Conservative party was greatly hampered by its incapacity to answer publicly the mounting indictment of Gladstone and his colleagues. Peers were not allowed to make speeches during an election campaign. This constitutional usage not only silenced the Prime Minister but three of his best speakers, Salisbury, Cairns and Cranbrook. The leading figures on the Conservative side in the Lower House were not distinguished for effective oratory. Northcote was too mild and courteous, W. H. Smith was dull, and Cross, whose style was once compared to that of a Chairman of Quarter Sessions charging a jury of tenant farmers, was harsh and monotonous. They were outgunned even by the lesser Liberal artillery, Hartington, Harcourt, Bright; and they could not begin to stand up to Gladstone. A contemporary observer, William Saunders, did some statistical research into comparative rhetorical output during the election. Hartington made twenty-four major orations, Gladstone fifteen, Bright and Harcourt six each. Against these could be put a mere six by the leader of the House who was howled down during one of them, six by W. H. Smith and

[1] ibid., 124.

nine by Frederick Stanley.[1] But Stanley needed all his eloquence to counteract the well-publicized conversion of his brother, Lord Derby, to the Liberal party, news fraught with such alarming possibilities in Lancashire that Cross, once one of Derby's closest friends, felt obliged to remind electors that the ballot was secret. It was symptomatic of the way the tide was flowing that there was far more rowdyism at Conservative than at Liberal meetings, and several ministers found it on occasions difficult to get a hearing, among them Lord John Manners, who was bombarded at Melton Mowbray with eggs filled with gas tar.

Disraeli does not seem to have been much worried about the result, although Corry warned him, as the campaign progressed, that the Central Office was being over sanguine. The party managers reckoned on a loss of sixteen to eighteen seats. This would leave them with a majority of between fourteen and eighteen over all other groups combined, which would be enough though not comfortable. The pro-Government Press was wildly optimistic, such papers as the *Daily Telegraph*, the *Standard*, and the *Morning Post* taking victory for granted. Even the cautious *Times* wept crocodile tears about the damage to the two-party system likely to result from another Liberal defeat, and 'the helpless condition' to which that party would be reduced. The Liberal Press, to begin with, was noncommital, but the party leaders expected victory from an early stage. Harcourt told Chamberlain after consulting all the party managers that the Liberals would have an absolute majority of not less than thirty.[2] On the eve of the poll Adam, the Liberal Chief Whip, was quite confident of winning. But no one on either side predicted the landslide that ensued.

Meanwhile there was little for Disraeli to do, at all events little that he did. Salisbury, who had gone with his wife to recover health in the south of France, invited him to treat Hatfield as his own. Thither he repaired at the end of March to stay with the rest of the Cecil family for the election period. While Gladstone cut down trees at Dalmeny, Disraeli was engaged in the less strenuous pastime of drinking Salisbury's 'Grand Château Margaux of 1870'. The only snag was that his host, doubtless reluctant to waste a rare vintage on the less discriminating palates of his youthful and numerous

[1] Quoted, *Annual Register, 1880*, 51. For some reason Cross is omitted from this comparison. He made numerous speeches and the campaign in Lancashire was largely a personal duel between him and Hartington.

[2] Garvin, *Chamberlain*, i, 276.

progeny, had instructed the butler to offer it only to Disraeli. 'I feel awkward,' he told Lady Bradford, 'but forget my embarrassment in the exquisite flavor. All this because I once mentioned my detestation of hosts who give you an inferior claret at dinner when alone sensible men drink wine, and reserve their superior *crus* for after the repast.' Disraeli's frequently expressed dislike of this barbarous custom will be applauded by the modern oenophile.

Alas, it was not long before he needed all the pleasures of Château Margaux to console him for the dismal news which began to pour in from the polls. On the first day, March 31, voting occurred in sixty-nine boroughs and the Government was down on balance by 15 seats. This was serious though not fatal, but the next few days saw a rapid deterioration. By the end of Saturday, April 3, when the last of the urban constituencies polled, the Conservatives had lost 50 seats. 'It seemed,' noted Gladstone after cutting down a tree, 'as if the arm of the Lord had bared itself for work that He has made His own.' It was clear that the Government was out and Disraeli returned to London that day to await with apprehension the county results as they came in during the next week.

A fortnight earlier Cranbrook noted in his diary that Disraeli 'had his doubts about the counties, which surprised me. He often has means of judging which others have not.'[1] Disraeli was well aware of the agricultural distress and the threat of separate farmers' candidates. Indeed he always sensed the electoral atmosphere in the Home Counties and London more accurately than in the great cities of the north or Scotland which were for him unfamiliar territory to the end of his life. His doubts were well justified. The swing to Liberalism was almost as big in the country as in the town, and if the Liberals had put up more candidates they might have made even greater inroads on these traditional Tory strongholds. For example in North Lincolnshire the only Liberal, fighting against two Conservatives, had given up his canvass and proposed to withdraw. At the last moment he was induced to hand in his nomination papers and was returned head of the poll. The Conservatives lost 27 English county seats, reducing their representation to 116 while the Liberals rose to 54. When all the results were in, the magnitude of the Liberal triumph became obvious. They had almost exactly reversed the situation in the old Parliament. The figures were as follows, with figures at the dissolution given in parentheses: Liberals

[1] Gathorne Hardy, ii, 129.

353 (250); Conservatives 238 (351); Home Rulers 61 (51). In all the
Liberals had gained 121 seats and lost only 18. Their leaders were
as amazed as their rivals at such a great change. 'The downfall of
Beaconsfieldism', wrote Gladstone, 'is like the vanishing of some
vast magnificent castle in an Italian romance.'

The Conservatives did badly almost everywhere. In Scotland all
their gains of 1874 were wiped out. They fell from 19 to 7, leaving
the Liberals with 53 seats. Gladstone won Midlothian by 211 votes.
In Wales they did even worse, retaining only 2 seats in the whole of
the Principality. In Lancashire, where Disraeli's manifesto might
have been expected to rally the Orange vote, they suffered heavy
losses. The defection of Derby may well have been an influence
there. Only in the south did they to some extent reverse the trend,
gaining Greenwich, Gladstone's old seat, and 3 out of the 4 seats
for the City of London. They also managed to hold nearly every
constituency in Kent, an achievement which, Disraeli told the
Queen, merited a step in the peerage for Lord Sondes, 'a most
worthy man & one of Yr Majesty's most powerful subjects. We owe
to him the almost entire support of Kent in County & Boroughs.
Cantia Invicta!'[1]

Inadequate statistics and the complications caused by independent candidates and uncontested seats makes any accurate calculations of 'swing', such as are so familiar to our modern psephologists,
impossible. But Professor Hanham, taking a sample group of fifty-
two constituencies which were the subject of straight fights in all
three elections since the 1867 Bill, has produced figures suggesting
that in these the swing was about 5 per cent to the Liberals. The
swing to the Conservatives had been roughly the same in 1874, and
so it seems that the party was back where it had been in 1868.[2] A
feature of the election which aroused contemporary comment was
the low number of uncontested seats compared with past practice,
but even so it is clear that although the Liberals fielded twenty-two
more candidates than they had in 1874, they would have done
better still if they had left even fewer Tory seats unfought. Altogether the Conservatives were allowed to take 56 seats without a
struggle and, though this was far less than the figure for 1874 (127)

[1] Royal Archives, C.35.105, Disraeli to the Queen, April 8.
[2] Hanham, 192–3. See also J. P. D. Dunbabin, 'Parliamentary Elections in Great
Britain 1868–1900: A Psephological Note', *English Historical Review* lxxxi (1966),
82–99, who suggests that the swing in 1880 was rather lower, and that the Conservatives did better in the big towns than they had in 1868.

or even 1868 (90), they were lucky that it was as high as it was.

All accounts agree that Disraeli bore the blow of defeat with an air of dignified imperturbability. He blamed no one, and refused to allow the Central Office managers who had advised in favour of a dissolution to be made scapegoats. He told Lord Barrington, who lunched with him at Downing Street on Sunday, April 4, when all hope of victory had vanished, that he was not sorry to have some rest and that he looked forward to spending spring and summer among the woods of Hughenden – something he had never been able to do before. 'He chiefly deplored his fall from power,' wrote Barrington, 'on account of M. Corry, who in his opinion was fitted to fill any *Cabinet* office. This was said with genuine warmth.' Barrington concluded his memorandum of their talk:

> It is pleasing to see how well D. is, and with what charming temper he takes this evil stroke of fortune in the sunset of his great career. So many of his friends, especially ladies, send to enquire how he is. 'As well as can be expected', says he as if he had been confined![1]

But it would be wrong to suppose that Disraeli felt indifferent on the matter. Privately he was bitterly disappointed and the process of winding up the Government filled him with gloom:

> . . . as hard work as forming one [he told Lady Bradford] without any of the excitement. My room is filled with beggars, mournful or indignant, and my desk is covered with letters like a snow storm. It is the last and least glorious exercise of power, and will be followed, wh: is the only compensation, by utter neglect and isolation . . . Discomfited, defeated, and, if not disgraced, prostrate, by a singular anomaly and irony of fate I pass my life now in exercising supreme power – making peers, creating baronets, and showering places and pensions on a rapacious crew.[2]

Disraeli did his best for his party and his friends. There were peerages for Sir Laurence Palk, Sir Ivor Guest, Sir Arthur Guinness and one for Baillie-Cochrane, who had been angling for it for years. There was an earldom for Lytton as a sign of defiance at his treatment by the Liberals. Lord John Manners received 'the Red Ribbon'

[1] M. & B., vi, 524.
[2] ibid., 531.

along with his pension. There was just time to appoint the evangelical Dean Ryle to the newly-created See of Liverpool, for which 'the Tories subscribed the whole endowment', Disraeli claimed to the Queen. 'Lord Sandon says his seat at Liverpool depends on the appointment being made by your Majesty's present advisers.'[1]

Then there was the problem of Lord Henry Lennox. Having refused various offices as beneath him he now became alarmed. Time was short, but a gleam of hope appeared. Lord Hampton opportunely died and his Civil Service Commissionership became vacant. Undeterred because Gladstone had made both the creation of the post and Lord Hampton's appointment to it the object of particular obloquy during the first Midlothian campaign, Disraeli submitted Lord Henry's name to the Queen. This was too much even for Sir Stafford Northcote. The appointment of such a flibbertigibbet could never be defended in the House. Reluctantly Disraeli withdrew the submission.

But there was one personal friend whom he was resolved to reward, Monty Corry. Nothing better illustrates what might be called the Arabian Nights aspect of Disraeli's character than his treatment of his faithful secretary. Corry was forty-one and had played no part at all in public life, But Disraeli was determined to make him a peer. The snag was that peers – or at any rate Tory peers – were expected to have an estate adequate to their dignity, and Corry, though grandson of two earls had, like so many younger scions of the peerage, the most exiguous of incomes. True, he had expectations from a rich childless widowed aunt, Lady Charlotte Lyster, who was eighty-one and owned Rowton Castle and a large estate in Shropshire. But nothing definite had been settled and wealthy old ladies are notoriously addicted to capricious willshaking.

Disraeli decided to bring things to a head. He sent Corry to see her, and at the same time wrote a letter to her himself:

April 7, 1880
Downing Street

Dear Lady Charlotte,
    Monty will tell you about the plan which is on the tapis for his welfare and elevation.
    Nothing can be done without your approbation and assistance. I have advised him to consult you at once.

[1] *The Letters of Queen Victoria*, 2nd Series, iii, 78.

I would not of course make the proposal to the Queen, nor could Her Majesty entertain it unless I could show that a becoming estate would eventually become his.

Yours, dear Lady
Charlotte,
sincerely,
Beaconsfield[1]

The letter did the trick. Lady Charlotte, who was fond of her nephew, did not perhaps mind having the matter decided for her. She signed an irrevocable deed giving him the reversion of her estate which was estimated in the New Domesday to consist in 1883 of 6,300 acres producing £5,600 p.a. Disraeli at once wrote to the Queen but his well-known account is, as so often, not quite in accord with the facts. Corry, he told her, 'has come into possession of Rowton Castle and a domain of seven thousand acres in Shropshire. His income will exceed ten thousand per annum.' He went on to praise Corry's talents. 'Is it possible that such a man will be content to fall back into the crowd of dismissed private secretaries?', and he suggested, not unaware of the Queen's aversion to society, 'He will probably become absorbed in that fashionable world where he is a favourite'. Would the Queen make him a peer? 'He knows nothing of the request.'[2]

Corry, of course, was well aware of the request, his future income was a good deal less than £10,000, and he was not destined to inherit the estate for another nine years. But the version was near enough to the truth for Disraeli; the Queen, a little hesitantly, agreed to confer the honour. And so with a wave of the old magician's wand the gay young man, who had sung a comic song at Raby sixteen years before, became Baron Rowton of Rowton Castle and heir to a fortune.

The peerage was not without its critics. In Liberal circles it caused almost as much merriment as that of Lady Beaconsfield and the famous comment, often applied subsequently to an eccentric appointment, namely that there has been nothing like it since Caligula created his horse a consul, was first made by Gladstone on hearing of Corry's elevation. But, although there was the 'Lothario' aspect of Lord Rowton's character which lent some justice to the Queen's one-time view that he was 'a man of pleasure', there was a

[1] Corry Papers.
[2] M. & B., vi, 529–30.

serious side to him too. He was not Lord Shaftesbury's grandson for nothing, as his philanthropic ventures culminating in the so-called Rowton Houses clearly show. In the 1890s Salisbury regarded him as a possible candidate for the Berlin embassy. He was not a man of intellect or ideas but he was a most capable and devoted private secretary to whom Disraeli owed a great debt; and Disraeli believed in gratitude.

One of Disraeli's problems was to soothe the feelings of the Queen. He had naturally done nothing to prepare her for a result which he never expected, and she had departed to Baden-Baden just before the election confident that the Conservatives would be returned 'stronger than ever'. But on April 2 Disraeli informed her that there was no doubt of his defeat. 'This is a terrible telegram,' she minuted to Ponsonby, and as the news became worse her lamentations became louder. Disraeli was the only Prime Minister since Melbourne who had been her personal friend and she found the prospect of parting dismal indeed. Knowing the importance she attached to her personal plans Disraeli assured her that she need not leave Baden till the 15th, 'I take the responsibility on myself'. Disraeli dwelt on his own sorrow. 'His separation from your Majesty is almost overwhelming. His relations with your Majesty were his chief, he might almost say his only, happiness and interest in this world.' The Queen replied in the first person and hoped that, 'when we correspond – which I hope we shall on many a *private* subject and without anyone being astonished or offended, and even better without anyone knowing about it', Disraeli would do the same.[1] She asked what honour she could confer on him and again offered to settle a barony upon his nephew Coningsby, but Disraeli refused, as he had in 1878.

The Cabinet now had to consider whether to resign or meet Parliament, but after such a resounding slap in the face there could be little argument. Northcote tentatively favoured delay – but the other ministers preferred to resign and on April 15 the decision was taken in principle, although the formal resignation was held up for a week. Meanwhile the Queen, now back in England, was consulting Disraeli about the succession. On April 18 he had an audience at Windsor and advised her to send for Hartington, 'in his heart a Conservative, a gentleman, and very straightforward in his conduct'.[2] It has been suggested, rightly, that Disraeli had no inten-

[1] M. & B., vi, 527.   [2] ibid., 534.

tion of smoothing the way for Gladstone, but it is only right to say that his advice was constitutionally correct, whatever his personal feelings may have been. Gladstone had resigned the leadership in 1875. The Queen would have been treating Hartington and Granville less than courteously if she had not sent for one of them in the first instance. As for the choice, it is arguable that it should have been Granville who was the senior of the two, but Disraeli knew that the Queen had not forgiven him for opposing the Royal Titles Bill. Hartington's liaison with the Duchess of Manchester and intimacy with the Marlborough House set, though defects in her eyes, were not so serious – and in Disraeli's not defects at all.

The Queen raised the question of her right to veto certain persons who were obnoxious to her but might be suggested for places, in particular Lowe and Dilke. Disraeli detested Lowe but thought that his earlier and abject apology to the Queen purged his offence. Dilke's republicanism was another matter. 'He thought I shd object – but if I did allow him to enter the Govt, it must be in some inferior position in wh: he wd not be brought into contact with me & that I *must* insist on a written apology.'[1] The Queen was very firm, verbally, on Gladstone. 'I said that it would be impossible for me to send for Mr. Gladstone as I could only say that I cd not trust him or give him my confidence.'[2] This would certainly have been an unpromising start. Earlier and to those to whom she could vent her real feelings the Queen had been more violent. 'She will sooner *abdicate* than send for or have any *communication* with *that half mad firebrand* who wd soon ruin everything & be a *Dictator*', she told Ponsonby on April 4. 'Others but herself *may submit* to his democratic rule but *not the Queen*.'[3]

There were influential Liberals like Harcourt who favoured Disraeli's solution, but the Queen was not destined to escape. Both Hartington and Granville saw that a government which did not include Gladstone was impossible, and it soon became clear that the Grand Old Man had not fought his two titanic campaigns in order to serve either under Hartington, who had not been born when he first entered Parliament, or under Granville whose nickname, 'Puss', was a good index of his character.

On April 21 Disraeli held his last Cabinet meeting. The atmosphere was relaxed and friendly, so Cranbrook tells us. Disraeli

---

[1] Royal Archives, C.34.65, Memo. by the Queen, April 18, 1880.
[2] loc. cit.   [3] Ponsonby, 184.

thanked his colleagues for all they had done, and on their behalf
Lord Cairns reciprocated. The formal decision was taken to resign
and Disraeli went to Windsor to convey it. But although his
political responsibility was now ended, he remained as the Queen's
personal adviser during the next forty-eight hours while the Government of the country was in a state of suspense and there was no
Prime Minister. He counselled her what to say to Hartington, and
she sent him a long account 'one of the most interesting state papers
he has ever perused' of her interview. When the Liberal leaders
decided, as Disraeli put it, to 'shrink from the responsibility of their
position', he advised her what to say to Gladstone. She should
simply ask him whether he was ready to form a government.

> Lord Beaconsfield would advise your Majesty in the first instance
> to confine yourself to this question. Mr Gladstone will probably
> be diffuse in his reply, which will give your Majesty advantage in
> ascertaining his real intentions.
>   If he be not diffuse, then your Majesty, if he replies in the
> affirmative, may proceed to enquire as to the policy here com-
> mends and the persons he will propose to carry it into effect.[1]

Gladstone for once was not diffuse and accepted promptly. The
Queen could only console herself by telling Disraeli how decrepit he
appeared. 'Mr Gladstone looks very ill, very old and haggard and
his voice feeble . . . he said twice he looked to his not being long
in office as it was too much for him.'[2] She was, one suspects, more
influenced by what she hoped for than by what she saw. Gladstone
was one of the most robust statesmen in our history. The Queen
would not have been amused, had she known that he was to be an
active political figure for the next fourteen years, and to take office
in 1892 for the fourth time at the age of eighty-two.

3

It is difficult enough, with all our modern resources for investigating
public opinion, to say exactly why contemporary general elections
have gone the way they have. To pontificate about elections eighty
years or more ago would indeed be rash. Any verdict must be at
best a good guess. There is no means of being certain. Gladstone
thought he had won because he aroused the moral sense of 'the

---

[1] M. & B., vi, 538–9.
[2] loc. cit.

nation' against 'Beaconsfieldism', by which he meant gaudy, expensive foreign and imperial policies; and this has come to be the accepted verdict of history. But it does not follow, because a particular issue is given great prominence by one or other party, that it is necessarily the determining factor with the electorate. Nor was Gladstone's the only explanation given at the time. Joseph Chamberlain, for example, attributed the Liberal victory to good Liberal organization, the 'caucus'. Gorst attributed it to bad Conservative organization. Another theory was that the clergy had let the party down, as Salisbury was told 'either by actively voting against us or at least by sulking. I wonder whether it is true: & if so what is the cause. Is it the Public Worship Bill – or the Eastern Church – or Temperance.'[1] But Disraeli and most Conservatives thought they lost because of the agricultural and industrial depression.

On April 2, he had written to Salisbury

> I wish my visit [to Hatfield] had brought good fortune to your historic walls instead of a discomfiture alike vast and without an adequate cause. 'Hard Times', as far as I can collect, has been our foe and certainly the alleged cause of our fall.
>
> My own opinion is that any delay in the dissolution would only have aggravated the mal-disposition of the towns and would probably have landed us at the same time with an insurrection of our old and natural friends, the farmers. They were preparing for it in all directions with their Clubs and Councils, and Candidates of their own order, but this is a class that moves and conspires slowly, and tho' we shall not get off scot-free I still believe the damage tho' sore will be limited.[2]

He was writing before he knew the county results which were probably worse than he feared, but he was right in that they would have been worse still if the election had been postponed.

There is probably some truth in each of the varying explanations given for the *débâcle*. Perhaps no single cause can be isolated for Disraeli's defeat. Could he have done anything to avert it? The answer must be, very little. He could have dissolved earlier and might have done rather better. He could have chosen a more convincing theme for his election address. He might have said something about social reform. But at worst his errors were marginal, affecting the extent not the fact of his downfall. If he was right in

---

[1] Salisbury Papers, Salisbury to Lady John Manners, April 18, 1880.
[2] ibid.

thinking that the depression played a bigger part than external policy – and electoral experience in general suggests that it probably did – then there was not much that his or any government operating within the accepted limits of governmental intervention at that time could have done. *Laissez faire* was still the order of the day. Politicians regarded the economic climate as scarcely more in their control than the weather.

This economic fatalism enabled Disraeli to bear his defeat with a certain stoic equanimity, but the outlook must have been very depressing. Once again the Conservatives seemed to have relapsed into the position which they had occupied ever since 1830, or at least, since 1846, that of a permanent minority party. The great victory of 1874 appeared now as a mere flash in the pan. The normal forces of British politics had reasserted themselves. The Liberals seemed set for many years of tranquil power. No one could have predicted the strange convulsion that was soon to transform the political scene. No one could have guessed that Gladstone's personal return, which had in appearance so marvellously resuscitated the Liberal party, was destined within six years to shatter it for a political generation, perhaps in a deeper sense for ever. No one could have foreseen that well before the turn of the century the Conservatives would become the dominant party and in spite of set-backs hold that general position till after 1960. In 1880 the picture looked very different. Salisbury must have spoken for many Conservatives when he wrote to Lady John Manners: 'I was not sorry for the prospect of defeat simply. But such a defeat as this is quite another matter. It is a perfect catastrophe – & may I fear break up the party altogether.'[1]

In all the circumstances Disraeli might well have retired from the scene. He was an old man now and his health was far from good. It was scarcely conceivable that he could lead the party at the next general election which might not occur until 1886. But politics was the breath of his life, and he possessed a tenacity and courage equalled by few statesmen, surpassed by none. On May 19 a party meeting of peers and MPs was held in Bridgewater House. Lord Rowton described it in a letter to Queen Victoria.[2] Disraeli addressed the assembly and citing the precedent of the rapid decline of Grey's ministry after 1832 urged them not to be too pessimistic

[1] ibid., April 18, 1880.
[2] M. & B., vi, 575–7.

about their prospects. He advised MPs to watch with special vigilance the left wing of the Liberal party now amounting to perhaps a hundred or more. The Conservatives should always support the Government against them and would only gain in public esteem by doing so. 'The policy of the Conservative Party is to maintain the *Empire* and preserve the *Constitution*.' He said that if the result of the election had been different he might have retired. As it was, he felt it his duty to place his services at their disposal. He spoke for an hour and forty minutes and sat down to immense applause. Carnarvon then rose and said that, whatever his past differences, he was determined to support Disraeli and the party now. The meeting ended on a resounding vote of confidence in Disraeli. Two days later he wrote an account to Lord Lytton. It is one of his best letters and its form and content go far to explain why Disraeli led the party and why the party still wished to be led by him.

I am a wretched correspondent but I am sure you have never for a moment doubted my entire confidence in yourself and my approval of all you have done in dealing with some of the most considerable and critical affairs which have ever engaged the solicitude of statesmen.

Whatever philosophers may say, there is such a thing as luck & fortune – & the reverse – & that it should have fallen to my lot to govern England for a series of years with a decaying commerce & the soil stricken with sterility presents an issue which, I believe, no calculation could have foreseen or baffled.

The distress of this country is the cause & the sole cause of the fall of the government over wh: I presided. Had the dissolution been postponed for a few months the consequences wd have been still more serious, for we shd have lost all our counties.

The farmers are ruined, & I have little confidence myself in what is called the revival of trade. The stir was an American spirit & already languishes. The revenue offers no rally & the evil is too deep to be cured by a good harvest even if we have one.

At the solicitation of the Queen & the unanimous entreaty of our party, Lords & Commons assembled at Bridgewater House, I have consented to relinquish my purpose of retiring at present from public life. It is not in my humor ever to leave my friends in adversity but I think, tho' generous, they err in still wishing me to represent them. The situation requires youth & energy. When they are found – & they will be found – I shall make my bow. In the meantime I must act as if I were still young & vigorous, & take all steps in my power to sustain the spirit & restore the discipline of the Tory party. They have existed for more than a century & a half as an organized political connection & having survived the loss of the American colonies, the first Napoleon, & Lord Grey's Reform Act, they must not be snuffed out.

In this great undertaking I count on the cordial assistance of my late colleagues & especially of yourself, for you will have a great opportunity in the House of Lords – you see I prophesy as becomes one in the sunset of life – or rather I sh'd say the twilight of existence.[1]

[1] Knebworth Papers, May 31, 1880.

CHAPTER XXXI

Endymion; Falconet

1880

1

Disraeli left Downing Street on April 25 and stayed at Hatfield till his farewell audience with the Queen on the 27th. He then passed a few days at Lord Beauchamp's London house, for he no longer had a town house of his own, and departed to Hughenden on May 1 'in a state of coma', as he told Lady Bradford. He remained there for the rest of the year apart from forays to London for party councils or debates in the House of Lords. On these occasions he had the use of a suite of rooms in Alfred de Rothschild's house at Number 1 Seamore Place. His host, tactful as well as generous, left him alone to come and go as he pleased – a civility which Disraeli much appreciated.

At Hughenden he led an uneventful summer. His letters frequently refer to the pleasure of being in the country in those months – an experience which politics had forbidden him for most of his life. 'Tomorrow I go up for a House of Lords Division but shall return here on Wednesday,' he writes to the Queen on June 14. 'I cannot resist the fascination of the voice of the cuckoo, so mysterious and sultry, the wood-pigeons' cooing, and the sweetness and splendor of the May-blossom. Deign, Gracious Lady, to pardon this weakness (remembering that I never was before in the country in this month) of your Majesty's ever grateful and devoted Beaconsfield.'[1]

Disraeli stayed at Windsor on three occasions during 1880[2] and he continued to correspond with the Queen directly. In all, he wrote twenty-two letters after he had ceased to be Prime Minister. Ponsonby disapproved – or rather would have disapproved, had he known. He himself refused a suggestion that he should keep in touch with Disraeli through Corry, but the Queen merely by-passed him telling Disraeli that Corry should write to Prince Leopold or Captain Edwards, groom-in-waiting, or Miss Stopford, a

---

[1] Royal Archives, B.64.3.
[2] May 17–18, July 15–16, December 8–10.

woman of the bedchamber, 'all QUITE SAFE'.[1] In fact, the correspondence did no great harm. Nothing that Disraeli could say was likely to make the Queen detest Gladstone any more than she already did. Only on one occasion did he give advice that could have been seriously misleading. This was when the Queen who strongly objected to the Government's decision at the end of 1880 to evacuate Kandahar asked whether Sir William Harcourt was right in telling her that the Queen's speech which contained this announcement was not her's but her ministers'. Disraeli replied January 11, 1881 that 'the principle of Sir W. Harcourt . . . is a principle not known to the British Constitution. It is only a piece of Parliamentary gossip'.[2] But for the most part Disraeli avoided political advice and gave the Queen what she really wanted, sympathy, gossip, affection, tact.

> *May* 30 . . . No man has been more faithful to me in my fallen fortunes than the fisherman [John Brown who had caught a salmon sent from Balmoral to Hughenden] and I rejoice that his sport this year has been so favorable – I shall write him a little line to thank him and to tell him so.[3]
>
> *July* 22 . . . [refusing an invitation to a Ball at Marlborough house where the Queen was to be present] I am more hopeless than Cinderella. She might remain at a Ball till midnight, but I begin to die an hour before that time and am buried by twelve.
>
> The impending marriage of an old and faithful Servant of your Majesty, Lord Malmesbury, will not take place. It appears that the lady was married last April and her second husband is alive. Strange that one so experienced in feminine nature should have been so compromised, but I fear it proves what I have often felt, that the brown sex is no match for the fair.[4]
>
> *Christmas Day* . . . Oh Madam and most beloved Sovereign. What language can express my feelings when I beheld this morning the graceful and gracious gifts upon my table. Such incidents make life delightful and inspire even age with the glow and energy of youth.[5]

Disraeli seems to have been concerned in one delicate matter which was connected with royalty and came to a head very soon after his resignation. This was the possible marriage of his old friend Lord Rosslyn's stepdaughter, Miss Maynard, the future Lady

---

[1] Elizabeth Longford, *Victoria, R.I.* (1964), 436.
[2] *The Letters of Queen Victoria*, 2nd Series, iii, 181.
[3] Royal Archives, B.64.2.
[4] ibid., B.64.5.
[5] ibid., B.64.19.

Warwick, to Prince Leopold. Miss Maynard, then aged eighteen, was granddaughter and sole heiress of the third and last Viscount Maynard who had bequeathed to her on his death in 1865 estates worth £20,000 p.a. Her father had died earlier that year and in 1866 her mother married Lord Rosslyn. Corry, keeping Disraeli closely informed, acted as a go-between and carried on a three-cornered negotiation with the Queen at Windsor, Prince Leopold at Clare-mont, and the Rosslyns. Disraeli is said to have been anxious to promote the marriage, and the Queen was by no means opposed. She did not object in principle to her children marrying commoners. There was, it is true, a problem about the Prince's health – he was a haemophiliac – but this does not appear to have been regarded as a bar. As for the Rosslyns they were presumably in favour of a royal match, although Lady Rosslyn, a pushing and ambitious woman, was determined to secure what she regarded as a proper title and status for her daughter.

The Queen wanted matters to be brought to a head. Miss Stopford on May 5 sent a message on her behalf to Corry '. . . if they feel disinclined it would be better to say so *before the Prince goes to Canada* and not allow the matter to be hanging on, and for him to be refused in the end, for this the Queen could *not allow*, and wishes you therefore to put it very strongly'.[1] She met the conditions about rank. On May 7 Corry told Disraeli, 'I am now bearing to them a perfectly satisfactory assurance from the Queen as to *that*, and I foresee that in an hour I shall be en route to Windsor with an acceptance.'[2]

He was to be disappointed. Miss Maynard sent a refusal. 'The final letter leaves no opening for further pleading', he told Disraeli on May 11. The following day Corry went to 'the Fairy's home' where he had prolonged talks with the Queen and Prince Leopold.

> The annoyance and anger about the affair I will report to you I hope tomorrow (though late!). I succeeded in averting any irritating messages by showing that they would provoke revela-tions not desirable, or else misrepresentations, and that nothing has occurred which may not be explained so as to clear the young gentleman – a visit – a gracious invitation in return etc.
>
> The fairy readily took this view (which is the safest one I feel sure when one has to deal with an hysterical tigress) – but 'how

[1] Corry Papers, Miss Stopford to Lord Rowton.
[2] ibid.

angry Lord B. will be!' and does 'he think that I ought to insist on the return of my autograph letter to the Mother' arranging for delay?

In July Miss Maynard became engaged to Lord Brooke, equerry to the Prince and heir to the earldom of Warwick.[1] They were married on April 30, 1881, and the Prince stood as godfather to their eldest son born in September of the following year.

There was evidently no ill feeling on his part. It is not clear quite what really happened to stop the match. Lady Warwick wrote two books of memoirs which contain incompatible accounts. In one she said that her parents refused on her behalf without even telling her of the proposal. In the other she says that the proposal was rejected because she had already fallen in love with Lord Brooke, and that the Prince did not mind as he was in love with someone else. The second version seems more likely to be true and is more compatible with Corry's letters. Both stories have in common the claim that Disraeli was the matchmaker. He was certainly interested, and the Queen's remark suggests that he was disappointed at the outcome, but his papers throw no light on the matter. Anything from Queen Victoria to Disraeli about the future Lady Warwick would have been burnt by King Edward VII. The Queen's letters were returned to him in 1907 by Lord Rothschild. The private family ones were destroyed. The remainder were sent back and are now at Hughenden.

Disraeli took a gloomy view of politics throughout the year. His letters to the Queen were cautious but to the two sisters abounded with jeremiads. He regarded Gladstone whom he regularly calls the 'A.V.' (Arch Villain) as sold out to advanced radicalism and committed to a major assault on the landed interest. Certainly the prospects for that class looked dark enough in 1880. The election had been a disaster, and everyone knew that sooner or later the urban franchise of 1867 would have to be extended to the counties, in which case an indefinite vista of Liberal supremacy loomed ahead. The agricultural depression had divided even the element in the counties that was traditionally Tory. The farmers were fighting the gentry, and the Government's Game Bill was seen through Tory

[1] As Lady Brooke (after 1893 Lady Warwick), she was famed as one of the most beautiful members of the Marlborough House set. She was mistress of the Prince of Wales and later of Lord Charles Beresford. In 1895 she became converted to Socialism by Robert Blatchford and devoted much of her time and fortune to this cause. She was Labour candidate for Warwick in 1923, being defeated by Anthony Eden. She died in 1938.

eyes as a device to exacerbate that conflict. The repeal of the Malt Tax which was the main feature of Gladstone's supplementary budget in 1880 seemed to be part of the same policy: it was certainly mortifying that Gladstone who had assumed the Chancellorship of the Exchequer along with the Premiership should have managed at once to remove this long standing grievance of the farmers, which had remained unredressed for seven consecutive Tory budgets.

But, although Disraeli was alarmed at these and other manifestations of the new Liberal policy, he was determined to act cautiously. The Liberals had an overwhelming majority in the House of Commons and he saw no sign of decline in their prestige in the country. True, the Government early became enmeshed in a series of labyrinthine procedural complications partly arising from Irish obstruction, and partly from the Bradlaugh incident brilliantly exploited by Lord Randolph Churchill and the Fourth Party. But Disraeli did not take these too seriously. 'The Ministry seems in all sorts of difficulties', he wrote to Lady Chesterfield on May 24, 'but I don't think scrapes signify to a Government in their first year'.[1]

In these circumstances he thought it unwise for the Conservatives to overplay their hand in the House of Lords and court a constitutional struggle which they might well lose. He strongly advised against tampering with the Game Bill or the Employers Liability Bill, both popular measures in the country though detested, especially the former, by most Conservatives. He was opposed by a group of what would later have been called 'Die-hard' peers led by Lord Redesdale[2] who, in Disraeli's words 'has many excellent qualities and talents but who is narrow-minded, prejudiced, and utterly unconscious of what is going on in the country'.[3] Redesdale was easily defeated. Disraeli's attitude to the Game Bill is well summed up in a passage from his speech on August 30

I would most earnestly hope, if there are to be differences between the two Houses of Parliament, that as far as your Lordships' House is concerned, those differences should be upon subjects of great national interest . . . I feel confident that if you exercise your great authority with becoming firmness and discretion, you may defy Democrat and Demagogue, because you will be supported by the sympathy of the great body of the

---

[1] M. & B., vi, 579.

[2] 2nd Baron and 1st Earl, 1805–86, a redoubtable supporter of the Protestant and Tory cause.

[3] M. & B., vi, 589, Disraeli to Lady Bradford.

people. You will not have that support if you choose this occasion to try the relative strength of the two Houses of Parliament.[1]

In a situation where the normal minority party in the country was the perpetual majority party in the Upper House it was essential for the leader to possess and exercise a restraining authority. Disraeli had it and used it, like Wellington and Derby before him, and Salisbury after him. It was a disaster for the Tories and for the House of Lords, though not necessarily for the nation that no one was in that position after 1906.

Disraeli was, however, convinced that the House of Lords ought to take a stand on matters of deep importance. Two which he singled out were the rights of landed proprietors and the union with Ireland. Both were threatened by the Government's Compensation for Disturbance Bill which would have imposed a temporary embargo against Irish landlords evicting without compensation tenants who failed to pay their rent. Disraeli decided to muster all the forces of the Conservative party against the measure which was, indeed, far from popular with the Liberals. The second reading in the House of Commons was only carried by the votes of Irish members, some fifty Liberals abstaining and twenty voting with the Opposition; and Lord Landsdowne, himself an excellent Irish landlord, resigned from the Government in protest against a step which he regarded as a threat to landed property everywhere.

The Compensation for Disturbance Bill (Ireland) was justified by the extraordinary conditions that prevailed in a country dependent exclusively on agriculture and far worse hit than England by the slump of the late 1870s. But Disraeli, in spite of his clairvoyant oratorical epitome of the Irish problem thirty-five years earlier,[2] was at heart wholly out of sympathy with the Irish, and, excepting certain proposals in 1852 and 1859 made essentially for tactical purposes, he never did or said anything helpful to them. In terms of political tactics in 1880 his resistance to the Bill was shrewd enough. The Conservative party, as he saw it, was essentially the English party – and its fate in Wales and Scotland at the late election seemed a further confirmation of this belief. The Irish were most unpopular in England and voted Liberal anyway. The threat to landed tenure upset the Whigs as well as the Tories. All in all, it was as good an issue on which to give Gladstone a buffet as one

[1] *Hansard*, cclvi (1880), 620.
[2] See above, 169.

could find. Moreover Disraeli really did believe, along with the great majority of the landlord class, that the Bill was a menace to their whole position, and that its consequences could not be confined to Ireland. On August 3 it was thrown out by 282 to 51; more Liberals voted against it than for it, and the Whig peers made the running during the debate.

Although Disraeli's leadership of the party in the Lords was virtually unchallenged, this was by no means the case with North-cote's in the House of Commons where the Fourth Party[1] was beginning to create something of a sensation. On August 25 Disraeli escorted by Arthur Balfour paid a visit to the House to see them in action. He also observed 'Mr. Chamberlain who looked and spoke like a cheesemonger' and 'Mundella who looked like an old goat on Mount Haemus, and other dreadful beings'.[2] It is sometimes said that he actively encouraged Lord Randolph and his friends, but a closer look suggests the opposite. He did, it is true, tell Drummond Wolff that he would not have quitted the House of Commons had he foreseen Gladstone's return, and that he appreciated their feelings. 'But you must stick to Northcote. He represents the respectability of the party. I wholly sympathize with you because I was never respectable myself . . . Don't on any account break with Northcote but defer to him as often as you can. Whenever it becomes too difficult you can come to me and I will try to arrange matters. Meanwhile I will speak to him.'[3]

Disraeli was evidently uncomfortable about some of the activities of the four rebels. He did not wish to discourage their brilliance, energy and gadfly qualities which no doubt reminded him of Young England and his own forays against Peel, but he certainly did not wish them to damage 'the Goat', as they disrespectfully nicknamed Sir Stafford. It was a part of Disraeli's chameleon-like tact as well as his natural character that Gorst could write, speaking of a conversation with him later in the year at Hughenden: 'Lord B. was in his talk anything but Goaty.'[4] Yet Gorst's own account of what Disraeli said shows how anxious he was to preserve party unity. He assured Gorst that Northcote was not, as rumoured, planning a coalition with Derby and that he had not supported

---

[1] A small group of Tory *frondeurs* consisting of Lord Randolph Churchill, A. J. Balfour, John Gorst and Sir Henry Drummond Wolff.

[2] M. & B., vi, 588, Disraeli to Lady Bradford.

[3] Winston S. Churchill, *Lord Randolph Churchill* (new edition, 1951), 131.

[4] ibid., 129.

Derby in the late Cabinet; he told him that Northcote would not
make any further pledges to support the Government if it proposed
coercion in Ireland and would oppose suggestions for changing the
procedure of the House.

True, Gorst reports Disraeli as saying that 'just at present we
need not be too scrupulous about obeying our leader'. But this
remark is sandwiched between advice to tell Northcote in advance
of all their intentions, listening 'with respect and attention to anything he may say', and a firm expression that 'an open rupture
between us would . . . be most disastrous.'[1] After the interview
Disraeli wrote to Northcote, 'I have had Gorst down here and have
confidence in his future conduct. I will assist you as much as I can
in looking after the Fourth Party.'[2] But the path of the peace
maker is seldom smooth. Northcote was not wholly reassured.
Referring to the next session he wrote to Cross on November 29:
'We shall find the Fourth Party extremely violent and troublesome;
and I am secretly uneasy lest they should receive a little too much
encouragement from quarters which I need not now mention.'[3]

On September 20 Queen Victoria wrote a *very secret* letter to
Disraeli in which *inter alia* she observed: 'I *never* write except on
formal official matters to the Prime Minister;' and after asking his
opinion on foreign policy enclosed for his comment an extract from
a letter of Granville's about the state of the parties at home. Granville referred to 'the want of discipline in the two Houses. . . . The
Liberal party has never been remarkable for this quality. But Sir
Stafford Northcote has lost all authority over a portion of the
Conservative MPs, while Lord Beaconsfield has no longer the same
authority over the extreme Tories in the Lords.'[4] Disraeli was not
going to take this lying down, and, observing that 'Lord Granville's
view of the state of the parties is highly exaggerated and quite
superficial,'[5] he sent a memorandum giving his own opinion of the
political situation.

A Ministry that has been signally defeated at a General Election
and has become an Opposition in the House of Commons with
very reduced numbers must be guided with an easy rein. In a
balanced state of parties with the prospect of power, Discipline

[1] ibid., 130.
[2] M. & B., vi, 589.
[3] British Museum, Add. MSS, 51265, f. 20.
[4] *The Letters of Queen Victoria*, 2nd Series, iii, 143, n.
[5] ibid., 145, September 22.

is not difficult to maintain; but where there is not that prospect, restless and able spirits will seek, in personal distinction, a substitute for party discipline. But tho' this always happens, it never extends far. There is scarcely half a dozen men, now, who would seriously question the counsel of Sir Stafford Northcote, and if I called the party together and exerted myself, I would answer for that half dozen. Lord Randolph, Mr. Gorst, and their companions, do no harm. They are a safety valve and tend to disorganise the ministerial ranks.

As regards the House of Lords, I went up a month ago, when I was told all was chaos. I was deprived, by their absence, of the assistance of my two ablest colleagues, Cairns and Salisbury, and the head of my staff, Lord Lathom, was at Homburg! I had to do everything myself, not only hold meetings but give continuous interviews. If I had held up my hand the Game Bill would have been defeated by as a great a majority as the Irish Disturbance Bill; the Employers' Bill by a large majority; and I could even have retained Ld. M^tEdgecombe's amendment to the Burial Bill, which wd have killed that measure. But I thought it for the advantage of Your Majesty and your Realm that these three measures having been brought forward with the authority of yr Majesty's ministers and being approved by the Ho: of Comm: should substantially pass; and they did pass, tho' such men as the Dukes of Buccleuch and Beaufort said they consented only in deference to my authority.

What I feel about the Ho: of Lords is, not that my authority is reduced, but that it is too great and may from circumstances become unpopular with my brother peers. Its exercise is most painful to me. The prospect is that the present Ministry will bombard the Ho: of Lords with measures which the Peers disapprove, and yet measures with so plausible a surface and so specious a pretext, that it will frequently be my duty to advise the Ho: of Lords to consent to their second reading, that is, to sanction their general scope. As for Lord Redesdale and the dozen men, or so, who would follow him, I look upon all that as mere fun. I could have them all, their leader included, in my pocket tomorrow if I cared to do so.

At the same time having made this truly candid statement, I do not deny that I sh^d be glad if I could place the leadership of the Ho: of Lords in other hands; but, hitherto, I have not seen my way to such a result.

With regard to an appeal out of doors, I have no reason to believe, that an appeal to the country at the present moment, would be materially different in its result from that recently ascertained. The fire and fervor of the general election have evaporated – the Country is perplexed and bewildered about Foreign and Indian affairs; to a certain degree, alarmed; but too much confused to act. The domestic measures of the Ministry have tended to their popularity. They have not only satisfied their own followers but to a certain extent they have detached the farmers from their natural allies, and tho' this last will ultimately find the repeal of the Malt Tax a heavy blow to them, and the Game Bill a mere phantom, yet to realize all this will require some little time.[1]

B

He may have overrated Northcote's authority in the lower house, but he did not exaggerate his own in the Lords. There, and indeed in the whole Tory party, his position remained impregnable until his death.

2

Politics was not Disraeli's only preoccupation that summer. With the indefatigable vitality which was one of his most extraordinary characteristics he decided to finish the novel which he had begun ten years earlier after the publication of *Lothair*. On October 15, 1878, he had given Monty Corry a glimpse of it when he deposited it in the new strong room at Hughenden, the very first item to be put there. He told Corry that he hoped to add another hundred pages but that the theme was already far enough advanced for the book to be published in case he did not live to finish it. He left a note of how the plot was meant to end, as he told Corry later when the book came out, 'leaving it to me to add the "hundred pages" lacking, with my own hand if I thought proper, and to publish the whole under his name.'[2] Trust in a private secretary could scarcely go further, and Disraeli's confidence is the more surprising in view of the high qualities which he himself considered were necessary in a writer of novels. At the same time that he told Corry of the existence of the manuscript he made some comments on the task of an author

'The greatest stretch of intellect in the world is to write a first rate work of fiction. It requires first rate "narrative power", first rate descriptive and first rate dramatic power and above (all) a sense of humor.'
    As a general rule Lord B. would lay it down to be more difficult to be a great writer of fiction than a great speaker. Certainly his

[1] Royal Archives, A.77.39, n.d., but must be September 23, 1880.
[2] Corry Papers, memorandum by Corry, October 15, 1878, with further addition, October 21, 1882.

experience is that a great effort to be the former is the most exhausting.[1]

The new novel was of course *Endymion*, one of the most mellow, delightful, and engagingly improbable romances to issue from his pen. It must have been something like three-quarters, perhaps four-fifths completed when Disraeli put it away in October 1878. Rather more than half the book had been written before he returned to office in 1874, and very probably before his wife died at the end of 1872. *Lothair* came out in the spring of 1870, and the ensuing two and a half years seems to be the time when the greater part of *Endymion* was written. But it is quite clear, contrary to the usual version of the matter, that Disraeli wrote a fair amount, at least one fifth, of the book while he was Prime Minister and probable that most of this part was written in the late summer and autumn of 1878.[2] The remainder was completed in the summer of 1880.

As with *Lothair* Disraeli was most secretive. In October 1878 Corry was the first person to know that he had begun a new novel, and remained the only one until the time came to negotiate with the publishers. Not a hint did Disraeli give, even to Lady Bradford or Lady Chesterfield. He rapidly completed his hundred pages during the early summer. By the middle of July things were far enough advanced for Corry to enter into negotiations with Longmans. Their first offer was £7,500 but it was made on the basis that *Lothair* had brought in only £6,000, and Corry was able to point out that this estimate ignored substantial American sales.[3] The publishers reconsidered this offer. During the early hours of August 4 while the Duke of Argyll was speaking in the House of Lords on the Compensation for Disturbance Bill, an observer might have seen Lord Rowton rise from his place beside Disraeli who was due to reply, and return a few moments later with a note which he passed to his chief.

There are things too big to impart in whispers! So I leave your side, just to write those words.
    Longman has today offered *Ten Thousand Pounds* for Endymion.
    I have accepted it! I cannot tell you what a pleasure it is to me to see my ardent ambition for you gratified!

[1] loc. cit.
[2] For a full discussion see Robert Blake, 'The Dating of Endymion', *Review of English Studies*, New Series, xvii, 66, May 1966, 177–82.
[3] Hughenden Papers, Box 94, B/XX/Co/143, Corry to Disraeli, July 21, 1880.

And you have an added honor which may for ever remain without precedent.[1]

Longman had not yet even read the book – nor for that matter had Corry. The publisher agreed to pay £2,500 on delivery of the manuscript and the balance on April 1, 1881. It was believed to be the largest sum ever paid for a work of fiction: the modern equivalent would be at least £60,000. Corry read the manuscript for Disraeli at Hughenden during August. 'Read it once my dear fellow for the purpose of seeing if the story and the work in general be fit to publish. If you condemn it I will burn it. And then I would ask you to read it a second time to see if it be in English; and then again a third time to review the spelling and punctuation.'[2] This task accomplished – for there was little danger of Corry condemning it to the flames – Mr Norton Longman was invited to Hughenden for the week-end to examine the manuscript with the help of Corry. On September 14 he paid a second visit to collect the book and pay over his cheque. His amusing account of this strange evening is well known:[3] how Disraeli was quite alone but for the servants, whom he wished to keep in ignorance; how curiously agitated he seemed to be; his air of mystification and secrecy; the care he took to deceive his valet, Baum, who was not allowed even to light the candles in the study; the appearance of the three volumes in three red dispatch boxes; the problem of where to conceal them in Longman's bedroom for the evening, the publisher choking back just in time the suggestion 'my Gladstone bag'; and finally the signing of the cheque.

Endymion was published on November 26. The short interval, barely over ten weeks between delivery and publication, must fill the modern writer with envy. At first it looked as if Longman had been over sanguine. The book sold well, but not well enough to justify such an unprecedented sum. Disraeli was uneasy. He feared, he told Lady Bradford on publication day, that the transaction 'will prove rather the skill of Monty's diplomacy than Mr. Longman's acumen. If so my conscience will force me to disgorge.'[4] In March he offered to cancel the agreement and accept instead a royalty of 10s in the £ on all copies sold. Longman in reply admitted that the

[1] M. & B., vi, 552.
[2] Corry Papers.
[3] Quoted, M. & B., vi, 552–4.
[4] ibid., vi, 569.

three volume edition of *Endymion* had not gone as well as *Lothair*, but he firmly refused to take advantage of Disraeli's generosity. Luckily, the cheap six-shilling edition launched early in the new year sold well. Longman was not out of pocket, and the story of a transaction, by no means typical of relations between authors and publishers, had a happy ending, as Corry's note shows:

> Mr Longman visited me at 19 Curzon St, a few days before Lord Beaconsfield's death, and authorized me to inform Lord B: – who heard the intelligence with extreme satisfaction – that his firm had just turned the corner and was beginning to make a profit out of the bargain.
> I believe that this was the last piece of business on wh: he and I spoke together.
> After so many! and such![1]

Endymion, despite the disapproval of Archbishop Tait who finished it 'with a painful feeling that the writer considers all political life as mere play and gambling',[2] had a better reception both from the critics and from Disraeli's friends than *Lothair*. Yet for all its qualities it is not such a good book, although one can see why contemporaries preferred it. *Endymion* contains many excellent things. The fireworks blaze away as gaily as ever. But it lacks that fascinating yet faintly disturbing ambiguity which in *Lothair* and the trilogy of the 1840s so often leaves us uncertain whether the author is mocking or accepting the political beau-monde of which he was master in both fiction and reality. This subtle blend of irony, satire and romance which gives Disraeli's best novels a flavour unlike anything else in literature is found to perfection in *Lothair*,-and it pervades *Coningsby*, *Sybil* and much of *Tancred*. It is not absent from *Endymion* but there is less of it, and not enough to mask the absurdity of the plot and the implausibility of the principal characters. The style, too, has a certain languor and tiredness about it. One might have guessed, if one did not already know, that the author was an old man.

The theme of the novel is the influence of women upon a political career. Disraeli as usual was thinking of himself. He liked to maintain, as he put it to Lady Bradford once, 'I owe all to women' – on any objective assessment a gross exaggeration even when allowance is made for Mrs Austen, his sister Sarah, Mary Anne, Mrs Brydges

[1] Corry Papers.
[2] M. & B., vi, 568, quoting Tait's journal.

Willyams, and Queen Victoria. Endymion Ferrars born in 1819 is the son of a financially ruined Tory politician manqué forced to retire to a remote country house, Hurstley (clearly Bradenham) in order to economize. The father gets Endymion a clerkship in a dim government office at the age of sixteen. Endymion is frankly a stick. He is good looking, kind hearted, hard working, discreet, and dull; 'prudent and plastic', he 'always did and said the right thing'. Disraeli told Sir Charles Dilke who apparently took it as a compliment that he had been the model for Endymion, though it is hard to see any resemblance. This is a very unDisraeliesque hero, and, as described by the author he scarcely seems likely to come to much. Yet the book ends with him at the age of forty, leader of the Whig party and Prime Minister of England.

Of the women who have wrought this improbable transformation the most important is Myra, his devoted beautiful and formidable twin sister who 'never cried in my life except in a rage', and who is determined through her adored brother to restore the shattered family fortunes. She marries first Lord Roehampton (Palmerston), then King Florestan (Napoleon III) – not a bad 'double' for a penniless girl to bring off. Next comes Berengaria Lady Montfort, the great Whig hostess, an amalgam of Lady Palmerston, Mrs Norton, and Lady Normanby. Lord Montfort (Lord Hertford), a milder version of the Monmouth who dominates *Coningsby*, opportunely dies leaving her his huge fortune, and though presumably far older she marries Endymion. Her rival political hostess, Zenobia, is Disraeli's old friend Lady Jersey. There are the inevitable Rothschilds – but dehebraicized, rather surprisingly, and given Swiss ancestry under the name of Neuchatel. Their mansion, Hainault House, is an enlarged version of Gunnersbury. Their beautiful daughter Adriana is in love with Endymion and makes him an anonymous gift of £20,000 in Consols at a crucial moment in his career but she marries Waldershare (George Smythe) through whom Disraeli good-humouredly laughs at Young England and some of his own beliefs – or professions of belief – nearly forty years earlier. Many other women play their part in helping Endymion to the top of the greasy pole. Some of them come alive but Myra carries no conviction: she is as unlikely as Endymion himself.

Disraeli, as we saw, lacked the power to create characters. He usually peopled his novels with persons whom he had known. *Endymion* seems particularly conspicuous for this, but perhaps the reason is that by the time he came to write it he knew a greater number of more famous figures than ever before, and so his characters are easier to identify. However that may be, the novel is a portrait gallery of the past. Not only do Palmerston, Louis Napoleon, Lady Palmerston, Lady Jersey, the Rothschilds, and George Smythe appear in their disguise but we have Bismarck (Count Ferrol) Metternich (Baron Sergius) Persigny (the Duke of St Angelo), the Bulwer brothers (Mr Bertie Tremaine and Mr Tremaine Bertie), Cobden (Mr Thornberry). Cardinal Manning reappears as Nigel Penruddock, the Archbishop of Tyre, but this time in a much more flattering guise than in *Lothair*, explicable perhaps by the fact that since then he had quarrelled with Gladstone over the Vatican Decrees and had given Disraeli the gratifying information that he thought Gladstone 'the most revengeful man he ever knew'.[1]

Most of the portraits in *Endymion* are drawn with a kindly pen. There is one exception, Thackeray who is caricatured as St Barbe, the egotistic envious radical writer always complaining at the success of his rival, Gushy, and sneering behind their backs at the noblemen whom in their presence he toadies shamelessly. Thackeray had been dead for seventeen years and, although he had in 1847 published a parody of Disraeli in 'Punch's Prize Novelists' – 'Codlingsby by B. De Shrewsbury Esq'[2] – it was felt by many people that there was something undignified in Disraeli's belated riposte. As a picture of Thackeray, St Barbe is grotesque. Even if we regard him as a character in his own right, he does not compare with the immortal Rigby; but he has his good moments all the same. Endymion tells him he should belong to a club. He replies:

'So I was told by a friend of mine the other day – one of your great swells. He said I ought to belong to the Athenaeum,[3] and he would propose me, and the committee would elect me as a matter of course. They rejected me and selected a bishop. And then people are surprised that the Church is in danger!'

Many people, among them Queen Victoria, were puzzled that Disraeli made his hero a Whig rather than a Tory. But the reasons

[1] ibid., 584. Disraeli passed this on to Northcote, who records it in his diary.

[2] See *Punch*, xii (1847), 166, 198–9, 213–14 and 223. It is not very subtle and plays up to the anti-Semitism which disfigures *Punch* all too often when referring to Disraeli, but is otherwise inoffensive.

[3] Thackeray had been defeated for the Athenaeum in 1850, but was elected in the following year.

are not hard to guess. First the novel is not about political creeds, it is essentially the story of an ascent: how Endymion rises from clerk to private secretary, to MP, to under-Secretary, to the Cabinet, to the top. We never learn what he meant to do when he got there, or why he was a Whig. Hence no doubt the head shakings of the Archbishop and of other grave personages. Secondly Disraeli wanted for particular reasons to set his story in the years of his own youth and early middle-age. Unlike his other political novels this one is quasi-historical. It is as if an elderly statesman in 1966 published a novel which began with the Marconi scandal and ended with the resignation of Neville Chamberlain. The first real historical event in *Endymion* is the death of Canning, the last the fall of the Aberdeen coalition. But if the story was to be one of ascent through the various grades of the political *cursus honorum* the hero had to belong to the majority party, and therefore could not be a Tory: the Conservatives were in office too little, and they had sunk into a very dejected condition at the time when the novel ends.

No one need regret Disraeli's decision to set his story in that particular period. It gave him a wonderful chance of recreating the grand world which had constituted the background of his own astonishing career; his comments upon the changing scene and the parliamentary events of those years are the best part of a book which contains some of Disraeli's most celebrated excursions into political history and is also a gold mine for the historian of manners and 'society'. With the exception of the character of St Barbe, Disraeli's retrospect is essentially kindly and urbane. It is, in keeping with the title,[1] a landscape by the light of the moon, the full harvest moon on a warm night softening and romanticizing all that is harsh and familiar, lending magic to the ordinary, poetry to the humdrum. Thus, for all its defects, *Endymion* remains one of the most charming and readable of Disraeli's novels – and it is readable not simply because of what it tells us about the author but for its own sake, an enchanting fantasy, witty, gay and good-humoured. The final paragraph of the notice in the *Edinburgh Review*, if we disregard the somewhat priggish last sentence, sums it up admirably.

---

[1] Endymion was in classical mythology the human lover of Selene goddess of the moon. It has been suggested that Disraeli intended some sort of allusion to Lady Bradford (Selina), but the title was invented before that romance began, and Corry's story seems more likely, viz. that the novel was named after a supposed ancestor of Lady Beaconsfield, Endymion Porter, 1587–1649, Groom of the Bedchamber to Charles I and a patron of literature and art.

Upon the whole we close these volumes not without gratitude to the author for the amusement he has afforded us. It may be suspected that he is laughing all the time at society, at politics, at his readers. But what then? We can laugh with him. To take such a book *au grand serieux*, as the French say, would be a mistake; but as a satirical picture of life, with the transformations of a Christmas pantomime, it has the merit of entertaining an enormous number of readers, from the cabinet minister at Whitehall, who throws aside his despatches to devour it, to the Californian miner or Australian shepherd, who will imagine that he finds in these pages some traces of what is happening in another hemisphere, though in this he might be a little mistaken. These are but the coloured shadows from the magic-lantern of life; the lamp within shines, we trust, with a purer and steadier light.[1]

Having finished *Endymion* Disraeli promptly settled down to write yet another novel. Seldom did the *Vivian Gray* side of his character show itself more strikingly than in this final gesture of his old age a few months before his death. For his new romance was nothing less than an attempt to caricature his old enemy Gladstone. Alas, it extends only to nine chapters and the first paragraph of a tenth, but they are enough to show that death cut short what might have been a highly entertaining book, though no doubt Archbishops would have shaken their heads more sadly than ever.

The novel has no title but it is reasonable to guess that like all Disraeli's books it would have been called after its principal character, *Falconet*.[2] Joseph Toplady Falconet, is a younger son of Mr Wilberforce Falconet, a wealthy merchant of evangelical propensities living at Clapham Common. The scene appears to be set in the very recent past, and some of the characters from *Lothair*, including the hero of that book reappear. It has been suggested by Philip Guedalla that the Christian names were symbolic: Joseph is intended to remind us of Joseph Surface, the immortal hypocrite in *The School for Scandal*, and Toplady[3] is the name of the anti-Methodist Anglican divine who wrote 'Rock of Ages'. Incidentally, though Guedalla does not make this point, Gladstone had in 1839 translated 'Rock of Ages' into Latin – a fact of which Disraeli must

---

[1] *Edinburgh Review*, cliii, 129. The article was written by Monckton Milnes. See Pope-Hennessy, *Monckton Milnes*, ii, 217.

[2] First published in *The Times* in three instalments, January 20, 21, 23, 1905, and then as an appendix in M. & B., v, 531–60.

[3] Augustus Montagu Toplady (1740–78), an extreme Calvinist and a vituperative controversialist who in 'More Work for Mr. Wesley' accused his foe of 'satanic guilt' and 'satanic shamelessness'.

have been aware. The story begins with young Falconet's adoption for a pocket borough belonging to Lord Bartram who like Lord Roehampton in *Endymion* is evidently a version of Palmerston. Falconet makes an eloquent speech at the hustings on the revival of the slave trade in the Red Sea. 'True it was that it subsequently appeared that there had been no revival of the slave trade in the Red Sea, but that the misapprehension had occurred from a mistake in the telegraph, manipulated by a functionary suffering from *coup de soleil* or *delirium tremens*. But this did not signify . . .' However, Lord Bartram at a subsequent dinner with the Falconets to celebrate Joseph's election is against pursuing the matter. ' "I think I would leave the Red Sea alone," said the Earl. "It was a miracle that saved us being drowned in it before." Mrs. Falconet looked grave and her husband quickly turned the conversation . . .'

Disraeli had come to view Gladstone with greater detestation than ever, since the general election. Indeed his remarks if taken seriously are almost as unbalanced as those of Queen Victoria. 'If he were younger the Crown would not be safe,' he told Lady Chesterfield. And to Lady Bradford, 'I think the A.V. so wicked a man that he would not hesitate to plunge us into a great war to soothe and salve his maniacal vanity.' Therefore he must have enjoyed delineating young Falconet 'arrogant and peremptory'; as a boy 'scarcely ever known to smile', with 'a complete deficiency in the sense of humour', a prodigy at school and university where he was 'the unrivalled orator of its mimic Parliament'; 'his chief peculiarity was his disputatious temper and the flow of language which even as a child was ever at his command to express his arguments.' 'Firm in his faith in an age of dissolving creeds he wished to believe that he was the man ordained to vindicate the sublime course of religious truth.' His powers of oratory make him an immediate success in the House and his humourlessness is no barrier. He 'was essentially a prig, and among prigs there is a freemasonry which never fails. All the prigs spoke of him as the coming man.'

It is intriguing to speculate upon the fate destined for this unattractive hero. Already the female cast is in evidence: Claribel, Lord Bartram's young second wife who is much interested in Falconet, Lady Ermyntrude her daughter, Angela Hartmann, daughter of a rich Nihilist. He was surely going to be entangled with one or more of them. As for the male characters, it is noticeable how

Queen Victoria and Disraeli at High Wycombe station on her visit to Hughenden,
December 15, 1877

Hughenden Manor today

Disraeli in old age
One of a series of photographs by Jabez Hughes
taken at Osborne by command of Queen Victoria

many appear to be dominated by varieties of Nihilistic belief, not only Hartmann, but the Buddhist missionary, Kusinara, and Lord Bartram's heir, Lord Gaston whose faith has been sapped by attending an Oxford college ruled by 'one of those distinguished divines who do not believe in divinity' – a palpable hit at Jowett's Balliol. Finally there is a mysterious 'Unknown' whose name is not revealed and who discusses with Hartmann their common programme of 'the destruction of the species'.

Disraeli, as Buckle suggests, may well have been influenced by the assassination of Alexander II in St Petersburg on March 13, 1881[1] – an event which was the culmination of a series of nihilist conspiracies. How Joseph Toplady was to fit into all this remains a matter of surmise. Perhaps one of these Nihilists was destined, partially or temporarily, to convert him from his stern and unbending Toryism. Disraeli was obsessed with what he regarded as Gladstone's destructionism of and hostility to the old territorial influences. There may be a clue in the Unknown's remark to Hartmann. 'Destruction in every form must be welcomed. If it be only the destruction of a class it is a step in the right direction.' Nine short chapters are too small a base from which to conjecture. The novel shows no signs of failing talent. It is in Disraeli's most characteristic vein, and one can only regret that it was never finished.

[1] Hartmann may even be named after the Russian Nihilist Leo Hartmann, whom the Russian authorities had vainly endeavoured to extradite from Paris a year earlier.

CHAPTER XXXII

The End

1880–1

At the time that Disraeli began *Falconet* there seemed no reason why he should not live to complete it. Although he had a bad attack of asthma and gout in October and early November, he was in exceptionally good health during the last weeks of 1880. Always sensitive to weather, he enjoyed to the full one of those rare prolongations of summer which occasionally soften the approach of the English winter. 'Here after a slight rime which soon vanishes almost with the faeries,' he wrote to Queen Victoria on November 3, 'we have & have had for some days, the climate of Cannes, or Nice, or the Riviera, cloudless skies, westerly breezes and almost scorching suns, so that at noon I can sit on the southern terrace for a couple of hours & feel like Egypt. But alas! the sun sets at four! There is nothing like the magic of long days.'[1]

True, life had its inconveniences. Monty Corry's sister was seriously ill, and it was alleged that the cure was a visit to Biarritz. He took her there in November and was intending to return, but she promptly became even iller, and the experts now declared that Algeria was the only place. As a result, Corry had to cancel all his plans, and Disraeli was bereft. 'If she had gone to Bournemouth she would probably be well by this time,'[2] he grumbled to Lady Bradford. Then Disraeli decided to visit Dr Kidd in London. 'If he continued his visits to Hughenden I should have to execute a mortgage on my estate; if indeed land be any longer a security.'[3] But he arrived there only to encounter a black fog which prevented him from even inspecting a house in Curzon Street which he was on the point of buying, and he hastily returned to Hughenden where it was 'radiant and balmy'. The purchase was just the sort of negotiation for which Corry was invaluable, the owner of the house, Lord Tankerville, being notoriously difficult. 'I shall never feel

[1] Royal Archives, B.64.16.
[2] Zetland, ii, 299, to Lady Bradford, November 21.
[3] M. & B., vi, 592, to Lady Bradford, November 15.

assured with so uncertain a vendor, that it is mine until all is signed and sealed,' wrote Disraeli to Lady Chesterfield.[1] Luckily there was no hitch. His offer was accepted and the proceeds of *Endymion* enabled him to acquire a seven year lease of 19 Curzon Street, which he intended to be his base for the coming parliamentary struggle.

Corry's absence made it essential to find a substitute as secretary. He selected Lord Barrington who was personally congenial. 'He is not a Monty, but he has good talents, great experience of the pol. world, having been priv. secy to Ld Derby, and one too on whose honor and devotion I can rely.'[2] Barrington was an Irish Viscount who sat for Eye in Suffolk from 1866 until 1880 when Disraeli conferred a UK barony on him in the resignation honours. He was Vice-Chamberlain of the Household from 1874 to 1880. He owned over 6,000 acres with a rent roll of £17,000 p.a.

Affairs were pressing. The Government had decided to start the 1881 session on January 7 – far earlier than usual – in order to carry an urgent Irish Coercion Bill. On December 31 Disraeli left Hughenden which he was not destined to see again, and passed a fortnight at Alfred de Rothschild's while his new house which would have been ready in ample time for a normal session was being put in order. 'I wish to . . . use myself to the human face divine,' he wrote on December 27 to Salisbury who was at Nice. 'It is no easy thing to step out of the profound solitude in which I live – often not speaking to a human being the whole day – and walk into the House of Lords and make a speech on a falling Empire.'[3]

In the debate on the Address, Disraeli supported Irish coercion but reminded his audience of his warning about Ireland before the election. On the wider issues he deplored the Government's policy of 'perpetual and complete reversal of all that has occurred'. He had chiefly in mind foreign and imperial policy, and it is true that, since his return to office, Gladstone had, to an unusual degree, attempted to undo the policies of his predecessor – not always with happy results. But Granville could justifiably reply that, in view of the huge majority which had condemned the previous government the new one could scarcely be expected to follow feebly in its footsteps.

Disraeli complained to Lady Bradford that he had been physically incapacitated from saying all that he wished. This is one of

[1] Zetland, ii, 298, November 19.
[2] M. & B., vi, 594, Disraeli to Lady Bradford, December 17.
[3] ibid., vi, 596.

several indications that his health at, or a little before, this time was beginning to deteriorate. As late as December 21 he could write from Hughenden to the Queen.

> . . . tho' I generally shrink from an egotistic bulletin even in deference to gracious command, I might perhaps be pardoned this day in saying that for some years I have not felt in such good health & that I have just returned from a walk of three miles in a hilly country & with no other companion than a dog, without the slightest feeling of weariness. Life indeed in such a climate as this year gives to us would be delightful, had we not to put on our night-caps at three o'ck.[1]

He was never to talk in this vein again. The weather which had been so beneficial almost up to Christmas suddenly changed. The next four months were a period of quite abnormal severity, snow, frost and biting east winds. On arriving in London at the end of the year Disraeli was in a state of semi-collapse and remained in his rooms at Seamore Place till the debate. Dr Kidd notes that 'during the winter of 1880 his condition became more and more anxious'.[2] In addition to bronchial trouble he began to suffer from mild uraemia which may explain the drowsiness of which he now complains for the first time. It may account too for the silence and seeming deafness into which he could sometimes sink even during the numerous dinner parties which he regularly attended almost to the very last. His social life, involving as it did frequent breaks in his dietetic régime and drives through London late at night in icy weather, cannot have been good for his health. But he was by no means always in a depressed condition. He would often be as witty and sardonic as in the past, and wherever he went he could be sure, whether silent or articulate, of being the centre of attention, the embodiment of his own self-created myth, a legend in his lifetime.

Conscious of his declining powers, Disraeli seems to have been genuinely anxious to pass on the leadership of the party in the House of Lords to Salisbury. But what he called the 'Epiphany Session' threw out these plans. Salisbury was in the south of France, and it was impossible to make the necessary arrangements before Parliament met. There was one welcome but short-lived development; Corry returned from Algiers in time for the session. But to

---

[1] Royal Archives, B.64.18.

[2] Joseph Kidd 'The last illness of Lord Beaconsfield', *The Nineteenth Century*, 26 (July, 1889), 68.

Disraeli's annoyance the invalid sister soon suffered another relapse. On February 12 he wrote to Lady Bradford. 'Alas! Alas! Monty leaves me again, and for quite an indefinite time . . . my correspondence alone will overwhelm me. It is impossible to teach a new secretary his work.'[1] It is perhaps significant of the change in Disraeli that he did not write again to Lady Bradford for a whole month – and then only two more letters before his final illness set in on March 23. The last letter that he wrote to Lady Chesterfield was on January 26. 'The weather has completely upset me,' he began, 'And I really cannot fight against it any more.'[2]

It would probably be wrong to see in this remark any real element of premonition. Disraeli was soon in a more buoyant mood, dining with the Granvilles and with Lady Lonsdale, summoning a Tory meeting at his house – he moved into 19 Curzon Street on January 15 – endeavouring to decide tactics over the Government's proposal for the closure – or *clôture* as it was called to emphasize its un-English nature. The Irish party's obstructionist tactics had convinced all other sections of the House that something of the sort was necessary, even before the famous forty-one-hour sitting which began on January 31 and was ended only by the Speaker taking the law into his own hands. But Disraeli was determined to restrict the closure to the essential minimum, and he was anxious to prevent Sir Stafford Northcote yielding to Gladstone who 'is trying it on with every art of Jesuitry on his former pupil', Disraeli told Corry, who was at Sandringham and he added nostalgically

> It was easy to settle affairs with Palmerston because he was a man of the world, and was therefore governed by the principle of honor: but when you have to deal with an earnest man, severely religious and enthusiastic, every attempted arrangement ends in unintelligible correspondence and violated confidence.[3]

On March 1 Disraeli dined at Windsor Castle. It was the last time that the Queen was to see him. Three days later he made a major speech in the House of Lords, attacking the Government's decision to evacuate Kandahar. It contained the phrase 'the key of India is London', which Disraeli borrowed from the Russian Ambassador who had called on him the previous day, though Disraeli used it to support the opposite policy to that favoured by Russia. Disraeli

[1] M. & B., vi, 602.
[2] ibid., 600.
[3] ibid., 601, January 29.

took the opportunity to make some acid observations on Derby: 'I do not know that there is anything that would excite enthusiasm in him except when he contemplates the surrender of some national possession.'

On March 10 he gave his first and only dinner party in his new house. There were seventeen guests, among them Lord Bradford, Lady Chesterfield, Lord and Lady Granville, Alfred de Rothschild, the Duke and Duchess of Sutherland and Sir Frederick Leighton, the President of the Royal Academy. Lady Bradford could not come as she was away from London at the time. The last survivor of the party was Lord John Manners' son Henry, the 8th Duke of Rutland, who died forty-four years later. Disraeli had been ill during the previous two days and received his guests leaning on a stick. Drugs kept him going through the evening. 'The dinner yesterday went off, I believe, very well,' he told Lady Bradford. 'As the gentlemen smoked after dinner tho' not long, that gave me an opportunity of inhaling some of my poison in the form of a cigarette, and nobody found it out.'[1]

Shortly after this he had to deal with a political crisis whose gravity he somewhat overstated when writing to the Queen. Gladstone tried to apply the new rules of closure intended for extraordinary obstruction to the ordinary business of supply. It was certainly something of a try on, but hardly, as Disraeli termed it, 'the greatest revolution in the country since 1688'.[2] Fortunately on this occasion Northcote stood firm and Disraeli was able to frustrate his old enemy. On March 15 he spoke for the last time in the House of Lords, to support a vote of condolence to the Queen on the assassination of the Tsar.

He continued his social life; in Lytton Strachey's immortal phrase, 'moving still, an assiduous mummy from dinner party to dinner party'. But the weather remained inexorable. At one of these parties he told Mrs Goschen 'I am blind and deaf. I only live for climate and I never get it.' It was the climate which killed him in the end. Returning to his house on the night of Tuesday, March 22, one of the worst of the year, he was caught for a minute by the sleety blast of the east wind. Next day the chill had developed into bronchitis, and from then onwards he gradually declined.

At first there seemed no special cause for alarm. He was able to

[1] ibid., 606.
[2] ibid., 607, Disraeli to Queen Victoria, March 12.

discuss politics with Cairns, Salisbury and Cranbrook on March 27, and on the 28th Barrington brought in Sir Charles Dilke to see him. The same day he wrote his last letter to the Queen, a shaky but legible pencilled note in reply to her inquiry, ending 'At present I am prostrate though devoted – B'. The Queen became anxious and pressed Barrington, who was dining that night at Buckingham Palace, to secure a second opinion. This was not too easy, Kidd being a homoeopath, for the rules of medical etiquette forbade orthodox practitioners to join in consultation with heretics of that persuasion. However, Barrington and Sir Philip Rose persuaded Dr Quain, a leading specialist in chest diseases, that refusal would be disloyalty to the Queen. On the afternoon of the 29th he examined the patient and at once arranged for a trained nurse to live in; Disraeli hitherto had been nursed by his valet Baum and by Mrs Baum. A second trained nurse and another chest specialist, Dr Bruce, were called in a few days afterwards to provide constant attention.

It is unlikely, given the treatment available in those days, that anything could have saved Disraeli, and he seems to have been convinced from early on that he would not recover. 'I feel I am dying,' he told Rose. 'Whatever the doctors may tell you, I do not believe I shall get well.' But his characteristic ironical wit did not desert him. 'Take away that emblem of mortality,' he said when given an air cushion to lie on, and on March 31 when correcting his last speech for *Hansard*: 'I will not go down to posterity talking bad grammar.' It was suggested to him that he might like to be visited by the Queen. 'No it is better not. She would only ask me to take a message to Albert.' Disraeli was much in the Queen's thoughts. She sent him spring flowers and before departing for Osborne wrote on April 5 her last letter, with instructions that it should be read to him if he was not well enough to read it himself. Disraeli held it in his hand for a moment as if in deep thought. 'This letter ought to be read to me by Lord Barrington, a Privy Councillor,' he said – and it duly was.

The fearful spasms of coughing which were the worst symptom of his illness gave him a great deal of pain. 'I have suffered much. Had I been a Nihilist I would have confessed all.'[1] These words which have inspired various esoteric conjectures have a simple and distressing explanation. The murder of the Tsar by the Nihilists was

[1] Wilfrid Meynell, *The Man Disraeli*, 278.

in everyone's mind. It was well known that the Russian authorities had used torture to extract admissions from the assassins; Disraeli's meaning is clear enough.

Corry, who had been told of the bad news, hastened back from Algiers, arriving on April 7. But Disraeli was so worn out and shattered in nerve that he could not at first bear the strain of an encounter. Three days later Corry wrote to Lady Bradford in a sombre vein. 'God grant I am wrong! It *may* well be! for the doctors are by no means hopeless. But somehow I feel as if I knew better than they! . . . He still shrinks from seeing me . . . I have seen *him* often, and do not see any bad change in his face, but the weakness! . . .'[1] The meeting occurred quite naturally and quietly soon afterwards. From then onwards Corry was constantly at his bedside and did all in his power to help and soothe the last days of his old chief. Among other things he was able to give him the good news about *Endymion*. Corry told the doctors that as soon as they knew the case to be hopeless it was their duty to tell their patient. They never told him. Perhaps they never knew until too late.

The old statesman's struggle for life was watched with intense interest and increasing anxiety by the public. Great numbers called at Curzon Street to inquire, among them Gladstone. 'May the Almighty be near his pillow,' he wrote in his diary on March 29. Letters, postcards and telegrams of sympathy poured into the house. By the beginning of April it was widely known that he was very seriously ill, and those who read between the lines of the bulletins had little hope. But in the middle of the week before Easter the weather suddenly became milder and on Thursday, April 14, Disraeli took a turn for the better. For the rest of the week bulletins were more cheerful. The improvement was only fleeting. The bitter east wind returned and whether or not for that reason he began once more to fail. April 17 was Easter Sunday. Those aware that Disraeli always received the Sacrament at Easter suggested that he should be reminded of the day and given the opportunity. Corry and Barrington readily agreed, but Quain interposed an emphatic veto. He feared that Disraeli would assume his condition to be hopeless, and give up the struggle. Quain should not be blamed, but it was a wrong decision nevertheless. Disraeli's last authentically recorded words were, 'I had rather live but I am not afraid to die'.

By now his condition had become very bad. Uraemia was affect-

[1] M. & B., vi, 615.

ing him seriously, his bronchial tubes were almost choked, fits of coughing left him totally exhausted and strained his heart. Towards the end his mind was beginning to be confused. Bouts of extreme restlessness were followed by heavy coma. He lingered on through Sunday and Monday, but at about midnight it became obvious that the end was near. He passed into the calmer sleep which often precedes death. At one o'clock Corry, who had been watching with Dr Kidd and Dr Bruce, sent for Rose and Barrington, and for Dr Quain. Corry and Barrington held one of his hands, Kidd the other. Just after a quarter past four their silent vigil was broken by a strange movement from the dying man. He half lifted himself from his pillows and leaned forward with the same gesture which he had used on countless occasions in the past when he rose to reply in debate. His lips moved but no sound came to the intently listening group around his bed. He sank back and died peacefully ten minutes later at half-past four in the morning.[1]

And so there were no last words for his friends.

He often said he knew he had no chance [wrote Corry in deep distress to Lady Bradford] and seemed to wish almost that the doctors would tell him so. But they did not know – or would not tell him, and so he glided on till the ship of his life got among the clouds and the breakers, and he began to sink without knowing where he was. And so it came that he had not the opportunity of sending a word to some, to whom, as I thought, he would have sent a loving message had he known what was so near. I never doubted what the end must be. I knew too well how little of reserve force for long past was left in him.[2]

The news of Disraeli's death was at once telegraphed to the Queen, the Prince of Wales and the Prime Minister. The Queen was for the moment overwhelmed. She wrote with her own hand the announcement of the death in the Court Circular, and she sent touching letters of sympathy to Corry and Barrington. The letter to Corry shows the full measure of her grief.

Osborne   April 19, 1881

Dear Lord Rowton,

I cannot write in the 3rd person at this terrible moment when I can scarcely see for my fast falling tears. I did *not* expect this very rapid end tho' my hopes sank yesterday very much. Since

[1] ibid., 617.
[2] loc. cit.

Thursday *till yesterday* the improvement seemed so steady. Alas! it was but the flickering up of the light before it went out.

I feel deeply for *you* – who loved him and devoted yourself to him as few sons ever do! How thankful I am that you were with him so much that last week!

I hardly dare trust to speak of myself. The loss is so *overwhelming. Just a year ago* he came to see me *before* his resignation took place and *then* when I suffered and also at Baden at the thought of losing him as my Minister – and how *he* felt this separation. But then he was well – and so well afterwards I thought I should yet see him my Minister again – but the ever returning asthma tried him very much when he had to speak, and I fear he was not prudent afterwards.

Never had I *so* kind and devoted a Minister and very few such devoted friends. His affectionate sympathy, his wise counsel – *all* were so invaluable even out of office. I have lost *so* many dear and valued friends but none whose loss will be more keenly felt. To England (or rather Gt. Britain) and to the *World* his loss is *immense* and at such a moment. God's will be done! I have learnt to say this but the bitterness and the suffering are not the less severe. As yet I cannot realize it.

I long to see you and hear all and talk of many things. *He* told me how much I could rely *on you* in future times and when he was no more and I shall claim your assistance and am sure I can rely on you for help for *you* knew *all* his thoughts and views.

My poor faithful Brown was quite overcome when he had to tell me. His sad and tearful face had too plainly told that a heavy blow had fallen.

> Ever
> Yours
> Very sincerely
> V.R.I.

I will write to Ld. Barrington to-night. You will no doubt know all about *his* wishes. You must be greatly exhausted.[1]

The news of Disraeli's death was received with all the usual manifestations of grief in the Victorian Age: flags were flown everywhere at half-mast on public buildings and at the political headquarters of both parties in the big cities; muffled peels were tolled at cathedrals; dinners were cancelled; blinds were drawn over the windows of the great London clubs. Disraeli had inspired such intense animosity in some circles that it would probably be wrong to utter the stock cliché about universal sorrow. Yet it is true that, except in the minds of implacable partisans, there was a real sense of regret at the

---

[1] Corry Papers.

passing of such an extraordinary figure from the political scene. In his last years Disraeli had come to be regarded with genuine affection by the mass of his countrymen. His death removed something of the colour and excitement of political life. It was widely felt – probably with justice – that there would never be anyone quite like him again.

On receiving the news at Hawarden where he was staying for the Easter recess, Gladstone at once decided that a public funeral would accord with the sense of the nation and be what Disraeli would have wanted. He telegraphed accordingly to the executors, and on the same morning Dean Stanley called at Curzon Street to offer a funeral at Westminster Abbey. Corry and Rose repaired that afternoon to Hughenden to examine Disraeli's will, and found as they expected specific orders to the contrary

> I DESIRE and DIRECT that I may be buried in the same Vault in the Churchyard of Hughenden in which the remains of my late dear Wife Mary Anne Disraeli created in her own right Viscountess Beaconsfield were placed and that my Funeral may be conducted with the same simplicity as hers was.

Such categorical instructions could not have been overridden and the Queen, though strongly in favour of a public funeral, felt bound to defer to the executors.

Accordingly the funeral which took place on April 26, was private. Although a great concourse of people came to Hughenden the limited space in the church was kept for those invited. Most of the leading figures of the day were there: the royal family in the persons of the Prince of Wales, the Duke of Connaught, and Prince Leopold who represented the Queen; the whole of the late Conservative Cabinet, except Cranbrook who was in Italy; Lytton, lately Viceroy of India; Derby in spite of recent political and personal estrangement; Lord Abergavenny, unrivalled former manager of the party machine; Hartington, Harcourt, and Rosebery for the Liberals – Granville was ill and Gladstone implausibly pleaded pressure of work; Leighton and Millais for the arts – no literary figures were asked. On the personal side Corry, Barrington, Bradford and Lennox were there together with Sir Philip Rose and Sir Nathaniel de Rothschild; and the presence of the young Duke of Portland with whom Disraeli was to have spent that Easter made a suitable epilogue to the strange and still slightly mysterious story, beginning thirty-five years earlier, of Disraeli's relations with the House of Bentinck.

The family mourners were Ralph Disraeli and his son Coningsby who was the heir to Hughenden and then a Charterhouse schoolboy of fourteen. Disraeli's coffin was carried from the house by tenants of the estate and he was buried, as he had ordered, in the vault outside the east end of the church where his wife, his brother James, and Mrs Brydges Willyams already lay.

Protocol forbade the Queen from attending in person the funeral of one of her subjects. The first breach of that rule occurred eighty-four years later when Queen Elizabeth II went to the funeral of Sir Winston Churchill in St Paul's Cathedral. Queen Victoria sent two wreaths of fresh primroses to Hughenden with the inscription: 'His favourite flowers from Osborne, a tribute of affection from Queen Victoria.' A story has grown up that 'his' meant the Prince Consort's, but, whatever the origin of the primrose as a link between her and her favourite minister, she meant what common sense would suppose she meant. 'The sight of the primroses He loved so well and she is so fond of make her now very sad,' she wrote to Corry. 'They will ever recall Him to her mind, but nothing is *needed* to do that.'[1] In the context in which this was written no one except Disraeli could have been intended.

Although she would not go to the funeral the Queen was determined to visit the grave. It would be a compensation for that 'last look' which she so much regretted missing.[2] To modern minds the Victorians had an almost morbid preoccupation with death – and no one more so than the ruler who gave her name to the era. Yet perhaps the emotionalism, the tears, the locks of hair, the keepsakes, the plumed hearses, crape, black-edged paper and the rest provided a relief which our stiff upper lips and requests for no mourning and no flowers do not quite give. We laugh at Victorian inhibitions about sex. Are we not equally inhibited about death?

The Queen made a point of driving from Windsor by the same rather unusual route through Sir Philip Rose's grounds near Penn, east of Wycombe, which Disraeli had happened to take – for no particular reason except that he was lunching with Rose – on the last occasion when he had made the journey, December 10. The vault was reopened and she laid a china wreath of flowers on the

[1] ibid., Queen Victoria to Corry, April 21.
[2] ibid., April 23.

coffin. Afterwards she took tea in the library, even as she had when
she visited Disraeli in 1877 at the height of the eastern crisis.
Corry who was host gave her as a memento a little dagger which
Disraeli had brought back from Constantinople half a century
before.[1]

The Queen wished to commemorate her affection for her minister
in permanent form. She had a marble monument erected in Hughenden Church above the seat in the chancel which Disraeli used to
occupy. The inscription on it ends with a quotation from Proverbs,
'Kings love him that speaketh right'.

A notable absentee from the funeral had been the Prime Minister.
His plea of business was not regarded as convincing, and there was
much private criticism. The truth was that Disraeli's death had
thrown him into a state of no little mental perturbation. He could
not believe that Disraeli's preference for a private funeral was
sincere. He thought it was conscious affectation, a last theatrical
gesture. Gladstone's private comment was, for him, singularly lacking in magnanimity. 'As he lived so he died – all display without
reality or genuineness.'[2] It must have cost him an effort to write a
suitable letter to Queen Victoria, although he did manage to do so.
But the big hurdle remained. He would have to say something in
the House of Commons when moving a resolution to set up a
national memorial to his old rival in Westminster Abbey.[3] Gladstone had a passion for sincerity and he really believed that
Disraeli's influence in public life had been almost wholly bad. What
was more he knew that a great many people knew that this was his
belief. Worry brought on a sharp attack of diarrhoea. But in the
end all was well. Gladstone prayed for guidance, and his speech
which silenced the critics was a model of its kind. He did not
comment on Disraeli's policies, but he pointed out that constitutionally Disraeli had just as much authority to do what he did as
the present government had. He did not say that his death was a
loss to the nation. But he did single out many of the qualities which
Disraeli's admirers would have chosen, too: '. . . long sighted
consistency of purpose . . . his remarkable power of self-government; and last but not least, his great parliamentary courage – a
quality in which I, who have been associated in my life with some

---

[1] *The Letters of Queen Victoria*, 2nd Series, iii, 217–18, Queen's Journal, April 30.
[2] Magnus, *Gladstone*, 281.
[3] Only five Prime Ministers had been thus honoured: Chatham, William Pitt,
Canning, Peel, and Palmerston.

scores of Ministers, have, I think, never known but two whom I could pronounce his equal.'

Under Disraeli's will his landed property and personalty were entailed for life upon his nephew Coningsby at the age of twenty-five with the usual provisions in default of male heirs. The will directed that whoever inherited should take the name of Disraeli. The executors were Sir Philip Rose and Sir Nathaniel de Rothschild (later the first Lord Rothschild). His literary executor was Corry who had absolute discretion over the preservation, publication or destruction of the papers. There were no legacies and no provision for any other members of the family.

Disraeli's finances were in a better state than most people expected. It is true that Andrew Montagu's mortgage on Hughenden, a sum of £57,000, was still outstanding. But since the intervention of this kindly, if eccentric, benefactor in 1862, Disraeli had inherited over £30,000 from Mrs Brydges Willyams and £5,000 from his brother James. Moreover he had made very nearly £20,000 from *Lothair, Endymion* and the collected edition of his novels. Most of this sum was invested in Consols – £40,000 at his death, and he had used some of the remainder to enlarge the Hughenden estate. There was a successful – though to Queen Victoria highly distressing – sale of his effects at Sotheby's in July, which brought in over £3,000 on the first day. In the end his will was proved at £84,000. By the time Coningsby came into the estate in 1892, the mortgage had been paid off and the property was in good condition, clear of all encumbrances. It was rumoured in the Press at the end of 1881 that the generosity of the Rothschild family had contributed to the paying off of the mortgage. There is nothing to confirm this, but it is true that, if Sir Nathaniel de Rothschild had wished to be a secret benefactor, he was in an excellent position to do so.

There was some discussion about the possibility of conferring an hereditary title on either Ralph or Coningsby in order to perpetuate the fame of the great man. Disraeli had on three occasions refused the Queen's offer to settle a barony on Coningsby by special remainder, presumably on the ground that the Hughenden estate was not large enough to 'keep up' a peerage. The suggestion now was a baronetcy, which did not require such extensive property as a peerage. Ralph would have liked it, and the Queen was agreeable. Gladstone did not oppose but pointed out that there was no precedent for thus honouring collateral heirs and wondered whether

Coningsby 'with a much smaller income (as Mr. Gladstone sup-
poses) than that which country gentlemen commonly enjoy' would
really want such a title when he came of age.[1] Corry was consulted
and advised delay till the will was proved.[2] In the end no title was
conferred.

Perhaps it was just as well. The baronetcy would have been
extinct long ago by now. Coningsby was the last in the male line of
the Disraeli family and he was not very distinguished. He sat as
Member for Altrincham from 1892 until 1906 when along with many
Tory MPs he was engulfed in the landslide. He did not return to
politics and lived on quietly at Hughenden till his death in 1937.
He had no children, and the estate was soon afterwards sold. In
1949 it was acquired by the National Trust.

Strangely enough the family of Disraeli's illustrious rival has
lasted longer than his own. The descendants of the man whom
Disraeli regarded as the great threat to the landed class are still
securely in possession of Hawarden Castle, while Hughenden belongs to an institution. Disraeli relished the ironies of events, but he
would not have appreciated this one.

In all but the strictly legal sense of the word, Corry was Disraeli's
true heir. Queen Victoria rightly said that he had devoted himself
to his chief 'as few sons ever do' and it was to Corry that Disraeli
entrusted all the really delicate tasks arising from his death. The
Queen too relied on his advice for many years to come, asked him
constantly to Windsor or Osborne, and valued him as a go-between
in important political negotiations, hearing perhaps in his words an
echo of her old friend's from beyond the grave: indeed Corry's letters
to her are at times couched in language almost as hyperbolic as that
of his master.

His role did not go unnoticed. He strongly supported Lord Salisbury against Lord Randolph Churchill and was sufficiently conspicuous in the manoeuvres following the latter's resignation to be
described in an anonymous letter to the *Pall Mall Gazette*, said to be
written by 'a Privy Councillor', as 'a political busybody in the guise
of an irresponsible court favourite'. But Corry could console himself
with the reflection that Disraeli would certainly have backed Salisbury against Lord Randolph in a crisis like this. Salisbury thought
highly enough of Corry to consider him seriously for the Berlin

[1] Corry Papers, Gladstone to Queen Victoria, May 18 (copy).
[2] ibid., Corry to the Queen, May 20 (draft).

embassy in 1895, although in the end he chose a professional diplomat. Philanthropist, man of fashion, repository of political secrets, raconteur of innumerable Disraeliana, friend of *both* the Queen and the Prince of Wales – in itself no mean feat – Lord Rowton was a favourite and conspicuous figure of the late Victorian social scene. He toyed for years with the idea of writing the life of his chief but he lacked the power of concentration. His career after Disraeli's death, like the vapour trail left by an aeroplane in a blue sky, gradually grew diffuse and melted into the surrounding air. He died in 1903, still unmarried, and the barony of Rowton, like the earldom of Beaconsfield, became extinct.

Epilogue

Disraeli is not likely to be forgotten. No one would deny him a place in history. Yet there is still no agreement as to where that place should be. Was he an insincere charlatan, a dreamer, an opportunistic adventurer, a sphinx without a riddle – like Louis Napoleon? Or was he a patient far-sighted political genius who purged his party of the aridities of Peelism and in the end brought it to grips with the new world of empire and democracy? Was his rise due to luck or was it the result of extraordinary talents? What if anything did he really believe? What would have been different if he had never lived?

It would be presumptuous to give a dogmatic or even a confident answer to these questions, but some possible replies emerge. Up to a point, Disraeli *was* an adventurer. It is very hard to discern any consistent purpose in his political activities from 1832 to 1846, indeed beyond save an unrelenting, though by no means unerring determination to get to the top. It is impossible to believe that he would have attacked Peel as he did, if he had been given the minor office which he wrongly expected in 1841. People knew this and it was the reason why his onslaughts were so bitterly resented, although his language was not more violent or more wounding than Bentinck's. Distrust of his sincerity was increased when he tried to back-pedal on protection. He was of course right. Protection was indeed dead and damned. But MPs could not easily stomach such words from Disraeli. There was an ornate effrontery about him, which provoked intense dislike among his opponents and much mistrust among his supporters. He might perhaps have blurred this impression had he been willing to make some concessions to the spirit of humbug. But as in the case of the Bulgarian atrocities his hatred of cant made him refuse the least move in that direction; and so, he often seemed more cynical, more heartless, more on the make than he really was. His reputation was not helped by the rumours current about his youthful escapades: debts and duns, *Vivian Grey*, Henry Stanley, Lady Sykes, Lord Lyndhurst, the circumstances of his marriage – a side of his career largely suppressed by his official

757

biographers. The rumours were often exaggerated and sometimes false, but the reality was none too savoury.

The particular combination of his qualities and defects goes some way to explain why he spent so little of his long career in office; only eleven out of thirty-five years after 1846, and of those eleven five were in short-lived minority governments without real power. The sole parliamentarian of genius, and for many years the only one of even ordinary talent on his side of the House, he was yet the object of deep distrust among the elements which he and Derby had to win over if they were ever to hold office except by virtue of their opponents' temporary divisions. Thus for long years he remained an indispensable liability to his party; in Gladstone's phrase 'at once Lord Derby's necessity and his curse'. The party could not throw him over without displaying to all the world its intellectual bankruptcy, but at the same time his presence aroused an inextinguishable repugnance among those moderate, serious, high-minded, middle-of-the-road men who needed to be convinced of the respectability of the Conservatism that had rejected Peel. Disraeli, as he himself said, was never 'respectable'.

For here was the first important point where Disraeli's personality and behaviour affected events. The logic of the Conservative position after 1832 dictated the policy of accommodation with the business and commercial interests followed by Peel. The landed classes were on too narrow a political basis to rule alone, though the moderation of the first Reform Act masked the reality of the situation and, by giving them a disproportionate share of parliamentary representation, encouraged them in the illusion that they could somehow convert their substantial minority into a majority, without making concessions. Disraeli, detesting Peel and devising a romantic but basically unrealistic Tory philosophy of his own, was responsible more than anyone else for the fall of Peel and the temporary repudiation of Peelism. He could not have done it single-handed, but without him it would probably not have been done at all. Yet when the dust settled, it became clear enough that, though Peel had fallen, the party was not going to get anywhere if it continued to repudiate Peelism. Disraeli saw this very early. He never abandoned or denied his own 'philosophy' but it had little effect on his actions – quite rightly, for no one in his senses would have tried to lead the Conservative party after 1846 by reference to the principles of Young England. Disraeli's actual policy was essentially Peelite, but his very presence as a leader made the sort of consensus achieved by Peel extraordinarily difficult. Memories were too bitter for him alone, or even for Derby with him as adjutant, to play that role. In the end it fell to Palmerston who, but for a sixteen-month interlude, ruled with no real challenge for a whole decade.

During those years Disraeli did very little. If he had died or retired in 1865 or 1866 his influence on his country and his party would have seemed to the historian to be as negative as that of Charles James Fox. But the death of Palmerston and the advent of Gladstone gave him an opportunity for a second time to imprint his personality upon his party and to shape the course of events. The occasion was not, as is often said, the Reform Act of 1867. This was largely Derby's responsibility and was essentially the outcome of tactical needs rather than a far-sighted implementation of Tory democracy. Some Bill, not greatly dissimilar, would have been carried anyway at about that time, and Disraeli's own part is mainly significant for the parliamentary brilliance which, though it raised the cry of 'betrayal' from a few, consolidated his hold on the great mass of the party and ensured his succession to Derby. Disraeli's real opportunity came later with the waning of Gladstone's star from about 1872 onwards.

For Gladstone's great reforming ministry frightened the forces of property, landed or otherwise, even as the Whig–Radical alliance had frightened them in the 1830s. Disraeli exploited this situation with cautious adroitness, mending the party machine, waiting shrewdly upon events, and above all attacking Gladstonianism for its radical implications. The old feuds in the party were forgotten, though not by everyone, and Disraeli became, even as Peel had been, the leader around whom moderate opinion began to crystalize. The analogy should not be pressed too far. There was something about Disraeli, which those who constitute that mysterious but nevertheless recognizable entity, 'the establishment', could never quite countenance, whereas they were usually happy with Peel. Perhaps they sensed Disraeli's deep inner scepticism about their own values. Probably they were disconcerted by his foreign manner and his rococo language. Certainly they distrusted his levity and doubted his sincerity. But there can be no doubt that to the majority of 'society', of the upper, and of the middle class, he seemed a pillar of commonsensical, if slightly cynical, moderation, a much-needed contrast to the strenuous, relentless, moralistic rhetoric of his great rival.

No doubt any Conservative leader, for example the 15th Earl of Derby or Sir Stafford Northcote, would have profited from this reaction, but Disraeli added certain features peculiarly his own to the pattern with which he was to stamp the Conservative party, and these enhanced the contrast with Gladstonian liberalism: belief in empire; adoption of a tough, 'no nonsense', foreign policy; assertion of Britain's or, as he would have said, England's, greatness in the world. Disraeli was unsympathetic to all forms of nationalism except English nationalism – this was quite compatible with being most unEnglish himself – and he saw no reason, whether in Ireland or the Balkans or elsewhere, to allow what he considered English interests to be overridden by the supposedly higher moral law that encourages the emancipation of nations 'rightly struggling to be free'. Most Conservatives have followed him along this course ever since. It has been both the strength and weakness of the party.

It was in some ways a new departure. Under Derby the party had not been empire-minded or in favour of gun-boat diplomacy. Disraeli himself had once called the colonies 'millstones round our necks'. In their spasmodic efforts to oppose Palmerston the Conservative front bench had on occasion assumed almost a Little Englander tone. The early prophets of Imperialism were largely Liberals. Disraeli changed all that, partly because Gladstone for a host of reasons which included Christian ethics and a passion for Treasury economy, was hostile to any sort of forward policy, foreign or imperial, partly because he saw that jingoism might be a vote winner, mainly because his own temperamental instincts pointed that way. His attitude decisively orientated the Conservative party for many years to come, and the tradition which he started was probably a bigger electoral asset in winning working-class support during the last quarter of the century than anything else, though he himself did not live to see its fruits. If Disraeli and Gladstone had not been the men they were this particular line of cleavage might not have developed as it did. But in the event they polarized political opinion, and something of their respective attitudes has continued to colour the outlook of the Right and the Left in Britain from that day to this.

Their conflict was not accompanied by any trace of that mutual respect which is usually to be found among rival leaders. 'Lord

Beaconsfield and Mr. Gladstone are men of extraordinary ability; they dislike each other more than is usual among public men,' wrote Granville to Queen Victoria.[1] In the Edwardian era when the issues dividing the parties were far graver, it was quite possible for the leaders to meet socially at country houses and elsewhere, but only the most reckless hostess would have dared to ask Disraeli and Gladstone to the same dinner table, let alone the same house party. This personal hatred – it is not too strong a word – was even more bitter among their adherents. In the autumn of 1878 Henry Loch, Governor of the Isle of Man, wrote to Lord Lytton:

> I have never known such strong feeling to exist on any question as on this [Afghanistan] and the Turkish question – friends of years standing become bitter foes – members of the same family don't speak one to the other – and when the questions are discussed, which they are morning noon and night by all classes and by both sexes there is an intensity of excitement that frequently breaks out into the most violent language – and it is all *purely personal*, the divergence of opinion not being so much upon the merits of the questions which seem seldom understood, but upon the feelings that are entertained either towards Lord Beaconsfield or Mr. Gladstone . . .[2]

These passions have been carried far beyond the grave and it is only fairly recently that people have at last been able to praise one of the great rivals without feeling obliged to damn the other. The truth surely is that both were extraordinary figures, men of genius, though in widely differing idioms, and that, like most men of genius operating in a parliamentary democracy, they inspired a great deal of dislike and no small degree of distrust among the bustling mediocrities who form the majority of mankind. Not only among mediocrities. Nearly thirty years after Disraeli's death Lord Cromer could take the opportunity of reviewing Monypenny's first volume in order to present his own picture of Disraeli as a meretricious Oriental charlatan devoid of principle or purpose, and there are those who think of him in this light today; they have their counterparts among those who still regard Gladstone as a humourless humbug, a sanctimonious hypocrite claiming the authority of the Almighty when producing the ace of trumps from his sleeve.

The charge of insincerity and lack of principle has often been

---

[1] *The Letters of Queen Victoria*, 2nd Series, iii, 86, April 24, 1880.
[2] India Office Library, Letters from England, 1878, vi, November 21.

made against Disraeli. Yet there is little justification for it. He was perhaps unlucky or unwise in adumbrating any Tory 'philosophy' at all, however imprecisely, however much in the language of an artist rather than a thinker. For it gave his enemies the opportunity of pointing out that he did very little to carry it into practice when in power, while his supporters have too often tried to justify their hero by twisting his later policies into some sort of fulfilment of the 'Tory idea' of the 1840s, and interpreting his attitude towards the monarchy, the extension of the franchise, and social reform as a realization of the ideals of *Coningsby* and *Sybil*. It suited someone like Lord Randolph Churchill, himself in rebellion against the Tory establishment as represented by Northcote, to see Disraeli's whole career in terms of the ideas which he had held when he, too, was in rebellion against the establishment then represented by Peel. The myth began with the Fourth Party and has its adherents even now.

But Disraeli, however vividly he painted the contrast between the two nations, was not a sort of baroque version of Lord Shaftesbury; nor, however much he praised the virtues of popular monarchy, was he an exponent of royal absolutism. He was a practical politician – in spite of his own definition of that figure as one who practices the errors of his predecessors. The truth is that Disraeli had principles when he led the party and believed in them sincerely, but they were not the 'principles', if that word can be used at all, of Young England. It is easy to underestimate Disraeli's innate conservatism. He believed passionately in the greatness of England – not in itself a Tory monopoly. But he also believed no less deeply that England's greatness depended upon the ascendancy of the landed class. All the rest was 'leather and prunella'. This does not mean that he wished to set class against class. On the contrary he proclaimed the doctrine of one nation and asserted that if the Conservative party was not a national party it was nothing. But he did sincerely think that the nation would decline with the decline of the landed interest. Like Gladstone he was 'an out-and-out inequalitarian'. He believed in a hierarchical ladder which certainly should not be inaccessible to men of talent – after all he was himself a marvellous example of successful climbing – but which should on no account be laid flat or broken or removed. He thought that under such a dispensation people of all classes would enjoy greater freedom and happiness than they would get under the dead hand of a centralizing Benthamite bureaucracy, however 'democratic'. Most of his specific attitudes can be traced to this sort of conservatism: support of Crown, Church, Lords; dislike of Irish separatism with its threat to the land; anxiety to preserve the rule of the JPs in the counties; acceptance of cautious social reform in those geographical or metaphorical areas where the landed interest was least affected. Economic factors were soon to bring about the decline of the land more effectively than any political measures, and were indeed already doing so in his lifetime; but he did not live to see the full consequences.

Disraeli believed in the aristocratic principle, and thought of himself as an aristocrat, but to most of his contemporaries he must have seemed an odd character to identify himself with that class. When he reached the top in 1868 he was not the first middle-class man to have done so, but if there can be degrees of 'middle-classness', he was the most middle class. This was what Queen Victoria meant when she referred to him as 'a man risen from the people'. Addington was the first middle-class Prime Minister, Peel the second. But Addington's father, who was a successful doctor with the assets of a large income, a landed estate, and Lord Chatham as patient and friend, sent his son to Winchester and Brasenose. Peel inherited great wealth, had a father who was a baronet and MP, and enjoyed an education at Harrow and Christ Church. Disraeli possessed none of these advantages. We may agree with the Duke of Argyll that the impediments in his way have often been exaggerated and that some of them were self-imposed. It is true that he had from the first a foot on the ladder that could lead to the top in nineteenth-century England, even if it was only a toe-hold on a low rung. The fact remains that he had farther to go than any other Prime Minister of his century. The fact remains, too, that in spite of all the democratization of the past hundred years there have been only two occupants of Number Ten Downing Street since Disraeli, who neither inherited substantial wealth nor went to a famous public school, nor attended an ancient university—and those were Lloyd George and Ramsay MacDonald, in their way almost as 'foreign' as Disraeli himself.

This is not the place to discuss the merits of Disraeli's belief in aristocracy – a belief which was by no means peculiar to him. The point is that his life cannot be understood unless it is given full weight. To think of him as a prisoner of the Tory party, a would-be Radical struggling to be free, is quite wrong. It is easy to misinterpret the famous three-hour interview which H. M. Hyndman had with him a few weeks before his death and his often-quoted words, 'It is a very difficult country to move, Mr. Hyndman, a very difficult country indeed, and one in which there is more disappointment to be looked for than success'. But it does not follow that Disraeli wanted to move it. He was merely warning his enthusiastic visitor that democratic empire federation and the socialization of property were not policies which he could expect to carry through the medium of the Conservative party, as Hyndman appears to have hoped.

Disraeli had learned long ago that the art of politics is the art of the possible, though he had not, perhaps, learned that lesson when he first adumbrated the 'Tory idea'. After he became leader he had to make as many concessions and compromises and reversals as ever Peel had had to make, but he was a more skilful politician than Peel. This is why he has had a better Press from the politicians of both sides than from the administrators or the academic historians. He lacked the administrative and legislative ability which the former appreciate, and rightly find in Peel, Gladstone or Balfour. At the same time he lacked the logic, the precision, the clarity which academics naturally look for and respect. Of course he had brilliant and prescient ideas, and he could sum up a situation in lapidary sentences, but these flashes were often mingled with mere nonsense and rhodomontade. His mind was like a catherine wheel shooting out sparks. Most of them fell on damp earth. Every now and then one would reach the dry grass, set it ablaze and illuminate the night.

Where Disraeli excelled was in the art of presentation. He was an impresario and an actor manager. He was a superb parliamentarian, one of the half dozen greatest in our history. He knew how much depends upon impression, style, colour; and how small a part is played in politics by logic, cool reason, calm appraisal of alternatives. This is why politicians appreciate him. They realize that a large part of political life in a parliamentary democracy consists not so much in doing things yourself as in imparting the right tone to things that others do for you or to things that are going to happen anyway. They know how much of the art of politics lies in concealing behind a façade of rigid adherence to immutable principle those deviations or reversals which events and responsibility so often force upon governments. Form can at times be more important than content. Nothing better illustrates Disraeli's genius as a politician than the way he presented the Reform Bill of 1867. The contrast with Peel's handling of the Corn Law crisis is one of the most remarkable and instructive in British politics. Many people in the history of the Conservative party have worked harder and done more than Disraeli ever did: yet none has left a deeper impression upon it.

Disraeli was in many ways a very 'unVictorian' figure. Of course there existed in that era as in most periods a dissident minority of those who did not accept the orthodoxy of the day, but it was rare to find a party leader among them. Disraeli was a sceptic and a romantic. Optimistic and cheerful about his own career which he saw as a colourful adventure story, he was less optimistic about the extent to which human endeavour could improve the lot of humanity. His views were the opposite to those of Macaulay. The spirit of strenuous moral effort, belief in progress, faith in the efficacy of representative institutions, confidence in material prosperity struck no echo in his mind. 'Progress to what and from where? . . . the European talks of progress, because by an ingenious application of some scientific acquirements he has established a society which has mistaken comfort for civilisation.'

This scepticism makes Disraeli a less 'dated' figure than almost any contemporary politician. Morally and intellectually Gladstone was his superior. In courage, great though Disraeli's was, Gladstone was certainly not his inferior. But he was, far more than Disraeli, a man of his times. It is hard to imagine him living in any other period, whereas it is quite easy to envisage Disraeli living either today or in the era of Lord North. It is this timelessness that gives his best novels their lasting fascination, and makes his wit as good now as it was a hundred years ago. There is a champagne-like sparkle about him which has scarcely ever been equalled and never surpassed among statesmen. No Prime Minister has received and deserved more space in the dictionaries of quotations. He also had a rare detachment, an extraordinary ability to survey the scene from outside and to wonder what it was all about.

But his very detachment, his indifference to the conventions of the age had its drawbacks. Disraeli did some dubious things in his career but not more than many other people. He was an opportunist, but politicians have to be, unless they are willing to become antediluvian survivals incapable of affecting events. He differed from the rest, largely because he was more candid – some would say more brazen – in avowing his own motives. 'The people have their passions

and it is even the duty of public men occasionally to adopt sentiments with which they do not agree, because the people must have
leaders.' Thus he spoke in 1834 standing for High Wycombe as an
Independent secretly backed by the Tory party fund to the tune of
£500. Few men have given more handles to their enemies from
Vivian Grey onwards.

Moreover, Englishmen instinctively distrust wits and cynics, and
are uneasy if they encounter irony or fancy – anyway in politics. If
Disraeli had simply been a romantic worshipper of England's traditions, institutions and grandeur, he would have had an easier
passage. One side of him was indeed that, but another was a
slightly mocking observer surveying with sceptical amusement the
very stage upon which he himself played a principal part. When
Archbishop Tait finished *Endymion* 'with a painful feeling that the
writer considers all political life as mere play and gambling' he hit
on a half-truth which was widely held. Disraeli's inner pessimism
about the ultimate ends of politics did often lead him to use just
that sort of language. To him, more than to most, politics avowedly
was 'the great game'. But the British – and this was particularly
true of the Victorian era – prefer public men to be serious figures
assuming their load of responsibility with conscientious reluctance
and sedate demeanour. As Disraeli himself wrote, 'The British
People being subject to fogs and possessing a powerful Middle Class
require grave statesmen'. Perhaps this was why he was so often in
opposition and so seldom in power. Disraeli never was a grave
statesman.

Appendices

Disraeli's letter to Mary Anne

'Park Street. Thursday night, Feb. 7, 1839.'[1]

I wd have endeavoured to have spoken to you of that which it was necessary you shd know, & I wished to have spoken with the calmness which was natural to one humiliated & distressed. I succeeded so far as *to be considered a 'selfish bully' &*[2] to be desired to quit your house for ever. I have recourse therefore to this miserable method of communicating with you; none can be more imperfect but I write as if it were the night before my execution.

Every hour of my life I hear of an approaching union from all lips except your own. At last a friend anxious to distinguish me by some unusual mark of his favor & thinking to confer on me a distinction of which I shd be proud, offers me one of his seats for our happy month. The affair was then approaching absurdity. There was a period, & a much earlier one, when similar allusions to the future & intimations of what must occur were frequent from your lips; as if you thought some daily hint of the impending result was necessary to stimulate or to secure my affection.

As a woman of the world, which you are thoroughly, you ought not, you cannot be, unacquainted with the difference that subsists between our relative positions. The continuance of the present state of affairs cd only render you disreputable; me it wd render infamous. There is only one construction which Society, & justly, puts upon a connection between a woman who is supposed to be rich & a man whom she avowedly loves & does not marry. In England especially there is no stigma more damning; it is one which no subsequent conduct or position ever permits to be forgotten. It has crushed men who have committed with impunity even crimes; some things may indeed be more injurious; none more ignominious.

This reputation impends over me. I will at least preserve that honor which is the breath of my existence. At present I am in the position of an insolvent whose credit is not suspected; but ere a few weeks I must inevitably chuse between being ridiculous or being contemptible; I must be recognised as being jilted, or I must at once sink into what your friend Lady Morgan has already styled me 'Mrs. Wyndham Lewis's De Novo.'

[1] See above, p. 156–7.
[2] The passages in italics are those that have not been hitherto published.

This leads me to the most delicat of subjects, but in justice to us both I will write with the utmost candor. I avow, when I first made my advances to you I was influenced by no romantic feelings. My father had long wished me to marry; my settling in life was the implied tho' not stipulated, condition of a disposition of his property, which wd have been convenient to me. I myself, about to commence a practical career, wished for the solace of a home, & shrunk from all the torturing passions of intrigue. I was not blind to worldly advantages in such an alliance, but I had already proved that my heart was not to be purchased. I found you in sorrow, & that heart was touched. I found you, as I thought, aimiable, tender, & yet acute & gifted with no ordinary mind – one whom I cd look upon with pride as the partner of my life, who cd sympathise with all my projects & feelings, console me in the moments of depression, share my hour of triumph, & work with me for our honor & happiness.

Now for your fortune: I write the sheer truth. That fortune proved to be much less than I, or the world, imagined. It was in fact, as far as I was concerned, a fortune which cd not benefit me in the slightest degree; it was merely a jointure not greater than your station required; enough to maintain your establishment & gratify your private tastes. To eat & to sleep in that house & nominally to call it mine – these cd be only objects for a penniless adventurer. Was this an inducement for me to sacrifice my sweet liberty, & that indefinite future wh: is one of the charms of existence? No; when months ago I told you there was only one link between us, I felt that my heart was inextricably engaged to you, & but for that I wd have terminated our acquaintance. From that moment I devoted to you all the passion of my being. Alas! It has been poured upon the sand.

As time progressed I perceived in your character & in mine own certain qualities, wh: convinced me that if I wished to persevere that profound & unpolluted affection wh: subsisted between us money must never be introduced. Had we married, not one shilling of your income shd ever have been seen by me; neither indirectly nor directly, wd I have interfered in the management of your affairs. If Society justly stigmatizes with infamy the hired lover, I shrink with equal disgust from being the paid husband.

You have branded me as selfish – Alas! I fear you have apparent cause. I confess it with the most heart rending humiliation. Little did I think when I wept, when in a manner so unexpected & so irresistible you poured upon my bosom the treasured savings of your affection, that I received the wages of my degradation! Weak, wretched fool! This led to my accepting your assistance in my trial; but that was stipulated to be a loan & I only waited for the bill which my agent gave me when you were at Bradenham as the balance of our accounts & which becomes due this very month, to repay it into yr bankers.

By heavens as far as worldly interests are concerned, your aliance cd not benefit me. All that society can offer is at my command; it is not the apparent possession of a jointure that ever elevates position. I can live, as I live, without disgrace, until the inevitable progress of events gives me that independence which is all I require. I have entered into these ungracious details because you reproached me with my interested views. No; I wd not condescend to be the minion of a princess; and not all the gold of Ophir shd ever lead me to the altar. Far different are the qualities which I require in the sweet participator of my existence. My nature demands that my life shall be perpetual love.

Upon your general conduct to me I make no comment. It is now useless. I will not upbraid you. I will only blame myself. *All warned me: public and private – all were eager to save me from the perdition into which I have fallen. Coxcomb to suppose that you wd conduct yourself to me in a manner different to that in which you have behaved to fifty others!*

And yet I thought I had touched your heart! Wretched Idiot!

As a woman of the world you must have foreseen this. And for the gratification of your vanity, for the amusement of ten months, for the diversion of your seclusion, could you find the heart to do this? Was there no ignoble prey at hand that you must degrade a bird of heaven? Why not have let your Captain Neil have been the minion of your gamesome hours with^t humiliating & debasing me. Nature never intended me for a toy & dupe. But you have struck deep. You have done that which my enemies have yet failed to do: you have broken my spirit. From the highest to the humblest scene of my life, from the brilliant world of fame to my own domestic hearth, you have poisoned all. I have no place of refuge: home is odious, the world oppressive.

Triumph – I seek not to conceal my state. It is not sorrow, it is not wretchedness; it is anguish, it is the ENDURANCE of that pang which is the passing characteristic of agony. All that can prostrate a man has fallen on my victim head. My heart outraged, my pride wounded, my honor nearly tainted. I know well that ere a few days can pass I shall be the scoff & jest of that world, to gain whose admiration has been the effort of my life. I have only one source of solace – the consciousness of self-respect. Will that uphold me? A terrible problem that must quickly be solved.

Farewell. I will not affect to wish you happiness for it is not in your nature to obtain it. For a few years you may flutter in some frivolous circle. But the time will come when you will sigh for any heart that could be fond and despair of one that can be faithful. Then will be the penal hour of retribution; then you will recall to your memory the passionate heart that you have forfeited, and the genius you have betrayed.

D.

Writings of Benjamin Disraeli

(*Compiled by R. W. Stewart*)

1 COLLECTED EDITIONS

1. UNIFORM EDITION OF THE NOVELS, published by David Bryce, 1853. It was for this edition that Disraeli made drastic revisions of the texts, particularly of *Vivian Grey* and *The Young Duke*. The revised texts were used in Longmans' collected editions.

2. COLLECTED EDITION OF THE NOVELS AND TALES, 10 volumes, Longmans, 1870–1. Revised texts. [The first volume of this collection was the first one-volume edition (the eighth) of *Lothair*.]

3. HUGHENDEN EDITION OF THE NOVELS AND TALES, 11 volumes, Longmans, 1881.

4. YOUNG ENGLAND, edited by Bernard N. Langdon-Davies, illustrated by Byam Shaw, 4 volumes, Brimley Johnson, 1904. This edition includes *Vivian Grey*, of which the original text is printed, *Coningsby, Sybil* and *Tancred*.

5. VIVIAN GREY (2 volumes) and THE YOUNG DUKE, edited by Lucien Wolf, Moring, 1904–5. The original texts are printed. These two works appear to have been intended as part of a new edition of all the novels.

6. THE WORKS OF BENJAMIN DISRAELI, EARL OF BEACONSFIELD, EMBRACING NOVELS, ROMANCES, PLAYS, POEMS, BIOGRAPHY, SHORT STORIES AND GREAT SPEECHES, with a critical introduction by Edmund Gosse . . . and a biographical preface by Robert Arnot . . . London and New York, printed for subscribers only by M. W. Dunne, 20 volumes, 1904–5.

7. UNIFORM EDITION OF THE NOVELS, edited by the Earl of Iddesleigh, 9 volumes, John Lane, The Bodley Head, 1905–6.

8. THE BRADENHAM EDITION OF THE NOVELS AND TALES . . . with introductions by Philip Guedalla, 12 volumes, Peter Davies, 1926–7.

9. THE NOVELS, 11 volumes, John Lane, The Bodley Head, 1927–8.

2 BOOKS AND PAMPHLETS

1. *An Inquiry into the Plans, Progress, and Policy of the American Mining Companies*, 1825.
2. *Lawyers and Legislators: or, Notes, on the American Mining Companies*, Murray, 1825.
3. *The present state of Mexico: as detailed in a report to the General Congress by the Secretary of State for the Home Department and Foreign Affairs, at the opening of the session in 1825.* With notes and a memoir of Don Lucas Alaman, Murray, 1825. [The three 'mining pamphlets' were published anonymously.]
4. *Vivian Grey*, 2 volumes, Colburn, 1826. Published anonymously. *Vivian Grey*, volumes iii to v, Colburn, 1827.
5. *The Voyage of Captain Popanilla*, by the author of *Vivian Grey*, Colburn, 1828; Philadelphia, 1828.
6. *The Young Duke*, by the author of *Vivian Grey*, 3 volumes, Colburn and Bentley, 1831; New York, 1832.
7. *England and France, or a Cure for the Ministerial Gallomania*, Murray, 1832. Published anonymously.
8. *Contarini Fleming, a psychological Auto-biography*, 4 volumes, Murray, 1832; New York, 1832.
9. *The Wondrous Tale of Alroy* [and] *The Rise of Iskander*, by the author of Vivian Grey, *Contarini Fleming* etc., 3 volumes, Saunders and Otley, 1833.
10. *What Is He?*, by the author of *Vivian Grey*, Ridgway, 1833. Reprinted in *Whigs and Whiggism*.
11. *Velvet Lawn, a sketch written for the benefit of the Buckinghamshire Infirmary*, by the author of *Vivian Grey*, Wycombe, E. King, 1833.
12. *The Revolutionary Epick*, the work of Disraeli the Younger, author of *The Psychological Romance*, 2 volumes, Moxon, 1834. [A revised edition] Longmans, 1864.
13. *Vindication of the English Constitution in a letter to a noble and learned Lord*, by Disraeli the Younger, Saunders and Otley, 1835. Addressed to Lord Lyndhurst. Reprinted in *Whigs and Whiggism*.
14. *The Letters of Runnymede.* [The first edition, published at Exeter, was unauthorized.]
    The Letters of Runnymede, Macrone, 1836. [The volume includes 'The Spirit of Whiggism'.] Published anonymously. Reprinted in *Whigs and Whiggism*.

15. *Henrietta Temple, a love story,* by the author of *Vivian Grey,* 3 volumes, Colburn, 1837. [Actually 1836.]

16. *Venetia,* by the author of *Vivian Grey* and *Henrietta Temple,* 3 volumes, Colburn, 1837; Philadelphia, 1837.

17. *The Tragedy of Count Alarcos,* by the author of *Vivian Grey,* Colburn, 1839.

18. *Coningsby, or, the new generation,* 3 volumes, Colburn, 1844. [Fifth edition, with a preface by the author, 1849.] New York, 1844.

19. *Sybil, or, The Two Nations,* 3 volumes, Colburn, 1845; Philadelphia, 1845.

20. *Tancred, or, The New Crusade,* 3 volumes, Colburn, 1847; Philadelphia, 1847.

21. *Lord George Bentinck, A Political Biography,* Colburn, 1852. [Actually 1851.] Eighth edition, revised, Longmans, 1872.

22. *Lothair,* 3 volumes, Longmans, 1870. [Fifth edition, revised by the author, 1870. Seventh edition, revised and with a preface by the author, 1870.] New York, 1870.

23. *Endymion,* by the author of *Lothair,* 3 volumes, Longmans, 1880; New York, 1880.

3 ARTICLES IN NEWSPAPERS AND PERIODICALS

1. *'The Court of Egypt, a Sketch', by MESR, in *New Monthly Magazine,* June 1832.

2. *'The Speaking Harlequin', ibid., August 1832.

3. *'The Bosphorus, a Sketch', by MARCO POLO JUNIOR, ibid., September 1832.

4. *'Egyptian Thebes', by MARCO POLO JUNIOR, ibid., October 1832.

5. Letter [on a speech at Wycombe], in *The Times,* 13 November 1832.

6. *'Ixion in Heaven', in *New Monthly Magazine,* December 1832 and February 1833.

7. *'Ibrahim Pacha, The Conqueror of Syria', by MARCO POLO JUNIOR, ibid., February 1833.

8. *'Walstein, or a Cure for Melancholy', by the author of *Vivian Grey, Contarini Fleming* etc., in *Court Magazine,* July 1833.

9. *'An Interview with a Great Turk, From the Notebook of a recent Traveller', by the author of *Vivian Grey,* ibid., January 1834.

10. *'The Infernal Marriage', by Disraeli the Younger, in *New Monthly Magazine*, July to October 1834.

11. *'The Carrier-Pigeon', by the author of *Vivian Grey*, in *Book of Beauty* for 1835.

12. Letters between Disraeli and Morgan O'Connell, and Disraeli's Letter to Daniel O'Connell, in *The Times*, 6 and 8 May 1835.

13. †Leading Articles. 14 articles in *The Morning Post*, 22 August to 7 September 1835. [Written at the request of Lord Lyndhurst in defence of the House of Lords. Reprinted in *Whigs and Whiggism* under the title, 'Peers and People'.]

14. *'The Consul's Daughter', by the author of *Vivian Grey*, in *Book of Beauty* for 1836.

15. Letters to the Editor of *The Times*, 28, 31 December 1835, 9, 14 January 1836, and A Letter 'To Joseph Hume, Esq., M.P.', in *The Times*, 12 January 1836 [regarding allegations in the *Globe* newspaper about Radical support of Disraeli in his early elections].

16. †'The Letters of Runnymede' (19 articles), in *The Times*, 18 January to 15 May 1836. [See also section 2.]

17. †Leading article on Lord Lyndhurst's Speech, in *The Times*, 19 August 1836.

18. 'To a Maiden Sleeping after her First Ball', by the author of *Vivian Grey*, in *Book of Beauty* for 1837. [Verse.]

19. 'Calantha', by the author of *Vivian Grey*, ibid.

20. 'A New Voyage of Sindbad the Sailor, Recently Discovered' (11 articles), in *The Times*, 15 December 1836 to 10 February 1837.

21. †'To the Lord Lieutenant of Ireland', by RUNNYMEDE, ibid., 13 February 1837.

22. †'A Character' [Spring Rice] by SKELTON JUN., ibid., 7 March, 1837. [Verse.]

23. †'Open Questions, a Political Eclogue', by SKELTON JUN., ibid., 9 March 1837. [Verse.]

24. †'An Heroic Epistle to Lord Viscount Mel——e', by SKELTON JUN., ibid., 20 March 1837. [Verse.]

25. †'To Lord Viscount Melbourne', by RUNNYMEDE, ibid., 17 April 1837.

26. Review of '*England Under Seven Administrations*', by A. FON-BLANQUE, ibid., 17 May 1837.

27. Review of '*Society in America*', by HARRIET MARTINEAU, ibid., 30 May 1837.

28. *'A Syrian Sketch', by the author of *Vivian Grey*, in *Book of Beauty* for 1838.

29. †'Old England by Coeur-de-Lion' (10 articles), in *The Times*, 3 to 15 January 1838.

30. 'On the Portrait of the Lady Mahon', in *Book of Beauty* for 1839. [Verse.]

31. 'On the Portrait of the Viscountess Powerscourt', ibid. [Verse.]

32. †'To Lord John Russell', by LAELIUS, in *The Times*, 6 May 1839.

33. †'To the Queen', by LAELIUS, ibid., 13 May 1839.

34. †'To Lord Melbourne', by LAELIUS, ibid., 28 May 1839.

35. 'To the Duke of Wellington' [a sonnet] by B. DISRAELI, ibid., 29 August 1839. [*The Oxford Book of Victorian Verse*, 104.]

36. *'The Valley of Thebes', in *Book of Beauty* for 1840.

37. *'Munich', in *Book of Beauty* for 1841.

38. †'The State of the Case: In a Letter to The Duke of Wellington', by ATTICUS, in *The Times*, 11 March 1841.

39. *'Eden and Lebanon', in *Book of Beauty* for 1842.

40. *'The Midland Ocean', ibid., 1843.

41. 'Fantasia', in *The Keepsake* for 1845.

42. *'Shoubra', ibid., 1846.

43. †'Coalition' [the first leading article in *The Press*], 7 May 1853.

* Reprinted in *Tales and Sketches*, edited by J. Logie Robertson.
† Reprinted in *Whigs and Whiggism*, edited by W. Hutcheon.

4 SPEECHES

1. THE CRISIS EXAMINED, BY DISRAELI THE YOUNGER. [A speech at Wycombe.] Saunders and Otley, 1834. Reprinted in *Whigs and Whiggism*.

2. 'CHURCH AND QUEEN', FIVE SPEECHES DELIVERED . . . 1860–1864, EDITED, WITH A PREFACE, BY A MEMBER OF THE UNIVERSITY OF OXFORD [Frederick Lygon, MP], Palmer, 1865.

3. PARLIAMENTARY REFORM, A SERIES OF SPEECHES ON THAT SUBJECT DELIVERED IN THE HOUSE OF COMMONS . . . (1848–

1866), REPRINTED (BY PERMISSION) FROM HANSARD'S DEBATES, edited by Montagu Corry . . . Longmans, 1867.

4. THE CHANCELLOR OF THE EXCHEQUER IN SCOTLAND, BEING TWO SPEECHES DELIVERED BY HIM IN THE CITY OF EDINBURGH ON 29TH AND 30TH OCTOBER, 1867, Edinburgh, Blackwood, 1867.

5. SPEECHES ON THE CONSERVATIVE POLICY OF THE LAST THIRTY YEARS . . . edited, with an introduction, by John F. Bulley, Hotten, 1870.

6. ADDRESSES ON EDUCATION, FINANCES, AND POLITICS . . . ON THE OCCASION OF HIS VISIT TO GLASGOW . . . Hawksley, 1873.

7. SELECTED SPEECHES . . . arranged and edited with introductory and explanatory notes, by T. E. Kebbel, 2 volumes, Longmans, 1882.

8. TORY DEMOCRAT: two famous Disraeli speeches edited by Sir Edward Boyle, foreword by . . . Walter Elliot, Conservative Political Centre, 1950. [This contains the Manchester and Crystal Palace speeches of 1872.]

5 LETTERS AND OTHER WRITINGS

1. *Home Letters written . . . in 1830 and 1831* [edited by Ralph Disraeli], Murray, 1885.

2. *Lord Beaconsfield's Correspondence with his Sister, 1832–1852* [edited by Ralph Disraeli], Murray, 1886.

3. *Lord Beaconsfield's Letters, 1830–1852*, Murray, 1887. [The two previous volumes together, with some·additions. Reprinted, with an introduction by Augustine Birrell, Cassell, 1928.]

4. *The Letters of Disraeli to Lady Bradford and Lady Chesterfield*, edited by the Marquis of Zetland, 2 volumes, Benn, 1929.

5. *Letters from Benjamin Disraeli to Frances Anne, Marchioness of Londonderry, 1837–1861*, edited with an introduction by the Marchioness of Londonderry, Macmillan, 1938.

6. *Whigs and Whiggism, Political Writings* . . . edited, with an introduction, by William Hutcheon, Murray, 1913. [The contents of this volume are indicated in sections 2, 3 and 4 above. Some other

articles, of doubtful authorship, are included, and their attribution to Disraeli discussed.]

7. *The Radical Tory,* Disraeli's political development illustrated from his original writings and speeches, selected, edited and introduced by H. W. J. Edwards, with a preface by G. M. Young, Cape, 1937.

8. *Tales and Sketches* . . . with a prefatory memoir by J. Logie Robertson, Paterson, 1891. [The contents of this volume are indicated in section 3. It also includes *A True story* (a magazine article published in 1820, sometimes attributed to Disraeli), *Popanilla,* and the *Memoir* prefixed to the writings of his father.]

9. *The Revolutionary Epick and Other Poems* . . . edited by W. Davenport Adams, Hurst and Blackett, 1904. [This volume includes *Count Alarcos, The Dunciad of Today* (see below, 11), and a number of poems from the novels.]

10. *Falconet,* an unfinished novel. Published in *The Times,* 20, 21 and 23 January 1905. Reprinted in Monypenny and Buckle's *Life,* and with *Endymion* in Guedalla's edition of the novels.

11. *The Dunciad of Today, a Satire, and the Modern Aesop,* with an introduction by Michael Sadleir, Ingpen and Grant, 1928. [Two pieces from the *Star Chamber,* attributed by Sadleir to Disraeli.]

12. *Rumpel Stilts Kin,* by B. D. and W. G. M. [William George Meredith], The Roxburghe Club, 1952. [With an introduction by Michael Sadleir.]

13. *The Life of Paul Jones, from Original Documents in the Possession of John Henry Sherburne, Esq., Register of the Navy of the United States,* Murray, 1825. [An abridged version of the work originally published in the United States. Edited, with a preface by Disraeli.]

14. *Curiosities of Literature,* by Isaac Disraeli, with a view of the life and writings of the author, by his son. Fourteenth edition, 3 volumes, Moxon, 1849. [The memoir of his father, dated Hughenden Manor, Christmas 1848.]

15. *Ixion in Heaven,* decorated by John Austen, Cape, 1925. [See section 3.]

16. *The Infernal Marriage,* decorations by John Austen, Jackson, 1929. [See section 3.]

17. *Coningsby,* with an introduction by Walter Allen, *Chiltern Library,* John Lehmann Ltd, 1948.

18. *Sybil,* with an introduction by Walter Sichel, *World's Classics,* Oxford, 1926.

Select Bibliography

Index

Select Bibliography

A. MANUSCRIPT COLLECTIONS

Austen Papers in the British Museum
Brydges Willyams Papers owned by the Hon. Jacob Rothschild
Corry Papers owned by Mr Montagu Lowry-Corry
Cross Papers in the British Museum
Derby Papers owned by the Earl of Derby
Disraeli Papers at Hughenden Manor, Buckinghamshire, referred to as
    the Hughenden Papers
Gladstone Papers in the British Museum
Iddesleigh Papers in the British Museum
Lockhart Papers in the National Library of Scotland
Lytton Papers at Knebworth
Murray Papers owned by Sir John Murray, KCVO
Peel Papers in the British Museum
Royal Archives at Windsor Castle
Salisbury Papers at Christ Church, Oxford

B. PRINTED WORKS

The list does not purport to be comprehensive. It includes the books
mentioned in footnote references and a few others which seemed useful
or relevant. For a list of Disraeli's own works, see Appendix II.

Where a source is referred to repeatedly in the text a short title has
been given after its first appearance, e.g. M. & B. for Monypenny and
Buckle, Morley for Morley's *Life of Gladstone*. These books are marked
with an asterisk. See also note on sources, above, p. xxv.

ARGYLL, DUKE OF, *Autobiography and Memoirs* (2 vols, 1906)
BAGEHOT, W., *Biographical Studies* (1880)
BALFOUR, LADY BETTY, *History of Lord Lytton's Indian Administration*
    (1899)
BATTISCOMBE, GEORGINA, *Mrs. Gladstone* (1956)
BAXTER, MARY D., *In Memoriam. R. Dudley Baxter, M.A.* (1878)
BEELEY, SIR H., *Disraeli* (1936)

BENSON, A. C., and ESHER, VISCOUNT, *The Letters of Queen Victoria, 1837–61* (3 vols, 1907)

BIGNOLD, SIR R., *Five Generations of the Bignold Family* (1948)

BLAKE, ROBERT, 'The Rise of Disraeli', in H. R. Trevor-Roper (ed.), *Essays in British History presented to Sir Keith Feiling* (1964)

— 'The Dating of Endymion', *Review of English Studies*, New Series xvii, 66, (May 1966)

BRIGGS, ASA, *Victorian People* (1954)

BROUGHTON, LORD (J. C. Hobhouse), *Recollections of a Long Life* (6 vols, 1909–11)

BUCKLE, G. E. (ed.), *The Letters of Queen Victoria*, Second Series, 1862–86 (3 vols, 1926) [*See also* MONYPENNY, W. F.]

CAMPBELL, LORD, *Lives of the Lord Chancellors* (vol. viii, 1869)

CAZAMIAN, LOUIS, *Le Roman Social en Angleterre* (Paris, 1904)

CECIL, LORD DAVID, *Early Victorian Novels* (1934)

CECIL, LADY GWENDOLEN, *The Life of Robert, Marquis of Salisbury* (vols i and ii, 1921)

CHILSTON, VISCOUNT, *W. H. Smith* (1965)

CHURCHILL, W. S., *Lord Randolph Churchill* (new edition, 1951)

CLINE, C. L., 'Disraeli and Peel's 1841 Cabinet', *Journal of Modern History*, xi (1939)

CONACHER, J. B., 'Peel and the Peelites, 1846–50', *English Historical Review*, lxxiii (1958)

COUPLAND, SIR R., *Zulu Battle Piece* (1948)

COWLING, MAURICE, 'Lytton, the Cabinet and the Russians, August to November, 1878', *English Historical Review*, lxxvi (1961)

— 'Disraeli, Derby and Fusion, October, 1865 to July, 1866', *Historical Journal*, viii (1965)

CROSS, VISCOUNT, *A Political History* (1903)

DASENT, A. I., *John Thadeus Delane, Editor of 'The Times'* (2 vols, 1908).

DAVIDSON, R. T., and BENHAM, W., *Life of Archibald Campbell Tait* (2 vols, 1891)

DEVEY, LOUISA, *Life of Rosina, Lady Lytton* (1887)

DISRAELI, BENJAMIN, *Lord George Bentinck; a Political Biography* (1852)

D'ISRAELI, ISAAC, *The Curiosities of Literature* (new edition, 1881)

DISRAELI, RALPH (ed.), *Home Letters, 1830–31* (1885)

— *Lord Beaconsfield's Correspondence with his Sister, 1832–52* (1886)

DOWELL, S., *History of Taxation and Taxes in England* (4 vols, 1888)

DRUS, ETHEL (ed.), *A Journal of Events during the Gladstone Ministry, 1868–74*, by John, First Earl of Kimberley (Camden, 3rd Series, xc, 1958)

DUNN, W. H., *James Anthony Froude: a Biography* (vol ii, 1963)

ELLETSON, D. H., *Maryannery* (1959)

ESCOTT, T. H. S., 'Lord Carnarvon's Resignation', *The Gentleman's Magazine,* ccxii (1878)

EYCK, F., *The Prince Consort* (1959)

FABER, RICHARD, *Beaconsfield and Bolingbroke* (1961)

FONBLANQUE, E. B. DE, *Lives of the Lords Strangford* (1877)

FRASER, SIR WILLIAM, *Disraeli and His Day* (1891)

FROUDE, J. A., *Lord Beaconsfield* (1890)

GARDINER, A. G., *Life of Sir William Harcourt* (2 vols, 1923)

GARVIN, J. L., *Life of Joseph Chamberlain* (vols i and ii, 1932–3)

GASH, N., *Politics in the Age of Peel* (1953)

— *Reaction and Reconstruction in English Politics, 1832–52* (1965)

GATHORNE HARDY, A. E. (ed.), *Gathorne Hardy* First Earl of Cranbrook: a *Memoir* (2 vols, 1910)

GLADSTONE, W. E., *The Bulgarian Horrors and the Question of the East* (1876)

— *Lessons in Massacre; or the Conduct of the Turkish Government in and about Bulgaria since May, 1876* (1877)

GORST, H., *The Fourth Party* (1906)

GOWER, LORD RONALD, *My Reminiscences* (new edition, 1895)

GREGORY, SIR WILLIAM, *An Autobiography* (1894)

GRIERSON, H. J. C. (ed.), *Letters of Sir Walter Scott* (12 vols, 1932–7)

HAMER, F. E. (ed.), *The Personal Papers of Lord Rendel* (1931)

HAMILTON, LORD GEORGE, *Parliamentary Reminiscences and Reflections* (2 vols, 1916–22)

HANHAM, H. J., *Elections and Party Management; Politics in the Time of Disraeli and Gladstone* (1959)

— 'Political Patronage at the Treasury, 1870–1912', *Historical Journal* (1960–1), iii

HARDINGE, SIR A., *Life of Henry Fourth Earl of Carnarvon* (3 vols, 1925)

HENDERSON, G. B., *Crimean War Diplomacy and Other Historical Essays* (1947)

HILL, R. L., *Toryism and the People, 1832–46* (1929)

HUTCHEON, W. (ed.), *Whigs and Whiggism; political writings by Benjamin Disraeli* (1913)

JAMES, R. R., *Rosebery* (1963)

JENNINGS, LOUIS J., *Memoirs . . . of John Wilson Croker* (3 vols, 1884)

JERMAN, B. R., *The Young Disraeli* (Princeton, 1960)

JONES, W. D., *Lord Derby and Victorian Conservatism* (1956)

KEBBEL, T. E., *Lord Beaconsfield* (1888)

— *Lord Beaconsfield and Other Tory Memories* (1907)

— (ed.) *Selected Speeches of the Late Earl of Beaconsfield* (2 vols, 1882)

KIDD, JOSEPH, 'The Last Illness of Lord Beaconsfield', *Nineteenth Century*, 26 (July, 1889)

KITSON CLARK, G., *The Making of Victorian England* (1962)

LANG, ANDREW, *Life and Letters of J. G. Lockhart* (2 vols, 1896)

— *Life, Letters and Diaries of Sir Stafford Northcote, First Earl of Iddesleigh* (2 vols, 1890)

LAWSON-TANCRED, MARY, 'The Anti-League and the Corn Law Crisis of 1846', *Historical Journal*, iii, No. 2 (1960)

LAYARD, SIR H., *Autobiography and Memoirs* (1905)

LONDONDERRY, MARCHIONESS OF (ed.), *The Letters of Benjamin Disraeli to Frances Anne, Marchioness of Londonderry* (1938)

LONGFORD, ELIZABETH, *Victoria, R.I.* (1964)

LUCY, H. W. A., *A Diary of Two Parliaments* (1886)

LYTTON, EARL OF, *The Life of Edward Bulwer, First Lord Lytton* (2 vols, 1913)

MACDONELL, J. C., *The Life and Correspondence of William Connor Magee* (2 vols, 1896)

MCDOWELL, R. B., *British Conservatism, 1832–1914* (1959)

MACLAGAN, MICHAEL, *Clemency Canning* (1962)

MAGNUS, SIR PHILIP, *Gladstone; a Biography* (1954)

— *King Edward the Seventh* (1964)

MALMESBURY, EARL OF, *Memoirs of an ex-Minister* (2 vols, 1884)

MARTIN, SIR THEODORE, *Life of H.R.H. the Prince Consort* (5 vols, 1879)

— *A Life of Lord Lyndhurst* (1883)

MARTINEAU, J., *Life of Sir Bartle Frere* (2 vols, 1895)

MAUROIS, ANDRÉ, *La Vie de Disraeli* (Paris, 1928)

MAXWELL, SIR H., *Life and Letters of George William Frederick, Fourth Earl of Clarendon* (2 vols, 1913)

MEDLICOTT, W. N., *The Congress of Berlin and After* (1938)

MEYNELL, WILFRID, *The Man Disraeli* (revised edition, 1927)

MONYPENNY, W. F., and BUCKLE, G. E., *The Life of Benjamin Disraeli, Earl of Beaconsfield* (6 vols, 1910–20)

MORLEY, JOHN, *Life of W. E. Gladstone* (3 vols, 1903)

— *Life of Richard Cobden* (2 vols, 1913)

MOORE, DORIS LANGLEY, *The Late Lord Byron* (1961)

NEVILL, RALPH (ed.), *Reminiscences of Lady Dorothy Nevill* (1906)

NORTHCOTE, SIR STAFFORD, *Twenty Years of Financial Policy, 1842–61* (1882)

O'LEARY, CORNELIUS, *The Elimination of Corrupt Practices in British Elections, 1868–1911* (1962)

PARKER, C. S. (ed.), *Sir Robert Peel from his Private Papers* (3 vols, 1891–9)

PHIPPS, THE HON. E., *Memoir of Plumer Ward* (2 vols, 1850)

PONSONBY, ARTHUR, *Henry Ponsonby; his Life from his Letters* (1942)

POPE-HENNESSY, JAMES, *Monckton Milnes; the Years of Promise* (1949)
— *Monckton Milnes; the Flight of Youth* (1951)

RAMM, A. (ed.), *The Political Correspondence of Mr. Gladstone and Lord Granville, 1868–86* (4 vols, 1952–62)

RAMSAY, A. A. W., *Sir Robert Peel* (1928)

ROTH, CECIL, *The Earl of Beaconsfield* (New York, 1952)

RUSSELL, G. W. E. (ed.), *Malcolm MacColl, Memoirs and Correspondence* (1914)

RYE, W., *Norfolk County Families* (2 vols, 1911–13)

SADLEIR, MICHAEL, *Bulwer and his Wife; a Panorama, 1803–36* (1931)
— *Blessington – d'Orsay; a Masquerade* (1933)

SARKISSIAN, A. O. (ed.), *Studies in Diplomatic History and Historiography in honour of G. P. Gooch* (1961)

SCOTT, SIR WALTER, *Familiar Letters* (2 vols, Edinburgh, 1890)

SETON-WATSON, R. W., *Disraeli, Gladstone and the Eastern Question* (1935)
— 'Russo-British Relations During the Eastern Crisis' (unprinted letters), *Slavonic Review*, iv (1924–5) and v (1925–6)

SEYMOUR, C., *Electoral Reform in England and Wales* (1915)

SHANNON, R. T., *Gladstone and the Bulgarian Agitation, 1876* (1963)

SICHEL, W., *Disraeli; a Study in Personality and Ideas* (1904)

SMILES, SAMUEL, *Memoir of John Murray* (2 vols, 1891)

SMITH, GOLDWIN, *Reminiscences* (1910)

SMITH, SHEILA M., 'Willenhall and Woodgate: Disraeli's Use of Blue Book Evidence', *Review of English Studies*, New Series, xiii, 52 (November, 1962)

SOMERVELL, D. C., *Disraeli and Gladstone* (1938)

SOUTHGATE, D., *The Passing of the Whigs, 1832–1886* (1962)

STANMORE, LORD, *Sidney Herbert* (2 vols, 1906)

STEWART, R. W., 'The Publication and Reception of Vivian Grey', *Cornhill Magazine* (October, 1960)

STRACHEY, LYTTON, and FULFORD, ROGER (ed.), *The Greville Memoirs* (8 vols, 1938)

STUART, C. H., 'The Formation of the Coalition Cabinet of 1852', *Royal Historical Society Transactions*, 5th Series (1954)

SUMNER, B. H., *Russia and the Balkans, 1870–1880* (1937)

TAYLOR, A. J. P., *The Struggle for the Mastery in Europe, 1848–1918* (1954)
— *The Trouble Makers* (1957)

TEMPERLEY, H. W. V., 'Disraeli and Cyprus', *English Historical Review*, xlvi (July, 1931)

THOMPSON, F. M. L., *English Landed Society in the Nineteenth Century* (1963)

THOMPSON, G. C., *Public Opinion and Lord Beaconsfield, 1876–80* (1886)

[THE TIMES], *The History of The Times*, vol i, '*The Thunderer*' *in the making, 1785–1841* (1935)

— vol ii, *The Tradition Established, 1841–85* (1939)

TILLOTSON, KATHLEEN, *Novels of the Eighteen-Forties* (1954)

TORRENS, W. M., *Memoirs of . . . Viscount Melbourne* (new edition, 1890)

— *Twenty Years in Parliament* (1893)

TREVELYAN, G. M., *The Life of John Bright* (1913)

TROLLOPE, ANTHONY, *An Autobiography* (1946 edition)

VITZTHUM VON ECKSTAEDT, C. F., *St. Petersburg and London, 1852–64* (2 vols, 1887)

WAKE, JOAN, *The Brudenells of Deene* (1953)

WATERFIELD, GORDON, *Layard of Nineveh* (1963)

WEST, ALGERNON, *Recollections* (2 vols, 1899)

WHIBLEY, C., *Lord John Manners and his Friends* (2 vols, 1925)

WILBERFORCE, REGINALD, *Life of the Right Reverend Samuel Wilberforce, D.D.* (3 vols, 1881)

WILLIS, N. P., *Pencillings by the Way* (New York, 1835)

ZETLAND, MARQUESS OF (ed.), *The Letters of Disraeli to Lady Bradford and Lady Chesterfield* (2 vols, 1929)

Index